Access 2003 VBA
Programmer's Reference

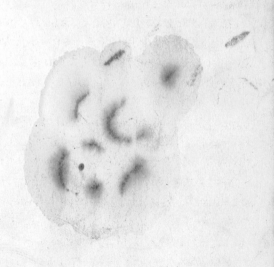

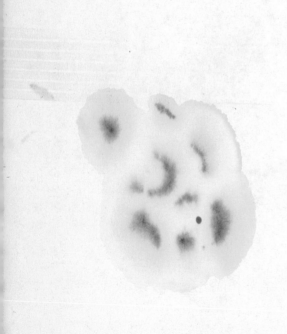

Access 2003 VBA
Programmer's Reference

Patricia Cardoza
Teresa Hennig
Graham Seach
Armen Stein

WILEY

Wiley Publishing, Inc.

Access 2003 VBA Programmer's Reference

Published by
Wiley Publishing, Inc.
10475 Crosspoint Boulevard
Indianapolis, IN 46256
www.wiley.com

Published by Wiley Publishing, Inc., Indianapolis, Indiana

Published simultaneously in Canada

ISBN: 0-7645-5903-6

Manufactured in the United States of America

10 9 8 7 6

To my husband Rob, together we can climb mountains. To my parents, who've given me the foundation to succeed in life; I love you.

—Patricia

To my family, for their unwavering love and encouragement. To the PNWADG, for the privilege of leading such a great group of developers.

—Teresa

I dedicate this book (or at least my chapters) to my beautiful wife Julie-Anne, for carrying the world on her shoulders so I could work uninterrupted, and for her unfailing support, encouragement, and sacrifice, despite illness and personal hardship. And to my children, Madeleine and Eli, who tried to understand why Daddy couldn't spend so much time with them. I am indeed a lucky man.

—Graham

Credits

Authors
Patricia Cardoza
Teresa Hennig
Armen Stein
Graham Seach

Executive Acquisitions Editor
Robert Elliott

Development Editor
Eileen Bien Calabro

Production Editor
Angela Smith

Copy Editor
TechBooks

Senior Production Manager
Fred Bernardi

Editorial Manager
Kathryn Malm

Vice President & Executive Group Publisher
Richard Swadley

Vice President and Executive Publisher
Robert Ipsen

Vice President and Publisher
Joseph B. Wikert

Executive Editorial Director
Mary Bednarek

Proofreading and Indexing
TECHBOOKS Production Services

About the Authors

Authors

Patricia Cardoza is an Exchange and Outlook Applications developer, writer, and Microsoft Outlook MVP. Patricia currently serves as Exchange Administrator and lead developer for Pacific Southwest Container, a large manufacturing company. She has authored two other books, *Special Edition Using Microsoft Office Outlook 2003* and *Absolute Beginner's Guide to Microsoft OneNote 2003*. She has also written numerous articles about Outlook, Exchange, and wireless devices for a variety of journals including *.NET Magazine* and *Tech Republic*. In her spare time, she loves to cook, read, watch movies with her husband, and spoil her three cats.

Teresa Hennig is the owner of Eade.com, which specializes in developing cost-effective Access applications. Her energy and enthusiasm are complemented by her ability to quickly grasp a situation and provide a solution. Her biggest rewards are being a partner with her clients and sharing their joy in their successes. Her site, www.DatabaseAnswerSite.com, is recognized as a resource for learning about relational databases by several universities and technical support organizations.

An avid Access aficionado, Teresa is the president of the two leading Access user groups in the US northwest: the Pacific Northwest Access Developers Group (PNWADG) and the Access Special Interest Group. She is also dedicated to helping the Spinal Cord Society raise money to find a cure for spinal cord injuries. And, she wishes that she had more time to enjoy dancing.

Graham Seach is Chief Development Officer for a Sydney-based database development company, Pacific Database (www.pacificdb.com.au). He has been developing applications in Access since version 1.0, has participated in the Microsoft Office 2003 beta program, and has presented at several Microsoft events, notably the Microsoft Office 2003 System launch in Sydney and Melbourne in 2003.

Graham holds an MCP in Access Development, master-level Brainbench certification in Access, and is recognized by Microsoft as an MVP (most valuable professional). He has received this award three times. He regularly provides worldwide Access developer support for Microsoft via the Microsoft newsgroups, and has been published in *MSDN Magazine*. Graham's technical focus is now on Access and the SQL Server integration, having provided many business solutions to a wide range of government, military, and private organizations.

Armen Stein is the owner and founder of J Street Technology, Inc., a team of database application developers in Redmond, Washington. He is President Emeritus of the Pacific Northwest Access Developers Group, and has contributed to *Access/Office/VB Advisor* magazine and *Smart Access*. He has taught database classes at Bellevue Community College and Seattle Central Community College and also developed and taught his own 1-day training class called *Access Development the J Street Way*. Armen earned a business administration/computer science degree from Western Washington University, and has been developing computer applications since 1984. His other interests include activities with his family, backgammon, cheering on the Mariners, and driving his 1969 Ford Bronco in the sun.

Contributors

Steve Clark is a Microsoft Access MVP, an MCP, and a Project Manager and Developer for the FMS Professional Solutions Group (www.fmsinc.com/consulting). As a developer, he specializes in database development and has produced Access, VB(.NET), and ASP(.NET) applications for clients from all elements of business, both nationally and internationally. He earned a bachelor's degree in computer science from the University of Cincinnati in 1994 and has been with FMS since 1998 and an Access MVP since 2001. When he's not managing or developing, he enjoys participating in all forms of motorcycle racing.

Brian M. Sockey is founder and president of Farsight Solutions, Inc. (DBA TeleVantage NorthWest), a Microsoft Business Solutions partner, and value-added reseller of Artisoft TeleVantage software-based business telephone systems. Before starting TeleVantage NorthWest, Brian worked in the Developer Support group at Microsoft, where he specialized in client/server development issues involving Microsoft Access and SQL Server. Brian enjoys the great outdoors, theater, and good food (almost everything except blue cheese).

Randall J. Weers, the founder and president of Procia, Inc., specializes in process and data management applications utilizing the Microsoft Office suite. His primary focus is to help people manage business processes and business rules through the appropriate application of process improvement and automation. Randall's experience includes everything from business process analysis to technical and training manual writing. Randall makes his home in Seattle, Washington, where he is the facilitator for IT WorkGroups, a Puget Sound-based alliance of senior-level independent information technology professionals.

Sam Radakovitz joined Microsoft in 1998 and was a member of the Access team for Access 2000, 2002, and 2003. A lot of his efforts were focused on wizards and security features. For Access 2003, Sam was thoroughly engaged in the new macro security. This made it a perfect fit for him to review this book's security chapters, especially the one on macro security. When creating Access applications, Sam enjoys going outside the box and adding a bit of creativity. So, being invited to provide applications that could demonstrate some of Access's new features seemed like an awesome opportunity to share his ideas with other developers.

Acknowledgments

We'd like to thank all the folks at Wiley who made this book possible. Bob Elliott worked with Patricia and Teresa to build the amazing team of authors present on this book as well as to get all the mounds of paperwork straight. Eileen Bien Calabro showed incredible patience formatting, organizing, and editing our chapters. She reassured us that we could get all this done and done well, in a remarkably short time, as long as we focused. Our technical editor, Michael Stowe, tirelessly checked all of our facts and gently steered us back on course when needed. Techbooks International Pvt. Ltd. worked incredibly hard to format all the pages and work with all of the figures in this book. Thanks everyone!

—The Group

Thanks to all who had to put up with me when I had to meet deadlines. My husband, Rob, endured many nights of takeout and several weekends when I was glued to my computer. My parents, Joe and Sally, have supported me in everything I do and I thank God for them every day.

I would not be where I am today in my career if it were not for the Microsoft Most Valuable Professional (MVP) program. I am honored to be included in that esteemed group of professionals.

Lastly, I'd like to thank Teresa Hennig. She handled the majority of the scheduling of chapters and helped me keep all of the information for this book organized. Coordinating four authors and several contributors takes patience and dedication. Thanks Teresa for all your hard work.

—Patricia

First, I'd like to thank Paul Eade for being such an incredible resource and wealth of knowledge. You are an amazing friend, and I cherish the opportunities to laugh and just be silly.

I can't say enough about the Microsoft Access Team, including Rita Nikas. Their passion and dedication has made Access an incredibly powerful program. A special note of appreciation to Bill Ramos, Tim Getsch, and Sanjay Jacob for investing so much of themselves into finding out what developers want, for making the ADE so awesome, and for being so responsive to all of our requests! I also want to thank Michael Kaplan for sharing his opinions and encouragement and for doing so much for the Access groups.

To everyone I've met through this book . . . thank you for an amazing opportunity to enjoy a new challenge and to help Access developers! Very special thanks go to Patricia Cardoza, who seems like Wonder Woman—balancing a career and family while writing multiple books. She not only wrote several elements, but also reviewed every chapter and helped us all in countless ways. And thanks to Randy Weers, who offered help when I needed it. Yes, work should be fun! And last thanks go to all the Mikes and Michaels. I can't imagine a world without Michaels!

—Teresa

Acknowledgments

Needless to say, I want to first thank my wife and children for their support, encouragement, and understanding throughout a very difficult and demanding time.

I want to thank Rita Nikas, my Microsoft MVP Lead, who first made me aware of the book, and whose resolute determination to solve problems and to source much needed information will always be appreciated.

I also want to thank Mike Gunderloy, who, despite the fact that we had never met, kindly sent pages from his own book, to help me with mine; a gesture I will never forget.

Finally, I would like to express my thanks to Professor Roger Box of Charles Sturt University, who gave me a 2-week extension on my final assignment, so I could make a book deadline.

—Graham

I would like to acknowledge the encouragement and support from my wife, Lori, and kids, Lauren and Jonathan.

—Armen

I'm glad that I could help Randy and Teresa. It is cool to feature some of my work on the book's Web site. I want to thank my girlfriend Denice and my parents for putting up with my long hours of work and extra work! Without everyone's support and understanding my daily life would be much more difficult!

—Steve

My thanks to Teresa Hennig for giving me the opportunity to contribute to this book and for cracking the whip when I was struggling to keep moving forward. My deep appreciation to Sam Radakovitz for the invaluable insight into the new security features of Access. Thanks also to the members in IT Workgroups who helped me deliver a better picture for the Access Security model. And most of all, in loving memory of my wife Lisa, I dedicate my efforts on this book.

—Randall

Contents

Contents

Contents

Contents

Contents

Contents

Contents

Contents

Foreword

When Teresa told me she was writing a book on Access VBA programming, I thought she was crazy. She's so busy with her database consulting business and running the Pacific Northwest Access Developers Group that I couldn't figure out where she would find the time to write. I'm glad she and the other authors found the time. As a coordinating lead author, she worked with Patricia and put together a team of authors that produced an excellent piece of work.

This book is clear, concise, approachable, and above all, easy to understand. In addition to providing a look at the new features of Access, it provides a good overview of Macros and how you might use them to automate your Access application. I know what you're thinking, "But this is a book on VBA, right?" Yes it is, and it jumps right into the subject in the following chapter. Here's where it gets good.

This book does a great job of progressing from fundamental topics to advanced topics. It moves smoothly from introducing VBA to automating forms and reports to working with APIs, SQL, and other Office applications. It then tackles advanced topics such as understanding client/server development, security, and working with the Windows Registry. If that weren't enough, the book provides a set of appendixes covering a variety of important topics such as the ADO and Access object models, API reference information, naming conventions, and VBA reserved words. Clearly, there is a lot of valuable information packed into this book.

If you've been using Access for some time and you're just beginning to roll up your sleeves to jump into the world of code, this book is for you. If you need to hone your VBA programming skills or need ideas on how to polish your application, this book is for you as well. At the very least, you should add this book to your library of Access books, especially next to the ones by John Viescas and Cary Prague. At most, you should have this book readily available as you work on your next project.

——Mike Hernandez

Author: *Database Design for Mere Mortals*®, *2nd Edition*

Co-author: *SQL Queries for Mere Mortals*®

Introduction

Welcome to the *Access 2003 VBA Programmer's Reference*. We wrote this book for Access users and programmers who want to increase the power of Access by adding the VBA (Microsoft Visual Basic for Applications) language. Access is Microsoft's leading consumer relational database management system for desktop applications. It's so popular because it's relatively easy to learn and very powerful. With wizards and detailed help files, users can easily create tables, queries, forms, and reports after only a brief introduction.

To utilize the power of Microsoft Access more effectively, you can add VBA code to your Access databases. By using VBA code, you can respond to application-level events, display forms and reports, manipulate toolbars, and even launch external applications or control certain aspects of Windows.

The Evolution of Access and VBA

Microsoft Access has had a rich history. Version 1.0 was the initial version of Access that ran on Windows 3.1. It was very quickly replaced by Version 1.1, which added a few new features and fixed many of the bugs introduced in the initial version. At this point in the history of Access, no one really took Access seriously as a database; it was buggy, there were a number of limitations in its feature set, and the database community just hadn't accepted that Microsoft could produce a quality database product.

In 1994, the first real version of Access was released: Access 2.0. Many database programmers using other software, such as FoxPro and dBase, decided to give Microsoft Access 2.0 a chance. Access 2.0 worked very well on both Windows 95 and Windows NT; however, it was missing much of the 32-bit API (application programming interface) and couldn't work with long filenames. Microsoft Access went through several more versions (95, 97, 2000, and 2002) before the current release, Access 2003.

Access 2003, released in October 2003, includes some additional enhancements, including the ability to open an Access 97 database without converting it to an updated format. Users of Access 2000 and Access 2002 were prompted to convert an Access 97 database to Access 2000 format before they could use the database. This often caused problems in corporate installations where often, multiple versions of the Microsoft Office software suite were installed on different computers or in different departments. Access 2003 can open certain Access 97 databases without converting them, thus allowing multiple versions to access the same database.

There have not been a large number of changes to VBA in Access 2003. However, the changes that have been made offer developers some distinct advantages. We've included an entire chapter (Chapter 3) about new features in Access 2003.

What Is VBA?

Microsoft Visual Basic for Applications (VBA) allows programmers to develop highly customized desktop applications that integrate with a variety of Microsoft and non-Microsoft programs. For example, all of the Microsoft Office System products support VBA. In addition, many third-party programs, such as drafting programs as well as WordPerfect, also support VBA.

VBA is actually a subset of the Visual Basic programming language and is a superset of VBScript (another in the Visual Basic family of development programs). VBA includes a robust suite of programming tools based on the Visual Basic development, arguably the world's most popular rapid application development system. Developers can add code to tailor any VBA-enabled application to their specific business processes. A manufacturing company can use VBA within Microsoft Access to develop sophisticated inventory control and management systems with custom toolbars, a back-end database, management reports, and security. Rather than purchasing an off-the-shelf Inventory Control product, usually at a great cost and with a very limited ability to customize, developers can take a product they already have installed (Access as part of the Microsoft Office 2003 System) and build a robust application with no additional expense other than time. Once the application is in place, the developer can respond to customization requests quickly and effectively, rather than waiting for another company to work the customization into their development cycle.

You might be wondering why you should develop in VBA rather than the more robust Visual Basic 6.0 or Visual Basic .NET. Both are robust, popular, and capable programming languages. However, using VBA within Access gives you some key benefits: First, you can take advantage of a built-in Access object library. This means you can take full advantage of a wide variety of Access commands, including executing any command from any toolbar in Access. Second, VBA is included in all Microsoft Office System applications. To develop in Visual Basic, you'll need to purchase Visual Basic 6.0 or Visual Basic .NET either alone or as part of the Visual Studio or Visual Studio .NET suite. It could get very expensive if multiple developers in your organization need access to the Visual Basic development tools.

Despite the advantages of VBA, there are definitely circumstances in which you'll want to use Visual Basic. If you need to deploy an application to a wide variety of computers, especially those without a full installation of Microsoft Access, Visual Basic might be your best bet. We will examine the three languages in the Visual Basic family and why you might want to use each of them.

Access 2003 VBA Programmer's Reference

This book is separated into two sections. The chapters provide tutorial information and the numerous appendices provide the reference material you'll need to write VBA code within Access. While the chapters are designed to build upon one another to give you a detailed guide to VBA in Access, each chapter can be read and applied separately from the rest of the book.

What Does This Book Cover?

This Programmer's Reference book covers a wide variety of programming topics. A brief introduction to VBA is included, although this book assumes the reader has at least some basic familiarity with the VBA programming language. Likewise, an entire chapter is devoted to changes in Microsoft Office Access 2003, covering both new wizards and GUI (graphical user interface) features that previously required VBA code, as well as the new VBA features included with Access 2003. You'll learn how to create and name variables, how to use Data Access Object (DAO) and ActiveX Data Object (ADO) to manipulate data both within Access and within other applications, proper error handling techniques, and advanced functions such as creating classes and using APIs. There are two important chapters on Security and Macro Security as well as a chapter on the Access Developer Extensions (ADE). Finally, we'll explore a bit of the relationship between Access and SQL (Structured Query Language) Server, as well as how you can use VBA in Access to control and enhance other Office applications.

How to Use This Book

The initial chapters are written in a tutorial format with detailed examples. True to the Wrox Programmer's Reference standard format, we've included numerous reference appendices with details on the various object models you might use when writing VBA code in Access. We've also included a detailed primer on the Windows Registry and a listing of common API functions you might want to use in your code.

Real world examples will be given for many, if not most, of the programming topics covered in this book. Some typical topics include the following:

❑ How to hide fields on a form based on database login information.

❑ How to show or hide entire sections of reports based on information entered on a form.

❑ How to use VBA to transfer information between Access and other Office programs such as Outlook, Word, and Excel.

❑ How to configure custom menus for your Access database applications.

Throughout the book we've also included tips and tricks we've discovered during our programming experiences.

Introductory and Background Material

Chapters 1 through 5 provide some background reference material you'll need if you're new to Access or VBA. After a detailed look at the new features in Access 2002 and 2003, we've provided information on the building blocks of VBA, such as objects, properties, methods, and events. An introduction to the VBA Editor and its various debugging tools follows.

Accessing Data

After the introductory material, Chapters 6 and 7 focus on accessing data by using VBA. Both DAO and ADO provide methods for accessing data in Microsoft Access and other external data sources such as Informix and SQL Server.

Executing and Debugging

Chapters 8 and 9 provide detailed information on executing and debugging VBA code. Every development project needs some debugging, even if you're an expert developer. We'll show you some easy ways to debug your code as well as provide some tips and tricks to make the tedious process of debugging a bit easier.

Working with Access Objects

Two Access objects in particular, Forms and Reports, can make heavy use of VBA (Chapters 10 and 11). You can write VBA code to respond to a variety of events from the controls on a form or even from the form itself. You can write code to show or hide certain sections of a form or report in response to information entered on the form or even the particular user logged on to Windows at the time.

Advanced VBA Programming

The next three chapters (12–14) provide information on creating classes in VBA, using APIs, and using SQL and VBA. They are designed to give you a thorough tutorial on these subjects so you can design your own classes, implement some common APIs in your code, and use SQL to access data.

Miscellaneous Material

Calling Chapters 15 through 20 miscellaneous is not really fair to the extremely thorough content presented. Chapter 15 shows you how to use VBA to transfer information between Access and the other Office programs. You'll learn how to create tasks and e-mail in Outlook, perform a mail merge in Word, and export data to an Excel spreadsheet. We'll even show you how to take information from Access, create a graph, and insert that graph into PowerPoint.

Chapter 16 provides a detailed study in security. It seems every week there's a new security hole in a computer program, which can expose your computer to malicious code. When developing a database, you can implement security in your database to prevent users from seeing the code, or you can even prevent access to certain tables or queries in your database.

Chapter 17 examines working with client/server development and Chapter 18 examines the Windows Registry. Next, we provide an in-depth look at a new set of tools, the Access Developer Extensions. These tools help you automate many common tasks in Access.

Chapter 20 focuses on macro security. Access 2003 introduces some new concerns related to macro security. We'll introduce you to Sandbox mode and let you know how to properly work with these new security features.

Appendices

Appendix A provides information on upgrading to Access 2003 from previous versions. Appendix B shows you how to create and use references within your VBA code. We've provided extensive information on the DAO, ADO, and Access Object Models in Appendices C, D, and E, respectively. Rounding out the mix are appendices on common API calls, proper naming conventions, VBA reserved words, and the Windows Registry. Finally, we've included a wonderful appendix full of tips and tricks you can use to develop professional applications.

Other Access/VBA Sources

Just as no man (or woman) is an island, no book can be all things to all readers. No matter how many times you read this book, it can't tell you the meaning of life any more than it can tell you everything you need to know about VBA within Microsoft Access. There are several other resources you'll want to utilize while writing your VBA code. Some of our favorites are:

❑ Microsoft Newsgroups—Microsoft maintains a news server (msnews.microsoft.com) and has a wide variety of Access and VBA newsgroups to choose from. Currently there are more than 25 Access newsgroups for you to choose from. They all begin with microsoft.public.access. You can access newsgroups through a newsreader such as Outlook Express or through the Web at: http://support.microsoft.com/newsgroups/default.aspx.

- ❑ MVPS.ORG (http://www.mvps.org/)—This is your jumping-off point to a number of interesting offerings being provided for you by a few folks associated with the Microsoft Most Valuable Professional (MVP) program.

- ❑ Microsoft Access Support Center (http://support.microsoft.com/default.aspx?scid=fh;en-us;acc&x=16&y=16)—This provides information about current issues, downloads, updates, and of course ways of obtaining product support.

- ❑ Microsoft on Google (http://www.google.com/microsoft)—This harnesses the power of Google and limits the searches to Microsoft-related sites.

- ❑ Microsoft Developer Network (http://msdn.microsoft.com)—The Developer Center for Access provides a myriad of articles and tutorials on key issues. You can also find links to usergroups, newsgroups, and other valuable resources.

- ❑ Microsoft TechNet (http://www.microsoft.com/technet)—This site allows you to access Microsoft Knowledge Base articles, security information, and many other technical articles and tips.

Conventions Used in This Book

We've used several different styles of text in this book to help you understand different types of information. Some of the styles we've used are listed here:

> **When there's a mission critical piece of information or a tip we've found particularly valuable in our development, we include it in a box such as this.**

Advice, hints, and background information comes in this type of font.

Important words or phrases are in *italic*.

Words that appear on the screen, such as menu commands or toolbar buttons are in a font such as `File`.

Keys that you press on the keyboard, like *Ctrl*, are in italics.

Code within the text is styled like the following: `For I = 1 to 10`

Any new or important code is offset with shading similar to the following sample:

```
SELECT TeamID, TeamName, StadiumName FROM tblFootball;
```

Code you've seen before is in the same font, without the shading, as shown here:

```
Dim strText as String
```

Source Code

As you work through the examples in this book, you can choose either to type in all the code manually, or use the source code files that accompany this book. All of the source code used in this book is available for download at www.wrox.com. Once at the site, simply locate the book's title (either by using the Search box or by using one of the title lists) and click the Download Code link on the book's detail page to obtain all the source code for the book.

> *Because many books have similar titles, you may find it easiest to search by ISBN; for this book, the ISBN is 0-7645-590-6.*

After you download the code, just decompress it with your favorite decompression tool.

Tell Us What You Think

We've tried to make this book as complete as possible. We're all active programmers and have included tips and tricks that we've used in our everyday lives. Programming books can often be dry and boring. We've tried to liven our book up a bit with some interesting examples. If you liked the book (or even if you didn't), we encourage you to send us your feedback. You can contact us via e-mail at support@wrox.com (be sure to include the book's title) or through the Wrox Web site.

Customer Support

We've done our best to make sure that every code sample is complete, debugged, and well commented. However, if there are samples or topics you just can't quite grasp or need a little more help with, there are places you can turn. You can e-mail your questions to Wrox at support@wrox.com (again, be sure to include the book's title) or visit the Microsoft Newsgroups. Most of us hang around the Access newsgroups and will attempt to answer your questions as quickly and completely as possible. You can also e-mail any of us directly (patricia@mvps.org, teresa@eade.com, gseach@pacificdb.com.au, and armen@JStreetTech.com). Thanks for reading!

Introduction to Microsoft Access

What is Microsoft Access? If you're reading this book, hopefully you know that Access is a relational database management system (RDBMS). An RDBMS means that you can store data that's related in multiple ways. For example, you can store a table of products related to a table of customers. Each customer can have multiple products. For each customer, you can store multiple shipping locations or billing records. A basic database is nothing more than a collection of data that's related. However, databases can be much more than just a collection of related data. You can add sophisticated code to your database to display only the data you want in the precise way you want it. You can display different data to each user of your database. You can even write a front-end program for your database, using Visual Basic or Visual C++.

A Microsoft Access database consists of a variety of objects to help you manage your data. Tables allow you to store your data in easy to understand rows and columns. Queries allow you to manipulate data within tables and display information from multiple tables in the result set. Forms allow you to create a pleasant and easily understood graphical user interface (GUI) so that users can enter data in your tables. Reports allow you to output data from tables and queries in a variety of different ways. You can sort and group data, create charts, add images, and even customize a report with programming. Data Access pages allow you to view formatted data through Internet Explorer. Macros string a series of commands together and run all of them with little or no user intervention. Finally, modules store VBA code to further automate your database.

Why Use Microsoft Access?

Ask a variety of database programmers why they think you should use Microsoft Access and you'll get answers ranging from "it's the best darn piece of software out there" to "it's a robust piece of software that won't break the bank and doesn't take a degree in rocket science to use." While we don't necessarily think Access is the best darn piece of software out there, we do think it's very good at what it does—allowing users with a range of abilities the opportunity to create databases to store information. We do think Access is a pretty darn good piece of software. It's relatively easy to use, even for a beginner, and it comes with a robust sample database (Northwind) that a new user can play around with and learn many of the basics. New users can learn a lot from simply going through the various tables, queries, forms, and reports in the Northwind database.

There are also a number of books on Microsoft Access available for purchase. You can buy books from beginner to advanced level and easily create simple databases within a few hours. In particular, any of the following titles will help you learn Microsoft Access 2003:

❑   *Access 2003 Bible*, Cary N. Prague, Michael R. Irwin, Jennifer Reardon, ISBN: 0764539868, Wiley Publishing, Inc.

❑   *Access 2003 All-in-One Desk Reference for Dummies*, Alan Simpson, Margaret Levine Young, Alison Barrows, ISBN: 0-7645-3988-4, Wiley Publishing, Inc.

For example, you can use databases to inventory DVD collections, track weekly cycling miles and durations, and even to log the hours spent on various projects at the office.

Is Access the Only Database I'll Ever Need?

The simple answer to this question is no. Access is not the only database product on the market, nor is it the only database product available from Microsoft. There are times when you might want to use a different type of database such as SQL Server or Microsoft Development Environment (MSDE). If you've only ever used Microsoft Access for your database needs you might be wondering why you'd need another type of database program. Well, there are several reasons that are detailed in the following paragraphs.

Microsoft Access

Microsoft Access works very well for single-user applications. You can get by with Access for multiuser applications; however, you need to be aware of how record-locking options affect your data. It's also possible that you'll encounter users who like to open the database exclusively, thus locking out other users from the application. If you have multiple users with differing versions of Access trying to use the same database, you'll probably end up with some compatibility issues as well. In addition to the single-user and multiple-user scenarios, Access works very well when you have multiple users but a single code base that makes all of the requests to the database. For example, a front-end application written in Visual Basic can take advantage of ADO to make calls to the back-end Access database. This type of application works very well in a single- or multiuser environment as the only time the data is touched is when an ADO call is made to the database.

MSDE

The Microsoft SQL Server Desktop Engine (MSDE) is actually a database server, very much like SQL Server. In fact, it's actually a scaled-down SQL Server installation aimed at desktop environments. If you have a desktop application that needs the features of SQL Server, you can use MSDE in place of a full SQL Server installation. Designing your application against MSDE is also a good idea if you think eventually your application will grow large enough to need the full features of SQL Server. If you're designing a desktop application that needs a database and have the MSDE package that's included with Visual

Studio, you can freely distribute MSDE. The redistribution license is included with Visual Studio. You can also redistribute MSDE with the Access Runtime included with Access 2003. There are some distinct advantages to MSDE. It's more robust, accommodating databases up to 2GB in size. Jet databases are limited to 2GB in size; however, databases larger than 1GB often suffer performance issues. It is possible for a Jet database to grow to 2GB; however, if you're designing a Jet database that large, you'll need to be very careful with building proper indexes and building in a regular compact and repair cycle. So, why not use MSDE for everything? Well, for one thing, you have more administrative and security concerns with MSDE than with Access. MSDE is a database server. Thus it can often behave in ways the users won't understand. For example, if disk space becomes an issue, MSDE will often take a table offline. A typical computer user won't know how to remedy that situation.

Along with administrative issues, you also need to worry about security. As a slightly scaled-down version of SQL Server, MSDE suffers the same security vulnerabilities as SQL Server. MSDE was recently vulnerable to the SQL Slammer worm. If you're writing an application that installs MSDE, you'll need to keep on top of security issues that affect SQL Server and MSDE.

SQL Server

If you're designing a large-scale professional application that requires a back-end database, you should consider using SQL Server as your database. SQL Server is the most robust of the databases listed in this chapter, but it also costs the most and has the highest learning curve. You cannot distribute SQL Server freely, nor can it be installed on a typical desktop class machine. SQL Server requires Windows NT, Windows 2000 Server, or Windows 2003 Server. One of the advantages to both SQL Server and MSDE is that code written for one will work equally well with the other. The two products use the same API and SQL language. However, there are several distinct advantages to SQL Server. SQL Server supports larger databases and more users. In addition, it has many features that are not found in MSDE, such as full-text searching, replication, failover, and Query Analyzer. From a developer's perspective, SQL Server allows you to script the creation of a database. MSDE doesn't support this functionality.

If you're not sure which type of database to create for your application, ask yourself the following questions:

- ❑ Does your application need to be accessed by multiple users?
- ❑ Does your application need to create databases via code?
- ❑ Will your database grow beyond 2GB?
- ❑ Will your application need replication or full-text searching?

Even answering these questions won't tell you for sure every time which type of database you should use for your application. You'll have to use the answers to these questions as well as some common sense and research to determine which type of database application to use. For example, if you need a database that promises to grow to around 1.5GB and needs to be accessed by multiple users on a central server, you can utilize either MSDE or SQL Server. However, using SQL Server gives you some added benefits, including the capacity beyond 2GB in size for future growth. If money is an issue, you'll want to lean toward using an MSDE database, as the license is included with Visual Studio.

Whatever database you choose, be sure to research your options before making your decision. If you do choose SQL Server, you'll need to do some research on server sizing and performance based on your application's size and number of users.

Automating Microsoft Access Without VBA Code

This book is about automating Access with VBA code; however, not everything you need to do with your database should be accomplished via code. Part of being a good programmer is knowing when to write code and when to let someone else do it for you. The someone else can often be Microsoft Access itself. Access is a powerful application that includes a variety of wizards and built-in commands that can help automate your application without writing even one line of code. This section will go into some detail about how you can automate your application without writing any code at all.

The Database Wizard

If you need to create a database and don't know where to start, you can use the Database Wizard to create several different types of business and personal databases. Some of the different types of databases you can create include:

❑   Asset tracking

❑   Contact management

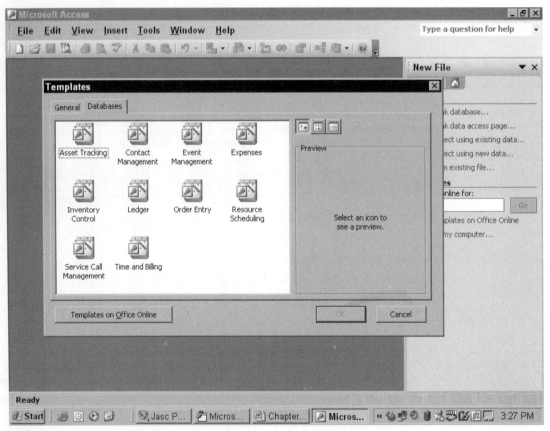

Figure 1-1

- ❑ Event management
- ❑ Inventory control
- ❑ Order entry
- ❑ Time and billing

To create a new database using the Database Wizard, open Access and select New from the File menu to display the TaskPane. Choose On my computer from the Templates section and click the Databases tab in the dialog box that appears (Figure 1-1).

Choose the type of database you want to create and click OK. Enter the filename for your database and click Create. Access will display the various screens of the Database Wizard. The particular screens you see and questions the wizard asks will depend on the type of database you selected. We'll detail the steps for creating a database for Inventory Tracking.

The first screen you'll see details the steps Access takes to create your new database. Click Next (see Figure 1-2).

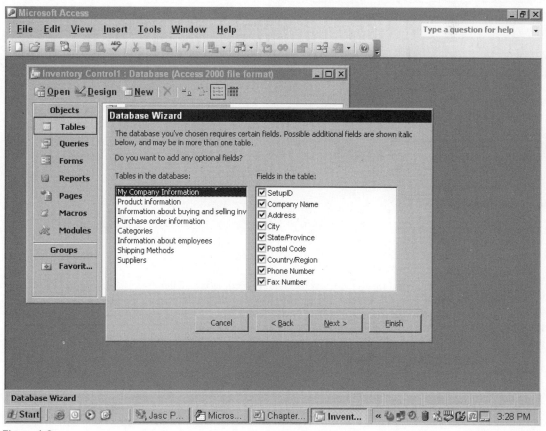

Figure 1-2

Each database type requires specific tables and fields. You can choose to add fields beyond the required fields by choosing the table from the left-hand column and by examining the fields in the right-hand column. All checked fields will be included in the selected table. If you attempt to remove a required field, Access will inform you of the field's requirement and leave the box checked. When you're done manipulating the fields in your tables, click Next (see Figure 1-3).

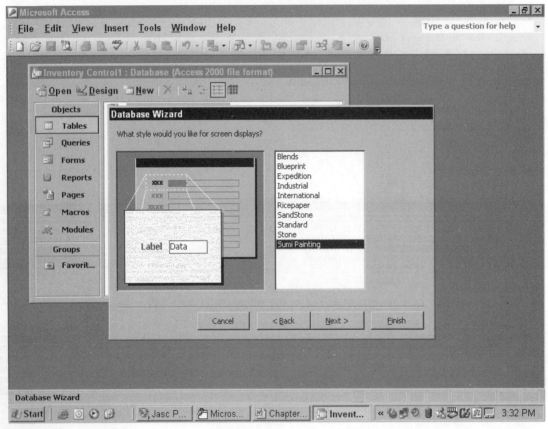

Figure 1-3

Choose the style you want for the various forms in your database. Click Next to configure a style for the reports in your database. Click Next again and give your database a title. This title can be different from the filename you assigned to your database. Click Next and then Finish and Access will build your database.

When the wizard completes, Access displays your database. You can then further customize your database.

If you need to create a database and just don't know where to start, using the Database Wizard can help you get started. Even if you don't use all of the tables and reports the wizard creates, using the Database Wizard can give you some ideas of what tables you need in your database.

Once you've completed the Database Wizard you'll see there are many automatic features you can utilize within your database. Switchboards, such as the one in Figure 1-4, provide a launch point for data entry, reports, and graphs you can use within your database. The Switchboard for the Inventory Tracking database allows you to enter data, view that data, preview reports, customize the switchboard, or exit the database. You can configure switchboards to launch a specific report, open a form for data entry, run a query or macro, or display a security warning about unauthorized access to the database. If the switchboard designed by the Database Wizard doesn't meet your needs, you can create your own.

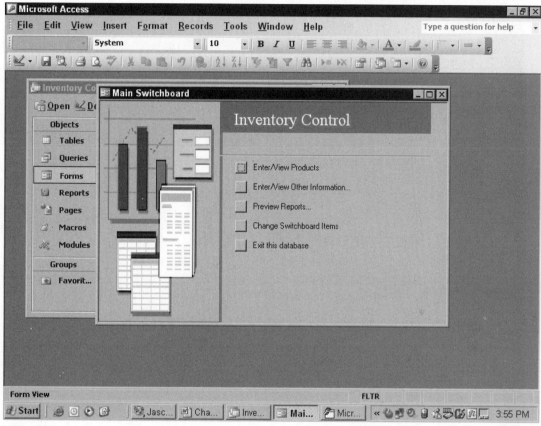

Figure 1-4

Creating a Switchboard for Your Database

Creating a Switchboard form is as simple as creating a form and configuring the form to launch when the database loads. Once you've created the form, add some command buttons to perform various actions you think your users might want to perform. We'll look at creating a switchboard from scratch in the following pages. Along the way, we'll use some of the other built-in wizards you can use to automate Access without code.

Begin at the Beginning

To create a switchboard, you'll first need to create a new form. Choose Forms from the Access bar and click the New button to launch the New Form dialog box. For a switchboard form you don't need to choose a table or query for the form's data source, just choose Design View from the list box and click OK.

You can give switchboard forms a nice title and maybe a couple of lines of text to serve as a brief explanation to users. After you've added these elements to the form, it might look similar to Figure 1-5. Any number of elements can be added to the form, including images, text, frames, fields, or other graphics. But what good is a form if it doesn't *do* anything?

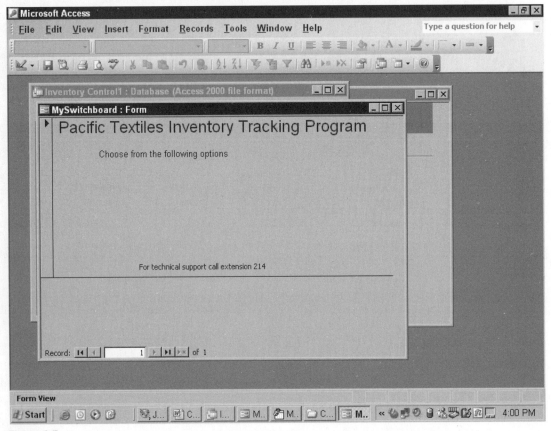

Figure 1-5

In order for your form to *do* something, you'll need to add command buttons to the form. To add a new command button, choose the command button tool from the Control Toolbox and click anywhere on your form to insert the command button and start the Command Button Wizard. The first screen you'll see in the wizard (Figure 1-6) allows you to choose the type of action to perform.

We typically start designing the database's switchboard by adding two command buttons: One to launch the main data entry form (or forms as the case might be) and one to exit the database. The following steps

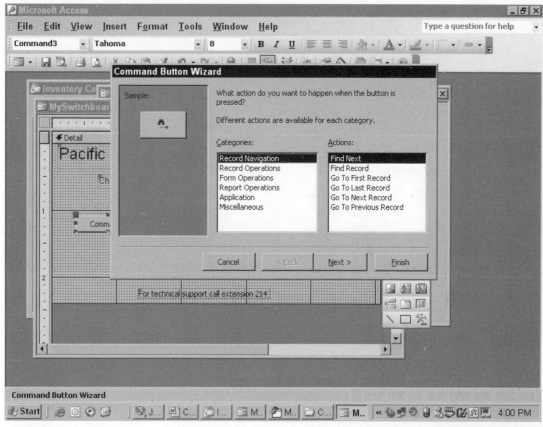

Figure 1-6

will create a command button to launch the MySwitchboard form for data entry:

1. Choose Form Operations from the Categories list box.

2. Choose Open Form from the Actions list box and click Next (see Figure 1-7).

3. Access displays a list of all forms available in your database. Choose the appropriate form and click Next again.

4. You can open the form and display all records or choose a specific record to display. Click Next to continue.

5. The next step in configuring your command button allows you to associate text or an image with the button. In most cases, we choose to display text on the button rather than an image. However, if you are designing a multilanguage application, you might want to stick with universally recognizable images, rather than text. Enter the text of the button in the text box, as shown in Figure 1-8, and click Next.

6. The final step in the wizard is naming your command button. Access suggests a default name of "Command" followed by a number. You should enter a meaningful name for your command button and click Finish.

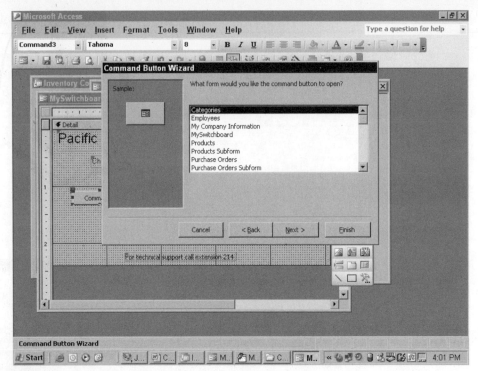

Figure 1-7

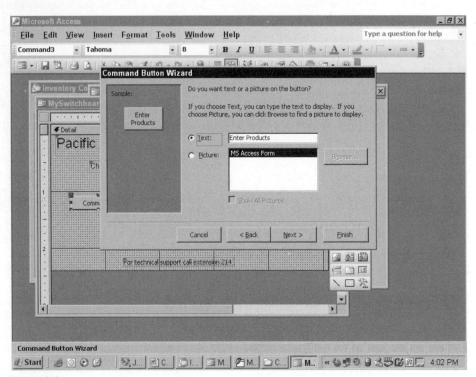

Figure 1-8

While it's tempting to just accept this name and move on, it's against all common programming recommendations. You should always give your command buttons (as well as your other controls such as text boxes, labels, combo boxes, and image controls) a meaningful name. Even if you don't follow established naming conventions, such as cmdfrmPurchaseOrder), you should still ensure the name you give to your objects is meaningful, otherwise you could be left editing code that's almost unreadable because none of your objects have recognizable names. Just imagine trying to edit code for a command button that launches a particular form when you have 100 command buttons on your form and you can't remember whether you were looking for Command53 or Command91.

You can create multiple command buttons using the previous steps. When you're done, your form might look something like Figure 1-9. Save your form and close it. The next step in creating your switchboard is configuring your form to launch when you start your database. Use the following steps to configure a start-up form.

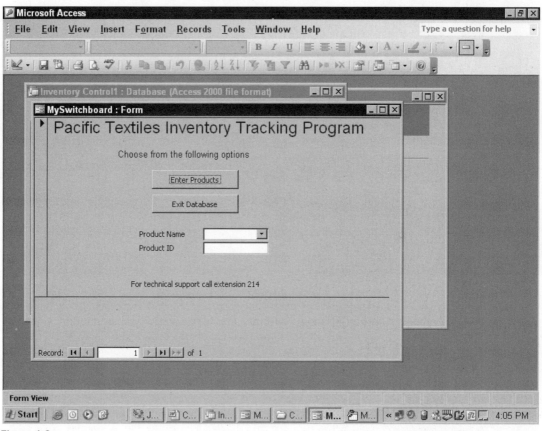

Figure 1-9

1. Choose Startup from the Tools menu (see Figure 1-10). The dialog box that is displayed allows you to enter a title for your entire application, specify an application icon, a customized menu bar, and specify a startup form.

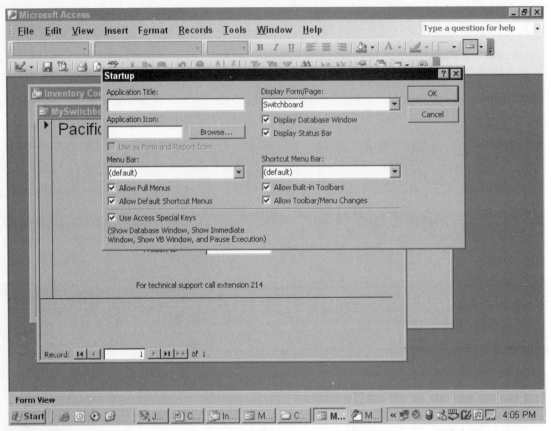

Figure 1-10

2. Use the drop-down box marked `Display Form/Page` and choose the switchboard form you created previously.

3. You can also choose whether users will see the Database Window and Status Bar or whether they will only see your custom switchboard form. If you're worried about users fiddling with the tables, forms, and reports in your database, it's often helpful to hide the Database Window. Savvy users can still access the Database Window (unless you take further steps to secure the database), but hiding the Database Window through the startup form at least makes it a little less tempting to fiddle.

4. Click OK to save your changes.

The next time you launch your database, the `MySwitchboard` form will automatically load for your users. You can have several switchboards within your application. For example, you might want to have a main switchboard that allows your users to explore various aspects of the application such as data entry, reporting, and application options (such as toolbar customizations or security options). When your users select the reporting button, you can launch a separate reporting switchboard with buttons for all of the reports in your application.

Create a Switchboard through the Switchboard Manager

There's another easy way to create a switchboard for your application. You can use the Switchboard Manager to create a new switchboard or edit an existing switchboard. Choose Database Utilities from the Tools menu and select Switchboard Manager from the popout menu (see Figure 1-11).

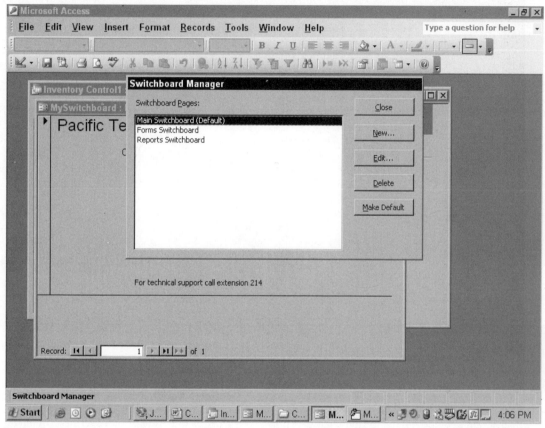

Figure 1-11

To create a new switchboard, click the New button. Enter a name for your new switchboard. Once you've created your switchboard, click Edit to control the items displayed on your switchboard. For a new switchboard, there won't be any items on the switchboard. Now click New (Figure 1-12). You can enter the text displayed on your switchboard and choose a command from the drop-down menu. You can choose from eight different commands including opening a form in add or edit mode, exiting the application, running a report, or running code or a macro. Depending on the command you choose, the third drop-down menu will change and allow you to choose a particular form, report, or macro.

Once you've added all of the necessary commands to your switchboard form, click Close to return to the Switchboard Manager. If you want your new switchboard to launch when the database loads, select it in the Switchboard Pages box and click Make Default. When you're done manipulating your switchboards, click Close.

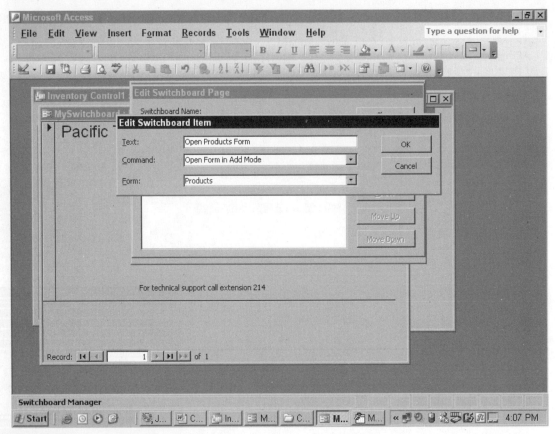

Figure 1-12

Add and Configure Controls Using Wizards

In addition to the command button wizards, you can use wizards to populate list boxes and combo boxes on your form. The Combo Box Wizard allows you to control the data within your combo box, as well as how the combo box is displayed. To launch the Combo Box Wizard, click the `Combo Box` icon in the `Control Toolbox` and click your form to place the combo box on your form. The first step of the Combo Box Wizard, shown in Figure 1-13, prompts you to choose where the data for your combo box comes from.

If you choose to type in the values you want, Access allows you to enter the data directly in the wizard. You can enter as many values as you need in multiple columns. Don't worry if you can't think of every option you want in your combo box, you can always go back and enter more options later.

If your combo box values are stored in a table or query, the second step of the Combo Box Wizard (shown in Figure 1-14) allows you to choose a table or query as the source of your combo box. Click `Next` to choose the fields in the table you want displayed in your combo box. The next step allows you to specify a sort order for your combo box. Click `Next` again to configure the column width of your combo box. Click `Next` one last time to give your combo box a label. Click `Finish` to save your combo box.

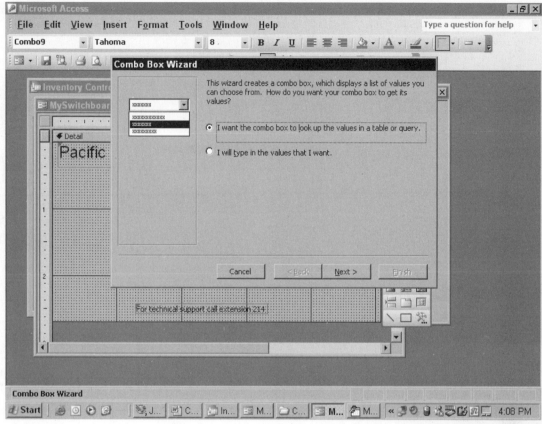

Figure 1-13

The Combo Box Wizard doesn't allow you to enter a name for your combo box. A generic name, such as Combo5 is used instead. As previously mentioned, it's best to rename your combo box with some sort of meaningful name such as cboProducts.

If you create a combo box on a form that displays records in a table or query, you can choose one additional option when creating your combo box. You can choose to find a record on your form based on the value selected in the combo box. If you do this, Access actually adds code behind your combo box.

Building Automation into Your Project

Access can help you build a quick macro in response to a control's event. There are two ways you can build an event:

❏   Click the Build button on the toolbar (it looks like a magic wand).

❏   Click to select the control and choose its properties. Click the Event tab of the Properties dialog box. When you click the event you want, an Ellipses icon will appear next to the event. Click the icon to launch the builder, as shown in Figure 1-15.

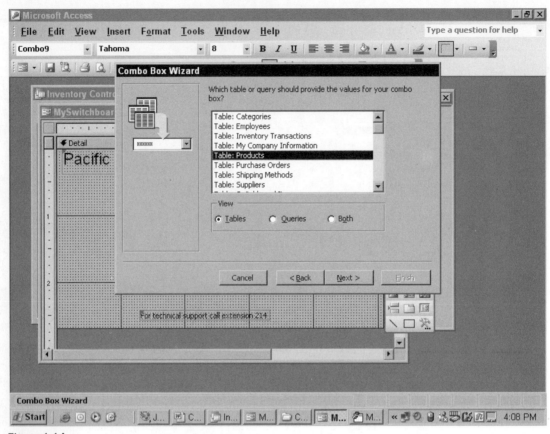

Figure 1-14

You can choose the Expression Builder, the Macro Builder, or the Code Builder. Choosing the Expression Builder displays Figure 1-16.

Using Expression Builder

The Expression Builder does just that—allows you to build an expression with the various fields and controls in your database. For example, in response to the click event of a command button, you can populate a text box on your form with the name of a particular product from the Products table. To build your expression, double-click the Tables branch of the tree in the bottom-left pane of the Expression Builder. Choose the Products table and all of the fields from that table appear in the middle pane of the Expression Builder. Double-click the ProductName field. You can perform a conditional and comparison operations within the Expression Builder as well. For example, you could enter the following in the Expression Builder:

```
=MsgBox("Enter a Product ID between 1 and 10")
```

This code displays a message box informing the user what sort of data to enter in a text box. You can put this code in one of the events of the txtProductID text box. There are a variety of types of expressions

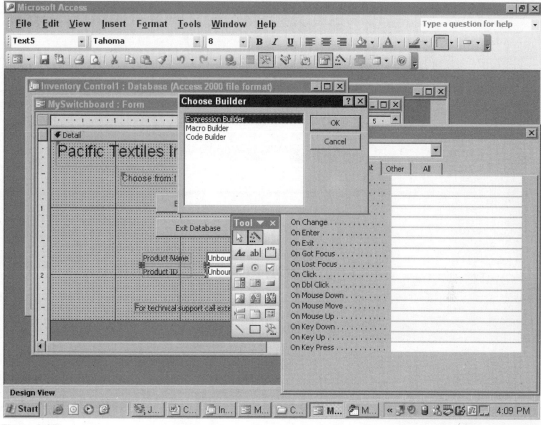

Figure 1-15

you can build. Access includes a variety of built in functions you can use within the Expression Builder, including mathematical functions, financial functions, and text comparison functions.

Using the Macro Builder

The Macro Builder opens a new blank macro for you to work with. Before you can work with your macro, you'll need to enter the macro's name. Click OK to save your blank macro. You can now choose from a variety of actions to include in your macro. Click the first line of the Actions column to choose an action from the drop-down menu. Depending on the action you choose, you might have to enter additional information to complete your macro. For example, if you choose RunApp from the Actions combo, you'll need to enter the command line used to start the application. To launch Outlook in response to the click of a command button, choose RunApp from the Actions menu and enter outlook.exe in the command line box. The second column in the macro window allows you to enter a description for any macro action you choose.

You can choose several macro commands to run in the same macro. Simply enter each command on its own line in the Actions column and continue to pay attention to the additional required parameters.

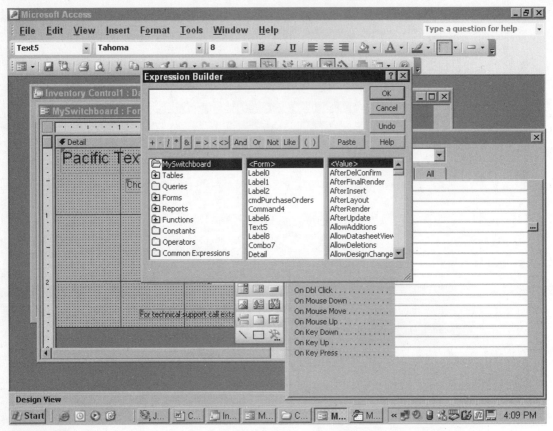

Figure 1-16

When you're done creating your macro, close it and return to your form. Unlike the `Expression Builder`, the macro you create through `Macro Builder` can be used anywhere without recreating it each and every time. Simply click in an event in the `Properties` dialog box and choose your newly created Macro from the drop-down list.

Using the Code Builder

We won't go into much detail about the `Code Builder` in this chapter. All the `Code Builder` does is open up the Visual Basic Editor and takes you right to the specific procedure you choose. For example, if you invoke the code builder for the Click event of a command button named `cmdOpenProducts`, you'll see the following in the Visual Basic Editor:

```
Private Sub cmdOpenProducts_Click()
End Sub
```

From here it's up to you to write the code you want to run in response to the click event of your button.

Summary

The various sections in this chapter detail a few of the ways you can automate your Access application without writing any code. However, this is a book about Access 2003 VBA, so you're probably wondering when we're going to write some code. Stay tuned. Chapter 2 introduces you to the basics of VBA development. If you're experienced in VBA you can probably skip this chapter; however, if you are new to VBA development, or you just want a refresher course in some of the basics, be sure to read Chapter 2. The rest of the book breaks down VBA in Access into manageable topics, going into detail about each one.

2

Access, VBA, and Macros

If you've read the first chapter, you've examined the various wizards available in Access to add automation to your database and probably you're not satisfied. Your database needs more. It's just about time to write some VBA code to work with your Access database. Before you do this, you'll need a basic understanding of VBA and how it's used within Access. This chapter covers the differences between VBA and macros within Access, as well as a bit about using VBA within Access. We'll also provide information about the differences you'll find between Access VBA and other forms of VBA, such as VBA in Excel or VBA in Word.

VBA within Access

If you're reading this book, you've made the decision to use VBA within Access to develop your application. VBA within Access can be implemented in several places, such as writing VBA code within modules and behind controls on forms and reports. We'll take a quick look at both types of code in this section. Later chapters will provide in-depth coverage of VBA within forms and reports as well as the many different uses of VBA within modules.

Writing Code within Modules

A module is a container for code. You can store various subs, functions, and declarations within a module. To view all modules currently available in your Access database, click the Modules tab of the Access action pane. To view a module, select the module and choose Design from the database window's toolbar (see Figure 2-1).

We'll go into details on the various components of the VBA Editor in the Chapter 4, "VBA Basics," but you'll notice that by default, the VBA Editor contains a Project Explorer, a Properties dialog box, and the main code editor. If you have various modules available in your project, they will be listed in the Project Explorer in the upper-left corner of the screen. The Properties dialog box displays the properties for the currently selected object (either the module itself, or a control or form within the module).

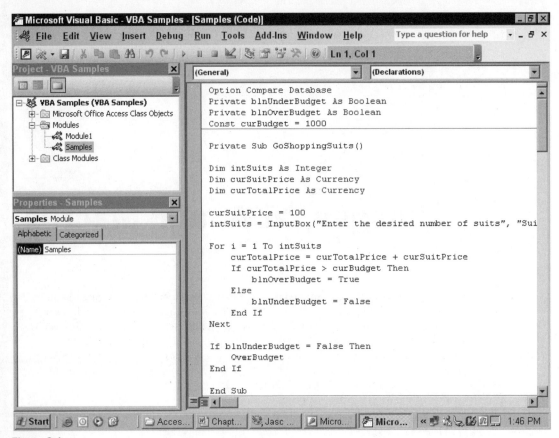

Figure 2-1

Writing Code Behind Forms and Reports

Chapter 4 goes into detail about the VBA Editor within Access. But before you dive head first into VBA, you might want to get your feet wet by writing some basic code within a form. Every object on a form has a number of events you can respond to through VBA. Most objects or controls have a click event, a change event, and enter and exit events, just to name a few. You can add code to any of these events and that code will run in response to a user's actions on your form. Chapter 1 introduced you to the Build Event option, a way to build macros, expressions, or code. We'll cover this topic in a bit more detail here. Open an Access database and view a form in design mode. To build code in response to a control's event, click once to select the control. Display the Properties dialog box by clicking the Properties icon on the toolbar or right clicking the Control and choosing Properties. Once you have the Properties dialog box visible, click the Event tab. Choose the control's event in the Properties dialog box and click the Ellipses button (...) next to the Event box. Choose Code Builder from the dialog box that appears to display the VBA Editor, as shown in Figure 2-2.

You'll notice two differences between Figure 2.1 and Figure 2.2. First of all, the Properties dialog box shows all of the properties for the control you selected on your form. From this dialog box you can change any number of properties of the form including size, ControlTipText, and TabIndex. The second difference is subtle, but if you examine the Project Explorer in the upper-left corner of the window,

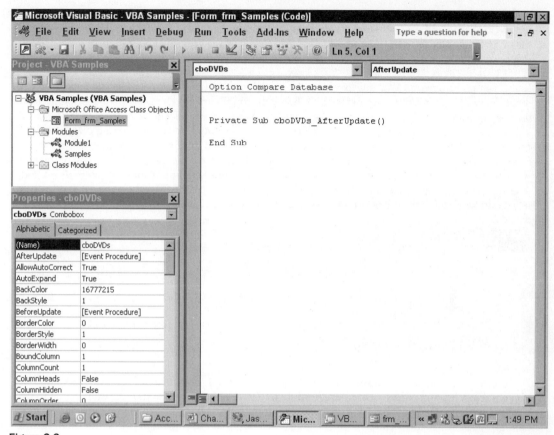

Figure 2-2

you'll notice that there's a new heading, Microsoft Office Access Class Objects. Under that heading is the name of the currently loaded form that contains the control you're currently working with.

The code window displays the name of the control you're working with and the event you chose. Whenever you choose to build code, a subroutine (sub) is created for you automatically. A function, the other main type of code block you'll write, is used when your code needs to return a value. Since you're writing code in response to an event on the form, you're not actually returning a value. You might update the value of the control on the form within the sub, but the actual sub itself doesn't return a value.

Other than the differences listed previously, the VBA Editor used to build code in response to a control's event is identical to that available in a module. The next chapter will go into detail about the various programming components you'll need to work within VBA.

VBA versus Macros in Access

Now that you've seen a little about how VBA works within Access you might be chomping at the bit to get started. However, there's one other scenario you should consider before jumping into Access programming without looking back: a macro. You can create a macro—a saved series of commands. Unlike in Word and Excel, where you can record your own macros, in Access you'll have to create the macro yourself, step-by-step. A macro enables you to perform a variety of operations within Access in response to the click of a command button or any other programmable event on a form or report.

If you've programmed in Word or Excel, you know that you can create a macro by starting the macro recorder and performing the desired steps. When you stop the macro recorder, all of the operations you've performed, from mouse clicks to keyboard strokes to menu selections, are recorded and saved in VBA code. You can then run the macro at a later time by selecting it from the `Macros` dialog box or in response to a keyboard or menu shortcut. Once you've recorded your macro, you can examine the VBA code behind the macro by simply choosing `Edit` from the `Macros` dialog box. This is one of the easiest ways to learn some VBA code within Word or Excel. For example, if you want to know the VBA code to insert three lines of text at the end of your Word document, just create a Word document start recording a macro, and type your three lines of text. You'll end up with code that looks similar to the following:

```
Sub InsertName()
' InsertName Macro
' Macro recorded 9/21/2003 by Patricia Cardoza
    Selection.TypeText Text:="Patricia Cardoza"
    Selection.TypeParagraph
    Selection.TypeText Text:="MIS Application Specialist"
    Selection.TypeParagraph
    Selection.TypeText Text:="Pacific Southwest Container"
    Selection.TypeParagraph
End Sub
```

As you can see, there are some keywords you need to know before you can program Word to do what you want in VBA. Recording a macro in Word first, then perusing the commands can help you to figure out how to write more sophisticated code directly in the VBA Editor. As shown in the previous code listing, `TypeText` is the method of the `Selection` object that allows you to enter your own text within the document. `TypeParagraph` inserts a carriage return in the document. These are just two of the many methods you can use with the `Selection` object. While very few programmers ever need to use every method of an object, you can write better VBA code by familiarizing yourself with some of the most frequently used methods of the objects you'll be dealing with.

While Word and Excel have the ability to record macros, Access doesn't have this capability. To write VBA code in Access, you'll have to just jump right in and code. However, if you aren't quite ready for VBA code yet, you can still create detailed macros using the Macro Editor in Access. The only limitation is that you can't record a macro; you must create it yourself step-by-step. This book is the *Access 2003 VBA Programmer's Reference* so we won't spend much time on Macros, but we'll provide a very brief tutorial on creating and using macros in Access here.

Macros in Access 2003

This section provides an introduction to using macros in Access 2003. Not much has changed in the last several versions of Access with respect to macro recording, but if you're just picking up Access 2003 for the first time, this section is for you.

You can use macros for a variety of tasks in Access. Even though it might sound a bit crazy, we usually prefer to write code rather than create a macro. However, that's not always the easiest or most logical method of automation. Access 2003 includes 55 built-in macro commands. Many have additional conditions that can be set. For example, if you choose the `OpenDataAccessPage` macro action, you'll need to select an existing Data Access Page in your database. You can also choose whether to open the Data Access Page in `Browse View` or `Design View`. Other macro actions have similar additional required arguments.

To create a new macro, navigate to the `Macros` tab of the Access 2003 `TaskPane` and click `New`; Access displays the new Macro window, see Figure 2-3. The default name for your new macro is `Macro1`, but you should change the name when you save the macro. There's nothing inherently wrong with naming your macro `Macro1`, but it doesn't give you very much of a clue about what the macro is for. It's better to give your macro a descriptive name, such as `mcr_OpenForm` (which follows the Reddick naming conventions) or even something as simple as `GoToRecord` (which can be the name of the action the macro performs). Whatever you name your macro (and whether or not you choose to follow Reddick's conventions or create your own conventions) make sure you can easily discern the purpose of the macro when you're looking at your Access 2003 database objects.

When I started programming in Access I didn't have a book like this to learn from. So I created many queries with the name Query1, Query2, Macro1, Macro2, and so on. While the queries and macros I created worked just fine, when I then had to update those databases years later, I couldn't remember what

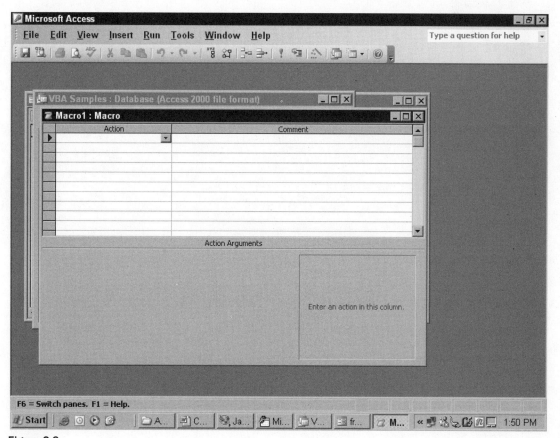

Figure 2-3

each individual query and macro did. I had to go through each query and macro one-by-one and rename them according to their purpose before I could update the database. Don't make the same mistakes I did when I started Access development.

Now that you've opened up a blank macro, click the first line of the Action column to display the Actions drop-down menu shown in Figure 2-4.

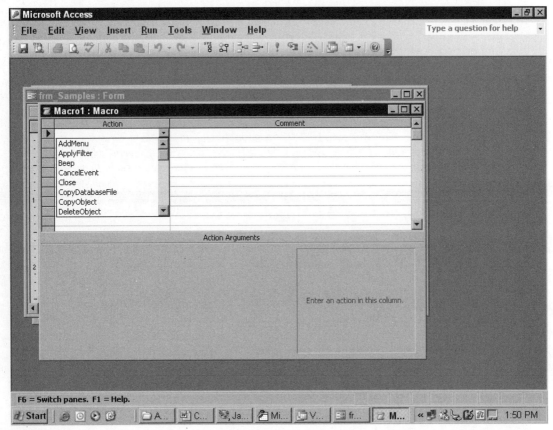

Figure 2-4

To implement an action, click the Action name to add it to your macro. Depending on the action you choose, you'll see additional criteria appear in the Action Arguments section of the window. Not all actions have arguments. In particular the Beep, CancelEvent, FindNext, Maximize, Minimize, Restore, ShowAllRecords, and StopMacro actions don't have arguments. Figure 2-5 shows a macro with several different actions. The Action Arguments is shown for the OpenForm action.

For readability, some Access programmers like to group their actions in a macro, leaving a blank line between groups of actions. There's nothing wrong with this practice; however, there's no advantage to it either.

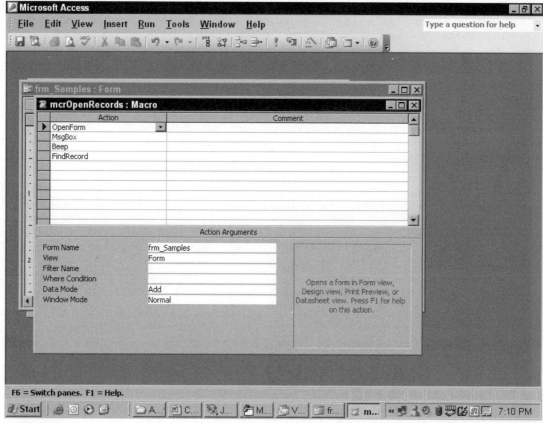

Figure 2-5

Now that you've completed your macro, save you changes and exit. However, what good is a macro if you don't have a way to call it? One of the common uses for a macro and one of the easiest ways to use one is in response to the click event of a command button on a form. To associate a macro with the click event of a command button, use the following steps:

1. Within the design of your form, choose a command button.

2. Click the `Properties` toolbar button to display the properties window for the command button.

3. Click the `Event` tab of the `Properties` dialog box.

4. Click in the `OnClick` line of the `Properties` dialog box to display the drop-down arrow.

5. From the drop-down list choose the name of your macro. All macros in your database are listed in the drop-down list.

6. Save and run your form. Clicking the command button will run each action in the macro sequentially.

You can also call macros from within your code. You might wonder why you would ever call a macro from within code. After all, you're already writing code, why not just write code to accomplish the steps in the macro? Well, we can't give you a definitive answer to that question, except to say that if you already have a perfectly good macro that does what you need, why not use it? Writing code to duplicate a working macro is like taking two steps backward for every one step forward. On the other hand, sometimes you just want everything in one place. If so, go ahead and duplicate your macro actions within code.

Advantages to Using VBA over Macros

While macros are perfectly acceptable and even recommended in certain situations, there are some key advantages to using VBA instead of a macro. The following is a list of some of the advantages you'll enjoy using VBA instead of a macro.

❑ *Error Handling*: If a macro encounters an error, it just stops. For example, a macro created to open a form will fail if the form can't be found. While Access will provide a fairly detailed error message informing you the macro failed, you can't add any error handling. If you're writing a macro to add a menu item to the menu bar, how can you be sure the code only runs once? If the code were to run twice, you could end up with two instances of the same menu listed on your menu bar. Using VBA code for this task is more appropriate as you can test to see if the menu has already been added. If not, the code runs; if so, the code does not run or displays a graceful error message. In some circumstances, running your macro could even crash the entire Access application.

❑ *Speed*: A one-action macro will probably execute faster than the equivalent VBA code. However, running a complex macro with 10 or 12 actions usually takes significantly longer than the equivalent code. VBA code within Access is fast. If you're designing an end-user application, you definitely need to be concerned with speed. If your users see the hourglass for even more than 5 or 6 seconds, their perception will be that your application is slow.

❑ *Functionality*: With 55 macro actions, how could you ever miss functionality? We're being facetious, of course—if all Access programming were limited to 55 actions, there wouldn't be very many applications written in Access. How would you ever display a custom error message, play a sound other than the default "beep" or open an HTML file in response to a button click? VBA provides so much more functionality than Access macros. Some of the key functionality is the ability to interact with other applications. Using VBA, you can open Word or Excel files, send e-mail from Outlook, open an Internet Explorer browser and navigate to a particular Web site, or open almost any file stored on your computer or a network drive. External application access isn't limited to Microsoft products either. You can add a reference to any number of applications through the References dialog box in Access VBA. Once you've added a reference, you can control other applications such as Adobe Acrobat, VMWare, or Yahoo Messenger. You can also take advantage of many Web services such as MapPoint and CarPoint.

❑ *Control*: With VBA, you can exercise almost complete control over your code. Instead of working with macros where you are must let the chosen macro actions perform the work, you can control each step of the process in VBA. Macros can't ask for a variety of variables to input into an equation. They can't dynamically create an ADO connection based on user input. They also can't run a different set of actions for each user of your application. VBA can accomplish all of these tasks with ease.

❑ *Interaction with other applications*: When using VBA within Access you're not limited to merely programming Microsoft Access. You can add references to other object libraries such as Word, Excel, Outlook, and even non-Microsoft programs including accounting packages, drafting programs, and even graphics programs.

Summary

This chapter covered the basics of VBA within Access, creating some basic macros within Access, and finally, why you might want to use VBA instead of a macro within Access. If you're going to use VBA however, you'll need to understand the various components of VBA programming. Chapter 3 covers what's new in Access 2003. Chapter 4 covers properties, methods, and events as well as goes into detail about the interactions between the three. If you're an experienced VBA programmer, you can skip the next chapter. However, if you're a self-taught programmer (and there are many out there) or just want a refresher course on the basics, take a look at Chapter 4, "VBA Basics."

3

New Features in Access 2003 (and 2002)

This chapter is different than the others. Instead of focusing on one topic or providing a tutorial on how to do things, this chapter is intended to highlight the powerful new features in Access.

Between Access 2002 and 2003, there are some very cool features that will save a lot of time and give you more power, flexibility, and reach. We'll cover:

- ❑ Easy upgrading
- ❑ Key benefits for developers
- ❑ Wizards and builders
- ❑ Changes in Jet—install Service Pack 8
- ❑ Macro security
- ❑ End-user benefits
- ❑ Integrating with SharePoint
- ❑ XML support
- ❑ Access Developer Extensions

Easy Upgrading

First and foremost, developers need to know about the issues surrounding upgrading and converting. Fortunately, it is very easy and painless to upgrade from Access 2000 or Access 2002 to Access 2003. In fact, 2002 and 2003 have the same file format. The only real differences between 2002 and 2003 are the several new features. And converting from the Access 2000 file format to 2003 is as easy as selecting `Convert` on the `Convert/Enable` dialog window. This is covered in detail in

Appendix A. But the fact is that you can use Access 2003 to make design changes in both Access 2000 and Access 2002–2003 files. So, if a 2002 database was saved as an Access 2000 file format, Access 2003 can be used to make design changes and the file will still open with Access 2000.

You can use Access 2003 to make design changes in both Access 2000 and Access 2002–2003 format files.

The important message here is that upgrading is managed quite effectively by Access—one might say, "even seamlessly." And with the click of the mouse, you can even convert from 2003 back to Access 2000 or 97. To convert a database to Access 97, 2000, or 2002–2003 file format, start by clicking `Tools`, and select `Database Utilities`. Then, click `Convert Database` and select the file format. Then, respond to the dialog boxes to select and convert the database. As an extra precaution, the converter ensures that the original file is retained, and it will not let you replace the existing file with the newly converted file. So, unless the developer deletes or changes the original file, it will be there. After all, it may be needed as a reference to make an MDE or for any number of other reasons.

Not to keep beating this drum, but this is unprecedented. We can do development work in Access 2003 and, when we think the application is ready, save a copy in the previous version's file format and test it on the oldest platform that will host the application. For example, you may need to accommodate some people using Windows 98 and running Access 2000. Then, after everything is tested and running smoothly, use the older version of Access to make the MDE from the file created with Access 2003. That's because although Access 2003 will save a file to a previous version's format, it will only make MDEs with the 2002–2003 file format. However, all that development time was gloriously spent in 2003!

If there are any errors encountered when converting a database, Access conveniently records the information in a `Conversion Errors` table. This table displays the Object Type, Object Name, and Error description. Just having confidence that various versions can be upgraded and/or work together isn't enough to justify upgrading. But, being able to save time and develop with the other powerful new features in Access 2003 is very enticing. Next, we will look at some of the features that will save a considerable amount of time while helping to build stronger applications.

Database Structure and Management Tools for Developers

As developers, we are always seeking ways to improve and leverage our skills. And, Access 2003 has many new tools that are specifically designed to help efficiently develop powerful applications.

Find Object Dependencies

As a database grows it can be difficult to keep track of object dependencies. For example, several forms could be relying on one query, or a subform could be associated with more than one form. After a while, a developer can become wary of changing or deleting objects, even if he or she is the only developer associated with that database. Things can be even worse if you inherit an application. Talk about proceeding with trepidation. You can now shelve those fears; Viewing Object Dependencies has come to the rescue.

Viewing object dependencies allows you to view what the object depends on as well as what objects depend on it. For example, by selecting a query, you could see what forms and reports are using it and you could also see if it was relying on a form or other queries. The tree view will show tables, queries, forms, and reports that are in the database. However, it will not show macros, VBA code, Data pages, SQL-specific queries, and Access projects. Figure 3-1 shows how to select a table to view the objects that depend on it. By selecting the other option, it will list the objects that it depends on. So, with a couple of clicks, you can look at both types of object dependencies.

The Object Dependencies feature only applies to MDB files.

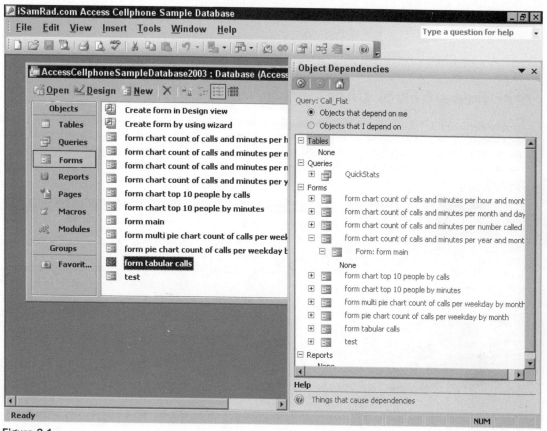

Figure 3-1

The Object Dependencies feature employs the functionality of tree view. As shown in Figure 3-1, you can drill into the dependencies. Actually, this feature will allow navigating up to four levels. However, since the information is based on the name maps maintained by the Name AutoCorrect feature, the tracking function of Name AutoCorrect must be turned on; please note that this does not require Name AutoCorrect to be enabled, but merely turned on. Another nice thing is that if Name AutoCorrect was not turned on before requesting to see the dependencies, a dialog box will prompt you to turn it on. Then, if you choose to turn it on, Access will proceed to display the requested dependency information.

> In order for Object Dependencies to be viewed, the Name AutoCorrect feature needs to be turned on. However, it does not have to be enabled.

To view Object Dependencies, from the View menu item select Object Dependencies. At that point, if Name AutoCorrect was not turned on, there will be a prompt to turn it on so as to view the dependencies. To view Hidden Objects, the Show-Hidden Objects will need to be selected on the View tab of the Options dialog box (under Tools | Options).

A word of caution here: Don't rely solely on the dependency lists when deciding to delete database objects. There are several objects that will not show up on the dependency view. Access Help "About Object Dependencies" provides detailed information about which dependencies are shown as well as what types of objects are not included.

Form/Report Error Checking

If you are an independent developer, you might think of this as your on-call quality assurance team. All developers know that a fresh set of eyes can be very effective at finding errors that are overlooked. And, it saves a lot of time to catch them early in the process. Well, this feature can flag common errors as they are made. You can't get more timely feedback than this. In addition to flagging errors, the process will even offer solutions.

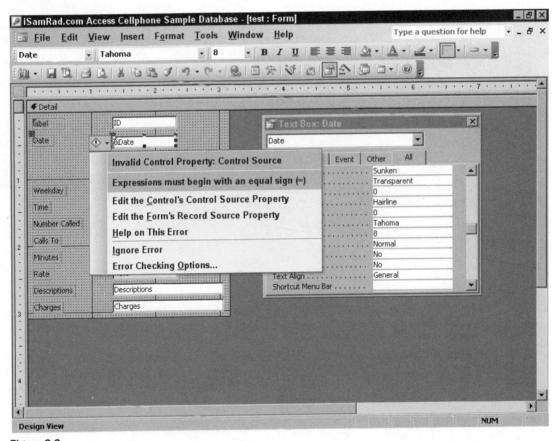

Figure 3-2

Since multiple errors can simultaneously occur on the same object, the errors will be ranked from highest to lowest priority. By clicking the error indicator, you can correct or ignore each error. Figure 3-2 shows an example of multiple errors on one control.

Sometimes you just don't want to hear about everything that Access thinks is an error. Access provides the options to not only turn error checking on and off but to specify the settings. This allows you to limit the types of errors that are flagged. You can even select the color used to flag errors. To set these options, once again, choose `Options` from the `Tools` menu and then select `Error Checking`. Figure 3-3 shows how to specify which errors should be flagged.

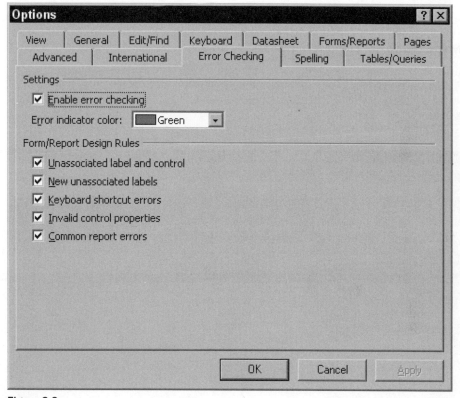

Figure 3-3

The common error scenarios that are flagged include the following.

❑ Unassociated label and control—When a label and a control are selected but they are not associated with each other.

❑ New unassociated label—If a label is added to a form or control and it is not associated with any control.

❑ Invalid control source—The control source property is not a valid expression or field name, the expression specified does not start with "=", or the expression refers to the control itself—a circular reference.

❑ Duplicate Option values—The Option value property is not unique in the option group.

❏ Keyboard shortcut errors—Such as an unassociated label with a keyboard shortcut, a label or control that has a shortcut that is already associated with another label or control, and a space character as a shortcut key.

❏ Invalid sorting and grouping definitions for a report.

❏ Report width greater than page width.

Propagate Field Properties

Changes to field properties can quickly and easily cascade to corresponding properties of controls on forms and reports. And as always, there are a few caveats, such as, this is feature does not apply to Access projects and the control property will not be updated if:

❏ The control already has a different value specified in the property sheet

❏ The control is on a Data Access Page

❏ The field property is changed in a linked table

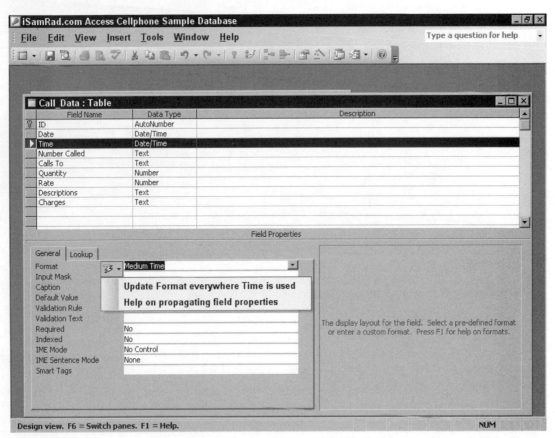

Figure 3-4

When an inheritable property is updated, the New `Property Update Options` button will appear, as shown in Figure 3-4.

Clicking the button opens the `Updates Properties` dialog box (see Figure 3-5). This allows you to choose to update the corresponding controls that are bound to that field. You can conveniently see all of the places that the control can be updated and select/unselect all or specific locations to be updated. Again, the Access team has provided the information and given the developer the final decision.

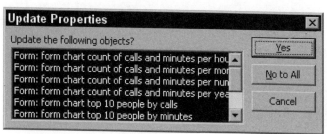

Figure 3-5

Customize SQL Font

Finally, you can choose the font for SQL and Query Views. Of course, there is reason to be judicious when selecting a font. Not everyone would be happy looking at script in their queries. But, using special fonts can give a bit of personality to screen shots. Notice that the font appears in both the query grid and the SQL view. Thankfully, it does not appear that changing the font used in queries will affect the appearance of the database sheet views.

When giving a presentation, you could have fun by customizing the SQL font, and even changing the font to suit the audience.

To change the font, click `Tools` on the menu bar, and then click `Options`. This will open the `Options` dialog window. The query design font is on the lower left of the `Table/Queries` tab. The font type and size can be quickly changed via the `Options` menu. The `Query Design Font` is on the lower left of the `Tables/Queries` tab. Figure 3-6 shows how changing the font can affect the readability of the SQL view. The selected font will also be used in the query grid. Figure 3-7 shows what Chiller font looks like in the query grid. So when you are preparing a presentation, keep in mind that changing the font to make it larger, easier to read, or even just more striking is certainly something worth considering.

Did you know that you can also change the font used by the Zoom Wizard?

You can also modify the font when using the Zoom feature. To do this, right-click in a query criteria field and then select `Zoom`. In the lower right, click the font and you'll see the familiar dialog box for selecting a custom font. This cool feature was added by Michael Kaplan. Figure 3-7 shows how to change the zoom font as well as the effect of selecting a font such as Kristen. And, as expected with a really good tool, you get to see what the font will look like before it is applied. Now that demonstrates the benefit of having a developer add features. They are one of us so they know what will help.

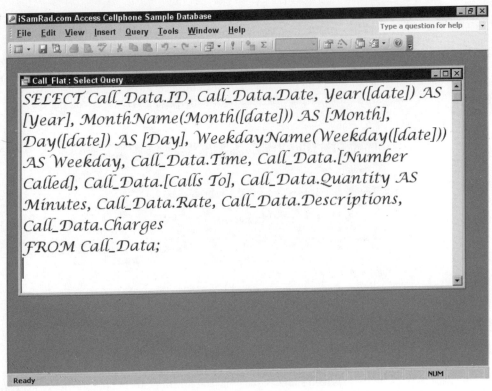

Figure 3-6

Get Context-Sensitive SQL Help

When you are working in Access (not the VBE) and need help with a SQL statement, the natural instinct may be to click Help. In the past, this typically led to a futile search, followed by opening the VBE window and starting the search all over again. With Access 2003, you can get help with your code without opening the VBE. There are several ways to get SQL help from within Access.

❑ The most convenient is typically to hit *F1*: From the SQL view put the cursor on the keyword that you want help with and then hit *F1*. Voila, the answer to the question!

❑ The next most obvious way is to open Access Help and type in the SQL Keywords.

❑ Alternatively, open Access Help and type in Aggregate Functions, VBA Functions, or Access Functions.

❑ And, there is also Access Help's Table of Contents. This is impressively extensive, especially if it includes online help. You can just keep drilling. There are at least six layers. Now that's organized.

> Note: If you're working in an ADP, you'll still need to use the VBE to get help with SQL.

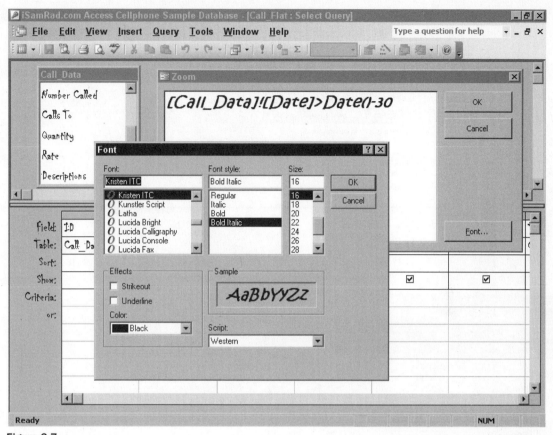

Figure 3-7

To get help from the Table of Contents, open Access Help and click Table of Contents. Under the Creating and Working with Databases and Objects folder, click Database objects, and then click Queries to display the Microsoft Jet SQL Reference folder. Keep going because there are still at least two more levels. It would take more than a day to study all the material just in this folder alone. Figure 3-8 shows the Table of Contents opened to display Help with Access functions.

It is important to note that the Microsoft Jet SQL Reference folder does not include the links to Data Access Object (DAO) reference topics and examples. It would be a little too confusing to have DAO and ActiveX Data Object (ADO) in the same folder. However, help with DAO is provided in a couple of other folders that are at the bottom of the Table of Contents. Obviously, it would be in the folder Microsoft DAO 3.60. And, it is also in the Microsoft Jet SQL Reference folder that is just below the DAO 3.60 folder.

> **If you are looking for help with DAO, you need to look in the folders named Microsoft DAO 3.60 or Microsoft Jet SQL Reference.**

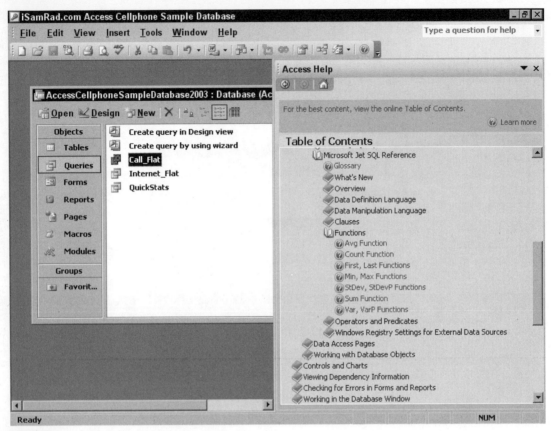

Figure 3-8

Backup Database/Project

Finally, a consistent, fast, and easy way to save your work. We can't tell you how many times we've either closed and zipped a database, or copied and renamed a database object to test some changes. Pretty soon the database window is filled with nonfunctional objects. And heaven forbid that someone forgets if `Name AutoCorrect` was on, which can result in the code referring to the wrong object.

Again, the Access team felt the developer's pain and provided an awesome solution. You don't even have to worry about specifying where to save the file or giving the file a unique name. The backup command will automatically (1) default to the folder that contains the database and (2) give the file a unique name, based on the current file name with a suffix of the current date. And, if a backup already exists for that date, an incrementally numbered extension will be added to the date. Figure 3-9 shows the `Save Backup As` dialog window.

It only takes three mouse clicks to create a backup. Click `File` on the main menu and then click `Backup Database`. In the `Save Backup` window, click `Save`. You can also expend the energy for four mouse clicks if you take the path of `Tools, Database Utilities,` and then click `Backup Database`. And for the hot key fanatics, just use *Alt+F+K+S*. This feature is going to save so much time and reduce database bloat by eliminating unneeded objects. Similarly, using a wizard can save time.

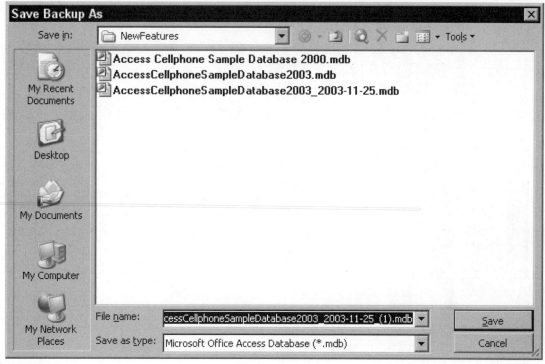

Figure 3-9

Sorting Option on Lookup Wizard

In the past, many developers found the Combo Box Wizard to be a great tool for starting a combo box, but then needed to modify the SQL to accommodate additional fields, to include criteria or for any number of other reasons. Now the combo box, list box, and Lookup Wizards allow you to specify the sort order on up to four fields. Figure 3-10 shows the Combo Box Wizard sort order dialog box. Combo Box Wizard not only provides about as many options as the Report Wizard, but it also allows you to preview the data and drag the columns to their desired widths.

Figure 3-11 shows how easy it is to set the column widths.

Speaking of combo boxes and list boxes, in Access 2002 AddItem and RemoveItem methods were added. Now these work more like they do on Microsoft Visual Basic and Visual Basic for Applications (VBA) forms. The methods are available only when the RowSourceType property is set to Value List.

Copy and Paste Linked Table as Local Table

Most developers work with a lot of linked tables. Occasionally, it would be nice to also work with the table locally. Sometimes it is handy to use the local copy as a temporary worktable, to quickly crunch and manipulate data without putting the "real" data at risk and without being concerned about network connections.

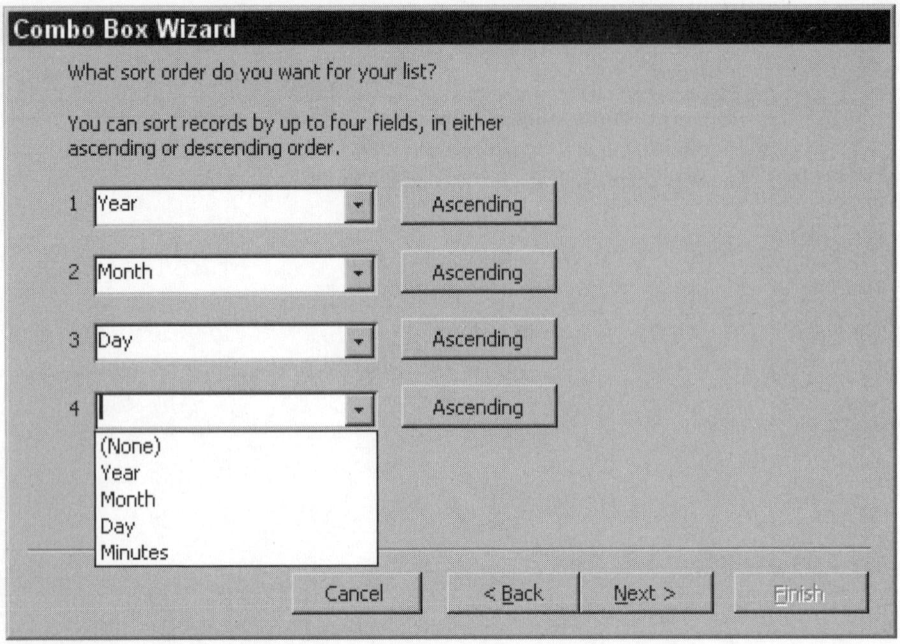

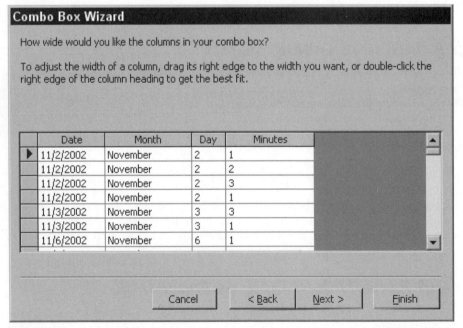

Figure 3-10

Figure 3-11

You no longer have to go through the steps of file, import, and then browse to where ever the data is stored. Now, it is as easy as right-click the linked table, select copy, and then paste with or without the data. Figure 3-12 shows the `Paste Table As` window that you'll see when you are pasting a linked table. It is just copying and pasting a local table; it will not show the references to linked and local.

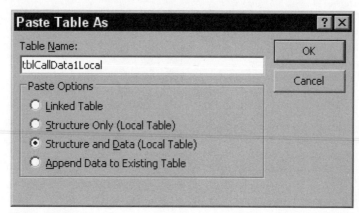

Figure 3-12

By right clicking a linked table, several more actions are listed, such as going directly to the `Linked Table Manager` or exporting the table. The shortcut menus put a lot of options at your fingertips. That covers several of the major new tools for working with tables and data. Given space and time constraints, the following section provides briefer descriptions of several other new features that deserve checking out. Again, these are only highlights and this is not intended to be an exhaustive list.

Notable Mention

There are countless other improvements that you will quickly notice. In fact, there are too many to mention. However, this section will quickly group and summarize some more noteworthy enhancements. This is heavily swayed toward features added in 2003. Since development starts with the table structure, it will be discussed first. The new file format was introduced in Access 2002. This file format has been maintained in Access 2003 and it is now called Access 2002–2003 file format. Access 2002 defaulted to save in the Access 2000 file format. And, it did not require files to be converted to 2002 except to make an MDE. As always, the file format has to match the application version to make an MDE, which means that you have to use the 2002–2003 file format to make an MDE using Access 2003 or Access 2002. Since one version of Access can open multiple file formations, the caption on the database window conveniently and prominently displays the current file format. Figure 3-13 also shows the caption for a 2003 database in the 2003 file format. Reviewing the options provided on the datasheet tab gives you a good idea about how much control you now have over the look and feel of the Access environment.

Forms and reports have such an extensive list of enhancements that all of them cannot be covered here. Obviously, PivotTable and PivotChart views are new. And it is important to know that the report format now allows levels to be expanded or collapsed. Plus, you can save forms and reports as Data Access Page (DAP). Saving to DAPs was added in 2002 and it was greatly improved with the enhanced XML features of 2003. Suffice it to say that working with Web pages is getting easier with each release. This is only fitting since the Internet is critical to our clients and therefore to developers. There are several other new properties and events for both forms and reports. Developers will love the multiple levels of undo and

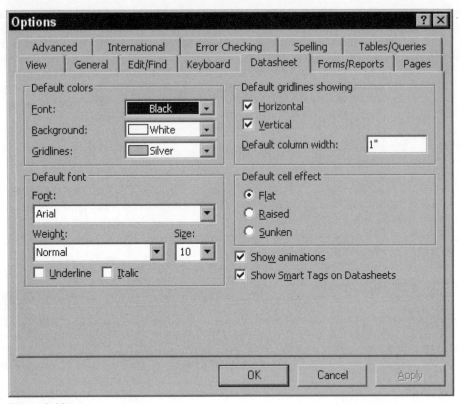

Figure 3-13

redo. In fact, there are so many new events for both forms and reports that you really just need to see them all in Appendix E, "The Access Object Model." You can also find out more about forms in Chapter 10 and about reports in Chapter 11. These chapters emphasize and demonstrate some of the really cool features, controls, tools, and events that are now available in forms and reports.

The Printer object and Printers collection make it easier to programmatically control printing. You can now use the Printer object and Printers collection to specify a specific printer, paper size, tray, and special features without having to open the report, select the printer, and save the report. This is covered in more detail in Appendix E.

Access Projects provide a way of connecting to SQL Server. There have been extensive upgrades and enhancements with regards to ADP and working with SQL Server or the Microsoft Development Environment. This list is indeed too long to enumerate, but let us pique your curiosity with updatable views, batch update as an Access form property, using disconnected recordsets for ADP objects, and even the ease of using the linked table manager to link to SQL Server; Chapter 17, "Understanding Client-Server Development with VBA," is devoted to working effectively with SQL Server.

Compact and repair has been combined into one command and it works better than ever at recovering broken forms and reports. Not only that, but it can even reduce a file size by as much as 70 percent. Talking about reducing file size is a reminder that the regular use of Compile and Save can go a long way toward preventing problems. So, when working in the VBE, make it a habit to click `Debug`, `Compile` at least hourly.

Missing references–Speaking of code, if references are missing, the new message will be more informative and actually tell you what file (reference) it cannot find. So, when you move or open a new database, it is easy to find out if it is necessary to update or correct references. It is so much nicer to fix references before trying to use the application. A lot of developers were frustrated with having to peck through references to figure out what was missing or to get them in the right priority. Thankfully, Access pretty much handles the priority issues. So, when a database is converted from an earlier version of Access, it does a pretty good job of automatically updating references to Microsoft components. There is more about this in Appendix B, "References for Projects."

Speech recognition was introduced in Access 2002 and was improved in 2003. It can be used for both commands and data input. It is not, however, available in Design View. But, who would be brave enough to talk the computer through placing controls on a form. Thinking back to school exercises when we had to tell someone how to draw something, it never came out looking like the original drawing. So, you can only imagine how a dictated form would look.

Multilingual support is provided for both text and graphics. We definitely have a global economy, so our applications need to support the international needs of our clients. Now, you can display multilingual text in tables, forms, and reports if the required fonts are installed. And the multilingual text can be preserved when the data is output to RTF, HTML, text, XML, and Excel file formats. Third party ad-ins are available to assist with extensive conversions into other languages.

In fact, special languages and fonts don't have to be installed for you to start benefiting from the multilingual features in Access. There are already several language dictionaries to choose from on the `Spelling` tab of the `Options` menu. And, the `International` tab allows changing the default cursor direction from moving left-to-right to moving right-to-left. It's pretty easy to see the `International` and `Spelling` tabs of the `Option` window.

Now, it is time to move on to learn about some of the tools that Access provides to do the work for you—specifically, the wizards, builders, and managers. Developers should not be taking these for granted.

New Wizards and Builders and Managers

As developers, we employ the proven engineering principle of building on established technology and techniques. So, even a dyed-in-the-wool coder should at least check out what the wizards, builders, templates, and other add-ins can do. After all, if Access provides a tool or resource, you owe it to yourself to be aware and use it when appropriate. Even if the results need to be modified, these tools can often save precious development time. There are so many tools included in Access 2003 that you can get a jump-start on nearly every object, including the database itself. But, if you don't know what is available, it's not very likely that you will look for it or try to use it. Appendix K provides a fairly comprehensive list of the current wizards, builders, and managers. Since some features are not installed during a typical installation, the tables also use an asterisk after the name to indicate whether the wizard is only installed if the `Additional Wizards` component is selected during set-up. If you don't at least select `Typical Wizards`, the only wizards that will be installed are the `Color Builder`, the `Expression Builder`, and the `Query Builder`.

> Again, our advice is that you should go for the gusto and do a custom install by selecting to have everything run from your computer! Why wait? You know that you will want to at least check out the extra features.

A Wizard for Every Occasion

As you already know, we are aficionados of wizards. And, even if they don't create exactly what you want, wizards lay a foundation that can easily be modified. As mentioned, there were so many new or improved wizards in Access 2002 or Access 2003 that it seemed prudent to provide a complete list. With that in mind, there is a table in Appendix K that lists the currently available wizards. Note the term currently available, because this is a new day for Access at Microsoft. So, there is anticipation that the Access team will continue to add and improve features and wizards.

Although you may not need to use every wizard, it is handy to know what is available and to take advantage of the ones that might be applicable. Fortunately, it typically isn't necessary to search for wizards, because they are strategically placed or programmed to be where they are needed. Builders are equally handy resources for developers.

Available Builders

Wizards are there to do the work behind the scenes and provide a finished product. Builders, on the other hand, are there to guide the developer through a process rather than to do it. We probably use the `Query Builder` more than any other. It makes creating queries fast and intuitive. In fact, it is so easy, that we teach a lot of clients how to use it and give them a separate database just for working with ad hoc queries. The other builder that most developers would not want to be without is the `Expression Builder`. This can even be used in conjunction with a wizard.

Combining the use of builders and wizards is a convenient way to gain some tips and learn about writing code.

In addition to Access-specific builders, there are also some that are pretty much universally available in Microsoft Office, such as the `Color Builder`. There are several other builders that you may benefit from knowing about. The list of builders and what they do is provided in Appendix K.

Once installed, builders can be accessed from the toolbars and shortcut menus. Even though you may not need all of them now, it is often helpful to have them installed from the beginning. In fact, just to use the ODBC (Open Database Connectivity) Connection String Builder requires installing the "Additional Wizards" component. As developers work with more external data sources, the ODBC Connection String Builder will increase its value tenfold.

Most developers are familiar with Smart Tags. They have been used extensively in Word and Excel. So, user awareness can be leveraged as Smart Tags are incorporated into Access applications. They were available in Access 2002, so it is definitely time for them to become more prevalent. In addition to the Smart Tags that ship with Access, more Smart Tags are available on the Internet and you can create your own tags.

As mentioned earlier, it is possible to combine the power of wizards and builders. One example is to use the builder to create a table and then use the Lookup Wizard to set the properties for a look-up field. This is not an endorsement for rampant use of table-level look-up fields. And, that's as far as this discussion will go on table structure. There are entire books dedicated to that subject and there are camps ready to voice an opinion on the right way to manage tables and fields. And, that leads to the discussion of managers.

Managers

You may think of these as wizards, but managers are truly managers. They make things work or, more specifically, they manage how things work together. The linked table manager may be the most familiar manager. This manager makes it fast and easy to link the user interface to various data files. It is also a convenient tool for relinking tables when a database is moved, tables are updated, or an application is repurposed. The list of managers, what they do, and how to find them is given in Appendix K.

The Add-In Manager installs and uninstalls Microsoft and third party add-ins. It also assists developers in creating and adding their own wizards, builders, and menu ad-ins. There is additional information about creating your own add-ins at http://msdn.microsoft.com.

In addition to new features and tools that make work easier for developers, Access 2003 has some changes behind the scenes that you need to know about. All developers and users will need to learn about Service Pack 8 and how to work with macro security and digital signatures.

Changes to Jet

There have not been any major enhancements to jet, but one or two service packs may need to be installed, depending on when Jet was installed. Those using Access 2003 need to install Service Pack 8. This is so important that it will be repeated.

Also, if you plan to use Jet Replication Manager with Jet 4.0 SP7 or later and you do not have Mstran40.exe version 4.0.6508.0, you must also download and install Jet4Repl.exe. The Microsoft Knowledge Base article 321076 provides additional information about how to obtain Jet4Repl.exe.

Service Pack 8

For new installations of Access, it is likely that Jet was not already on the system and therefore, Service Pack 8 (SP8) would not be installed already either. In that case, the first thing to do after installing Office and Access is to download and install Office updates and SP8. All developers know that drill by now. SP8 needs to be installed to work with the new security features. The security messages will quickly become irritatingly familiar. So much so that even developers who seldom dealt with security settings on their personal files will learn how to create a digital signature and to digitally sign a file or macro project. This will be briefly explained in the following discussions as well as thoroughly dissected in Chapter 20, "Macro Security."

> **SP8 needs to be installed in order to block unsafe expressions without affecting common functionality. You can learn more about the Sandbox mode in Chapter 20.**

When installing DLLs that contain code to work with new features in Access of other programs, the following occurred:

❑ Jet 4.0 SP8 fixes the following past problems:

❑ Access quits unexpectedly when linked Oracle table is left inactive.

❑ Access causes an error when you export fields with data type single or double to Oracle.

❑ Performance problems occurred when certain pass-through queries were run.

❑ Microsoft Access unexpectedly quit when you tried to upsize a database where the tables contained triggers. Although the service pack prevents Access from quitting, it still does not permit tables with triggers to be upsized.

❑ Invalid argument error message occurred when you tried to create a linked table by using DAO code after the installation of Jet 4.0 SP7.

❑ An access violation occurred when you ran certain queries that used linked Paradox tables.

❑ Oracle integer field appeared as double in Access.

❑ When you tried to create links to dBase files, you received an access violation or nothing occurred; that is, no link was created and you did not receive an error message.

❑ When you refreshed a linked table, you were prompted to select a DSN even though you were still using the same DSN, and all the connection information was correct.

Security and Related Features

Access 2003 provides several new security features to protect users from malicious code. It may seem strange to have this termed Macro Security, but that's what it is. Developers, users, database administrators, and network administrators are all going to need to get up to speed quickly in learning how to work with macro security and digital signatures. The following is a brief introduction to these topics. Please read Chapter 20 for more detailed explanations.

What Is Macro Security? And Why Are We Talking about Macros?

In this instance, the term *macro* is not referring to macros in the sense of automating some tasks. Instead, it refers to security settings and certifications for VBA and other executable code associated with Access databases and projects.

To avoid macro warnings, attach a digital signature to each macro project and add that signature to your list of trusted sources. If the macros are already signed and if you are willing to trust all macros signed with that certificate, add the signer to your list of trusted sources. This will stop macro warnings when your security setting is set to High or Medium.

A less secure option is to change the security level to Low. When your macro security level is set to Low, Microsoft Access will not provide warnings about macros. To reduce your risk of getting a macro virus infection on your computer, run specialized antivirus software that is up-to-date and thatcan check files and add-ins for macro viruses and use macros only from trusted sources.

> The presence of a certificate does not guarantee that a macro is safe. You should review the details of the certificate to confirm that the Issued to and Issued by fields contain recognized and acceptable entities and check the Valid from field to determine if the certificate is current.

Although Office has four security levels, Access only has three. If the security level is set to the highest possible, which is called Very High, Access cannot open any Access database or Access project files. So, this might be added to the list of things to check when someone suddenly cannot open any databases. The three levels applicable to the Access environment are:

❑ *High Level*: This is the default security mode for Office Applications other than Access. Files and signatures/certificates are evaluated prior to the file being allowed to be opened. Criteria include, the file being from a trusted source, the signature being valid, the author is known, and the certificate is current. Files with current, valid, and accepted signatures are automatically opened. Only signed and/or trusted files can be opened. Files with an unsigned macro (code) can be opened only if the user chooses to trust the author and the certification authority. Files will not be opened if they have incompatible encryption or when the signature is invalid, has expired, or has been revoked.

❑ *Medium Level*: This is the default security mode for Access—with Sandbox mode not enabled. Files and signatures/certificates are evaluated prior to the file being allowed to be opened. Criteria include the file being from a trusted source, the signature being valid, the author is known, and the certificate is current. Files from a trusted source with a valid signature are automatically opened. If the signature is invalid, it cannot be validated; if the signature has expired or has been revoked, the user will be warned and has the option of canceling or opening the file.

❑ *Low Level*: This setting essentially shuts off macro security because all macros are treated equally and opened without prompting for a signature validation. This can be a convenient setting for development on a personal computer if you are confident that you are not getting malicious macros from elsewhere.

To review security levels and the list of trusted publishers and signatures, click Tools on the menu bar, then Macros, and then click Security. This will open the Macro Security window, as shown in Figure 3-14. The Macro Security window allows you to specify the security level and to see the list of trusted publishers and prior trusted sources if some signatures have expired or become invalid. If the Security command does not appear on the Macro fly out menu, you may need to customize the toolbar to add it. (To customize the toolbar go to Tools, then Customize, and then Commands. In the Categories list, click Tools, and then in the Command list click "Security." Remember, this is not to be confused with User-Level Security.)

When using a medium security setting and a database that contains VBA or macros is opened (if it is not your own file and it does not have an authenticated digital signature), two dialog boxes will need to be responded to before the database can be opened. The first dialog box provides a link to the Windows Update site for downloading SP8. If you click Yes to open the file, you will get the second dialog box. The second dialog box is the macro security warning. You can click Yes to open the database or you can cancel. If you respond Yes and open the database without enabling its functionality, it is unlikely that the application will function properly, if at all. After SP8 has been installed and Sandbox mode enabled, only the macro security warning dialog box will display when opening a database without a digital signature

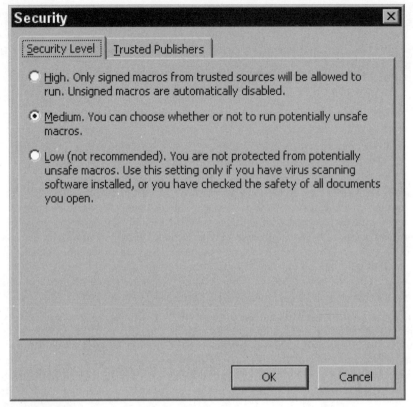

Figure 3-14

under medium security settings. Figure 3-15 shows the standard Security Warning dialog box along with the quick help pane.

> `Trust installed add-ins` **on the macro security dialog is enabled by default. This is why wizards do not produce a security dialog box when they are opened. However, if you uncheck** `Trust installed add-ins` **then launching a wizard will prompt you with a security dialog box.**

Digital Signatures

Digital signatures are essentially like seals; they are to indicate that the item remains intact as delivered by the sender/signer. That is why code with trusted signatures is opened and used without warnings. A digital signature only applies to the parts of the database that could be modified to do malicious things, such as VBA code, macros, action queries, and properties of ActiveX controls. If any of these are modified after the file or macro project has been signed, the digital signature will be removed, and the file will no longer open under medium or high security.

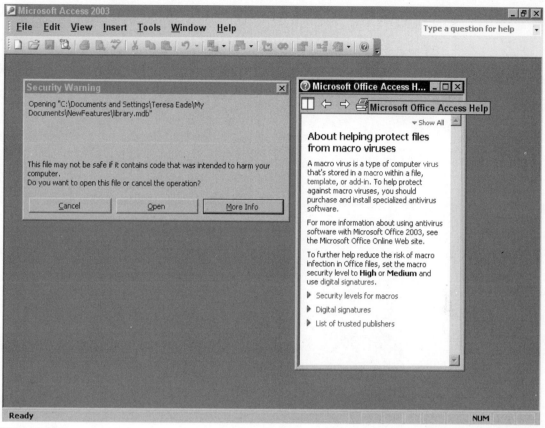

Figure 3-15

Access automatically resigns databases when they are in low security. Remember that in low security, all macros and projects are trusted. The reason that a new signature may be needed is that if a file has been modified in an earlier version of Access (or the signature is for some other reason invalidated), it will trigger a virus-warning message when it is reopened in Access 2003. One way to fix or prevent this annoying warning on your own files is to change to a low security setting, open and modify some part of the code, and then close the file. This will force the signature to be re-signed.

Access automatically re-signs databases that have been modified when they are in low security. For the sake of convenience and productivity, it is recommended that a project not be signed until it is ready to send to someone else or deploy. Doing development work on a signed database can cause extra database bloat. But, the effect of that can be minimized by frequently running Compact & Repair—which in general is a good idea, anyway. And, if you have a certificate for a security of a high level (that is, prompts for password before signing) then you may have to enter the password all the time.

If you have existing digital signatures, you can easily sign a VBA project. Go to the VBE window and click Tools, then Digital Signature; this will open the Digital Signature window as shown in Figure 3-16. One signature will cover VBA Code, Macros, Action Queries, and ActiveX control properties on Forms/Reports.

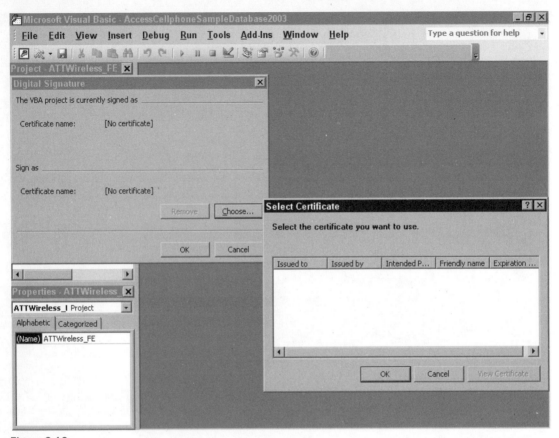

Figure 3-16

Expression Sandbox

The Expression Sandbox enables Jet to block unsafe expressions while still allowing Access 2003 to be fully functional. Installation of SP8 is required for the Sandbox mode to work with Access. As previously mentioned, you will need to install SP8 as soon as you install Access 2003.

Access 2003 uses the Microsoft Jet Expression Service to evaluate expressions in forms, reports, and queries and elsewhere to identify unsafe expressions. Unsafe expressions are those that contain methods or functions that could be exploited by a malicious user.

Sandbox mode can be turned on and off if the macro security level is set to Medium or High. To change the setting for Sandbox mode, open Access, then click Tools, then Macro, and then Security. Select either Medium or High level. This will open a Security Warning message box. In the message box, click Yes to enable Sandbox mode. After you click OK, Access will close. Then you open Access, the Sandbox mode will be enabled. Although we don't recommend this approach, setting the macro security level to low will disable the Sandbox mode. Chapter 20, "Macro Security," contains a detailed explanation of the Expression Sandbox.

If you are feeling a bit overwhelmed with the security things, then it is probably time to turn back on the enthusiasm and review features that are sure to excite the end users. Particularly managers and data crunchers who want to get at the data that they want, when and how they want it. The next section describes some of the new, powerful features that are focused on enriching the end-user experience.

End-User Enhancements

Access 2003 provides a seemingly endless list of new features and enhancements that benefit both the developer and the end user. Since these features are primarily in the user interface, they are grouped together as end-user enhancements. This is not to say that developers do not benefit tremendously. In fact, Pivot charts, XML, and integration with SharePoint services are prime examples of features that really leverage the developer skills to create impressive applications.

Pivot Charts

Pivot charts were introduced in Access 2002. Amazingly, they are like golden nuggets hiding under a rock; they have not been publicized and exploited. Anyone who is struggling with cross tab queries should take a look at PivotTable and PivotChart views for forms.

These incredibly powerful views allow users to look at data in countless ways. It can be drilled into, grouped by criteria, limited to the top X, expanded, sorted, totaled, subtotaled, charted, diagramed, and the list of criteria is seemingly endless. The number of chart options is absolutely amazing, and developers can let the user interact with the data and even change the chart type on the fly.

Although there are wizards for creating PivotCharts and PivotTables, most people find them rather intuitive, especially after doing a couple of experiments. And, they are so easy to modify after they are setup that you will want the ability to change them. There are several ways to create a PivotChart. In addition to using the wizard or creating a form in Design View, you can open an exiting form and switch to PivotChart view to see what it would look like. Of course, it may be prudent to take the conservative approach of making a copy of a form and using that to experiment, rather than risk unintentionally making changes to a functional form. Alternatively, this would be a good time to employ the nifty new database backup feature.

Once you have created a PivotChart, it is remarkably easy to add filters, replace fields, or expand and collapse the details. As shown in Figure 3-17, with a right-click of the mouse you can even select a different type of chart. Any manager will appreciate the ease of changing both the detail and the display format on the fly.

Windows XP Theming

Finally, Access applications will look more like the rest of Office applications. However, in Access 2003, most forms controls can inherit the Windows theme. So, buttons, options groups and the like will suddenly have the softer features that have become familiar to users. Again there are caveats, such as the operating system must be set up to use theming and the desktop cannot currently be set to use Windows XP with Windows Classic theme selected. Controls that do not inherit the Windows theme are labels, images, object frames, subforms, lines, and rectangles. And, of course, customized controls will retain their custom settings.

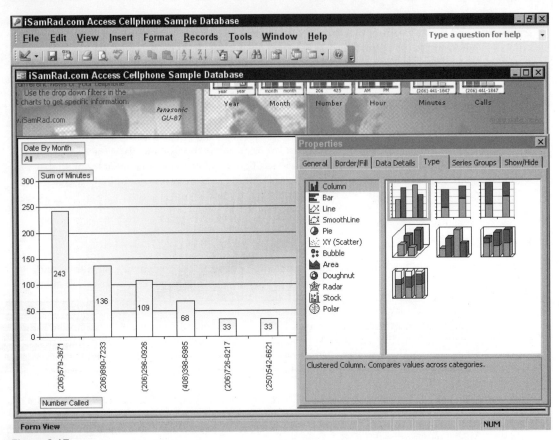

Figure 3-17

It takes only four mouse clicks to specify whether or not Access should adopt the Windows theme. On the `Tools` menu, click `Options`. In the `Options` window, open the `Forms/Reports` tab, and then select or clear the `Use Windows Themed Controls on Forms` check box.

> **To change the Windows theme, open the** `Display` **window in** `Control Panel`**. On the** `Themes` **tab, select a theme other than** `Windows Classic` **in the** `Themes` **list box.**

Forms, dialogs boxes, and wizards will all inherit the current Windows theme. And, Data Pages will also display the Windows theme when viewed in Access as well as when viewed with Internet Explorer. Regretfully, the theme required for this book's screen shots does not allow the Window's theme to influence Access. But, this is certainly a feature worth experimenting with.

Templates

Templates deserve mentioning, even if developers don't want to take a lot of credit for using templates. But at a minimum, templates can be great tools for building demonstration projects and for learning aids.

For instance, it may be worthwhile starting with a common Access template when preparing a presentation for a user group or other organization. That way, when the participants get back to work, they will be able to use their template to apply what they just learned. Access 2003 installs at least 10 MDB templates. These relate to a variety of businesses, such as asset tracking, event management, time and billing, order entry, and service call management. To create a database using a template it takes only a few steps. If the new file task pane is not open, on the `File` menu, click `New` to open the new `TaskPane`. On the lower section of the pane, under `Templates`, click `On my computer`. This will display the templates window. You can also obtain more templates online.

The following is a sample of the Access database templates available from Microsoft Office:

- ❑ Photograph database
- ❑ Music collection database
- ❑ Video collection database
- ❑ Wine collection database
- ❑ Book collection database
- ❑ Workout history database
- ❑ Membership database
- ❑ Inventory management database

Smart Tags

Smart Tags are available in Microsoft Office XP. In general, they allow you to provide addition information about a record or specific data point (see Figure 3-18) or to perform an action that would typically require opening another program to perform. Access 2002 relied on tags that were in Word and Excel data; however, Smart Tags are now directly supported in Access 2003.

Smart Tags can be used on tables, queries, forms, reports, and Data Pages. They can also be exported to HTML, and work on Data Pages through Internet Explorer.

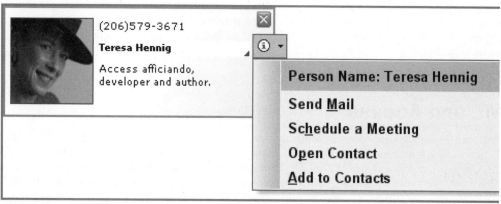

Figure 3-18

Smart Tag can be added to a control, by setting the Smart Tag property on the control. Then, when the Smart Tag Action button appears, activate the control, and select from the available options. Several Smart Tags ship with Access and there are more available on the Internet. Plus developers can create Smart Tags. Access `Help` provides additional information about Smart Tags, and MSDN (The Microsoft Developer Network) is also a good resource.

AutoCorrect Options Buttons

Most users are probably familiar with AutoCorrect options because these have been around for a few versions of Word. Basically, Office, or for our purposes, Access will try to intelligently and automatically correct what it interprets as spelling errors. As soon as a word is autocorrected, the `AutoCorrect Options` button will appear immediately after the work. The icon will change to a button icon when you point to it. Clicking the button provides options such as to undo the change, stop making the change, and to open the `AutoCorrect` window so that more preferences can be set. Since you are probably familiar with this feature in Word, we'll move on without providing an example.

Better Accessibility

As with other Office programs, Access 2003 has new features that make Access easier for people with disabilities. Some of the key improvements are due to having the Access forms and dialogs function more like Windows dialog boxes. So standard accessibility aides will function more effectively and require less customization to work well with Access. Additional improvements are in the areas of speech recognition and the use of keyboard shortcuts.

Speech recognition continues to improve. It can be used for both commands and data entry. And, since the Access Forms and Controls behave more like standard Windows dialog boxes, they are more familiar and intuitive for users to master. Additionally there are seemingly hundreds of keyboard shortcuts. Access not only recognizes the standard shortcuts of other Office menu commands, but there are fairly intuitive keyboard shortcuts for menu and toolbar items. Plus, as was mentioned in the error checking, developers can confidently create keyboard shortcuts for any (and all) command buttons on their forms.

For a list of Access keyboard shortcuts, go to Access `Help`, and in the `Table of Contents`, go to `Startup and Settings`, `Accessibility`, and then `Using Accessibility` features in Access. Figure 3-19 shows a partial list of general keyboard shortcuts for navigating and for working with menus.

XML and Access

XML can be used to send, store, and display data, and even related tables, via an Internet or intranet. Think of using your browser to view Access data and even the schema or data structure. With Access 2003, you can import and export XML data and transform data to other formats using XML related files. This works with both a database (.mdb) and an Access project (.adp). To build on familiar ground, we'll start with the similarities between XML and HTML.

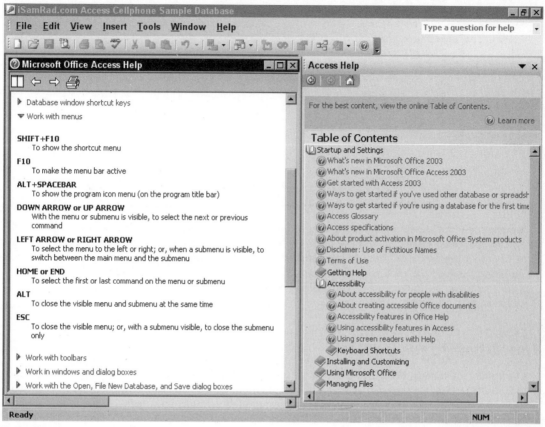

Figure 3-19

Relating XML to HTML

XML stands for eXtensible Markup Language. Extensible—as in being extendable and flexible at the same time. Extendable because the language can be extended to contain any value, and flexible because there are very few limitations. To help understand how XML is useful to the programming community, it may be useful to examine *HTML*, a markup language that has been around for quite a while. HTML stands for HyperText Markup Language. It contains the instructions that a Web browser, such as Microsoft Internet Explorer, uses to display the information contained in an .htm or .html file. An .htm file is simply a text file that contains special markups, also known as tags. The tags instruct the browser where to start an instruction and where to stop. Let's relate HTML to something that Access developers are more familiar with, such as VBA. Both languages provide intrinsic functionality. HTML uses tags and VBA uses statements such as If, Do, or Stop.

When the Web page is rendered, the text is translated from plain text characters to the rich presentation layout, based on the instructions contained within the tags. Tags are denoted by the text, which are enclosed between the Greater Than (<) and the Less Than (>) symbols. The HTML of any Web page can be displayed by choosing View/Source from the main menu of Internet Explorer. The following example displays an HTML source file:

```
<IMG height=10 src="Investing Lessons_files/1p-trans.gif" width=400
    border=0> </TD><!----------------------RIGHT SIDE MARGIN------
------------------>
    <TD vAlign=top align=middle width=180 bgColor=#ffffff>
      <TABLE cellSpacing=0 cellPadding=7 bgColor=#ffff99 border=0>
        <TBODY>
        <TR>
          <TD vAlign=center align=middle bgColor=#ffff00><FONT
            face="verdana, arial, helvetica, sans-serif" size=1><B>MORE
            INFORMATION</B><BR></FONT></TD></TD>
        <TR>
          <TD><BR><FONT face="verdana, arial, helvetica, sans-serif"
            size=2><B>More by this author...</B><BR>
```

In the previous code example, there are tags to instruct the browser to display a picture `<image>` `</image>`, place some data within a table `<td></td>`, and format the text in bold `<b></b>`. There are many other tags in the example, but the important thing to understand is that each tag can only perform one function. Just like VBA, which has reserved words such as Left, Date, or Mod, each HTML tag performs a specific function that is predefined in advance. Attempting to use the tag for any other function may produce an error or undesired results.

The Advantages of XML

As we just mentioned, HTML is a fixed language that is used to define how data should be displayed across the Internet. In contrast, XML is a flexible method of providing data storage that can be sent across the Internet. XML uses tags, but they do not have a predefined function. The flexibility lies in the ability of the developer to create any tag that is needed. The following example shows an example of an XML file:

```
<Products>
  <ProductID>1</ProductID>
  <ProductName>Chai</ProductName>
  <SupplierID>1</SupplierID>
  <CategoryID>1</CategoryID>
  <QuantityPerUnit>10 boxes x_20 ba,s</QuantityPerUnit>
  <UnitPrice>18</UnitPrice>
  <UnitsInStock>39</UnitsInStock>
  <UnitsOnOrder>0</UnitsOnOrder>
  <ReorderLevel>10</ReorderLevel>
  <Discontinued>0</Discontinued>
</Products>
```

In the XML sample, there are record-level and field-level tags. The tag `<Products>` defines the start of a new record, and each field name has its own tag. All tags also have an ending tag that signifies either the end of the field or the end of the record.

In Access 2000 and 2002, it was possible to export data to XML, but that was the extent of the export. With the enhanced XML support in Access 2003, you can specify a *transformation file* (.xsl—Extensible Style Language) when you import or export data using XML. This transformation file is used to define how the data should be used. To better understand this concept, review the earlier HTML file and consider how the text is displayed in the browser when it is surrounded by the bold tags, that is, <b> **This text would be in Bold**</b>. XML is the text and XSL adds value to the text or raw data by providing the formatting and extra instructions.

With Access 2003, a transformation file can be generated during the export, and subsequently applied during an import. When you import XML data, the transformation file will be automatically applied to the data as soon as the data is imported, before a new table is created or before any data is appended to an existing table. So, the user sees only the formatted data. You may also notice *XSD files*. XSD is the XML Schema standard approved by the World Wide Web Consortium (W3C) for describing the type and structure of XML documents.

A second feature that has been incorporated in XML with Access 2003 allows users to drill into data. If desired, related data tables can be automatically generated during an export. They will be recovered during the import, along with their relationships. For added convenience and control, predefined filters or sort orders can also be applied. One easy way to learn about exporting using XML is to right-click a table, click Export on the shortcut menu, and select the file type of XML. Then, click Export. In the Export XML dialog box, click More Options. This will open the Export XML window shown in Figure 3-20. As you can see, it is easy to then apply filters and set several other options.

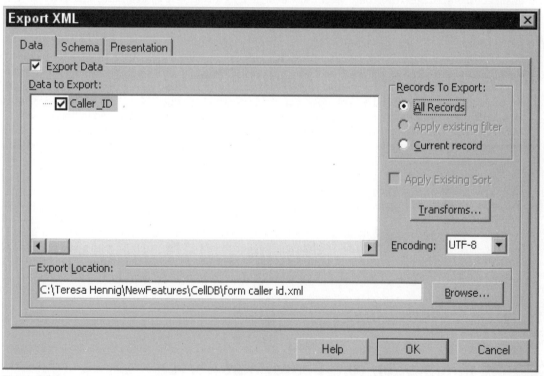

Figure 3-20

XML is the new standard for data transfers, and like HTML, it will be used for years to come. Learning to harness the flexibility and usefulness can be a tremendous benefit to your clients. They will be able to import data from a variety of sources and share data that will be consistently formatted. And if they want to, they can even allow the viewer to drill down for more details. The Access online help files and the

MSDN Web site provide additional information and detailed instructions on how to work with XML and how to create XSL style sheets. Another way of extending Access's reach is through integration with SharePoint Services.

Using Access 2003 with SharePoint Services

Access 2003, when teamed with *SharePoint Portal Server* or *SharePoint Team Services 2.0* can provide some pretty awesome data sharing capabilities. Both flavors of SharePoint (Portal Server and Team Services) have the ability to share and track Microsoft Office documents among multiple users. And, with built-in document check-in/check-out, version tracking, subscription services, e-mail updates and alerts, *Windows SharePoint Services* (WSS) makes it easy to share and manage information. It can even be used to ensure that users are automatically kept up-to-date on their projects.

By making it easy to create a Web site that manages information in one central location, WSS dramatically improves team collaboration. And as it becomes more popular, companies will want to do more complicated things with the online data that is offered at a Web site. For example, printing mailing labels for a selected group of contacts. As you probably know, printing directly from a Web site has inherent challenges. But, Access reports are specifically designed for printing. By integrating Access with WSS, you have the best of both worlds. You can easily collect, store, and share data at a central location using WSS, and you can easily manipulate that data with Access.

So, if you are familiar with SharePoint capabilities, you can start getting excited about using Access to tap directly into its power and convenience. Using Access 2003, you can directly import from and export to or link a table to a SharePoint Services list. And, from SharePoint Services, you can export or link to a table in Access. If you're noticing the LINK option you're likely catching onto the potential here. Yes, this can be a dynamic connection so that changes in either location are immediately reflected in both places. However, when there are situations that it would be preferable to for the Access user to have static data, the import/export options take only seven steps to set up. Access 2003 makes it easy to have the best of both worlds.

Leveraging an Access developer's expertise to extend the functionality of a WSS Web site can result in extremely powerful solutions that were not previously possible. When Access tables are linked to data in WSS, the data is treated as though it is native to Access. So, data that was previously difficult to get into Access is now easily and quickly incorporated into the Access schema. Access can be used to analyze and/or scrub the data either locally or while it still resides on the WSS. And, Access can be used to modify and publish data to a WSS Web site. WSS and Access are an excellent example of how uniting two technologies can create a whole that is more valuable than the sum of its parts.

As previously stated, it is amazingly easy to import and export data from Access to and from a SharePoint server. In fact, it is just seven easy steps for either direction.

Export Information to a SharePoint Server

Access 2003 has the ability export tables or queries to lists on a SharePoint server. This is pretty easy to set up and a snap after that. You can use the Export to Windows SharePoint Services Wizard as shown in the following steps:

1. Select a table or query to export in the database window.

2. Select Export from the File menu.

3. In the Save as type drop-down box in the Export Table dialog box choose Windows SharePoint Services (see Figure 3-21).

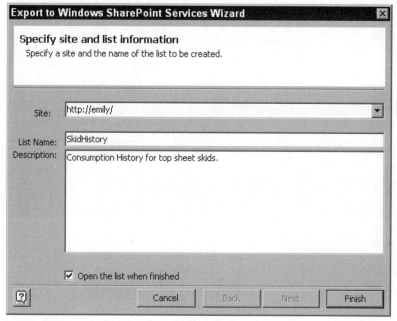

Figure 3-21

4. Enter the site URL for the SharePoint site you need.

5. You can enter a name for your list and a description.

6. If you don't want to view the list when the export is complete, uncheck the box marked Open the list when finished.

7. Click Finish to export your list. An Internet browser will open to your list.

Import Information From a SharePoint Server

In addition to exporting information from Access 2003 to a SharePoint server, you can also link to a SharePoint server or import information. To link an Access table to a SharePoint list use the following steps:

1. Select Get External Data from the File menu and choose Link Tables.

2. Choose Windows SharePoint Services (see Figure 3-21).

3. Choose your SharePoint server from the list or enter one not listed.

4. Click Next (see Figure 3-22).

5. Choose the appropriate list and click Next.

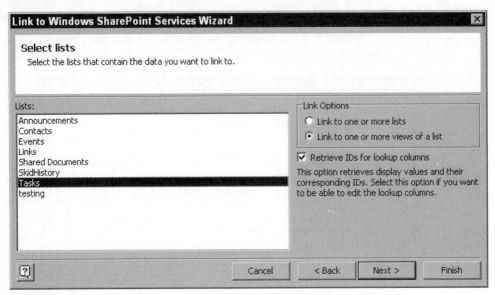

Figure 3-22

6. Select the view of the list you need and click Next.

7. Click Finish on the confirmation screen to perform the import.

In addition to linking an Access table to a SharePoint list, you can use similar steps to import a list from a SharePoint Server. SharePoint Services and Office 2003 provide a number of sharing opportunities to help you collaborate with your team and to share data with any number of entities. But not everyone will have a need for SharePoint. So let's move on to one of the most awesome packages that Microsoft has offered to Access Developers, the Access Developer Extensions.

Access Developer Extensions

Microsoft and in particular the Access program management went all out when they created and offered the Access Developer Extensions (ADE). This impressive set of tools offers an amazing set of cost-effective and stress-reducing features. Invest 5 minutes to breeze through this intro and you will certainly concur. As mentioned earlier, the ADE is part of Visual Studio Tools for the Microsoft Office System. So, when you get the ADE, you automatically have additional resources that will enable you to expand your development horizons even further.

The ADE makes it easy for developers to consistently and efficiently create MDE files and package them for deployment. The license agreement clearly states that it includes a royalty-free distribution of Access Runtime solutions. So developers can now package and deploy Access 2003 applications, and the clients do not need to worry about the cost of upgrading to Access 2003. This is going to not only save our clients a lot of money, but it will make it easier to explain the cost effectiveness of creating solutions in Access 2003. In addition to royalty-free distribution of the runtime, the ADE includes several other impressive tools. The ADE is required for creating Access 2003 MDE files. The Custom Startup Wizard makes the MDE file. Then, after the MDE is created, the Package Wizard makes it a snap to create a deployment package. You can supersize the package by combining or stacking installations together to create highly customized packages. And, that's not all. The ADE also includes the Property Scanner that can be used to ensure that changes to the name of a feature or object are cascaded throughout the entire database. But perhaps the most astonishing thing is that the source code is included. You can learn more about the ADE by reading Chapter 19.

> The ADE includes over 14,000 lines of source code.

The Property Scanner

The Property Scanner will search for custom strings throughout all of the properties or code in tables, queries, forms, reports, and modules. The search will look at essentially all Access objects. Then, the Property Scanner produces list of all the locations that the string was found. Developers can then click and go directly to the object in a specific string. Figure 3-23 shows the Property Scanner window and many of the options for setting search criteria.

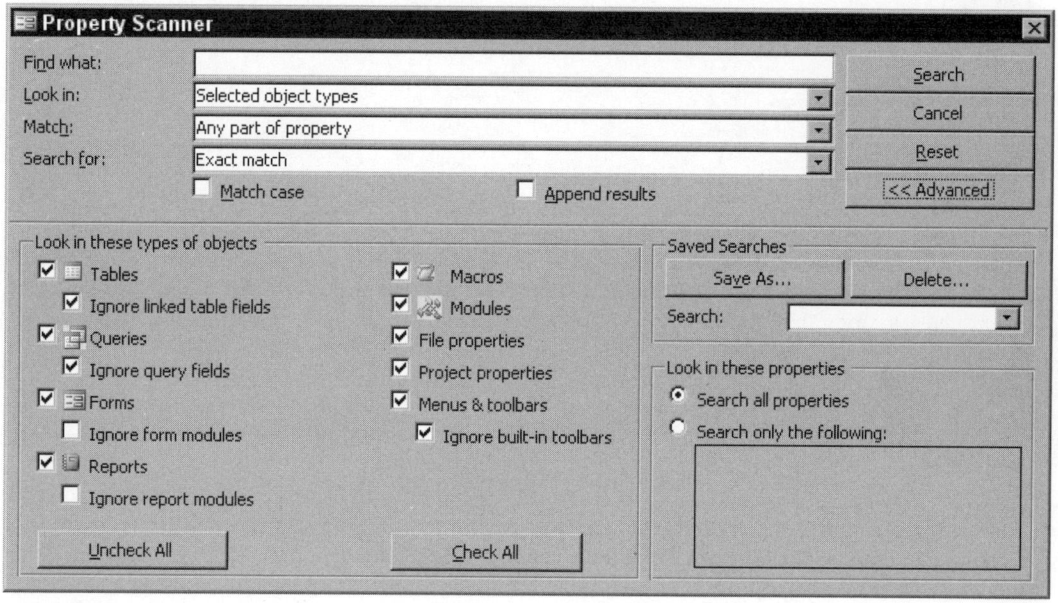

Figure 3-23

The Property Scanner also allows for advanced search criteria, for saving criteria, and for saving search results. You can find out how to use the Property Scanner in Chapter 19, "Using the ADE Tools."

The Custom Startup Wizard

The Custom Startup Wizard has an intuitive interface that allows developers to specify a multitude of startup settings as well as the options that will be implemented when the underlying MDB file is used to create an MDE file. Figure 3-24 shows how to specify many start-up options in second step of the Custom

Startup Wizard. In addition to being incredibly easy, the options are even explained in the description box at the bottom of the page. No need to worry or to wonder about the effect; the description provides instant assurance. And notice that the `Name AutoCorrect` is prominently listed so that it can easily be turned on or off.

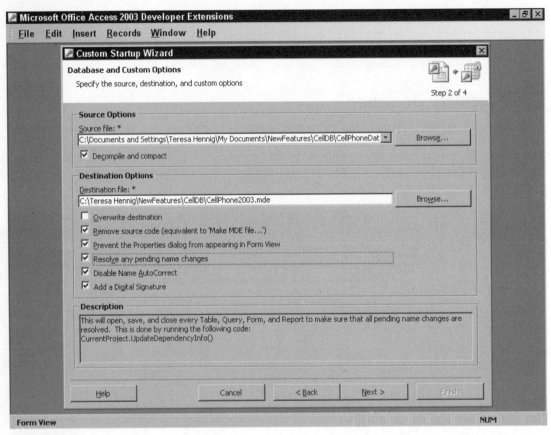

Figure 3-24

As shown in Figure 3-25, the next step allows you to test and find code that may not work. It will also check for potentially missing VBA references. How is that for thinking ahead! We keep telling you, the features in the ADE are power tools for the developer—try them once and you will certainly agree.

One of the great reliefs about using the Custom Startup Wizard to create the MDE is that the underlying MDB file is not affected. The wizard will create the MDE file and even save the settings as a template. So, the next time you want to create the same MDE or to create a MDE with similar settings, you can start with the saved template and reuse it as is or use it as the starting point to create a new template. It only takes a couple of clicks to give the name and location for saving the template. It will also create a batch file that can run through the Custom Startup Wizard without even opening the wizard. Creating MDE files is going to be so easy and stress free.

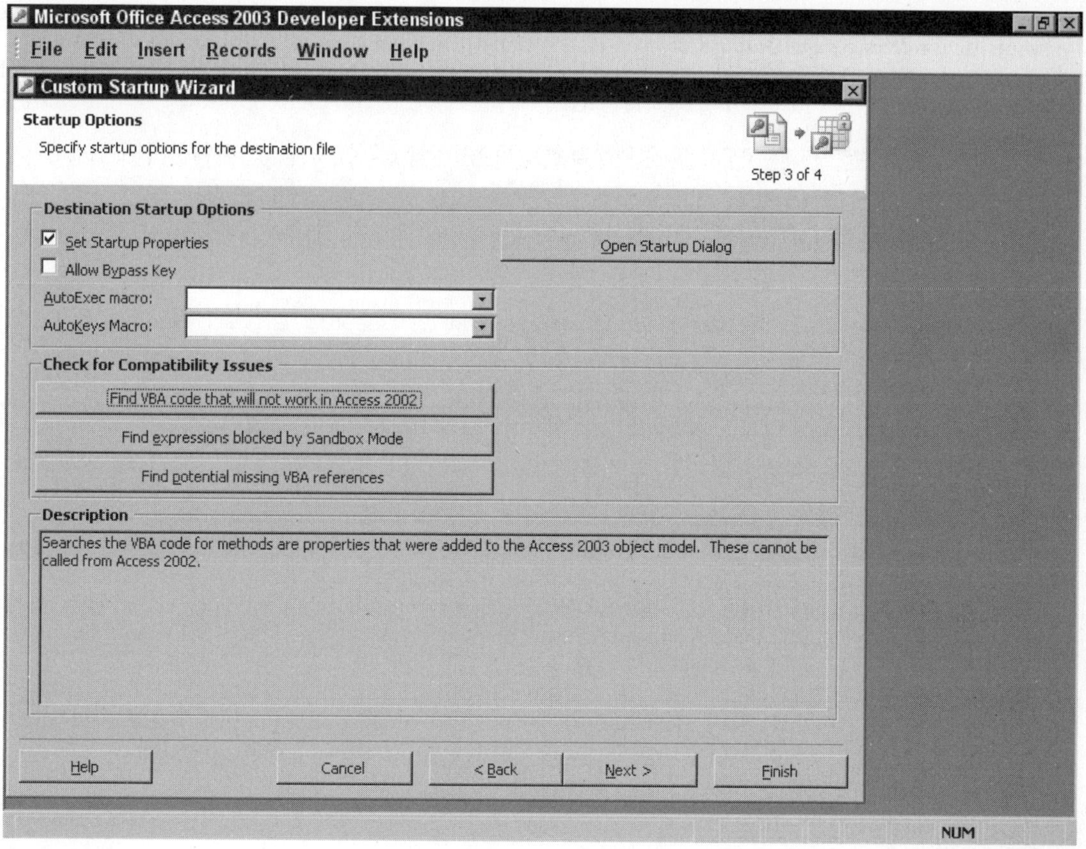

Figure 3-25

The Package Wizard

The Package Wizard is like the extra point after a touchdown. It produces incredibly professional-looking setup routines. Now you can deploy Access solutions with the same panache as Microsoft and all the other big guys. The Package Wizard builds the cabinet file (CAB) that includes Windows Registry Keys and even the digital certificate, if appropriate, that need to be included when deploying an Access solution.

The Package Wizard can automatically include the Access Runtime and any other files that are necessary to make up the complete solution delivery package. And, the setup routine will automatically create necessary shortcuts and even specify the correct Access EXE if there happens to be more than one installed.

The Package Wizard Welcome screen explains the remarkable things that it can do. This screen allows the developer to quickly select an existing template. From there, it is easy to modify the template and/or add additional templates or files and set other options.

This is where the deployment package can really be customized. You can put multiple Startup Wizard batch files together to essentially chain installations. So, the package could install a program, and then immediately install the update to some part of it, plus it could install the back end files and maybe even some MDE references. All of that from one installation setup file. Figure 3-26 shows how easy it is to open, read, and stack a batch file. You can edit the file so that several installations can be chained together into one setup routine. Just right-click the batch files, select Edit, and then copy and paste the entire file into an existing batch file.

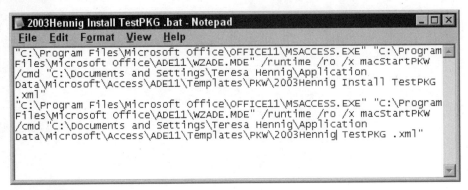

Figure 3-26

Having a custom image in the installation welcome screen can reinforce a developer's credibility and add pizzazz to the application. You can accomplish this by following our tip in Chapter 19 about how to incorporate a BMP file into the installation process.

Chapter 19, "Using the ADE Tools," includes excellent step-by-step instructions for working through the stages of the Custom Setup and Package Wizards. Creating professional-looking installation routines will be much easier and faster with the ADE.

Summary

You are now ready to read more so that you can start using Access 2003 to leverage your skills as a developer. You'll be honing up on working with code as you go through the next few chapters. There are some new features that everyone will need to know how to work with, such as the new macro security, which is covered in Chapter 20, and making MDEs, which is covered in Chapter 19.

4

VBA Basics

Now that you know a bit about automating Access, using macros, and how VBA fits into the Access automation picture, you're almost ready to write some code. All that's left is to spend a few pages reviewing VBA basics.

For experienced programmers, this chapter will be unnecessary; however, if you're just delving into VBA from another programming language or from VBScript, this chapter contains vital information you'll need to successfully use the subsequent chapters in this book. We'll cover the basic VBA programming objects, learn about variables and how to declare them, and review some additional VBA structures you'll use in your code. Along the way, we'll build a few procedures you can use directly in your application to perform various tasks.

VBA Objects

You can't program in VBA without understanding how the various components of VBA work together. All VBA code is comprised of individual statements. Those statements take objects and manipulate their properties, call their methods, and perform their events. This section will introduce the concepts of objects, properties, methods, and events.

Objects

VBA is an object-oriented programming (OOP) language. OOP is a type of programming in which programmers define a complete data structure, from data types to the operations that can be applied to the data structure. Programmers can create an entire object that contains both data and the operations that the object can perform. Programmers can also create relationships between objects.

There are a lot of objects you can access in VBA. The collection of objects exposed by a particular application is called an object library. There are many different object libraries you can access in VBA. For example, you can use VBA to manipulate the Access object library and work with objects such as tables, queries, forms, and reports. You can set references (which we'll cover in the next chapter) to other object libraries such as Microsoft Outlook, Adobe Acrobat, or Microsoft Word. Every time you set a reference to another application's object library, you have access to all of the objects within that library. An object is generally thought of as a physical thing. Let's say you're setting a reference to a car's object library. Once you set the reference to the object library for the car, you can access all of the car's objects, such as its tires, roof, carpet, steering wheel, and windows.

Properties

A property is a physical attribute of an object. Each property can have multiple values. For example, the properties for a car object include color (silver), doors (four), and cylinders (four). However, the car has objects of its own. The car's tire object has a brand property of Michelin. The car's carpet object has properties of style (plush) and clean (true). Some properties of an object can be easily changed. If you want to change the color of the car, all you need to do is find an auto detailer and choose another color. In as short as one day, the carpet's clean property can easily turn to false. However, you can't easily change the number of doors on the car (well, you could just take them off, but then you wouldn't have a complete car anymore). Short of completely replacing the engine, you can't change the number of cylinders. Objects in VBA have the same type of properties. Some can be changed and some cannot.

Every object in Access has properties as well. The form object, for example, has many properties including Border Style, Width, Height, and Caption. Each of these properties has many possible values. The Border Style property can be set to None, Thin, Sizable, and Dialog. Each choice presents the form object with a slightly different look. Before you start manipulating properties in VBA code, take a look at the object and examine some of its properties. In the case of a form, launch the form in design mode and change some of its properties. Then run the form and see how the properties you changed affect the display of the form.

Methods

A method is an action that can be performed by or on an object. When you're in your car, you can invoke the start method on the engine, invoke the release method on the parking break, invoke the shift method of the transmission, and invoke the press method of the gas pedal. All of these methods cause something to happen; in this case, they cause the car to go forward (or cause the drive method to be executed on the car itself). So, as you can see, an action or event that happens (driving) is made up of many other methods performed on many other objects.

Objects in VBA have methods as well. For example, you can invoke the `LoadPicture` method on a control within an Access form. This method causes a picture to be displayed within the control.

Events

An event is something that happens to an object. The car turns when you move the wheel. The horn blares when you press it. The door closes when you pull it. Turning, blaring, and closing are all events of the car. You might be wondering what the difference is between an event and a method. Well, they are definitely related. An event happens when the user *does* something. The actual doing is the method. So you invoke the move method on the wheel and the car invokes the turn event. Make sense? We hope so. If not, we'll examine the same relationship between the methods and events of an Access form.

When you open an Access form, you actually raise (or cause to happen) the `OnOpen` event. When you close the form, you raise the `OnClose` event. Within code, however, you can invoke the `Open` method of the form. Invoking the `Open` method causes the `OnOpen` event to fire. So, invoking a method causes an event.

Now that you know a bit about properties, methods, and events, we'll review briefly the fundamentals of VBA programming.

Variables and VBA Syntax

This section explores some fundamentals you need to know in order to successfully program in VBA. We'll go through them relatively quickly as most of them need only to be recapitulated. If you need more information about any of these topics, you might want to purchase a beginner's guide to VBA programming, such as *VBA For Dummies*, by John Paul Mueller (Wiley Publishing, Inc., ISBN: 0764539892).

Variables

One of the most important concepts in programming is the use of variables. A variable is a location in memory where you can store a value while your code is running. Throughout your code you'll need to declare, change, and fill variables. These variables will hold a variety of different types of data including strings, numbers, and objects. You use a variable in order to save time. For example, if you need to specify a particular state repeatedly in your code, it can be much faster and cleaner to create a variable `strState` than to repeatedly use "Maine" in your code. If you ever need to switch states and use California instead, all you have to do is change the value of your variable rather than find all the instances of Maine in your code. Declaring variables properly is likely one of the most important tasks you'll need to master to program in VBA. It's not hard, and we'll cover the major rules and recommendations in the next few sections.

Types of Variables

In VBA, you can declare many different types of variables. Each type of variable can hold different data. You should always make a point to declare your variables with their correct type. You can, however, choose not to declare a data type. If so, the variable is created as a variant. Variant variables require significantly more space in memory than other types of variables; so use them sparingly. The following table lists the various types of variables, the amount of memory they take up, and the data they can store.

Data Type	Size in Memory	Possible Values
Byte	1 byte	0 to 255
Boolean	2 bytes	True or False
Integer	2 bytes	–32,768 to 32,767
Long (long integer)	4 bytes	–2,147,483,648 to 2,147,483,647

Continues

Data Type	Size in Memory	Possible Values
Single (single-precision real)	4 bytes	Approximately −3.4E38 to 3.4E38
Double (double-precision real)	8 bytes	Approximately −1.8E308 to 4.9E324
Currency (scaled integer)	8 bytes	Approximately −922,337,203,685,477.5808 to 922,337,203,685,477.5807
Date	8 bytes	1/1/100 to 12/31/9999
Object	4 bytes	Any object reference
String	Variable length: 10 bytes + string length; fixed length: string length	Variable length: ≤ about 2 billion (65,400 for Windows 3.1) Fixed length: up to 65,400
Variant	16 bytes for numbers 22 bytes + string length	Number: same as double String: same as string
User-defined	Varies	

You'll notice that the VBA data types are similar but not exactly the same as the data types in an Access table. The major differences between Access data types and VBA data types are that there is no equivalent to the variant or object data types in Access Jet data types and the number data type in Access has a field size property that allows you to specify the field as byte, integer, long, single, decimal, or double.

Numeric Data Types

When working with numeric data, you have a choice of eight different data types. This section will provide a brief introduction to the data types available to you within your code and help you choose the proper data type for your needs.

Each different numeric data type provides a different level of accuracy; however, they also use differing amounts of space. There are some general rules of thumb you can follow when choosing the right data type for your variable:

- ❑ When creating a variable to store whole numbers, choose the long data type.
- ❑ When creating a variable to store fractional numbers, choose the double data type.
- ❑ If you need to store a negative value, you can use any data type except for the byte data type.
- ❑ If you need to store a value outside the range of −32768 to 32767, do not use the integer data type; it can't handle numbers that large.
- ❑ To control loops, always use an integer data type.

There are a few key differences between the single and double data types. The single data type allows you a precision level of 7 digits, while the double data type gives you approximately 15 digits of precision. Both data types allow you to work with numbers larger than 2 billion.

You should never use double or single data types to represent fractional numbers. These cannot do so with extreme accuracy. For example, take the following code:

```
Sub TestFractionalDivision()
'Do not actually run this code!
'If need be, use Ctrl+Break to stop code execution
Dim dblResult As Double
dblResult = 1 / 5
Do Until dblResult = 1
    'Do something interesting
    dblResult = dblResult + 1 / 5
Loop
End Sub
```

The loop will run forever, because the value of dblResult never actually equals 1. You'll have to use *Ctrl+Break* to end this code loop. This is why you're always better off using integers for looping operations.

The single and double data types are floating-point data types. This means that they can handle numbers with the decimal point in a variety of places. The currency data type is a fixed-point number. This means that there are always four decimal places in a currency number to handle most types of international currency. Just because the currency data type is generally used for dealing with dollars and cents, it's not limited to financial transactions. You can use the currency data type for any number with up to four decimal places. Because the decimal is always in the same place, VBA actually performs a little trick with currency calculations. To save time, VBA removes the decimal points, performs the calculation on the integer numbers, and then puts the decimal points back. This speeds up the calculation while retaining the four decimal place accuracy.

Other Data Types

In addition to numeric data types, there are a variety of other data types you can use. Boolean variables can take only two values, True and False. If you've ever used VBScript, you probably are familiar with using numeric values to represent True and False. If you haven't, it's important to note that when referring to a Boolean data type in VBScript, 0 is False and –1 is True. You can actually still use these values even with Boolean data types. VBA interprets zero as False. The difference is that any nonzero value is always interpreted as True. The following two code samples actually produce the same result.

```
Sub TestIfTrue()
Dim blnIsTrue As Boolean
blnIsTrue = True
If blnIsTrue = True Then
    MsgBox "True"
End If
End Sub
```

```
Sub TestIsTrue()
Dim blnIsTrue As Boolean
blnIsTrue = 2
If blnIsTrue = True Then
    MsgBox "True"
End If
End Sub
```

The Date Data Type

Remember the Y2K bug? Computers used to store dates with only two-digit years. This caused a problem when computers needed to start storing dates past the year 1999. After all, 01 could be a two-digit year code for 1901 or for 2001. Programmers scrambled for several years to fix the problem. So now computers store dates with a four-digit year. However, the problems didn't end there. Different countries represent dates in different ways. For example, the date 9/10/2003 could represent either September 10 or October 9 depending on the region of the world you live in. To work around this problem, VBA has a nifty way of dealing with dates. All dates are represented as a floating-point number (one with a flexible number of decimal places). When working with a date and time, the date portion is converted to an integer. The time is represented by the decimal portion of the number and is calculated as a percentage of a day. For example, noon would be half of a day and represented by 0.5. In order to determine the integer value for the date, an initial date is needed for calculations. That initial date is December 30, 1899. So counting that as day 0, March 1, 2004, would be represented as 38047, and 6:00 P.M. on that date would be represented as 38047.75.

So if you're working with dates in VBA, you will not have to perform conversions between 38047.75 and March 1, 2004, 6:00 P.M. VBA is aware of the regional settings specified in the user's Control Panel Regional Settings applet and will convert the date to the proper format. So, if you're in Australia, VBA will convert 38047.75 to 01/03/04. If you're in the United States, VBA will display 03/01/04 (or 03/01/2004 depending on your settings). VBA's use of a calculated number for dates ensures that dates will always be calculated correctly regardless of the specific regional settings used on the local computer.

There are a few quirks in VBA's date calculations that you should be aware of when you're working with dates. First, a variable declared as a date has an initial value of December 30, 1899 (or zero when converted to the floating-point decimal value). So the following code will produce a value of December 31, 1899.

```
Sub AddADay()
    Dim dtInitialDate As Date
    dtInitialDate = DateAdd("d", 1, dtInitialDate)
    Debug.Print dtInitialDate
End Sub
```

You can work with dates directly in VBA by assigning the literal date value to a date variable. To do this, use # to delimit your dates. For example, to assign a value of March 1, 2004, to the variable dtInitialDate, use the following code:

```
dtInitialDate = #03/01/2003#
```

This ensures that VBA will recognize the date properly no matter what your regional settings are.

If you're in a region of the world that enters dates with d/m/yyyy, you'll need to enter the literal date in the format m/d/yyyy when using the method described previously. Otherwise, VBA will not recognize it properly.

The String Data Type

The string data type is fairly straightforward. You use this data type for all types of alphanumeric data including names, sentences, or phrases. You can store numbers in a string data type. However, you can't perform operations on them in the same manner as you would if these were stored as numbers. Consider the following code:

```
Sub FunWithStrings()
    Dim strBikes As String
    Dim strCost As String
    Dim intBikes As Integer
    Dim curCost As Currency

    strBikes = "5"
    strCost = "100"
    intBikes = 5
    curCost = 100
    Debug.Print strBikes + strCost
    Debug.Print intBikes + curCost
End Sub
```

The first operation, `Debug.Print strBikes + strCost` produces a result of 5100. The operation is merely concatenating the two string variables. The second operation, `Debug.Print intBikes + curCost` actually performs the mathematical calculation and produces a result of 105.

When creating a string variable, the default value of the variable is a zero-length string. This isn't the same as a null value; it's more like an empty value. You can assign pretty much any value to the string variable. The trickiest problem you're likely to encounter while using string variables in VBA is dealing with quotation marks. For example, the following is a valid way to assign a string value to a variable:

```
strCustomerName = "ABC Textiles"
```

The same syntax works if you need to store a value with a single quote in the name, such as the following:

```
strCustomerName = "Johnny's Cycles"
```

However, what if you need to store a value with a double-quote character in the name? If you follow the same rules as the previous two examples, you'll end up with something like the following:

```
strCustomerName = "The "W" Hotel, New York City"
```

That might look like a valid line of code, but when you actually type that into your code, you'll get a compile error even before you run the code. The problem is that VBA sees the second double quote and thinks you want to end the string. VBA doesn't quite know what to do with the text that follows the double quote. In order to work around this issue, you'll need to use a double set of double quotes within your string. So your actual assignment statement should look like the following:

```
strCustomerName = "The ""W"" Hotel, New York City"
```

If you enter all strings with double quotes using that method, you'll get predictable results every time.

String Comparisons

You can't have a discussion about string variables without discussing how to work with strings. Some of the tasks you'll need to perform with strings include comparing two strings, finding matches to a partial string, or determining the length of a string. The next few paragraphs describe some of the tricks you can use to work with string variables.

When comparing two strings, you'll find that VBA is by default case insensitive. In other words, California and CALIFORNIA are considered to be the same string. You can change this default behavior by editing the first line of your VBA code. When opening a module in VBA, the first line is Option Compare Database. Changing this line to Option Compare Binary will have one immediate effect: All string comparisons are now case sensitive. See the following table for a summary of the various options you can select for the Option Compare statement in VBA.

Compare Statement	Definition
Option Compare Database	String comparisons are case insensitive. Local settings of the current database are used.
Option Compare Binary	String comparisons are case sensitive. Local settings of the current database are ignored.
Option Compare Text	String comparisons are case insensitive. Locale settings specified in Control Panel are used. This setting isn't often used.

Unless you have good reason to change the Option Compare statement, we suggest leaving it at the default value of Option Compare Database.

There are a variety of other string comparisons you can use besides comparing entire strings to each other. You can search for strings based on one or more characters in the string. For example, the following code sample illustrates a few of the types of string comparisons you can use within your code.

```
Sub CompareStrings()
    Dim strString1 As String
    Dim strString2 As String
    strString1 = "Microsoft"

    If strString1 Like "Micr*" Then
        Debug.Print "True"
    End If

    If strString1 Like "Mic*t" Then
        Debug.Print "True"
    End If

End Sub
```

Both of these comparison operations return True. The first returns True whenever the first four letters of strString1 are Micr. The second comparison returns True whenever the first three letters of strString1 are Mic and the last letter is t. The following table describes the variety of comparison operations you can use in VBA.

Comparison Expression	Strings that Match	Strings that Do Not Match
Like "Mi*"	Microsoft, Michigan	MapPoint, Monochrome
Like "sol*d"	Sold, solid	Solids
Like "s?t"	Sit, sat	Seat
Like "177#"	1776, 1777, 1778, and so on.	1977, 177, 1077
Like "s[ea]t"	Set, sat	Sit, seat
Like "s[!ea]t"	Sit	Set, sat

As you can see from the table, the rules are fairly straightforward. The last two rules are the most confusing. Using two characters (or more) within the brackets tells VBA that any of the characters within the brackets can be used within the string. Putting the exclamation point before the characters in the brackets tells VBA that any character except those within the brackets can be used to compare the string.

Variants

The variant data type is probably the most flexible data type within VBA. Unlike other variable types, which can only hold one type of data, the variant data type can hold many different types of data. You can use it to hold text, numbers, dates, and user-defined types. The only type of data a variant data type cannot hold is a fixed-length string. As previously explained, there is one very good reason to not use variant data types for everything. As tempting as it might seem to just use variant data types for all of your coding, this practice results in much higher memory use than using the proper data type. Just as an example, if you use a variant to hold a string of data, you're using 11 extra bytes of data for every string you store. Over the course of an entire application, these extra bytes can have a significant performance impact.

There are times, though, when you need to use a variant data type. For example, if you're not sure the type of information a variable needs to hold, use the variant data type. Typically this can be used when you're asking the users of your application for data. If you're not sure whether they will enter a date, a number, or a string, you can create a variant data type and store their answer in that variable.

Nulls

There's one last concept we should discuss when talking about variables: Null. When you first learn programming, you learn that Null is the value of a field with no data. If you create a field in a table and don't fill it with any data, the value of the field is Null. So what's Null? Null is nothing, but it's also something. That sounds a bit confusing. Well, it is actually. Here's an example:

```
Sub CompareNulls()
    Dim varValue1 As Variant
    Dim varValue2 As Variant

    varValue1 = Null
    varValue2 = Null

    If varValue1 = varValue2 Then
        Debug.Print "Nulls are not equal"
    End If
End Sub
```

If you run the previous code sample, you'll see that the phrase never prints in the Immediate window. But how can that be? You just set the two variables equal to the same value. Well, you might think you set them to the same value, but, really, two Nulls never equal each other.

There are a few rules of Null you need to be aware of. First, you cannot assign Null to anything other than a Variant data type. You can never have a null string; rather, you have a zero-length string. You cannot have a Null single or double; rather, you have a variable with value 0. The second rule of Null is that no two Nulls match. Null doesn't match zero; it doesn't match a zero-length string; it doesn't even match itself. The only comparison operation you can run on Null is to determine if it's null. But, as mentioned above, Null never equals Null. Well, this is where it gets really confusing. If you alter the previous code sample slightly, you get a completely different result, as shown in the following example:

```
Sub CompareNulls2()
Dim varValue1 As Variant
Dim varValue2 As Variant
varValue1 = Null
varValue2 = Null
If IsNull(varValue1) And IsNull(varValue2) Then
    Debug.Print "Both variables are Null"
End If
End Sub
```

This code sample will print the phrase in the Immediate window. This is because you can test for the Null condition by using the IsNull function. This function evaluates to True if the value of the variable is Null and to False if the value of the variable is not Null. Confused now? Just remember the two basic rules of Null. Null doesn't equal anything and Null equals nothing. Right.

Using Variables

Now that you've learned a bit about the different types of variables, you need to know how to use those variables within your code. You can use a variable by simply adding a statement like the following to your code:

```
strState = "Maine"
```

However, simply using variables in your code without first declaring them isn't a very good programming practice for a number of reasons. First, if you don't declare your variables in advance, when the variable is created by the previous statement, it's created as a variant data type. As we saw previously, the size of a variant variable holding a string value is 22 bytes plus the length of the string. The size of a string variable is only 11 bytes plus the length of the string. So what's the big deal about 11 bytes? Well, it might not be a big deal if you're only declaring three or four variables in your entire application, but if you have several hundred or even a thousand variables in your application, you'll unnecessarily eat up a whole lot of space by using variants instead of strings.

By always declaring your variables you'll know that you're minimizing the amount of space your variables need. If you're using a large number of variables in your application, it can be hard to remember to always declare your variables. If you're happily coding along, it's easy to forget that the last line of code you just typed contained a new variable. You can have VBA help you out a little by requiring you to declare all of your variables before you use them. Making one simple change to your VBA code causes VBA to produce an error when you run your code for every undeclared variable. This is important for two reasons. First, it's just a good programming practice to declare all of your variables. This ensures that your variables have the proper types and can speed code execution. Second, if you don't declare your variables, you can actually get yourself into trouble. The following code sample illustrates this.

```
Sub BuyNewBike()

curBikePrice = InputBox("Please enter bike price.", "Enter Bike Price")
If curVikePrice > 100 Then
    MsgBox "Don't Buy the Bike! It's too expensive!", vbCritical, "Bike
Purchase"
Else
    MsgBox "You can buy the bike. It's within your budget.", vbOKOnly,
"Bike Purchase"
End If

End Sub
```

This code sample looks simple enough. You enter the price of the bike in the InputBox that appears on the screen when you run this code. If the price of the bike is greater than $100, the program tells you not to buy the bike. If the price is less than $100, you can buy the bike.

However, this code won't actually work. If you examine the code carefully, you'll see that the variable that accepts the price of the bike, curBikePrice, isn't the same as the variable used in the If...Then statement, curVikePrice. A mistake like this is quite easy to make. You're typing along and you hit the wrong key. You probably wouldn't even notice it until you ran the code and nothing happened. As it's written, there's actually nothing wrong with the code. It won't produce any errors; it just won't produce the required results. There's one very easy way to prevent this type of mistakes from happening. You can add a single line of code to the General Declarations section of your code, Option Explicit. This line tells VBA that all variables used within your application must be declared before they can be used. If you force variable declaration, then typing the wrong name for a variable will cause VBA to display an error when the code is compiled, as shown in Figure 4.1.

Once the error message is displayed, VBA will highlight the undeclared variable, so you can see where your error might be. You can either correct the spelling of the variable to match the declared variable or add a new line of code to declare the variable in your code.

If you want to always use Option Explicit within all of your procedures, you can configure Access to do this for you. Choose the Tools menu from anywhere in Access and select Options. Choose the Editor tab and check the box marked Require Variable Declaration. Click OK to save your changes. Now, whenever you create a new module or build code behind any Access form or report, you'll always be prompted to declare your variables.

So far you've learned that it's better to declare your variables ahead of time, and always use the correct data type for your variables. Now you need to learn how to actually perform that variable declaration.

Declaring Variables

You declare a variable by use of the Dim (short for dimension) keyword, then the variable name, the word as, and the variable type. For example, to declare the state variable in your procedure, you can use the following statement:

```
Dim strState as String
```

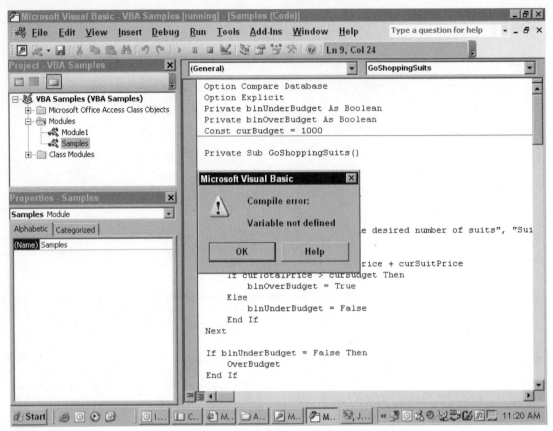

Figure 4-1

Once you dimension your variable, you can assign it a value anywhere in your procedure. For string variables such as `strState`, use the following statement to assign the value "Maine" to your variable:

```
strState = "Maine"
```

Now that your variable has a value, you can use it repeatedly within your procedure. Consider the following code segment:

```
Private Sub OpenDatabaseConnection()

Dim objConn As ADODB.Connection
Dim objRST As ADODB.Recordset
Dim strSQL As String
Dim strConn As String
Dim strState As String

'Create the ADODB Connection and Recordset Objects
Set objConn = CreateObject("ADODB.Connection")
Set objRST = CreateObject("ADODB.Recordset")
```

```
'Open your ADODB Connection
strConn = "Provider=Microsoft.Jet.OLEDB.4.0;Data Source=c:\ Cust.mdb;"
strSQL = "Select * from tblCust WHERE CustState = '" & "Maine" & "';"

objConn.Open (strConn)
objConn.Mode = adModeRead
objRST.Open strSQL, objConn, adOpenForwardOnly, adLockOptimistic
objRST.MoveFirst

'Print relevant customer information
While Not objRST.EOF
    Debug.Print objRST.Fields("CustName")
    Debug.Print objRST.Fields("CustState")
    Debug.Print objRST.Fields("CustCountry")
    objRST.MoveNext
Wend

objRST.Close
objConn.Close
'Release your variables
Set objRST = Nothing
Set objConn = Nothing
        End Sub
```

This code opens an ActiveX Data Objects (ADO) connection to an Access database. It then opens a recordset of all customers in Maine and prints their name, state, and country in the Immediate window. This is pretty simple code. You're only referencing the state in one place, so you really do not need to create a variable to hold the state name. If you know without a doubt that you'll never need to change your code and you won't need the same value later in your code, you can certainly just use the actual value. However, what if you needed to write code to allow users to input their own state name? If you've hard coded the state name in the procedure, you would have no way of switching states when the user needed to do so. You could adapt the previous code through the use of a variable and InputBox to allow users to select the state they need. After changing your code, it would read similar to the following:

```
Private Sub OpenDatabaseConnection()

Dim objConn As ADODB.Connection
Dim objRST As ADODB.Recordset
Dim strSQL As String
Dim strConn As String
Dim strState As String

'Create the ADODB Connection and Recordset Objects
Set objConn = CreateObject("ADODB.Connection")
Set objRST = CreateObject("ADODB.Recordset")

'Open your ADODB Connection
strConn = "Provider=Microsoft.Jet.OLEDB.4.0;Data Source=c:\ Cust.mdb;"
strState = InputBox("Please enter a state", "Enter State")
strSQL = "Select * from tblCust WHERE CustState = '" & strState & "';"

objConn.Open (strConn)
objConn.Mode = adModeRead
```

```
objRST.Open strSQL, objConn, adOpenForwardOnly, adLockOptimistic
objRST.MoveFirst

'Print relevant customer information
While Not objRST.EOF
    Debug.Print objRST.Fields("CustName")
    Debug.Print objRST.Fields("CustState")
    Debug.Print objRST.Fields("CustCountry")
    objRST.MoveNext
Wend

objRST.Close
objConn.Close
'Release your variables
Set objRST = Nothing
Set objConn = Nothing
End Sub
```

Using the preceding code, users can enter any state in response to the InputBox and your code will still run.

There's one key element missing from this procedure—error handling. If users enter Sacramento as a state, misspell Mississippi, or simply choose a state for which no records exist in your database, the preceding code will generate an error. We'll provide a brief introduction to error handling in Chapter 5 and more details on error handling in Chapter 9.

Naming Your Variables

There are only a few rules you need to follow when naming a variable:

❑ You can only use letters, numbers, and the underscore symbol (_). No other symbols are allowed.

❑ Variable names must start with a letter.

❑ You cannot use a reserved word for your variable name (reserved words are covered in Appendix H).

❑ Variable names must be less than 255 characters.

In addition to the rules you must follow when naming your variables, it's customary to follow some sort of naming convention when creating your variables. Which convention you choose is up to you; however, the most popular is the Reddick naming convention. We've provided a detailed appendix on this set of naming conventions as well as guidelines for creating your own naming conventions. You should make your variable names meaningful at the very least. If you create variables with names such as var1, var2, and var3, you'll have a hard time keeping track of which variable you need to use for which statement.

Throughout this book, you'll find that we stick pretty closely to Reddick's naming conventions. That means that our variables will usually contain a prefix that determines their data type. A string variable, for example, will have the str prefix, while a Boolean variable will have a bln prefix.

In addition to Reddick's naming conventions, there is one other convention some developers like to use for additional clarity in their code. You can add a prefix to all of your variable names to denote whether the variable is a global, private, or local variable. See the following table for the prefix used to denote variable scope and lifetime.

Prefix	Variable Scope	Usage
G	Global variable	Variables declared with the Public keyword
M	Private (module-level) variables	Variables declared with the Private keyword
S	Static variables	Local variables declared with the Static keyword

Variable Scope and Lifetime

The last two important variable concepts we'll cover in this chapter are the scope and lifetime of variables. The scope of a variable defines where in the program the variable is recognized. The lifetime of a variable describes how long it exists.

If you declare your variable within a sub or function, the variable's scope is limited to that sub or function only. If you use the same name for a variable in another sub or function, you won't have to worry about the two variables conflicting with each other. The variable's scope is limited to the sub or function. The lifetime of that variable is the same sub or function. The variable lives only while the sub or function is running. As soon as the procedure ends, the variable is destroyed and the memory used by the variable is released. A subsequent call of the procedure creates the variable again from scratch.

There might be times you want your variable to exist outside a particular sub or function. If you declare the variable in the General Declarations section of the module (located at the top of the module), your variable can have a longer scope and lifetime. You can declare the variable in two different ways. If you use the Private keyword, the variable is available to any and all procedures within the current module. Use of the Public keyword makes the variable available anywhere in the entire application. The following code sample illustrates how declaring your variables differently can affect their scope and lifetime.

```
Option Explicit    'Used to require variable declaration

Public txtCustomerName as String    'Scope is entire application
Private txtVendor as String    'Scope is any procedure in this module
Dim txtSupplier as String    'Scope is entire application

Private Sub GetCustomerName()
    Dim txtCustomer as String    'Scope is limited to this sub
End Sub
```

You might be wondering why the two statements that begin with Dim have different scopes. Use of the Dim keyword in the General Declarations section limits the scope of the variable to the procedure. Any variable declared with the Dim keyword in the General Declarations section has a scope of every procedure in the module.

In the previous listing, txtVendor and txtSupplier are both module-level variables. They can be used anywhere within the module and anytime the module is loaded. txtCustomerName is a global variable. It can be used anywhere within any procedure in your application.

The last keyword we'll cover in this section is the Static keyword. Use of the Static keyword allows you to create a local variable with an ongoing lifetime. Why would you want to do this? What if you needed to know how many times a particular procedure was run? You could simply declare a global variable and increment this variable every time the procedure runs. However, it's often easier to track the use of variables when they are declared within the procedure in which they're used. There's one big difference between using the Static keyword within the procedure and using the Public keyword in the General Declarations section to declare your variables. If you declare the variable with the Public keyword in the General Declarations section, you can use the variable anywhere within your application. If you use the Static keyword within a procedure, you can only use the variable within that procedure. However, every time you call that procedure, the variable isn't destroyed when the procedure completes. The variable remains and holds its value. You cannot use the Static keyword to create a variable within Procedure A and use it within Procedure B.

Overlapping Variables

When you're writing your code, you need to be careful of using the same variable name twice in different ways. If you declare a global variable of strString and then declare a variable within your procedure named strString, how is VBA supposed to know which one you want to use? VBA will always use the global variable, but if that's not what you intended, your code could produce unexpected results. For example, consider the following code listing.

```
Option Compare Database
Option Explicit

Public intQuantity As Integer
Public curPrice As Currency

Private Sub FindTotals()
    Dim intQuantity As Integer
    Dim curTotalPrice As Currency

    curPrice = InputBox("Please enter the bike price.", "Enter Bike Price")
    curTotalPrice = intQuantity * curPrice
    MsgBox curTotalPrice, vbOKOnly, "Total Price"
End Sub

Private Sub EnterValues()
    intQuantity = InputBox("Please enter the number of bikes you want to
buy.", "Total Bikes")
End Sub

Private Sub CalculatePrice()
    EnterValues
    FindTotals
End Sub
```

These three procedures illustrate how variables can overlap. If you run the CalculatePrice procedure, Access VBA will run the other two procedures in this listing: EnterValues and FindTotals. When this code is run, the `EnterValues` procedure will ask you for the total number of bikes you want to buy. The `FindTotals` procedure will ask you for the bike price and calculate the total purchase price (quantity of bikes multiplied by the purchase price). However, there's one problem here. There's an added line in the `FindTotals` procedure that causes the calculation to fail, `Dim intQuantity as Integer`. That one line tells Access VBA to create a local procedure-level variable with the same name as the public variable declared in the `General Declarations` section of the module.

If you want Access VBA to use the procedure-level variable, you can add the module's name before the variable name. The following code will work as expected.

```
Option Compare Database
Option Explicit

Public intQuantity As Integer
Public curPrice As Currency

Private Sub FindTotals()

Dim intQuantity As Integer
Dim curTotalPrice As Currency

curPrice = InputBox("Please enter the bike price.", "Enter Bike Price")
curTotalPrice = Module2.intQuantity * curPrice
MsgBox curTotalPrice, vbOKOnly, "Total Price"
End Sub

Private Sub EnterValues()
intQuantity = InputBox("Please enter the number of bikes you want to buy.",
"Total Bikes")
End Sub

Private Sub CalculatePrice()
    EnterValues
    FindTotals
End Sub
```

Adding the name of the module in front of the variable name you need is an easy way to tell Access VBA exactly which variable you need. Just as a general tip however, try to avoid this situation entirely. Utilize naming conventions and declare your variables with as narrow scope as you need. If you don't need to declare a public variable but can get by with a procedure-level variable, it's better to do so.

Other VBA Structures

There are a few other VBA components you'll use often within your code. These are comments, constants, and to a lesser extent, enums. This section provides a brief introduction to each and shows you how these components can be helpful within your code.

Comments

VBA programming consists of writing statements and comments. While comments are not explicitly required, uncommented code is hard to read and very difficult to understand, especially if someone else needs to work with your code. When working with the VBA Editor in Access, comments are prefaced with an apostrophe and appear in green. Comments are ignored during code execution. You can have one or many lines of comments in a procedure, and VBA will ignore them all. Comments don't slow down the execution of your code; so don't be afraid to use them liberally. At a minimum, your comments should list what the procedure is for and when it was written. Figure 4.2 shows a typical procedure with detailed comments.

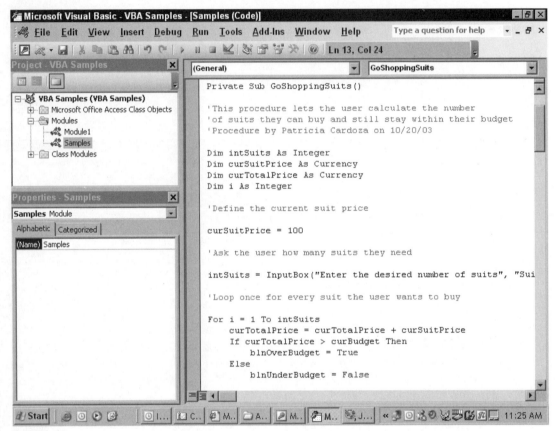

Figure 4-2

You might be wondering why you need to add comments to code you're writing for your own applications. Well, any time you write code, there's a chance that code will be used for more than one application. It's also possible that someone else will eventually inherit your code. What if you choose to leave your current position to take a new job? When your company hires a replacement programmer, they might need to make changes to your code. If you haven't added any comments to your code, they might have a hard time understanding your procedures. If you've ever had to examine another programmer's code and found it without comments, you'll understand the importance of comments.

Comments also help you understand why you might have used a particular piece of code. For example, if you hard coded certain values within your application, you might wonder why you chose to use those particular values. You can use comments to remind yourself why you used specific code.

Line Continuation

Many VBA statements are quite long. Take the following If . . . Then statement used to fill a variable with a value:

```
If (txtCustomerState = "CA" and txtCustomerZip = "95685") or
(txtCustomerState = "WA" and txtCustomerZip = "89231") then
    txtCustomerRegion = "Western US"
End If
```

As you can see, this code is a bit long. When printed in this book, even the conditional portion of the statement takes up several lines. When you write this code in VBA, all of the code will fit on one very long line; however, the line won't all display on the screen, as shown in Figure 4.3. This can make procedures difficult to read, as you need to not only scroll up and down to view the entire procedure but scroll left and right as well.

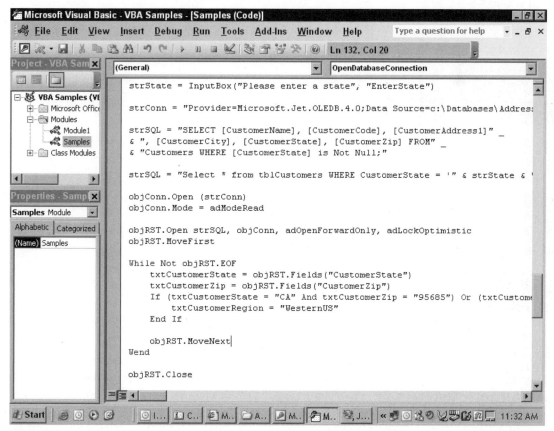

Figure 4-3

Instead of writing very long lines of code in VBA, use the line continuation character to break long lines of code. Ending a line of code with a space followed by an underscore signifies that the next line is a continuation of the current line as in the following code snippet, shown here and in Figure 4.4.

```
If (txtCustomerState = "CA" and txtCustomerZip = "95685") or _
(txtCustomerState = "WA" and txtCustomerZip = "89231") then
    txtCustomerRegion = "Western US"
End If
```

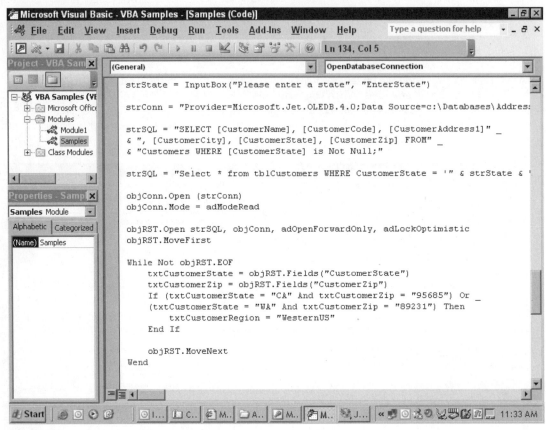

Figure 4-4

Isn't that easier to read? There's one limitation to the line continuation character though; you can't use it within literal strings. If you're using the line continuation character within a string, there's one way around this limitation. You can use the & symbol on the continued line and add extra quotation marks to work around this limitation. For example, if you need to open a recordset with an SQL statement, you could end up with a very long SQL statement in order to include all of the fields you need within your table. The statement might read something like the following:

```
strSQL = "SELECT [CustomerName], [CustomerCode], [CustomerAddress1],
[CustomerCity], [CustomerState], [CustomerZip] FROM Customers WHERE
[CustomerState] is Not Null;"
```

You can use the line continuation character along with the & symbol to turn that code into the following:

```
strSQL = "SELECT [CustomerName], [CustomerCode], [CustomerAddress1]" _
& ", [CustomerCity], [CustomerState], [CustomerZip] FROM" _
& "Customers WHERE [CustomerState] is Not Null;"
```

You should use the line continuation character any time you have a line of code longer than your screen width.

Constants

There are several different types of constants you can use in VBA: literal, symbolic, and built-in. Literal constants are numbers, strings, and dates that are hard coded in the procedure. For example, adding the following line of code to your procedure shows the use of a literal constant:

```
Public dtStartDate as Date = #12/25/2003#
```

A symbolic constant is very much like a variable. It is used for values that won't change in your code, and are fixed. They are usually declared at the beginning of your procedure and use the Const keyword instead of the Dim keyword. Specifying a constant for the width of a page is an example of a symbolic constant. Often the constant name is typed in all capital letters.

```
Const PAGE_WIDTH = 80
```

You can declare literal or symbolic constants in several ways. Later in this chapter, we'll cover variables, how they are declared, and when you can use them. Constants follow many of the same rules as variables. You can declare constants with either the Public or Private keyword. We'll go over the use of the Public and Private keywords when we discuss variables later in this chapter.

Built-in constants are defined within VBA. They can help you code by allowing you to learn the constant name rather than the number associated with the constant's value. For example, VBA provides constants for such uses as defining the types of buttons you'll see on a message box Rather than use the number that corresponds to the Yes or No button option in a message box, you can use the constant vbYesNo. Because the constant is named with a semi-intuitive name, it's easier to remember while you're coding. You can call a built-in constant by simply using its name. All built-in constants in VBA begin with the letters vb. There are approximately 700 built-in constants in VBA.

The following table lists some of VBA's built-in constants. As you can see, there are constants for all sorts of VBA operations. If you're really curious about the entire list of VBA constants, you can view them in the Object Browser. We'll cover the Object Browser Chapter 5.

Constant Name	Value	Purpose
VbFirstFourDays	2	Configures the first week of the year to be the first week with at least four days

Continues

Constant Name	Value	Purpose
VbFirstFullWeek	3	Configures the first week of the year to be the first full (7 day) week
VbOkOnly	0	Describes a type of message box with only an OK button
VbYesNoCancel	3	Describes a type of message box with three buttons: Yes, No, and Cancel
VbMonday	2	Constant used to specify Monday as the day of the week
VbWednesday	4	Constant used to specify Wednesday as the day of the week
VbHidden	2	Used to describe the hidden attribute of a file

Each object library you reference within your code contains its own set of built-in constants. For example, in Microsoft Access there are five built-in constants to specify a type of view. These constants are acViewDesign, acViewNormal, acViewPivotChart, acViewPivotTable, and acViewPreview. Using the built-in constants within your code is a lot easier than remembering that you need to specify the number 1 to open a form in design mode. All built-in constants in Access use the prefix ac. Each object library has its own prefix. When referring to Outlook built-in constants, the prefix is ol. Word constants begin with wd.

So how can you find out if there are constants you could use in your code? Well, the first way is to just start invoking properties, methods, and events. One of the great advantages of VBA is that once you start typing, VBA will help you along. So if you start typing the message box function, VBA will prompt you to choose the proper constant for the type of buttons you need. Figure 4.5 illustrates this feature. We'll discuss this feature more in Chapter 5.

Enums

Both Access and VBA contain another structure called an *enum*. Short for enumeration, this structure is a wrapper of sorts for a group of built-in constants—more of a way to categorize constants than actually do anything with them. You won't actually use the enum to do anything; rather, you'll use the constants declared within the enum instead of using their intrinsic values. Access has a number of built-in enums. The following enum describes the various constants that can be used to specify the view of a form.

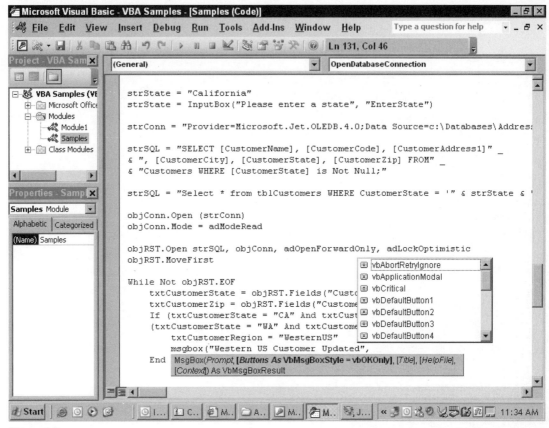

Figure 4-5

```
Enum AcFormView
    acNormal = 0
    acDesign = 1
    acPreview = 2
    acFormDS = 3
    acFormPivotTable = 4
    acFormPivotChart = 5
End Enum
```

You can browse any of the Access or VBA enums through the use of the Object Browser. We'll cover the Object Browser in Chapter 5.

Summary

In this chapter, we've refreshed your memory about some of the basics of VBA. Now, we'll move on to cover the VBA Editor. Chapter 5 goes into detail about the various panes of the VBA Editor and provides a brief overview of how to use each one.

5

Using the VBA Editor

You'll use the VBA Editor to write almost all of your VBA code. While you can simply enter the VBA Editor and start typing code, knowing a bit about the different components of the VBA Editor can help you properly structure and debug your code. In this chapter, we'll examine the major structural components of the VBA Editor as well as some basic code debugging techniques.

Anatomy of the VBA Editor

You can access the VBA Editor in several ways. From anywhere in Microsoft Access, click *Alt+F11* on the keyboard or choose `Tools, Macro, Visual Basic Editor`. You can also enter the VBA Editor from any Form or Report. From the `Properties` dialog box, click the `Events` tab, select the event you're interested in, click the `Ellipses` button (...), and choose `Code Builder`. When you first view the VBA Editor, you might be a little overwhelmed by the number of components you see on the screen. Let's view the VBA Editor within a user-created module, as shown in Figure 5-1.

The VBA Editor shown in the figure has the following components:

❑ `Project Explorer`: This window shows you all of the components of the current VBA Project. The various components can include three types of objects: form or report modules, class modules, and standard modules. Each type of component has its own icon. The `Project Explorer` in Figure 5-1 contains a class module, a source form, and a standard module. The VBA Project carries the same name as the current database. If for any reason, the `Project Explorer` isn't visible when you display the VBA Editor, click *Ctrl+R* to display it.

❑ `Properties` Window: This dialog box, typically shown on the bottom-left corner of the VBA Editor, lists all of the properties for the currently selected object. The object could be a module or a class module. You probably won't use the `Properties` window often when writing VBA code in Access 2003. This window is more helpful when working with user forms in Visual Basic.

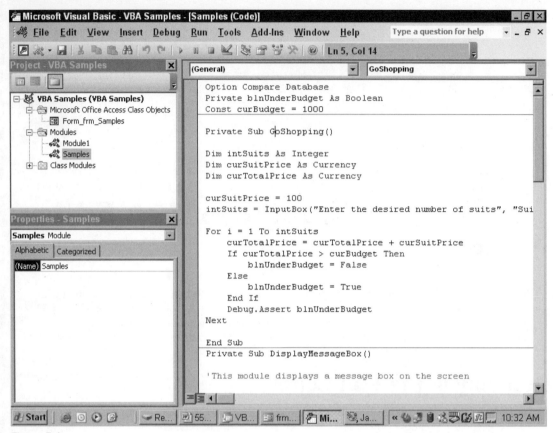

```
Microsoft Visual Basic - VBA Samples - [Samples (Code)]

File   Edit   View   Insert   Debug   Run   Tools   Add-Ins   Window   Help        Type a question for help

                                                             Ln 5, Col 14

Project - VBA Samples                    (General)                          GoShopping

  VBA Samples (VBA Samples)              Option Compare Database
    Microsoft Office Access Class Objects Private blnUnderBudget As Boolean
      Form_frm_Samples                   Const curBudget = 1000
    Modules
      Module1                            Private Sub GoShopping()
      Samples
    Class Modules                        Dim intSuits As Integer
                                         Dim curSuitPrice As Currency
                                         Dim curTotalPrice As Currency

                                         curSuitPrice = 100
Properties - Samples                     intSuits = InputBox("Enter the desired number of suits", "Sui

Samples Module                           For i = 1 To intSuits
                                             curTotalPrice = curTotalPrice + curSuitPrice
 Alphabetic  Categorized                     If curTotalPrice > curBudget Then
 (Name) Samples                                  blnUnderBudget = False
                                             Else
                                                 blnUnderBudget = True
                                             End If
                                             Debug.Assert blnUnderBudget
                                         Next

                                         End Sub
                                         Private Sub DisplayMessageBox()

                                         'This module displays a message box on the screen

 Start       Re...   55...   VB...   frm...   Mi...   Ja...              10:32 AM
```

Figure 5-1

❑ Code Window: This is where you'll actually write your code. By default, the Code window displays all subs and functions within the current module. You can change the display of the Code window and limit it to only the currently selected procedure by selecting Options from the Tools menu. In the Window Settings frame of the Editor tab, uncheck Default to Full Module View. Click OK to save your changes. The Code window has several components of its own.

   ❑ The Object list box allows you to choose from a variety of objects. When you're writing code inside a standard module, this list box will only contain the (General) option. When you're writing code within a class module associated with a form or report, the Object list box contains an entry for every object (text box, combo box, label, and so on) within the form or report.

   ❑ The Procedure list box displays different items depending on the type of module you're viewing. When viewing a class module associated with a form or report, the Procedure list box contains an entry for every event associated with the selected object. For example, if you choose a combo box on your form, the Procedure list box contains an entry for events such as the Click event, the BeforeUpdate and AfterUpdate events, and the LostFocus event, among others. If you're viewing a standard module, this list box contains an entry for every sub or function in your module. You'll use this drop-down list to select the specific procedure you need to edit. If you have a module with a large number of procedures, scrolling through the Code window to find the specific procedure can be a time-consuming and onerous task. Simply click the Procedure drop-down box to choose any available procedure in the current module or class module. All subs and functions are listed alphabetically. You can also use the Procedure drop-down box to jump directly to the General Declarations section.

❑   The Code window is where you'll actually write your code. You can include subs, functions, and general declarations.

In addition to these visible components, there are a number of components you can display to help you write your code and work with the Access 2003 Objects. Most of these components are available under the View menu within the VBA Editor.

Your Access Database and VBA Project—Better Together

You might wonder how a VBA Project and your Access database correlate. Well, in a nutshell, here's what you need to know. First, you get one VBA Project for every Access database you create. The objects in the Project Explorer shown in Figure 5-1 are present no matter where in your Access database you're writing code. You could be writing code behind a Form or Report, or in a module. Regardless, you'll see the same objects listed in the Project Explorer. Second, don't confuse the VBA Project with an Access Project. An Access Data Project (ADP) is a completely different entity, covered in Chapter 17.

Using the Object Browser

The Object Browser is probably one of the most powerful tools you'll use when writing VBA code. You can display the Object Browser by selecting Object Browser from the View menu of the VBA Editor or by clicking F2 within the VBA Editor. The Object Browser, shown in Figure 5-2, has a number of components.

When you load the Object Browser, you'll notice that you can still view the Project Explorer and the Properties window. The Object Browser appears directly over the Code window. You can return to the Code window at any time by selecting Code from the View menu or by clicking F7. There are several components of the Object Browser you'll use often.

❑   The Project/Library box shows all the available type libraries. We'll discuss how to add a type library to your Project later in this chapter. You can choose any available type library from the drop-down box or choose <All Libraries>. The type library you choose in the Project/Library box will dictate which objects you can browse with the Object Browser.

❑   The next drop-down box is the Search text box. You can enter search terms in that box and click the Search button (the icon of the binoculars) to search the selected type libraries for the particular term. Results of your search are displayed in the Search Results pane.

❑   The Search Results pane lists all of the results of your search. You can show or hide the Search Results pane by clicking the Show/Hide icon (two up or down arrows) next to the

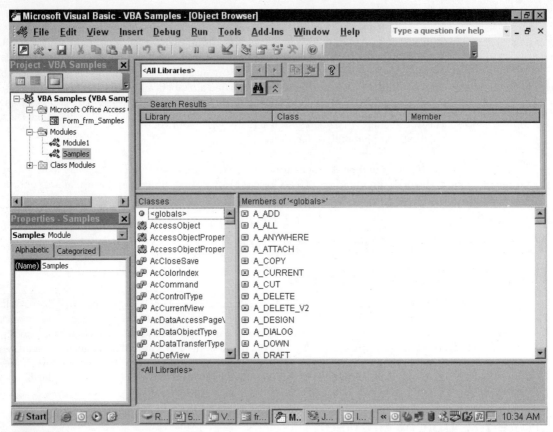

Figure 5-2

Search button. The Search Results pane lists the relevant library, class, and member of any object returned by your search. To display more information about any object displayed in the Search Results pane, click the object to display its full information in the Details pane.

❑ The Classes list displays all of the objects, enums, and collections in the currently referenced library. You can scroll through the Classes list and click to select any of the listed items. After you select an item, more details are displayed in the Members of list and the Details pane.

❑ The Members of list displays all of the properties, methods, events, and constants associated with the currently selected object in the Classes list. Select any of the items in the Members of list to display details in the Details pane.

❑ The Details pane of the Object Browser displays information such as the type of object, its data type, the arguments it needs, and the parent library or collection. For example, in Figure 5-3, the Details pane informs you that the constant vbOkOnly is a member of the Enum vbMsgBoxStyle, which is a member of the VBA object library. Its value is 0 and the other members of the Enum vbMsgBoxStyle include vbApplicationModal, vbCritical, vbExclamation, and many others.

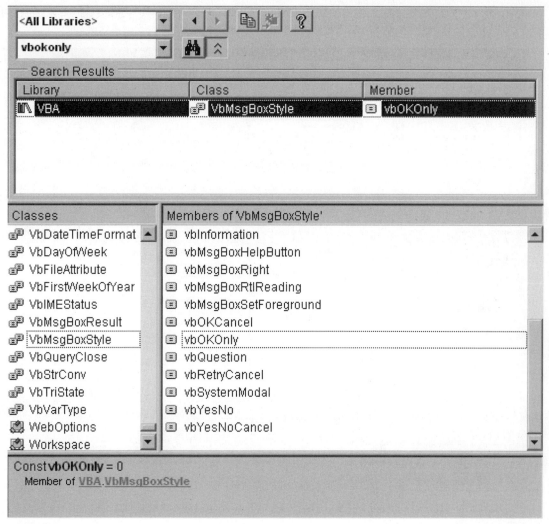

Figure 5-3

If a Help file is associated with the currently selected object, you can display a Help topic by clicking the item in either the Classes or Members of list, and then pressing *F1* or clicking the Help button in the upper-right corner of the Object Browser.

The buttons next to the Project/Library box allow you to scroll through the previous or next members of the current collection.

One of the advantages of the Object Browser is that you can actually use it to take you to anywhere in the code the current object is declared. For example, in Figure 5-3, I've searched the current database's object library (Samples) for the procedure CoffeeTime. The Search Results pane lists the library, class, and member for the CoffeeTime sub. You can click the View Definition button (the fourth button from the left next to the Project Library drop-down box) to return to the Code window and display the CoffeeTime sub, as shown in Figure 5-4.

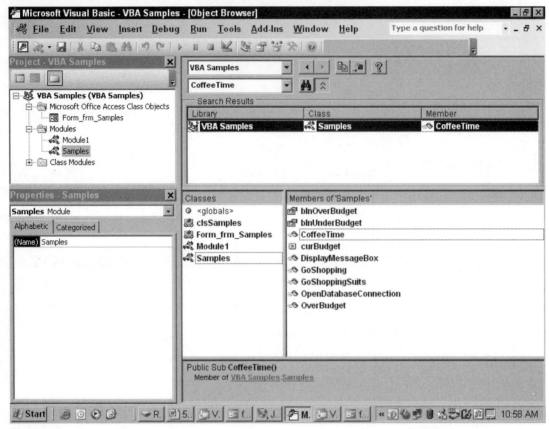

Figure 5-4

The rest of this chapter will explore the other components of the VBA Editor that can help you write and debug VBA code.

Testing and Debugging VBA Code

The Code window is where you'll actually write your code. Shown previously in Figure 5-1, it can contain subroutines, functions, and declarations. In addition to the Code window, there are other components of the VBA Editor you'll use to test and debug your code. We'll explore each of those components in the following sections.

When Should You Debug Your Code?

There are several schools of thought you can follow when deciding when to debug your VBA code. You could debug as you write, testing every few lines. This could be quite time-consuming. You'd have to run your code every few lines (possibly with incomplete procedures) and make heavy use of the tools in this section such as the Immediate window and Watch statements. The advantage to this method is that you'll always know the value of your variables and the likelihood of making a mistake is reduced. The alternative to this method is to write all of the code in your application and then debug your code. This method allows you to write entire procedures or even your entire application's code without debugging. This is a tempting method as it doesn't require you to stop your productive code typing to debug your application. However, you can easily end up with numerous errors in your code, some of which might require you to make major changes to your code as you discover them.

The best method of debugging falls somewhere between these two options. You should definitely debug at the end of each procedure. This allows you to be confident that each procedure produces the appropriate and expected values. Unless you're writing incredibly long procedures, this method should be sufficient to ensure you're not writing code with too many errors.

Immediate Window

The Immediate window can be displayed in the Visual Basic Editor to allow you to enter commands and view the contents of variables while your code is in break mode. Press *Ctrl+G* or choose Immediate Window from the View menu to display the Immediate window in the Visual Basic Editor, as shown in Figure 5-5.

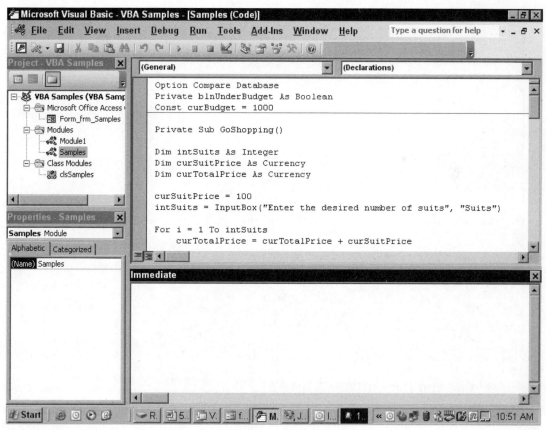

Figure 5-5

In the `Immediate` window, you can display the value of a variable by using the ? (`Debug.Print`) command. Just type ? along with the variable name and press *Enter*. VBA Editor will display the contents of the variable in the `Immediate` window. For example, typing the following and pressing *Enter* will display the value of the `intNumEmployees` in the `Immediate` window.

```
? intNumEmployees
```

This can be helpful troubleshooting your code if you're encountering unexpected results. Simply set a breakpoint in your code and test the value of a variable at any time. This can allow you to determine where in the code the value is being incorrectly calculated. The question mark is shorthand for typing `Debug.Print`. Instead of typing ? `intNumEmployees` you can also type `Debug.Print intNumEmployees` and click *Enter*. Both statements produce the same results.

In addition to displaying the value of variables, you can also execute VBA commands in the `Immediate` window. Just eliminate the ? character and type the entire command, followed by pressing the *Enter* key. Typing `msgbox("Replace with pithy message text.")` and pressing *Enter* will display the message as shown in Figure 5-6.

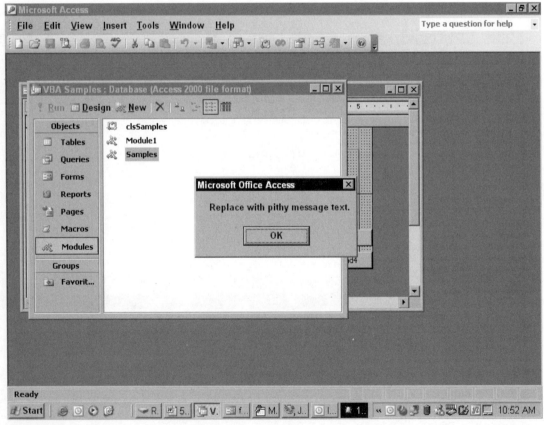

Figure 5-6

You can even perform calculations in the `Immediate` window such as

```
intTotalEmployees = intTempEmployees + intFullTimeEmployees.
```

The `Immediate` window can do more than just display some simple calculations. It is a powerful debugging tool for your applications. For more information about the `Immediate` window, see Chapter 8.

Using the `Immediate` window along with other aspects of the VBA Editor detailed in this chapter, such as breakpoints and stepping through code, is the most generally accepted method of debugging your code. However, there's another method that is often used, especially by beginning developers. This other method involves placing message box code throughout your code to test the values of certain variables or calculations. There's nothing technically wrong with this method, but it can be messy and cumbersome. After all, when you're done debugging your code, you'll need to comment or remove all those message box calls. This can be a lot of unnecessary work when you could have just used some of the more widely accepted debugging methods.

The Debug.Print Statement

We've already established that the ? character is short for `Debug.Print`. It's easy to use both of these statements directly in the `Immediate` window; however, that's not the only place you can use this statement. Consider the following code:

```
Sub FunWithStringsAndNumbers()
Dim strBikes As String
Dim strCost As String
Dim strCustomerName As String
Dim intBikes As Integer
Dim curCost As Currency
strBikes = "5"
strCost = "100"
strCustomerName = "The ""W"" Hotel, New York City"
intBikes = 5
curCost = 100
Debug.Print strBikes + strCost
Debug.Print intBikes + curCost
Debug.Print strCustomerName
End Sub
```

This code produces the following results in the `Immediate` window:

```
5100
105
The "W" Hotel, New York City
```

You can use the `Debug.Print` statement within any procedure to display results of calculations or values of variables in the `Immediate` window.

The Debug.Assert Statement

You might have noticed that when you were starting to type `Debug.Print`, you could have just as easily chosen to type `Debug.Assert`. This option conditionally suspends execution of code at the line where

Debug.Assert appears. For example, the following code uses the Debug.Assert statement to stop code execution when a specific condition is met:

```
Option Compare Database
Private blnUnderBudget As Boolean
Const curBudget = 1000
Private Sub GoShopping()
Dim intSuits As Integer
Dim curSuitPrice As Currency
Dim curTotalPrice As Currency
Dim i as Integer
curSuitPrice = 100
intSuits = InputBox("Enter the desired number of suits", "Suits")
For i = 1 To intSuits
    curTotalPrice = curTotalPrice + curSuitPrice
    If curTotalPrice > curBudget Then
        blnUnderBudget = False
    Else
        blnUnderBudget = True
    End If
    Debug.Assert blnUnderBudget
Next
End Sub
```

This code will break every time you go over budget on your shopping trip. You can use this statement when testing for specific conditions within your code. While Debug.Assert is a good debugging tool, you probably won't ever use it in live code.

Breakpoints

Breakpoints are simply places in your code that pause execution of code. For example, if you want to check the value of a variable curTotalCost midway through the following procedure, you'd need to use the Debug.Print statement or set a breakpoint.

```
Sub HowMuchCanWeSpend()
Dim curTotalPrice As Currency
Dim curUnitPrice As Currency
Dim intNumSocks As Integer
Dim i As Integer
curUnitPrice = 3.5
intNumSocks = InputBox("Please enter the number of pairs of socks you
want.", "Pairs of Socks")
For i = 1 To intNumSocks
    curTotalPrice = curTotalPrice + curUnitPrice

Next
Debug.Print curTotalPrice
End Sub
```

The preceding code prints in the Immediate window the amount you'll spend for the total sock purchase. That's great, but what if you want to see how your total expense is adding up as you go? You can certainly add a Debug.Print statement within the For...Next loop, but you can also set a breakpoint anywhere in the procedure. Once the breakpoint is reached, you can use the Immediate window to check the value of your variables. You can set a breakpoint on any line of code except for Dim statements and comments.

The simplest way to set a breakpoint is to click in the left margin of the Code window. A brick-colored dot will appear in the margin and the corresponding line of code is also highlighted. To clear a breakpoint, click the left margin again in the same spot. You can also set and clear breakpoints by placing your cursor in the desired line of code and select Toggle Breakpoint from the Debug menu or pressing F9. When you run the code, every time the breakpoint is reached, code execution stops and VBA waits for you to decide what to do next. You can choose from the following options:

❑ Check the value of variables in the Immediate window. When your code reaches a breakpoint, the value of all variables is retained. You can check the value of any variable by using the Debug.Print statement or the ? character within the Immediate window.

❑ Use your mouse to hover over any variable in the current procedure. The value of the variable is displayed close to the mouse cursor.

❑ Press F5 or select Continue from the Run menu to continue code execution. Execution proceeds until the end of the procedure or until the next breakpoint is reached.

When VBA encounters a breakpoint, it pauses execution immediately before the line of code is executed. The line of code that contains the breakpoint isn't actually executed unless or until you choose to step through your code using the F8 key.

Stepping through Code

In most cases, you design code to run with little or no user intervention. However, when you're testing code, sometimes you want to do more than insert a breakpoint or two or include a couple of Debug .Print statements. If you're running code with many variable changes or some intricate looping, it can sometimes be helpful to step through the code line by line. Doing this allows you to watch the value of variables after each line of code is executed. This can help you pinpoint any errors or logical mistakes in the code.

To step through your code, press F8 to begin the procedure (you can also press F8 after the code has entered break mode to step through the remaining code). When you first press F8 to begin code execution, the name of the sub or function is highlighted in yellow. Subsequent clicks of the F8 key move execution from line to line, highlighting the next executable line in yellow. Comment lines and Dim statements are skipped when stepping through code. As you press F8, the highlighted line is executed.

If the current procedure calls another sub or function, F8 will also execute the called procedure line by line. If you're confident that the called procedure doesn't contain any errors and you want code execution to process the entire called procedure and then return to line by line execution of the calling procedure, click *Shift+F8* to step over the procedure. Stepping over the called procedure executes the entire procedure and then returns to the calling procedure where code execution continues one step at a time. If you're within a called procedure, you can also click *Ctrl+Shift+F8* to step out of the current procedure. So what's the difference between stepping over and stepping out of the procedure? Well, if you're already in the called procedure, the two are exactly the same. However, let's assume you're stepping through the following code:

```
Option Compare Database
Private blnUnderBudget As Boolean
```

```
Const curBudget = 1000
Private Sub GoShopping()
Dim intSuits As Integer
Dim curSuitPrice As Currency
Dim curTotalPrice As Currency
curSuitPrice = 100
intSuits = InputBox("Enter the desired number of suits", "Suits")
For i = 1 To intSuits
    curTotalPrice = curTotalPrice + curSuitPrice
    If curTotalPrice > curBudget Then
        blnUnderBudget = False
    Else
        blnUnderBudget = True
    End If
Next
If blnUnderBudget = False Then
    OverBudget
End If
End Sub

Private Sub OverBudget()
Debug.Print "You've gone over budget."
Debug.Print "You need to work some overtime."
Debug.Print "Remember to pay your taxes."
End Sub
```

Use the *F8* key to step through the code until you reach the last If...Then loop (If blnUnderBudget = False Then). When the OverBudget line is highlighted in yellow (meaning it hasn't yet been executed), stepping over the OverBudget procedure returns execution to the line after the OverBudget call (in this case the End If line). If you step out of the procedure, the OverBudget procedure runs, your code returns to the GoShopping procedure and completes the procedure. If, however, you use the *F8* key to step through your code until you reach the first line of the OverBudget procedure, stepping out of the procedure returns you to the line after the OverBudget call (the End If line). Use the following table as a cheat sheet and create some simple procedures to test the various debugging techniques shown in this chapter.

Debugging Technique	Description	Shortcut Key
Step Into	Executes the next line of code in your procedure.	*F8*
Step Over	Executes code one line at a time within the current procedure. If a second procedure is called from within the first, the entire second procedure is executed at once.	*Shift+F8*
Step Out	VBA executes the entire current procedure. If executed within the second procedure, the entire second procedure is executed and execution returns to the line following the line in the first procedure that called the second procedure.	*Ctrl+Shift+F8*

Run to Cursor

Many times when you're executing code, you don't want to run every line of code line by line, but executing the entire procedure at once doesn't help you debug the procedure. If you have a long loop within the procedure, it can be very tedious to execute every line of the loop every time the loop needs to run. For example, consider the following code:

```
Sub CoffeeTime()
Dim curLatteAllowance As Currency
Dim curLattePrice As Currency
Dim intNumLattes As Integer
Dim curTotalExpenses As Currency
curLattePrice = 3.5
curLatteAllowance = InputBox("Enter the amount of money you have for
lattes." _
, "Latte Allowance")
While curTotalExpenses < curLatteAllowance
    intNumLattes = intNumLattes + 1
    curTotalExpenses = curTotalExpenses + curLattePrice
Wend
Debug.Print intNumLattes
MsgBox "You can purchase" & intNumLattes & "lattes.", _
vbOkOnly, "Total Lattes"
End Sub
```

If you have $350 to spend on lattes, the While...Wend loop will run 100 times. Pressing *F8* to step through that long of a loop can be very tedious. If you're not worried that the loop is producing incorrect data, you can place your cursor in the Debug.Print intNumLattes line and press *Ctrl+F8*. Your procedure will run until it reaches the Debug.Print line, then it halts. The line is highlighted. You can then press *F8* to execute the highlighted line of code or press *F5* to continue execution until the end of the procedure.

Locals Window

Sometimes it can be quite tedious to test the value of every variable when your code enters break mode. If you're stepping through code and need to test the value of seven different variables every step of the way, that's a lot of Debug.Print statements to keep track of in the Immediate window. You can use the Locals window to display all the variables in a procedure and their values. You can watch the variable values change as you step through the code. To display the Locals window, choose Locals Window from the View menu. Figure 5-7 shows the Locals window while stepping through the previous CoffeeTime procedure.

As you step through the procedure, the Locals window shows you the up-to-date values of all variables. Figure 5-8 shows the Locals window for the same procedure when you reach the last line of the procedure. Once you reach the end of the procedure and execution stops, the Locals window is empty again.

Watch Window

The last debugging tool we'll examine in this chapter is the watch window. This window allows you to watch a variable within your procedure. When the value of the variable changes or when the variable is

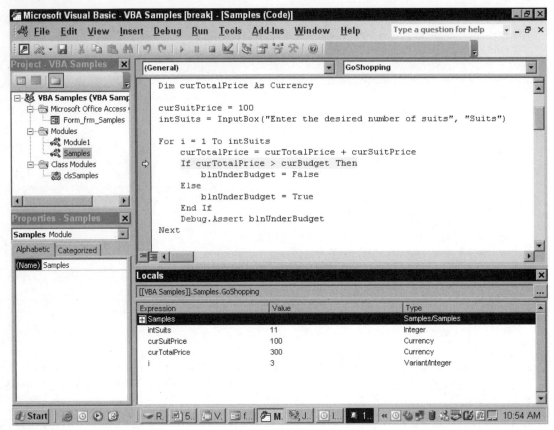

Figure 5-7

`True`, your code will enter break mode. To display the `Watch` window, select `Watch Window` from the `View` menu.

We'll return to the `CoffeeTime` procedure we've used in other places in this chapter. If you want to know when the value of the `intNumLattes` variable changes, you can add a watch for that variable. To add a watch, right-click in the `Watch` window and choose `Add Watch` (Figure 5-9).

Enter `intNumLattes` in the `Expression` text box. Choose whether you want to watch the expression, break when the value is `True`, or break when the value changes. Click `OK` to save your watch. When you run the `CoffeeTime` procedure, the procedure will enter break mode whenever the value of the `intNumLattes` variable changes. If you choose to simply watch the expression (rather than break), the `Watch` window behaves almost exactly like the `Locals` window except that only the watched variables are shown.

If you have a rather long loop to execute and you no longer need your watch, you can delete it while your code is in break mode. Simply right-click the watch and select Delete Watch. You can then press F5 to continue code execution.

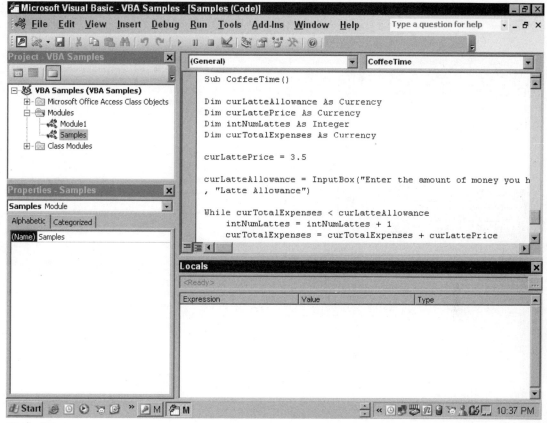

Figure 5-8

The `CoffeeTime` procedure isn't the best case study for the `Watch` window. If we alter the `GoShopping` procedure from earlier in this chapter just a bit, you can see the `Watch` window in action. Here's the revised code:

```
Option Compare Database
Private blnOverBudget As Boolean
Const curBudget = 1000

Private Sub GoShoppingSuits()
Dim intSuits As Integer
Dim curSuitPrice As Currency
Dim curTotalPrice As Currency
curSuitPrice = 100
intSuits = InputBox("Enter the desired number of suits", "Suits")
For i = 1 To intSuits
    curTotalPrice = curTotalPrice + curSuitPrice
    If curTotalPrice > curBudget Then
        blnOverBudget = True
```

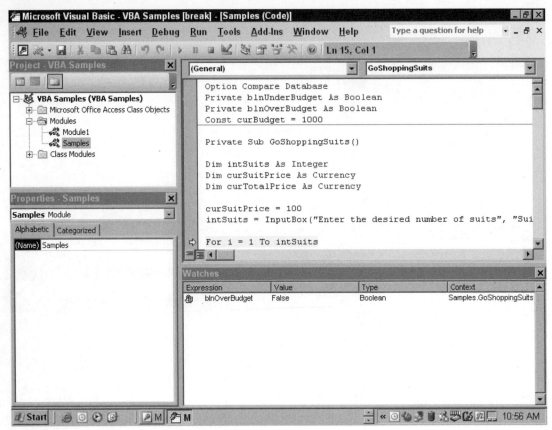

Figure 5-9

```
    Else
        blnOverBudget = False
    End If
Next
If blnOverBudget = True Then
    Msgbox "You're over budget!", vbExclamation, "Over Budget"
End If
End Sub
```

You can add a watch for the blnOverBudget and break when the value is True. As soon as your loop executes for the 11th time, the watch expression is triggered and the code enters break mode.

Summary

We've explored some basic VBA syntax, some of the uses of VBA within Access, and the basics of the VBA development environment. Now you're ready to create some code. The rest of the chapters address the techniques you'll need to extract data from other data sources, control Access forms and reports, secure your database, and provide you with enough tips and tricks to add some real pizzazz to your Access databases. Have fun!

Using DAO to Access Data

As you've seen from previous chapters, VBA is the programming language you use to programmatically interact with the Access object model. You use VBA to manipulate Access-specific objects, such as forms, reports, and so on. But since Access is a Relational Database Management System, you will undoubtedly find yourself also needing to programmatically interact with the data it contains, and indeed with the database design, or schema. Microsoft Access employs two data access object models: Data Access Objects (DAO) and ActiveX Data Objects (ADO). While Chapter 7 describes ADO, this chapter is solely concerned with examining the DAO model.

We'll begin this chapter with a brief history of DAO and an indication of when it might be most appropriate to use DAO in preference to ADO. We'll introduce the three most important objects in the DAO object hierarchy: the DBEngine, Workspace, and Database objects. We'll then talk about database properties and how to use them.

Before we start working with DAO objects to access our data, we'll take an in-depth look at how to use DAO to create and modify our database structure, including tables, fields, indexes, and relations. We'll then spend some time discussing the Jet (Joint Engine Technology) security model, and how you can create and manipulate security objects, such as users, groups, and of course, how to read and assign object permissions. Finally, we'll examine data access in detail using `QueryDefs` and `Recordsets`. This will include many examples of how to create data access objects, and how to find and manipulate their data.

Direct Access Objects

DAO is the programmatic interface between VBA and Jet databases, ODBC (Open Database Connectivity) data stores, and installable ISAM (Indexed Sequential Access Method) data sources, such as Excel, Paradox, dBase, and Lotus 1-2-3.

As is described in greater detail a little later in this section, DAO supports two different data access environments, or *workspaces*: Microsoft Jet and ODBCDirect. You use Microsoft Jet workspaces when you need to take advantage of Jet's unique features, such as the ability to link data from different database formats.

DAO was first released as a part of Visual Basic 2.0, and was known internally at Microsoft as *VT Objects*, which provided a limited set of options for interacting with ODBC data sources. In November 1992, DAO 1.0 was released as part of Access 1.0. It provided Access developers with a limited set of database objects for manipulating the Microsoft Jet data engine. Improvements in DAO version 2.0 (released with Access 2.0) meant that programmers were afforded almost complete control over creating and modifying database objects, as well as manipulating data using a variety of recordset types. DAO 2.5 was created for both 16- and 32-bit platforms, and was designed for use with ODBC Desktop Database Drivers 2.0.

In 1995, Microsoft simultaneously released DAO 3.0 in both Access 95 and Visual Basic 4.0, offering full 32-bit type libraries, plus several extra properties and methods to complete the object model. In addition, the new `Error` object was added to provide an easier way of accessing runtime error information.

DAO is implemented so that its objects (databases, tables, fields, queries, and so on) are organized into a hierarchy of collections. A *collection* is simply a container for a group of objects of the same type. Each object in the hierarchy contains one or more properties that define its characteristics, and one or more methods (programs) to carry out a variety of actions against those objects. DAO enables you to use a programming language to access and manipulate data in local or remote databases, and to manage those databases, their objects, and their structures.

But because DAO was specifically designed to interface with the Jet database, it has to translate calls to ODBC when using databases other than Access, thereby resulting in slower performance. To counter this, Microsoft briefly introduced RDO (Remote Data Objects), a model that attempted to offer performance advantages over DAO when accessing remote data sources. The problem was that RDO only shipped with Visual Basic Enterprise Edition, and required a Visual Basic runtime license to use it.

DAO 3.5 was released with a new feature—*ODBCDirect*. The ODBCDirect workspace uses RDO in the background to provide an alternative when you only need to execute queries or stored procedures against a back-end server, such as SQL Server, or when your application needs the specific capabilities provided by ODBC, such as batch updates or asynchronous queries. ODBCDirect allows you to access database servers through ODBC, without having to load the Jet database engine. Although it is the same technology, ODBCDirect was designed to provide the remote data access functionality that DAO didn't handle.

DAO 3.6, as shipped with Access 2003, is the newest offering that has been updated to use the Jet 4.0 database engine. The only real difference between DAO 3.6 and DAO 3.5 is that all Unicode interfaces are enabled, which means that data is now supplied in Unicode. Additionally, dBase and Paradox ISAMs now require that the Borland database engine be installed, and since Jet 4.0 does not provide a Visual FoxPro ISAM, you'll need to use the Visual FoxPro ODBC Driver instead. These changes don't affect $3.5x$ applications, because DAO $3.5x$ and 3.6 can coexist on the same computer.

Why Use DAO?

Visual Basic programmers highly recommend ADO as their preferred object model for accessing databases. Although ADO is an excellent model with its own unique benefits, in the context of Access databases, it doesn't have the benefit of native database connectivity, which is where DAO has the distinct advantage.

Applications written in other programming languages, such as Visual Basic, Delphi, and the like, must explicitly *connect* to the data source they intend to manipulate, and they must do so every time they need to manipulate the data or underlying schema. This is because, unlike Access, these applications do not have an inherent connection to the data source. When used in Access, DAO allows you to manipulate data and schema through an implicit connection that Access maintains to whichever Jet, ODBC, or ISAM data source it happens to be connected to.

As *linked tables* are a uniquely Jet-specific feature, DAO is quite simply the better alternative for accessing Jet databases. In fact, it is impossible to do so natively using any other data access model.

DAO has evolved right alongside Jet, and has become the best model for accessing and manipulating Jet objects and structure. Because of its tight integration with Jet, DAO also provides much faster access to Jet databases than does ADO or JRO. This may all sound like marketing hype, but to qualify the advantages of DAO over other models, consider the following:

- ❑ ADO connections can only be applied to one database at a time, whereas DAO allows you to link (connect) to multiple databases simultaneously.

- ❑ Using the OpenRecordset method's dbDenyWrite option, DAO allows you to open a table while preventing other users from opening the *same* table with write access. The ADO Connection object's adModeShareDenyWrite constant operates at connection level—not at table level.

- ❑ Using the OpenRecordset method's dbDenyRead option, DAO allows you to open a table while preventing other users from opening the table at all. The ADO Connection object's adModeShareDenyRead constant can only be set at connection level.

- ❑ You can create users and groups in DAO, but not in ADO, because you can't specify the PID (Personal IDentifier) in ADO.

- ❑ You can secure Access objects (such as forms, reports, and so on) in DAO, but not in ADO, because there are no suitable ADO constants to specify permissions for execute, read changes, and write changes.

- ❑ You can dynamically link an updatable ODBC table in DAO, but not in ADO.

- ❑ DAO allows you to create replica databases that prevent users from deleting records, whereas JRO does not.

- ❑ In DAO, you can return information about Exchange and Outlook folders and columns using the TableDef and Field Attributes properties. ADO does not pass this information on.

- ❑ Using the DBEngine's GetOption and SetOption methods, DAO allows you to set and change Jet options without requiring you to make Registry changes.

- ❑ DAO allows you to create, change, and delete custom database properties.

- ❑ You can force the database locking mode with the DAO.LockTypeEnum constants against CurrentDb, but you can't do the same thing in ADO using ADO.LockTypeEnum against CurrentProject.Connection.

- ❑ Using AllPermissions properties, DAO allows you to retrieve an object's implicit permissions, whereas ADO doesn't have an AllPermissions property, forcing you to enumerate the groups of each user.

- ❑ DAO allows you to run a separate Jet session, using PrivDBEngine, whereas ADO does not.

❑   The current version of DAO is a very mature, well-documented, and easy to use object model for accessing database services. You can use DAO from any VBA environment such as Word, Excel, and so on, and a variety of other programming languages such as Visual Basic, FoxPro, and C++.

Finally, I think it is safe to say that DAO will be around as long as Jet databases are used.

Referring to DAO Objects

In code, you refer to objects in the DAO hierarchy by working your way down the object hierarchy. The following format illustrates generally how to reference DAO objects:

```
DBEngine.ParentCollection.ChildCollection!Object.Method_or_Property
```

You might recall from earlier discussion that a collection is a container for a group of objects of the same type. Many DAO object collections contain still other collections, so it is sometimes necessary to drill down through several collections before you get to the object that you want to operate on. This provides a highly structured and predictable method for accessing data and schema.

With the exception of the DBEngine object, all DAO objects are contained within their own collections. For example, the TableDef object is part of a TableDefs collection, and the Group object is part of a Groups collection. As a way of distinguishing between collections and individual objects, those that are named in the plural (ending with the letter *s*) are collections, whereas those named in the singular are individual objects.

Collections provide an easy way to enumerate their members by allowing you to refer to them by their name or ordinal position. You can also populate a variable with the object's name and use it instead. For example, the following examples show how you can refer to the same object in different ways.

Syntax	Description	Example
Collection("name")	Literal string	DBEngine(0).Databases("myDB")
Collection(position)	Ordinal collection position	DBEngine(0).Databases(0)
Collection(variable)	String or variant variable	strVar = "myDB" DBEngine(0).Databases(strVar)
Collection![Name]	Object name	DBEngine(0).Databases!myDB

> Where the object name contains nonstandard characters, such as spaces, you must enclose the object name in square brackets [ ].

Finally, throughout this chapter, I have used the convention of capitalizing the first character of object and collection names, to highlight the difference between them and the casual use of the same word for other purposes. The following example illustrates this convention:

The Database *object is an instance of a connection to a database or other data source. It is a member of the* Workspace *object's* Databases *collection, which is a container for a group of* Database *objects that represent connections to one or more databases.*

Default Collection Items

Let's say you wanted to retrieve the DefaultValue property for a field called PaymentDate in a table called tblPayments. This is the long way of doing it:

```
DBEngine![#Default
Workspace#].Databases(0).TableDefs!tblPayments.Fields!PaymentDate.DefaultValue
```

As you can see, referring to objects, properties, and methods can sometimes result in quite long lines of code. This can get pretty tedious after a while, so you can also refer to objects by their parent collection's default item. Assuming tblPayments is the first table in the TableDefs collection, and PaymentDate is the first field in that table's Fields collection, here is the shortened version:

```
DBEngine(0)(0)(0)(0).DefaultValue
```

The default item for any DAO object collection is the item that occupies ordinal position 0. This is in contrast to VBA collections, in which the first member occupies position 1—an important fact to remember.

The following table lists examples of the two ways you can use to refer to DAO collection members.

Collection	Default Member	Example
Containers	Documents	DBEngine.Workspaces(0).Databases(0) .Containers(0).Documents(0) DBEngine(0)(0).Containers(0)(0)
Databases	TableDefs	DBEngine.Workspaces(0).Databases(0) .TableDefs(0) DBEngine(0)(0)(0)
DBEngines	Workspaces	DBEngine.Workspaces(0) DBEngine(0)
Groups	Users	DBEngine.Workspaces(0).Groups(0).Users(0) DBEngine(0).Groups(0)(0)
QueryDefs	Parameters	DBEngine.Workspaces(0).Databases(0) .QueryDefs(0).Parameters(0) DBEngine(0)(0).QueryDefs(0)(0)
Recordsets	Fields	DBEngine.Workspaces(0).Databases(0) .Recordsets(0).Fields(0) DBEngine(0)(0).Recordsets(0)(0)

Continues

117

Collection	Default Member	Example
Relations	Fields	DBEngine.Workspaces(0).Databases(0) .Relations(0).Fields(0) DBEngine(0)(0).Relations(0)(0)
TableDefs	Fields	DBEngine.Workspaces(0).Databases(0) .TableDefs(0).Fields(0) DBEngine(0)(0)(0)(0)
Users	Groups	DBEngine.Workspaces(0).Groups(0) .Users(0).Groups(0) DBEngine(0).Groups(0)(0)(0)
Workspaces	Databases	DBEngine.Workspaces(0) DBEngine(0)

The DBEngine Object

The DBEngine object is a property of the Access *Application* object, and represents the top-level object in the DAO model. The DBEngine object contains all the other objects in the DAO object hierarchy, yet unlike many of the other DAO objects, you can't create additional DBEngine objects.

The DBEngine object contains two major collections: Workspaces and Errors. These are described in this section because they relate so closely to the DBEngine object.

The Workspaces Collection

A *workspace* is a named user session that contains open databases and provides the facility for transactions and (depending on the type of workspace) user- and group-level security. As you can have more than one workspace active at any time, the Workspaces collection is the repository for all the workspaces that have been created.

As mentioned earlier, DAO maintains two different object models, depending on the type of data source you want to manipulate, and it is the Workspace object that determines which model you use: *Microsoft Jet* or *ODBCDirect*.

To access Microsoft Jet databases and ODBC or installable ISAM data sources through the Jet database engine, you use the Microsoft Jet workspace. To access ODBC data sources through DAO (bypassing Jet), you use ODBCDirect workspaces. The type of data source you connect to, and the DAO objects, properties, and methods you can use, depends on the type of workspace you create.

For a list of the collections, objects, and methods supported by Microsoft Jet and ODBCDirect workspaces, refer to Appendix C.

The Workspace object contains four different object collections. In Microsoft Jet workspaces, these are Databases, Groups, and Users. In ODBCDirect workspaces, they are the Databases and Connections collections. Each of these collections is described in later sections.

Creating a Workspace

When you first refer to a `Workspace` object, or one of its collections, objects, methods, or properties, you automatically create the default workspace, which can be referenced using the following syntaxes: `DBEngine.Workspaces(0)`, `DBEngine(0)`, or simply `Workspaces(0)`.

The default workspace is given the name #Default Workspace#. In the absence of user- and group-level security, the default workspace's `UserName` property is set to `Admin`. If security is implemented, the `UserName` property is set to the name of the user who logged on.

You don't have to do anything to begin using a Microsoft Jet workspace; Access creates one by default unless you explicitly create an ODBCDirect workspace. To use an ODBCDirect workspace, you either set the `DBEngine`'s `DefaultType` property to `dbUseODBC`, or set the `CreateWorkspace` method's `Type` property to `dbUseODBC`, when you create the workspace.

The basic procedure for creating a new workspace is as follows:

1. Create the workspace, using the `DBEngine`'s `CreateWorkspace` method.

2. Append the new workspace to the `Workspaces` collection.

You can use a workspace without appending it to the `Workspaces` collection, but you must refer to it using the object variable to which it was assigned. You will not be able to refer to it through the `Workspaces` collection until it is appended.

The following example demonstrates how to create both a Microsoft Jet workspace and an ODBCDirect workspace, and print their `Name` properties:

```
Dim wsJet As DAO.Workspace
Dim wsODBC As DAO.Workspace

'Create a new Microsoft Jet workspace
Set wsJet = DBEngine.CreateWorkspace( _
        "myJetWS", strUserName, strPassword, dbUseJet)

'Create a new ODBCDirect workspace
Set wsODBC = DBEngine.CreateWorkspace( _
        "myODBCWS", strUserName, strPassword, dbUseODBC)

'Append the workspaces to the collection
Workspaces.Append wsJet
Workspaces.Append wsODBC

'Print the names of all the workspaces
Debug.Print "wsJet.Name:  " & wsJet.Name        'myJetWS
Debug.Print "wsODBC.Name: " & wsODBC.Name       'myODBCWS

'Clean up
wsODBC.Close
wsJet.Close
Set wsODBC = Nothing
Set wsJet = Nothing
```

If you just want to use the default workspace, you can either refer to it as DBEngine(0), or create a reference to it in the same way you create references to other Access or DAO objects.

```
'Create a reference to the default workspace
Set wsJet1 = DBEngine(0)
Debug.Print "wsJet1.Name: " & wsJet1.Name      '#Default Workspace#
```

Since you're not creating a new workspace object, there is no need to append it to the Workspaces collection.

Finally, there is one other way to create a new workspace. To maintain compatibility with previous versions of DAO, Access 2003 still provides the DefaultWorkspaceClone method.

```
'Create a clone of the default workspace
Set wsJet2 = Application.DefaultWorkspaceClone
Debug.Print "wsJet2.Name: " & wsJet2.Name      '#Clone Access#
```

The DefaultWorkspaceClone method creates a clone (identical copy) of the default workspace, whatever it happens to be. The cloned workspace takes on properties identical to those of the original, with the exception of its Name property, which is set to #Clone Access#.

You would use the DefaultWorkspaceClone method where you want to operate two independent transactions simultaneously without needing to prompt the user again for the username and password.

Using Transactions

A *transaction* is defined as a delimited set of changes that are performed on a database's schema or data. They increase the speed of actions that change data, and enable you to undo changes that have not yet been committed.

Transactions offer a great deal of data integrity insurance for situations where an entire series of actions must complete successfully, or not complete at all. This is the all-or-nothing principle that is employed in most financial transactions.

For example, when your employer transfers your monthly salary from their bank to yours, two actions actually occur. The first is a withdrawal from your employer's account, and the second is a deposit into yours. If the withdrawal completes, but for some reason, the deposit fails, you can argue until you're blue in the face, but your employer can prove that they paid you, and are not likely to want to do so again. Similarly, your bank will not be too impressed if the withdrawal fails, but the deposit succeeds. The reality is that the bank will take the money back, and you still end up with no salary. Either way, you get shafted! If, however, the two actions are enclosed in a single transaction, they must both complete successfully, or the transaction is deemed to have failed, and both actions are rolled back (reversed).

You begin a transaction by issuing the BeginTrans method against the Workspace object. To write the transaction to disk, you issue the CommitTrans method, and to cancel, or roll back the transaction, strangely enough, you issue the Rollback method.

Normally, transactions are cached, and not immediately written to disk. But if you're in a real hurry to get home at five o'clock, and immediately switch off your computer before the cache is written to disk, your most recent changes are lost. In Microsoft Jet workspaces, you can force the database engine to immediately write all changes to disk, instead of caching them. You do this by including the `dbFlushOSCacheWrites` constant with `CommitTrans`. Forcing immediate writes may affect your application's performance, but the data integrity benefits may outweigh any performance hit in certain situations.

The following code segment demonstrates a typical funds transfer transaction using a Microsoft Jet workspace. As transactions operate at workspace level, you can use them in exactly the same way with ODBCDirect workspaces.

In the following example, and in other examples given throughout this chapter, we have deviated from the Reddick object-naming convention by varying the names for `Workspace`, `Database`, and `Recordset` object variables. We do this because it sometimes makes the code easier to understand. In the following example code, rather than extend the length of the two `Database` object names, we have given them the names dbC and dbX, for the current and external databases respectively. They could just as easily have been named dbsC and dbsX.

```
Public Sub TransferFunds()
    Dim wrk As DAO.Workspace
    Dim dbC As DAO.Database
    Dim dbX As DAO.Database

    Set wrk = DBEngine(0)
    Set dbC = CurrentDb
    Set dbX = wrk.OpenDatabase("c:\Temp\myDB.mdb")

    On Error GoTo trans_Err

    'Begin the transaction
    wrk.BeginTrans
        'Withdraw funds from one account table
        dbC.Execute "UPDATE Table1.....", dbFailOnError

        'Deposit funds into another account table
        dbX.Execute "INSERT INTO Table22.....", dbFailOnError

    'Commit the transaction
    wrk.CommitTrans dbFlushOSCacheWrites

trans_Exit:
    'Clean up
    wrk.Close
    Set dbC = Nothing
    Set dbX = Nothing
    Set wrk = Nothing
    Exit Sub

trans_Err:
    'Roll back the transaction
    wrk.Rollback
    Resume trans_Exit
End Sub
```

In the above example, changes to both databases either will complete as a unit, or will be rolled back as a unit.

You don't need to use transactions, but if you do, they can be nested up to five levels. It is also important to understand that transactions are global to the workspace—not the database. For example, if you make changes to two databases in the same workspace, and you roll back the changes to one of those databases, the changes made to the other database will also be rolled back.

The Errors Collection

The first thing to remember about the DAO Errors collection is that it is not the same as the VBA.Err object. The VBA.Err object is a single object that stores information about the last VBA error. The DAO Errors collection stores information about the last DAO error.

Any operation performed on any DAO object can generate an error. The DBEngine.Errors collection stores all the error objects that are added as the result of an error that occurs during a single DAO operation. Each Error object in the collection, therefore, contains information about only one error.

Having said that, some operations can generate multiple errors, in which case the lowest level error is stored in the collection first, followed by the higher level errors. The last error object usually indicates that the operation failed. Enumerating the Errors collection allows your error handling code to more precisely determine the cause of the problem, and to take the most appropriate remedial action.

When a subsequent DAO operation generates an error, the Errors collection is cleared and a new set of Error objects is added to the collection. This happens regardless of whether you have retrieved the previous errors' information or not. So you can see that unless you retrieve the information about an error as soon as it occurs, you may lose it if another error happens in the meantime. Each error obliterates and replaces its predecessor—a bit like politics really.

One last point to note is that an error that occurs in an object that has not yet been added to its collection, is not added to the DBEngine.Errors collection, because the "object" is not considered to be an object until it is added to a collection. In such cases, the error information will be available in the VBA.Err object.

To fully account for all errors, your error handler should verify that the error number returned by both the VBA.Err object and the last member of the DBEngine.Error object are the same. The following code demonstrates a typical error handler:

```
intDAOErrNo = DBEngine.Errors(DBEngine.Errors.Count - 1).Number

If VBA.Err <> intDAOErrNo Then
    DBEngine.Errors.Refresh
End If

For intCtr = 0 To DBEngine.Errors.Count - 1
    Select Case DBEngine.Errors(intCtr).Number
        Case 1
            'Code to handle error
        Case 2
            'Code to handle error

        'Other Case statements
```

```
          Case 99
               'Code to handle error
     End Select
Next intCtr
```

The Databases Collection

Using DAO, you can have more than one database open in Access at any time. If you're using an Access .mdb, you already have one database open (called the *current* database). Using the Workspace object's OpenDatabase method, as shown in the example in section on *Using Transactions*, you can open more than one database, and operate on them under the same workspace context. Indeed, if you were to define more than one Workspace object, you could have several databases open, each operating under a different workspace context. The choice is yours. The Databases collection contains and manages these databases.

The Default (Jet) Database

Unless you're working with an Access Data Project, when Access starts, it creates a default *Microsoft Jet* database for you to work with. This default database is automatically added to the Databases collection.

Among its properties and methods, the Database object contains five collections: TableDefs, Containers, QueryDefs, Recordsets, and Relations. Each of these collections and their respective objects and properties are discussed in later sections. In most cases, you will be working with the default Microsoft Jet database, which you can refer to using any of the following syntaxes:

```
DBEngine.Workspaces("#Default Workspace#").Databases(0)
DBEngine.Workspaces(0).Databases(0)
DBEngine(0).Databases(0)
DBEngine(0)(0)
CurrentDb()
```

The current user's default database is an object that you will use quite a lot. Although you can work with it using any of the reference methods listed above, in most cases it is often more convenient to assign it to an object variable.

```
Dim dbs As Database
Set dbs = DBEngine(0)(0)
```

But far and away the most common method is to use the CurrentDb() function, described below.

The CurrentDb() Function

Access only ever maintains a single permanent reference to the current database. The first member of the Databases collection is populated with a reference to the current database at startup. This reference, pointed to by DBEngine(0)(0), is fine under most circumstances, but when, for example, you are working on wizards, it is not always up-to-date. In these circumstances it is possible for the first database collection member to point to something other than the default database. The chance of this occurring in *normal* databases is negligible, but to ensure that you are working with the current database, you need to execute the Refresh method,

```
DBEngine(0).Databases.Refresh
Debug.Print DBEngine(0)(0).Name
```

that rebuilds the collection, placing the current database in the first position in the Databases collection. This of course can be a pain, not to mention the huge performance hit your code experiences every time you want to use the current database.

The solution that Microsoft came up with was to provide the CurrentDb() function. CurrentDb (the parentheses are optional) is not an object; it is a built-in function that provides a reference to the current user's default database. Although they do refer to the same database, it is essential that you understand two important concepts:

CurrentDb and DBEngine(0)(0) are not the same objects internally. Access maintains a single permanent reference to the current database, but CurrentDb temporarily creates a new internal object—one in which the collections are guaranteed to be up-to-date.

When CurrentDb is executed, Access creates a new internal object that recreates the hierarchy and refers to the current database. The interesting fact is that immediately after CurrentDb executes and returns a pointer, the internal object is destroyed.

For example, the following code will generate an error, because the reference to the current database is lost immediately after the line containing CurrentDb executes:

```
Dim fld As DAO.Field
Set fld = CurrentDb.TableDefs(0).Fields(0)
Debug.Print fld.Name
```

This is the case for most DAO objects. One notable exception to this is the Recordset object, for which Access tries to maintain the database reference. To use CurrentDb effectively, it is always wiser to assign the reference to an object variable.

```
Dim dbs As DAO.Database
Dim fld As DAO.Field
Set dbs = CurrentDb
Set fld = dbs.TableDefs(0).Fields(0)
Debug.Print fld.Name
dbs.Close
Set dbs = Nothing
```

Of course, you get nothing for free, and CurrentDb is no exception. The price you pay for the convenience and reliability of a function like CurrentDb is a considerable performance hit. CurrentDb is (in my tests) is roughly 60 times slower than DBEngine(0)(0). So why would you use it?

The reason you would use CurrentDb in preference to DBEngine(0)(0) is that you can rely on its collections being up-to-date. For the majority of cases, the performance hit experienced using

`CurrentDb` is not an issue, because it is highly unlikely that you will ever call it in a loop. The recommended method for setting a reference to the current database is as follows:

```
Private dbC As DAO.Database
Public Property Get CurrentDbC() As DAO.Database
    If (dbC Is Nothing) Then Set dbC = CurrentDb
    Set CurrentDbC = dbC
End Property
```

This `Property` procedure can be used in both class modules and standard modules, and relies on the existence of a `Database` object variable declared at module level. If you want, you can change it to a function instead; it will work just the same. The reason it checks `dbC` is that variables can be erased (and thus the reference lost) when an error occurs somewhere in your application, or if someone hits `Stop` in the IDE (integrated development environment).

Opening an External Database

Sometimes you need to work with data in another Access database, a dBase IV database, or Excel spreadsheet, but you don't want a permanent link. You can do so by opening a temporary connection to it with the `Workspace` object's `OpenDatabase` method.

Although this method belongs to the `Workspace` object, I am describing it in this section because the end result is that a new (albeit temporary) `Database` object is added to the `Databases` collection.

The `OpenDatabase` method is fairly straightforward.

```
Set dbs = wrk.OpenDatabase(dbname, options, read-only, connect)
```

The following table describes the `OpenDatabase` method arguments.

Argument	Description
dbname	A string value that represents the full path and filename of the database you want to open.
options	An optional Boolean True (−1) or False (0) that indicates whether to open the database in exclusive (True) or shared mode (False).
Read-only	An optional Boolean True (−1) or False (0) that indicates whether to open the database as read-only.
Connect	An optional Variant connection string that specifies how to prompt the user to establish a connection (ODBCDirect workspaces only).
	DbDriverNoPrompt The ODBC Driver Manager uses the connection string provided in the dbname and connect arguments. If you don't provide sufficient information, a runtime error occurs.

Continues

Argument	Description
DbDriverPrompt	The ODBC Driver Manager displays the ODBC Data Sources dialog box, which displays relevant information supplied in dbname or connect. The connection string is composed of the DSN selected by the user, or the default DSN if none is selected.
DbDriverComplete	(Default) If the dbname and connect arguments include sufficient information to complete a connection, the ODBC Driver Manager uses the string in connect. Otherwise it behaves as it does when you specify dbDriverPrompt.
dbDriverCompleteRequired	This option behaves like dbDriverComplete, except that the ODBC driver disables the prompts for any information not required to complete the connection.

The following example code demonstrates how to open several different databases using different techniques. Specifically, it opens the following databases from the following five sources:

❑   Microsoft Jet database

❑   dBase IV database using Jet

❑   SQL Server database using ODBC through Jet

❑   SQL Server database using ODBCDirect

❑   A second instance of an SQL Server database, using an existing connection

After opening each database, you'll notice that the code prints the name of the database, and a count of the respective Databases collection. Take particular notice of the database names and collection counts for the ODBCDirect databases.

You can see that the database name is that of the connection—not the database. This is because ODBCDirect has established a connection to the DSN, rather than the database; so it is the DSN's name that is returned.

```
Public Sub OpenSeveralDatabases(strUsrName As String, strPwd As String)
    Dim wsJet As Workspace
    Dim wsODBC As Workspace
    Dim dbJet As Database
    Dim dbdBase As Database
    Dim dbODBC As Database
    Dim dbODBCDirect As Database
    Dim dbODBCDirect1 As Database
    Dim cn As Connection
```

```
        'Create the Jet and ODBCDirect workspaces
        Set wsJet = DBEngine(0)
        Set wsODBC = DBEngine.CreateWorkspace( _
            "", strUsrName, strPwd, dbUseODBC)

        'Print the details for the default database
        Debug.Print "Jet Database "; wsJet.Databases.Count & _
            " - " & CurrentDb.Name

        'Open a Microsoft Jet database - shared - read-only
        Set dbJet = wsJet.OpenDatabase("C:\Temp\db1.mdb", False, True)
        Debug.Print "Jet Database "; wsJet.Databases.Count & _
            " - " & dbJet.Name

        'Open a dBase IV database - exclusive - read-write
        Set dbdBase = wsJet.OpenDatabase( _
            "dBase IV;DATABASE=C:\Temp\db2.dbf", True, False)
        Debug.Print "Database "; wsJet.Databases.Count & _
            " - " & dbdBase.Name

        'Open an ODBC database using a DSN - exclusive - read-only
        Set dbODBC = wsJet.OpenDatabase( _
            "", dbDriverComplete, True, "ODBC;DATABASE=myDB;DSN=myDSN")
        Debug.Print "Jet Database "; wsJet.Databases.Count & _
            " - " & dbODBC.Name

        'Open an ODBCDirect Connection using a DSN - read-only
        Set cn = wsODBC.OpenConnection( _
            "", dbDriverComplete, True, "ODBC;DATABASE=myDB;DSN=myDSN")
        'Get a reference to the default ODBCDirect database
        Set dbODBCDirect = wsODBC.Databases(0)
         'This could so be written as: Set dbODBCDirect = cn.Database
        Debug.Print "ODBCDirect Database "; wsODBC.Databases.Count & _
            " - " & dbODBCDirect.Name

        'Open a second database reference using the ODBCDirect connection
        Set dbODBCDirect1 = wsODBC.OpenDatabase( _
            "", dbDriverComplete, True, "ODBC;DATABASE=myDB;DSN=myDSN")
        Debug.Print "ODBCDirect Database "; wsODBC.Databases.Count & _
            " - " & dbODBCDirect.Name

        'Clean up
        cn.Close
        wsJet.Close
        wsODBC.Close
        Set dbJet = Nothing
        Set dbdBase = Nothing
        Set dbODBC = Nothing
        Set dbODBCDirect = Nothing
        Set dbODBCDirect1 = Nothing
        Set cn = Nothing
        Set wsJet = Nothing
        Set wsODBC = Nothing
End Sub
```

Closing and Destroying Database Object References

There has been a great deal of confusion about whether to explicitly close and destroy object references to the current database. Some of the most highly regarded experts in the field have publicly clarified this issue many times, but many still seem to cling to the fear that doing so will blow their database up. In this section, we will try to lay that argument to rest once and for all.

The problem stemmed from the fact that in Access 2.0, if you called the Close method against DBEngine(0)(0) or CurrentDb, the call would fail, but problems would occur with any open objects, specifically Recordsets. This resulted either in an application hang, or with Access refusing to close. Following the fix to this bug (where the internal "OK to close?" check routine was moved from the end of the method, to the beginning), calls to dbs.Close issued against either DBEngine(0)(0) or CurrentDb now do absolutely nothing to the permanent internal database object. Many people still believe that this long dead bug still exists, and warnings about it still resound in the halls of UseNet. However, although you can call Close if it gives you a warm fuzzy feeling inside, any attempt to do so against DBEngine(0)(0) or CurrentDb will literally do nothing. Therefore, dbs.Close is redundant.

Some people have experienced bugs with the DAO Recordset object, in particular, the RecordsetClone object, where an orphaned reference sometimes prevents Access from closing. There has never been any such bug with the Database object.

Destroying object references is a different affair. For the present, you still should set Database object variables to Nothing when you have finished with them, as you would with any other object reference. It is perfectly safe to do so, regardless of whether the reference came from DBEngine(0)(0) or CurrentDb.

Setting myObj = Nothing decrements the internal object reference count by one. When the reference count reaches zero, the object is destroyed. But since Access maintains a *permanent* internal reference to the current database, this will not destroy the internal object, and thus will never have any effect on it.

The Connections Collection

As you saw in the section entitled *Opening and External Database*, you can open an ODBCDirect database using the OpenDatabase method against an ODBCDirect workspace object. Similarly, you can also open an ODBCDirect connection using the OpenConnection method of the ODBCDirect workspace.

When you open an ODBCDirect Connection object, it is automatically added to the Connections collection, and a corresponding Database object is added to the ODBCDirect workspace's Databases collection. When you close the Connection object, both the Connection and Database objects are removed from their respective collections. You can refer to a Connection object as:

```
DBEngine(0).Connections("Connection name")
DBEngine(0).Connections(0)
```

Once a connection is established, you can open Recordsets, create QueryDefs and TableDefs, and just about anything else you can do using a Jet workspace.

DAO Object Properties

As you're no doubt already aware from previous chapters, every Access object (like forms and reports) has a collection of properties. In this section, we're going to examine some of those properties, and describe how to use them to change Access and DAO object behavior.

All the properties associated with an Access object exist from the moment you create the object. DAO object properties, however, exhibit quite different behavior. In DAO, depending on the object, not all its properties exist until you set its value. It is quite important, therefore, that you understand the differences between the types of properties used in DAO.

DAO Property Types

In contrast to Access object properties, there are three types of object properties: built-in, system-defined, and user-defined.

❑   *Built-in properties* exist when the object is created, and like most of their Access counterparts, define the characteristics of the object itself. For example, `Name` and `Type` are examples of built-in properties.

❑   *System-defined properties* are those that Access adds to the object's `Properties` collection when it needs the property in order to work its magic. These are not Jet properties, but are created and used by Access.

❑   A *user-defined property* can be added to an object's `Properties` collection when you explicitly set a value to it. For example, a field's `Description` property is a user-defined property. Although you can set a value to it when you define the table, Jet doesn't recognize that the property exists until after you've done so. In fact, after you've set its value, it appears in the field's `Properties` collection, but you still can't see it in the `Object Browser`, as shown in Figure 6-1.

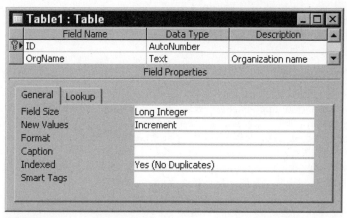

Figure 6-1

Creating, Setting, and Retrieving Properties

Without even thinking about it, you've been setting and retrieving properties for as long as you've been programming. Whenever you check the value of a `TextBox`, or set the `Enabled` state of a command button, you are working with object properties. In this section, we'll examine how to manipulate Access properties, object properties, and user-defined properties.

You can refer to built-in properties either directly through the object to which they belong or through the object's `Properties` collection. User-defined properties, on the other hand, do not form part of an object's type library, and thus are not available via that route, so you have to refer to them through the object's `Properties` collection.

Setting and Retrieving Built-In Object Properties

The built-in properties that you would be most familiar with are those that affect the way form and report controls work. Even DAO objects have properties that can be manipulated in the same way. For example, to change a `TextBox`'s `Enabled` property, you can refer to it in either of the following two ways:

```
Me!TextBox1.Enabled = False
Me!TextBox1.Properties("Enabled") = False
```

To check the name of a recordset's `Field` object, you retrieve its `Name` property. The following two examples are equivalent ways to check this property:

```
Debug.Print rst.Fields(0).Name
Debug.Print rst.Fields(0).Properties("Name")
```

All objects have a *default* property, which is the property that is referenced when you call the object itself. For example, when you test a `Field` object directly, you are actually referring to its `Value` property. The following lines of code all refer to the `Field` object's `Value` property:

```
rst.Fields(0)
rst.Fields(0).Properties("Value")
rst.Fields(0).Properties(0)
rst.Fields(0).Value
```

Creating Object Properties

You can only create user-defined properties for persistent DAO objects, such as tables and queries. You can't create properties for nonpersistent objects, like recordsets. To create a user-defined property, you must first create the property, using the `Database`'s `CreateProperty` method. You then append the property using the `Properties` collection's `Append` method. That's all there is to it.

Using the example of a table's `Description` property, the following code demonstrates just how easy it is:

```
Public Sub CreateTableProperty(strTableName As String, _
        strFieldName As String, _
        strPropName As String, _
        lngPropType As DataTypeEnum, _
        varValue As Variant, _
        Optional booIsDDL As Boolean = False)
```

```
      Dim dbs As Database
      Dim prop As Property

      Set dbs = CurrentDb

      'Create the property
      Set prop = dbs.CreateProperty(strPropName, _
lngPropType, varValue, booIsDDL)

      'Append the property to the object Properties collection
      dbs(strTableName)(strFieldName).Properties.Append prop

      Debug.Print
dbs(strTableName)(strFieldName).Properties(strPropName)

      'We don't need the property any more, so delete it
      dbs(strTableName)(strFieldName).Properties.Delete strPropName

      'Clean up
      Set prop = Nothing
      Set dbs = Nothing
End Sub
```

As a second example, you could even create a special user-defined property for a table in the same way. This approach can be used with all persistent objects.

```
Public Sub CreateSpecialTableProp(strTableName As String, _
        strPropName As String, _
        lngPropType As DataTypeEnum, _
        varValue As Variant)
      Dim dbs As Database
      Dim prop As Property

      Set dbs = CurrentDb

      'Create the property
      Set prop = dbs.CreateProperty(strPropName, _
        lngPropType, varValue, False)

      'Append the property to the object Properties collection
      dbs(strTableName).Properties.Append prop

      Debug.Print dbs(strTableName).Properties(strPropName)

      'We don't need the property any more, so delete it
      dbs(strTableName).Properties.Delete strPropName

      'Clean up
      Set prop = Nothing
      Set dbs = Nothing
End Sub
```

Setting and Retrieving SummaryInfo Properties

As we've already discussed, all objects in Access have properties. Properties come in two flavors: those that change the behavior of the object to which they refer, and those that represent something akin to metadata (information about information, or objects). As you've seen in the preceding sections of this chapter, DAO objects also have properties, and we have already discussed how to set and retrieve those properties. But there is one set of properties that we haven't looked at yet.

When you select `Properties` from the `File` menu, Access presents you with the `Properties` dialog box. This dialog box displays several built-in properties, some you can change, and some you can't. The `General` tab displays various information about the database, including its file location and size, creation date, and the dates it was last modified and accessed. The `Summary` tab allows you to enter your own properties, such as the document (database) `Title` (which is different from the Database Title, which you set from the `Tools | Startup` menu), `Subject`, `Author`, `Manager`, and so on. These two tabs contain the information the `Search` facility uses when you want to find a specific file, using `File |Open| Find`, as shown in Figure 6-2.

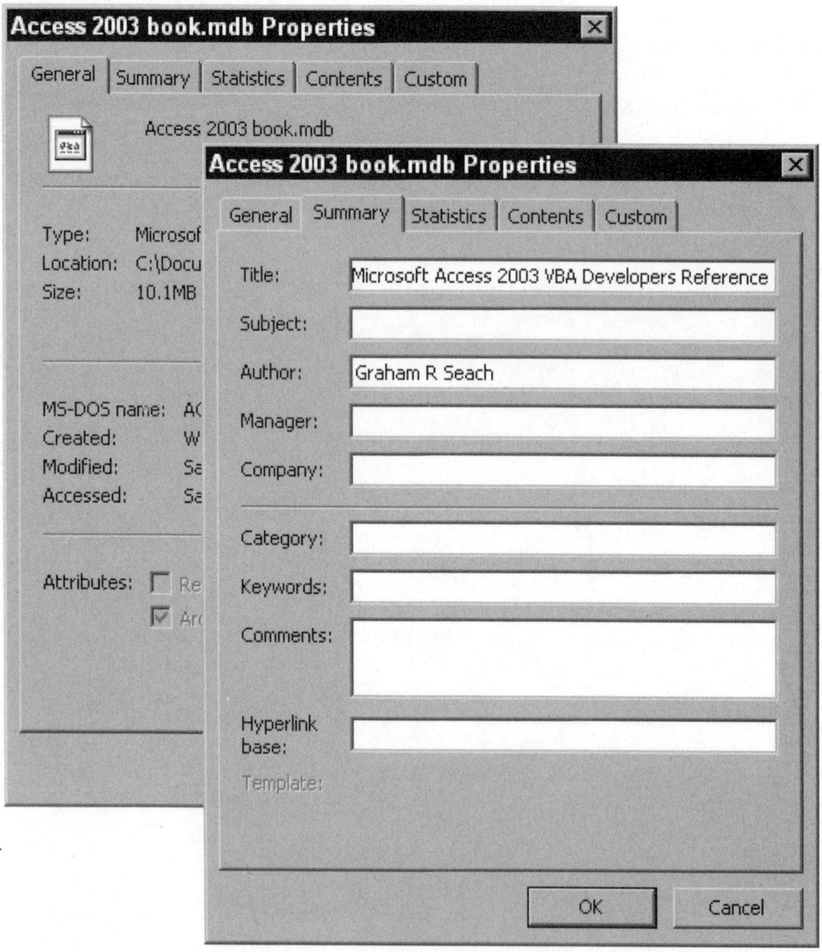

Figure 6-2

In code, specifically DAO code, you can set and retrieve the value of any of these properties from the `SummaryInfo` document of the Databases container, for the current database. Of course, you don't have to create these properties before using them. Access creates them automatically when you launch the database. The following example line of code illustrates how to access the `Subject` property shown in the `Properties` dialog box.

```
dbs.Containers("Databases").Documents("SummaryInfo").Properties("Subject")
```

Setting and Retrieving User-Defined Properties

You can also create and use user-defined properties for other purposes. We often use a custom database property to record the database version. We like to put it with the other custom properties, so it can be accessed in the two ways described below.

As with the example of a table's `Description` property, there are two ways to create a user-defined property: using the user interface, and through code.

To create such a property with the user interface, select `Properties` from the `File` menu. The `Properties` dialog box is displayed, as shown in Figure 6-3. Then select the `Custom` tab. Enter the property name into the `Name` box, select the appropriate data type, give it a value, and click `Add`.

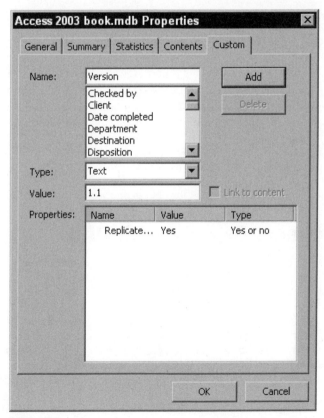

Figure 6-3

The following example shows how you can create the same property in code, and retrieve its value:

```
Public Sub SetVersion(strVersion As String)
    Dim prop As Property
    Dim dbs As Database

    'On Error Resume Next

    Set dbs = CurrentDb

    'Set the property's value
    'If it doesn't exist, an error 3270 "Property not found" will occur
    dbs.Containers(1)(3).Properties("Version") = strVersion
    If Err <> 0 Then
        'If the property doesn't exist, create it
        Set prop = dbs.CreateProperty("Version", dbText, strVersion)

        'Append it to the collection
        dbs.Containers(1)(3).Properties.Append prop
    End If

    'Now read the property
    Debug.Print dbs.Containers(1)(3).Properties("Version")

    'Clean up
    Set prop = Nothing
    Set dbs = Nothing
End Sub
```

First you must test that the property exists. In this example, we test it by attempting to set its value. If all goes well, the property must already exist, and its value is set. If an error occurs, you have to create the property—again by using the `CreateProperty` method at database level, and then appending it to the appropriate collection.

The `Debug.Print` line demonstrates how to retrieve the property's value.

Finally, the code cleans up, by destroying all the objects that were instantiated in the procedure.

Creating Schema Objects with DAO

Sometimes you need to create data access objects on the fly. For example, you might be creating objects that you will later delete, to fill a temporary need. Much of DAO's power lies in its ability to create things like tables and queries programmatically.

Let's say you inherit a manufacturing company from a long lost, yet recently deceased uncle. This company makes copper-plated widgets, but since he never actually sold any because of the absence of an invoicing system, you decide to implement one. Naturally enough, you'll want to create a database schema to record the details of the invoices you issue to your customers: one table for the invoice header, and one for the line items.

Like the man says "experience is the best teacher," so to learn how to do it, let's just jump right in and create our table schema in code.

The basic procedure for doing so is this:

1. Create the header table (tblInvoice), including its fields.

2. Create the line items table (tblInvItem), including its fields.

3. Create the indexes for both tables.

4. Create the relationship between the two tables.

Creating Tables and Fields

For our invoicing system, we have two tables to create. The basic procedure for creating a table in code is as follows:

1. Check if the table already exists, and if so, delete it.

2. Create the table object using the Database's CreateTableDef method.

3. Create the Field objects in memory, using the TableDef's CreateField method, setting each field's attributes as appropriate.

4. Append each Field object to the TableDef's Fields collection.

5. Append the TableDef object to the Database's TableDefs collection.

6. Refresh the TableDefs collection to ensure it is up-to-date.

The header table stores the basic high-level information about each invoice, such as the invoice number, date, and the customer ID. The following example demonstrates how to create a new table called tblInvoice and add four fields to it. First, let's declare all the objects needed to create the table.

```
Public Sub CreateInvoiceTable()
    Dim dbs As Database
    Dim tdf As DAO.TableDef
    Dim fldInvNo As DAO.Field
    Dim fldInvDate As DAO.Field
    Dim fldCustID As DAO.Field
    Dim fldComments As DAO.Field
    Set dbs = CurrentDb
    On Error Resume Next

    'If the table already exists, delete it
    dbs.TableDefs.Delete "tblInvoice"
    On Error GoTo 0

    'Create the table definition in memory
    Set tdf = dbs.CreateTableDef("tblInvoice")
```

At this point, you have created the new TableDef, but it only exists in memory. It won't become a permanent part of the database until you add it to the TableDefs collection. Before you do that, however, you need to add one or more fields to the table, because you can't save a table that has no fields.

```
'Create the field definitions in memory
Set fldInvNo = tdf.CreateField("InvoiceNo", dbText, 10)
fldInvNo.AllowZeroLength = False
fldInvNo.Required = True

'The InvoiceNo field could also have been specified thus:
'Set fldInvNo = tdf.CreateField()
'With fldInvNo
'      .Name = "InvoiceNo"
'      .Type = dbText
'      .Size = 10
'      .AllowZeroLength = False
'      .Required = True
'End  With

Set fldInvDate = tdf.CreateField("InvoiceDate", dbDate)
fldInvDate.Required = True

Set fldCustID = tdf.CreateField("CustomerID", dbLong)
fldCustID.Required = True

Set fldComments = tdf.CreateField("Comments", dbText, 50)
fldComments.AllowZeroLength = True
fldComments.Required = False

'Append the fields to the TableDef's Fields collection
tdf.Fields.Append fldInvNo
tdf.Fields.Append fldInvDate
tdf.Fields.Append fldCustID
tdf.Fields.Append fldComments
```

The fields have now been added to the table, but the table still needs to be added to the `TableDefs` collection to make it a permanent fixture. Once you've done that, you should refresh the `TableDefs` collection to ensure it is up-to-date, because in a multiuser application, the new table may not be immediately propagated to other users' collections until you do.

```
'Append the TableDef to the Database's TableDefs collection
dbs.TableDefs.Append tdf

'Refresh the TableDefs collection
dbs.TableDefs.Refresh

Set fldInvNo = Nothing
Set fldInvDate = Nothing
Set fldCustID = Nothing
Set fldComments = Nothing
Set tdf = Nothing
Set dbs = Nothing
End Sub
```

Next, we need to create a table to store the invoice line items, including the product ID, the number of items sold, and their individual unit price. Since the total invoice price and tax can be calculated at runtime, we won't violate normalization rules by creating fields for these items.

The following example creates a new table called `tblInvItem`, and adds five fields to it. It is based on the same basic procedure for creating tables, but includes an additional attribute definition, `dbAutoIncrField`, to create an *AutoNumber* field.

```
Public Sub CreateInvItemTable()
    Dim dbs As Database
    Dim tdf As DAO.TableDef
    Dim fldInvItemID As DAO.Field
    Dim fldInvNo As DAO.Field
    Dim fldProductID As DAO.Field
    Dim fldQty As DAO.Field
    Dim fldUnitPrice As DAO.Field

    Set dbs = CurrentDb
    On Error Resume Next

    'If the table already exists, delete it
    If IsObject(dbs.TableDefs("tblInvItem")) Then
        dbs.TableDefs.Delete "tblInvItem"
    End If

    'Create the table definition in memory
    Set tdf = dbs.CreateTableDef("tblInvItem")

    'Create the field definitions in memory
    Set fldInvItemID = tdf.CreateField("InvItemID", dbLong)
    'Make the field an AutoNumber datatype
    fldInvItemID.Attributes = dbAutoIncrField
    fldInvItemID.Required = True

    Set fldInvNo = tdf.CreateField("InvoiceNo", dbText, 10)
    fldInvNo.Required = True
    fldInvNo.AllowZeroLength = False

    Set fldProductID = tdf.CreateField("ProductID", dbLong)
    fldProductID.Required = True

    Set fldQty = tdf.CreateField("Qty", dbInteger)
    fldQty.Required = True

    Set fldUnitPrice = tdf.CreateField("UnitCost", dbCurrency)
    fldUnitPrice.Required = False

    'Append the fields to the TableDef's Fields collection
    tdf.Fields.Append fldInvItemID
    tdf.Fields.Append fldInvNo
    tdf.Fields.Append fldProductID
    tdf.Fields.Append fldQty
    tdf.Fields.Append fldUnitPrice

    'Append the TableDef to the Database's TableDefs collection
    dbs.TableDefs.Append tdf
```

```
        'Refresh the TableDefs collection
      dbs.TableDefs.Refresh

      Set fldInvItemID = Nothing
      Set fldInvNo = Nothing
      Set fldProductID = Nothing
      Set fldQty = Nothing
      Set fldUnitPrice = Nothing
      Set tdf = Nothing
      Set dbs = Nothing
   End Sub
```

Creating Indexes

Just creating the tables and fields isn't enough. Eventually the invoices tables are going to get pretty big, so querying against them will begin to take some time. The bigger the table,the longer it takes. To provide some measure of performance, you need to create indexes, because without proper indexes, the Jet engine must scan the entire table to find the records you want. The basic procedure for creating an index is as follows:

1. Create the `Index` object using the `TableDef`'s `CreateIndex` method.
2. Set the index's attributes as appropriate.
3. Create the index's `Field` objects using its `CreateField` method.
4. Append each `Field` object to the index's `Fields` collection.
5. Append the index to the `TableDef`'s `Indexes` collection.

Before you create your first index, there are three things you should be aware of. First, once an index has been appended to its collection, its properties are read-only. Therefore, if you want to change an index's property after you've created it, you must delete the index and re-create it with the new properties.

Second, although you can give an index any name you like, when you create a primary key using the `Access Table Designer`, it will be automatically named `PrimaryKey`. Therefore, to maintain consistency, it is wise to give code-created primary keys the same name.

Third, Jet databases do not support clustered indexes, so in Jet workspaces and other workspaces that connect to databases that use the Jet engine, the `Index` object's `Clustered` property is ignored.

Let's start the process of creating indexes by creating the primary key. When you create a primary key, Access automatically creates an index for it. The following procedure creates a primary key index for the specified table, which includes the fields supplied in the `ParamArray` argument. In the case of our invoice tables, that'll be only one field in each.

```
   Public Sub CreatePKIndexes(strTableName As String, _
         ParamArray varPKFields() As Variant)
      Dim dbs As Database
      Dim tdf As DAO.TableDef
      Dim idx As DAO.Index
      Dim idxFld As Variant
      Dim varPKey As Variant
```

```
    Set dbs = CurrentDb
    On Error Resume Next
    Set tdf = dbs.TableDefs(strTableName)

    'Check if a Primary Key exists.
    'If so, delete it.
    varPKey = GetPrimaryKey(tdf)
    If Not IsNull(varPKey) Then
        tdf.Indexes.Delete varPKey
    End If

    'Create a new primary key
    Set idx = tdf.CreateIndex("PrimaryKey")
    idx.Primary = True
    idx.Required = True
    idx.Unique = True
```

At this point, the index exists in memory, and will remain so until it is added to the `TableDef`'s `Indexes` collection. But before you do that, you must add the fields that make up the key to the index's `Fields` collection, and refresh the collection.

```
    'Append the fields
    For Each idxFld In varPKFields
        Set idxFld = idx.CreateField(idxFld)
        idx.Fields.Append idxFld
    Next idxFld

    'Append the index to the Indexes collection
    tdf.Indexes.Append idx
    'Refresh the Indexes collection
    tdf.Indexes.Refresh

    Set idx = Nothing
    Set tdf = Nothing
    Set dbs = Nothing
End Sub
```

The following function is called from the above `CreatePKIndexes` procedure, and returns the name of the primary key if one exists, and `Null` if there isn't one:

```
Public Function GetPrimaryKey(tdf As DAO.TableDef) As Variant
'Determine if the specified Primary Key exists
    Dim idx As Variant

    For Each idx In tdf.Indexes
        If idx.Primary Then
            'If a Primary Key exists, return its name
            GetPrimaryKey = idx.Name
            GoTo GetPrimaryKey_Exit
        End If
    Next idx

    'If no Primary Key exists, return Null
    GetPrimaryKey = Null
```

```
GetPrimaryKey_Exit:
End Function
```

You should run the `CreatePKIndexes` procedure to define the indexes for both the `tblInvoice` and `tblInvItem` tables. In fact, you can run this procedure in your own applications to create indexes on any table that doesn't have primary keys defined.

Finally, since Access is a relational database, you should set up relationships between the two tables, to tell Access how the information in one table relates to information in the other. This allows you to create related datasets in queries. The following section describes how to create those relationships in code.

Creating Relations

The basic procedure for creating a `Relation` is as follows:

1. Create the `Relation` object using the `Database`'s `CreateRelation` method.
2. Set the `Relation` object's attributes as appropriate.
3. Create the fields that participate in the relationship, using the `Relation` object's `CreateField` method.
4. Set the `Field` object's attributes as appropriate.
5. Append each field to the `Relation`'s `Fields` collection.
6. Append the `Relation` object to the `Database`'s `Relations` collection.

The following code creates a relationship whose name is specified by the `strRelName` argument, specifies its attributes, and adds the tables and fields that make up the relationship.

Note that you can name a relationship any way you like, but when you create a relationship using the `Relationships` window, Access names the relationship according to the names of the tables involved. For example, if you were to create a relationship between `tblInvoice` and `tblInvItem`, Access would name it `tblInvoicetblInvItem`.

```
Public Sub CreateRelation(strRelName As String, _
    strSrcTable As String, strSrcField As String, _
    strDestTable As String, strDestField As String)

    Dim dbs As Database
    Dim fld As DAO.Field
    Dim rel As DAO.Relation
    Dim varRel As Variant

    Set dbs = CurrentDb
    On Error Resume Next

    'Check if the relationship already exists.
    'If so, delete it.
    If IsObject(dbs.Relations(strRelName)) Then
        dbs.Relations.Delete strRelName
    End If
```

```
        'Create the relation object
        Set rel = dbs.CreateRelation(strRelName, _
                                     strSrcTable, _
                                     strDestTable)
```

The `Relation` object now exists in memory, but as with the `TableDef` and `Index` objects, it won't be a permanent part of the database until you append it to the `Database`'s `Relations` collection.

The following code segment defines the relationship's attributes. Notice that I have used three `Relation` attribute enum values: `dbRelationLeft`, `dbRelationUpdateCascade`, and `dbRelationDeleteCascade`. These, of course, define a `LEFT JOIN` relationship with referential integrity set to `Cascade Update` and `Cascade Delete`.

When you specify the `Attribute` property, use the sum of the enum values you want to include. This is generally accomplished using the logical `Or` operator, rather than the unary plus (+).

```
        'Set this relationship to:
        ' LEFT JOIN
        ' Referential integrity = Cascade Update and Cascade Delete
        rel.Attributes = dbRelationLeft Or _
                         dbRelationUpdateCascade Or _
                         dbRelationDeleteCascade
```

Once the `Relation` object has been created and its attributes specified, you then add all the fields that collectively form the relationship. Lastly, you add the new relationship to the `Database`'s `Relations` collection to make it permanent, and refresh it.

```
        'Append the field(s) involved in the relationship
        Set fld = rel.CreateField(strSrcField)
        fld.ForeignName = strDestField

        'Append the field to the relation's Fields collection
        rel.Fields.Append fld

        'Append the relation to the Database's Relations collection
        dbs.Relations.Append rel
        'Refresh the Relations collection
        dbs.Relations.Refresh

        Set rel = Nothing
        Set fld = Nothing
        Set dbs = Nothing
    End Sub
```

When you create your own relationships in code, they will not automatically appear in the `Relationships` window. To display the `Relationships` window, display the `Database` window, and then select `Relationships` from the `Tools` menu.

To display the new relationships you've created in code, you either add the related tables to the `Relationships` window, or click `Show All` from the `Relationships` menu.

Putting It All Together

When writing your own procedures to create DAO objects, you should include sufficient error handling code, and perhaps even wrap the whole lot in a transaction, and so if any part of it fails, you don't have orphaned objects that you will have to delete manually.

> **Remember that an orphaned object (one that remains alive in Access's memory space, but not in your application) can easily prevent Access from closing. The other side effect of having orphaned objects is that every object consumes system resources; if you have enough orphaned objects unnecessarily consuming resources, you can quite simply run out, and your application will fail without warning.**

You can use the following procedure to manage all the code we've just created, to test the creation of invoice tables, indexes, and relationships:

```
Public Sub CreateInvoiceSchema()
    CreateInvoiceTable
    CreatePKIndexes "tblInvoice", "InvoiceNo"
    CreateInvItemTable
    CreatePKIndexes "tblInvItem", "InvItemID"
    CreateRelation "Relation1", "tblInvoice", _
            "InvoiceNo", "tblInvItem", "InvoiceNo"
End Sub
```

Managing Jet Security with DAO

Security in Access is based on the *workgroup model*, which is conceptually similar to the *user-level security model* employed by the Windows operating system. In contrast to database-level security models employed by other desktop database systems, Jet workgroup information is stored in a file that can reside on a network share. Using this approach, the same security system can be shared by many databases, rather than having to create a separate security system for every instance of your database. Using this approach, you simplify security maintenance by adding or removing users and groups, or changing permissions in one centralized file.

> **Microsoft Jet security is always present and always enabled; it is not something that can be disabled. You just don't notice it because of the default workgroup and several default users and groups.**

Because DAO acts only as an interface to Jet security, a detailed discussion of the Jet security model is beyond the scope of this book. For those who want to learn about Jet security in greater detail, there are already several excellent books on the subject that you can read. Therefore, I will restrict this chapter to discussing those aspects of the DAO object model that directly relate to Jet security; specifically how to manage Jet users, groups, and permissions in code.

DAO deals with Jet security in two ways. First, the `Workspace` object maintains two security-related collections: `Groups` and `Users`. Each `Group` object maintains a `Users` collection that contains information about all the users who belong to that group. Similarly, each `User` object contains a `Groups` collection that lists the groups to which that user belongs. Second, Access and Jet objects (for example, tables, forms, and so on) each have a `Permission` object that stores information about the permissions a user has to that object.

Creating Security Objects

When you create a new Jet user or group account, either through the user interface or via code, you must supply a *Personal IDentifier* (PID). The PID is a case-sensitive 4–20 character string that Jet combines with the user or group name to create a unique *Security IDentifier* (SID). The SID is a unique identifier, which is similar to a public security key. Once you create the account, you can never view or change the SID. But (and this is why the SID is notable) if you ever delete the user or group account, and later decide to re-create it, you must use the same PID, because Access remembers it. If the resulting SID does not match, Access will not allow you to re-create the account. Therefore, whenever you create a new user or group account, save the SID offsite so you don't lose it.

When you create a new user account, you can also include a case-sensitive 1–14 character password, which the user must enter when they log on. The only user who can change the password is the user who owns it; however, members of the *Admins group* can clear any user's password.

Passwords and PIDs are encrypted and stored in the workgroup file, and thus, cannot be viewed by anyone. The following sections demonstrate how to create and modify user and group accounts, and includes code to add SIDs and passwords.

Managing Users and Groups

The `Workspace` object contains a `Groups` collection and a `Users` collection. The `Groups` collection contains all the `Group` objects used in the workgroup. A `Group`, as its name suggests, is a collection of `Users` to whom you want to assign the same privileges. You can enumerate the users and groups using the following code:

```
Public Sub EnumUsersAndGroups()
    Dim wrk As DAO.Workspace
    Dim grp As DAO.Group
    Dim usr As DAO.User

    Set wrk = DBEngine(0)

    'Enumerate the groups
    Debug.Print "Groups..."
    For Each grp In wrk.Groups
        Debug.Print vbTab & grp.Name
    Next grp

    'Enumerate the users
    Debug.Print "Users..."
    For Each usr In wrk.Users
```

```
        Debug.Print vbTab & usr.Name
    Next usr

    Set grp = Nothing
    Set wrk = Nothing
End Sub
```

The above code simply lists all the users and groups that exist in the system, but it doesn't show the relationship between them. If you want to find out which users belong to a specific group, you need to enumerate the `Users` collection for that specific group.

```
Public Sub EnumGroupUsers(strGroup As String)
    Dim wrk As DAO.Workspace
    Dim varUser As Variant

    Set wrk = DBEngine(0)

    Debug.Print "Users belonging to the '" & strGroup & "' group..."
    For Each varUser In wrk.Groups(strGroup).Users
        Debug.Print vbTab & varUser.Name
    Next varUser

    Set wrk = Nothing
End Sub
```

Similarly, you can list all the groups that a specific user belongs to by enumerating the `Groups` collection for that user.

```
Public Sub EnumUserGroups(strUser As String)
    Dim wrk As DAO.Workspace
    Dim varGroup As Variant

    Set wrk = DBEngine(0)

    Debug.Print "Groups to which user '" & strUser & "' belongs..."
    For Each varGroup In wrk.Users(strUser).Groups
        Debug.Print vbTab & varGroup.Name
    Next varGroup

    Set wrk = Nothing
End Sub
```

The Current User

The *current user* is defined as the user who is currently logged on to the database application. For most security-related operations, you need to know the name of the current user. DAO provides a convenient way of obtaining this information using the `Workspace` object's `UserName` property.

```
strMyName = DBEngine(0).UserName
```

Using this property, you can create a `User` object for the current user, without having to know their name, like so:

```
Dim usr As DAO.User
Set usr = DBEngine(0).Users(DBEngine(0).UserName)
```

Creating and Deleting Groups

Rather than assign access permissions to individual users, as mentioned above, you can create Groups to which one or more users can be assigned. Each Group can be assigned specific permissions to the database's objects, and every user who is assigned to that group will *inherit* the permissions of that Group. As we'll examine in this section, using DAO, you can create or delete Groups in code. The following code shows how to create a new group. The basic procedure is to create the group using the CreateGroup method, and then append it to the Groups collection.

```
Public Sub CreateUserGroup(strGroupName As String, _
     strPID As String)
   Dim wrk As DAO.Workspace
   Dim grp As DAO.Group

   Set wrk = DBEngine(0)
   On Error GoTo CreateUserGroupErr

   'Create the new group
   Set grp = wrk.CreateGroup(strGroupName, strPID)
   ws.Groups.Append grp

CreateUserGroupErr:
   Set grp = Nothing
   Set wrk = Nothing
End Sub
Deleting a group is even easier; just execute the  Groups collection's
Delete method.
Public Sub DeleteGroup(strGroup As String)
   On Error Resume Next
   DBEngine(0).Groups.Delete strGroup
End Sub
```

You can't rename a group once it has been created. If you need to rename a group, you have to delete it, and then re-create it. Remember, though, if you need to re-create a user or group, you must supply the same SID that you used to create it in the first place.

Creating and Deleting Users

Using DAO, you can create a new user account that can then be added to one or more groups. The following code shows how to create a new user. The basic procedure is to create the user with the CreateUser method, and then append it to the Users collection.

```
Public Function CreateUserAccount(strUserName As String, _
     strPID As String, strPassword As String)
   Dim wrk As DAO.Workspace
   Dim usr As DAO.User

   Set wrk = DBEngine(0)
   On Error GoTo CreateUserAccountErr
```

```
        'Create the new user
        Set usr = wrk.CreateUser(strUserName, strPID, strPassword)
        wrk.Users.Append usr

CreateUserAccountErr:
        Set usr = Nothing
        Set wrk = Nothing
End Function
```

As with deleting a group, deleting a user is quite simple; just execute the Users collection's Delete method.

```
Public Sub DeleteUser(strUser As String)
        On Error Resume Next
        DBEngine(0).Users.Delete strUser
End Sub
```

To rename a user account, you must delete the account, and then re-create it.

User and Group Operations

Before you can assign permissions that allow the user to access any of the Access or Jet objects, you must add the users to one or more groups.

There are two ways you can do this: by adding the user to the group, or by adding the group to the user. Although the following two procedures achieve exactly the same end, they demonstrate how to do it:

```
Public Sub AddGroup2User(strUser As String, _
        strGroup As String)
    Dim wrk As DAO.Workspace
    Dim usr As DAO.User
    Dim grp As DAO.Group

    Set wrk = DBEngine(0)
    On Error Resume Next

    'Create object references
    Set usr = wrk.Users(strUser)
    Set grp = usr.CreateGroup(strGroup)

    'Add the group to the user's Groups collection
    usr.Groups.Append grp
    usr.Groups.Refresh

    Set usr = Nothing
    Set grp = Nothing
    Set wrk = Nothing
End Sub
Public Sub AddUser2Group(strUser As String, _
        strGroup As String)
    Dim wrk As DAO.Workspace
    Dim usr As DAO.User
    Dim grp As DAO.Group
```

```
        Set wrk = DBEngine(0)
        On Error Resume Next

        'Create object references
        Set grp = wrk.Groups(strUser)
        Set usr = grp.CreateUser(strUser)

        'Add the group to the user's Groups collection
        grp.Users.Append usr
        grp.Users.Refresh

        Set usr = Nothing
        Set grp = Nothing
        Set wrk = Nothing
    End Sub
```

Similarly, if you want to delete a user from a group, you can delete the user's entry from the Groups collection, or delete the group from the Users collection. For simplicity, we'll only show you one method.

```
    Public Sub DeleteUserFromGroup(strUser As String, _
    strGroup As String)
        Dim wrk As DAO.Workspace

        Set wrk = DBEngine(0)
        On Error Resume Next

        wrk.Users(strUser).Groups.Delete strGroup

        Set wrk = Nothing
    End Sub
```

Determining if a User Belongs to a Specific Group

When determining if a user should have access to a particular object or function, you may need to determine whether the user belong to a specific group. Like most other functions, this is also fairly easy; just check if the name of the user exists in the group's Users collection, or if the group exists in the user's Groups collection.

```
    Public Function IsUserInGroup (strUser As String, _
            strGroup As String) As Boolean
        Dim wrk As DAO.Workspace

        Set wrk = DBEngine(0)
        On Error Resume Next

        IsUserInGroup = False

        'Check in the Users --> Groups collection
        IsUserInGroup = _
            (wrk.Users(strUser).Groups(strGroup).Name = strGroup)

        'You can also do it this way...
        'Check in the Groups --> Users collection
```

```
'IsUserInGroup = _
        (wrk.Groups(strGroup).Users(strUser).Name = strUser)

    Set wrk = Nothing
End Function
```

Managing Passwords

To change a user's password, you execute the User object's NewPassword method. You must provide both the old and new passwords; however, if you are a member of the Admins groups and are changing the password of another user, the old password argument is ignored.

```
Public Sub ChangePassword(strUser As String, _
    strOldPassword As String, strNewPassword As String)
    Dim wrk As DAO.Workspace
    Dim usr As DAO.User

    Set wrk = DBEngine(0)
    Set usr = wrk.Users(strUser)

    'Change the password
    usr.NewPassword strOldPassword, strNewPassword

    Set usr = Nothing
    Set wrk = Nothing
End Sub
```

The issue, of course, is that there is no way to view the password for any user.

Managing Permissions

Permission is what your parents denied you when you wanted to eat chocolates all day. In my house, permission to eat chocolates was granted only under certain conditions.

The notion of permission is the same in computer systems, except that computers don't keep chocolates in a cupboard; they keep objects and data, to which many would like access.

Computer systems grant or deny access to objects and data, based on the rights that users or groups of users, are granted by the system administrator. Further, specific users can be granted or denied special access in addition to the rights of the group to which they belong. This is like your mother ruling that all children under the age of 10 are permitted to snack on the fruit biscuits in the cupboard, but not the chocolates. The exception being that little Johnny (age 8) may also eat any chocolate he wants, but only from the red box (laxatives).

In Access, user and group permissions are defined in two places: Permissions relating to individual objects are stored in the Permissions property of Document objects. Permissions for future objects are stored in the Permissions property of Container objects.

Depending on the specific object, different permissions can be granted. The following tables list those permissions, and the constants that define them.

Object	Permission Constant	Value	Description
Container	DbSecNoAccess	0	No access to the object
	DbSecFullAccess	1048575	Full access to the object
	DbSecDelete	65536	Can delete the object
	DbSecReadSec	131072	Can read the object's security information
	DbSecWriteSec	262144	Can change the object's security information
	DbSecWriteOwner	524288	Can change the ownership of the object
Table	DbSecCreate	1	Can create new Document objects (valid only with a Container object)
	DbSecReadDef	4	Can read the table definition
	DbSecWriteDef	65548	Can modify or change the table definition
	DbSecRetrieveData	20	Can retrieve data from the Document object
	DbSecInsertData	32	Can add records
	DbSecReplaceData	64	Can modify records
	DbSecDeleteData	128	Can delete records
Database	dbSecDBAdmin	8	Assigns admin rights—can create replicas, change the database password, and set startup properties
	dbSecDBCreate	1	Can create new databases (valid only on the Databases container object in the Workgroup Information File
	dbSecDBExclusive	4	Can open the database exclusively
	DbSecDBOpen	2	Can open the database
Macro	AcSecMacExecute	8	Can run the macro
	AcSecMacReadDef	10	Can read the macro's definition
	AcSecMacWriteDef	65542	Can modify the macro's definition
	acSecFrmRptExecute	256	Can open the form or report
	acSecFrmRptReadDef	4	Can read the form's or report's definition and its module
	acSecFrmRptWriteDef	65548	Can modify the form's or report's definition and its module

Reading Permissions

As mentioned earlier, object permissions are stored in two main places: the Permissions property of Document objects, and the Permissions property of Container objects, the latter being where the permissions for future objects is defined. But before you get too carried away with this new found knowledge, you might be interested to know that object permissions are stored in a Long Integer bit field. To get at individual permissions, you need to perform a bitwise operation, which is not very difficult.

To determine the permissions that the current user has to Table1, for example, just read the Permissions property of its Document object.

```
Debug.Print dbs.Containers("Tables").Documents("Table1").Permissions
```

You should be aware that the Permissions property only returns *explicit* permissions, which are those that are explicitly defined for that particular user. *Implicit* permissions, which are returned by the AllPermissions property, are the sum of all the permissions the user has, whether explicitly granted, or the ones they inherited by virtue of their membership of one or more groups.

For example, let us suppose that Fred Nurk belongs to a group called Data Entry, and the Data Entry group has dbSecInsertData and dbSecReplaceData permissions to Table1, but that the administrator has explicitly granted him dbSecDeleteData permissions, but accidentally revoked his individual dbReplaceData permissions to the same table. Fred's total permissions are the sum of all permissions—dbSecInsertData + dbSecDeleteData.

To determine if the current user has particular permissions to an object, you must explicitly test for those permissions. The following example demonstrates this:

```
Public Function HasDeletePermissons( _
        strTableName As String, Optional strUser As String) As Boolean
    'Checks if the current user has Delete
    'permissions to a specific table
    Dim dbs As Database
    Dim doc As DAO.Document

    Set dbs = CurrentDb

    'Set a reference to the table's Document
    Set doc = dbs.Containers!Tables.Documents(strTableName)

    'Specify the user
    If strUser <> "" Then doc.UserName = strUser

    'Test for explicit permissions only
    HasDeletePermissons = _
        ((doc.Permissions And dbSecDeleteData) = dbSecDeleteData)

    'To test for implicit permissions,
    'uncomment the following line
    'HasDeletePermissons = _
        ((doc.AllPermissions And dbSecDeleteData) = dbSecDeleteData)

    Set doc = Nothing
    Set dbs = Nothing
End Function
```

The more observant reader might have noticed that you can, in fact, specify the user name. The default setting for the Document object's UserName property is that of the current user, but if you set the UserName property prior to reading the Permissions property, you can check the permissions for any user or group in the workgroup.

The following code shows how to determine the exact object permissions for a *specific* user or group:

```
Public Sub WhichPermissions( _
        strTableName As String, Optional strUser As String)
    'Determines the specific permissions a
    'specific user has to a specific table
    Dim dbs As Database
    Dim doc As DAO.Document
    Dim lngPermission As Long

    Set dbs = CurrentDb

    'Set a reference to the table's Document
    Set doc = dbs.Containers!Tables.Documents(strTable)

    'Specify the user
    If strUser <> "" Then doc.UserName = strUser

    'Retrieve the permissions
    lngPermission = doc.AllPermissions

    'Determine the user's implicit permissions
    Debug.Print "Permissions granted to " & _
            strUser & " for " & strTable
    If ((doc.AllPermissions And dbSecNoAccess) = _
            dbSecNoAccess) Then
        Debug.Print vbTab & "dbSecNoAccess"
    End If

    If ((doc.AllPermissions And dbSecFullAccess) = _
            dbSecFullAccess) Then
        Debug.Print vbTab & "dbSecFullAccess"
    End If

    If ((doc.AllPermissions And dbSecDelete) = _
            dbSecDelete) Then
        Debug.Print vbTab & "dbSecDelete"
    End If

    If ((doc.AllPermissions And dbSecReadSec) = _
            dbSecReadSec) Then
        Debug.Print vbTab & "dbSecReadSec"
    End If

    If ((doc.AllPermissions And dbSecWriteSec) = _
            dbSecWriteSec) Then
        Debug.Print vbTab & "dbSecWriteSec"
    End If
```

```
        If ((doc.AllPermissions And dbSecWriteOwner) = _
              dbSecWriteOwner) Then
          Debug.Print vbTab & "dbSecWriteOwner"
        End If

        Set doc = Nothing
        Set dbs = Nothing
    End Sub
```

So far, we've covered how to check the permissions for existing Jet and Access objects, but what about objects that will be created in the future? DAO provides a facility for this too. You can retrieve the default permissions that have been set for any new objects, by checking the `Permissions` property of the `Document` object's parent—the `Container` object.

```
    Debug.Print dbs.Containers!Tables.AllPermissions
    Debug.Print dbs.Containers!Tables.Permissions
```

Setting Permissions

Setting object permissions is similar to setting any other property, but it is worth mentioning that you can not only set the property, but can also simultaneously set multiple permissions, and add or remove one or more permissions.

To explicitly *set* the permissions for an object, you simply assign the permission to the object's `Permission` property. For example, to assign the permission for the current user to delete data from `Table1`:

```
    Set doc = dbs.Containers!Tables.Documents!Table1
    doc.Permissions = dbSecInsertData Or dbSecDeleteData
```

To *add* a permission to an object's existing permissions, you use the bitwise `Or` operator with the existing permissions. For example, to add permission for the current user to delete data from `Table1`:

```
    Set doc = dbs.Containers!Tables.Documents!Table1
    doc.Permissions = doc.Permissions Or dbSecInsertData
```

To *remove* one or more permissions from the object's existing permissions, you make use of the `And Not` operators. For example, to remove two permissions from `Table1`; the ability to modify and delete data:

```
    Set doc = dbs.Containers!Tables.Documents!Table1
    doc.permissions = doc.Permissions And Not ( _
          dbSecReplaceData Or dbSecDeleteData)
```

Data Access with DAO

Accessing data is the reason we use databases, and a large proportion of your programming will usually revolve around manipulating those objects that deal with data: queries and recordsets. In this section, we'll take a detailed look at how to access and manipulate your database data using DAO objects.

Working with QueryDefs

When you build a query with the graphical Query Designer, you are building a QueryDef object in the default *Jet workspace*. When you save the query, you are also appending a reference to it in the QueryDefs collection. You can also build a QueryDef in code, which is one of the purposes of this section.

In an *ODBCDirect* workspace, you can only create *temporary* QueryDefs, which cease to exist when you close the workspace.

You can think of permanent (Jet workspace) QueryDefs as SQL statements that are compiled the first time they are executed. This is similar in concept to the way code is compiled. Once compiled, permanent queries run marginally faster than their temporary, unsaved, counterparts, because Jet does not need to compile them before execution. Temporary QueryDefs are useful when you don't need to save them, as when you create their SQL statements during runtime. You would normally build and run SQL statements in line with your code when you need to change its clauses depending on current operating conditions or the value of some variable.

Creating a QueryDef

To create a QueryDef, execute the CreateQueryDef method against the Jet Database object, or in the case of ODBCDirect workspaces, the Database or Connection objects.

In Microsoft Jet workspaces, if you set a QueryDef's Name property to something other than a zero-length string, it is automatically appended to the QueryDefs collection, and saved to disk. Omitting the Name property, or explicitly setting it to a zero-length string, will result in a temporary (unsaved) QueryDef.

In ODBCDirect workspaces, QueryDefs are always temporary, and so, are unsaved. In ODBCDirect, the QueryDefs collection only ever contains open QueryDefs, which when closed, are automatically removed from the collection.

The following code demonstrates how to create a QueryDef in a Microsoft Jet workspace:

```
Public Sub CreateQuery (strName As String, strSQL As String)
    Dim dbs As Database
    Dim qdf As QueryDef

    Set dbs = CurrentDb

    'Create the QueryDef
    'If the user supplies a name, the QueryDef will be
    'automatically appended to the QueryDefs collection
    Set qdf = dbs.CreateQueryDef(strName, strSQL)

    Set qdf = Nothing
    Set dbs = Nothing
End Sub
```

You can create a pass-through query to an ODBC data source by setting the QueryDef's Connect property to a valid connection string, after the query has been created.

```
qdf.Connect = strConnectionString
```

Parameters

Although you can't add parameters to a `QueryDef` using DAO, you can retrieve information about them using the following construct:

```
db.QueryDefs("myQuery").parameters(0).Name
```

For example, you can retrieve the date the `QueryDef` was created, the date it was last updated, its SQL statement (so you can change it in code), a flag indicating whether the query is updatable, and so on.

You can also specify a query parameter's value in order to specify the value of criteria to filter the query's output, or the selected records on which the query operates. For example, the following procedure sets a reference to an existing query called `myActionQuery`, sets the value of its parameter (`Organisation`), and then executes the query.

```vba
Public Sub ExecParameterQuery()
    Dim dbs As Database
    Dim qdf As DAO.QueryDef

    Set dbs = CurrentDb
    Set qdf = dbs.QueryDefs("myActionQuery")

    'Set the value of the QueryDef's parameter
    qdf.Parameters("Organisation").Value = "Microsoft"

    'Execute the query
    qdf.Execute dbFailOnError

    'Clean up
    qdf.Close
    Set qdf = Nothing
    Set dbs = Nothing
End Sub
```

Modifying a QueryDef

Once you have created a `QueryDef`, you can modify its properties as easily as modifying any other DAO property.

```vba
Public Sub ModifyQuery(strName As String, _
        strNewSQL As String, lngPrepare As Long)
    Dim dbs As Database
    Dim qdf As QueryDef

    Set dbs = CurrentDb

    'Modify the QueryDef's properties
    With dbs.QueryDefs(strName)
        .SQL = strNewSQL
        .Prepare = dbQPrepare 'ODBCDirect workspaces only
    End With

    Set dbs = Nothing
End Sub
```

The `QueryDef` object's `Prepare` property is valid only in ODBCDirect workspaces, and specifies if the query is to be prepared on the server as a temporary stored procedure before it is executed.

Setting the `Prepare` property to `dbQPrepare` can slow the first execution of the query, but increases performance on all subsequent executions. Some queries, however, can't be executed as stored procedures, in which case, you must specify `dbQUnprepare`.

Deleting a QueryDef

Deleting a `QueryDef` is simple. Just issue the `Delete` method against the `QueryDefs` collection.

```
dbs.QueryDefs.Delete strName
```

Executing Queries

There are three ways to programmatically execute a query: using the `DoCmd.RunSQL` method, the `object.Execute` method, and the `OpenRecordset` method. Not all of these methods return records. The query argument for any of the following methods can either be the name of a permanent or temporary `QueryDef`, or a string expression that equates to a query:

```
DoCmd.RunSQL
```

Although not part of the DAO object model, you can execute the `RunSQL` method of the `DoCmd` object to run an action query:

```
DoCmd.RunSQL "UPDATE Table1 SET Field1 = 123"
```

or

```
DoCmd.RunSQL qryMyQuery
```

Running a query in this way will display a message box to confirm that you wish to make changes to the database. To eliminate this message box, set the `DoCmd` object's `SetWarnings` property to `False` prior to calling `DoCmd.RunSQL`, but remember to set it back when you've finished, otherwise all warning messages will thereafter be disabled.

```
DoCmd.SetWarnings False
DoCmd.RunSQL qryMyQuery
DoCmd.SetWarnings True
```

Any errors raised while executing the query will display a message box. You can disable the message box as described above, and you can trap the error using the `On Error Goto` construct. By default, the query will be included in an existing transaction, but you can exclude it by setting the `UseTransaction` property to `False`.

```
DoCmd.RunSQL qryMyQuery, False
object.Execute
```

You can use the `Execute` method of the `QueryDef` object, Microsoft Jet or ODBCDirect `Database` object, and ODBCDirect `Connection` object, to run an action query:

```
qdf.Execute  options
dbs.Execute qryMyQuery,  options
cn.Execute qryMyQuery,  options
```

With the `Execute` method, there is no need to set the `SetWarnings` property to disable change confirmation message boxes, because none are displayed. The `Execute` method operates directly on its parent object.

There are several major benefits to using the `Execute` method in preference to the `DoCmd.RunSQL` method:

❑ The `Execute` method runs faster than `DoCmd.RunSQL`.

❑ The `Execute` method can be included in an existing transaction, like any other DAO operation, without needing to specify an option to do so.

❑ You can specify several options that change the way the method works.

The following table lists the various constants that can be supplied as options for the `Execute` method.

Constant	Description
DbDenyWrite	Denies write permission to other users (Microsoft Jet workspaces only).
DbInconsistent	Executes inconsistent updates (Microsoft Jet workspaces only).
DbConsistent	Executes consistent updates (Microsoft Jet workspaces only).
dbSQLPassThrough	Executes an SQL pass-through query, which passes the query to an ODBC database for processing. (Microsoft Jet workspaces only).
DbFailOnError	Rolls back updates if an error occurs (Microsoft Jet workspaces only).
DbSeeChanges	Generates a runtime error if another user is changing data that you are editing (Microsoft Jet workspaces only).
DbRunAsync	Executes the query asynchronously (ODBC `Connection` and `QueryDef` objects only). This allows your code to keep running while the query is loading. In ODBCDirect workspaces, you can use the `StillExecuting` property to determine if the query has completed.
DbExecDirect	Executes the statement without first calling the `SQLPrepare` ODBC API function (ODBCDirect `Connection` and `QueryDef` objects only).

You can execute a query when you open a recordset. To do so, specify the query name in the `Database` object's `OpenRecordset` method to run a select or action query:

```
dbs.OpenRecordset(qryMyQuery)
```

Similarly, you can open a recordset based on a query, like so:

```
Set qdf = dbs.QueryDefs("qryMyQuery")
Set rst = qdf.OpenRecordset(dbOpenDynaset)
```

The following section on recordsets describes this in greater detail.

Working with Recordsets

When you need to access and manipulate data one record at a time, you must use a `Recordset` object. For this reason, *recordsets* are the workhorse of database programming. As you've already seen, there are five types of recordset available in DAO, one of which is for the ODBCDirect workspace. The one you use depends on the workspace you're using, where the data comes from, and what you want to do with it.

Creating a Recordset

You can create a recordset by using the `OpenRecordset` method of the `Database`, `TableDef`, or `QueryDef` objects.

```
Set rst = dbs.OpenRecordset( Source, Type, Options, LockEdits)
Set rst = object.OpenRecordset( Type, Options, LockEdits)
```

The `Source` argument specifies the name of a table or query, or a string expression that equates to an SQL query. For `dbOpenTable` recordsets, the `Source` argument can only be the name of a table.

The default recordset type that is opened if you omit the `Type` argument, depends on the type of table you're trying to open. If you open a Microsoft Jet recordset on a local table, the default is a *Table* type. If you open a Microsoft Jet recordset against a linked table or query, the default type is *Dynaset*. If you open an ODBCDirect recordset, the default type is *ForwardOnly*.

The `Type` argument values are specified by a number of constants. These constants and their values can be found in Appendix C. The following code examples demonstrate how to open different types of recordsets.

Opening a Recordset Based on a Table or Query

```
Dim dbs As Database
Dim rsTable As DAO.Recordset
Dim rsQuery As DAO.Recordset

Set dbs = CurrentDb

'Open a table-type recordset
Set rsTable = dbs.OpenRecordset("Table1", dbOpenTable)

'Open a dynaset-type recordset using a saved query
Set rsQuery = dbs.OpenRecordset("qryMyQuery", dbOpenDynaset)
```

Opening a Recordset Based on an SQL Statement

```
Dim dbs As Database
Dim rsSQL As DAO.Recordset
Dim strSQL As String

Set dbs = CurrentDb

'Open a snapshot-type recordset based on an SQL statement
strSQL = "SELECT * FROM Table1 WHERE Field2 = 33"
Set rsSQL = dbs.OpenRecordset(strSQL, dbOpenSnapshot)
```

Opening a Recordset That Locks Out All Other Users

```
Dim dbs As Database
Dim rsSQL As DAO.Recordset

Set dbs = CurrentDb

'Open a dynaset-type recordset based on a saved query
Set rsSQL = dbs.OpenRecordset("qryMyQuery", _
                dbOpenDynaset, dbDenyRead)
```

Opening a Recordset That Contains More Than One SELECT Query

In ODBCDirect workspaces, you can open one of the following recordset types that contain more than one SELECT query: Dynamic, Dynaset, ForwardOnly, Snapshot.

The following example demonstrates how to use such a recordset. We start by declaring all the variables and opening an ODBCDirect connection.

```
Dim wsODBC As Workspace
Dim cn As DAO.Connection
Dim rst As DAO.Recordset
Dim intCount As Integer
Dim booNext As Boolean

'Create ODBCDirect Workspace
Set wsODBC = CreateWorkspace("", "sa", "somepassword", dbUseODBC)

'The DefaultCursorDriver setting is required when using
'compound SQL statements.
wsODBC.DefaultCursorDriver = dbUseODBCCursor

'Open the connection (in this case, using a DSN)
Set cn = wsODBC.OpenConnection("myConnection", , , _
                "ODBC;DATABASE=myDB;DSN=myDSN")
```

Next, we open the ODBCDirect recordset, specifying two or more different SELECT queries, each separated by a semicolon (now you know what the semicolon is for).

```
'Open the recordset
Set rst = cn.OpenRecordset("SELECT * FROM Table1; " & _
                    "SELECT * FROM Table2", dbOpenDynamic)
```

As you would expect, the first dataset to be loaded into the recordset is the one that is specified first in the method call or SQL property, and you can cycle through each recordset in the same way you would with other recordsets.

If when you finish with one recordset, and there are more records that are pending (including an empty recordset), the next dataset is loaded into the recordset and the `NextRecordset` property returns `True`. When the last record of the last recordset has been read, this property returns `False`.

You can terminate a recordset, and move on to the next one, by using the `NextRecordset` method. In the example, this is done by prematurely exiting the `Do...Loop` construct after the first record is returned.

```
'Cycle through the recordset queries
booNext = True
intCount = 1
With rst
    Do While booNext
        Debug.Print "Contents of recordset " & intCount & "..."
        Do While Not .EOF
            Debug.Print , !Field1, !Field2

            'Terminate the first recordset early
            If intCount = 1 Then Exit Do
            .MoveNext
        Loop

        'Load the next query
        booNext = .NextRecordset
        intCount = intCount + 1
    Loop
End With

rst.Close
cn.Close
wsODBC.Close
```

As with other recordsets, you can flush the recordset with the recordset's `Cancel` method, but you should remember that this cancels the entire recordset, not just the current dataset.

Filtering and Ordering Recordsets

Whenever you work on records in a database, it is rare that you want to carry out an action on the entire table, although if you did, you would be best served by using an action query, because queries operate much faster on large numbers of rows than do row processing methods (recordsets). However, it is more likely that you'll want to do something with a subset of records, and that means you would need to filter your query to select only those records that you wanted to work on.

With recordsets, you have the additional opportunity to sort the records, so you can operate on them in a specific order, perhaps by ascending date, for example. This section is concerned with illustrating how to filter your recordsets and order their output.

Filtering Records

Filtering is simply a way of restricting the number of rows returned by a recordset, so that you can minimize the amount of data you have to wade through. The additional benefit of filtering is that it also reduces the amount of data that is sent across the network, thereby minimizing bandwidth usage.

As you've already seen, you can filter a recordset using a WHERE clause in a query on which the recordset can be based, or in its Source argument. For example:

```
Set rst = dbs.OpenRecordset( _
    "SELECT * FROM tblCustomers WHERE CustomerNo > 1234")
```

This filters the recordset as it is being created, and of course, you can't do this on table-type recordsets, because they load the entire table, but you can filter dynaset- and snapshot-type recordsets.

Another method of filtering a recordset as it is being created is to use the Recordset object's Filter property. You can't filter an existing recordset once it's been created, so the filter won't take effect until you create a new recordset that is based on the first.

For example, if we create a recordset like that shown above (filtered on CustomerNo), we can then further filter its records and place the output into a second recordset. We do this by setting its Filter property, by specifying the WHERE clause of an SQL query, without the word WHERE. For example:

```
rst.Filter = "[CustName] LIKE '*parts*'"
```

Then we create a new recordset that will be based on a subset of the rows in the first recordset that is defined by the Filter property, like this:

```
Set rsFiltered = rst.OpenRecordset
```

After doing so, rsFiltered contains only those rows from rst whose CustName rows contains the word *parts*. You might think that this is a rather inefficient way of doing things, and under normal circumstances I'd agree with you; however, there are circumstances in which this approach might be the better way to go.

For example, let's say you want your sales representatives to visit all the customers in a certain city, based solely on the city that was visited last. You don't know which city that might be, so in the following example code, we create a recordset that returns rows for all my customers who were last visited between 30 and 60 days ago. Once we have the record for the last customer visited within that time frame, we then extract the name of the city in which they reside, and create another filtered recordset (based on the first), and set their ToBeVisited flag to True. This lets the sales representatives know to visit them. Of course, there's nothing here that couldn't be done in an action query, but this example demonstrates how you could use this feature.

```
Dim dbs As Database
Dim rst As DAO.Recordset
Dim rstFiltered As DAO.Recordset
Dim strCity As String
```

```
Set dbs = CurrentDb
'Create the first filtered recordset, returning customer records
'for those visited between 30-60 days ago.
Set rst = dbs.OpenRecordset( _
    "SELECT * FROM Customers WHERE LastVisitDate BETWEEN Date()-60
AND Date()-30 ORDER BY LastVisitDate Desc")
'Begin row processing
Do While Not rst.EOF
    'Retrieve the name of the first city in the selected rows
    strCity = rst.City
    'Now filter the recordset to return only the customers from that city
    rst.Filter = "City = '" & strCity & "'"
    Set rsFiltered = rst
    'Process the rows
    Do While Not rsFiltered.EOF
        rsFiltered.Edit
        rsfiltered!ToBeVisited = True
        rsFiltered.Update
        rsFiltered.MovNext
    Loop

    'We've done what hat needed. Now exit.
    Exit Do
    End If
    rst.MoveNext
Loop
```

You may have noticed that I used the ORDER BY clause in the preceding example. The ORDER BY clause is explained in the next section.

Ordering Records

Ordering is a way of defining how the data returned in the recordset is to be sorted. For example, you might want to see, in ascending order of amount, a list of customers who owe you money.

There are three ways to sort recordsets: using the WHERE clause in a query on which the recordset can be based, or in its Source argument; using the Index property; or using the Sort property. You can only use the Index property on table-type recordsets, whereas the WHERE clause and Sort property only work with dynaset- and snapshot-type recordsets.

Ordering Using the WHERE Clause

When you specify the SQL statement on which a recordset is based, you can terminate the query with an ORDER BY clause. This clause specifies three things: the columns on which the sort will be based, the order of precedence for the sorting of those columns, and the actual order in which the data in those columns will be sorted. For example:

```
SELECT * FROM tblCustomers ORDER BY CustomerNo DESC, CustName
```

In the above query, the records returned will be ordered according to the criteria set up for both the CustomerNo and CustName columns. By virtue of their relative positions in the clause (CustomerNo appears *before* CustName), the recordset will first be sorted according to the criteria for CustomerNo, and then by CustName. As you can see, CustomerNo will be sorted in descending order.

Although you can specify ASC, for ascending order, the default is ascending, so there is no need to explicitly declare it.

Ordering Using the Index Property

Setting the Index property of a table-type recordset is quite simple to execute; however, you are restricted to the sort order already specified by the table's index. For example:

```
rst.Index = "CustomerNo"
```

will immediately reorder the recordset in CustomerNo order. If the CustomerNo index is defined in ascending order, that is how the recordset will be sorted.

Ordering Using the Sort Property

As with the Filter property discussed above, setting the Sort property will not affect the current recordset. Rather, it will only affect a new recordset that is created and based on the current one.

For example, if we create a recordset, filtered on CustomerNo, we then set this recordset's Sort property, by specifying the WHERE clause of an SQL query, without the word WHERE. For example:

```
Set rst = dbs.OpenRecordset( _
    "SELECT * FROM tblCustomers WHERE CustomerNo > 1234")
rst.Sort = "[CustomerNo] DESC, [CustName]"
```

Then we create a new recordset whose sort order is defined by the Sort property, like this:

```
Set rsOrdered = rst.OpenRecordset
```

Navigating Recordsets

Once you've opened a recordset, you'll probably want to get at its data, and unless you only ever want to see one record, you'll probably want to move from record to record.

DAO provides five methods and five properties to help you navigate through your recordsets. The five methods are MoveFirst, MovePrevious, MoveNext, and MoveLast. The five properties are AbsolutePosition, PercentPosition, RecordCount, BOF (beginning of file), and EOF (end of file).

RecordCount

Given its name, you might assume that the RecordCount property actually indicates the number of records returned by a recordset. This assumption is not quite accurate.

Recordsets do not always return their entire dataset immediately; they can take quite some time to populate; the more rows they have to return, the longer they take. DAO returns a pointer to the recordset early, so you can get on with doing whatever it is you want to do, assuming that the latter rows will have been returned by the time you get to them.

The RecordCount property actually returns the number of rows that the recordset has accessed so far.

Of course, if you issue the MoveLast method before checking RecordCount, the recordset does not return until all the records have been accessed, in which case RecordCount then reports the correct number of rows. In fact, that's how you get an accurate record count, by issuing a `MoveLast`, followed by checking the `RecordCount` property.

```
Set rst = dbs.OpenRecordset("SELECT * FROM Table1", dbOpenDynaset)
If rst.AbsolutePosition > -1 Then
    'Move to the last row
    rst.MoveLast

    'Now get the count
    lngCount = rst.RecordCount

    'If you want, you can now move again
    rst.MoveFirst

    '- - - -
    'Continue processing
    '- - - -

End If
```

> `RecordCount` **always returns the correct number of rows for table-type recordsets.**

In a single-user environment, once `RecordCount` has the correct number of rows, it keeps synch when rows are added or deleted. In a multiuser environment, however, things get a little trickier.

For example, if two users are modifying records in the same table, additions or deletions made by one user will not be reflected on the other user's computer until they access *that* record (or the place where a deleted record *used* to be). To ensure you have an accurate record count in a multiuser environment, you should:

❑   Use the recordset's `Requery` method (see the note below); or

❑   Use the `MoveLast` method again.

> **The `Requery` method is not supported on table-type recordsets. The `RecordCount` property for snapshot-type recordsets will not change once it has been created, and it certainly won't reflect changes made by other users.**

AbsolutePosition, PercentPosition

The `AbsolutePosition` and `PercentPosition` methods allow you to move the cursor to a specific row in the recordset. For example, if you wanted to move to the 127th row, you could issue the following method call:

```
rst.AbsolutePosition = 127
```

Similarly, if you wanted to move to (roughly) half-way through the recordset, you could issue this:

```
rst.PercentPosition = 50
```

Because you can also use these methods to determine where you are in the recordset, we usually use `AbsolutePosition` to determine if our recordset has any records in it.

```
Set rst = dbs.OpenRecordset(strSQL, dbOpenDynaset)
If rst.AbsolutePosition > -1 Then
    'The recordset contains records
Else
    'It does not
End If
```

You see if `AbsolutePosition` returns –1, its position is undetermined. You can't determine the cursor position of an empty recordset. But if the recordset contains records, its position is determinable, and therefore, must be greater than –1. If `AbsolutePosition = 0`, you must be located at the first row of the recordset.

`AbsolutePosition` does not equate to a row number, and although it does return the cursor's current position in the recordset, that position can change as you add or delete rows, or change your filtering and sorting. You can't use `AbsolutePosition` with table-type recordsets, and ForwardOnly recordsets don't support either `AbsolutePosition` or `PercentPosition`.

MoveFirst, MovePrevious, MoveNext, and MoveLast

The four methods for moving around in a recordset are `MoveFirst`, `MovePrevious`, `MoveNext`, and `MoveLast`. These methods constitute the workhorses of recordset navigation, particularly `MoveNext` and `MovePrevious`. As their names suggest, they allow you to move the cursor forward and backward from the current position.

The Move Method

The `Recordset` object's `Move` method allows you to move the cursor to another position relative to either the current position, or that specified by a `Bookmark`. The `Move` method provides two arguments:

```
rst.Move rows[, start]
```

The `rows` argument specifies the number of rows to move, and the direction: greater than zero indicates forward, less than zero means backward. The optional `start` argument specifies where to start the move from. When you supply a `Bookmark` for the `start` argument, DAO moves the cursor the appropriate number of rows from the position specified by the `Bookmark`. If you omit the `start` argument, DAO moves the cursor from the current position.

In ForwardOnly recordsets, the `rows` argument must be greater than zero, and you cannot specify a `Bookmark`.

BOF, EOF

If you move beyond the boundaries of a recordset, an error will occur. To avoid this rather unpleasant side effect of poor programming practice, you should test to see whether you have reached the beginning or end of the recordset. Make sense?

Before using `MoveNext` or `MoveFirst`, you should check the value of `BOF` and `EOF`.

```
    If Not rst.BOF Then rst.MovePrevious
```

or

```
    If Not rst.EOF Then rst.MoveNext
```

To help you understand the behavior of these properties, consider the following scenarios:

❑ If you issue MoveNext while the cursor is on the last row, EOF returns True. If you then issue MoveNext again, EOF remains True and an error occurs.

❑ If you issue MovePrevious while the cursor is on the first row, BOF returns True. If you then issue MovePrevious again, BOF remains True and an error occurs.

❑ As mentioned earlier, I use AbsolutePosition to test for an empty recordset, but as we've discovered, AbsolutePosition can't be used on ForwardOnly or table-type recordsets, so we need another method for determining whether a recordset contains any records.

❑ BOF and EOF are widely used when looping through recordsets, when you don't know how many records have been returned. Usually, row processing begins at the first row, and continues unil all the rows have been processed. Sometimes, however, processing begins at the last record, and continues backwards until the beginning of the recordset. BOF and EOF allow you to do this.

For example, the following code shows a standard forward looping construct:

```
Set rst = dbs.OpenRecordset("SELECT * FROM Table1", dbOpenDynaset)
Do While Not rst.EOF
    'Process the rows
    rst.MoveNext
Loop
```

The following example demonstrates a typical reverse-direction loop:

```
Set rst = dbs.OpenRecordset("SELECT * FROM Table1", dbOpenDynaset)
rst.MoveLast
Do While Not rst.BOF
    'Process the rows
    rst.MovePrevious
Loop
```

Testing for an Empty Recordset

As mentioned in the previous section, if you attempt to move beyond a recordset's boundaries, an error will occur. Similarly, if you attempt to execute any other recordset method on an empty recordset (one that has not returned any records), an error occurs.

Whenever you open a recordset, the first thing you need to know is, "did it return any records?" When you open a recordset, you usually want to do something with the data it returns. If the data is there, you can confidently take whatever actions you had planned. But if, for whatever reason, the recordset doesn't return any records, you will have to take some alternative action.

Testing for an empty recordset can be accomplished in several ways:

1. Test for `AbsolutePosition`, as described earlier.

2. Test for `BOF` and `EOF` together. If `BOF` and `EOF` are both `True`, the recordset is empty. For example:

```
Set rst = dbs.OpenRecordset("SELECT * FROM Table1", dbOpenDynaset)
If Not (rst.BOF And rst.EOF) Then
    'The recordset returned records
End If
```

3. If you need to loop through the recordset, create a condition test that can't be met in the event of an empty recordset. For example:

```
Set rst = dbs.OpenRecordset("SELECT * FROM Table1", dbOpenDynaset)
Do Until rst.EOF
    'The recordset returned records
Loop
```

4. Check the recordset's `RecordCount` property. If it is zero, you know there aren't any records. For example:

```
Set rst = dbs.OpenRecordset("SELECT * FROM Table1", dbOpenDynaset)
If rst.RecordCount > 0 Then
    'The recordset returned records
End If
```

Bookmarks and Recordset Clones

If you're anything like my 10-year-old daughter, you will read *Prisoner of Ascaban* in three days. As she was reading so constantly, the book was hardly out of her hands, so there was little need for a bookmark to keep her place so that she could return to it at a later time. In software terms, a Bookmark is the same thing.

A recordset `Bookmark` is a special marker that you place in your recordset, so you can quickly return or refer to it at some later stage. For example, if you wanted to move from your current position in the recordset to check or change a value in some other part of the same recordset, you could set a `Bookmark`, move to the other spot, make your changes, and then return to where you were in the first place.

When you open a recordset, every row is automatically assigned a unique internal `Bookmark`, and as you will soon see, creating a reference to a `Bookmark` is simply a matter of setting the value of a variable. So there is really no practical limit to the number of bookmarks you can set. When you close the recordset, the internal `Bookmarks` are lost, and any `Bookmarks` you have set become invalid.

Although recordsets based entirely on Jet tables always support `Bookmarks`, not all recordset types do. Recordsets based on external data sources may not allow them, for example, those based on linked Paradox tables that have no primary key. For that reason, you should always check the `Recordset` object's `Bookmarkable` property before attempting to use `Bookmarks` on non-Jet recordsets.

Using `Bookmarks` is much faster than using the other recordset navigation methods. The following procedure demonstrates how to use `Bookmarks` for record navigation:

```
Public Sub UsingBookmarks()
    Dim dbs As Database
    Dim rst As DAO.Recordset
    Dim varBookmark As Variant

    Set dbs = CurrentDb
    Set rst = dbs.OpenRecordset("SELECT * FROM Table1", dbOpenDynaset)
    If rst.AbsolutePosition > -1 Then
        'Force the entire recordset to load
        rst.MoveLast
        rst.MoveFirst

        'Move to the middle of the recordset, and print
        'the current cursor position, for reference
        rst.PercentPosition = 50
        Debug.Print "Current position: " & rs.AbsolutePosition

        'Set the bookmark
        varBookmark = rst.Bookmark

        'Move to the last record, and print its position
        rst.MoveLast
        Debug.Print "Current position: " & rs.AbsolutePosition
        '
        'Do whatever you came here to do
        '
        'Now move back, and verify the position
        rst.Bookmark = varBookmark
        Debug.Print "Current position: " & rs.AbsolutePosition
    End If

    rst.Close
    Set rst = Nothing
    Set dbs = Nothing
End Sub
```

Now What About Those Clones?

Scientists have cloned mice, sheep, fish, and a variety of plants, and it seems every new generation of politician is a poor quality clone of the ones that preceded them. It's a pity I can't clone my salary check! In terms of recordsets, a clone is a functional replica of the original. There are two clone methods: `Clone` and `RecordsetClone`. `Clone` is a method of the `Form` object, whereas `RecordsetClone` is a method of the `Recordset` object. Both are identical in function, except for the following issues: The `Clone` method is not supported for ForwardOnly-type recordsets, and you can't set the `Filter` or `Sort` properties for recordsets created using the `RecordSetClone` method.

Microsoft states in the online help that the recordset returned by the `Clone` method has no current position when it is first created. Calling `AbsolutePosition` straight after creating the clone indicates that it does; however, I'd be inclined to take Microsoft at their word and not rely on a clone having a current position until after I had executed one of the `Move` methods.

If you use the `Clone` or `RecordsetClone` method to create a copy of the original recordset, all the bookmarks are identical, because, rather than creating a new recordset from scratch, the two clone methods simply point an object variable at the original set of rows. The clone operates on exactly the same data as the original, so any changes made in one are reflected in the other. But (and here's the nifty part), although the data and bookmarks are identical, you can operate on the clone independently of the original; that is, you can change the cursor position in the clone (by using any of the navigation methods) and have no effect on the cursor position in the original. It is for this reason that recordset clones and bookmarks are usually mentioned together.

Let's say you are designing a data entry form for customers. Let's also say you want to allow the users to type in a customer number, and have the form immediately display the record for the customer with that number. There are several ways you can do this, not all of them satisfactory.

You could use `DoCmd.ApplyFilter` or reopen the form using a filter with `DoCmd.OpenForm`, but at best, they would return only one record, and your form navigation buttons would then be useless. At worst, they would return an empty recordset. What good is that? The answer is to use a bookmark and recordset clone together. In the `AfterUpdate` event of your Customer Number text box, you could add the following code:

```
Private Sub txtEnterCustNo_AfterUpdate()
    Dim rsClone As DAO.Recordset
    Dim strCustNo As String

    'Remove leading and trailing spaces
    strCustNo = Trim(Me.txtEnterCustNo)

    'Check that the text box contains a value
    If strCustNo <> "" Then
        'Create a clone of the form's recordset
        Set rsClone = Me.RecordSetClone

        'Search for the customer's record
        rsClone.FindFirst "[CustNo] = """ & strCustNo & """"
        'The FindFirst method is explained in the following section

        'Test the result of the search
        If rsClone.NoMatch Then
            'NoMatch returned True (not a match)
            DoCmd.Beep
            MsgBox "Customer not found."
        Else
            'NoMatch returned False (found)
            '
            'The clone's bookmark is now set to its
            'current position, which is the row
            'returned by the FindFirst method
            '
            'Move the form's current cursor position
            'to the one pointed to by the clone's bookmark
            Me.Bookmark = rsClone.Bookmark
        End If
    End If
```

```
        'Clean up
        On Error Resume Next
        rsClone.Close
        Set rsClone = Nothing
    End Sub
```

Examining the above code, you can see that the real work is done in no more than four lines.

1. Create a clone of the form's recordset.

```
Set rsClone = Me.RecordsetClone
```

2. Search for the record using the clone (leaves the original recordset untouched).

```
rsClone.FindFirst "[CustNo] = """ & strCustNo & """"
```

3. Check if the search failed. If so, we return a message box to inform the user. If the search passes, we execute line 4.

```
If rsClone.NoMatch Then
```

4. Change the form's Bookmark.

```
Me.Bookmark = rsClone.Bookmark
```

Finding Records

As you saw in the preceding section on bookmarks and recordset clones, we often need a way to find a specific record when working with recordsets. In fact, I used one way in the example to find the right customer.

DAO provides two ways to find a specific record: Find and Seek. Which one you use depends entirely on the type of recordset you want to use it on.

The Seek Method

The Seek method is the fastest way to find a specific record, but it can only be used on table-type recordsets, because it specifically relies on the table's indexes. Naturally, the table must have at least one index for it to search on. Trying to call Seek against a non-table-type recordset will earn you a runtime error.

> **Syntax:** rst.Seek comparison, key1, key2. . .key13

To use Seek, you must specify three things: the name of the index to use (you can only specify one index at a time), a comparison operator string (which can be <, <=, =, =>, or >), and one or more values that correspond to the value of the key you're looking for. You can specify up to 13 different key values.

For example, the following code shows how to search the `tblCustomers` table to find a customer whose CustomerNo is 123:

```
Set rst = dbs.OpenRecordset("tblCustomer", dbOpenTable)
rst.Index = "CustomerNo"
rst.Seek "=", 123
```

You might recall from the section on creating table indexes that the primary key index is called `PrimaryKey` by default, but you can name it anything you like. So if you want to use the table's primary key index, you must know its name.

To use `Seek` effectively, you need to understand how it works. If you specify =, =>, or > as the comparison operator, Access starts its search at the beginning of the recordset and works its way forward to the end. If you use any of the other operators, Access starts at the end of the recordset, and moves toward the beginning. With that knowledge, you can see that using `Seek` within a loop is essentially pointless.

You must specify a key value for each column in the index, particularly if you're using the = comparison operator. The reason is that some of the key fields may default to `Null`, and since nothing can "equal" `Null`, your `Seek` method will usually not find what you're looking for.

The `Seek` method is not supported for any recordset type in ODBCDirect workspaces, and you can't use `Seek` on linked tables. But all is not lost, the following code demonstrates how to use `Seek` on a linked table:

```
'Open the database that contains the table that is linked
Set dbs = OpenDatabase(strMyExternalDatabase)
'Open a table-type recordset against the external table
Set rst = dbs.OpenRecordset("tblCustomers", dbOpenTable)
'Specify which index to search on
rst.Index = "CustomerNo"
'Specify the criteria
rst.Seek "=", 123
'Check the result
If rst.NoMatch Then
    MsgBox "Record not found."
Else
    MsgBox "Customer name: " & rs.CustName
End If
```

What this does (if you haven't already figured out) is open the external database that contains the table that is linked in the current database. It then creates a table-type recordset on the table in that database. In that way, you are operating directly on the table you want to search. The code then searches the table, and finally, checks to see if the search failed. You should never assume that the search is successful; instead, always use the recordset's `NoMatch` property to determine the result.

Even doing things this way, in most circumstances, the `Seek` method is still faster thanthe `Find` methods.

The Find Methods

There are four `Find` methods: `FindFirst`, `FindPrevious`, `FindNext`, and `FindLast`. Their purpose is self-evident, given their names, and you can use them on all recordset types.

The Seek method always uses a table's indexes to execute the search, and although the Find methods will too (if they can), they can just as easily use a table scan to find the right record; it just depends on the type of search, and amount of data being searched. Not surprisingly then, the Find methods are usually far slower than using Seek.

Notwithstanding, the Find methods can be used on filtered dynaset and snapshot recordsets, which minimizes the number of records that have to be searched.

In addition, since you have FindNext and FindPrevious methods at your disposal, you don't have to start at the beginning or end of the recordset to find subsequent matches; you can just keep searching until you find the record you want.

All four methods have the same syntax:

```
rs.[FindFirst | FindPrevious | FindNext | FindLast] criteria
```

The criteria argument can be any valid SQL WHERE clause, without the word WHERE. For example, the following code demonstrates how to find the first and second instances of a customer having the word *parts* in his or her name.

```
'Search for the first matching record
rst.FindFirst "[OrgName] LIKE '*parts*'"
'Check the result
If rst.NoMatch Then
MsgBox "Record not found."
Else
    MsgBox "Customer name: " & rs.CustName
    'Search for the next matching record
    rst.FindNext "[OrgName] LIKE '*parts*'"

    'Check the result
    If rst.NoMatch Then
        MsgBox "Record not found."
    Else
        MsgBox "Customer name: " & rs.CustName
    End If
End If
```

Not a very object-oriented piece of code, but it serves to illustrate how to use these methods.

Once a matching record is found, any subsequent search begins from the *current* cursor position, not the start or end of the recordset, like in the Seek method. As with the Seek method, always follow the search with a check of the recordset's NoMatch property, to determine the result of the search.

Working with Recordsets

So far we've looked at navigating our way through recordsets, setting and using bookmarks, creating recordset clones, and finding specific records. All this has been done so that we can get to the exact record that we intend to do something with.

So what can we do with recordsets? In addition to the methods we've already covered, the following sections answer that question.

Retrieving Field Values

We have already covered this topic without ever having given it a thought. On an open recordset, you return a field value by simply referring to it. There are, of course, several ways to do this.

The first method is to refer to the field by name, as in the code below.

```
Set rst = dbs.OpenRecordset("tblMyTable")
MsgBox rst!CustomerNo
'or
MsgBox rst("CustomerNo")
```

Don't forget that the field name you use depends entirely on the table or query on which the recordset is based. For example, if the customer number is contained in the `CustomerNo` field, and the recordset gets its data directly from `tblCustomers`, then `rs!CustomerNo` would suffice.

However, if the recordset gets its data from a query in which the `CustomerNo` field is renamed (using the `As` keyword) to `CustNo`:

```
SELECT CustomerID, CustomerNo As CustNo, CustName FROM tblCustomers
```

then you would use `rs!CustNo`.

You can also refer to a field by the recordset's `Field` object, as in the following example:

```
MsgBox rst.Fields!CustomerNo
MsgBox rst.Fields("CustomerNo")
MsgBox rst.Fields(2)
```

In Appendix C, you will find a section entitled *Undocumented Tools and Resources*. Within this appendix, a subsection entitled *Recordset.Collect* shows the comparative speed of these value retrieval methods, which you might find both interesting and useful.

Adding, Editing, and Deleting Rows

Not all recordsets are editable, and the same can be said about some rows. Snapshot recordsets are never editable, and user permissions and record locks can result in recordsets or individual rows that you cannot edit. In addition, join in some recordsets that are based on multiple tables can render the entire recordet uneditable.

Adding Rows

The procedure for adding rows to a recordset is quite simple: open the recordset, issue the recordset's `AddNew` method, make the additions, and then issue the `Update` method. Here's an example:

```
'Open the recordset
Set rst = dbs.OpenRecordset("tblCustomers", dbOpenynaset)
With rst
```

```
        'Begin the editing session
        .AddNew
            'Make the additions
            !CustName = "Fred Nurk"
            !DOB = DateSerial(1956, 11, 5)
            !LastVisited = Date()
            '
            'Make other additions if you wish
            '
            'Commit the changes
        .Update
End With
```

If using an Autonumber field, there is no need to specify it as Access will automatically calculate and enter it for you. In fact, if you try to specify a value for an Autonumber field, Access will give an error.

Editing Rows

The procedure for editing recordset data is quite simple: move to the row you want to edit, issue the recordset's `Edit` method, make the changes, and then issue the `Update` method. The following example demonstrates how:

```
    'Open the recordset
    Set rst = dbs.OpenRecordset("tblCustomers", dbOpenynaset)
    With rst
        'Find the record you want to edit
        .FindFirst "[CustomerNo] = 123"
        If Not .NoMatch Then
            'Begin the editing session
            .Edit

                'Make the change(s)
                !LastVisited = Date()
                '
                'Make other changes if you wish
                '
            'Commit the changes
            .Update
        Else
Else
    MsgBox "Record not found."
    End If

    End With
```

Deleting Rows

Deleting rows is even simpler; you simply move to the row you want to delete, and then issue the `Delete` method.

```
    'Open the recordset
    Set rst = dbs.OpenRecordset("tblCustomers", dbOpenynaset)
    With rst
        'Find the record you want to edit
        .FindFirst "[CustomerNo] = 123"
```

```
    If Not .NoMatch Then
        'Delete the row
        .Delete
    Else
    MsgBox "Record not found."
    End If

End With
```

An important point to note when deleting rows is that as soon as you delete one, all the rows *above* it shift down one position. This is of real consequence only if you are moving *upwards* through the recordset (toward the end), deleting rows as you go. For example, if you wanted to delete a contiguous set of rows, you would end up deleting every *second* row. This is because when you delete the current row, the cursor does not move, but the rows *above* it move *down* one position to compensate. So, as in Figure 6-4, if you were on row 6 when you delete it, the cursor hasn't changed position, but you will then be on row 7.

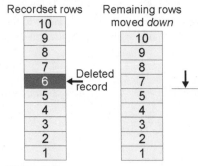

Figure 6-4

The recommended procedure for deleting contiguous rows is to move *downwards* (from the end to the beginning) through the rows, rather than *upwards*.

```
rst.MoveLast
Do Until rst.BOF
    rst.Delete
Loop
```

Cancelling an Edit

If you change your mind and decide not to continue adding, editing, or deleting records, you can cancel the update using the `CancelUpdate` method. You can only the cancel changes between the `AddNew...Update` or `Edit...Update` methods. For example:

```
With rst
    .AddNew
    !OrgName = strOrgName
    !Address = strAddress

    'If some criteria is met, update the record
    If IsFinancial(lngOrgID) Then
        .Refund = curRefundAmt
        .Update
```

```
        Else
            'If the criteria test fails, cancel the update
            .CancelUpdate
        End If
End With
```

Using Arrays with Recordsets

Sometimes you may choose to populate an array with data from a recordset. Perhaps you're intending to pass the array to a Windows API, and since APIs do not accept recordsets as parameters, this is the only way you can do it. Normally, you would define the array, and then loop through the rows, appending data to the array as you went.

```
Dim varMyArray() As Variant
Dim varField As Variant
Set rst = dbs.OpenRecordset("Table1", dbOpenSnapshot)
rst.MoveLast
ReDim varMyArray(rst.RecordCount, rst.Fields.Count)
rst.MoveFirst
Do While Not rst.EOF
    For Each varField In rst.Fields
        varMyArray(rst.AbsolutePosition, _
                varField.OrdinalPosition) = varField
    Next varField

    rst.MoveNext
Loop
```

But DAO provides a nifty little method to do all this for you—GetRows. GetRows returns a two-dimensional array containing all the column data for the specified number of rows, with the first element specifying the row and the second specifying the column.

```
Dim varMyArray As Variant
Set rst = dbs.OpenRecordset("Table1", dbOpenSnapshot)
varMyArray = rst.GetRows(120)
```

You don't have to define the array's rows; in fact, you don't even have to declare it as an array; just define it as a variant. Access takes care of the rest.

After you call GetRows, the recordset's cursor position is set to the next unread row. You can specify the number of rows to return, but if you specify more rows than that exist, Access only returns the number of rows that were actually present in the recordset.

Be a little judicious when using this technique, because Access will return *all* the recordset columns, regardless of their data type. You could end up with Memo and OLE (object linking and embedding) data in your array. It is wiser to filter the recordset, so you only have the data you actually need.

Summary

In this chapter, we took a detailed peek into the world of DAO. By now you should have a fairly good understanding of when to use DAO, and how to refer to its objects. You should have a good working knowledge of the main objects in the hierarchy, such as the DBEngine, Workspace, Error, Database, and `Recordset` objects, and their associated collections. Although very few people can remember every single property and method of every object, you should have gained enough exposure to them by now, to be able to start writing some reasonably sophisticated software. In any case, Intellisense can help you out when you're unsure.

Now that you've mastered DAO, the next chapter seeks to undermine your confidence by introducing a whole new object model—*ActiveX Data Objects*.

7

Using ADO to Access Data

In the last chapter, you were introduced to one of the two data access models that Access supports: Data Access Objects (DAO). In this chapter, we will closely examine the other model: ActiveX Data Objects (ADO).

Recall from Chapter 6 that DAO was the default data access technology in the early versions of Access. In fact, Access was bound so closely to the Jet database engine by the fact that developers used Access as both the front-end user interface and the back-end data store that they rarely felt a need for anything else. As applications design evolved from standalone to client/server architectures, the need to connect to and access data from disparate data sources became more and more important. Although Microsoft made several attempts at evolving DAO into a remote data access technology, its real forté was in accessing data from local Jet databases. This is where ADO comes in. When you need to connect to external data sources, you need to start using ADO, because ADO is specifically designed to connect to a wide variety of external data sources.

ADO is a part of Microsoft's data access vision of the future, called *Universal Data Access* (UDA), in which a single method is used to retrieve data from any data source, which may include relational databases, the mainframe indexed sequential access method/virtual storage access method (ISAM/VSAM), hierarchical databases, e-mail, disk files, graphical data, and so on.

OLE DB (Object Linking and Embedding Databases) is the interface that enables UDA. ADO is a development interface for OLE DB and replaces both DAO and RDO.

OLE DB sees the world in terms of data *providers*, which act as an interface between the data source and the *consumer* of the data. Although OLE DB was written for procedural programming models, ADO sits atop OLE DB, providing programmers with an object-oriented model they can use to access and manipulate the data sources.

When you use Access 2003 to create a standard Jet database (MDB), by default, Access uses the Jet *OLE DB provider* to manage the connection to the data store. Confirm this by entering the following line of code in the Visual Basic Editor's Immediate window:

```
?CurrentProject.Connection
```

You'll see the returned connection string begins with the following:

```
Microsoft.Jet.OLEDB.4.0;
```

Similarly, Access uses the Access OLE DB provider when you create an *Access Data Project* (ADP) against the SQL Server or MSDE. The same property call returns a connection string that begins thus:

```
Microsoft.Access.OLEDB.10.0;
```

Ambiguous References

In versions prior to Access 2000, the DAO object library was selected by default when a new database was created, allowing developers to write code using DAO.

Access 2000 selected the ADO object library by default (supposedly expecting developers to write using ADO), but this move generated much heartache, because Microsoft didn't adequately advise anyone of the change. Since average Access developers didn't know the difference between the two object models, the first they learned about it was when their applications started generating errors in code that had previously worked.

By the time Microsoft realized the ramifications, Access 2002 was already in beta, and the ADO preselection remained, but the issue is resolved in Access 2003. In Access 2003, *both* object libraries are preselected.

That being the case, writing unambiguous code has never been more important, because, for the first time, the very real possibility exists that a novice developer could inadvertently write ambiguous code. So what does this all mean? Consider the following:

```
Dim db As Database
Dim rs As Recordset
```

Nothing terribly strange there, except for two things: First, only DAO has a `Database` object—ADO has none. Second, DAO and ADO both have `Recordset` objects. If both DAO and ADO object libraries are selected, to which object model does the above recordset declaration refer?

If you have only one library referenced, Access chooses that one, but if you have two, Access encounters the ambiguity and lets you know about it in what can seem to be very strange ways.

We have seen code written by professional Access developers, in which both DAO and ADO objects had been used interchangeably, and they could not understand why their code failed to work.

Therefore, to ensure that Access (and you) know which object refers to which object library, you need to disambiguate your code. The following example demonstrates this principle:

```
Dim db As DAO.Database
Dim cn As ADODB.Connection
Dim rsDAO As DAO.Recordset
Dim rsADO As ADODB.Recordset
```

Doing this can also make your code run a tad faster, because Access doesn't have to examine the library list to figure out which library to use.

Referring to ADO Objects

When you refer to ADO objects, you do so in the same way you would using DAO, but the difference is that ADO does not have a native connection like DAO.

Recall that in DAO you can use the `DBEngine(0)(0)` object or the `CurrentDb()` function to return a reference to the current database. ADO does not have a current database. In fact, it doesn't know anything about dataset; it only knows about data sources through a provider. Therefore, in ADO, you must always implement a connection to an external data store through a provider.

Default Collection Items

As you may recall from Chapter 6, an object's parent collection can have a default member that you can refer to. The following table lists the default members for those ADO objects that have them.

Object library	Collection	Default member	Example
ADODB	Command	Parameters	cmd(0)
	Record	Fields	rcADO(0)
	Recordset	Fields	rsADO(0)
ADOX	Catalog	Tables	cat(0)
	Table	Columns	cat.tables(0)(0) cat(0)(0)

Connecting to a Data Source

The `Connection` object is considered to be the top-level object in the ADO object model. Although it doesn't contain all the other ADO objects, like the DAO `DBEngine` object, you must specify the connection that the other ADO objects will use to carry out their functions.

The `Connection` object represents a single connection to an OLE DB provider, but, of course, you can create several connection objects, each connecting to a different provider. There are two ways to create a connection: implicitly and explicitly. To create an *implicit* connection, you supply the connection string when creating a child object, such as a `Recordset`:

```
rsADO.Open strSQL, strConnectionString
```

This creates a temporary connection that is destroyed when you close the recordset. To create an *explicit* connection, you must declare it, instantiate it, supply it with the various properties it needs, and then open it:

```
Dim cn As ADODB.Connection

Set cn = New ADODB.Connection

With cn
    .ConnectionString = CurrentProject.Connection
    .CursorLocation = adUseClient
    .Atributes = .Attributes Or adXactCommitRetaining
    .Open
End With
```

The above example used the `CurrentProject.Connection` property to supply the connection string information for the connection. In DAO, you would have used `DBEngine(0)(0)` or `CurrentDb()`. Since ADO does not have a `Database` object, use the `CurrentProject` object instead.

If you are creating a connection within an ADP to the default data store, that's all you need, and it doesn't matter whether Access is connected to a Jet back end, SQL Server, or Oracle.

However, if you are creating a connection to an external data source from an MDB or ADP, you need to build your own connection string. Issue the `CurrentProject.Connection` method in the Immediate window to see what an actual connection string looks like. Both the Access help file and the section entitled *Rolling Your Own Connection String* also provide some guidance.

Specifying a Cursor Location

In contrast with DAO, when you create an ADO connection, you should specify a *cursor*, which is a database element that controls record navigation, data updateability, and the tracking of changes made by other users.

There are two types of cursor: *client side* and *server side*. Choose the cursor you want to use by setting the `Command` or `Recordset` object's `CursorLocation` property to one of the following two constants, before you open the connection or recordset:

```
rs.CursorLocation = adUseClient 'Default. Use a client-side cursor
rs.CursorLocation = adUseServer 'Use a server-side cursor
```

As with most things in life, the choice comes complete with a tradeoff. In most cases, server-side cursors are a bit faster; however, client-side cursors offer a little more functionality. For example, you need to specify `adUseClient` if you intend to use the `Sort` method.

When you set the `CursorLocation` at connection level, you are specifying the cursor location that will be used by default when you create recordsets against that connection. You can override this setting at recordset level, however.

Server-Side Cursors

Using a server-side cursor (which, by the way, is the default in ADO), the records contained in the recordset are cached on the server. The major benefit of this is that network traffic is significantly reduced, thus improving application performance. The downside is that server resources are consumed for every active client; the more clients (and the more data being cached), the more server resources are consumed. It is important, therefore, to plan ahead to ensure your server has sufficient resources to do the job. Server-side cursors allow you to use both keyset and dynamic cursors, and also support direct positional updates, which are fast and avoid update collisions.

You can also use each connection for more than one operation. For example, you can have a recordset open and still execute multiple update queries without having to open an additional connection. Server-side cursors are best for inserting, updating, and deleting records, and they also allow you to have multiple active statements on the same connection.

Client-Side Cursors

If the data source you're connecting to doesn't support server-side cursors, you'll have no choice but to use a client-side cursor. With nonkeyset client-side cursors, the server sends the entire recordset to the client across the network. Since the client must now provide and manage the resources necessary to cache the records, this places a significant load on both the network and the client. Needless to say, this reduces your application's overall performance.

One benefit of using client-side cursors is that, once the data is cached, subsequent access to the data is much faster than with client-side cursors, because the data resides locally. A second benefit to using client-side cursors is that the application is generally more scalable, because the resources required to run the application are distributed among many clients, rather than loading down a single server.

Rolling Your Own Connection String

The following is the output of the `CurrentProject.Connection` property for the *NorthWind* (Jet) sample database. To shorten the file paths for this example, we moved the database to a different folder.

```
Provider=Microsoft.Jet.OLEDB.4.0;
User ID=Admin;
Data Source=C:\myDatabase\Northwind.mdb;
Mode=Share Deny None;
Extended Properties="";
Jet OLEDB:System database=C:\myDatabase\System.mdw;
Jet OLEDB:Registry Path=
Software\Microsoft\Office\11.0\Access\Jet\4.0;
Jet OLEDB:Database Password="";
Jet OLEDB:Engine Type=5;
Jet OLEDB:Database Locking Mode=1;
Jet OLEDB:Global Partial Bulk Ops=2;
Jet OLEDB:Global Bulk Transactions=1;
Jet OLEDB:New Database Password="";
Jet OLEDB:Create System Database=False;
Jet OLEDB:Encrypt Database=False;
Jet OLEDB:Don't Copy Locale on Compact=False;
Jet OLEDB:Compact Without Replica Repair=False;
Jet OLEDB:SFP=False
```

When you write your own connection string, you only really need to supply the following parameters:

- ❑ Provider (including version)

    - ❑ User ID

    - ❑ Password or database password (if applicable)

    - ❑ Data source

    - ❑ System database (if applicable)

The following connection string is from the *NorthWind* ADP, where all the other information is contained within the Data Link.

```
Provider=Microsoft.Access.OLEDB.10.0;
Persist Security Info=False;
Data Source=(local);
Integrated Security=SSPI;
Initial Catalog=NorthwindCS;
Data Provider=SQLOLEDB.1
```

Creating and Using a Data Link

Instead of using `CurrentProject.Connection` to set your connection string, or writing your own, you can use a Data Link.

You can specify a filename as a parameter of the `Connection` object, but you have to create a UDL file first. To create a custom data link, do the following:

1. Open `Windows Explorer` and select `File | New | Text Document`.

2. Rename the file to something meaningful, and change its file extension to `.UDL`.

3. Click `Yes` in the message box that Windows subsequently displays.

4. Then double-click the file; the `Data Link Properties` dialog box is displayed, as in Figure 7-1.

5. For the purpose of demonstration, select *Microsoft Jet 4.0 OLE DB Provider*, and click `Next`.

6. Browse and select an *Access database* (*.mdb).

7. Enter your username and password (if applicable), remembering that the default username for an unsecured Access database is `Admin`, with a blank password. If you want to avoid having to enter your password every time you make a connection, tick the `Allow saving password` check box.

8. Click `Test Connection`. If all went well, the message box is displayed, as in Figure 7-2.

9. Select the `Advanced` tab and examine the permissions you can set for this link. For this demonstration, accept the default settings. If you want, you can select the `All` tab and change the settings manually.

10. Click `OK`.

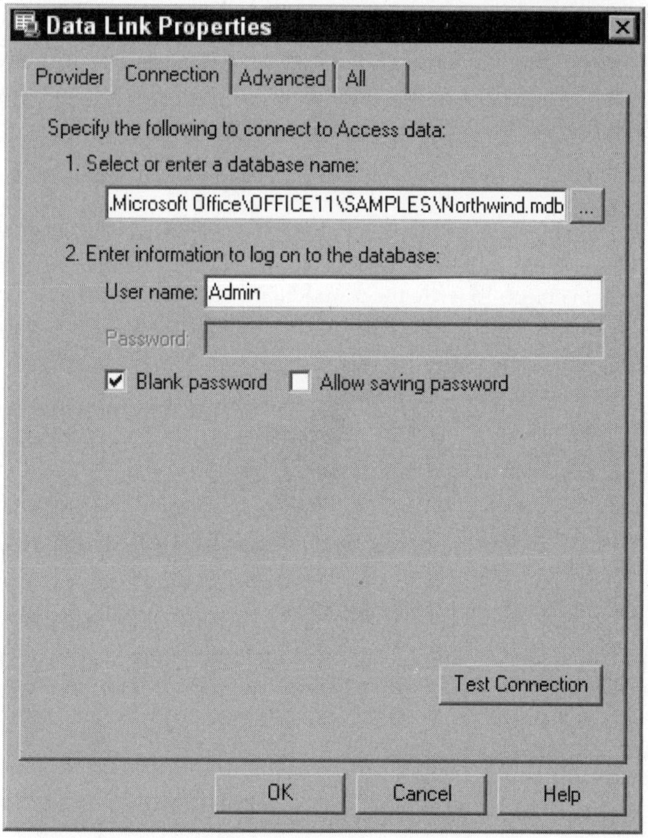

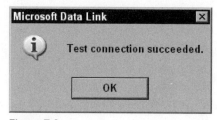

Figure 7-1

Figure 7-2

You can then specify the connection string by supplying the filename and path to the data link file just created.

```
Dim cn As ADODB.Connection
Set cn = New ADODB.Connection
cn.Open "File Name=C:\myDatabase\myDataLink.udl"
```

Using Transactions

As discussed in Chapter 6, a *transaction* is a delimited set of changes that are performed on a database's schema or data. These changes increase the speed of actions that change data, and enable you to undo changes that have not yet been committed.

In DAO, transactions operate under the context of a Workspace, whereas ADO transactions operate under the context of a `Connection`.

Just as with a DAO transaction, you begin an ADO transaction by issuing the `BeginTrans` method against the `Connection` object. To write the transaction to disk, issue the `CommitTrans` method. But instead of issuing a `Rollback` method as you would in DAO, the ADO counterpart is the `RollbackTrans` method.

Not all providers support transactions, so you need to verify that the provider-defined property `Transaction DDL` is one of the `Connection` object's properties. The following line entered in the Immediate window checks the value of this property:

```
?CurrentProject.Connection.Properties("Transaction DDL")
```

If no error occurs, the provider supports transactions.

The following code demonstrates a typical funds transfer transaction using an ADO transaction.

```
Public Sub TransferFunds()
    Dim cn As ADODB.Connection
    Set cn = New ADODB.Connection

    On Error GoTo trans_Err

    With cn
        .ConnectionString = CurrentProject.Connection
        .Open
    End With

    'Begin the transaction
    cn.BeginTrans
        'Withdraw funds from one account table
        cn.Execute "UPDATE Table1....."
        'Deposit funds into another account table
        cn.Execute "INSERT INTO Table22....."

    'Commit the transaction
    cn.CommitTrans

trans_Exit:
    'Clean up
    cn.Close
    Set cn = Nothing
    Exit Sub

trans_Err:
```

```
        'Roll back the transaction
        cn.RollbackTrans
        Resume trans_Exit
   End Sub
```

In the above example, changes to both databases will either complete as a unit or will be rolled back as a unit.

You can nest ADO transactions, but in contrast with DAO transactions, you can return an ADO transaction's nesting position when you create it. A return value of 1 indicates that it occupies the top-level position in a virtual *collection*. A value of 2 indicates that it is a second-level transaction, and so on.

When you call `CommitTrans` or `RollbackTrans`, you are operating on the most recently opened transaction. To resolve higher-level transactions, you must close or roll back the current transaction.

When you call `CommitTrans` or `RollbackTrans`, the appropriate action is taken, and the transaction is closed. If you set the Connection object's `Attributes` property to `adXactCommitRetaining`, a new transaction is created after you issue `CommitTrans`. If you set it to `adXactAbortRetaining` (you can set both), the same occurs after issuing `RollbackTrans`.

Data Access with ADO

Accessing data is the reason why we use databases, and a large proportion of your programming will usually revolve around manipulating those objects that deal with data: views, stored procedures, and recordsets.

The ADO Object Model

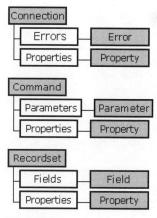

Figure 7-3

ADO actually supports two additional objects not shown in Figure 7-3: the `Record` and `Stream` objects.

The `Record` object can be seen as a single-row recordset. Although records have a limited functionality when compared to recordsets, they relieve you of the overhead of having to instantiate the more complex recordset. In addition, they have different properties and methods that can be quite useful.

The `Record` object can also manipulate data such as folders and files in a file system, e-mail messages, and so on. That means the source of data for the `Record` object can be the current row of a recordset, a Uniform Resource Locator (URL).

The `Stream` object reads, writes, and manages a stream of bytes. This byte stream can be text or binary, and is limited in size only by the available system resources.

You would typically use an ADO stream object to contain the text or bytes of a file or message supplied using a provider such as the *Microsoft OLE DB Provider for Internet Publishing*.

The data source for a stream object can be a file whose location is specified by a URL, a field in a record or recordset that contains a stream object, a resource field containing the URL of a file, a BLOB field in a recordset, or a custom-designed stream that exists in memory.

Unfortunately, an in-depth study of these objects is beyond the scope of this book. So if you wish to examine these objects in greater detail, consult your provider's documentation and the Access help.

Executing Action Queries

An *action query* is a query that carries out some action on a set of data, without returning any rows. There are two ways to programmatically execute an action query, both of which involve using the `Execute` method.

The Connection.Execute Method

```
connection.Execute CommandText [, RecordsAffected] [, Options]
```

You can use the `Execute` method of the `Connection` object. Just instantiate a connection and issue its `Execute` method—it's that simple!

```
Dim cn As New ADODB.Connection
Dim lngRA As Long, lngOptions As Long

lngOptions = adCmdUnspecified And adAsyncExecute

cn.Open CurrentProject.Connection
cn.Execute strSQL, lngRA, lngOptions
```

The `CommandText` argument can be an SQL statement: the name of a table, the name of a stored procedure, or a provider-specific text or command. The `RecordsAffected` argument, if supplied, is populated with the number of records affected by the operation, when the operation completes.

The `Options` argument can be a combination of the `CommandTypeEnum` values or `ExecuteOptionEnum` values that affect the way the `Execute` method works. Appendix J contains a list of all the available `CommandTypeEnum` and `ExecuteOptionEnum` values.

The Command.Execute Method

You can also execute an action query by calling the Execute method against a Command object.

```
cmd.Execute RecordsAffected, Parameters, Options
```

Simply set the command object's CommandText, CommandType, and ActiveConnection properties; then call the Execute method. The Parameters property can be populated by a variant array of parameter values passed with an SQL statement. The Options property defines the provider how to evaluate the CommandText property (refer to previous table).

```
Dim cn As New ADODB.Connection
Dim cmd As New ADODB.Command
Dim strSQL As String
Dim RA As Long

'Open the connection
cn.Open CurrentProject.Connection

'Setup the SQL statement
strSQL = "UPDATE Suppliers SET Region = 'None'"

With cmd
    .CommandText = strSQL
    .CommandType = adCmdUnknown
    .ActiveConnection = cn
    .Execute RA
End With

Debug.Print RA & " records were updated."

cn.Close
Set cmd = Nothing
Set cn = Nothing
```

Specifying Command Parameters

Instead of specifying the Command object's parameters in the SQL statement, you can also set them using the Command object's Parameter object.

For example, the following function updates the prices of all products of a given category by calling an SQL Server stored procedure, which returns a count of the products that were updated.

```
Public Function UpdatePrices( _
        strCategory As String, _
        curNewPrice As Currency) As Integer

Dim cmd As New ADODB.Command
Dim RA As Long

'Build the Command object
With cmd
```

```
    'Set the connection
    .ActiveConnection = CurrentProject.Connection

    'Set other properties
    .CommandText = "qryUpdatePrices"
    .CommandType = adCmdTable
```

To be able to refer to the parameters by name (for providers that support it), you must first refresh the `Parameters` collection; otherwise you'll need to refer to them by ordinal position.

```
    .Parameters.Refresh
    .Parameters("Category") = strCategory
    .Parameters("Price") = curNewPrice

    'If we were specifying parameters for a
    'stored procedure, we would use the "@"
    'predicate.
    '.Parameters("@Category") = strCategory
    '.Parameters("@Price") = curNewPrice

    'Execute the query
    .Execute RA
End With

    Debug.Print RA & " products were updated."
    UpdatePrices = RA

    Set cmd.ActiveConnection = Nothing
    Set cmd = Nothing
End Function
```

Creating Your Own Parameters

If you're attempting to execute an Access stored query (one that has been saved to disk), you can provide values for its parameters in two ways.

First you can rewrite the query, like

```
Dim cmd As ADODB.Command
Dim rs As ADODB.Recordset

Set cmd = New ADODB.Command
Set rs = New ADODB.Recordset

'Setup the Command object
With cmd
    .CommandText = "SELECT * FROM qrySuppliersByCity WHERE City = 'London'"
    .CommandType = adCmdUnknown

    'Associate the Command object with a connection
    .ActiveConnection = CurrentProject.Connection
```

```
    'Request the recordset
    Set rs = .Execute
End With
```

But that involves wrapping the stored query in a hard-coded SQL statement every time you want to run it, and using a WHERE clause. But that's not the same as supplying a parameter value. Additionally, if the stored query is a *parameter query*, the above method does not provide you a way to supply values to the parameters.

At this point, you might be thinking that you can simply use the Parameter object's Refresh method to supply a parameter, as was demonstrated above. You would be correct, but not if you intend to do it against a parameter query in Access database. In an Access database, you can't refer to a parameter in a query's Parameters collection by name.

The second method is to create parameters in the Command object, which match those specified in the parameter query. The following code segment demonstrates how to do this.

```
Dim cmd As ADODB.Command
Dim rs As ADODB.Recordset

Set cmd = New ADODB.Command
Set rs = New ADODB.Recordset

'Setup the Command object
With cmd
    .CommandText = "qrySuppliersByCity"
    .CommandType = adCmdUnknown

    'Create the parameter
    .Parameters.Append .CreateParameter( _
            "City", adVarChar, adParamInput, 50)

    'Set the parameter's value
    .Parameters("City") = "London"

    'Associate the Command object with a connection
    .ActiveConnection = CurrentProject.Connection

    'Request the recordset
    Set rs = .Execute
End With
```

Just to round out the ways in which you can create parameters, an alternative method is to create the parameter as an object in its own right, and append that object to the Parameters collection, like

```
Dim prm As ADODB.Parameter
Dim cmd As ADODB.Command
Dim rs As ADODB.Recordset

Set prm = New ADODB.Parameter
Set cmd = New ADODB.Command
Set rs = New ADODB.Recordset
```

```
'Setup the Command object
With cmd
    .CommandText = "qrySuppliersByCity"
    .CommandType = adCmdUnknown

    'Create the parameter
    Set prm = .CreateParameter ("City", adVarChar, adParamInput, 50)
    .Parameters.Append prm
    'Set the parameter's value
    .Parameters("City") = "London"

    'Associate the Command object with a connection
    .ActiveConnection = CurrentProject.Connection

    'Request the recordset
    Set rs = .Execute
End With
```

Creating ADO Recordsets

ADO recordsets are basically the same as DAO recordsets, with a few notable differences, as explained below.

Creating a Standard Recordset

In DAO you would create a recordset, like this

```
Set rs = db.OpenRecordset( source,   options)
```

But in ADO, you could do it like this:

```
rs.Open Source, ConnectionString,
CursorType, LockType, Options
```

The Source argument can be an SQL statement, the name of a table, the name of a stored procedure, a URL, or a provider-specific text or command. The ConnectionString argument can be a Connection object or a Connection string. Appendix J contains a list of all the available CursorType, LockType, and Options values.

You can supply more than one Options value by using the AND operator, for example:

```
rs.Options = adCmdStoredProc And adAsyncFetchNonBlocking
```

Creating a Recordset from a Command Object

Suppose you need to create a recordset that is based on a parameter query. Most often, you won't know what values to supply until you get to that point in your code. The problem is, of course, how to supply those values?

The answer is to base your recordset on a Command object, which itself is based on the Parameter query. How does this solve your dilemma? The following is a typical example.

```
Dim cmd As New ADODB.Command
Dim rs As New ADODB.Recordset

'Build the Command object
With cmd
    .ActiveConnection = CurrentProject.Connection
    .CommandText = "qryPrices"
    .CommandType = adCmdTable
    .Parameters.Refresh
    .Parameters("City") = strCityVariable
    .Parameters("ProductID") = lngProductID
End With

'Create the Recordset
Set rs = cmd.Execute
MsgBox rs!UnitPrice

rs.Close
Set rs = Nothing
Set cmd = Nothing
```

Since the Recordset object does not have a Parameters collection, you can see that the Command object is what executes the query and passes its dataset to the Recordset when the Recordset is created. The Command object does have a Parameters collection, so you can supply the query's parameters to it.

If you wanted to pass parameters to a stored procedure in an ADP, you would need to make the following changes:

```
'Build the Command object
With cmd
    .ActiveConnection = CurrentProject.Connection
    .CommandText = "spPrices"
    .CommandType = adCmdStoredProc
    .Parameters.Refresh
    .Parameters("@City") = strCityVariable
    .Parameters("@ProductID") = lngProductID
End With
```

Opening a Shaped Recordset

A very useful feature of ADO is that you can create *shaped recordsets*. *Data shaping* allows you to define the columns of a recordset, the relationships between them, and the manner in which the recordset is populated with data. These columns can contain data from a provider, such as Access or the SQL Server, references to another recordset, values derived from a calculation on a row, and so on.

Let's take a simple example. In the *NorthwindCS* sample database (an ADP), there are two tables, organized into a parent-child relationship: Orders, which contains the header information for customer orders, and `Order Details`, which contains the individual line items for each order. Figure 7-4 shows this relationship at work.

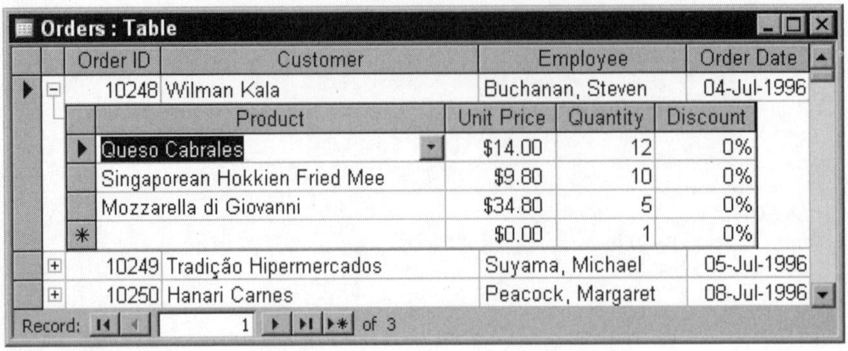

Orders : Table

Order ID	Customer	Employee	Order Date
10248	Wilman Kala	Buchanan, Steven	04-Jul-1996
10249	Tradição Hipermercados	Suyama, Michael	05-Jul-1996
10250	Hanari Carnes	Peacock, Margaret	08-Jul-1996

Product	Unit Price	Quantity	Discount
Queso Cabrales	$14.00	12	0%
Singaporean Hokkien Fried Mee	$9.80	10	0%
Mozzarella di Giovanni	$34.80	5	0%
*	$0.00	1	0%

Record: 1 of 3

Figure 7-4

Let's say you wanted to populate a list with the details of a select set of orders. In the past, you would have created a recordset based on a query very much like the following:

```
SELECT O.OrderID, O.CustomerID, O.OrderDate,
       D.ProductID, D.UnitPrice, D.Quantity, D.Discount
FROM Orders As O
INNER JOIN [Order Details] As D ON D.OrderID = O.OrderID
WHERE Year(O.OrderDate) = 1996
AND OrderID BETWEEN 10248 AND 10250
ORDER BY O.OrderDate DESC
```

The above query returns a dataset that contains all the orders in 1996 where the `OrderID` is between 10248 and 10250, in descending date order. Such a recordset would return the following rows (Figure 7-5).

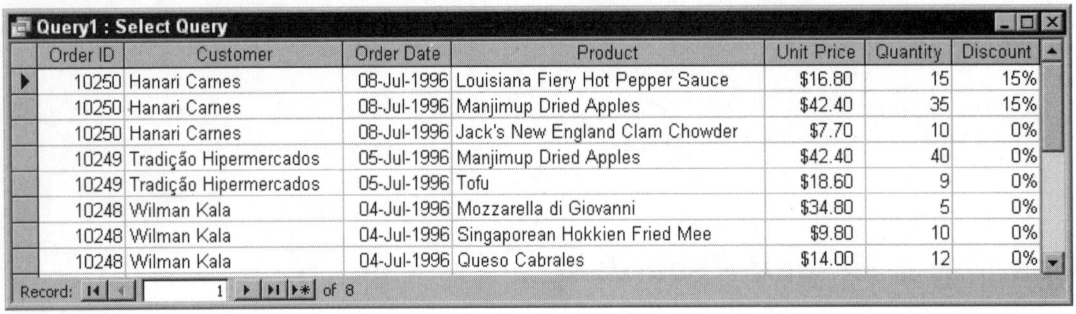

Query1 : Select Query

Order ID	Customer	Order Date	Product	Unit Price	Quantity	Discount
10250	Hanari Carnes	08-Jul-1996	Louisiana Fiery Hot Pepper Sauce	$16.80	15	15%
10250	Hanari Carnes	08-Jul-1996	Manjimup Dried Apples	$42.40	35	15%
10250	Hanari Carnes	08-Jul-1996	Jack's New England Clam Chowder	$7.70	10	0%
10249	Tradição Hipermercados	05-Jul-1996	Manjimup Dried Apples	$42.40	40	0%
10249	Tradição Hipermercados	05-Jul-1996	Tofu	$18.60	9	0%
10248	Wilman Kala	04-Jul-1996	Mozzarella di Giovanni	$34.80	5	0%
10248	Wilman Kala	04-Jul-1996	Singaporean Hokkien Fried Mee	$9.80	10	0%
10248	Wilman Kala	04-Jul-1996	Queso Cabrales	$14.00	12	0%

Record: 1 of 8

Figure 7-5

You'll notice that the columns from the `Orders` table (`OrderID`, `CustomerID`, and `OrderDate`) are repeated unnecessarily for every row of data returned from the `Order Details` table. Wouldn't it be nice if you could return only one row of `Orders` data for each group of related rows from `Order Details`? Closely examine the following ADO code, paying particular attention to the SQL statement:

```
Dim cn As New ADODB.Connection
Dim rsOrders As New ADODB.Recordset
Dim rsDetails As New ADODB.Recordset
Dim strSQL As String

'Define and create the connection
cn.CursorLocation = adUseClient

'We have to use this provider
cn.Provider = "MSDataShape"

'Open a connection to SQL Server
cn.Open "Data Provider=SQLOLEDB;" & _
        "Integrated Security=SSPI;Database=NorthwindCS"
```

Now we need to create the SQL statement that will do all the work.

```
'Create the SQL statement that does all the work
strSQL = "SHAPE {SELECT DISTINCT OrderID," & _
                            "CustomerID, OrderDate" & _
            "FROM Orders" & _
            "WHERE Year(OrderDate) = 1996" & _
            "AND OrderID BETWEEN 10248 AND 10250" & _
            "ORDER BY OrderDate DESC}" & _
        "APPEND ({SELECT OrderID, ProductID, UnitPrice," & _
                    "Quantity, Discount" & _
            "FROM [Order Details]}" & _
        "RELATE OrderID TO OrderID)"
```

Once the SQL statement is formed, open a recordset based on it.

```
'Create the recordset for the orders table
rsOrders.Open strSQL, cn

Do While Not rsOrders.EOF
    'Print out the header rows, one at a time
    Debug.Print rsOrders!OrderID, _
                rsOrders!CustomerID, _
                rsOrders!OrderDate
```

Now return the child records in a second recordset. If you examine the above SQL statement, you'll see that the child dataset is aliased as `Details`. The `Details` column is actually a reference to a child recordset.

```
    'Create the child recordset
    Set rsDetails = rsOrders("Details").Value

    Do While Not rsDetails.EOF
        'Print out the child records, one at a time
        Debug.Print vbTab & rsDetails!ProductID, _
                            rsDetails!UnitPrice, _
                            rsDetails!Quantity, _
                            rsDetails!Discount

        rsDetails.MoveNext
    Loop

    rsOrders.MoveNext
Loop
```

This is what would be returned by the above code. The obvious difference between the data returned here and what you see in Figure 7-4 is because the `CustomerID` and `ProductID` columns are designed using Access lookups, and although Access displays the lookup values, the provider used to shape the recordsets does not.

10250	HANAR		07/08/1996
41	7.7	10	0
51	42.4	35	0.15
65	16.8	15	0.15
10249	TOMSP		07/05/1996
14	18.6	9	0
51	42.4	40	0
10248	VINET		07/04/1996
11	14	12	0
42	9.8	10	0
72	34.8	5	0

When you return the value of a column that contains a reference to another recordset, ADO returns an actual recordset represented by that reference. Recordsets such as this are called *hierarchical recordsets*. Hierarchical recordsets exhibit a parent-child relationship, in which the parent is the container recordset and the child is the contained recordset. The reference to the child recordset is actually a reference to a subset of the child, called a `Chapter`. A single parent may reference more than one child recordset.

The `Shape` statement allows you to create a shaped recordset, which you can then access programmatically or through a visual control. You can issue the `Shape` statement like any other ADO command text.

This simple example demonstrates only a fraction of what can be accomplished using the `Shape` statement. Unfortunately, an in-depth examination of SQL is outside the scope of this book; refer to the Access help for more information.

Verifying the Options That a Recordset Supports

Check which options a specific recordset supports by using the *Supports* method. The method returns `True` if the option is supported, and `False` if not . The following table lists the options you can test for.

With this constant...	You can do this...
AdAddNew	Use the AddNew method to add records.
AdApproxPosition	Use the AbsolutePosition and AbsolutePage properties.
AdBookmark	Use the Bookmark property.
AdDelete	Use the Delete method to delete records.
AdFind	Use the Find method to locate a specific record.
AdHoldRecords	Move the cursor position without committing any changes to the current record.
AdIndex	Use the Index property to set an index.
AdMovePrevious	Use the MoveFirst, MovePrevious, and Move methods to move the cursor position backwards.
AdResync	Use the Resync method to resynchronize the recordset with its underlying data.
AdSeek	Use the Seek method to locate a specific record.
AdUpdate	Use the Update method to commit changes to the current record.
AdUpdateBatch	Use the UpdateBatch and CancelBatch methods.

A typical example of how to test for, say, AbsolutePosition functionality is as follows:

```
booResult = rs.Supports(adApproxPosition)
MsgBox "This recordset does" & _
       IIf(booResult = True,"", "not") & _
       "support AbsolutePosition and AbsolutePage"
```

Referring to Recordset Columns

As with DAO recordsets, you can refer to ADO recordset columns in a variety of ways:

```
rs.Collect(1)
rs.Collect("myField")
rs!myField
rs(1)
rs.Fields(1)
rs.Fields!myField
rs("myField")
rs.Fields("myField")
```

If you're interested in the relative performance characteristics of each method, refer to the end of Chapter 6.

Filtering and Ordering Recordsets

As with DAO recordsets, you can filter a recordset's output by specifying its source using a WHERE or HAVING clause, or by setting its Filter property. Similarly, setting the ADO recordset's Sort property will change its sort order, just like in DAO.

Since we have already covered these topics in Chapter 6, there is no need to repeat them here.

Navigating Recordsets

SQL queries operate on many records at the same time, but recordsets are designed to allow you to operate on records one-at-a-time. Therefore, to use recordsets effectively, you must be able to navigate from record to record. The following sections describe the various ways in which you can move around in your recordset.

RecordCount

You might recall that the RecordCount property in DAO returns the number of rows that the recordset has accessed so far. In ADO, the RecordCount property returns the actual number of rows in the recordset, without first having to force a count by moving to the last row.

For example:

```
rs.Open "SELECT * FROM Table1", CurrentProject.Connection
If rs.AbsolutePosition > adPosUnknown Then
    'Get the count
    lngCount = rs.RecordCount

    '- - - -
    'Continue processing
    '- - - -

End If
```

AbsolutePosition, AbsolutePage

Assuming the provider supports absolute positioning, the AbsolutePosition property allows you to move the cursor to a specific row in the recordset, just as in DAO. For example, if you wanted to move to the 127th row, you could issue the following call:

```
rs.AbsolutePosition = 127
```

ADO provides three constants you can use to verify the current cursor position, two of which obviously replace the BOF and EOF properties found in DAO.

❏   adPosUnknown—The recordset is empty, or the provider doesn't support absolute positioning.

❑ adPosBOF—True if the current cursor position is before the first record.

❑ adPosEOF—True if the current cursor position is after the last record.

The ADO-specific `AbsolutePage` property indicates the page on which the current record resides.

```
lngCurrentPage = rs.AbsolutePage
```

You might also recall that the DAO object model provides a `PercentPosition` property, with which you can move to a relative position in the recordset by specifying a percentage value. ADO does not support this property, but you can accomplish the same thing by calculating the percentage and supplying it to the `AbsolutePosition` property. For example, if you wanted to move to (roughly) halfway through the recordset, you could do this:

```
rs.AbsolutePosition = 0.5 * rs.RecordCount
```

MoveFirst, MovePrevious, MoveNext, MoveLast, and Move

These five methods work in exactly the same way in ADO as they do in DAO.

Bookmarks and Recordset Clones

`Bookmarks` and `Recordset` clones in ADO are exactly the same as in DAO. For more details on using `Bookmarks` and `Recordset` clones, refer to Chapter 6.

Finding Records

As you saw in the Chapter 6 section on *Bookmarks and Recordset Clones*, we often need a way to find a specific record when working with recordsets. DAO provides two ways to find a specific record: `Find` and `Seek`.

The Seek Method

The ADO `Seek` method, although a little different from its DAO cousin, is still the fastest way to find a specific record, but it can only be used with server-side cursors on tables that have been opened as `adCmdTableDirect`, because it specifically relies on the table's indexes (and the indexes reside on the server—not on the client). Naturally, the table must have at least one index for it to search on.

Syntax: `rs.Seek KeyValues, SeekOption`

To use the ADO `Seek` method, you must specify three things: the name of the index key to use (although an index can be made up of multiple columns, you can only specify one index at a time), a variant array whose members specify the values to be compared with the key columns, and a `SeekEnum` constant that defines the kind of `Seek` to execute. The `SeekOption` constant can be one of the following.

Constant	Value	Description
AdSeekFirstEQ	1	Locates the first key that is equal to the value specified in KeyValues.
AdSeekLastEQ	2	Locates the last key that is equal to the value specified in KeyValues.
AdSeekAfterEQ	4	Locates the key that is equal to the value specified in KeyValues, or the key just after it.
AdSeekAfter	8	Locates a key that is just after where a match with a value specified in KeyValues would have occurred.
AdSeekBeforeEQ	16	Locates the key that is equal to the value specified in KeyValues, or the key just after where it would have occurred.
AdSeekBefore	32	Locates a key that is just before where a match with a value specified in KeyValues would have occurred.

For example, the following code shows how to search the tblCustomers table to find a customer whose Customer No. is 123:

```
Set rs = db.OpenRecordset("tblCustomer", dbOpenTable)

rs.Index = "CustomerNo"
rs.Seek 123, adSeekFirstEQ

If rs.EOF Then
    'A matching record was found
Else
    'A matching record was not found
End If
```

Primary key indexes in Jet databases are called PrimaryKey, whereas primary key indexes in the SQL Server are called PK_tablename by default, but you can name them anything you like. So if you want to use the table's primary key index, you must know its name.

You must specify a key value for each column in the index. The reason is that some of the key fields may default to Null, and since nothing can *equal* Null, your Seek method will usually not find what you're looking for.

In contrast with the DAO Seek method where you would check the NoMatch property to see if the search succeeded or failed, the ADO Seek method has no such property. If the method finds a record that matches the criteria, the Recordset object's cursor is moved to that row, if not, to the end of the recordset. So if no matching record is found, the Recordset object's EOF property is set to True.

The Find Method

Unlike DAO, ADO only has one Find method. The Find method has the following syntax:

```
rs.Find Criteria, SkipRows, SearchDirection, Start
```

The `Criteria` argument can be any valid SQL WHERE clause, without the word WHERE. The `SkipRows` argument is the number of rows to skip when searching for the next or previous match. The `Start` argument is a bookmark that you can use as a starting point for the search. And lastly, the `SearchDirection` argument can be either `adSearchForward` or `adSearchBackward`, the function of which is fairly obvious.

Unless otherwise specified, all searches begin at the current row, so it's a good idea to always issue the `MoveFirst` method before attempting `Find` when you first open a recordset.

The following code demonstrates how to find the first and second instances of a customer having the word *parts* in their name.

```
'Search for the first matching record
rs.Find "[OrgName] LIKE '*parts*'", , adSearchForward
rs.MoveFirst

'Check the result
If rs.NoMatch Then
    MsgBox "Record not found."
Else
    MsgBox "Customer name:" & rs.CustName

    'Search for the next matching record
    rs.Find "[OrgName] LIKE '*parts*'", 1, adSearchForward

    'Check the result
    If rs.NoMatch Then
        MsgBox "Record not found."
    Else
        MsgBox "Customer name:" & rs.CustName
    End If
End If
```

Notice that the `SkipRows` argument is specified in both searches. This is because you have to skip the current row too. Unfortunately, you can only specify a single column name in the search criterion. The `Find` method does not support multicolumn search.

Two interesting points to note are that literal string values can be specified either within single quotes or within hash characters. For example:

```
"State = 'NY'" or "State = #NY#"
```

Also, the use of the asterisk as a wildcard character is restricted. You can specify it at the end of the criterion string, or at the beginning AND end. You cannot use the asterisk at the beginning (without one also being at the end), or in the middle. The following truth table illustrates this point.

State LIKE '*York'	Illegal
State LIKE 'New*'	OK
State LIKE '*ew Yor*'	OK
State LIKE 'New *ork'	Illegal

Once a matching record is found, any subsequent search begins from the current cursor position, not from the start or end of the recordset, like the Seek method. As with the Seek method, always follow the search with a check of the recordset's NoMatch property to determine the result of the search.

Editing Data with Recordsets

As in DAO, you edit data in recordsets using the AddNew, Update, and CancelUpdate methods.

You'll notice that we didn't mention the Edit method; that's because it doesn't exist in ADO. In DAO, when you leave a record, any changes are discarded. By contrast, when you leave a record in ADO, the changes are immediately committed. In addition, the ADO Update method is optional. You don't need to use it; however, you'll earn yourself a runtime error if you attempt to close a recordset without committing or cancelling any changes, so I recommend you explicitly use it anyway.

```
With rs
    .Open "Shippers", cn, _
        adOpenDynamic, adLockOptimistic, adCmdTable

    'Check that a record exists
    If .AbsolutePosition > adPosUnknown Then
        'ADO does not have an "Edit" method
        !Phone = "555-5554"
        .Update
    End If

    'Add a new record
    .AddNew
    !CompanyName = "Ollivanders"
    !Phone = "555-5555"

    If booOK2Save = True Then
        .Update
    Else
        .CancelUpdate
    End If
End With
```

Using the above technique, you can edit records and send the updates to the database one at a time. Of course, you can edit a bunch of records and send the updates all at once, like

```
With rs
    .Open "Shippers", cn, _
        adOpenDynamic, adLockOptimistic, adCmdTable

    'Check that a record exists
    If .AbsolutePosition > adPosUnknown Then
        'Edit several records
        !Phone = "555-5554"

        .MoveNext
        !Phone = "666-6666"
```

```
            .MoveNext
            !Phone "777-7777"
            .Update
        End If
End With
```

ADO also allows batch updates, which allows you to edit multiple records and then send them all to the OLE DB provider to be saved as a single operation. To use this feature, you must use a client-side cursor and open the recordset using the `adLockBatchOptimistic LockType` property.

```
With rs
    .CursorLocation = adUseClient
    .CursorType = adOpenKeyset
    .LockType = adLockBatchOptimistic
    .Open "Customers", cn

    'Find the right record to edit
    .Find "Country = 'USA'"
    Do While Not .EOF
        'Edit the current record
        !Region = "AA"

        'Skip over the current record to
        'find the next matching record
        .Find "Country = 'USA'", 1
    Loop

    'Commit all the changes
    .UpdateBatch
End With
```

Persistent Recordsets

In DAO, a recordset exists only within the scope of its object variable, after which it is destroyed. The same can be said of ADO recordsets; however, ADO also provides you with a way to save your recordsets to a file on the disk. This allows you to create a recordset, save it to disk, reopen it at some point in the future, make changes to it, and save it again.

Saving a Recordset to a File

To do all this, you use the `Recordset` object's `Save` method. The following examples demonstrate how to save, reopen, modify, and then resave a recordset. Not all providers allow you to save a recordset to a file. You're safe with the Jet OLE DB provider, but to be certain with other providers, open the recordset using a client-side cursor.

```
Dim rs As ADODB.Recordset
Dim strADTGFile As String
Dim strXMLFile As String

Set rs = New ADODB.Recordset

'Open the recordset
rs.CursorLocation = adUseClient
```

```
rs.Open "Customers", CurrentProject.Connection, _
adOpenStatic, adLockOptimistic, adCmdTable

'Specify the output files
strADTGFile = "c:\Temp\Customers.adtg"
strXMLFile = "c:\Temp\Customers.xml"
```

You'll get a runtime error if you try to save a recordset to a file that already exists, so we have to delete any existing file first. But if you try to delete a file that doesn't exist, you'll still get a runtime error.

```
On Error Resume Next
Kill strADTGFile
Kill strXMLFile
Err.Clear
On Error GoTo 0
```

Now use the Save method to save the recordset to disk. You have two options with regard to file formats: *Advanced Data Tablegram* (ADTG), which is a proprietary Microsoft format, or the *Extensible Markup Language* (XML) format.

Saving the recordset in the XML format is great if you intend to exchange data with another application that supports XML, but the ADTG format will produce a smaller file size.

```
'Save the recordset to disk as an ADT file
rs.Save strADTGFile, adPersistADTG

'Just to show that it can be done, save
'the recordset to disk as an XML file
rs.Save strXMLFile, adPersistXML

'Clean up
rs.Close
Set rs = Nothing
Set cn = Nothing
```

We'll leave both files on the disk for now, because we haven't finished with them yet.

If we were to continue working with the recordset, adding and deleting rows, or modifying data, the changes would be reflected in the database, not in the file. Any changes you want reflected in the file must be explicitly saved to the file—remember, this recordset is bound to the database by a connection.

Creating a Recordset Based on a File

The next example shows you how to reopen the recordset we saved to the disk in the preceding section, make a change to it, then resave it.

```
Dim rs As ADODB.Recordset
Dim strADTGFile As String

Set rs = New ADODB.Recordset

'Specify the output file
strADTGFile = "c:\Temp\Customers.adtg"
```

When you want to open a recordset using a file as its source, you must do so without specifying a connection. This creates a *disconnected recordset* (which we'll explain a bit later). Once the recordset is open, you can work with it just like any other recordset, but the recordset will be bound to the file—not the database. If you want to bind the recordset to the database, you must then set the recordset's `ActiveConnection` property.

Our example reconnects to the database, but also resaves the recordset to the file.

```
'Open the recordset with a client-side cursor,
'but NO connection!
rs.CursorLocation = adUseClient
rs.Open strADTGFile, , adOpenStatic, adLockOptimistic

'Now set the recordset's connection
rs.ActiveConnection = CurrentProject.Connection

'Make a change and save it again
rs!Fax = "555-1234"
rs.Update

Kill strADTGFile
rs.Save strADTGFile, adPersistADTG

'Clean up
rs.Close
Set rs = Nothing
```

Our final example opens the file again to demonstrate that we have indeed accomplished our goal of saving a modified recordset, after which the two output files are deleted, since we don't need them any more.

```
Dim rs As ADODB.Recordset
Dim strADTGFile As String
Dim strXMLFile As String

Set rs = New ADODB.Recordset

'Specify the output file
strADTGFile = "c:\Temp\Customers.adtg"

'Open the recordset with a client-side cursor,
'but NO connection!
rs.CursorLocation = adUseClient
rs.Open strADTGFile, , adOpenStatic, adLockOptimistic

'Now prove that the data had changed since the last operation
Debug.Print rs!Fax

'Clean up
rs.Close
Set rs = Nothing
Kill strADTGFile
Kill strXMLFile
```

Disconnected Recordsets

Ever wanted to use a recordset to store temporary data, but been forced to use a multidimensional array because DAO recordsets are always bound to the database? A disconnected recordset is one that is not bound to a database, file, or other data source. It is completely independent. You can add and delete columns, rows, indexes; all without affecting the data in your database.

To create a disconnected recordset, just open it without a connection.

```
Dim rs As ADODB.Recordset

'Instantiate the recordset
Set rs = New ADODB.Recordset

'Append some fields
rs.Fields.Append "CustomerID", adInteger
rs.Fields.Append "CustName", adVarChar, 20
rs.Fields.Append "Phone", adVarChar, 15
rs.Fields.Refresh

'Add some data
With rs
.Open
.AddNew
    !CustomerID = 1
    !CustName = "Ollivander"
    !Phone = "555-5555"
.Update
End With

'
'Now do whatever you want with this
'temporary, disconnected recordset
'
'Clean up
rs.Close
Set rs = Nothing
```

You can also create a disconnected recordset by removing the connection from a bound recordset. For example:

```
Dim rs As ADODB.Recordset

'Instantiate the recordset
Set rs = New ADODB.Recordset

'Give it a client-side cursor, and set its attributes
rs.CursorLocation = adUseClient
rs.LockType = adLockBatchOptimistic
rs.CursorType = adOpenKeyset

'Open the recordset, getting its data from the database
rs.Open "Customers", CurrentProject.Connection
```

```
'Now disconnect the recordset
Set rs.ActiveConnection = Nothing

'Print out the data to prove we still have it
Debug.Print rs!CustomerID, rs!CompanyName

'Clean up
rs.Close
Set rs = Nothing
```

Because the default cursor in ADO is server side, you must use a client-side cursor for this to work, because once you disconnect, there is no server. Any changes you make to the data while the recordset is disconnected will not be reflected in the database until you reconnect it and issue the `Update` or `UpdateBatch` methods (depending on how many records you changed).

If you intend to use `UpdateBatch`, the recordset's `LockType` must be set to `adLockBatchOptimistic`, as shown above.

```
'Change the data
rs!CompanyName = "who cares"

'Reconnect to the data source
rs.ActiveConnection = CurrentProject.Connection
'Update the data
rs.UpdateBatch

'Prove it worked
Debug.Print rs!CustomerID, rs!CompanyName
```

Opening a Recordset Containing More Than One SELECT Query

As in DAO, you can create a recordset containing more than one `SELECT` query.

The following example demonstrates how to create and use such a recordset. Start by creating a *stored procedure* to do the job:

```
CREATE PROCEDURE dbo.MultiSelect AS
    SELECT * FROM Invoices
    SELECT * FROM Customers
```

or specify a hard-coded query:

```
strSQL= "SELECT * FROM Invoices SELECT * FROM Customers"
```

In the example that follows, we have used a stored procedure. You might recall from the same section in Chapter 6 that each SQL statement is separated by a semicolon. As you can see, that's not the case in ADO; just separate the statements by a space (or in the case of a stored procedure, by a line break). Next, we create a procedure to demonstrate how it's done.

```
Dim cmd As New ADODB.Command
Dim rs As ADODB.Recordset

'Setup the Command object
```

```
With cmd
    .ActiveConnection = CurrentProject.Connection
    .CommandText = "MultiSelect"
    .CommandType = adCmdStoredProc
End With

'Open the first set of data
Set rs = cmd.Execute
```

When we create the recordset, the first dataset to be loaded is the one that is specified first in the stored procedure or SQL statement (if hard-coded), and you can cycle through each recordset in the same way you would with other recordsets.

```
Do While Not rs Is Nothing
    Do While Not rs.EOF
        Debug.Print rs.Fields(0).Name, rs.Fields(0).Value
        rs.MoveNext
    Loop
```

The `Recordset` object's `NextRecordset` method retrieves subsequent sets of data. The recordset is set to `Nothing` when there are no more recordsets available.

You can terminate a recordset and move on to the next one by issuing the `NextRecordset` method.

```
    'Open the next set of data
    Set rs = rs.NextRecordset
Loop

'Clean up
'There is no need to close the Recordset object
Set cmd = Nothing
```

As with other recordsets, you can flush the recordset with the recordset's `Cancel` method, but remember that this cancels the entire recordset, not just the current dataset.

Creating Schema Recordsets

You're no doubt familiar with using recordsets to access and manipulate data. But ADO also allows you to open recordsets that contain information about your database's tables. Of course, you can get at this information using ADOX, but some details are more readily accessed using ADO schema recordsets.

To open a schema recordset, you issue the `OpenSchema` method against the `Connection` object. The `OpenSchema` method has three parameters you can use to specify more options.

```
connection.OpenSchema Schema, Restrictions, SchemaID As Recordset
```

The `Schema` parameter specifies the type of information to return. Its values are defined in Appendix J.

The optional `Restrictions` parameter allows you to filter the output. For example, you can filter the recordset to return only a single table or view. The available values are listed in Appendix J.

The `SchemaID` parameter is only required when the `Schema` parameter is set to `adSchemaProviderSpecific`, when you must also supply a *globally unique identifier* (GUID) that identifies the provider schema to return. These are shown as `Constants` in the example code at the end of this section. For example, the following code prints the details of every table and view in the current database.

```
Dim rs As ADODB.Recordset
Dim fld As ADODB.Field

'Create the recordset
Set rs = CurrentProject.Connection.OpenSchema(adSchemaTables)

'Loop through the recordset rows
Do Until rs.EOF
    For Each fld In rs.Fields
        'Loop through the fields in ach row
        Debug.Print fld.Name
        Debug.Print vbTab & Nz(fld.Value, "** Null **")
    Next fld

    rs.MoveNext
    Debug.Print String(20, "-")
Loop

'Clean up
rs.Close
Set fld = Nothing
Set rs = Nothing
```

To restrict the output of the `OpenSchema` method, you must supply an array of values from the `Restrictions` list. In other words, where the above example code prints a list of all the tables and views in the database, the constraint columns for an `adSchemaTables` recordset are

- ❑ TABLE_CATALOG
- ❑ TABLE_SCHEMA
- ❑ TABLE_NAME
- ❑ TABLE_TYPE

The array values must be specified in the same order that they appear above:

```
Array(TABLE_CATALOG, TABLE_SCHEMA, TABLE_NAME, TABLE_TYPE)
```

So, to restrict the output to a single table with a TABLE_NAME of `Categories` and a TABLE_TYPE of `Table` this would be the resulting array

```
Array(TABLE_CATALOG, TABLE_SCHEMA, "Categories", "Table")
```

Therefore, this is what you end up with:

```
Set rs = CurrentProject.Connection.OpenSchema( _
        adSchemaTables, Array(Empty, Empty, "Categories", "Table"))
```

The Jet provider also provides eight provider-specific schema recordsets in two broad categories. The following example demonstrates how to use them.

```
'Access object security GUIDs
Public Const JET_SECURITY_FORMS = _
        "{c49c842e-9dcb-11d19f0a-00c04fc2c2e0}"
Public Const JET_SECURITY_REPORTS = _
        "{c49c8430-9dcb-11d1-9f0a-00c04fc2c2e0}"
Public Const JET_SECURITY_MACROS = _
        "{c49c842f-9dcb-11d1-9f0a-00c04fc2c2e0}"
Public Const JET_SECURITY_MODULES = _
        "{c49c8432-9dcb-11d1-9f0a-00c04fc2c2e0}"

'Jet OLE DB provider-defined schema rowsets
Public Const JET_SCHEMA_REPLPARTIALFILTERLIST = _
        "{e2082df0-54ac-11d1-bdbb-00c04fb92675}"
Public Const JET_SCHEMA_REPLCONFLICTTABLES = _
        "{e2082df2-54ac-11d1-bdbb-00c04fb92675}"
Public Const JET_SCHEMA_USERROSTER = _
        "{947bb102-5d43-11d1-bdbf-00c04fb92675}"
Public Const JET_SCHEMA_ISAMSTATS = _
        "{8703b612-5d43-11d1-bdbf-00c04fb92675}"
```

The following code lists all the currently logged-on users.

```
Public Sub WhosOn()
    'Print the details of all currently logged-on users
    Dim rs As ADODB.Recordset
    Dim fld As ADODB.Field

    'Create the recordset
    Set rs = CurrentProject.Connection.OpenSchema( _
            adSchemaProviderSpecific, , JET_SCHEMA_USERROSTER)

    'Loop through the recordset
    Do Until rs.EOF
        For Each fld In rs.Fields
            'Loop through the Fields collection
            Debug.Print fld.Name
            Debug.Print vbTab & Nz(fld.Value, "-NULL-")
        Next fld

        rs.MoveNext
    Loop

    'Clean up
    rs.Close
    Set fld = Nothing
    Set rs = Nothing
End Sub
```

Using ADO Events

The ADO `Connection` and `Recordset` objects support several events for a variety of operations. These events won't interrupt your code, and can be more accurately pictured as *notifications*, which are actually a call to an event procedure that you define in your code, much like a text box's `AfterUpdate` event.

ADO object events aren't always so important for synchronous operations, because your code waits for the operation to complete before proceeding. They can be very important for asynchronous operations, however, because there's no way of telling when the operation will complete.

For example, let's say you execute the following code to open an asynchronous connection against an SQL Server database that resides on the other side of the country. Just for fun, let's also say the network runs at 9600 baud. With such a slow network speed, getting connected takes considerable time. Naturally enough, an error will occur when you try to open the recordset, because the connection will not have opened by the time you execute the recordset's `Open` method.

```
Dim cn As New ADODB.Connection
Dim rs As New ADODB.Recordset

'Open an asynchronous connection
cn.CursorLocation = adUseServer
cn.Open CurrentProject.Connection, , , adAsyncConnect
rs.Open "vwSomeView", cn
```

To account for this possibility, you can use the `Connection` object's `ConnectComplete` event. But before you do that, you must declare the `Connection` object using the `WithEvents` keyword.

```
Private WithEvents cn As ADODB.Connection
```

Remember though that the `WithEvents` keyword can only be issued in a class module. That being the case, the above code could be written as follows:

```
'Open an asynchronous connection
cn.CursorLocation = adUseServer
cn.Open CurrentProject.Connection, , , adAsyncConnect
```

Then you wait for the connection attempt to succeed or fail, as the case may be. You trap the event with the following event procedure.

```
Private Sub cn_ConnectComplete(ByVal pError As ADODB.Error, _
                    adStatus As ADODB.EventStatusEnum, _
                    ByVal pConnection As ADODB.Connection)
    Dim rs As New ADODB.Recordset

    'Check the connection status and take the appropriate action
    Select Case adStatus
        Case adStatusOK
            'Indicates that the operation succeeded without error
            rs.Open "Invoices", cn

        Case adStatusErrorsOccurred
            'The operation failed due to an error
```

```
                'Display the error message
              MsgBox "Error: " & pError.Number, pError.Description
      End Select

      rs.Close
      cn.Close
      Set rs = Nothing
      Set cn = Nothing
   End Sub
```

Within the event procedure, you can also set adStatus to any of the following values to specify certain behaviours.

❑   adStatusCantDeny—Specify that the operation can't request cancellation of the pending operation.

❑   adStatusCancel—Cancel the operation.

❑   adStatusUnwantedEvent—Do not allow any more notifications for the duration of the event procedure.

The Connection object also exposes other events such as WillConnect, ConnectComplete, and Disconnect. The Recordset object exposes other events. Refer to Appendix 7 for a list of all the available events for the Connection and Recordset objects.

Testing the State Property

If you choose not to rely on events, you can always test the object's State property. The State property returns a value that indicates the current status of the operation currently being carried out. For example, the following code segment tests the current state of a Connection object's Open operation.

```
cn.Open CurrentProject.Connection, , , adAsyncConnect
Do Until cn.State = adStateOpen
    DoEvents
Loop

rs.Open "Invoices", cn
```

Not what we'd call a professional approach, but every programmer is different, and you might like to do such things. The State property can return the following values.

Constant	Value	Description
AdStateClosed	0	The object is closed.
AdStateOpen	1	The object is open.
AdStateConnecting	2	The object is connecting.
AdStateExecuting	4	The object is executing a command.
AdStateFetching	8	The object is retrieving rows.

Creating Schema Objects with ADOX

So far we've been working with the ADODB library, which is the library to use when you want to work with database data. The ADOX library is the one you use when you want to work with the database schema, such as tables, views (queries), indexes, and so on.

To implement ADOX, you need to add a reference to it. Open any code module by pressing *Alt+F11*, and select References from the Tools menu. The References dialog box is displayed. Locate and select *ADO Ext. 2.7 for DDL and Security*, and click OK.

The ADOX Object Model

As you can see from Figure 7-6, the ADOX model contains one top-level object, the Catalog object, which contains five collections: Tables, Groups, Users, Procedures, and Views.

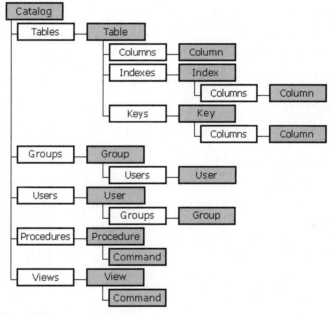

Figure 7-6

Each of the Table, Index, and Column objects also has a standard ADO Properties collection, as shown in Figure 7-7.

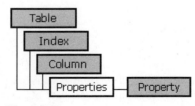

Figure 7-7

Working with Queries (Views)

Since ADO is part of Microsoft's UDA strategy, it was felt that the term *query* failed to adequately describe the mechanism for retrieving data from a source that could be almost anything. As described earlier, ADO can retrieve data from many different sources, not just the Jet database engine, so the term *view* was adopted in ADO to more accurately describe a view, or perspective, of the data, regardless of where it came from.

To simplify things while working with the Jet database engine, Microsoft has maintained the existing terminology by referring to them externally as queries; however, this nomenclature changes to views when working with external data sources such as the SQL Server.

If this seems a little confusing, don't worry. Just remember that ADO is a different object model that simply refers to the same objects in a different way, and by (sometimes) different names. When working with queries, just replace the DAO-specific keywords query and QueryDef with the new ADO keyword view. That's all you need to do.

Whenever you work with other data access objects, such as Recordset and Command objects, you can also use a View object to specify the SQL operation that should be used. Exactly how you do that is explained in the relevant sections on Recordset and Command objects.

As with DAO QueryDefs, you can also build ADO views in code.

Creating a View

The process of creating an ADO View is the same as in DAO. To create a view in ADO:

1. Create a Catalog object and define its ActiveConnection property.

2. Create a Command object and define its CommandText property.

3. Append a new View object to the Views collection, using the Command object as its argument.

```
Dim cat As New ADOX.Catalog
Dim cmd As New ADODB.Command

'Open the Catalog
cat.ActiveConnection = CurrentProject.Connection

'Create the Command object that represents the View
cmd.CommandText = "SELECT * FROM tblCustomers WHERE"

'Create the View
Cat.Views.Append "AllCustomers", cmd

'Clean up
Set cat.ActiveConnection = Nothing
Set cat = Nothing
Set cmd = Nothing
```

You might recall from the section on *DAO QueryDefs* that you could set the value of any parameters in code. In ADO, you set the parameter values in the Command object. We'll demonstrate this in the section *Command Object*.

Modifying a View

To modify an existing view, you can reassign its `Command` object.

```
'Create the Command object that represents the View
cmd.CommandText = "SELECT * FROM tblCustomers WHERE City = 'Boise'"

'Create the View
Cat.Views("AllCustomers").Command = cmd
```

Deleting a View

Deleting a `View` is simple. Just issue the `Delete` method against the `Catalog` object's `Views` collection.

```
cat.Views.Delete strViewName
```

Creating Tables and Columns

Let's replicate the design of the two invoicing system tables we created in Chapter 6. The basic procedure for creating a table in ADO is as follows:

1. Create a `Catalog` object and define its `ActiveConnection` property.
2. Create a `Table` object.
3. Check if the table already exists, and if so, delete it.
4. Create the table object in memory using the `New` keyword.
5. Create the `Column` objects in memory, using the table's `Append` method, setting each column's attributes as appropriate.
6. Append the `Table` object to the catalog object's `Tables` collection.
7. Refresh the `Tables` collection to ensure it is up-to-date.

The header table stores the basic high-level information about each invoice, such as the invoice number, date, and the customer ID. The following example demonstrates how to create a new table called `tblInvoice` and add four fields to it.

First, let's declare all the objects needed to create the table.

```
Public Sub CreateInvoiceTable()
    Dim cat As ADOX.Catalog
    Dim tbl As ADOX.Table

    'Create and connect a Catalog object
    Set cat = New ADOX.Catalog
    cat.ActiveConnection = CurrentProject.Connection

    On Error Resume Next

    'If the table already exists, delete it
    cat.Tables.Delete "tblInvoice"
    On Error Goto 0
```

```
        'Create the table definition in memory
        Set tbl = New ADOX.Table
        tbl.Name = "tblInvoice"
```

At this point, you have created a new `table` object, but it only exists in memory. It won't become a permanent part of the database until you add it to the catalog object's collection. Before you do that, however, you need to add one or more columns (called `fields` in DAO) to the table, because you can't save a table that has no columns.

```
        'Create the new columns
        tbl.Columns.Append "InvoiceNo", adVarChar, 10

        'The InvoiceNo column could also have been specified thus:
        'Dim col As ADOX.Column
        'Set col = New ADOX.Column
        'With col
        '      .Name = "InvoiceNo"
        '      .Type = adVarChar

        '      .DefinedSize = 10
        'End With
        '
        'tbl.Columns.Append col

        'Create the remaining columns
        tbl.Columns.Append "InvoiceDate" adDBDate
        tbl.Columns.Append "CustomerID" adInteger
        tbl.Columns.Append "Comments" adVarChar, 50
```

The columns have now been added to the table, but the table still needs to be added to the catalog's `Tables` collection to make it a permanent fixture. Once you've done that, you should refresh the `Tables` collection to ensure it is up-to-date, because in a multiuser application, the new table may not be immediately propagated to other users' collections until you do.

```
        'Append the new table to the collection
        cat.Tables.Append tbl
        cat.Tables.Refresh

        'Clean up
        cat.ActiveConnection = Nothing
        Set tbl = Nothing
        Set cat = Nothing
```

Next, we need to create a table to store the invoice line items, including the product ID, the number of items sold, and their individual unit prices. Since the total invoice price and tax can be calculated at runtime, we won't violate normalization rules by creating fields for these items.

The following example creates a new table called `tblInvItem`, and adds five fields to it. It is based on the same basic procedure for creating tables, but includes an addition attribute definition, `dbAutoIncrField`, to create an `AutoNumber` field.

```
Public Sub CreateInvItemTable()
    Dim cat As ADOX.Catalog
    Dim tbl As ADOX.Table

    'Create and connect the Catalog object
    Set cat = New ADOX.Catalog
    cat.ActiveConnection = CurrentProject.Connection

    On Error Resume Next

    'If the table already exists, delete it
    cat.Tables.Delete "tblInvItem"
    On Error Goto 0

    'Create the table definition in memory
    Set tbl = New ADOX.Table
    tbl.Name = "tblInvoice"

    With tbl.Columns
        .Append "InvItemID", adInteger
        .Append "InvoiceNo", adVarChar, 10
        .Append "ProductID", adInteger
        .Append "Qty", adSmallInt
        .Append "UnitCost", adCurrency
    End With
```

Once you've appended a column to the table, you can set its Access-specific properties. For example, to make a column (in this case, the InvItemID column) the AutoNumber column, you must first set its ParentCatalog property, and then set its AutoIncrement property.

```
    With tbl.Columns("InvItemID")
        .ParentCatalog = cat
        .Properties("AutoIncrement") = True
    End With

    'Append the new table to the collection
    cat.Tables.Append tbl
    cat.Tables.Refresh

    'Clean up
    cat.ActiveConnection = Nothing
    Set tbl = Nothing
    Set cat = Nothing
```

Creating Indexes

The basic procedure for creating an index is as follows:

1. Create a Catalog object and define its ActiveConnection property.

2. Create a Table object and instantiate it.

3. Create an `Index` object.

4. Check if the primary key already exists, and if so, delete it.

5. Create the index using the `New` keyword, and set its attributes as appropriate.

6. Append the index's columns to the `Columns` collection.

7. Append the index to the table's `Indexes` collection.

Remember three things when creating indexes in ADO. First, not all providers support all index attributes. Check the provider's documentation for those it does support. Second, Jet databases do not support clustered indexes. Third, although you can give an index any name you like, when you create a primary key using the Access `Table Designer`, it will be automatically named `PrimaryKey` for Jet databases, and `PK_tablename` for SQL Server databases. Therefore, to maintain consistency, it is wise to give code-created primary keys the same name.

Let's create the primary key. The following sub creates a primary key index for the specified table, which can include multiple fields whose names are supplied in the `ParamArray` argument. In the case of our invoice tables, there will be only one field in each.

```
Public Sub CreatePKIndexes(strTableName As String, _
        ParamArray varPKColumns() As Variant)
    Dim cat As ADOX.Catalog
    Dim tbl As ADOX.Table
    Dim idx As ADOX.Index
    Dim varColumn As Variant

    'Create and connect the Catalog object
    Set cat = New ADOX.Catalog
    cat.ActiveConnection = CurrentProject.Connection

    Set tbl = cat.Tables(strTableName)

    'Check if a Primary Key exists. If so, delete it.
    For Each idx In tbl.Indexes
        If idx.PrimaryKey Then
            tbl.Indexes.Delete idx.Name
        End If
    Next idx

    'Create a new primary key
    Set idx = New ADOX.Index
    With idx
        .Name = "PrimaryKey"
        .PrimaryKey = True
        .Unique = True
    End With
```

At this point, the index exists in memory, and will remain so until it is added to the table's `Indexes` collection. But before you do that, you must add the columns that make up the key to the index's `Columns` collection and refresh the collection.

```
            'Append the columns
            For Each varColumn In varPKColumns
                idx.Columns.Append varColumn
            Next varColumn

            'Append the index to the collection
            tbl.Indexes.Append idx
            tbl.Indexes.Refresh

            'Clean up
            Set cat.ActiveConnection = Nothing
            Set cat = Nothing
            Set tbl = Nothing
            Set idx = Nothing
        End Sub
```

You should run the `CreatePKIndexes` procedure to define the indexes for both `tblInvoice` and `tblInvItem` tables.

Finally, relationships must be set up between the two tables.

Creating Relations

The basic procedure for creating an index is as follows:

1. Create a `Catalog` object and define its `ActiveConnection` property.

2. Create a `Key` object to act as the foreign key (the *many* side of the relationship).

3. Supply the `RelatedTable` property, which is the name of the primary table (the *one* side of the relationship).

4. Supply the `RelatedColumn` property (which is the name of the matching column in the primary table) for each column.

5. Set the other key attributes as appropriate.

6. Add the key to the table's `Keys` collection.

The following code creates a foreign key relationship between the `tblInvoice` table and the `tblProducts` table.

Note that you can name a relationship any way you like, but when you create a relationship using the `Relationships` window, Access names the relationship according to the names of the tables involved. For example, if you were to create a relationship between `tblInvoice` and `tblProducts`, Access would name it `tblInvoicetblProducts`.

```
Dim cat As New ADOX.Catalog
Dim ky As New ADOX.Key

'Create and connect the Catalog object
cat.ActiveConnection = CurrentProject.Connection
```

```
'Define the foreign key
With ky
    .Name = "ProductID"
    .Type = adKeyForeign
    .RelatedTable = "tblProducts"
    .Columns.Append "ProductID"
    .Columns("ProductID").RelatedColumn = "ProductID"
    .UpdateRule = adRICascade
End With

'Append the foreign key
cat.Tables("tblInvoice").Keys.Append ky

'Clean up
Set cat.ActiveConnection = Nothing
Set cat = Nothing
Set ky = Nothing
```

Managing Jet Security with ADO

Managing Access security in DAO was discussed in Chapter 6, and since the same methodology is used in ADO, we won't labor the point here. However, we will highlight the properties and methods available in ADO that aren't available in DAO.

The first thing to be aware of is that the ADO security objects are children of the Catalog object. For example, the Users and Groups collections are both accessed thus:

```
Dim cat As New ADOX.Catalog

cat.ActiveConnection = CurrentProject.Connection

Debug.Print cat.Groups(0).Name
Debug.Print cat.Users(0).Name
```

Creating Groups and Users

Once you've instantiated a Catalog object, you can create a new group in ADO by simply declaring its name as you append it to the Catalog object's Groups collection:

```
cat.Groups.Append "MyNewGroup"
```

To create a new user, all you need to do is to create a User object, set its name, and password, and then append it to the Catalog object's Users collection. The following example demonstrates just how easy it is to create a new group, a new user, and then add the user to a group.

```
Dim cat As ADOX.Catalog
Dim usr As ADOX.User

'Create the Catalog
Set cat = New ADOX.Catalog
cat.ActiveConnection = CurrentProject.Connection
```

```
'Create the new user
Set usr = New ADOX.User
usr.Name = "Doris Crockford"
usr.ChangePassword "", "sherbert_lemon"
```

To change the password at some later stage, just reissue the `ChangePassword` method using the following syntax:

```
userobject.ChangePassword oldpassword, newpassword
```

At this point we have a fully qualified `User` object. Now we append it to the `Catalog` object's `Users` collection.

```
'Append the new user to the collection
cat.Users.Append usr
```

A valid user account isn't much good to anyone if they don't belong to any groups, so let's add Doris to both `Admins` and `Users` groups.

```
'Add the new user to the Admins and Users groups
usr.Groups.Append "Admins"
usr.Groups.Append "Users"

'Clean up
Set cat.ActiveConnection = Nothing
Set cat = Nothing
```

How hard is that? Of course, to rename a user account, you must delete it, and then re-create it.

Managing Permissions

Setting permissions in ADO is even easier than it is in DAO. The `Catalog` object's `Users` and `Groups` collections manage permissions:

```
GroupOrUser.SetPermissions ObjectName, ObjectType, Action, Rights [,
Inherit] [, ObjectTypeID]
```

The `ObjectTypeID` parameter is an optional variant value that specifies the GUID for a provider object type that isn't defined by the OLE DB specification. This parameter is only used if you set `ObjectType` to `adPermObjProviderSpecific`. You should refer to the provider documentation for the specific GUID to use. The remaining parameter values for the `SetPermisions` method are listed in Appendix J. But, for now, let's take a look at how it works.

```
Dim cat As New ADOX.Catalog
Dim lngPermit As Long

'Create the Catalog
Set cat.ActiveConnection = CurrentProject.Connection
```

For this test, we want to remember the original permissions for the `Customers` table.

```
'Get the original permissions, so we can
'restore them when we've finished
lngPermit = cat.Users("Doris Crockford").GetPermissions( _
        "Customers", adPermObjTable)

Debug.Print "The original permissions were: " & CStr(lngPerm)
```

OK, so now we know what permissions Doris had. Let's play with her permissions for a while.

```
'Revoke all permissions to the Customers table
cat.Users("Doris Crockford").SetPermissions _
        "Customers", adPermObjTable, adAccessRevoke, adRightFull

Debug.Print "Permissions revoked. They are now: " & _
        CStr(cat.Users("Doris Crockford").GetPermissions( _
                "Customers", adPermObjTable))

'Now grant the Admin user full rights on the Customers table
cat.Users("Doris Crockford").SetPermissions _
        "Customers", adPermObjTable, adAccessSet, adRightFull

Debug.Print "Full permissions granted. They are now: " & _
        CStr(cat.Users("Doris Crockford").GetPermissions( _
                "Customers", adPermObjTable))
```

OK, she's had enough. She wants to get back to work, so let's restore her permissions for the table.

```
'Finally, restore the original permissions
cat.Users("Doris Crockford").SetPermissions _
        "Customers", adPermObjTable, adAccessSet, lngPermit

Debug.Print "Permissions restored: " & _
        CStr(cat.Users("Doris Crockford").GetPermissions( _
                "Customers", adPermObjTable))

'Clean up
Set cat.ActiveConnection = Nothing
Set cat = Nothing
```

Note: *We can do exactly the same thing to an entire group, using exactly the same code, but replacing* `cat.Users` *with* `cat.Groups`. *Now isn't that cool?*

Summary

In this chapter, you learned about the ADO object model, which included both the ADODB library, for manipulating data, and the ADOX library, for manipulating database schema.

By now you should have a fairly good working knowledge of creating and using ADO connections and transactions, and be able to create and execute queries using both `Connection` and `Command` objects. You should be able to confidently create and filter ADO recordsets, navigate your way around their rows, find specific records, and edit their data. We also covered persistent and disconnected recordsets, and examined the use of multiple SELECT clauses, shaped queries, and schema recordsets. You should also be fairly confident of your understanding of ADO events.

Specifically relating to ADOX, we undertook an in-depth tutorial on creating queries (views), tables and columns, indexes, and relations to help you create and modify entire databases from the ground up. Finally, we examined how to work with the Jet security model in ADO, creating groups and users, and managing object permissions.

In the next chapter, we'll examine VBA in some detail, which will add a great deal of context to what's been covered in Chapters 6 and 7.

8

Executing VBA

In the old days of programming, *procedural* languages ruled, meaning that the overall program execution traveled from top to bottom. The main body of any of these programs had to cover every possibility: display a screen to the user, gather input, perform edit checking, display messages, update the database (or simple files in those days), and close when everything was done. The main program also had to cover every option or side request that the user might make. This made it difficult to understand the entire program, and it was tough to make changes because everything had to be retested when a modification was made. These lumbering beasts included COBOL, RPG, Pascal, and earlier forms of Basic. Millions of lines of code were written in these languages.

Fortunately, those days are over for VBA programmers. VBA is an *event-driven* language. In every Access form and report there are a variety of events that are waiting for you to use. They are available when the form opens and closes, when records are updated, even when individual fields on the screen are changed. It's all there at your fingertips. Each event can contain a procedure, which is finally where we get back to our procedural roots. Although each procedure runs from top to bottom, just like in the old days, it only runs when the event *fires*. Until then, it sleeps quietly, not complicating your logic or slowing down your program.

Event-driven programming makes it much easier to handle complex programming tasks. By only worrying about events in your coding when they actually happen, each procedure is simpler and easier to debug.

In this chapter, we'll explore the nature of VBA events and show how the most common events are used, and we'll look at how two different sections of your VBA code can run at the same time. We'll also provide some guidelines about when and how to use Public and Private procedures, class modules, and data types. Finally, we'll outline structural guidelines for procedures, show some common string and date handling techniques, and also how to prevent rounding errors in your calculations.

When Events Fire

Events are at the heart of event-driven programming—which is no surprise. What can be surprising to novice programmers is the sheer number of events available to use. They all beg to have some code behind them. In reality though, very few events are used on a consistent basis. Most of them have absolutely no code behind them, and never will in normal usage. The trick is to know which ones are important and commonly used, and which ones are obscure and hardly ever used. They all look equally important in Access Help.

Common Form Events

To cut to the chase, here's a list of commonly used events and how you might want to use them. If you know how to use this basic set of events, you're most of the way there to understanding event-driven programming in Access VBA.

❏ Form—On Open: The Open event for a form fires before the Load event, and before the recordset is evaluated for the form. This means you can use this event to change the recordset (by changing the Where or Order By clause) before the form continues to load. This event can be cancelled, which means the form will not continue to the Load event.

❏ Form—On Load: The Load event for a form fires after the recordset for the form has been evaluated, but before the form is displayed to the user. This offers you an opportunity to make calculations, set defaults, and change visual attributes based on the data from the recordset.

❏ Form—Before Update: If you want to perform some data edits before the user's changes are updated in the database, this is the event to use. All the field values are available to you, so you can do multifield edits (such as HireDate must be greater than BirthDate). If something doesn't pass your validity checks, you can display a message box and cancel this event. This event also fires before a new record is inserted, so you can place edits for both new and changed records here.

❏ Form—On Double Click: This is a strange one. If you build a continuous form to display records in a read-only index format, your users will expect to drill down to the detail of the record by double-clicking anywhere on the row. But what if they double-click the record selector (the gray arrow at the left side of each row)? The event that fires is the Form's double-click event. By using this event, you can run the code that opens your detail form. This gives your user a consistent experience and the confidence that your applications work no matter what they do.

❏ Form—On Unload: This event can be used to check data validity before your form closes. It can be cancelled, which will redisplay your form without closing it.

❏ Form—On Current: This is one of the most overused events by novice programmers, but it does have some good uses. It fires every time your form's "current" record changes, that's the one that the record selector (the gray arrow on the left side of each record) points to. It also fires when your form first loads and positions to the first record in your recordset. One good place to use On Current is on a continuous form where one of the buttons below is valid for some records but not for others. In the On Current event, you can test the current record and set the Enabled property of the button to True or False as appropriate. Because this event fires so often, it can be hard to control and cause performance issues. Use it sparingly.

❏ Form—On Delete: This event fires after each record is deleted, but before the delete is actually finalized. This allows you to ask an Are You Sure message and cancel the delete of just that record if the user wants to. Use this in conjunction with the `Before Delete Confirm` event.

❑ Form—`Before Delete Confirm`: This event fires before a group of deletes is finalized. If you cancel this event, none of the records are actually deleted. This event also has a `Response` parameter; it can be used to suppress the normal Access message asking the user if they want to delete the group of records.

Common Control Events

Here are some events on form controls (such as text boxes, combo boxes, command buttons, etc.) that are commonly used.

❑ Control—`On Click`: This one is obvious; it fires when the control (most likely a command button) is clicked. This is where you put the code to run when the user clicks a button.

❑ Control—`Before Update`: The `Before Update` event is very useful for controls that contain values, such as text boxes and combo boxes. It fires just before a change to the control is committed, so you have a chance to edit the new value of the field. If this event is cancelled, the control will revert to its previous value.

❑ Control—`After Update`: This event fires after a change to the control is made. This is a handy time to control the next field to receive the focus or to update other fields in response to this one. This technique is explained in the section *Cascading Combo Boxes* in Chapter 14, "SQL and VBA."

❑ Control—`On Double Click`: This event fires when a control is double-clicked. This is useful when you want to provide a method of drilling down to a detail form from a read-only index form. Make sure you add the code to open the detail form to every double-click event of every field in the detail section.

Common Report Events

Here are some events on reports that are commonly used. These events can run code to customize and display reports so that they are much more flexible for your users.

❑ Report—`On Open`: This fires before the recordset is evaluated for the report. Just as with forms, you can use this event to change the recordset (by changing the `Where` or `Order By` clause) before the report continues to load. This can be especially useful when you use a form to prompt the user for selection criteria before the report continues to load. This technique is described in detail in Chapter 14. This event can be cancelled by setting the Cancel parameter to `True`, which will prevent the report from continuing to open.

❑ Report—`On Activate`: This event fires after the `On Open` event, and just as the report window is displayed to the user. The main thing this event is used for is to maximize the Access windows using `DoCmd.Maximize`. This allows the user to see more of the report. However, you'll probably want to restore the Access windows to their previous sizes when the report closes, which brings us to the `On Close` event.

❑ Report—`On Close`: As you might guess, this event fires when the report closes. A common line of code to include here is `DoCmd.Restore` to restore the sizes of your form windows that were maximized in the `On Activate` event.

❑ Report—On No Data: The On No Data event fires after the On Open event when the report evaluates the recordset and discovers that there are no records. This can easily happen if you allow your user to specify the criteria for the report and they choose a combination of values that doesn't exist in the database. In the On No Data event, you can display a message box to the user, then set the Cancel parameter to True, which will close the report.

Asynchronous Execution

Sometimes, Access runs two areas of your VBA code simultaneously, even though you've placed the code into different events or even in different forms and reports. This ability for Access to start running one procedure of code before another one is finished is called *asynchronous execution*. Most of the time asynchronous execution happens without you (or your user) really noticing, but it can sometimes cause problems, so you should know when it happens and what to do about it.

OpenForm

The most common asynchronous execution you'll encounter is when you open a form using the OpenForm command. Most of the time you won't notice it, but here's what really happens: When the OpenForm statement runs, the form you ask for starts to open, along with all of its Open, Load, and On Current events. However, your code after the OpenForm command also continues to run at the same time. Usually, not much happens at this point, so there's no harm done.

There are times, however, when you would like the execution of the code in the calling form to stop until the user is done with the form you open. This can happen when you are prompting the user for selection criteria during the Open event of a report (see Chapter 14), or when you open a form to add a new record from an index form.

In this latter case, you normally want to requery the index form to show the record that was just added, but you have to wait for the user to finish adding it. If you perform a requery right after the OpenForm, your code will continue merrily along and requery your first form, only within milliseconds after your second form has started to open. No matter how fast your user is, that's not enough time for them to add the new record. So your requery will run before the new record is added, and the new record will not appear on your index form.

There is a simple solution to the normal asynchronous execution of the OpenForm command. It's called *Dialog Mode*.

Dialog Mode to the Rescue

To prevent asynchronous execution when a form opens, use Dialog Mode. Instead of

DoCmd.OpenForm FormName:="frmMyForm"Specify Dialog Mode instead:

```
DoCmd.OpenForm FormName:="frmMyForm", windowmode:=acDialog
```

Dialog Mode accomplishes two things:

❑ It opens the form in Modal Mode, which prevents the user from clicking on any other Access windows until they are done with this form.

❑ It stops the execution of the calling code until the newly opened form is either closed or hidden.

This second feature of Dialog Mode is what is so helpful in preventing Access from trying to run two areas of your code at once.

Notice that the code stops until the form is *closed* or *hidden*. This is the basis for many clever uses of Dialog Mode where values from the called form are used elsewhere. If you just hide the form (by setting its `Visible` property to `False`), the values on the form are still there and ready for you to reference, even though the code in the calling form now continues to run. This is the technique for gathering selection criteria and building SQL statements, which is described in Chapter 14.

VBA Procedures

Now that we've discussed the events of VBA and how to use them, we'll cover how to use the different types of VBA procedures and to employ good practices in their design.

Function or Sub?

A common area of confusion among novice VBA programmers is whether to write a Function or a Sub (short for "subroutine"). Many developers create functions for every procedure they write, in the belief that they are better in some way. They aren't. Functions and Subs are just two kinds of procedures, and they both have their purposes. A quick way to determine which one is more appropriate is to ask this question: Does my procedure *do* something or *compute* something?

If the purpose of your procedure is to compute or retrieve a value and return it to the calling procedure, then by all means use a function. After all, functions are designed to return a single value to the calling procedure. They do it efficiently and easily, and they can be used directly in queries and calculated controls on forms and reports. They can even be used directly in macros, but you don't use macros, do you? (After all, you're reading this book.)

Functions will tend to have names that are *nouns*, like `LastDayOfMonth` or `FullAddress`. For example, a control on a report might have a control source property of

```
=LastDayOfMonth(Date())
```

This field would display the results of calling some function called `LastDayOfMonth` with the parameter value of today's date.

On the other hand, if the main purpose of your procedure is to do some action and there is no clear-cut value to return, use a Sub. Many programmers think that they must return something, even if they have to make some artificial return code or status. This practice can make your code harder for others to understand.

Subs will tend to have names that are *verbs*, like `LoadWorkTable` or `CloseMonth`. In practice, your code will look like this:

```
LoadWorkTable
```

Pretty easy, right? Any developer looking at this line of code can see the obvious: a Sub called `LoadWorkTable` is being called, and it doesn't return a value.

Public or Private?

Another decision that you have to make when you create procedures is whether to make them Public or Private. By default, Access will make procedures you create Public, but that's not necessarily what you want.

If you are working in a Module, the rules are a little different than if you are working in code that resides in a form or report. Forms and reports are intrinsically encapsulated as class modules, so their Public procedures aren't as public as you might expect. Let's cover procedures in Modules first.

Public and Private Procedures in Modules

Public Functions and Subs in Modules are just that—public property. Every area of your application can see them and use them. In order to do that, Public procedures in Modules have to have a unique name. Otherwise, how would your code know which one to run? If you have two Public procedures with the same name, you'll get a compile error.

Private procedures in Modules are very shy—they can't be seen or referenced by any code outside their own Module. If you try to reference a Private procedure from a different module or another form or report, Access will insist (at compile time) that no such procedure exists.

This hidden nature of Private procedures is their best feature. Because they are hidden, only their names need to be unique within their own module. Therefore, you can name them whatever you want—you don't have to worry about them conflicting with other procedures in your application.

This feature reallycomes into play when you reuse code by importing modules into other databases, maybe even ones you didn't create. If most of your module procedures are Private, you'll have a minimum of naming conflicts, since the rest of the application can't even see them. The Public procedures will still need to have a unique name, which is why many procedures that are meant to be imported have interesting prefixes like the author's initials or the company name.

Public and Private Procedures in Forms and Reports

Private procedures in Form and Reports behave just like Private procedures in modules. They are very private—they can't be seen or referenced from outside the form or report. The event procedures that Access automatically builds behind your forms and reports are automatically set to Private. This makes sense, as `Form_Open` and `OnClick` events are useful only inside that particular form or report. Also, these procedures need to have standard names, so it would seem that there would be a big mess with duplicate names across all your forms and reports if they were Public.

In reality, this problem wouldn't occur. The code behind your forms and reports isn't like the code in a normal module. Under the covers, it is really a *class module*, which is covered later in this chapter. You can see this in the Visual Basic Editing window, as shown in Figure 8-1.

It turns out that even a Public procedure that you build in the code behind a form can be named the same as a procedure in another form. This is because class modules require that you specify the name of the class object (in this case, the form name) before the name of the procedure if you want to call it from outside the form. However, this is rarely done. One possible situation might be some form initialization code that you want to run from outside the form, such as `InitializeForm`. If you want to do it, here's the syntax:

```
Form_frmMyFormName.InitializeForm
```

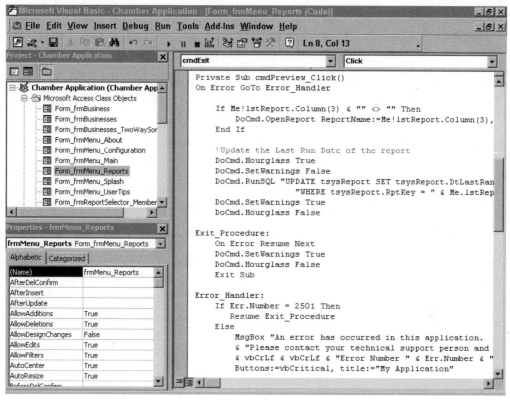

Figure 8-1

Notice that the prefix `Form_` and the name of the form qualifies the `InitializeForm` procedure name. Since many forms could have the same procedure name, you need to tell the code which form's procedure you want to run.

Coupling and Cohesion

Here's a topic that isn't specific to VBA, but bears mentioning while we are working with procedures. The design of your procedures is very important to delivering understandable, readable code. Two principles that guide the logical design of procedures (functions or subs) are *coupling* (bad) and *cohesion* (good).

Coupling is the tempting tendency to write long, complex procedures that do lots of things; in other words, *coupling* together multiple tasks into one procedure. It should be avoided. As a guideline, try to write procedures that compute one value or perform just one task. Some signs that you might have coupling tendencies in your procedures include:

❑   Procedure names that include multiple ideas, like `ComputeValuesAndReloadWorkTables`

❑   Procedure with large blocks of code that have section header comments that explain what this next section does

❑   Procedures that include "modes," with parameters that tell the procedure what to do

If your procedure couples multiple tasks together, you can run into problems like these:

❑ Your procedure is too complicated, making it harder to write and debug.

❑ The different tasks in your procedure can't be used separately; it's an all or nothing deal.

❑ If you make a change to your procedure, the whole thing needs to be retested. You can't trust that your little change didn't mess up other parts of the procedure. Remember the programmer's lament: "But all I changed was…"

If you find yourself writing long procedures with these coupling problems, take a deep breath and step back from it for a minute. Try to identify chunks of code that do something simple and *cohesive*. As a rule, procedures should do or calculate one thing, and should do so independently using parameters that are passed to them. They can also retrieve information from tables or queries to get the information they need.

You may wonder how to build procedures that really need to be complex. Sometimes there is no way to avoid complexity. However, you can hide a lot of complexity by breaking up your logic into smaller functions and subs, then calling them where appropriate. That way, each one of your procedures can be written and debugged separately. If you are working in a team environment, these can even be written by different developers.

Cohesion is related to coupling, but it's a good thing. It just means that each procedure should perform one function, and should be able to do its thing without a lot of help or knowledge from outside the procedure. It shouldn't rely on global variables or other objects to exist. Some signs of a poor cohesion are:

❑ Procedures that include duplicate blocks of code

❑ Procedures that expect forms or reports with specific names

❑ Use of global variables, especially when they are expected to retain their value for a long time

❑ Hard coding of system environment information like file paths

❑ Hard coding or special handling of certain records or values in tables

> **Hard coding is the practice of using values in code that would be more appropriate in a configurable lookup table or some other easy-to-change place, for example, many poorly written applications hard code paths to files. The moment these applications are moved to another computer, they break. Another more insidious example is the use of values lists for combo boxes in forms. These seem so easy to set up, but they are just another form of hard coding that will make your application less robust and harder to change over time. A better approach for a list of values that you don't think will change (or that you need to code against) is to put them in a table that doesn't have a maintenance form. This prevents your user from adding or removing these critical values your code depends on, but allows you flexibility over time. You can use a specific naming convention for these "values list" tables, like `tval` instead of `tlkp`.**

To improve cohesion, think of the old black box principle of programming, which specified that you should need no knowledge of how a procedure produces its result, only that given valid input, it would produce the correct output. Along the same lines, the procedure should have little knowledge of the world outside in order to do its job. Each procedure you write should perform one task or calculation. It should have a minimum of special knowledge from outside its own boundaries. The best way to send information into a procedure is through parameters, not by using global variables or by referring to specific forms or reports.

All this being said, cohesion is a spectrum, not a final black-or-white goal. Using VBA in Access sometimes calls for the use of global variables in controlled scenarios, or referring to an open form, or duplicating some code. It's best to be aware of coupling and cohesion principles so that you can make good coding decisions.

Error Handling

All of your procedures should have at least a minimum level of error handling. There are easy ways to implement simple error handling that can help you debug your code and protect your users from errors (both expected and unexpected). This topic is covered in much greater detail in Chapter 9, "VBA Error Handling."

Class Modules

Class modules are special modules within VBA that allow you to build code objects that have all the abilities of built-in Access objects: methods, properties, multiple instances, and data persistence. These special capabilities of class modules are interesting, but they are rarely needed in normal application programming. However, if you're familiar with class modules, you'll find times when they come in very handy. One reason to use class modules is their ability to remember data across multiple times they are called. This can also be done using the Static keyword when dimensioning variables in regular modules, or by using Global variables, but using a class module is a cleaner way.

A related benefit to this great memory that class modules have is that you can set multiple properties of an instance of a class, then ask it to do something with a method. These sound very technical, but in reality a class module uses a property Let procedure to merely remember a value in a variable. And a method is really just a procedure that does something—similar to the Subs we've already covered. The best way to show how class modules work is with a simple example.

Class Module Example: Using a Multilevel Hourglass

This is a very simple example, but one that you might actually need to use sometime. If you have time-consuming processing in your application, you may want to turn on the Hourglass so that the user knows that you're working on something and they should wait patiently.

However, sometimes multiple time-consuming functions and subs have to run in succession or in a nested structure, and sometimes one procedure is run without the others. Keeping track of the Hourglass status can be difficult in these cases. You need to be sure that it is on while the processing is occurring, but also that it is turned off at the end.

A good approach is to keep track of how "on" the Hourglass is. Every time a procedure needs the Hourglass, it increases the hourglass level—1 means that one procedure turned it on, 2 means that two nested procedures have turned it on, and so on. As each procedure finishes, it decrements the level by 1. When the hourglass level reaches 0, the Hourglass itself is turned off.

This class module, called `MultiLevelHourglass`, demonstrates how you can use class modules to remember the state of an object (in this case, the hourglass level) and manipulate it over time. It consists of three procedures:

- ❏ `TurnOn`—This increments the hourglass level and turns the Hourglass on, if necessary
- ❏ `TurnOff`—This decrements the hourglass level and turns the Hourglass off if necessary, plus an override parameter to force the Hourglass off regardless of level
- ❏ `IsOn`—This is a property that returns whether the Hourglass is currently on

Here's the code from the class module called `MultiLevelHourglass`. First, note the local module level variable. This keeps track of the current level. Because this is a class module, this variable's value will be retained across multiple uses of the object.

```
Option Compare Database
Option Explicit


Private mintHourglassLevel As Integer
```

The following is the simple property, called a `Property Get` in a class module. It merely sets the `IsOn` property to `True` if the level is greater than 0 or `False` if it isn't.

```
Public Property Get IsOn() As Boolean
    IsOn = (mintHourglassLevel > 0)
End Property
```

The following method turns the Hourglass on, or to be more accurate, increases the level of the Hourglass. If the hourglass level becomes 1 during a call to this procedure, the Access Hourglass itself is turned on. If the level is already greater than 1, there's no need, because the Access Hourglass is already on.

```
Public Function TurnOn()
    On Error GoTo Error_Handler

    'Increment the hourglass level.
    mintHourglassLevel = mintHourglassLevel + 1
    'Turn on the hourglass if the level is exactly 1
    If mintHourglassLevel = 1 Then
        DoCmd.Hourglass True
    End If

Exit_Procedure:
    Exit Function
Error_Handler:
    MsgBox "An error has occurred in this application. " _
    & "Please contact your technical support person and tell them this
information:" _
    & vbCrLf & vbCrLf & "Error Number " & Err.Number & ", " &
Err.Description, _
    Buttons:=vbCritical, title:="My Application"
    Resume Exit_Procedure
    Resume
End Function
```

Finally, here is the method that lowers the hourglass level, and actually turns off the Hourglass if level 0 is reached. Note the optional parameter to force the Hourglass off. This is really just a safety valve—you shouldn't really need it if each procedure you run is consistent about decreasing the level using `TurnOff` when it is finished. However, if you know that you are at the end of a long-running process and you want to be sure, you can use `ForceOff:=True` to ensure that the Hourglass isn't stuck on.

```
Public Function TurnOff(Optional ForceOff As Boolean)
On Error GoTo Error_Handler

    'Decrement the hourglass level.
    mintHourglassLevel = mintHourglassLevel - 1
    'Turn off the hourglass if the level is less than or equal to zero
    'or if it is being forced off regardless of level
    If mintHourglassLevel <= 0 Or ForceOff Then
        mintHourglassLevel = 0
        DoCmd.Hourglass False
    End If

Exit_Procedure:
    Exit Function
Error_Handler:
    MsgBox "An error has occurred in this application. " _
    & "Please contact your technical support person and tell them this
information:" _
    & vbCrLf & vbCrLf & "Error Number " & Err.Number & ", " &
Err.Description, _
    Buttons:=vbCritical, title:="My Application"
    Resume Exit_Procedure
    Resume
End Function
```

That's it for the class module called `MultiLevelHourglass`. Now all we need is some code to test it out.

```
Option Compare Database
Global objHourGlass As New MultiLevelHourglass

Public Sub HourglassTest()

    objHourGlass.TurnOn
    'lots of time consuming code here
        objHourGlass.TurnOn
            objHourGlass.TurnOn
            objHourGlass.TurnOff
        objHourGlass.TurnOff
    'any called functions should also use .TurnOn and .TurnOff
    Debug.Print objHourGlass.IsOn 'just for debugging purposes
    objHourGlass.TurnOff ForceOff:=True 'all done

End Sub
```

If you want to use this technique, you can call `objHourGlass.TurnOn` and `objHourGlass.TurnOff` to control the Hourglass throughout your application. You'll need to make sure that no other procedures are controlling the Hourglass directly by using `DoCmd.Hourglass`, because that would be circumventing this multilevel approach.

Using Variables

When using variables in your VBA code, there are several things to remember to ensure that your code runs smoothly. Choosing the appropriate data type for each variable is critical, and it's also important to use global variables correctly.

Naming conventions for variables are very important. In Appendix G, "Naming Conventions," the Reddick naming conventions for variables are described. If you get into the habit of consistently naming your variables, your code will be easier to maintain over time, faster to debug, and will look more professional.

Using Appropriate Data Types and Sizes

First, make sure that your variable types will handle the size of data they are expected to store. Many overflow errors occur because an `AutoNumber` key value from a table was stored in a variable defined as an `Integer`. This may work fine during testing, because an integer can store numbers with values up to 32,767. Then, when a user starts adding more data, the application breaks on an overflow error.

It's a good idea to define variables with the maximum size that is possible to occur. `AutoNumber` fields should be stored in variables defined as `Long` (which is the same as the `Long Integer` in Access tables). Defining a field as String will allow it to store very long strings, whether they are defined as `Text` or `Memo` in a table.

If a variable can possibly contain a Null, then you must define it as a Variant, in which case it will be able to store just about anything that you throw into it—a messy approach, and one that takes Access a bit longer to process. It's usually better to decide what kind of data each variable is going to hold, then set the appropriate data type so that Access doesn't have to figure out what's in there every time it uses the variable. However, sometimes it's useful to allow a variable to contain a Null, especially when there might not always be data to load into the field. If you do use a Variant data type, use it because there's a specific reason that it might contain a Null, not because you don't know what type to make it.

If you don't specify a variable's data type, it will be a Variant by default. A common error is to define more than one variable on a single line of code, like this:

```
Dim strCallingForm, strReportTitle as String
```

Many novice VBA programmers think that both variables in this example will be defined as Strings, but they won't be. VBA requires that each and every variable have its data type defined. In this example, `strCallingForm` will be defined as a Variant because its data type wasn't mentioned.

A correct way to define the two string variables on one line is like this:

```
Dim strCallingForm as String, strReportTitle as String
```

This style is technically correct (both variables are defined as Strings), but the second variable is easy to miss when you are looking at your code. The clearest and most consistent style for defining variables is to give each one its own line:

```
Dim strCallingForm as String
Dim strReportTitle as String
```

This may take an extra line of code, but it is much easier to read and understand.

Using Global Variables

Global variables are variables that retain their value until they are changed or until the application stops. They can be very handy, but they should be used in specific ways to avoid problems. To define a global variable, simply use Global instead of Dim, like this:

```
Global gstrCallingForm As String
```

Notice the naming convention: g for Global, str for String, then the variable name.

A global can be defined in any module; it doesn't matter which one. You can refer to it and set its value from anywhere in your application (that's why it's called Global). However, you will probably want to designate a module to store all your main reusable application code, which is where you can define your global variables. You may want to name this module basGlobal or something similar.

There's a problem with global variables, however. If your code is interrupted, after an error for example, the global variables are cleared out. There are two ways to reduce the impact of this little problem. The best way is to use the value in global variables for a very short time, like a few milliseconds. Globals can be used like parameters for objects that don't accept true parameters, such as forms. For example, the form *daisy-chaining logic* given in Appendix I, "Tips and Tricks," uses a single global variable to pass the name of the calling form to the called form, but the called form immediately remembers the name in a local module variable for safekeeping.

Another way to work around global variables' tendencies to forget their values is to create a wrapper function that first checks to see if the global variable has a value. If it does, it merely returns it, no problem. If it doesn't have a value (which will happen the first time the function is called, or if the value has been reset), the function then computes or retrieves the value, sets the global variable, and returns the value. This can be a good way to retrieve or compute values that take some time, like connection string properties or other application-wide values that are retrieved from tables. You get the speed of a global variable and the reliability of computing the values when necessary.

Evaluating Expressions in VBA

Expressions are one of the basic building blocks of any programming language. There are several ways to evaluate expressions in VBA so that you can control the flow of your procedural logic.

If .. Then

It seems like every programming language has some way of asking If, and VBA is no exception. The If .. Then structure is one of the most commonly used in VBA. Its usage is straightforward, but there are a couple of issues that warrant extra attention. First, the expression you are using needs to be formed correctly and completely. One common mistake is to use an expression like this:

```
If intOrderStatus = 1 Or 2 Then
    'some interesting code here
End If
```

The problem here is that a complete Boolean (true or false) expression needs to be on both sides of the Or. The literal way to interpret this expression is "if intOrderStatus = 1, or if "2" is True, then". Of course, this makes no sense. The value "2" is not "True". In fact, in Access VBA any value other than –1 is False, so the value 2 will always be false. So, this If statement has a big problem—the interesting code will run if the order status is 1, but it will never run if it is 2.

The correct way to write this line of code is

```
If intOrderStatus = 1 Or intOrderStatus = 2 Then
    'some interesting code here
End If
```

It's repetitive, but you have to tell VBA exactly what you want to do.

Instead of using multiple "Or" in SQL statements, you can use a much easier syntax: the In statement. In SQL, the equivalent to "Where OrderStatus = 1 or OrderStatus = 2" is merely "Where OrderStatus In (1,2)". That's so much easier to read and understand, and it only gets better the more values you have to compare.

Checking for Nulls

Another common area of confusion is checking for Null. This statement is not correct:

```
If varCustomerKey = Null Then
    'even more interesting code here
End If
```

An interesting fact about Null: It never equals anything. It is, by definition, unknown and undefined. A variable containing a null can't "equal" anything, including Null. In the above example, the interesting code will never run, no matter how null the customer key field is.

In order to check for a Null in a field, you must use the IsNull function, like this:

```
If IsNull(varCustomerKey) Then
    'even more interesting code here
End If
```

The IsNull function is the only way to look into a variable or recordset field and determine if there's a null in there. The "=" just can't do it. By the way, this is true in Access SQL too—you need to use IsNull to test for Nulls in the Where clauses of queries and recordsets.

Nulls and Empty Strings

Sometimes, you want to check to see if a field is either Null or contains an empty string (also known as a "zero-length string"). Empty strings can creep into your tables if you specify Yes to "Allow Zero Length" in the field definition during table design. If you want to be sure you are checking for either one, use a line of code like this:

```
If IsNull(BusinessName) or BusinessName = "" Then
```

What a hassle—you have to type the name of the field twice, and the line is confusing to read. There's a much easier way:

```
If BusinessName & "" = "" Then
```

This technique uses the concatenation behavior of the "&" operator to our favor. The & operator concatenates two strings together, even if one of them is null (see the section *String Handling Techniques* later in this chapter). In this case, it concatenates an empty string ("") onto the end of BusinessName. If BusinessName is null, the result will be an empty string. If BusinessName has any string value in it, it will remain unchanged by tacking on an empty string. This behavior allows us to quickly check if a field has either a null or an empty string.

Select Case

Another way to evaluate expressions and run code based on them is the often under-utilized Select Case structure. It allows you to test for multiple values of a variable in a clean, easy to understand structure, then run blocks of code depending on those values. Here's an example of a Select Case structure:

```
Select Case intOrderStatus
    Case 1, 2
        'fascinating code for status 1 or 2
    Case 3
        'riveting code for status 3
    Case Else
        'hmm, it's some other value, just handle it
End Select
```

Notice that there is no need for nested and indented If statements, and each Case block of code doesn't need a beginning or ending statement. Just to show the difference, the equivalent code using plain old If statements looks like this:

```
If intOrderStatus = 1 Or intOrderStatus = 2 Then
    'fascinating code for status 1 or 2
Else
    If intOrderStatus = 3 Then
        'riveting code for status 3
    Else
        'hmm, it's some other value, just handle it
    End If
Endif
```

This code is harder to read and understand. If you need to choose among multiple blocks of code depending on an expression's value, then Select Case is the preferred method.

Using Recordsets

Recordset operations are one of the cornerstones of Access VBA. They are a direct way to read, update, add, and delete records in Access tables and queries. We cover them in the following sections.

Opening Recordsets

Opening a recordset is easy, using either DAO or ADO (for more details about DAO and ADO refer to Chapters 6 and 7). To open a recordset, you first need a reference to the current database, usually named db, and a recordset object. This is accomplished this way

```
Dim db as Database
Set db = CurrentDB
Dim rec as DAO.Recordset
```

Now, you need to actually open the recordset. There are three basic ways to open a recordset: by table, by query, and by SQL statement. Here's the way to use a table directly:

```
Set rec = db.OpenRecordset("tblMyTableName")
```

If you have a query that already has some joined tables, selection criteria, or sort orders, you can use it to open the recordset instead of using a table.

```
Set rec = db.OpenRecordset("qryMyQueryName")
```

Finally, you can open a recordset using your own SQL statement instead of using a preexisting query. Access will evaluate and run the query string on the fly.

```
Set rec = db.OpenRecordset("Select * from tblMyTableName")
```

Now, you're probably thinking, "why is that last way any better than opening a table directly?" Your question is justified in this simple example. But using a recordset based on a SQL statement is much more flexible than using a table or query directly because you can modify the SQL statement in VBA code, for example like this:

```
Set rec = db.OpenRecordset("Select * from tblMyTable Where MyKey = " _
    & Me!MyKey)
```

Now we're seeing some flexibility. This example will open a recordset limited to only those records that match the MyKey field on the form that contains this code. You can use values from your open forms or other recordsets as selection criteria, set flexible sort fields, and so on.

Looping Through Recordsets

When your recordset opens, it automatically points to the first record. One of the most common uses for a recordset is to loop through the records, top to bottom, and perform some action for each one. The action could be sending an e-mail, copying child tables, or whatever you need to do. Following is some example code to loop through all of the records in tblBusiness:

```
Dim db As Database
Dim recBusiness As DAO.Recordset

    Set db = CurrentDb
```

```
        Set recBusiness = db.OpenRecordset("tblBusiness", dbOpenDynaset)

        Do While Not recBusiness.EOF

            'do some code here with each business

            recBusiness.MoveNext
        Loop
```

Notice that the EOF (End of File) property of the recordset object will become True when there are no more records in the recordset. It will begin with a True value if there are no records in the recordset at all.

Remember to include the .MoveNext method before the Loop statement. If you omit it, your code will drop into an infinite loop, repeatedly processing the first record, and not moving to the next one.

Don't use recordset looping and updating to simply update a group of records in a table. It is much more efficient to build an update query with the same selection criteria to modify the records as a group.

If you need to perform an action on some of the records in a recordset, try to limit the recordset using a Where clause when you open it. Avoid testing the records with If statements inside your loop to determine whether to perform the action. It is much more efficient to exclude them from the recordset to begin with, rather than ignoring certain records in your loop.

Adding Records

To add a record using a recordset, the recordset type needs to be capable of updates. In DAO, you need to specify dbOpenDynaset for the Type, like this:

```
    Set rec = db.OpenRecordset("tblMyTable", dbOpenDynaset)
    With rec
        .AddNew
        !MyField1 = "A"
        !MyField2 = "B"
        .Update
    End With
```

The .AddNew method of the recordset object instantiates the new record in the table, and if the table is in Access, also assigns a new AutoNumber key to the record if the table contains one. Don't forget the final .Update, because without it your record won't be added.

Finding Records

To find a record in a recordset, use the FindFirst method. This is really just a way to reposition the current record pointer (cursor) to the first record that meets some criteria you specify. The criteria is specified just like a Where clause in a SQL statement, except that you omit the word "Where." It looks like this:

```
    rec.FindFirst "CustomerKey = " & Me!CustomerKey
```

After you perform a `FindFirst`, you can check the `NoMatch` property of the recordset to determine whether you successfully found at least one matching record.

> Don't use the **Seek** method of a recordset. It doesn't offer any real advantages over the **FindFirst** method, and it won't work on a linked table.

Updating Records

The code for updating records in a recordset is almost the same as adding them, including the need to specify the dbOpenDynaset Type. You may also need to find the correct record to update using `FindFirst`. If you find it successfully, you can update it.

```
Set rec = db.OpenRecordset("tblMyTable", dbOpenDynaset)
With rec
    .FindFirst "CustomerKey = " & Me!CustomerKey
    If Not .NoMatch Then 'we found the record
        .Edit
        !CustomerName = "ABC Construction"
        !CustomerStatus = 1
        .Update
    End If
End With
```

The `With` statement is purely a programming convenience. Instead of typing the name of the object every single time, you can use `With <objectname>`. After that, and until you use `End With`, any references with no object name, just a dot (.) or bang (!), will be assumed to belong to the `With` object. You may want to improve the clarity of your code by not using it when you are trying to keep track of multiple recordsets, as in the next example.

Using Multiple Recordsets

You can easily keep track of multiple open recordsets at once. Each one needs to be defined with a `Dim` statement and opened using `OpenRecordset`, and they are kept completely separate by Access. Each recordset has its own current record pointer (often called a *cursor*), End of File (`EOF`), and Beginning of File (`BOF`) values, and so on.

This technique is necessary to perform the following trick: Copy a parent record and all of its child records into the same tables.

Copying Trees of Parent and Child Records

This is a task that can stump an Access programmer when trying to tackle it for the first time. The problem is as follows: There are two tables, tblPC and tblSpecification. Each (parent) PC has many (child) Specifications. Many PCs have almost identical Specifications, but with slight variations. You need to write some code to copy one PC to another, along with all of its Specifications. The user will then manually update the copied PC's Specifications.

At first, you might think that this seemingly simple problem can be performed using only queries. However, you soon run into a problem—you need to know the key of the newly copied PC so that you can assign the copied Specifications to it.

You can solve the problem by using multiple recordsets. Let's say that you have a continuous form showing a list of PCs and a Copy button at the bottom of the form. The desired functionality is to copy the PC record (with "Copy of" as a prefix of the new PC) and also copy over all of its Specification records to the new PC.

```
Dim db As Database
Dim recPC As DAO.Recordset
Dim recSpecFrom As DAO.Recordset
Dim recSpecTo As DAO.Recordset
Dim lngPCKey as Long

Set db = CurrentDb

If Not IsNull(Me.PCKey) Then

    Set recPC = db.OpenRecordset("tblPC", dbOpenDynaset)

    'copy the parent record and remember its key
    recPC.AddNew
    recPC!PCName = "Copy of " & Me!PCName
    recPC.Update
    recPC.Bookmark = recPC.LastModified
    lngPCKey = recPC!PCKey

    recPC.Close
    Set recPC = Nothing

    Set recSpecTo = db.OpenRecordset("tblSpecification", dbOpenDynaset)
    Set recSpecFrom = db.OpenRecordset("Select * From tblSpecification
Where PCKey = " & Me!PCKey)

    Do While Not recSpecFrom.EOF

        recSpecTo.AddNew
        recSpecTo!PCKey = lngPCKey 'set to the new parent key
        recSpecTo!SpecificationName = recSpecFrom!SpecificationName
        recSpecTo!SpecificationQty = recSpecFrom!SpecificationQty
        recSpecTo.Update

        recSpecFrom.MoveNext
    Loop

    recSpecTo.Close
    Set recSpecTo = Nothing
    recSpecFrom.Close
    Set recSpecFrom = Nothing

    Me.Requery
End If
```

```
Exit_Procedure:
    On Error Resume Next
    Set db = Nothing
    Exit Sub
Error_Handler:
    MsgBox "An error has occurred in this application. " _
    & "Please contact your technical support person and tell them this
information:" _
    & vbCrLf & vbCrLf & "Error Number " & Err.Number & ", " &
Err.Description, _
    Buttons:=vbCritical, title:="My Application"
    Resume Exit_Procedure
    Resume
```

This code has several key things to understand:

❑   The variable lngPCKey stores the key of the newly created copy of PC record. It's defined as a
    Long because our example assumes we are using AutoNumber keys, which are Long Integers.

❑   To find the record that was just created, you can use the LastModified property of the recordset.
    This returns a Bookmark to the record that was added, which you can use to find the new key.

❑   Setting the Bookmark property of a recordset positions it to that record.

❑   Use Me.Requery to requery the form's recordset so that the newly added record will be shown.

*If your backend database is Access (Jet), there's a simpler way to find the AutoNumber key of a newly
added record. Anywhere between the .AddNew and the .Update, the AutoNumber key field of the table
has already been set, so you can save it into a variable. Using this method, you don't need the Bookmark
or LastModified properties. However, use caution here: if your back-end database is SQL Server or
another ODBC database, the key won't be set after the .AddNew, and your code won't work. The
technique shown here works for both Jet and ODBC databases.*

> **Some developers are tempted to find the key with the highest value immediately after
> adding a record, thinking that this is a good way to find the new record. Don't do it!
> There are two problems with this approach. First, it will fail in a multiuser environ-
> ment if another user just happens to add a record before your code finds the "highest"
> value. Secondly, you shouldn't write code that depends on an AutoNumber key to have
> any certain value or sequence. If your database is ever switched over to random keys
> (which can happen if it is replicated), this technique will fail.**

Using Bookmarks and RecordsetClones

In the previous example, there's one annoying behavior. After the form is requeried, the record selector is
repositioned to the very top of the list. This is disconcerting and can make it difficult to find the record
that was just created.

It's easy to reposition the form to the new record—after all, we already know its key. Just after the
Me.Requery, we add some code to find the new record in the just-requeried recordset and reposition the
form to it.

To reposition the form, we use a `RecordsetClone`. This is a strange concept to developers when they first use it. Think of a `RecordsetClone` as a "twin" of the main recordset that the form is bound to. The nice thing about a `RecordsetClone` is that it has its own record cursor (with separate `FindFirst`, `EOF`, et cetera), but it uses the exact same set of records as the form. The way to synchronize the two "twin" recordsets is using a `Bookmark`, which is essentially a pointer to an exact record in both recordsets.

If you find a record using a form's `RecordsetClone`, you can use the `Bookmark` to instantly reposition the form to that record. Here's the same code, with the extra repositioning section.

```
Dim db As Database
Dim recPC As DAO.Recordset
Dim recSpecFrom As DAO.Recordset
Dim recSpecTo As DAO.Recordset
Dim lngPCKey as Long

Set db = CurrentDb

If Not IsNull(Me.PCKey) Then

    Set recPC = db.OpenRecordset("tblPC", dbOpenDynaset)

    'copy the parent record and remember its key
    recPC.AddNew
    recPC!PCName = "Copy of " & Me!PCName
    recPC.Update
    recPC.Bookmark = recPC.LastModified
    lngPCKey = recPC!PCKey

    recPC.Close
    Set recPC = Nothing

    Set recSpecTo = db.OpenRecordset("tblSpecification", dbOpenDynaset)
    Set recSpecFrom = db.OpenRecordset _
    ("Select * From tblSpecification Where PCKey = " & Me!PCKey)

    Do While Not recSpecFrom.EOF

        recSpecTo.AddNew
        recSpecTo!PCKey = lngPCKey 'set to the new parent key
        recSpecTo!SpecificationName = recSpecFrom!SpecificationName
        recSpecTo!SpecificationQty = recSpecFrom!SpecificationQty
        recSpecTo.Update

        recSpecFrom.MoveNext
    Loop

    recSpecTo.Close
    Set recSpecTo = Nothing
    recSpecFrom.Close
    Set recSpecFrom = Nothing

    Me.Requery
```

```
        'reposition form to new record
        Set recPC = Me.RecordsetClone
        recPC.FindFirst "PCKey = " & lngPCKey
        If Not recPC.EOF Then
            Me.Bookmark = recPC.Bookmark
        End If
        recPC.Close
        Set recPC = Nothing

    End If

Exit_Procedure:
    On Error Resume Next
    Set db = Nothing
    Exit Sub
Error_Handler:
    MsgBox "An error has occurred in this application. " _
        & "Please contact your technical support person and tell " _
        & "them this information:" _
        & vbCrLf & vbCrLf & "Error Number " & Err.Number & ", " _
        & Err.Description, _
        Buttons:=vbCritical, title:="My Application"
    Resume Exit_Procedure
    Resume
```

Notice that you can reuse the `recPC` recordset object for the repositioning logic, because we are finished using it from earlier in the code, and it has an appropriate name. Of course, we need to close it and set it to `Nothing` again when we are done.

Cleaning Up

Although Access VBA is supposed to automatically clean up local objects when a procedure ends, there is a history of errors and exceptions to this. So, programmers have learned that the safest practice is to clean up everything themselves. It's boring, but it shows an attention to detail that is missing in many novice applications. To clean up recordsets, make sure that you:

❑   Close the recordset using the `.Close` method.

❑   Release the recordset object by setting it to `Nothing`.

These two easy steps will prevent strange problems and, more importantly, help you gain the respect of your peers.

Using VBA in Forms and Reports

Much of the power and flexibility of applications built using Access comes from the VBA code that you can use behind your forms and reports. Although code-less forms and reports can provide a lot of good functionality, they really shine when VBA coding techniques are added.

Access Wizards provide a first look at VBA code behind forms and reports. However, Wizard-built code is just scratching the surface. Here are some guidelines and techniques that will help you build extra functionality into your Access applications.

All About "Me"

Me is a very special word in Access VBA. It is a reference to the form or report that your code running in. For example, if you have some code behind the form frmBusiness, then anytime you use Me in that code, you get a reference to the form object of frmB-usiness.

This is a beautiful thing because there are many times that you need a reference to your own form or report, like when you need to make it visible. You could refer to it directly, like this:

```
Forms!frmBusiness.Visible = True
```

Or, you can use the Me reference instead:

```
Me.Visible = True
```

Obviously, the Me reference is much shorter and easier to type. But there is a far greater reason to use Me. It allows you to move code from one form or report to another, where it automatically adapts to its new home.

The Me object is a full reference to a form object. Not only can you refer to it, but you can also pass it to other functions as a parameter. All you have to do is define a function with a parameter with a Form data type, and you can pass the Me reference to it. This technique is used in the Better Record Finder technique shown in Appendix I, "Tips and Tricks."

It's good that you can pass Me as a parameter, because it doesn't work outside a form or report's code. Remember, Me refers to the form or report that the Me references lives in, not the form or report that's currently active. So Me will not work in a stand-alone module.

Referring to Controls

A *control* is any object that is placed on a form or report, like a label, text box, combo box, image, checkbox, and so onet cetera. To refer to a control (for example, a bound textbox named BusinessName) from the code behind a form or report, you use

```
Me!BusinessName
```

So, if you want to clear out the BusinessName control, you use

```
Me!BusinessName = Null
```

There has long been confusion in the VBA world about when to use a "!" (bang) and when to use a "." (dot). There are more technical ways to describe it, but for the average VBA programmer there's a quick rule that works most of the time: If you (or any programmer) named it, you can use a bang. If Access named it, you use a dot. Now, before all the VBA experts reading this get upset, please realize that this is a general guideline only, but it does help.

Now that we've just said that, here's an exception. In the last few versions of Access, you can use either a bang or a dot when referring to controls on forms or reports, even though you named them. This is because of a little trick Access does: it turns all of your controls into properties of the form or report, so they can be referred to with dots. This has a handy benefit: Access uses Intellisense to prompt you with the possible properties and methods that are available for an object. So, in the above example with `Me!BusinessName`, if you type `Me` and then `<dot>`, Access will prompt you with every method and property for the object `Me`, which includes your control `BusinessName`.

Note that the little trick about using a dot instead of a bang for controls on forms and reports does not extend to fields in a recordset. You still need to refer to those using bang, like this: `recMyRecordset!BusinessName`.

Referring to Subforms and Subreports

One of the most common questions about referring to controls on forms and reports is how to refer to controls on a subform or subreport from code behind the *parent* form or report. The parent form or report is the form or report than contains the subform or subreport control. Let's say that you have a form named `frmBusiness` and on it you have a continuous subform named `fsubPayments`. Each Business record may have many Payments. You need to refer to a value of the calculated field `txtSumPaymentAmount` on the subform.

The correct way to refer to `txtSumPaymentAmount` is

```
Me!fsubPayments.Form!txtSumPaymentAmount
```

Let's break this down into pieces:

```
Me
```

This refers to the parent form where this code is running, which in our example is `frmBusiness`.

```
!fsubPayments
```

This refers to the control that contains the subform (it's name usually defaults to the name of the subform object itself, but some programmers rename it).

```
.Form
```

This is the tricky piece. You need to "drill down" into the form that's in the control, since that's where the controls in the subform live. The control on the main form named `fsubPayments` is just a container—it doesn't contain the control you're looking for. However, it does have this Form reference to use to get down into the subform itself.

```
!txtSumPaymentAmount
```

Finally, we have the control we want. You can even refer to controls that are on subforms on subforms (two levels down). Remember that you need to use the Form reference to "get into" the form that's in the subform control "container." Let's say `frmA` contains subform `fsubB`, which contains subform `fsubC`, which has control `txtC`. The full reference looks like this:

```
Me!fsubB.Form!fsubC.Form!txtC
```

You can also shift into reverse and refer to controls above a subform, using the Parent property. If, in the previous example, some code in fsubC (at the bottom) needed to refer to control txtA on frmA (at the top), it would look like this:

```
Me.Parent.Parent!txtA
```

Note that you don't need the "Form" reference here, because the Parent reference is already a Form reference.

Sizing Reports

Here's a quick tip about viewing reports. Most of the time you'll want your reports to run maximized inside the Access window, because that gives more room to see the report, and the preview mode automatically resizes the report and allows you to zoom in and out.

However, Access treats all of its child windows (both forms and reports) equally. They're all maximized or they're all restore-sized—there's no mixing allowed. The dilemma is that most developers want to run Access forms in Restore size, so they can control the look of the form and not have extra gray space on the edges of the form. This is especially a problem with modern high-resolution screens with all that extra screen real estate.

The way to solve this problem is to run your forms in Restore size mode, and only switch to Maximized size when you run a report. In the On Activate event of each report, add the following line:

```
DoCmd.Maximize
```

In the On Close event of each report, add the line:

```
DoCmd.Restore
```

When your report activates (which is the last event that runs before you actually see the report displayed), Access will maximize all open child windows. Even though this will maximize all your visible forms, it doesn't matter because your open report will hide them from view.

When your report closes, it restores all the Access child windows to their former size just before you see them, so when the report disappears your forms are waiting there as if they had never undergone the indignity of being maximized and restored while you were looking at your report.

Why not maximize the report during the On Open event? The reason is timing. During the On Open event, the report isn't yet visible, so your forms are still showing. If you maximize everything then, your user will see your forms expand into maximized size for a brief moment before your report obscures them. By waiting until the Activate event, you ensure that the report will mask the forms' maximized display.

Closing Forms

If you want to use a button to close a form in Access instead of clicking the X button, you need to write VBA code to close the form. The basic way to do this is by using the following code:

```
DoCmd.Close
```

This method of the DoCmd object will close the active object, like your form. It doesn't get much simpler than that. Unfortunately, there is an obscure situation that will cause this code to fail to close the correct form. If you read the help documentation on DoCmd.Close, you'll see that if you don't provide any parameters, it closes *the active form*. You might assume that the active form is the one containing this code; after all, you just clicked the Close button, so the form must be active. However, there are situations where another form is the active one.

One case is where you have a hidden form on a timer that periodically does something. This is a technique that is often used in automatic log-off functionality, where a hidden form uses a timer to periodically check a table to determine whether it should exit the application. The problem is, when that timer fires and the code in the form checks the table, it becomes the active form. If you're unlucky enough for that to happen right when the Close button is clicked, the wrong form (the hidden one) will close.

Another situation is when the code in your closing routine reaches out and runs code in another form; this can make the other form active at that moment. The solution is to clarify the DoCmd.Close statement, like this:

```
DoCmd.Close ObjectType:=acForm, ObjectName:=Me.Name
```

This specifies that a form be closed, specifically the form that this code belongs to. If you get into the habit of using this syntax, the intended form (this one) will always close correctly.

Debugging VBA

Programming in VBA isn't easy. No matter how skilled you are there are times when you need help figuring out what the code is actually doing. Fortunately, VBA provides a rich and powerful debugging environment. You can stop the code at various times and for various reasons, view values of variables (and even change them), and step through your code line-by-line until you understand what's going on.

Responding to Errors

The main reason you'll need to debug your code is because Access has displayed an error message. Hopefully you've put error handling in your code, which can make this activity easier. This topic is covered extensively in Chapter 9.

Let's say you've coded a cool copy routine like the one shown earlier in this chapter. However, when you try it, Access displays an error. If you don't have error handing, a message box will be displayed, as shown in Figure 8-2.

If you do have error handling, good job! Your error handling message box will be displayed, as shown in Figure 8-3.

When Access displays your handled error message box, your code execution is suspended. To get the opportunity to debug your code, press *Ctrl-Break* on your keyboard to interrupt code execution and display the dialog box shown in Figure 8-4.

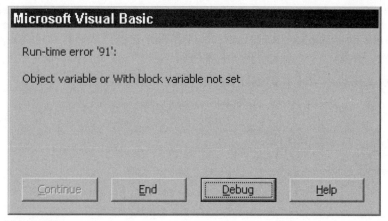

Figure 8-2

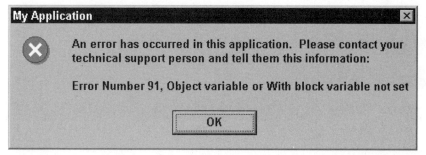

Figure 8-3

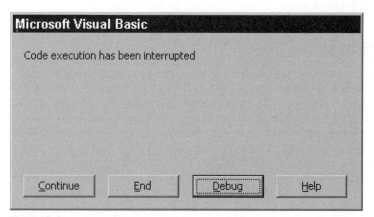

Figure 8-4

Whichever way you get there, you can finally click the Debug button. When you do, your code appears in the VBA code window. If you are not using error handling, the line of code that caused the error will be highlighted in yellow. If you are using error handling with an extra Resume statement as described in Chapter 9, you can reposition to the line that caused the error, as shown in Figure 8-5.

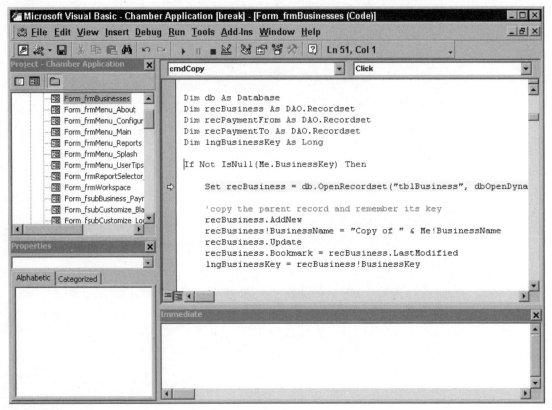

Figure 8-5

Investigating Variables

Now that you can see your code and the line that might be causing the problem, it's time to investigate. The error "Object variable or With block variable not set" is a clue, but it doesn't tell you exactly what the problem is. The first step is to check the current values of the variables near the line that caused the error. Remember, your code is suspended, so all your variables are intact and able to report their values.

The quickest and easiest way to determine the value of a variable is to hover your mouse pointer over the variable name in the code window when your code is suspended. However, if the variable is part of a longer phrase, hovering may not work. For example, the variable Me.BusinessKey is simple enough to be hoverable (see Figure 8-6).

Since BusinessKey has a reasonable value, it doesn't seem to be the problem. In order to check variables or objects that are part of a more complex statement, you need to highlight the portion you are interested

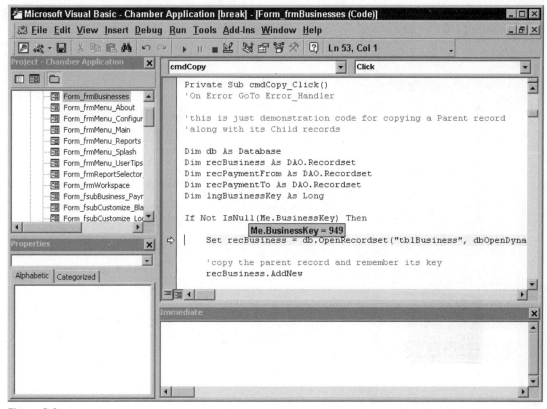

Figure 8-6

before you hover over it. In our example, just hovering over the object name "db" doesn't display anything, but after selecting it the hovering will give you a value, as shown in Figure 8-7.

By checking the value of db, you can see that it is currently set to Nothing. This is Access's way of telling you that the db object reference hasn't been set to any value yet. Sure enough, when you look at your code, you can see that although you defined db using the line Dim db as Database, you forgot to include the line Set db = CurrentDB. Adding this line before the OpenRecordset line will resolve the problem.

When Hovering Isn't Enough—Using the Immediate Window

There are times when having a variable's value pop up by hovering over it isn't sufficient. Perhaps the value doesn't fit in the pop-up, or maybe you need to copy the value to use it somewhere else. Or maybe you just want to look at it longer than the limited time the pop-up value displays. In these cases, you can use the Immediate Window (instead of hovering) to view variable values.

If the Immediate Window isn't already displayed, you can use *Ctrl-G* or select View..Immediate Window from the menu. Once you have it showing, you can ask Access to display the value of a variable using ?, like this:

```
?Me.BusinessKey
```

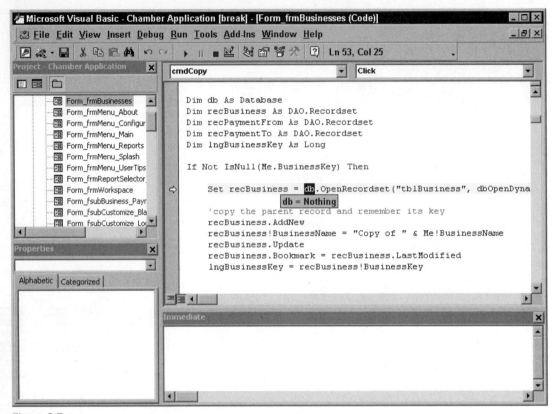

Figure 8-7

When you press *Enter*, Access will return the value:

```
?Me.BusinessKey
949
```

No matter how long this value is (it could be a very long string, for example) Access will display it here so that you can study it or even copy it into the clipboard to use somewhere else. This comes in very handy when the variable contains a long SQL string that you want to try out by pasting it into a new query.

Setting Breakpoints

Sometimes, your code doesn't actually produce an error, but it still doesn't work correctly. In these cases, you'll need to stop the code yourself using breakpoints.

The easiest way to set a breakpoint is to click the gray area to the left of a line of code where you would like the code to suspend execution. This will place a red dot to remind you where the breakpoint is set. Just before that line runs, your code will suspend and the code window will be displayed with that line highlighted in yellow, as shown in Figure 8-8.

At this point, you can investigate variable values as discussed previously in this chapter.

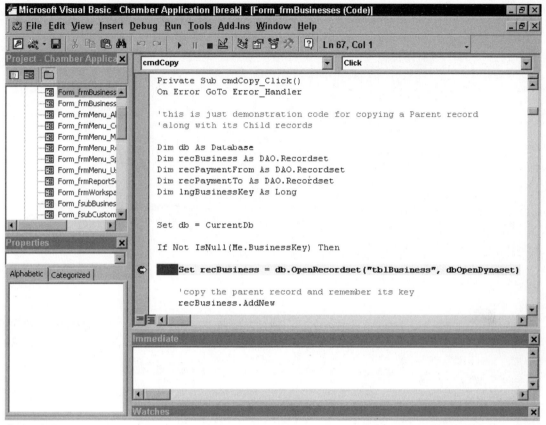

Figure 8-8

Setting Watch Values

Sometimes you have no clue where the problem lies, so you don't know where to set the breakpoint. However, you may want to suspend your code and investigate whenever a certain variable is set to a certain value. To do this you can use a watch value.

A watch value allows you to suspend execution of your code whenever a variable or object (or expression using a variable or object) changes or has a certain value. This is very powerful in complex code scenarios where you are having trouble finding where your logic is going wrong. You create watch values using the Add Watch window (see Figure 8-9), which you can request using Debug..Add Watch or by right-clicking in the Watches window.

Note that you can watch a single field, or you can type in an expression that uses multiple variables or values. Also, you can widen the context; it defaults to the procedure you are in, but you can widen it to include all procedures. Finally, you can choose to merely watch the expression, to break (suspend your code execution) when the expression becomes true (for example, BusinessKey = 949), or to break every time your expression changes. After you add your watch, it will appear in the Watches window, as shown in Figure 8-10.

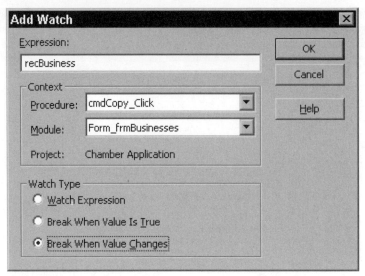

Figure 8-9

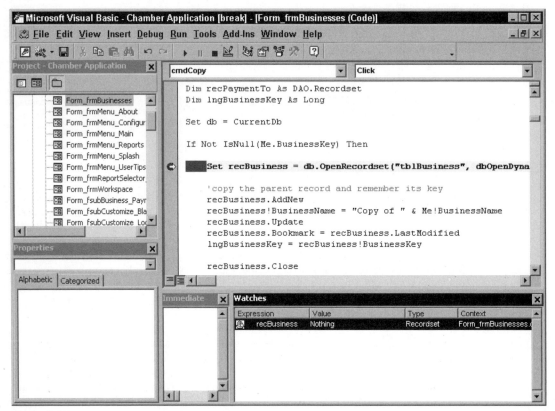

Figure 8-10

When the break condition you specified occurs, your code is displayed in the window. However, now you have an additional window, the `Watches` window. You can add more watch expressions here too, and if you specify an object to watch (like a form, report, recordset, et cetera), you can even drill down to all of its properties using the plus sign (+) next to the object name.

Stopping Runaway Code

We've all done it. We've created code that created an infinite loop. That's where your Access application just freezes, consuming all available computer power while it runs around the little race track that you accidentally created.

To stop your code in mid-execution use *Ctrl-Break* on your keyboard. This will suspend your code and drop you into the code window on whatever line that happens to be executing at that moment.

Stepping Through Your Code

Sometimes the only way to figure out a problem in your code is to actually run it line-by-line until you see where it goes wrong. You can use any of the methods above to stop your code, but there's nothing like getting your mind right into the logic by stepping through the code one line at a time.

The basic way to step through code is to use `Debug..Step Into` (*F8*). This debug command is the most common one to use because it's so basic. It runs the line of code that is highlighted, displays the next line that will be run, and awaits your next command. The `Step Into` (and other Step commands) is shown in Figure 8-11.

Sometimes the basic nature of `Step Into` is a problem. If the highlighted line of code is a call to another procedure (either a Function or a Sub), `Step Into` will do just that—it will dive into that procedure and highlight its first line.

Now, maybe this is just what you want. But if you are following good programming practices, like the coupling and cohesion guidelines earlier in this chapter, you have lots of small, fully tested functions that will be supremely boring and laborious to step through. After all, you know the error isn't in one of those, right?

The answer to this little problem is to use a cousin of `Step Into`, called `Step Over` (*Shift-F8*). This name isn't quite accurate, because when you use it the highlighted line of code isn't really stepped *over*, it's actually stepped *through*. The line of code that's highlighted will run, even if it is a call to one of your functions or subs, and then the next line will be highlighted. The entire function or sub will run without stopping, so you don't have to step through all that boring code.

Also note that `Step Over` works exactly the same as `Step Into` for a normal line of code (not a call to another procedure). This means that you can get into the habit of leaning on the *Shift* key when you use *F8*, and you'll never need to step through called procedures unless you want to.

What if you forget to use `Step Over` and use `Step Into` by accident? Hope is not lost. By using the often-forgotten `Step Out` (*Ctrl-Shift-F8*), you can run the remainder of the current procedure without stopping, and automatically stop on the very next line after your code returns to the calling procedure.

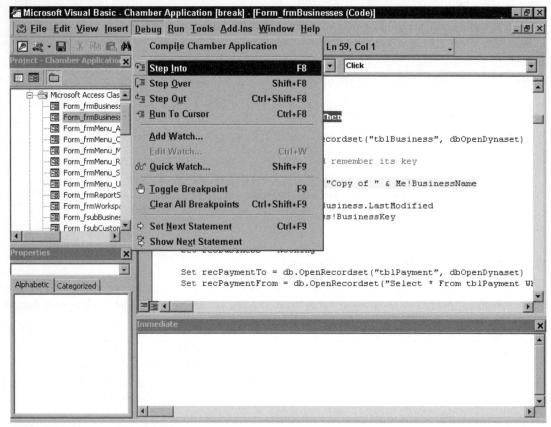

Figure 8-11

Common VBA Techniques

There are some VBA challenges that every Access developer will face at some point. There are simple and easy ways to handle drilling down to detail records, date math, rounding issues, and tricky string concatenation problems.

Drilling Down with Double-Click

It's a good design practice to use read-only continuous forms to display multiple records and then allow your user to drill down to the detail of a single selected record. This action should have a button at the bottom of the form (called `Detail`, for example) that opens the detail form for the currently selected record.

For convenience and to comply with Windows standards, it's also good to allow the user to drill down using double-click. Since you already have code behind the `Detail` button that opens the detail form, you can easily reuse that code.

```
Private Sub cmdDetail_Click()
On Error GoTo Error_Handler
    Dim stLinkCriteria As String
```

```
    If IsNull(Me!BusinessKey) Then
        EnableDisableControls
        GoTo Exit_Procedure
    End If

    gstrCallingForm = Me.Name
    stLinkCriteria = "[BusinessKey]=" & Me![BusinessKey]
    DoCmd.OpenForm FormName:="frmBusiness", _
        wherecondition:=stLinkCriteria
    Me.Visible = False

Exit_Procedure:
    On Error Resume Next
    Exit Sub
Error_Handler:
    MsgBox "An error has occurred in this application. " _
    & "Please contact your technical support person and tell " _
    & "them this information:" _
    & vbCrLf & vbCrLf & "Error Number " & Err.Number & ", " _
    & Err.Description, _
    Buttons:=vbCritical, title:="My Application"
    Resume Exit_Procedure
    Resume

End Sub
```

Since this code is already written and tested anyway, all you need to do is call it when the user double-clicks on a record. This is quite simple to do: all you need is to add a `Double-Click` event to each textbox on your detail form and add one line of code to each `Double-Click` Procedure.

```
Private Sub txtBusinessName_DblClick(Cancel As Integer)
On Error GoTo Error_Handler

    cmdDetail_Click

Exit_Procedure:
    On Error Resume Next
    Exit Sub
Error_Handler:
    MsgBox "An error has occurred in this application. " _
    & "Please contact your technical support person and tell " _
    & "them this information:" _
    & vbCrLf & vbCrLf & "Error Number " & Err.Number & ", " _
    & Err.Description, _
    Buttons:=vbCritical, title:="My Application"
    Resume Exit_Procedure
    Resume

End Sub
```

Here's a case where your actual code (1 line) is a lot shorter than all the error handling. But this line of code allows you to reuse the code you already have behind the `Detail` button.

> Just because Access creates and names an event procedure (**cmdDetail-Click** in this case) doesn't mean you can't use it yourself. Just call it by typing its name as a statement in VBA.

To support double-click all the way across your row, you need to add this same code to each field's Double-Click event. That way, whichever field your user double-clicks, they'll drill down to the detail record.

Now, there's only one more thing to add. Users will often double-click the Record Selector itself (the gray arrow to the left of the current record) when they want to drill down to the record's detail. Surprisingly, the event that fires in this case is not related to the detail section of the continuous form; instead, the Form's double-click event will fire. To support double-click the Record Selector, you can use this code behind the Form's On Double Click event:

```
Private Sub Form_DblClick(Cancel As Integer)
On Error GoTo Error_Handler

    cmdDetail_Click

Exit_Procedure:
    On Error Resume Next
    Exit Sub
Error_Handler:
    MsgBox "An error has occurred in this application. " _
    & "Please contact your technical support person and tell them this
information:" _
    & vbCrLf & vbCrLf & "Error Number " & Err.Number & ", " &
Err.Description, _
    Buttons:=vbCritical, title:="My Application"
    Resume Exit_Procedure
    Resume

End Sub
```

Date Handling

The way Access stores and manipulates dates can be a source of confusion to developers, especially those who remember the older database methods of storing days, months, and years in date fields. Access handles dates in an elegant, easy-to-use way.

How Access Stores Dates and Times

Access stores a particular date as the number of days that have elapsed since an arbitrary starting "zero date" (which happens to be December 30, 1899). You can prove this to yourself by typing the following in the Immediate Window (you can bring up the Immediate Window in Access using *Ctrl-G*).

```
?CLng(#12/31/1899#)
1
```

The `CLng` function converts an expression to a `Long Integer`. To this question, Access will answer with 1, meaning that 1 day elapsed since December 30, 1899. Of course, Access can handle dates before this date; they're stored as negative integers. If you want to see how many days have elapsed since that special zero date, try this:

```
?CLng(Date)
```

Access can perform date math very easily, because internally it doesn't store a date as days, months, and years. It just stores the number of days since the zero date and converts that value to an understandable date format only when the date needs to be displayed. But the date storage technique that Access uses goes even farther. Access can also store the time of day in the same date field. To do this, Access uses the decimal portion (the numbers after the decimal point) to store a fraction of a day. For example, 12 noon is stored as `.5` (half way through the day), and 6 A.M. is stored as `.25`. Again, you can see this for yourself by typing this into the `Immediate` Window:

```
?CDbl(Now)
```

Notice a couple of things about this example to see the internal date and time value. One is that you now need to use `CDbl` (Convert to Double Precision Number) so that you can see the decimal portion (the time portion) that is returned by the `Now` function. Also notice that each time you run this command, you'll see that the decimal portion changes, because time is elapsing.

> When you are storing the current date in a table, be sure to use the **Date** function. If you use **Now**, you'll also get a time component, which may cause incorrect results when you use dates in your query criteria. For example, if your query selects records where a date field is < = 4/28/2003, then any records with a date of 4/28/2003 should be returned. However, if they were stored with a decimal time component (by using **Now** instead of **Date**), they'll be fractionally greater than 4/28/2003 and won't be returned.

Simple Date Math

To add or subtract calendar time from a date field, use the `DateAdd` function. For example, to add 1 month to today's date, use

```
?dateadd("m",1,Date)
```

To subtract, use a negative number for the second parameter, `Number`. You can use different units of calendar time for the Interval parameter, like "d" for days, "ww" for weeks, "q" for quarters, and so on. Be careful when adding or subtracting years; you have to use "yyyy", not just "y". The Interval of "y" is Day of Year, which acts just like Day in the `DateAdd` function.

Date Math Example

Here's an example of date math that you can use. It computes the last day of a month by finding the first day of the next month, then subtracting 1 day.

```
Public Function LastDateofMonth(StartDate As Date)
On Error GoTo Error_Handler
    Dim dtNextMonth As Date
    Dim dtNewDate As Date
```

```
        'add a month to the start date
        dtNextMonth = DateAdd("m", 1, StartDate)

        'build a date
        dtNewDate = CDate((DatePart("m", dtNextMonth)) & _
            "/01/" & (DatePart("yyyy", dtNextMonth)))

        'subtract a day
        LastDateofMonth = dtNewDate - 1

Exit_Procedure:
    Exit Function
Error_Handler:
    MsgBox "An error has occurred in this application. " _
    & "Please contact your technical support person and tell " _
    & "them this information:" _
    & vbCrLf & vbCrLf & "Error Number " & Err.Number & ", " _
    & Err.Description, _
    Buttons:=vbCritical, title:="My Application"
    Resume Exit_Procedure
    Resume
End Function
```

Note the use of `Cdate`, which converts any expression that can be interpreted as a date into an actual date data type. You can use the `IsDate` to check whether an expression can be interpreted as a date. Also note how the `DatePart` function is used to break up a date into string components for Month, Year, and so on.

Handling Rounding Issues

Some of the more difficult to understand and debug errors in Access are rounding problems. These usually occur when adding up money values, but they can also happen in any math where a series of values is expected to add up correctly.

Rounding of Sums

One basic issue is not Access-related at all, but rather an issue whenever you add up a list of rounded numbers. For example, take a list of numbers that each represent one third of a dollar. If you add them up, you'll get 99 cents because the value of each portion (`.33333333...`) was truncated to .33.

```
 .33
 .33
 .33
 .99
```

A common place for this to show up is in a list of percentages that are supposed to sum to 100%. They often don't, because some precision was lost in the list. Then, you are faced with a decision—add up the actual numbers and show a total that's not 100, or just hard-code 100% so that it looks right. Most of the time you will want to use 100%, even though close observation will show that the numbers don't actually add up to 100. You may need to explain this kind of rounding error to your users.

Rounding Errors Caused by Floating Point Numbers

Another kind of rounding error comes from the way Access stores numbers in floating point fields. These fields cannot store certain numbers without losing some precision, so totals based on them may be slightly wrong. The best way to avoid these kind of rounding errors is to use the Currency data type for fields when they need to hold money values (as you might expect), or any numeric values that you want to use in calculations. The Currency data type is somewhat misnamed; it really can hold any decimal value.

> Access uses the word Currency for both a data type and a format. This is unfortunate, because they really are two different things. The Currency data type is a method of storing the numeric values in the table. The Currency format only affects the display of numeric data. The two can be used independently or together.

Access Rounding Functions

Access has a built-in function (Round) to round numbers, but it may not work the way you expect. Most people think that any decimal ending in 5 should round up to the next higher number. However, Access uses a form of scientific rounding that works like this:

❑ If the digit to be rounded is 0 through 4, round down to the lower number

❑ If the digit to be rounded is 6 through 9, round up to the higher number

❑ If the digit to be rounded is 5, round up if digit to the left is odd, and round down if the digit to the left is even.

This last rule is what surprises a lot of developers. Using this rule, Round gives the following results:

```
?round(1.5)
 2
?round(2.5)
 2
```

Yes, that's right. Both 1.5 and 2.5 round to 2 using the built-in Round function in Access VBA, because 1 is odd (round up) and 2 is even (round down). Here's another example:

```
?round(1.545,2)
 1.54
?round(1.555,2)
 1.56
```

Notice in this example that .545 rounds down, but .555 rounds up, for the same reason as described above. Since this can cause some trouble in business applications, developers have taken to writing their own rounding functions that behave the way business people expect. Here's an example of a function that rounds a trailing 5 upward to a specified number of decimal places:

```
Public Function RoundCurr(OriginalValue As Currency, Optional
NumberOfDecimals As Integer) As Currency
On Error GoTo Error_Handler
```

```
'returns a currency value rounded to the specified number of decimals of
the Original Value

    If IsMissing(NumberOfDecimals) Then
        NumberOfDecimals = 0
    End If

    RoundCurr = Int((OriginalValue * (10 ^ NumberOfDecimals)) + 0.5) _
    / (10 ^  NumberOfDecimals)

Exit_Procedure:
    Exit Function
Error_Handler:
    MsgBox Err.Number & ", " & Err.Description
    Resume Exit_Procedure
End Function
```

This function can be placed in any module in your application and used whenever you want the business-style rounding that most users expect. Note that if you don't specify the number of decimals you would like, the function will assume that you want none and will return a whole number.

String Concatenation Techniques

Sooner or later, you'll need to join (concatenate) two strings together. The operator for performing concatenation is "&". You may be tempted to say "and" when you see this symbol, but it really means "concatenate with." A classic example is joining First Name with Last Name, like this:

```
strFullName = FirstName & " " & LastName
```

This will result in the First Name and Last Name together in one string, like "Tom Smith."

The Difference Between & and +

There are times when you may need to concatenate something to a string, but only if the string actually has a value. For example, you may want to include the Middle Initial in a person's full name. If you write code like this

```
strFullName = FirstName & " " & MiddleInitial & " " & LastName
```

you will have a small problem. People with no middle name (it is null in the table) will have two spaces between their first and last names, like this:

```
Tom Smith
```

Fortunately, there is another concatenation operator: "+". The technical explanation of this operator is "concatenation with null propagation." That's a great phrase to impress your friends with at parties, but an easier explanation is that it concatenates two strings like the "&" operator, but *only if both strings have a value*. If either one is Null, the result of the whole concatenation operation is Null.

Using our FullName example, the goal is to have only one space separating First and Last names if there is no Middle Initial. Using +, we can tack on the extra space only if the Middle Name is not null:

```
MiddleName + " "
```

The whole thing looks like this:

```
strFullName = FirstName & " " & (MiddleInitial + " ") & LastName
```

Notice that you can use parentheses () to ensure that the operations happen in the correct order. In this case, the inner phrase (MiddleInitial + " ") will evaluate to the Middle Initial plus a space, or to null (if there is no middle initial). Then, the rest of the statement will be performed.

String Concatenation Example

Here is an example you can use in your code. It concatenates the city, state, postal code (ZIP code), and nation into one text field. This can be handy if you want to show a simulation of an address label on a form or report.

```
Function CityStZIPNat(City As Variant, State As Variant, ZIP As Variant,
Nation As Variant) As Variant
On Error GoTo Error_Handler

    CityStZIPNat = City & (", " + State) & (" " + ZIP) & _
    (IIf(Nation = "US" Or Nation = "CA", "", (" " + Nation)))

Exit_Procedure:
    Exit Function
Error_Handler:
    MsgBox Err.Number & ", " & Err.Description
    Resume Exit_Procedure
    Resume
End Function
```

You can try it out by calling it in the Immediate Window like this:

```
?CityStZIPNat("Seattle", "WA", "98011", "US")
Seattle, WA 98011
```

Notice that this code also tacks on the Nation at the end of the string, but only if it isn't US or CA (the ISO standard nation codes for USA and Canada, respectively). This allows you to use this function for both domestic and foreign addresses.

Summary

The only way to really learn how to execute VBA in your Access applications is to jump in there and try it. Using the techniques explained in this chapter—how to prevent problems with asynchronous execution, how class modules work, using recordsets and recordsetclones, debugging VBA, and more—you can tackle many of the common programming tasks that your users will need.

VBA Error Handling

When programmers use the term *error handling*, they really mean graceful or planned error handling. After all, Access will take some kind of action for any error that it encounters in your code. Graceful error handling includes the following:

❑   Quietly absorbing expected errors, so the user never sees them.

❑   For unexpected errors, displaying a "friendly" message to the user, and closing the procedure properly.

Error handling in Access VBA involves adding code to every procedure (both subs and functions) to take specific action when Access encounters an error. This is called handling or trapping the error.

Some developers call the encounter with an error *throwing* an error. Error handling is the code that *catches* the error and handles it properly, either by hiding it from the user or by explaining it to them.

In this chapter, we'll cover techniques to handle several types of expected and unexpected errors, so that your applications look and feel more professional to your users. But first, we'll address why you should use error handling at all. Since many Access developers see it as a mundane chore, we want to present good reasons for including error handling in every procedure you write.

Why Use Error Handling?

If you leave out error handling, Access will treat all errors equally, by displaying a nonfriendly error message and abruptly ending the procedure. Even worse, if you are using the runtime mode of Access, the entire application will close. This is not what you want users to experience.

Figure 9-1 shows an example of an error message that Access will display if you attempt to divide a number by zero in your application. Sure, technically it indicates what happened, but what is the user supposed to do about it? And what if they click the Debug button? They'll be looking at your code!

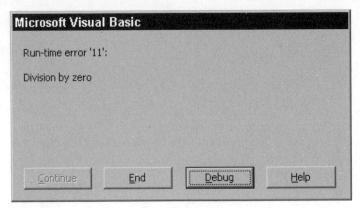

Figure 9-1

Also, when Access encounters an error, it abruptly ends the procedure. It does not run another line of code; it just terminates the function or sub that contains the error. So, it can often leave things hanging—open objects, open forms, the hourglass pointer, warnings turned off.

Amateur or Pro? When your code is being evaluated by another programmer, one of the easiest things for them to check is whether you have proper error handling. No matter how good your code is, without error handling you may look like a beginner. It's worth making sure that every procedure has error handling.

Now for the good news: Error handling isn't difficult. By using some easy techniques and code templates, you can make sure that your application never suffers an unhandled error. If you establish a standard way to handle errors, you can make it easy to implement in every procedure you write. It may not be fun or glamorous, but it will certainly make your application better.

Two Kinds of Errors: Unexpected and Expected

All errors that your Access application may encounter fall into one of two categories: *unexpected* errors and *expected* errors. In this section we'll describe these two categories and what your application should do when errors in each category occur.

Handling Unexpected Errors

Unexpected errors are errors that you have no way of predicting, and that under normal circumstances should not occur. When your application encounters an unexpected error (for example, divide by zero or a missing object), and no error handling is in effect, Access will display an error message like the one above, and then abruptly end the procedure.

The goal of error handling in this case is not to solve the problem the error is indicating; there's nothing you can do about it now. Your code has tripped on an error and fallen down.

The only thing you can do is let the user know what happened calmly and in plain language. Figure 9-2 is an example of what your error message might look like.

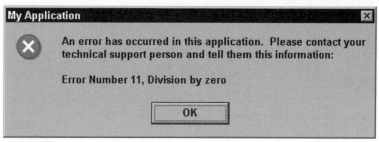

Figure 9-2

There are several differences between the error message Access shows and the "handled" error message you can show:

❑ The title of the message box can be specified by you instead of displaying "Microsoft Visual Basic" or "Microsoft Access."

❑ You can show an icon to have a stronger impact.

❑ You can add an explanation and text. You can even mention your phone number or other contact information.

❑ You can format the error message with blank lines, commas, and so on.

❑ Your user can't enter debug mode.

Absorbing Expected Errors

Some errors can be expected during normal operation. One error that you can safely predict will happen in your application is when the On Open event of a report is cancelled. This can happen when you display a form to prompt the user for selection criteria during the On Open event, and the user decides to cancel the report. This technique is described in Chapter 14.

There are other errors that you can expect. Maybe you expect a certain file to be on the hard drive, but it isn't. Maybe you expect a form to be open, but somehow it has been closed. These kinds of errors can be absorbed by your application if possible, never allowing the user to see them.

In these situations, your code should just ignore the error and keep going. To do this, you add an If statement to check if the error number matches the number you expect. If it matches, you can just Resume Next to continue to the next line of code. If it doesn't match, you can drop into your normal error handling.

Now we'll move into some basic error handling code that can be used for handling both expected and unexpected errors in your application.

Basic Error Handling

Let's start with the basics. Here is some code that you could add to every procedure to build in easy, no-frills error handling.

```
Public Function MyFunction
On Error GoTo Error_Handler

    'your function code goes here

Exit_Procedure:
    Exit Function

Error_Handler:
    MsgBox "An error has occurred in this application. " _
    & "Please contact your technical support person and " _
    & "tell them this information:" _
    & vbCrLf & vbCrLf & "Error Number " & Err.Number & ", " _
    & Err.Description, _
    Buttons:=vbCritical

    Resume Exit_Procedure
End Function
```

Here is an explanation of some important lines in the code.

```
On Error GoTo Error_Handler
```

The On Error GoTo statement in VBA tells the code to jump to a particular line in the procedure whenever an error is encountered. This statement sets up this directive, which remains true until it is replaced by another On Error statement or until the procedure ends. In this case, when any error is encountered, the code execution will jump to the line named Error_Handler.

> In the early days of Basic and other procedural languages, lines were numbered, not named. For example, your code might have a line GOTO 1100. In VBA, we still have the GoTo statement, but instead of numbering the lines, we can give them meaningful names like Exit_Procedure.

```
Exit_Procedure:
    Exit Function
```

If no error occurs throughout the main body of the procedure, the execution of the code will fall through to this point, where the Exit Function will run. As its name implies, the Exit Function statement exits this function immediately, and no lines below this one will be executed. Note that if this procedure is a sub instead of a function, you'll need to use Exit Sub instead.

This same Exit_Procedure line is also executed after any unexpected errors are handled.

```
Error_Handler:
    MsgBox "An error has occurred in this application. " _
    & "Please contact your technical support person and " _
    & "tell them this information:" _
    & vbCrLf & vbCrLf & "Error Number " & Err.Number & ", " _
    & Err.Description, _
    Buttons:=vbCritical
```

If an error does occur, execution jumps to the Error_Handler line, where a message box is displayed to the user.

```
Resume Exit_Procedure
```

When the user clicks OK (their only choice), the code execution is redirected back up to the `Exit_Procedure` line, which then exits the procedure as shown above.

With this technique, execution of the code will fall through to the `Exit_Procedure` code and the function will exit normally, as long as there are no errors encountered. However, if an error is encountered, the execution will be redirected to the error handling section.

> *In early versions of Access, the labels for the `Exit_Procedure` and `Error_Handler` sections had to be unique in the entire module. This forced programmers to use labels like `Exit_MyFunction` and `Error_MyFunction`. In recent versions of Access, these labels may be duplicated in different procedures. This is a great improvement, because now error handling code can be copied and pasted into each procedure with almost no modification.*

This is the most basic error handling you can include in your code. However, there's *one word* that you can add to make your code much easier to debug. Yes, it's just one word, but it can work wonders when you are trying to make your code work just right.

Basic Error Handling with a Twist

One of the problems with basic error handling is that when an error does occur, you have no easy way of knowing the exact line that caused the error. After all, your procedure may have dozens or hundreds of lines of code. When you see the error message, the execution of your code has already jumped to your error handler routine and displayed the message box; you may not be able to tell which line caused the problem. Many programmers rerun the code, using debug mode, to step through the code to try to find the offending line.

But there is a much easier way to find that error-producing line of code: Just add a `Resume` line after the `Resume Exit_Procedure`.

You're probably thinking: Why would I add an extra `Resume` right after another `Resume Exit_Procedure`? The extra `Resume` will never run! Well, you're right. It will never run *under normal circumstances*. But it will run if you ask it to. If your application encounters an error, you can override the next line that will run. In debug mode, you can just change the next line to be executed to your extra `Resume`. The `Resume Exit_Procedure` statement is skipped entirely. The following code is identical to the basic code shown previously, but with that one extra `Resume`.

```
Public Function MyFunction()
On Error GoTo Error_Handler

Dim varReturnVal As Variant

    'your function code goes here

Exit_Procedure:
    Exit Function        'or Exit Sub if this is a Sub

Error_Handler:
    MsgBox "An error has occurred in this application. " _
    & "Please contact your technical support person and tell them this
information:" _
```

```
            & vbCrLf & vbCrLf & "Error Number " & Err.Number & ", " _
            & Err.Description, _
            Buttons:=vbCritical, title:="My Application"

        Resume Exit_Procedure
        Resume

    End Function
```

Note the extra `Resume` just before the `End Function` statement.

Under normal operation, the extra `Resume` will never run, because the line before it transfers execution of the code elsewhere. The `Resume` only comes into play when you manually cause it to run. To do this, you can do something that is rarely done in debug mode: move the execution point in the code to a different statement.

Example of the Extra Resume

Here's how the extra `Resume` works. Let's say your code is supposed to open a report, but there's a problem: the report name you specified doesn't exist. Your code might look like this:

```
    Private Sub cmdPreview_Click()
    On Error GoTo Error_Handler

        If Me!lstReport.Column(3) & "" <> "" Then
            DoCmd.OpenReport ReportName:=Me!lstReport.Column(3),
    View:=acViewPreview
        End If

        'Update the Last Run Date of the report
        DoCmd.SetWarnings False
        DoCmd.RunSQL "UPDATE tsysReport " _
        & "SET tsysReport.DtLastRan = Date() " _
        & "WHERE tsysReport.RptKey = " & Me.lstReport
        DoCmd.SetWarnings True

    Exit_Procedure:
        On Error Resume Next
        DoCmd.SetWarnings True
        Exit Sub

    Error_Handler:
        MsgBox "An error has occurred in this application. " _
        & "Please contact your technical support person and " _
        & "tell them this information:" _
        & vbCrLf & vbCrLf & "Error Number " & Err.Number & ", " &
    Err.Description, _
        Buttons:=vbCritical, title:="My Application"
        Resume Exit_Procedure
        Resume
    End Sub
```

When you run your code, an error message appears, as shown in Figure 9-3.

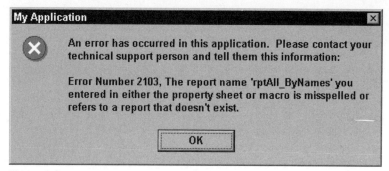

Figure 9-3

Instead of clicking OK like your user would do, press *Ctrl-Break* on your keyboard. You'll see a Visual Basic dialog box, as shown in Figure 9-4.

> This extra Resume technique won't work in an Access runtime application, because in runtime mode no design modes are allowed, including VBA code. It also won't work in an Access MDE, because all VBA source code is removed from an MDE application.

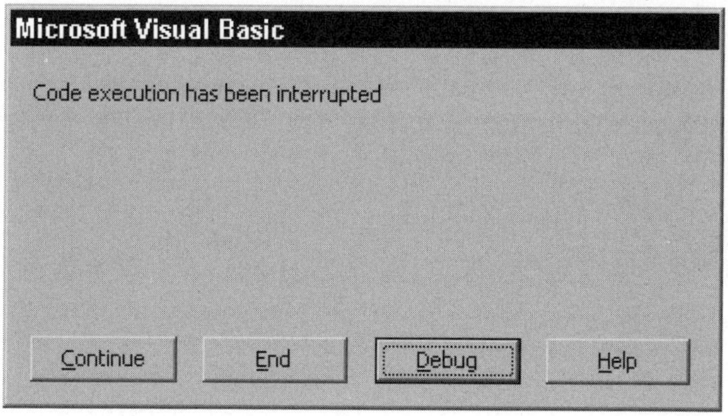

Microsoft Visual Basic

Code execution has been interrupted

| Continue | End | Debug | Help |

Figure 9-4

Now click the Debug button. Your code will display in the Code window, as shown in Figure 9-5.

The Resume Exit_Procedure statement will be highlighted in yellow. This is the statement that will execute next if you continue normally. But instead of letting it run, now you need to take control. Using your mouse, drag the yellow arrow down one line to the extra Resume line. By doing this, you are indicating that you want the Resume line to run next. Or, you can click or arrow down to the Resume line, and then use Debug..Set Next statement (*Ctrl-F9* on your keyboard). As usual in Access, there are several ways to do the same thing. Now, the yellow arrow will be pointed at the Resume statement, as shown in Figure 9-6.

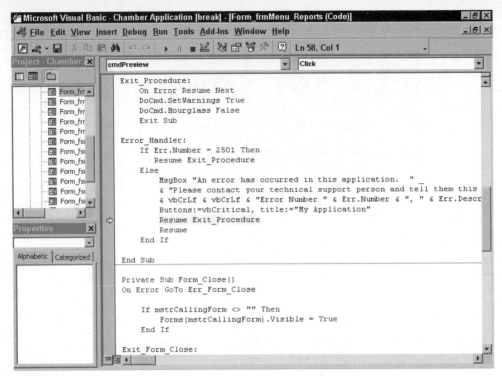

Figure 9-5

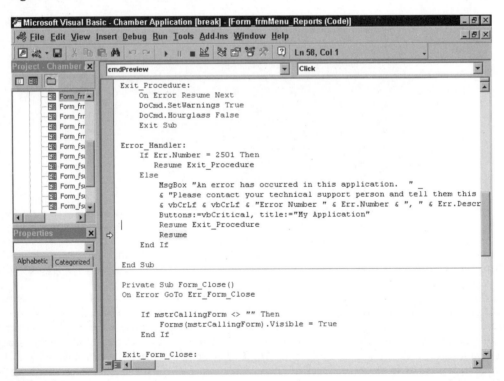

Figure 9-6

Now, you want the `Resume` statement to run, which will reposition to retry the statement that caused error. Press *F8* to run the next line of code (your `Resume`) and stop. Or, you can choose `Debug..Step Into` from the menu.

The exact line that caused the error will now be highlighted in yellow, as shown in Figure 9-7. That was easy, wasn't it?

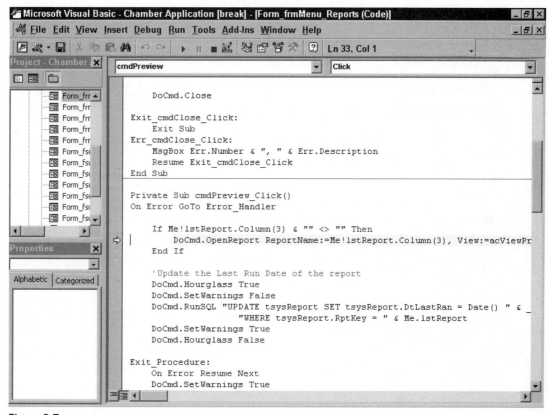

Figure 9-7

Now, admittedly, this is a very simple example. You probably could have figured out which line caused the error just by looking at the error description. However, when your procedures contain pages of code, often with coding loops, complex logic, and similar statements, this extra `Resume` technique comes in very handy. It can save you many hours of time while you are debugging your VBA code.

The extra `Resume` doesn't cause any harm in your code, so you can leave it in every procedure even when you deliver your application. Also, if a technically savvy client encounters an unexpected error, you can walk the client through this process to help determine what caused the problem in the client's environment. As you know, what works on your PC doesn't always work when your user is running it.

Cleaning Up After an Error

Errors often occur in the middle of a lengthy procedure, when all kinds of things are happening. Many settings or values persist after an error occurs, and it's up to you to make sure they are reset back to their appropriate values. For example, these situations may be true when an unexpected error occurs in your procedure:

❑   Objects are open

❑   The hourglass is on

❑   You have set the status bar text or a progress meter

❑   Warnings are off

❑   You are in a transaction that should be rolled back if an error occurs

Although your code may clean up all these settings under normal circumstances, a common mistake is to leave a mess when your code encounters an error. You don't want to leave a mess, do you?

Neglecting to clean up can cause problems, ranging in severity from annoying to serious. For example, if you don't turn the hourglass off, it will remain on while your user continues their work in Access. That's just annoying.

More seriously, if you don't turn DoCmd.SetWarnings back to True, any action queries (like an Update or Delete query) will modify or delete data without any warning. Obviously, that can cause some serious problems that neither you nor your user will appreciate.

> *Have you ever seen an Access application that won't close? Even when you click the "X" button, or run a DoCmd.Quit in your code, Access just minimizes instead of closing. This can be quite mysterious. Many reasons have been identified for this behavior, but one of them is related to cleaning up. Normally, Access will automatically close and release objects when they fall out of scope, typically when your procedure ends. However, some versions of Access have issues where this normal cleanup doesn't occur. Since Access won't close if it thinks that some of its objects are still needed, it just minimizes instead. To prevent this, make sure you close the objects you open, then set them equal to Nothing.*

The way to prevent these issues is to make sure your code cleans everything up even if it encounters an error. Even as it is failing and exiting the procedure, its last actions can save you some trouble. Here's an example:

```
Public Function MyFunction
On Error GoTo Error_Handler

Dim varReturnVal as Variant

    'your function code goes here

Exit_Procedure:
    Exit Function
```

```
Error_Handler:
    On Error Resume Next
    DoCmd.Hourglass False
    DoCmd.SetWarnings True
    varReturnVal = SysCmd(acSysCmdClearStatus)

    MsgBox "An error has occurred in this application. " _
    & "Please contact your technical support person and " _
    & "tell them this information:" _
    & vbCrLf & vbCrLf & "Error Number " & Err.Number & ", " _
    & Err.Description, _
    Buttons:=vbCritical, title:="My Application"

    Resume Exit_Procedure
    Resume

End Function
```

Note that the first line in the `Error_Handler` section is `On Error Resume Next`. This overrides the normal error handling and forces the code to continue even if an error is encountered.

Programmers have different styles and preferences when cleaning up after an error. For example, some programmers prefer to put all the cleanup code in the `Exit_Procedure` section, because they know that section will run whether the procedure ends normally or abnormally. Other programmers prefer to clean everything up as they go along in the main body of the code, then add additional cleanup code in the `Error_Handler` section. Either style is fine. The important thing to remember is that your procedure won't necessarily end normally. Look through your code to see what will happen if an error occurs, and make sure it is cleaned up.

One last point: Don't let your error handling trigger an infinite error loop. When your code is already in an error handling situation, or if it is just trying to finish the procedure, set your error trapping to `On Error Resume Next`. That way, your code will just continue, ignoring any errors that occur. If you don't add this statement, you might end up in an infinite loop where an error in your error handler triggers the error handler again... and so on.

More on Absorbing an Expected Error: Example

As stated earlier in this chapter, sometimes a normal activity in your application will result in Access encountering an error. For example, if the code behind a report cancels the `On Open` event, Access will display an error message. This is common when you display a form to gather selection criteria during the `On Open` event of a report. If the user clicks `Cancel` on the dialog box, the `Cancel` parameter is set to `True` and the `Open` event of the report is cancelled. This technique is described in Chapter 14.

Since this is a normal event, your user shouldn't see an error message. Your application should just continue as though nothing happened. The code in the `Open` event of the report will look something like this:

```
Private Sub Report_Open(Cancel As Integer)
On Error GoTo Error_Handler
```

```
        Me.Caption = "My Application"

        DoCmd.OpenForm FormName:="frmReportSelector_MemberList", _
        WindowMode:=acDialog

        'Cancel the report if "cancel" was selected on the dialog form.
        If Forms!frmReportSelector_MemberList!txtContinue = "no" Then
            Cancel = True
            GoTo Exit_Procedure
        End If

        Me.RecordSource = ReplaceWhereClause(Me.RecordSource,
    Forms!frmReportSelector_MemberList!txtWhereClause)

    Exit_Procedure:
        Exit Sub

    Error_Handler:
        MsgBox "An error has occurred in this application. " _
        & "Please contact your technical support person and " _
        & "tell them this information:" _
        & vbCrLf & vbCrLf & "Error Number " & Err.Number & ", " _
        & Err.Description, _
        Buttons:=vbCritical, title:="My Application"

        Resume Exit_Procedure
        Resume

    End Sub
```

An open selection criteria form is shown in Figure 9-8.

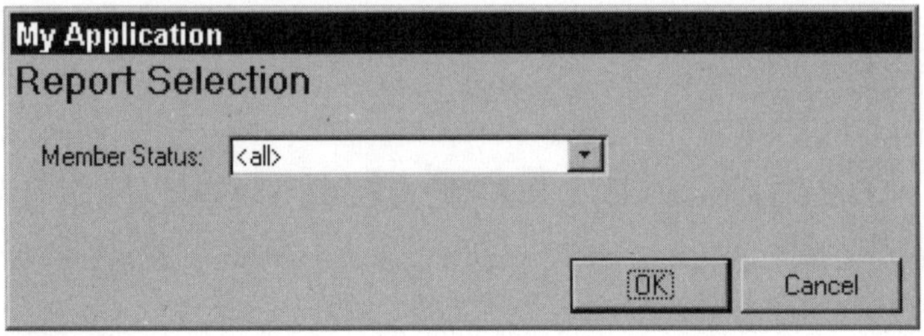

My Application
Report Selection

Member Status: `<all>`

OK   Cancel

Figure 9-8

If the user clicks OK, the form is hidden and the report's On Open code continues. It adds the selection criteria to the report's RecordSource property and displays the report. However, if the user clicks Cancel, the form sets a hidden Continue text box to "no" before it is hidden. If the report sees a "no" in this text box, it cancels itself by setting Cancel = True.

If you set the Cancel parameter to True in a report's On Open procedure, an error will be returned out to the calling code, and if it isn't handled you'll see an error, as shown in Figure 9-9.

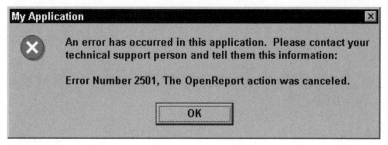

Figure 9-9

Now this is one ugly error message. For Access to continue without inflicting it on your poor user, you must check for this particular error (in this case, 2501) and absorb it by doing nothing but exiting the procedure. The following code shows how to absorb this error:

```
Private Sub cmdPreview_Click()
On Error GoTo Error_Handler

    If Me!lstReport.Column(3) & "" <> "" Then
        DoCmd.OpenReport ReportName:=Me!lstReport.Column(3), _
        View:=acViewPreview
    End If

    'Update the Last Run Date of the report
    DoCmd.Hourglass True
    DoCmd.SetWarnings False
    DoCmd.RunSQL _
    "UPDATE tsysReport SET tsysReport.DtLastRan = Date() " & _
    "WHERE tsysReport.RptKey = " & Me.lstReport
    DoCmd.SetWarnings True
    DoCmd.Hourglass False

Exit_Procedure:
    Exit Sub

Error_Handler:
    If Err.Number = 2501 Then
        Resume Exit_Procedure
    Else
        On Error Resume Next
        DoCmd.SetWarnings True
        DoCmd.Hourglass False
        MsgBox "An error has occurred in this application. " _
        & "Please contact your technical support person and " _
        & "tell them this information:" _
        & vbCrLf & vbCrLf & "Error Number " & Err.Number & ", " _
        & Err.Description, _
        Buttons:=vbCritical, title:="My Application"
        Resume Exit_Procedure
        Resume
    End If
End Sub
```

In the above code, you are telling Access that if error 2501 is encountered, it should be ignored. Access will not display an error message, and will instead exit the procedure immediately. However, if any errors other than 2501 occur, the code will continue through to the Else statement and use your normal error handling logic.

If you have several expected error codes that you want to quietly absorb, you can either add them to the If statement using Or, like this:

```
If Err.Number = 2501 Or Err.Number = 2450 Then
```

Or, if you want to take different actions for each error, you can use a Select Case statement, like this:

```
Select Case Err.Number
    Case 2501 'report was cancelled
        Resume Exit_Procedure
    Case 2450 'form is no longer loaded
        Resume Next
    Case Else
        ...normal error handling
End Select
```

In this example, when the report is cancelled (error 2501) Access will jump directly to Exit_Procedure, but if it encounters a form that is not loaded (error 2450), it will use Resume Next to ignore the error and continue with the next line of code.

While you are getting familiar with including error handling in every procedure, or if you aren't sure which error numbers need special handling, just include the basic error handling with the extra Resume. As specific expected errors pop up during your development and testing, you can add the code to handle and absorb them.

Error Handling with Logging

Some developers write code to insert an error log record into a table when an error occurs. The idea is to be able to analyze when and where errors have occurred by querying this table long after the errors happened. However, this technique has some issues.

❑   Access does not provide a way to determine the name of the procedure that is currently running. Since any error logging routine needs to know which procedure caused the error, you would need to manually code the name of the current procedure into each error routine. This is labor-intensive and prone to errors.

❑   The benefit of error logging is questionable, since few errors should be happening after your code has been tested and delivered. Errors should be rare enough that your users will let you know when they happen. You can always ask them to capture a screenshot if you want to see the details.

The bottom line is that we don't recommend spending the time to log unexpected errors to a table. This is one of those cases where the benefits usually don't outweigh the costs.

Error Handling That Sends E-mail

Another interesting way to track the errors that are occurring in an application is to add code to the error handling routines that "phone home" when an error occurs. Specifically, the application will build and send an e-mail to you (the developer) whenever an unexpected error occurs. This is usually done with the SendObject method, although there are other ways to utilize MAPI (mail application programming interface) directly.

This approach has the same problems listed in the previous section (*Error Handling with Logging*), and also has a few more:

❑　Your code needs to be able to send an e-mail using an installed e-mail client. There is always a possibility that there is no e-mail client installed, or it is not compatible with your e-mailing code.

❑　Some e-mail clients (for example, Microsoft Outlook) have code to protect against viruses using the e-mail program to propagate themselves to other computers. If an outside program (in this case, yours) tries to send an e-mail, a warning message will display alerting the user that a virus may be attempting to send e-mail. This isn't what you want your user to see when your application is running.

As with error handling with logging, this technique to automatically send e-mail when your application encounters an unexpected error is probably more trouble than it is worth.

Summary

Every procedure you write in Access VBA should have error handling. As we've shown in this chapter, to keep error handling simple and easy to implement, you can copy and paste the code shown previously in *Basic Error Handling with a Twist*. Then do a few quick steps if necessary to adapt the error handling to your procedure:

❑　Change Exit Function to Exit Sub if the procedure is a sub

❑　Add code to quietly absorb expected errors, if any

❑　Make sure you perform any necessary cleanup if an error occurs

By following these error handling guidelines, you'll build VBA code that is easier to debug and maintain, so you can focus on building great features into your application.

10

Using VBA to Enhance Forms

When most users hear that they need to utilize VBA to perform a task in Access, they typically think of programming. Unfortunately, this conjures images of grunts and trolls locked away in a dank basement chained to a mainframe terminal feverishly pounding the keyboard and laughing maniacally at hexadecimal displays. Fearing this, most users would rather allow their VCR to blink "12:00 A.M." rather than suffer the wrath of becoming a programmer. Although VBA technically *is* programming, it's really more about the ability to automate processes rather than inventing new operating systems or other complex algorithmic solutions. Most times, even Microsoft refers to it as Office Automation, hoping to tone down the fear of users. Although the stress here is automation, the developer will not be referred to as an automater—developer, programmer, or creator is still the norm.

So, now that your fears are subdued, turn your focus to the automation concept with this simple example. Suppose that a salesperson acquires a customer lead, and would like to send that lead an informational brochure. For the inexperienced Access user or developer, he or she may open the table (or worse, an Excel spreadsheet), enter the data, and close the table. Next the salesperson may create a query to extract that one entered lead, bind that query to a label report, and then print it. Then he or she opens a Word Document, types a cover letter to the lead, and prints that as well. From there, the salesperson gathers the label and the cover letter from the printer, applies the label to the shipping envelope, stuffs the cover letter and brochure into the envelope, and places it into the outgoing mailbox. It's almost exhausting just thinking about it.

If this were a real daily process for a salesperson, especially one paid on commission, he or she just may go hungry, as most of the day would be spent executing the process of business, rather than focusing on the objective of business.

Imagine now the automation of this simple operation. The user opens a data entry form and enters the new contact (or even an entire batch of contacts). Upon completion of the entry, the user can signal completion of the entry by clicking a button. The application then takes over—extracts the e-mail from each of the entered contact(s) and creates an e-mail with the electronic brochure attached.

This is the idea of VBA programming, especially with Form Automation. Utilizing simple snippets of code, the programmer can easily alleviate the user of mundane processes in a daily routine. When the user is doing work, and not working to do, then you know you have achieved the goal of automation. Now that you're in the proper mindset, becoming proficient with VBA is a less daunting task.

Although the focus of this chapter is the enhancement of forms, keep in mind that the concepts and techniques discussed will apply to reports as well. Although both are different objects, with completely different functionalities, the automation paradigm is the same.

Concept Review

Previous chapters introduced objects, methods, events, and properties. To recap the differences between these programming concepts, refer to the following table, as well as whenever necessary during the learning process. Understanding the differences between them will increase your ability to learn and understand VBA programming.

Concept	Definition	Examples
Object	An entity that can be manipulated with code	`Form, Report, Text box, Combo box, Command button, DoCmd, Debug`
Method	Any intrinsic (built-in) functionality already assigned to an object	`Form.Requery, Report..Print, TextBox.SetFocus, ComboBox.Dropdown, DoCmd.OpenForm, Debug.Print`
Event	An action associated to an object that executes when triggered by the user	`Form.Open, Report.NoData, TextBox.AfterUpdate, ComboBox.NotInList, CommandButton.Click`
Property	An attribute of an object that defines its characteristics (such as size, color, or screen location) or an aspect of its behavior (such as whether it is hidden)	`Form.BackColor, TextBox.ControlSource, ComboBox.RowSource, CommandButton.Picture, Report.Recordsource`

As you can see, VBA has a very robust object model for manipulating and enhancing the `Form` and `Report` objects, and also the controls placed upon them. When learning VBA, it is very helpful to determine what object functionality already exists, so that you do not attempt to write code to perform the same task. Acquiring this knowledge requires a little memorization, a lot of repetition, and the know-how of when to read the on-line help.

Armed with these tools, the remainder of this chapter covers the basics of properties, the `Me` object, navigation from an object event property to the corresponding event procedure, and finally some code examples for common user activities.

Properties

All forms have a set of properties that are specific to them, and each *control* (text box, command button, and so on) on the form has its own properties as well. There are many properties that share a common name between a form and the controls contained on it, but each object retains its own values. For example, a form and a text box both have a visible property, but the text box property may be set to `False`, while the form property is set to `True`. For review, the following table displays a list of example properties. A longer list can be found in Appendix E.

Object	Property	Description
Form	Caption	A string expression that appears in the title bar of the form
	Recordsource	A string expression that defines the source of data
	AllowEdits	Boolean value that specifies if the user can edit records on the form
Text box	ControlSource	A string expression identifying the name of the field in the Form's `Recordsource` that the text box should push/pull data.
	Visible	Boolean value that specifies if the control is visible to the user
	InputMask	A string expression that defines the way data is entered
	StatusBarText	A string expression displayed at the bottom of the Access window while the cursor is in the control
Combo box	RowSource	A string expression that defines the source of data
	LimitToList	Boolean value that restricts the user's selection to only values in the combo box
	Tab Index	Numerical value that specifies the order in which the cursor should travel from one field to the next

Event Properties

Event properties are the driving force behind the automation of a form. These properties are the reaction to a situation triggered by the user. Examples include clicking a command button, updating a text box, or entering a value that does not exist in a combo box. Anytime the user triggers one of these actions, the programmer must react appropriately to perform tasks such as opening another form (or report), sending an e-mail, and/or data validation. The possibilities of what can be performed are endless, but they all start with an event property.

The following table displays some of the frequently used event properties and what causes them to be executed. Some of these properties will be demonstrated in the code samples later in the chapter.

Property	Triggers when...
On Open	The form is opened (can be cancelled)
On Close	The form is closed
On Load	The form loads
On Unload	The form unloads (can be cancelled)
On Click	A section of the form or a control is clicked, once, by the mouse
On Dbl Click	A section of the form or a control is clicked, twice, by the mouse
On Current	A record is loaded into the form (think of it as 'On Current Record')
On Dirty	The user makes any modification to the current record
Before Update	Before the update is committed to the form or control (can be cancelled)
After Update	A form record or an individual control is updated
On Change	A value on a control is modified
On Timer	The TimerInterval property reaches a specified value
Not In List	The user enters a value that is not in a combo box
On Mouse Move	The mouse is moved over a section of the form or a control
On Enter	The user physically places cursor into the control. This can be accomplished with the *Tab* or *Enter* key, or by a click of the mouse

Just like the regular properties (that is, BackColor, Visible, or AllowEdits), Forms have their own set of event properties, and each control on that Form has its own as well. The items in the list above represent a cross section of event properties that exist for Forms and Controls. Not all controls have the same event properties as a Form, and depending on the type of control, it may have additional event properties to handle specific situations that only exist for that control. For example, a combo box (a control with which the user can select an existing value, or enter one not available) has a LimitToList property that restricts the user to only selecting a value that exists. If the user does not select or enter a valid value from this property, then the NotInList event property will trigger, and the programmer can add code to react to it.

Knowing *what* event properties are available and knowing *when* they will execute is the heart of VBA programming. Another tidbit to launch you forward is that some event properties can be cancelled, while others may not. Learning these three elements will take some time, but just knowing that they are there is a good start.

Associating Code to an Event Property

When you are ready to begin associating VBA code to an event property, you can start from either the Design View of the Form or the VBA Editor window itself. Both methods are useful, and when you utilize them will depend on your current location (form or editor) at the time that you need to start a new procedure.

From the `Form Design` window, click to highlight the desired control, then choose `View/Properties` from the main menu. (You can also press *F4* or just double-click the control to open the `Properties` window.) Once opened, click the tab called `Event`, open the combo box associated to the desired event property, and choose `[Event Procedure]`, as shown in Figure 10-1. Performing this step signifies to Access that you want to execute a VBA event procedure when the user triggers the event. Notice in Figure 10-1 that a macro can also be assigned to an event property. This is why there is a selection for event procedure. The reason it is in square brackets is that it will always be the first item in the combo box.

> *Note: To speed the selection of `[Event Procedure]`, when you enter the combo box of an event property, press the Left Square Bracket key "[," or just double-click the combo box. (Double-clicking a second time will select the next value in the list.)*

Figure 10-1

After the selection of `[Event Procedure]`, click the button that is just to the right of the combo box "opener." (The button has the Period of Ellipses [...] on it.) This action will cause the `VBA Editor` window to open. When the event procedure for the event property is opened for the first time, a new sub procedure is created for it. If a sub procedure already exists for the form or control event property, then that existing sub procedure is opened.

From the `Module` window itself, use the combo boxes at the top of the `Code` window to select the desired control, and then the subsequent event property. The combo box on the left has a value for the form, and all controls on the form. The combo box on the right has all of the possible event procedures based on the selection from the left combo box.

Figure 10-2 shows the `Control` and `Event Property` combo boxes, as well as a sample event procedure structure that is created for you. Notice that the procedure is a `Sub`, which means that it cannot return a value. It is also dimensioned as `Private`, which means that other modules in the database cannot see or utilize it. The last thing to notice in the picture is that the sub procedure has the `Cancel` parameter. The use of the `Cancel` parameter is described later in this chapter.

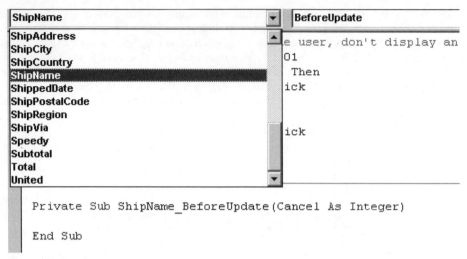

Figure 10-2

Using a naming convention comes in handy when viewing the Control combo box in the VBA Editor. All controls are listed alphabetically, so voluntarily adding a prefix to each control name will sort each control type together (that is, txt, cbo, cmd, and so on).

You Talking to Me?

Programmers are typically self-obsessed beings, so on your journey to learn about Form Automation, it is important to understand that "It's all about Me!" No, Me is not about You, Me *is* about the currently active Form. If you want to know anything about the Form, you can request information from the Me object. Using Me will expose all of the events, properties, and controls associated to it. To utilize Me in your code, enter Me. (dot or period) and then select the desired value from the IntelliSense combo box, which automatically appears. See Figure 10-3.

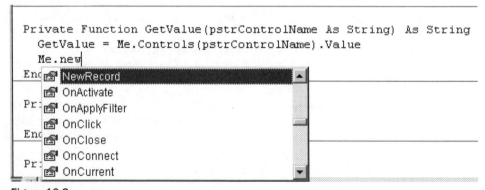

Figure 10-3

An example of using Me is if you want to know whether the user edited anything about the current record, you can inquire with the following:

```
If Me.Dirty then
```

Or, if you would like to change the caption of the current form, you could use the following command to change the `Caption` property:

```
Me.Caption = "Employees Form - Edited"
```

Finally, there may be times when you need to examine a value about a form but have no knowledge ahead of time what the "about" may be. There are many *collections* contained within the Me object that you can expose, even with very little information about the collection contents.

For example, suppose you need to reference the value of a certain control, but you don't know the name of the control before it happens. The ability to refer to that control in code using the specific name (that is, `txtFirstName`) will not work, so you may need a generic procedure, and need the flexibility to send it a variety of information like the following:

```
Private Sub DoSomething(pstrControlName As String)
   If Me.Controls(pstrControlName).Value > 50 then
      ...'Do something
   Else
      ...'Do something else
   End If
End Function
```

This type of programming begins to scare the faint of heart, but it demonstrates not only a practical use of the Me object, but also the power and flexibility that VBA possesses. In the above example, the Me object contains a collection called `Controls`, which is the same as referencing a control name directly. To this collection, a parameter can be passed in the shape of either a literal value (that is, `"txtFirstName"`, quotes required), a variable that contains the value (that is, `pstrControlName`), or an ordinal value (that is, zero (0) represents the first value in the collection).

The Me object is a very important and useful tool that can be used in any of the many event procedures that are written.

Event Property and Procedure Examples

The remainder of this chapter will apply all of the information covered in the previous sections to get you started on the automation of Access Forms. The examples are in no particular order and do not rely on each other for reader comprehension. In case an example is associated to another, it will be noted. This allows for the reading of only the property examples that are pertinent to you.

Form_Open(): Passing the OpenArgs Parameter

The `Form Open` event property triggers whenever a form is opened. Each form is only opened once, so this event should theoretically trigger only one time. ("Theoretically" is used here because there are cases when events should fire only once, but they end up firing more than once. Don't take this warning too seriously, but if you suddenly have trouble with a procedure, trace it and see if this is happening.)

In the `OpenForm` method of the `DoCmd` object, there is a parameter called `OpenArgs` that will allow you to pass a string to the called Form. There is no structure to the parameter value, other than it needs to be a string.

For example, the following will open the form called `Orders` and pass it the string value.

```
Docmd.OpenForm "Orders", OpenArgs:="CallingProc | MainMenu"
```

When the form opens, you can examine the `OpenArgs` property using the `Me` object. See the earlier section *You Talking to Me?* for more information. The following example will examine the `OpenArgs` property of the form, and react to it.

```
Private Sub Form_Open(Cancel As Integer)
  If Len( Me.OpenArgs) > 0 Then
    'Do Something
  Else
    Cancel = True
  End If
End Sub
```

In the previous code example, the application checks to see if a value was provided for the `OpenArgs` property. This is accomplished by checking the length of the value of the property. The `Len()` function will return the length of any string.

So, if the length of the `OpenArgs` property is more than 0, then a value has been supplied. If this is true then some processing will occur, otherwise the `Cancel` variable will be set to `True`.

Previously during the discussion on properties, it was mentioned that some event procedures could be cancelled. The `Open` event procedure is one of them. When the `Cancel` value is set to `True`, the event property will not complete the operation. In this example, the `Open` property will not complete, meaning that the Form will not finish opening. So, if the `OpenArgs` value is not provided, then the form will not open. This is a sneaky way of preventing users from opening a form on their own from the `Database` window.

OnTimer(): Performing an Action on an Interval

The `On Timer` property is an event that executes at a time specified by the Form's `TimerInterval` property. This is not a time like 5:34 P.M.; it is entered in milliseconds, which is 1/1000 of a second. So, if you want the `On Timer` property to execute every 3 seconds, then you would set the `TimerInterval` to 3000.

One practical use of the `On Timer` event property is to trigger code to notify users that they are to exit the application, perhaps for maintenance or an update. It is not uncommon to open a form, keep it hidden, and then execute `On Timer` to check a flag set by the administrator.

```
Private Sub Form_Timer()
  If DLookup("Kickout", "ztblAppInfo") = True Then
    MsgBox "The application must be closed", _
```

```
            vbInformation, "Administrative Request"
        ApplicationExit 'Custom Procedure to exit application
    End If
End Sub
```

The above example assumes that there is a table called `ztblAppInfo`, which has a Boolean field called `Kickout`. Using the `DLookup` function, the code will examine the `Kickout` field, and if it is true, it will display the message and exit the application.

OnClick(): Open a Form Based on Value on Current Form

The `On Click` event is triggered when you press the mouse button. The colloquial terms for mouse button actions are left click and right click, but the official Windows terminology is primary and secondary. The `On Click` event will only respond to the primary or the left click action. The same is true for the `On Dbl Click` event property as well. If you have selected to switch your mouse button, then these properties will trigger when the right mouse button is pressed.

As you can imagine, the `On Click` property is heavily used, as there is typically at least one command button on every form. Close the form, exit the application, print a report, or open another form are all common examples of `On Click` use.

For example, suppose that there are two forms, `frmCustomer` and `frmOrder`, which display information about customers and orders respectively. As you are browsing the customer information, perhaps you would like to quickly browse the order information, on `frmOrder`, that pertains only to the current customer. With the help of a command button, and some VBA code, this possibility is an easy reality.

The final pieces of information that complete this puzzle are the field names that correspond between the `frmCustomer` `CustomerID` and the `frmOrder` `CustomerID`. Typically, the table for each of these entities contains the field called `CustomerID`. Also, the name of the control that is bound to the `CustomerID` on `frmCustomer` is needed. So, assume that it is called `txtCustomerID`.

Put all of this together, and you can add the following type of code to any form to open another, where a dependency exists.

```
Private Sub cmdShowOrders_Click()
    If Not Me.NewRecord Then
        DoCmd.OpenForm "frmOrder", WhereCondition:="CustomerID=" & txtCustomerID
    End If
End Sub
```

The example above starts with the name of the command button. Following a standard naming convention, the prefix `cmd` signifies that this is a command button, and not a toggle button. Since the button will show the `Orders` form, the remainder of the name `ShowOrders` will make debugging and the maintenance of the code easy to recognize in the future. Finally, the event property is `On Click`.

The `NewRecord` property is a Boolean value that signifies if the user is on the New Record of the form. (In Access, all records are added on the New Record.) If the user is entering a new customer, then there should not be any existing orders, thus there is no need to open the `Orders` form.

The OpenForm method will open the form called frmOrder, and issue a Where clause to specify which records to display in the form. Some people call this a filter, others a query; either way, the records on the form will be restricted to only those that meets the criteria. In this case, the criteria specified will restrict the data to only those customer IDs that match the value in the text box called txtCustomerID. For clarification, the field name on the left of the "equals to" symbol (=) refers to the field on the opened object. The field name on the right refers to a field on the calling object.

To take this example one step further, suppose that each order has one invoice printed for it. When you are viewing the Order record, you can print the invoice for the order. The code is nearly identical, except that a Report is being opened.

```
Private Sub cmdShowInvoice_Click()
  If Not Me.NewRecord Then
    DoCmd.OpenReport "rptInvoice", WhereCondition:="OrderID=" & txtOrderID
  End If
End Sub
```

OnCurrent(): Opening Existing Records as "Read-Only"

The On Current event property triggers each and every time a record is accessed. Thus, adding a Procedure to this event will increase the load time for the user, so utilize this procedure with caution. If the user is accustomed to instantaneously browsing through multiple records, and you add a procedure that causes a noticeable delay, expect to receive a nasty e-mail.

For this example, suppose that you want to always start a record in a read-only state, and when the user is ready to edit the record, he or she must click a command button. The idea of this example is that you want to protect the user from accidentally making a change, or worse yet, an unauthorized deletion. This methodology could be implemented as a part of your security system, as only authorized users can see the Edit command button.

To do this, the On Current procedure can be used to set the form into the read-only state. A command button and its On Click procedure can be used to prepare the form to allow data modifications.

```
Private Sub Form_Current()
  'When user navigates to an existing record, disable the
  'ability to Add, Edit, and Delete.
  'For new records, enable all modification abilities.
  Dim fStatus As Boolean
  'Determine if user is on the NewRecord
  fStatus = Me.NewRecord
  'Set the modification abilities for the Form
  Me.AllowEdits = fStatus
  Me.AllowDeletions = fStatus
  cmdEdit.Enabled = Not fStatus
End Sub
```

This procedure would be associated to a Form's On Current event property. It would execute every time the user moves to a different record. The NewRecord property is examined to determine if the user is on the New Record. In Access all new records are added at the New Record. It can be accessed by clicking on the New Record button on the record navigation bar, or going one record past the last existing record.

The `NewRecord` property of the `Me` object returns a Boolean value that signifies if the user is currently on the New Record. If the user is on this record, then allow them to Add, Edit, or Delete the record. Otherwise, it would mean that they are on an existing record, so restrict their editing capabilities.

The `AllowEdits` and `AllowDeletions` are Form (`Me`) properties that specify whether or not the user can edit and delete records. Properties similar to these are `AllowAdditions` and `DataEntry`. The `AllowAdditions` property specifies if new records can be added. The `DataEntry` property sets the form into a mode in which the user can only enter new records or edit the records that they have just entered.

It stands to reason that for the completion of this example, there would need to be an Edit command button that would set the edit capabilities to allow edits to occur. (If you're not familiar with the On Click event, please review the sample code for it.) There isn't any logic needed for this event procedure, for a couple of reasons. First, if the user is on the New Record, then the Edit button is not enabled (or disabled). When the user clicks the Edit button, it is assumed that he or she only wants to do one thing, which is to gain the ability to edit the record.

```
Private Sub cmdEditRecord_Click()
  'When user clicks this button
  'Disable the Edit Button, Enable the Edit capabilities

  'Set the modification abilities for the Form
  Me.AllowEdits = True
  Me.AllowDeletions = True
  'It is not possible to disable the active control.
  'Doing so will result in an error. To avoid the error,
  'set the focus to any another control.
  txtFirstName.Setfocus
  cmdEdit.Enabled = False
End Sub
```

This example requires that a field called `txtFirstName` exist on the form. When the user clicks the button, the `AllowEdits` and `AllowDeletion` properties would be turned on, and after passing the control to the First Name field, the Edit button would be disabled.

BeforeUpdate(): Performing Data Validation

The `BeforeUpdate` property is triggered before a change or entry to a form or control is committed. This step allows for intervention between the time the user sets the value and when the value is actually saved.

In the following example, a sample of performing data validation is demonstrated. Data validation is the process of ensuring that the value entered by the user is logical and/or does not validate other business rule logic.

```
Private Sub txtEndDate_BeforeUpdate(Cancel As Integer)
  'Len returns the length of the values entered in the control
  'i.e. Len("Abcdef") = 6
  'If one of them is zero, then the product will be zero
  If Len(txtEndDate) * Len(txtStartDate) > 0 Then
    'Verify that the Start Date is before the End Date
```

```
    If txtEndDate > txtStartDate Then
        'Alert the user and Cancel the update
        Cancel = MsgBox("Start Date must be before the End Date", _
            vbInformation, "Data Validation Failure")
    End If
End If
```

This less than orthodox example starts with verification to ensure that both the Start Date and the End Date have been entered. (Unless you enforce the order in which fields are entered, the user may enter information in ways you've never imagined.) So, you would not want the error message to appear if the user had not entered the Start Date. Thus taking the length of both fields and multiplying them together will either result in 0 or a value greater than 0. When greater than 0, it means that both fields have a value.

It is assumed for this example that the format of the date entry is handled somewhere else. One method would be to use the InputMask. Assuming that if there is an entry, it will be a date, then all that remains to validate is whether or not the Start Date value is less than the End Date value.

Finally, if the validation fails, then the error message is displayed using the MsgBox function, and the Cancel parameter is set at the same time. The trick utilized here plays on the fact that the MsgBox function always returns a value greater than 0. In Access, 0 is the same as False, but any other value is considered to be True. So, combining the setting of the Cancel parameter and the execution of the MsgBox makes for clean, concise VBA code.

If the Cancel parameter does get set to True, then the BeforeUpdate event property is not finished, which prevents the save of the End Date.

AfterUpdate(): Synchronizing Two Combo Boxes

The AfterUpdate property is triggered after the form or control is updated. If you have not read about the BeforeUpdate property, it is important to know that the BeforeUpdate property must trigger and pass, then the record is saved (which may have issues due to constraints contained within the database itself), and only then can the AfterUpdate property trigger. But, after some values are updated, you may need to react to the newly saved value.

In this example, a common problem with combo boxes is addressed. There are times when you display the values in one combo box based on a value selected in another combo box.

```
Private Sub cboCategory_AfterUpdate()
    'Create a new rowsource for the Product Combo Box
    'after a category is selected
    'Verify that the user selected a category
    If Len(cboCategory) > 0 Then
        With cboProduct
            'Set the Product Rowsource to find
            'only products in the selected category
            .RowSource = _
                "SELECT ProductID, ProductName " & _
                "FROM Products WHERE CategoryID = " & cboCategory
            'Repopulate the Product Combo Box
```

```
        .Requery
        'Add Dazzle by displaying list for the user
        .SetFocus
        .Dropdown
      End With
    End If
  End Sub
```

The example above assumes that there are two combo boxes, `cboCategory` and `cboProduct`. `cboCategory` has a `rowsource` that uses the `Category` table (straight from the table or a query), and retains the `CategoryID` as the `BoundColumn`.

`cboProduct` can initially be based on the entire `Product` table, but after you select a value from `cboCategory`, then the `rowsource` for `cboProduct` is recreated. After `cboCategory` is updated, there is a check to ensure that a nonblank value is chosen (don't forget that updating a value from something to nothing is still an update), and then an SQL statement is created to extract only the records that contain a `CategoryID` that matches the `CategoryID` from `cboCategory`. (If you are not familiar with creating SQL statements, see Chapter 14 for more information.)

After the `rowsource` property of the dependent combo box is created and set, the work is not completed. You still need to instruct Access to repopulate the data, which is the job of the `Requery` method. If you omit this step, then the combo box will continue to display the same information as it did before.

Finally, for an extra touch of fun and excitement for the user, the dependent combo box is opened to display the new population of `Product` items. One thing to note is that the `DropDown` method can only be executed on the combo box that has the focus.

OnChange(): Late Bind a Subform on a Tab Control

The degradation of performance is a never-ending battle for the Access developer as users want more and more information, on the same form no less. But, no matter how accommodating you are to satiate their every need and desire, the smallest of performance hits causes your phone to ring and e-mail inbox to overflow with complaints. Even when you tell them ahead of time!

The reduction of Access performance sometimes sneaks up on you slowly, other times it's instantaneous. In case you're new, the instantaneous ones are a blessing, as you can quickly reverse whatever change you just made. The sneaky ones are typically a combination of a myriad of causes, of which you can spend several hours trying to revert, reprogram, or find a suitable workaround to restore the application to a usable performance level.

Now, with this kind of introduction, you might assume that this section is going to discuss some incredibly complex topics such as benchmarking, timing execution, or some other such fancy methodology. Unfortunately, that is the farthest thing from the truth. The objective of this particular example is to demonstrate how to work around a very typical performance drain.

In Access, with multiuser applications, it is not feasible to have data remain on each user's local machine, as the synchronization of the data would be very difficult. So, the next obvious step is to place a single database file (`.mdb`) on the network, and let all users share it. If you have ever done this, you have learned about the concept of corruption and know that it doesn't take long for users to begin complaining about the performance. The next step a developer can take is to split all of the user interface (UI) objects from the data into separate database files. Then each user can have a copy of the UI.mdb on his or her local machine, and only the data is shared. This action causes a significant increase in performance as form, query, and report definitions no longer need to pass from the network to each user machine. This reduction of network traffic is a significant factor in the increase. So, when all of these steps are taken, the only thing remaining to cause performance problems is the retrieval of data from the network.

When a form is fairly small, lightly populated with few controls, the ability for that form to load is fairly snappy. But as users ask for more, you find yourself adding a combo box here, a subform there, and the next thing you know, the form requires 30 seconds just to open. Of course your development machine has both databases on your local hard disk, so all of your tests don't net the same results. You might argue with the user about their sense of time, then physically walk to their machine, dramatically snap your arm to display your calculator wristwatch, and start your stopwatch as they try to open the form. You stare in horror as your regular load time is surpassed then abused, and you start looking for the nearest fire alarm to cause a distraction while you slip back to your office.

Don't let this be you.

It is not uncommon to create a tab control, and on each tab, place a different subform. In even the simplest of forms, the number of subforms can quickly increase. For example, customers can have multiple addresses, telephone numbers, e-mail addresses, contact journal entries, payment history, and of course the orders themselves. If a subform is made for each of these data points, you can imagine that the form is going to begin to get sluggish.

One final note to bring this point home is that maybe not every tab is used during every data entry session. There may be one set of users who only use one subset of the tabs, while another set of users uses a different subset. Also, in the example of surveys, there may be some tabs that are skipped if a question is answered a certain way.

For all of these reasons, never assume that all subforms need to be populated every time the form is opened. On the basis of this concept, it stands to reason that there is a way to prevent the data from being loaded to the subform. Being able to prevent it first requires you to understand how it works.

A subform control is just as generic of a control as a text box or combo box, but has no functionality until several properties are set. The following properties are necessary for a subform to load and display the data.

Property	Description
SourceObject	The name of the form to be displayed in the subform control
Link Child Field	The name of a field (or fields) on the subform that matches a field on the main form
Link Master Field	The name of a field (or fields) on the main form that matches a field on the subform

If the only way that you have created a subform on a main form is by using the Form Wizard, the Subform Control Wizard, or by dragging and dropping a form object from the Database window to the main form, then you may not have ever had the need to populate these properties. As you can see from the numerous techniques, Access does a very good job of insulating a user from having to deal with the minute details. This is good for development in speed and ease of use, but not so good when it is time to crawl under the hood and figure out what makes the motor run.

When a main form loads, and it encounters a subform, the SourceObject property is examined, and then *all* of the event procedures of that form (the subform) have to be executed. When it is finished, the main form returns to finish any remaining load tasks. Imagine having 10 subforms, each based on a complex query, and each with some code that needs to execute during the Load, Open, and/or Current event procedures. You can see that the ticks of the clock will quickly add up to a nasty e-mail from an unhappy user.

So, suppose there was a way to prevent the data from loading, and any of the event procedures from triggering, until such a time that the user absolutely needed to view that data. With each subform located on a separate tab, then the On Change event of the tab control itself could be used to implement an On Demand load system for the form.

Imagine the joy of the user when they go from 45 seconds of load time to only 5 seconds. (It has been done.) They'll think you're a genius. The remainder of this chapter will demonstrate how to implement a rather generic On Demand subform retrieval system that utilizes the concept of binding the subform when needed, and not automatically. This concept is also known as Late Binding, and can also be applied to combo boxes, list boxes, OLE bound object frames, charts, and any other object that requires data retrieval or has code associated to it.

The following sub procedure is a generic routine that binds a subform to the main form and then resets the LinkChildField property.

```
Sub BindSubform( _
   psfrm As SubForm, _
   pstrSourceObject As String, _
   pstrLinkChildField As String)
   'Generically Bind a Subform to a Main Form
   'Example Proc Call: BindSubform(sfrmTest, "frmSome_Test", "TestID")
   With psfrm
      'Only Bind if not previously bound
      If Len(.SourceObject) = 0 Then
         'Specify the name of the subform
         .SourceObject = pstrSourceObject
         'Set the Link Child Field
         .LinkChildFields = pstrLinkChildField
      End If
   End With
End Sub
```

It's important to note that for this workaround (to save load time) to be successful, all of the subforms that are placed on the main form must not have a value entered for the SourceObject properties. (During development, this is not needed, but just before deployment, be sure to remove the entries.) By not having the subforms connected, there is no load time incurred against their existence. A caveat to this is that you may have one or two subforms on the first tab that the user absolutely insists on displaying the first tab. If that is the case, then populate it or them via the normal method.

In the code sample above, there is a check to see if the SourceObject has been populated. If not, then it gets populated, which will cause the loading of the subform data to be executed. This generic procedure can be called any number of times from within the forms, and saves the repetition of the same code being written for every subform that needs to be bound.

The code to handle the call to the BindSubform procedure, when the user changes the Tab on the Tab control, is in the next example.

```
Private Sub tabProj_Change()
  'This procedure handles any needs of the user after
  'they select a different tab on a tab control
  'Using the control name of each tab, determine what needs to
  'happen on that tab.
  Select Case tabProj.Pages(tabProj.Value).Name
    Case "pgStates"
      'Perform data validation that prevents loading this tab
      'until all data entry is correct on Tab1
      If IsValidate_Tab1 Then
        'Bind the States subform
        BindSubform sfrmStates, "frmProject_States", "ProjectID"
      End If
  Case "pgLocations"
    'Bind Locations
    BindSubform sfrmLocation, _
      "frmProject_Locations", "ProjectStateID"
    Case Else
      'Performing any special processing for other tabs
      '...
    End Select
End Sub
```

This example starts with the declaration of the On Change event procedure for a tab control that is named tabProj. The prefix tab specifies that the control is a tab control. A Select...Case...End Select structure is used, because there may be many subforms on the main form, so an If...Then...Else...End If structure would become quite convoluted.

The Select structure examines the Pages collection of the tab control. tabProj.Value is the number value found in the PageIndex property of the tab. By using that number as the index for the Pages collection, it is the same as referring directly to the tab itself. From there, the inspection of the Name property returns the tab's assigned control name.

What is gained by taking this route is the ability to refer to the assigned tab name, instead of a number, which adds to the readability and debug-ability of the code. For starters, the PageIndex value starts at 0, which can be easily forgotten, or overlooked, and cause a problem. Next, the PageIndex of a tab can change, as it specifies the order of the tabs, but the Name stays the same. So, if you base your code on the name and then if you decide to move the order of the tabs, your code does not need to be changed to retain the same functionality.

The call to the BindSubform procedure requires some manual intervention in that you need to know the exact names of the subform control, the source object form that is to be bound, and the LinkChildField to be used.

This example is very long, and probably difficult for even intermediate developers to understand completely. But, hopefully the knowledge that there is this kind of control over a seemingly uncontrollable situation may change your outlook of Access and VBA programming. Knowing that you are in control may make other programming challenges easier for you to master.

NotInList(): Adding a Value to a Combo Box at Runtime

The NotInList event property is triggered when you enter a value into a combo box that is not contained within the list. This event property and procedure works in conjunction with the LimitToList property, which is a Boolean property of a combo box that instructs Access to restrict selections to values in the list.

This example comes from the need to add a new value to the underlying table used to populate a combo box list. Because a combo box was designed to display values from a table, it means that the value must already be in the table in order to be displayed.

In some combo boxes, it may be important to restrict the data to a finite list; for example, hotel room numbers. You would not want to allow a customer to be assigned to a room number that doesn't physically exist. If the hotel were to build another wing, then the new room numbers would be added by the administrator, for the use of the desk clerk.

On the other hand, there may be situations where it is not feasible or cost-effective to stop data entry and request that the Admin enter a new value. Instead, the combo box is used to increase data entry speed, but only to limit excessive similar entries from being added. For example, job titles are sometimes very common, but other times outrageously unique. Receptionist, Administrative Assistant, and Project Manager are all standard values that are repeatable values, but Senior Herbal Fragrance Arranger may be a less common choice.

You would not like to restrict the user from being able to enter the unique titles, but on the other hand, you would like to try to prevent a myriad of permutations of similar values from being entered. For example, Admin Asst, Administrative Asst, and Admin Assistant all convey the same information. So, given these constraints, you should not lock down the list, but you can at least try to prevent the endless variety of entries, by presenting the user with those common values, so that they can quickly choose one and move to the next field, without a second thought.

This is the premise of the example, and the following code provides a method to perform this type of action. There are two functions supplied in the excerpt: AddItem_Prompt and AddItem_ToTable. The prompting routine is only called once from the data addition procedure, but supposing that there are other procedures that called the prompt routine would be reason enough to separate it.

```
Private Function AddItem_Prompt( _
   pstrItemType As String, pstrNewData As String) As Boolean
   'Prompt the user to add a new value to the combo box
   'strItemType - Type of Item to be added(Customer, Category, Product)
   'varNewData - NewData from Combo Box
   Dim strMsg As String
   'Create a custom prompt for the type of data to be collected
   strMsg = "'" & pstrNewData & "' is not in the list." & _
      vbNewLine & vbNewLine & _
      "Would you like to add it?"
```

```
      'Show the prompt, and get response
      If vbYes = MsgBox(strMsg, vbYesNo + vbQuestion, _
        "Unknown " & pstrItemType) Then
        AddItem_Prompt = True
      End If
   End Function

   Public Function AddItem_ToTable( _
      pstrNewData As String, pstrTable As String, _
      ParamArray pastrFields()) As Integer
      'This routine will prompt the user to add data when an
      'unknown value is entered into a Combo Box
      'ENTRY:
      '    strItem      = Unknown data entered by user
      '    strTable     = Lookup Table
      '    strFields(0) = Prompt for Input Box
      '    strFields(1) = Field Name in table
      'Call Example 1: Add 'FMS, Inc.' to Company Table
      'AddItem("FMS, Inc.", "tblCompany", "Company Name", "CoName")
      'Example 2: Add 'IS' & "Information Systems" to Department Table
      'AddItem("IS", "tblDepartment", "Department Code", _
        "DeptCode", "Department Name", "DeptName")
      'Example 3: Add 'Clark' & User entered First Name and Middle Initial
                  to Customer Table
      'AddItem("Clark", "tblCustomer", _
        "Last Name", "LName", _
        "First Name","Fname", _
        "Middle Initial", "MI")
      Dim strMsg As String
      Dim i As Integer
      Dim varVal As Variant
      Dim rs As New ADODB.Recordset
      'Begin by setting the default response to be to show the
      'standard error message
      AddItem_ToTable = acDataErrDisplay
      'Prompt the user to add the new value
      If AddItem_Prompt(CStr(pastrFields(0)), pstrNewData) Then
         'Store the number of parameters passed in procedure call
         intMax = UBound(pastrFields(), 1) + 1
         'Create a recordset based on the tablename provided
         'in the procedure call
         If OpenADORecordset(rs, pstrTable, _
           adLockOptimistic, , adCmdTable) Then
           With rs
             'Start an new record
             .AddNew
             'Write the data to the specified field
             .Fields(pastrFields(1)) = pstrNewData
             i = 2
             'Repeat this process for each parameter passed
             Do While i < intMax
                'Prompt the user for any additional information
                varVal = _
                  InputBox("Enter " & pastrFields(i), "Add Item to List")
```

```
            'Store the additional information
            .Fields(pastrFields(i + 1)) = varVal
            i = i + 2
        Loop
        'Save the new record
        .Update
    End With
    AddItem_ToTable = acDataErrAdded
    End If
  End If
End Function
```

The explanation of this example starts with the return values that are assigned to the `AddItem_ToTable` procedure. Although it is declared as an integer, it is really an intrinsic constant value that is native to Access.

An intrinsic constant is simply a variable that is supplied natively with Access and assigned a permanent value. It is something that is easier to remember than a number like 1, 64, or 256. The following table lists the possibilities for the value.

Intrinsic Constant Name	Description
AcDataErrContinue	Suppresses the standard error message
AcDataErrAdded	Suppresses the standard error message, and refreshes the entries in the combo box
AcDataErrDisplay	Displays the standard error message

Looking through the code, you will notice that only two of the intrinsic constants are used. The third, `AcDataErrContinue`, is not used. When the custom routine above finishes, either the error message will show, or the data will be added, and the data is refreshed. Now that you understand what these values mean, you need to know where the value is applied. To understand that, refer to the following code:

```
Private Sub cboTitle_NotInList(NewData As String, Response As Integer)
    Response = AddItem_ToTable(NewData, "tblTitle", _
        "Title", "Title")
End Sub
```

The code above is the declaration of the `NotInList` event procedure for a combo box. It is important to examine the two parameters that are exposed to the developer. The two values are `NewData` and `Response`.

NewData

Remember that the object of this event procedure is to execute code when the value entered is not in the list. With this in mind, it makes sense that the `NewData` parameter is that unknown value. It is exposed to the developer for your convenience. Strangely enough, you can write to this parameter, but doing so will lose the unknown value.

Response

On the other hand, the Response parameter, which was covered in the table above, is used to instruct Access what action to take when the procedure terminates. In the code, you can see that the Response parameter is set to the value returned by the AddItem_ToTable function. If you review the code to this function, you will see that initially, the function is set to acDataErrDisplay. At the end of the function, when the function is successful, meaning that the unknown value was added to the data table, the parameter is set to acDataErrAdded.

ParamArray

Continuing with the exploration of the AddItem_ToTable function, notice that there is a procedure parameter that starts with the reserved word ParamArray. The ParamArray is an *Array* (a data storage mechanism in memory) that can accept any number of parameters. The Array is always set to the Variant datatype, and it is unlimited as to the number of values that it can receive. So, much like the OpenArgs parameter of the form, this is a way to pass anything you could possibly think of or ever need.

In the case of this particular procedure, the ParamArray is used to assist in the capture of even more data than just the one value that was entered in the combo box. Implementing this gives the ability to enter a second, third, or *n*th piece of information pertaining to the new data value. For example, suppose a new department code is added, you code-prompt the user for the new department name as well. If you capture only the code, then it would require for someone to return to the Department Table (or a form that displays the table's data) to update the Department Name. So, it is a luxury to this process, but quite useful. You should refrain from prompting for too many values, as the user really does want to finish the work at hand, not answer prompts all afternoon. After two prompts, it may be a better idea to require the opening of an entire data entry form to capture the information.

Included in the code is a call to a custom procedure called OpenADORecordset. This is a function that takes care of setting a connection string, issuing the appropriate lock, and then populating the recordset that is passed to it. Your code may not compile due to this procedure, so feel free to either replace it or create your own to fulfill the need.

The rest of the procedure is spent stepping through each of the parameter values, prompting for needed values, entering the value into the table in the accompanying field name, and then returning either a success or failure value to the calling procedure.

On Close(): Save a Setting to the Registry

In case you are unfamiliar with Windows, there is a very important database called the registry. In Windows 3.1, the registration database stored OLE registration information and file associations, while program settings were stored in initialization (.ini) files. With the introduction of Windows 95 and later versions, the registry became the central repository for all this information.

As you have read, the registry database is vital to the operation of all applications installed on your computer. Along with its everyday operation, you can also use it to store any information that you need to retain about your own application—for example, simple things like user preferences, state and/or status of scheduled routines, or even the location or sizes of screens.

Before proceeding, a little more background may be necessary to understand the need for storing information into the registry. In most cases, your custom Access Application resides in two separate databases, `data.mdb` and `application.mdb`. During the life of the application, users will request changes, which will require an update to the UI objects contained within it.

To perform the changes, you will want to make them on a development machine, without affecting any live data or existing functionality. Once the changes are completed, and tested thoroughly, you will need to deploy the new application version to all users. The easiest way to do this is to copy the new `application.mdb` to the user's machine. Here is where the registry is useful.

If there are any personalization settings stored within the `application.mdb`, perhaps in a local table, then there would need to be a mechanism to copy those values from the old version of the application to the new version. As you can imagine, it can be a hassle to perform, maintain, and control the execution of the process. So, to make a long story short, if there is some other place to store these settings that would not be overwritten with each update, then using it may save you some time, effort, and headaches.

To make it easy for you to create, retrieve, and delete values to the registry database, VBA offers the following functions:

Function	Description
SaveSetting	Saves or creates an application entry in the application's entry in the Windows Registry
GetSetting	Returns a key setting value from an application's entry in the Windows Registry or (on the Macintosh) information in the application's initialization file
GetAllSettings	Returns a list of key settings and their respective values (originally created with SaveSetting) from an application's entry in the Windows Registry or (on the Macintosh) information in the application's initialization file
DeleteSetting	Deletes a section or key setting from an application's entry in the Windows Registry or (on the Macintosh) information in the application's initialization file

When a setting is written to the registry, it is done in a directory structure that is similar to Windows Explorer. The base directory for all settings created by the `CreateSetting` function is

```
My Computer\HKEY_CURRENT_USER\Software\VB and VBA Program Settings\
```

Stored within this base folder, you create `Application`, `Section`, and `Key` names. Inside the `Key` names are the actual settings. So, when you execute the `CreateSetting` function, the rest of the registry setting is created like the following:

```
Application Name\Section Name\Key Name\Setting Name
```

For example, the following statement would create a new value in the registry that contains the text `"MySetting"`:

```
SaveSetting "MyApp", "MySection", "MyKey", "MySetting"
```

The following statement would be stored in the registry, and displayed as shown in Figure 10-4.

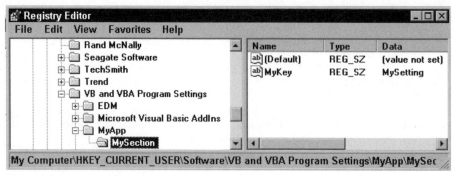

Figure 10-4

To summarize this example, a folder called "My App" is created under the "VB and VBA Program Settings" folder. A folder called "MySection" is created below the application name. Contained within "MySection" folder, the "MyKey" key holds the actual setting, which in this case is "MySetting".

For a real example, suppose that when users interact with a particular form, they are allowed to move and resize the form as they wish. When they reopen that form, it would be nice to be able to position it in the same place with the same size. This functionality can be implemented with the help of the registry. By storing the values when the form is closed, then the same values can be applied when the form is opened.

The following code is an example of saving the form attributes to the registry:

```
Private Sub Form_Close()
  'Save user form preference to the Windows Registry Database
  Const cstrAppName As String = "MyApplication"
  Dim strSectionName As String
  'Create a registry section based on the name of the Form
  strSectionName = Me.Name
  'Write Settings to the Windows Registry Database
  SaveSetting cstrAppName, strSectionName, _
    "WindowHeight", Me.WindowHeight
  SaveSetting cstrAppName, strSectionName, _
    "WindowLeft", Me.WindowLeft
  SaveSetting cstrAppName, strSectionName, _
    "WindowTop", Me.WindowTop
  SaveSetting cstrAppName, strSectionName, _
    "WindowWidth", Me.WindowWidth
End Sub
```

In the following code example, a constant variable is created for use throughout the remainder of the procedure. If you prefer to use an application global value, that would work as well. Next, the form name is used to create a Section in the registry. This will facilitate finding the values later in code. Within each Section, the form's Height, Left, Top, and Width are written to the respective keys.

```
Private Sub Form_Open(Cancel As Integer)
  'Reset the window to the saved settings
  Const cstrAppName As String = "MyApplication"
  Me.Move _
      GetSetting(cstrAppName, .Name, "WindowLeft", 1000), _
      GetSetting(cstrAppName, .Name, "WindowTop", 1000), _
      GetSetting(cstrAppName, .Name, "WindowWidth", 3000), _
      GetSetting(cstrAppName, .Name, "WindowHeight", 3000)
End Sub
```

Figure 10-5 displays the result of the registry after the user values are saved.

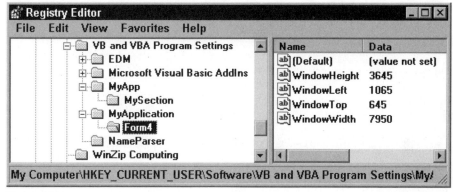

Figure 10-5

Creating Forms and Controls with VBA

Access has built-in functions for creating new form and control objects programmatically. These are the same functions that the wizards use to create new objects and work the same regardless of whether you are using an MDB or ADP file.

The CreateForm method creates a form and returns a Form object.

```
CreateForm([database[, formtemplate]])
```

The CreateForm method has the following arguments.

Argument	Description
database	A string expression identifying the name of the database that contains the form template you want to use to create a form. If you want the current database, omit this argument.
formtemplate	A string expression identifying the name of the form you want to use as a template to create a new form. If you omit this argument, Microsoft Access bases the new form on the template specified by the Forms/Reports tab of the Options dialog box, available by clicking Options on the Tools menu.

Add code similar to the Click event of a command button:

```
Private Sub cmdCreateNewForm_Click()
  Dim frmNewForm As Access.Form
  Set frmNewForm = CreateForm()

  'Form is created in a minimized state.
  DoCmd.Restore

  ' Set caption, resize and reposition.
  frmNewForm.Caption = "My New Form"
  DoCmd.MoveSize 500, 500, 8000, 4000

  ' Save new form
  DoCmd.Save acForm, frmNewForm.Name
End Sub
```

The following is the CreateControl function:

```
CreateControl(formname, controltype[, section[, parent[, columnname[, left[,
top[, width[, height]]]]]]])
```

The CreateControl function to create controls has a few more arguments.

Argument	Description
Formname	A string expression identifying the name of the open form or report on which you want to create the control.
controltype	One of the following intrinsic constants identifying the type of control you want to create.

Constant	Control type
acBoundObjectFrame	Bound object frame
acCheckBox	Check box
acComboBox	Combo box
acCommandButton	Command button
acCustomControl	ActiveX control
acImage	Image
acLabel	Label
AcLine	Line
acListBox	List box
acObjectFrame	Unbound object frame

Continues

Argument	Description	
	acOptionButton	Option button
	acOptionGroup	Option group
	AcPage	Page
	acPageBreak	Page break
	acRectangle	Rectangle
	acSubform	Subform
	AcTabCtl	Tab control
	acTextBox	Text box
	acToggleButton	Toggle button
Section	One of the following intrinsic constants identifying the section that will contain the new control	

Constant	Section
AcDetail	(Default) Detail section
AcHeader	Form or report header
AcFooter	Form or report footer
acPageHeader	Page header
acPageFooter	Page footer
acGroupLevel1Header	Group-level 1 header (reports only)
acGroupLevel1Footer	Group-level 1 footer (reports only)
acGroupLevel2Header	Group-level 2 header (reports only)
acGroupLevel2Footer	Group-level 2 footer (reports only)

Argument	Description
Parent	A string expression identifying the name of the parent control of an attached control. For controls that have no parent control, use a zero-length string for this argument, or omit it.
columnname	The name of the field to which the control will be bound, if it is to be a data-bound control
	If you are creating a control that won't be bound to a field, use a zero-length string for this argument.
left, top	Numeric expressions indicating the coordinates for the upper-left corner of the control in twips.
width, height	Numeric expressions indicating the width and height of the control in twips.

The following code can add a control to the above form:

```
Private Sub cmdCreateControl_Click()
  Dim frmNewForm As Access.Form
  Dim ctlNewControl As Access.Control

  ' Form1 is the default name of the form create earlier
  Set frmNewForm = Application.Forms("form1")

  ' Create the new control
  Set ctlNewControl = CreateControl(frmNewForm.Name, acTextBox, _
    acDetail, , , frmNewForm.WindowLeft + 250, _
    frmNewForm.WindowTop + 250, 1400, 500)

  ' Name it & save the form
  ctlNewControl.Name = "txtNewTextbox"
  DoCmd.Save acForm, frmNewForm.Name
End Sub
```

Managing Multiple Form Instances

Handling multiple instances of the same form is not as straightforward as it might seem. The reason is that the default opening behavior of a form is all the same *instance* of the form. Understanding the concept of an instance is as simple as counting to 1. There is only one form, and every time that form is opened, it is the same form. The form opens and displays the data specified in the Recordsource property.

This limitation is not typically a problem for the average application, as a user is happy to view data in this manner. For example, opening the customer form, based on the Customers table or a query thereof, displays all customers in the data source. The customer can navigate to the desired customer, and perform any maintenance. Now, imagine that there is a data entry form for stock market ticker symbols and their daily closing prices. With only one form, comparing two or more stocks may be rather difficult. Performing a side-by-side comparison of the vital statistics of two or more stocks would be challenging when only one can be displayed at a time.

So, now that a need has been identified, the discussion turns to the execution of multiple instances of the form. (Just in case you are thinking about expanding this same concept for reports, please understand that it is *not* possible. The report preview window is controlled outside of Access and therefore there is nothing you can do to work around its limitations.) The way to create more instances of a form is to create an object variable based on the desired form. The following code example performs this step:

```
Private Sub CreateFormInstance()

  'Declare the variable to be an existing form
  Dim frmTest1 As Form_Orders

  'Set the variable to a new instance of the form
  Set frmTest1 = New Form_Orders

  'Show the Form, as setting it does not make it visible
End Sub
```

Notice that the visible property of the form must be explicitly set to True, because the form is not visible by default using this opening method. Something also to note is that using this method would cause the form to only blink across the screen momentarily when the code is run. This occurs because the scope of the variable is local to the procedure in which it is declared. To allow the form to be more persistent requires that the variable be declared in the general declarations section of a module. Variables defined in this Global section will stay in scope throughout the life of the application. The scope in the above procedure is only until the procedure ends, which causes the flicker, as the variable is destroyed at the End Sub statement.

The following code is an example of the creation of multiple instances of the same form that persist throughout the life of the application:

```
    'Declare the first instance
    Dim frmTest1 As Form_Orders

    'Declare the second instance
    Dim frmTest2 As Form_Orders

Private Sub cmdOpenForms_Click()
    'Create the first instance
    Set frmTest1 = New Form_Orders

    'Create the second instance
    Set frmTest2 = New Form_Orders

    'Make both instances visible
    frmTest1.Visible = True
    frmTest2.Visible = True

End Sub
```

The above code declares the global variables, instantiates them, and makes them visible. Before you run off and try to program your next stock market application, you should understand that this example presents limited usefulness, because it requires knowing how many instances are required in advance of execution. This is also known as *hard-coding*, which does not bode well in dynamic situations. If the number of times that the form needs to open is unknown (that is, the number of stocks that you would like to compare at once), then the hard-coded solution may include too many instances or not enough.

The next step in the multi-instance ladder is maintaining a *collection* of form objects, created on demand by the user. To understand the concept of a collection, think about a stamp, marble, or baseball card collection. You have a binder for stamps, bag for marbles, and a shoebox for cards. A collection is the empty container, awaiting items to be placed within it. The following code demonstrates the creation of the collection, and the addition of members to it:

```
    'Create the global collection
    Dim colTest As New Collection

Private Sub cmdOpenForms_Click()
    'Declare an object variable as an existing form
    Dim frmTest As Form_Orders
```

```
    'Set the object to a new instance of the form
    Set frmTest = New Form_Orders

    'Add the form instance to the collection
    colTest.Add frmTest

    frmTest.Visible = True

End Sub
```

Each time the above code is executed a new instance of the form is added to the collection, and then the form is displayed to the user. This may accomplish your goal, but it is very important to understand that every instance that is created requires some amount of memory of the computer. If you continue to create instances, eventually all of the memory is allocated and strange but interesting error messages from Access and Windows are displayed. To avoid creating a form instance landfill inside the machine, proper housekeeping procedures must be implemented.

Housekeeping, with regard to VBA programming, is the proper destruction and reallocation of free memory throughout the life of the application. Just like in your home, if you open it, close it; if you get it dirty, clean it; if you turn it on, then turn it off. The same applies to created objects, because failing to close or destroy them can lead to memory leaks or other undesirable results.

So, if a form instance is closed by a user, then the memory allocated to the use of that object variable is still retained. The collection also maintains the form within its population as well. Therefore, the creator of the instance must make provisions to destroy the instance.

The ideal place to remove an object instance from the collection is within the On Close event procedure of the form instance. Just as the collection has an Add method, it also has a Remove method. It is used to destroy the instance from memory. In order to know which instance to destroy requires knowing where it is within the collection. Collection items can be referred to using an ordinal value, but it only relates to the sequential order in which the forms were instantiated. This is typically not useful when users are allowed to randomly open and close the instances (that is, user opens stock XYZ, ABC, and RRR. He or she decides against ABC and closes the form. It would be time then to destroy the ABC instance.)

To facilitate the specific reference of an instance, you may specify a unique index during the call to the Add method of the Collection object. The Key parameter is a string expression that can optionally be added for the direct reference to the instance within the collection. It is important to note that the supplied text value must be unique from any other Key value within the collection. Otherwise, destroying one instance would destroy all instances with the same name.

Specifying a unique string value presents an interesting challenge, as there needs to be some mechanism to create it. As each form opens, you need to determine something about that form instance that is unique from any other instance. In the case of the stock market example, the stock ticker symbol could be used. If motor vehicles are the basis of the form, then perhaps the VIN number could serve this purpose.

In the following example, multiple instances of an Order form are displayed. As most OrderID values are generated with an autonumber, this value is an obvious choice to use as unique index for the collection. To visually assist the user when multiple instances are opened, the caption can be modified to display the OrderID as well.

```
Public colOrders As New Collection
Private Sub cmdShowOrder_Click()
  Dim frmOrder As Form_Orders
  Dim strOrderID As String
  'Retrieve the desired OrderID
  strOrderID = Me!sfrmOrders.Form!txtOrderID
  'Open a new Orders form
  Set frmOrder = New Form_Orders

  'Set the form filter criteria
  frmOrder.Filter = "OrderID = " & strOrderID
  frmOrder.FilterOn = True

  'Set the caption to reflect the unique id
  frmOrder.Caption = "Order: " & strOrderID

  'Add the form instance to the Collection.
  ' Specify the Caption property for the 'Key' parameter
  ' The order number is used as the unique index
  colOrders.Add frmOrder, strOrderID

  'Display the form instance
  frmOrder.Visible = True

End Sub
```

The code example above creates the collection in the global declarations section. When the Show Order command button is clicked by the user, a new instance of the form is created in memory. On the subform is the desired OrderID to be displayed on the form. Therefore, when the form is opened, a filter is applied to show only that record. The caption is updated to visually enhance the user experience, by specifying the order that is being displayed. The instance is added to the collection, using the OrderID as the unique key index. Finally, the form instance is displayed. To better understand the use of this code, see Figure 10-6.

Figure 10-6 displays an order selection form. The user places the cursor on the desired record and then clicks the Show Orders button. Each time the button is clicked, a new instance of the form is opened.

The following code demonstrates the ability to destroy a specific instance of a form, within a collection, based on the unique Key value in the collection. For obvious reasons, the execution of this code is from the On Close event procedure of the form instance that is closing.

```
Private Sub Form_Close()
  'Remove the instance of this form from the collection
  Form_dlgViewOrders.colOrders.Remove CStr(OrderID)
End Sub
```

The above code example executes the Remove method of the colOrders collection. To specify the exact collection, the code module name must be supplied, so that there is no ambiguity as to which collection is to be used. In this case, the View Orders dialog box (dlgViewOrders) contains the collection. The Remove method is executed with the OrderID, converted to a string, and passed as the Key Index parameter.

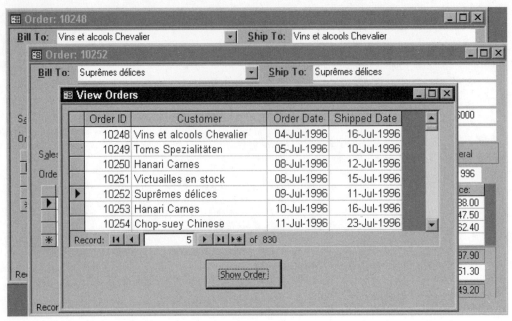

Figure 10-6

When Not to Use VBA

There are times when you will attempt to solve a problem with VBA, only to find out that VBA is *not* the answer. The following example is such a case. Over time, you will learn to identify what can be solved with code, with a query or multiple queries, and also via the use of controls on a form.

Syncronized Subforms

Subforms are one of the more convenient features of Access. When one form (a subform) is nested inside another form (a main form), Access can keep the subform's data synchronized with the main form by using a common field to relate the two. In a typical example, the main form might be based on a Customers table and a subform could be based on an Orders table. As records are scrolled in the main form, Access filters the subform so that only relevant orders are displayed for that particular customer.

A subform can also be synchronized with another subform. This technique is demonstrated in the Customer Orders form of the Northwind.mdb sample file and illustrated in Figure 10-7.

The first subform is based on order data and is linked to the main form by CustomerID. The second subform contains order details data and is linked to the first subform by the OrderID field. The mechanism Access uses to synchronize a subform relies on the Link Child Fields and Link Master Fields properties of the subform control. Although a wizard can be used to set up a nested subform that is linked to its parent form, subforms that link to another subform must be set up manually to synchronize. In this case, the Link Master Fields property should be the following:

```
[Customer Orders Subform1].Form![OrderID]
```

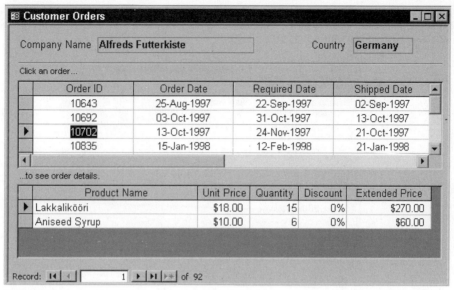

Figure 10-7

Note that [Customer Orders Subform1] refers to the name of the subform *Control*, not the name of the form that the control is based on.

It is also possible (and sometimes preferable) to handle the synchronization programmatically instead of relying on Access to do it for you. This gives you added flexibility when manipulating the subform's behavior. As an example, modify the Customer Orders form (shown above) to synchronize programmatically.

As you've learned, there was no need to write any VBA code to make this operation functional. So, do not always look to VBA code to solve the problem first. Keep in mind that within Access, there are many ways to solve problems—be sure to explore all options before making a final decision.

Displaying Data in a Treeview Control

One of the powerful features of Access development is the ability to add an ActiveX control to any UI. Adding such controls, like the Calendar and Treeview controls, is a great way to add functionality and a pizzazz to any application, with minimal effort on your part.

The Treeview control is used to display any information that exists within a hierarchy of information. A hierarchy can involve any data contained within a one-to-one or one-to-many relationship. For example, Customers have Orders and Orders have line items that Northwind defines as Order Details. This section demonstrates how to add a Treeview control to a form and also how to populate and display the information based on user interaction with it.

To begin this example, start a new blank form. It does not need to be based on a recordsource, as the data population will occur only within the Treeview control. After the form is created, insert the

ActiveX control in the form by choosing Insert/ActiveX Control... from the main menu, as shown in Figure 10-8. The figure displays the ActiveX Control selection dialog box. For this example, the Treeview control is from Visual Basic 6, SP 6.

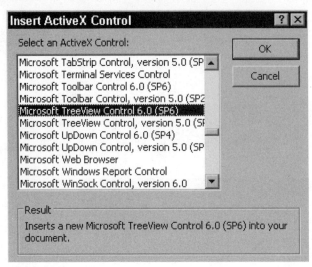

Figure 10-8

Select the desired control from the ActiveX Control dialog box, and it will be added to the form. Depending on the type of control selected, it may need to be moved, resized, or have its properties modified. It is important to note that an ActiveX control has properties that are displayed in the standard properties window, but a control can also possess another set of custom properties that were added by the control creator. In Figure 10-9, both the standard and custom property windows are displayed.

In order for a Treeview control to be operational, you must create an ImageList control. The ImageList control is a storage area for pictures that the Treeview uses when it displays the data. In this example, two images are used. One is an open folder to represent a selected entity, the other image is a closed folder, for nonselected ones.

To add an ImageList control to the form, use the ActiveX Controls selection dialog box and select the Microsoft ImageList control. After the control is added to the form, add images to the control using the custom property window. Right-click on the inserted ImageList control, select ImageListCtrl object from the submenu, then select the Properties choice. These steps open the ImageListCtrl Properties dialog box, which is where the images and their properties are defined.

On the General tab, first select the size of the icons, as this value cannot be changed after images are inserted. The 16 × 16 size is a good starting point, and is used for this example. The Images tab contains the inventory of icons. To add an image to the inventory, click on the Insert Picture button. This opens the standard Windows File Open dialog box to allow the user to browse for image files. The pictures used for this example are shipped with Visual Basic 6.0. Each image in the list has an Index, Key, and Tag property. When the Treeview opens, each data item is closed, so the closed image is used by default. When the data item is selected, then the open image will be used. The following properties are used for this example.

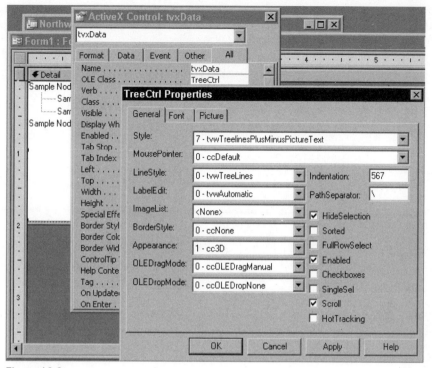

Figure 10-9

Image	Index	Key	Tag
Closed.bmp	1	Closed	Closed
Open.bmp	2	Open	Open

After defining the icons in the `ImageList`, the final setup step is to set the `ImageList` property of the `Treeview` control to the name of the `ImageList` control. Perform this step in the `Custom` property window of the `Treeview` control. To perform this step, right-click the `Treeview` control, choose `TreeCtrl` object, then `Properties`, and finally select the `ImageList` control name for the `ImageList` property.

The next step is to populate the data within the `Treeview`. Each item of data in a `Treeview` is considered a *node*, and resides with the `Treeview` `Nodes` collection. The following code example demonstrates the addition of a data node to the collection of `Treeview` nodes.

```
tvx.Nodes.Add _
    Key:="C105", Text:="Acme Supply Co.", _
    Image:= 1, SelectedImage:=2
```

The previous code example adds a new node to the collection of `Treeview` nodes. The node is defined with a unique key of C105, a display name of Acme Supply Co., and is set to use the image with the key of 1 by default, and the image with the key of 2 when selected.

Note: The `Key` property of every node is of type text, it must start with a letter, and it must be unique.

The `Treeview` control that is created in this section is designed to populate when the form is first loaded. During the `Form Load` event procedure, the `Treeview` is populated with one node for every customer from the `Northwind` example database. The following code demonstrates this population routine:

```
Private Sub Form_Load()
   'When the form loads, populate the Treeview with the Customer Data

   'Notice that MSComctlLib must be used
   Dim tvx As MSComctlLib.TreeView
   Dim rst As ADODB.Recordset

   'Notice that .Object must be used to enable IntelliSense
   Set tvx = tvxData.Object
   Set rst = New ADODB.Recordset

   With rst
      'Open the Customer Lookup Query
      .Open "qlkpCustomers", _
         Application.CurrentProject.Connection

      Do While Not .EOF
         'Make Key = "C" & CustomerID, and Display the Customer Name.
         tvx.Nodes.Add , , "C" & !CustomerID, !CompanyName, 1, 2
         'Go to next Customer
         .MoveNext
      Loop

   End With

End Sub
```

The previous code sample defines the `Treeview` control, and opens a recordset based on the `Customers` table. The query used is comprised of only the `CustomerID` and `CompanyName`. As the code loops through the customer records, nodes are added to the `Treeview` at the top level. The first two parameters of the `Add` method are omitted intentionally because this instructs that the nodes are added to the highest level of the `Treeview`.

The design concept of this `Treeview` example is to allow the user to select a customer, which will then trigger the `Treeview` to display the associated orders placed by that customer. To this point, only the customer data has been added. If all of the order data was populated at the same time, then the load time for the form would be horribly slow. This may not be the best solution, as the user of the `Treeview` may never click on a particular customer, thus, there is no need to load the subsequent orders for the non-selected customer. Instead, an on-demand data retrieval model can be implemented to minimize the overall loading of related data. A third model could be to load only those customers that are frequently used by a certain user.

To perform the population of the order data within the `Treeview` control, custom event procedures must be utilized, as Access is unaware of the functionality that is contained with a custom ActiveX control. To assist with the capture and execution of events on the `Treeview`, there are two event procedures exposed to handle the desired execution of this functionality. These events are the `NodeClick` and `Expand` event properties. It is important to understand that the `Treeview` control has both a `Click` and a `NodeClick` event procedure. The `Click` event is used for the entire `Treeview`, not a particular node, so it would not be the optimal choice for this example. To trap the event for a selected node, you must use `NodeClick`.

In the following code example, notice that the `Expand` and `NodeClick` procedure headers both expose a `Node` as a parameter. This node can be explored to determine which data has been selected. This node will be used after a customer is selected.

```
Private Sub tvxEmployees_Expand(ByVal Node As Object)
Private Sub tvxEmployees_NodeClick(ByVal Node As Object)
```

Because the `Treeview` is an ActiveX control, the procedure header for the `NodeClick` event cannot be generated from the standard `Form` property window. Instead, it must be started from within the `VBA Code Editor` window. First select the `Treeview` control name from the `Object` combo box on the left side, and then select the desired event procedure, either `Expand` or `NodeClick`, from the `Event` combo box on the right side.

The final step is to populate the child nodes for a customer, which will represent the orders. Previously, the `.Add` method was used, and all nodes were instructed to be created at the highest level of the `Treeview`. This method will not be effective for the child nodes, as they only have meaning in the context of the parent node; therefore, additional data must be supplied during the creation of the child node to ensure a proper match between the parent and child node.

To accomplish this, the previously omitted parameters of the `Add` method must now be supplied. These required parameters are the index of the related node, and the type of relationship to create between the two. This means that any type of relationship can be created, not just a parent to child relationship. The following code sample demonstrates the creation of a child node to a parent node.

```
tvx.Nodes.Add nodParent.Index, tvwChild, _
    "O1234", "1234 - 12/12/2003", 1, 2
```

In this example, the index of the parent node is specified, and the relationship is defined using the intrinsic constant `tvwChild`. (Because all of the intrinsic constants for a `Treeview` control have a prefix of `tvw-`, the `Treeview` variables used in this section use `tvx`, to help differentiate between the two.)

In the next code segment example, a procedure called `ShowOrders` is used to populate and display the orders for a selected customer. The routine is very similar to the population of the Customer Nodes, except that the Parent Node and relationship type must be supplied for the creation of each of the children.

```
Private Sub tvxData_NodeClick(ByVal Node As Object)
   ShowOrders Node
End Sub

Sub ShowOrders(pnod As Node)

  Dim tvx As MSComctlLib.TreeView
  Dim cnn As ADODB.Connection
```

```
     Dim cmd As ADODB.Command
     Dim rst As ADODB.Recordset
     Dim intPos As String
     Dim strParentID As String

     Set tvx = tvxData.Object
     Set cnn = Application.CurrentProject.Connection
     Set cmd = New ADODB.Command

     'Check if Parent has already been populated
     If pnod.Children = 0 Then
        'Even if no children, we may have attempted
        'to populate previously
       If Len(pnod.Tag) = 0 Then
         'Extract the ParentID from .Key
         strParentID = Mid$(pnod.Key, 2)

         'Prepare a Query to extract children data
         Set cmd.ActiveConnection = cnn
         cmd.CommandType = adCmdText
         cmd.CommandText = _
            "SELECT OrderID, OrderDate FROM Orders WHERE CustomerID = '" &
   strParentID & "'"

         Set rst = New ADODB.Recordset
         With rst
           'Retrieve Child data for this Parent
           .Open cmd
           Do While Not .EOF
             'Make Key = O + OrderID
             'and Display OrderID and Order Date
             tvx.Nodes.Add pnod.Index, tvwChild, _
               "O" & !OrderID, _
               !OrderID & " - " & !OrderDate, 1, 2
               'Go to next Child
               .MoveNext
           Loop

         End With

         'Mark node as populated
         pnod.Tag = "X"
         If pnod.Children > 0 Then
           'Ensure that first child is visible
           pnod.Child.EnsureVisible
         End If 'pnod.Children > 0
       End If 'pnod.Tag = vbNullString
     End If 'pnod.Children = 0

   End Sub
```

The techniques used in this procedure requiring further explanation are the need for marking the node as populated, and creating a unique key for each node while incorporating the EmployeeID for later reference.

To prevent reprocessing a parent node that has already been expanded, the tag property of the node is marked set to X. The actual character used is irrelevant, as the validation that occurs simply checks for the existence of the property having a length greater than 0. This technique is included because a parent node can be selected, but the result of the population does not yield any child nodes. Therefore, the check for nod.children being greater than 0 could result in reprocessing.

When a parent node is passed to the ShowOrders procedure, you need to know the parent CustomerID, so that the query that is created will only find the records related to that customer. So, adding the CustomerID to the Node key is simply a convenient way of retaining the information for later use.

The following table is a reference for the properties and methods used in the code.

Property/method	Description
.Index	Unique number assigned to a node by VBA
.Key	Unique value assigned by developer, must start with a letter
.Children	Number of child nodes associated to a parent node
.Child	The first child node of a parent
EnsureVisible	Force node to be visible in current window

Figure 10-10 displays the results of this entire example. Although the task is completed, there are many other features that could be implemented. For example, the selection of the OrderID could result in the Orders form being opened to display that order. With minimal programming and effort, adding Treeview control to an application adds an extra level of professionalism and pizzazz that many users will appreciate.

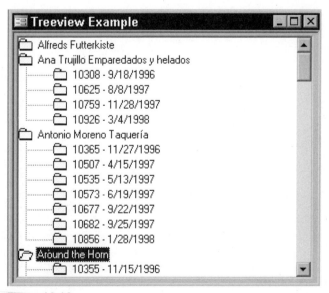

Figure 10-10

Summary

In this chapter, you have been exposed to many different facets of VBA programming within the Form environment. The examples supplied in this chapter were designed to demonstrate both the theory of how to approach a solution, and also provide a coding starting point for many common problems that occur in many different Access custom applications. Understanding the theory and code behind each example can assist all levels of developers with current and future projects. For more help about the specific property, methods, and procedures utilized in the examples, visit the Access online help files and/or the MSDN Web site.

In the next chapter, you will be introduced to coding VBA in the Report environment. It is very similar to coding in the Form environment, so many of the techniques that you have learned in this chapter will benefit you in the Report environment as well.

11

Enhancing Reports with VBA

This chapter focuses on the ability to modify Access Reports using VBA programming. If you have read the chapter about enhancing forms, then in this chapter you will recognize many of the same concepts that occurred there. There are many similarities, in that each object has its own properties, which can execute an event procedure. For example, the `Form` object has an `Open` event procedure and the `Report` object has one as well. Once you learn how to utilize an event procedure for one object, using that same event procedure in another becomes very simple.

When programming for a form, there are certain issues to worry about, such as application flow, searching for data, entry of data, and data validation. Almost none of this needs to occur when programming for a report. By the time a report executes, the data should already exist within the tables, and the report is just a printed copy of the information.

The examples contained within this chapter will get you on the road to solving challenging reporting problems that you may come across. It will start with a discussion of the available event properties, and will then move to specific examples. The specific examples are structured to demonstrate functionality that can be added to an event procedure. Specifically, the `Open`, `No Data`, `Format`, and `Print` event procedures are addressed. After these techniques are understood, the common problem of computing a running balance is addressed. The last example demonstrates how to solve a reporting problem without using VBA.

Event Properties

Event properties are used in reports, much the same way that they are in forms. The difference is that there are no properties that the user can initiate. Everything is done by the developer. There are no buttons to click, no combo boxes to open, or no data validation to perform.

Figure 11-1 and the following table display the extent of the event properties, and what causes them to be executed for a report. Some of these properties will be demonstrated in the code samples later in the chapter.

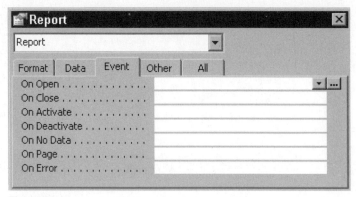

Figure 11-1

Property	Triggers When...
On Open	The report is opened
On Close	The report is closed
On Activate	The report preview window is activated
On Deactivate	The report preview window is deactivated
On No Data	The recordsource of the report contains no records
On Page	After a page is formatted, but before it is printed
On Error	An error occurs during the execution of code

Associating Code to an Event Property

When you are ready to begin associating VBA code to an event property, this is how you instruct Access to use your VBA code: You can start from either the Design View of the Report or from the VBA Editor window itself. Both methods are useful, and the times at which you utilize them will depend on your current location (Report or Editor) at the time that you need to start a new procedure.

From the Report Design window, click to highlight the desired control, and then choose View/Properties from the main menu. (You can also press *F4* or just double-click the control to open the Properties window.) Once opened, click the Event tab, open the combo box associated to the desired event property, and choose [Event Procedure], as shown in Figure 11-2. Performing this step signifies to Access that you want to execute a VBA event procedure when the user triggers the event. Notice in Figure 11-2 that a macro can also be assigned to an event property. This is why there is a selection for event procedure. The reason it is in square brackets is that it will always be the first item in the combo box.

To speed the selection of [Event Procedure] when you enter the combo box of an event property, press the *Left Square Bracket* key "[", or just double-click the combo box. (Double-clicking a second time will select the next value in the list.)

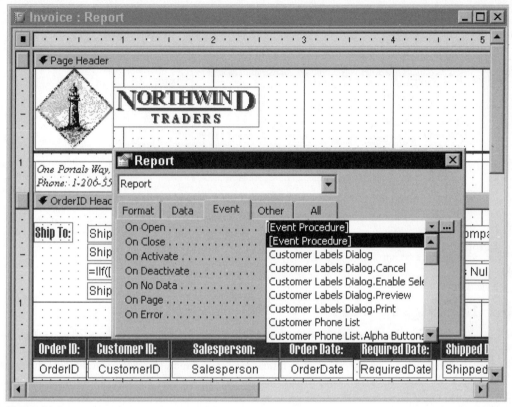

Figure 11-2

After the selection of [Event Procedure], click the button that is just to the right of the combo box "opener" (the button has the Period of Ellipses [...] on it). This action will cause the VBA Editor window to open. When the event procedure for the event property is opened for the first time, a new sub procedure is created for it. If there already exists a sub procedure for the report or control event property, then that existing sub procedure is opened.

From the Module window itself, use the combo boxes at the top of the Code window to select the desired control, and then the subsequent event property. The combo box on the left has a value for the report, and all controls on the report. The combo box on the right has all of the possible event procedures based on the selection from the left combo box.

Figure 11-3 shows the Control and Event Property combo boxes, as well as a sample event procedure structure that is created for you. Notice that the procedure is a Sub, which means that it cannot return a value. It is also dimensioned as Private, which means that other modules in the database cannot see nor utilize it. The last thing to notice in the picture is that the sub procedure has the Cancel parameter. The use of the Cancel parameter is described later in this chapter.

> Note: Using a naming convention comes in handy when viewing the Control combo box in the VBA Editor. All controls are listed alphabetically, so voluntarily adding a prefix to each control name will sort each control type together (that is, txt, cbo, cmd, and so on).

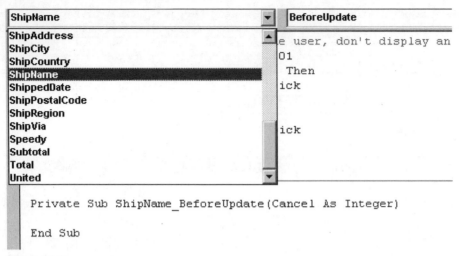

Figure 11-3

You Talking to Me?

Programmers are typically self-obsessed beings, so on your journey to learn about Form Automation, it is important to understand that "It's all about Me!" No, Me is not about You, Me *is* about the currently active Report. If you want to know anything about the Report, you can request information from the Me object. Using Me will expose all of the events, properties, and controls associated to it. To utilize Me in your code, enter Me. (dot or period) and then select the desired value from the IntelliSense combo box, which automatically appears.

Figure 11-4 shows the IntelliSense combo box as it applies the Me object.

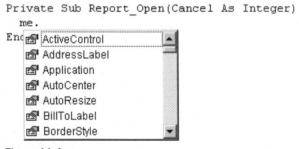

Figure 11-4

An example of using Me would be if you wanted to change the caption of the current report, you could issue the following command to change the Caption property:

```
Me.Caption = "Report: Invoice"
```

There may also be times when you need to examine a value about a report, but have no knowledge ahead of time what the "about" may be. There are many *collections* contained within the Me object that you can expose, even with very little information about the collection contents.

For example, suppose you need to reference the value of a certain control, but you don't know the name of the control before it happens. The ability to refer to that control in code using the specific name (that is, txtFirstName) will not work, so you may have a need for a generic procedure, and need the flexibility to send it a variety of information like the following:

```
Private Sub DoSomething(pstrControlName As String)
   If Me.Controls(pstrControlName).Value > 50 thenz
      ...'Do something
   Else
      ...'Do something else
   End If
End Function
```

This type of programming begins to scare the faint of heart, but it demonstrates not only a practical use of the Me object, but also the power and flexibility that VBA possesses. In the above example, the Me object contains a collection called *controls*, which is the same as referencing a control name directly. To this collection, a parameter can be passed in the shape of either a literal value (that is, "txtFirstName", quotes required), a variable that contains the value (that is, pstrControlName), or an ordinal value (that is, zero (0) represents the first value in the collection).

The Me object is a very important and useful tool provided to the developer that may be used in any of the many event procedures that are written.

Event Property and Procedure Examples

The remainder of this chapter will apply all of the information covered in the above sections to get you started on the automation of Access Reports. The examples are in no particular order and possibly do not rely on each other for reader comprehension. In case an example is associated to another, it will be noted. This allows for the reading of only the property examples that are pertinent to you.

Report_Open(): Execute a Query Before Report Displays

The On Open event procedure works just like the On Open event procedure of forms, in that it is triggered when the form is opened. The functionality that can be placed within this event procedure is unlimited, but it is important to keep in mind that the code will trigger only once. If there is a repetitive task that needs to execute throughout the report, then the code should be moved to a different event procedure.

There are many things that may need to happen when a report is opened, but one task could be the preparation of data, just prior to printing. It is not uncommon in Access to base a report on a table that is used specifically for the report. There could be some complex calculations or last minute processing that need to be done before the report can print correctly.

For example, suppose that you need to execute a Delete Query, an Append Query, and an Update Query prior to printing a report. The Delete Query would be used to empty any previous data from the report table, the Append Query would retrieve the new base data, and the Update Query would finish the data population effort.

So, when the form is opened, completing the described operation is as simple as issuing the necessary OpenQuery statements. The following example demonstrates this technique:

```
Private Sub Report_Open(Cancel As Integer)

    'Show a message in the Status Bar
    DoCmd.Echo True, "Preparing Report Data...Please Wait"

    'Turn off the Warning Messages
    DoCmd.SetWarnings False

    'Populate the report table
    DoCmd.OpenQuery "qryInvoices_0Empty"
    DoCmd.OpenQuery "qryInvoices_1AddData"
    DoCmd.OpenQuery "qryInvoices_2UpdateTotals"

    'Reset the Warning Messages
    DoCmd.SetWarnings True

End Sub
```

In the above example, the code starts by showing a message in the status bar, by using the Echo statement. (Note that if the first parameter is set to False, then the screen will not refresh.) Next, the standard Access error messages are suppressed by issuing the SetWarnings statement with the parameter of False. From there, the queries to empty, add, and update the data are executed. (Notice the naming conventions used, which keep the queries in a logical order.) At the end of the procedure, the standard warning messages are turned on again.

This technique is quite useful in ensuring that the data is always up to date when the report executes, but also be aware that it will add significant processing time to the report generation time, especially in Preview mode.

Report_NoData(): What to do When There Is No Data to Display

The On No Data event property is triggered when there is no data to display in the report. Now, this may sound odd, because why would anyone create a report that has no data? The answer comes from the fact that any report can be called from code. When the report is opened, parameters can be supplied to allow for the report to be opened with different cross sections of the data.

The following code example opens a report, and passes query criteria to the report using the Where parameter.

```
Docmd.OpenReport "rptInvoice", Where := "OrderID = 1234"
```

Another method of opening a report with different data is by using a `FilterName`:

```
Docmd.OpenReport "rptCustomerDetails", _

    FilterName := "qryCustomersInUSA"
```

In the first example, the `Where` clause is used to restrict the data to be displayed to only those records where the `OrderID` is equal to the number `1234`. In the second example, a query called "qryCustomersInUSA" is used to override the Report `RecordSource` property. Both of these techniques are very useful, and offer the developer options and flexibility that do not require the recreation of the same report layout with different RecordSources. As you can imagine, there are some developers that didn't know this, and in their databases you find:

❏ rptMonthly_January

❏ rptMonthly_February

❏ rptMonthly_March

As you can imagine, that developer did a lot more work than was necessary, but give them credit, as they got the job done. So, that should be enough background to realize why the `On No Data` event property can be useful. Refer back to the first example, and imagine what would happen if for some reason `OrderID 1234` had been deleted. If you executed the statement to open the Invoice report, then Access would still try to create the report, but would only produce a blank page, or even more strange results like #Name or #Error.

It is possible to verify that there is data for a report, prior to opening it, using a function such as `DCount()`. With this method, you can attempt to ascertain if there are any records prior to making the call to open the report. For example,

```
If DCount("*", "qryInvoices", "OrderID = 1234") > 0 then
   Docmd.OpenReport "rptCustomerDetails", Where := "OrderID = 1234"
End If
```

The above example is an extreme case, because the criteria is a hard-coded value, meaning that if any other `OrderID` is needed, the code would have to be changed to accommodate it. That is not so much the point of this exercise; instead, it is to demonstrate that having to check for records before a custom opening a report would add a significant amount of development time to each project.

Instead, the `On No Data` takes care of verifyingthat there is data, and allows for the cancellation of the report when there is no data found (see the following example).

```
Private Sub Report_NoData(Cancel As Integer)
   Cancel = MsgBox("No Records Found", vbInformation, Me.Caption)
End Sub
```

The previous example is very generic, because there are no hard-coded values. Because of this, and the simplicity of it, this code can be placed in every report in the database. The code itself sets the `Cancel` parameter, which is used to prevent any processing from occurring after the current procedure, to the result of the message box. Because the message box will only return a positive integer value (1, 2, 4, 8, and so on), the `Cancel` value will always be set to `True` when the `No Data` event procedure is executed.

(In Access, a True value is anything not equal to zero.) Finally, the Caption property of the Me object is an easy way to display information about the form in the message box.

As you step your way through VBA programming, be sure to take advantage of all aspects of the programming environment. The On No Data event property is one such property that can save you some development time and effort.

{Section}_Format(): Dynamically Display Page Numbers

The Format event procedure executes between the occurrences of when Access determines what data belongs in a report section, but before that data is formatted for printing. This procedure is suitable for making changes that affect page layout, such as displaying or hiding controls or for the creation of complex running calculations that span multiple groupings.

It is important to note that this event procedure executes for every section, including any sections that are not printed. To contrast this point, note that the Print procedure executes only when sections are printed. Unprinted sections will not execute, which may cause a problem for calculated running totals. Be sure to validate all numbers that are generated when performing a calculation on any report.

When using the Format procedure, the section (Detail, Header, or Footer) that is used will not only dictate when the event procedure should execute, but also what data is exposed at the time of execution. *Exposed* is a term that specifies that it is available for use by the developer. The following table describes these differences.

Section	Executes	Data Exposed
Detail	Just before each record is formatted	Current record
Group Header	Just before each new Group Header is formatted	Data in the group header First record of the Detail ection
Group Footer	Just before each new Group Footer is formatted	Data in the group footer Last record of the Detail section

In the following sample code, the format procedure is used to change an attribute about the report page footer section.

```
Private Sub PageFooter_Format(Cancel As Integer, _
   FormatCount As Integer)
   If Me.Page Mod 2 = 0 Then
     'Display the even page number on the Right Side
     Me.txtPageOdd.Visible = False
     Me.txtPageEven.Visible = True
   Else
     'Display the odd page number on the Left side
     Me.txtPageOdd.Visible = True
     Me.txtPageEven.Visible = False
   End If
End Sub
```

In the above sample, it is assumed that there are two text box controls placed within the `Page Footer`. They are identical in their data properties, as both have the following controlsource:

```
="Page " & [Page]
```

When the word `"Page"` is used on a report, it refers to the current page number. (This is what is known as a reserved word, and should only be used for the intrinsic purpose.) For the expression specified as the controlsource, it concatenates the literal word `"Page"` to the number of the current page of the report.

```
i.e. Page 1
```

As far as formatting of the two text boxes are concerned, `txtPageOdd` is placed on the left side of the page footer, and is left-justified. `txtPageEven` is placed on the right side, and is right-justified. With this setup, turn your focus back to the code in the event procedure, and notice that sometimes the odd page number is visible, and other times the even page number is visible. The effect that this gives is that the page number will either be on the left or right side of the page, depending if the number is odd or even.

The way that this is controlled is through the use of the `Mod` operator. The keyword mod is short for modulus and returns only the remainder of a division calculation between two expressions. As applied in this situation, the page number is divided by the number 2, and the remainder is compared to zero. If a number is divided by 2, and has a remainder, then it is not an even number. The converse is that the number is even. So, the code determines if the page number is odd or even and then displays the proper text box to show the page number on the appropriate side of the page.

Section_Print(): Conditional Formatting of a Text Box

The `Print` event procedure executes after the data in a report section is formatted for printing, but before the section is printed.

This procedure is suitable for calculating running page totals that are printed in the page header or footer or for making changes that affect page layout, such as displaying or hiding controls. It is important to note that the `Print` Procedure executes only when sections are printed. Unprinted sections will not execute this procedure, which may cause a problem for calculated running totals. Be sure to validate all numbers that are generated when performing a calculation on any report.

When using the `Print` Procedure, the section (`Detail`, `Header`, or `Footer`) that is used will not only dictate when the event procedure should execute, but also what data is exposed at the time of execution. Exposed is a term that specifies that it is available for use by the developer. The following table describes these differences.

Section	Executes	Data Exposed
Detail	Just before each record is printed	Current record
Group Header	Just before each new Group Header is printed	Data in the group header First record of the Detail section
Group Footer	Just before each new Group Footer is printed	Data in the group footer Last record of the Detail section

In the following sample code, the `Print` Procedure is used to change an attribute about the report, which resides within the `Detail` section.

```
Private Sub Detail_Print(Cancel As Integer, PrintCount As Integer)
   'Determine the number of items in Stock
   If txtUnitsInStock > 100 Then
     'Alert the reader with Red Text
     txtUnitsInStock.ForeColor = vbRed
   Else
     'Use Black for non-alerted values
     txtUnitsInStock.ForeColor = vbBlack
   End If
End Sub
```

In the previous example, the code determines if the current `In Stock` value of a product is greater than 100. If it is, then it changes the code to red for that record. If it is not, it returns the color back to black. It is very important to remember to return the color back to the original setting, or else after the first time the color is set to red, it will stay that way until the end of the report.

Compute a Running Balance

To apply what you have learned, the following example is a known problem for many users in all sectors of business. There are times when a user needs to compute a running balance based on a single column of numbers. This example uses a typical bank account, because most people can associate to it. The technique that is conveyed can be modified to pertain to invoices, mileage, weights, or anything else in your business model that would require a running balance. To start, suppose that there exists a table that stores bank account transactions, which may resemble Figure 11-5.

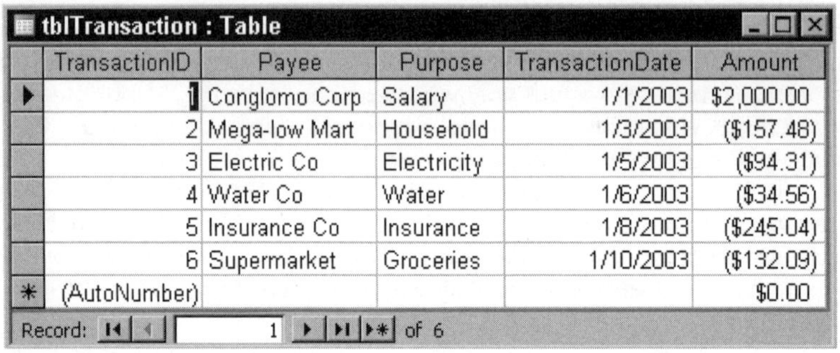

TransactionID	Payee	Purpose	TransactionDate	Amount
1	Conglomo Corp	Salary	1/1/2003	$2,000.00
2	Mega-low Mart	Household	1/3/2003	($157.48)
3	Electric Co	Electricity	1/5/2003	($94.31)
4	Water Co	Water	1/6/2003	($34.56)
5	Insurance Co	Insurance	1/8/2003	($245.04)
6	Supermarket	Groceries	1/10/2003	($132.09)
(AutoNumber)				$0.00

Record: 1 of 6

Figure 11-5

In the screenshot, there is an example data table, in which the `Payee`, `Purpose`, and `Transaction Date` fields are self-explanatory. For clarification, the `Amount` field retains the dollar figure for each transaction, where positive values are deposits and negative values are withdrawals. (Your paper checkbook may have different columns for each, but the same principle would apply.)

When new developers are faced with the running balance task, they initially try to solve the problem within the table itself. They add a new column to the table, call it `Balance`, and then attempt to populate the data with a query. This technique works, but only for the sort order in which the query was executed.

For example, suppose that the developer decided to create the running balance based on `Transaction Date`. Figure 11-6 displays the results of the query technique.

TransactionID	Payee	Purpose	TransactionDate	Amount	Balance
1	Conglomo Corp	Salary	1/1/2003	$2,000.00	$2,000.00
2	Mega-low Mart	Household	1/3/2003	($157.48)	$1,842.52
3	Electric Co	Electricity	1/5/2003	($94.31)	$1,748.21
4	Water Co	Water	1/6/2003	($34.56)	$1,713.65
5	Insurance Co	Insurance	1/8/2003	($245.04)	$1,468.61
6	Supermarket	Groceries	1/10/2003	($132.09)	$1,336.52
(AutoNumber)				$0.00	$0.00

Record: 14 4 [1] ▶ ▶I ▶* of 6

Figure 11-6

This would appear to be a logical way to do it, but just for the sake of confusion, suppose that the user decided to sort the data by the `Purpose` column, and/or filter the data based on the `Payee`. (For the filter example, it is assumed that there are multiple months of transaction data.) If the user were to perform the sort, then the data, including the balance field, would be sorted. It would look like Figure 11-7.

TransactionID	Payee	Purpose	TransactionDate	Amount	Balance
3	Electric Co	Electricity	1/5/2003	($94.31)	$1,748.21
6	Supermarket	Groceries	1/10/2003	($132.09)	$1,336.52
2	Mega-low Mart	Household	1/3/2003	($157.48)	$1,842.52
5	Insurance Co	Insurance	1/8/2003	($245.04)	$1,468.61
1	Conglomo Corp	Salary	1/1/2003	$2,000.00	$2,000.00
4	Water Co	Water	1/6/2003	($34.56)	$1,713.65
(AutoNumber)				$0.00	$0.00

Record: 14 4 [1] ▶ ▶I ▶* of 6

Figure 11-7

Notice that the balance column retains the values that were assigned to it when it was populated by the query. To the unsuspecting user, they would either get confused, or worse, they would simply use the last number in the column as the final balance. This would not reflect graciously on any of the parties involved.

If this field and technique are utilized, then it requires that the developer recalculate the running balance values every time the data is sorted, filtered, or queried. This would be very time-consuming for the developer. It would also decrease the end-user performance for each of their data operations.

Another way to solve the running balance problem is with a report. Some developers may find this to be an easier way to display the data, because the report can perform the necessary data recalculations when it is executed. In case the sort order is modified, then the calculated balances are always correctly calculated. And, since a report can be displayed on the screen, it does not require the user to physically print the data in order to view it.

Figure 11-8 is a graphical representation of a running balance solution.

Checking Account

Starting Balance
$1,234.56

Payee	Purpose	Date	Amount	Balance
Conglomo Corp	Salary	1/1/2003	$2,000.00	$3,234.56
Mega-low Mart	Household	1/3/2003	($157.48)	$3,077.08
Electric Co	Electricity	1/5/2003	($94.31)	$2,982.77
Water Co	Water	1/6/2003	($34.56)	$2,948.21
Insurance Co	Insurance	1/8/2003	($245.04)	$2,703.17
Supermarket	Groceries	1/10/2003	($132.09)	$2,571.08
			Ending Balance:	$2,571.08

Figure 11-8

In the previous picture, the Balance column begins with a `Starting Balance` of $1234.56, which is then added to the first Transaction Amount, and then carried over to each of the remaining individual transactions. At the end of the report, the final balance is restated, for a quick-glance reference of the value.

Running Sum Property

As new report developers attempt to solve the running balance task, they soon learn about the `Running Sum` property of a text box. It appears rather straightforward and a logical approach to utilize this property to perform the calculation. What they don't know is that this property only performs 98 percent of the work at hand, but doesn't finish the job. In Figure 11-9, the report looks exactly the same, but it uses the `Running Sum` property for the `Balance column`.

Checking Account

Starting Balance
$1,234.56

Payee	Purpose	Date	Amount	Balance
Conglomo Corp	Salary	1/1/2003	$2,000.00	$2,000.00
Mega-low Mart	Household	1/3/2003	($157.48)	$1,842.52
Electric Co	Electricity	1/5/2003	($94.31)	$1,748.21
Water Co	Water	1/6/2003	($34.56)	$1,713.65
Insurance Co	Insurance	1/8/2003	($245.04)	$1,468.61
Supermarket	Groceries	1/10/2003	($132.09)	$1,336.52
			Ending Balance:	$1,336.52

Figure 11-9

The previous picture displays the running balance of all of the transaction records. The `Balance` field uses the same controlsource as the `Amount` field, but the `Running Sum` property for `Balance` is set to `Over All`. (The choices for this property are `Over Group`, `Over All`, and `No`.) At first glance, anyone could be fooled that this data is accurate, but compare the first report picture with the second, and you can see that the report is significantly incorrect. Although the Running Sum property can perform the task of adding the previous value to the current value, it cannot incorporate the starting balance from the top of the report. Without the use of the starting balance, the ending balance will always be incorrect.

The Report Design

Now, to understand the code needed to perform the running sum task, it first involves understanding the construction of the report itself. It is assumed that you understand each of the different sections of the report generator. To help you understand the construction of the report, take a look at Figure 11-10.

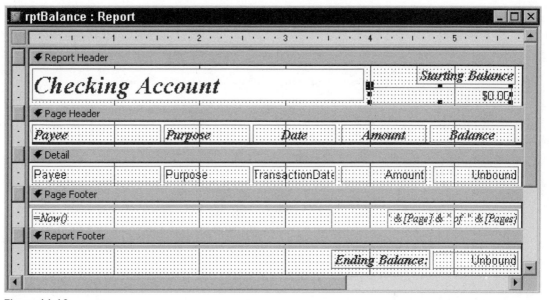

Figure 11-10

Figure 11-10 shows the report designer for a running balance report. There are several important controls that are used in the VBA code of the report. These fields are listed in the following table.

Control	Property	Setting	Description
txtAmount	Controlsource	Amount Column	Bound to Amount Column in data table
txtBalance	Controlsource	Unbound	Value is set by the VBA code
	Running Sum	No	Do not use the running balance.
txtBalance_Starting	Controlsource	Unbound	Retrieves previous ending balance from a function
txtBalance_Ending	Controlsource	Unbound	Value is set by the VBA code

The other properties of these controls are inconsequential to the remainder of the functionality of this example. Further, it is important to note that the Running Sum property is mentioned only to avoid any confusion, that it should be used for this example. The Starting Balance calls a VBA function to return the previous ending balance. As there may be many factors to the retrieval of this data, it is not discussed further, but instead assumed to retrieve the correct starting value for the example.

VBA Code Behind Report

Once the theory and controls, as described in the previous paragraphs, are understood, the only thing that remains is to examine the code itself, which resides in the Report's code module. The code is designed to use a module-level variable to maintain the running balance. At points throughout the report execution, the variable is either incremented or displayed.

In this example, all of the procedures for this code are displayed as one segment. It may appear overwhelming to a new developer, but understand that this is one of the code views that can be selected when developing in the VBA environment. (The other view displays only one procedure at a time.)

The example procedures are arranged top-down in the order in which they are executed after the report is opened. This is not required, but has been done to add to assist with reading comprehension. VBA is an event-driven language and does not require any specific order to the procedures. (Some procedural languages require that called procedure occur prior to the calling procedure.)

The final benefit of viewing this code in its entirety is that it demonstrates the importance of having clean, readable, and simple code. It is important to understand that programming does not stop when the functionality is complete. At some point, either you or another programming will be required to read, enhance, or worse, fix your code. As you view the code example, take note of the subtle difference that it makes when techniques such as a naming convention, indentations, and readable comments are included.

```vba
'Create a variable to hold the running balance.
Dim mdblBalance As Double

Private Function GetStartingBalance()
   'Get Starting Balance
   'Could be obtained via other dynamic methods
   GetStartingBalance = 1234.56

End Function

Private Sub Report_Open(Cancel As Integer)

   'Initialize the running balance to previous balance
   mdblBalance = GetStartingBalance

   'Set the starting balance in the Report Header
   txtBalance_Starting = mdblBalance

End Sub

Private Sub Detail_Print(Cancel As Integer, _
   PrintCount As Integer)
```

```
    'Increase the balance by the current transaction amount
    mdblBalance = mdblBalance + txtAmount

    'Set the balance value to the new running balance amount
    txtBalance = mdblBalance

End Sub

Private Sub ReportFooter_Print(Cancel As Integer, _
    PrintCount As Integer)

    'Set the ending balance to the final balance amount
    txtBalance_Ending = mdblBalance

End Sub
```

In reviewing this code, the first thing that you should notice is that there are no more than 10 lines of actual code that you would have to write. All of the procedure headers and footers are created for you, and without the inclusion of developer comments, the coding effort is minimal. It is important to note that many facets of VBA do not require hundreds of lines of code, when designed correctly. In this case, the mixture of a few controls with a little bit of code offers a significant amount of functionality. If you find that you are coding with significant more effort than this, then you may want to rethink your methodology.

The code in the above example starts by declaring a module-level variable to hold the running balance. The variable must remain in scope throughout the life of the entire report, or else the running value would be lost. There is no need to declare the balance variable as Public (or Global) unless you need to refer to it outside of the report.

GetStartingBalance() is a procedure that is exposed to all other procedures within the report module. It is there to retrieve the previous ending balance from perhaps the last month. There are multiple paradigms that could be used for implementation, but for this example, a hard-coded value is supplied. In practice, you could store the previous balance in a table, or calculate it at the time the report is executed. It really depends on what functionality is supplied to the user when executing the report. For example, can they select a date range to print the report, or is it hard-coded by month?

The Report_Open() procedure executes one time when the report opens. In this example, the balance variable is initialized during this procedure, as it only needs to be initialized one time. You may have an example where a running balance needs to be reset at certain times throughout the execution of the report. If this is the case, then the variable initialization would need to occur in an event procedure that is executed multiple times throughout the generation of the report. An example of this would be a group header or footer. Also, the starting balance text box is populated with the initial value.

The processes of incrementing the running balance and displaying it on the report are both executed from the Detail section Print event procedure. Both of these steps are performed here, because at the time the value is computed, it needs to be printed. Separating these two steps between other event procedures can lead to the balance being increased at undesired intervals, and cause the wrong value to be written on the report.

The last section that is printed for a report is the Report Footer. This is commonly used for printing grand totals. For example, a sum of the Amount field would net the sum of the detail items for only the current report. In the example, the ending balance is displayed in the footer. This could be as a convenience to the user, or by their request.

When Not to Use VBA

There are times when you will attempt to solve a problem with VBA, only to find out that VBA is *not* the answer. The following example is such a case. Over time, you will learn to identify what can be solved with code, with a query or multiple queries, and also via the use of controls on a report.

When developing a report, there are things that you can do that don't require programming. Instead, with a properly placed control, or with the use of a grouping section, the desired functionality can be achieved. In this example, an index letter can be added to the start of each Alphabetical value in the report. This can be helpful for easy recognition of data by the user. Figure 11-11 demonstrates the desired effect.

G

Product Name:

Geitost

Genen Shouyu

Gnocchi di nonna Alice

Gorgonzola Telino

Grandma's Boysenberry Spread

Gravad lax

Gudbrandsdalsost

Gula Malacca

Gumbär Gummibärchen

Gustaf's Knäckebröd

I

Product Name:

Ikura

Inlagd Sill

Ipoh Coffee

Figure 11-11

In this report, each product is listed alphabetically. Where one letter ends, and the next begins, the starting letter is printed to assist the reader with locating their desired value. This functionality could be programmed in the report writer, but is easily implemented with just a text box control and a group.

Figure 11-12 displays the report called `Alphabetical List of Products`, which comes with the `Northwind` database example.

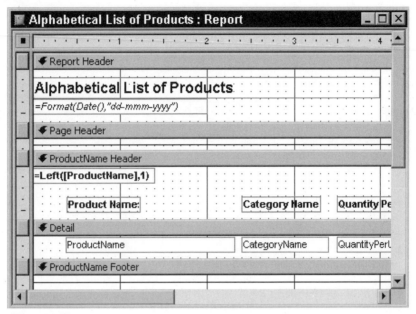

Figure 11-12

In Figure 11-12, notice that there is a report section called `ProductName Header`. This is the start of a grouping for the field called `ProductName`. Typically, group headers are a good place to put specific labels that may apply only on the group level. As seen here, the labels for `Product Name`, `Category Name`, and the `Quantity Per Unit` are displayed.

Along with those static labels is a text box. Although it looks the same as the labels, it reveals that it is a textbox by the fact that it displays a "=" sign as the first character. This is a method of populating a text box at the time of generation. So, rather than execute VBA code to populate this text box, the "=" sign instructs Access to evaluate (or calculate) the value before showing the report. The text box displays the following expression:

```
=Left([ProductName],1)
```

This expression is used to extract the first character from each `Product Name` (that is, `Left("Apple")` = `"A"`). Thus, every time the group header is printed, the first character is printed for each `ProductName`.

Now, if you're familiar with reports, at this point you may be a little confused. It would stand to reason that for every product in the table this text box should be displayed. After all, the grouping is by the `ProductName`. If that were the case, then the report would look like Figure 11-13.

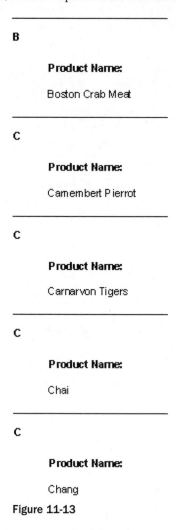

Figure 11-13

Figure 11-13 demonstrates what Access should produce, based on the fact that the header should print with every product name. The way to prevent this is to use a property of the Group called `Group On`. The `Group On` property has two settings, which are `Each Value` and `Prefix Characters`. The value used in the most recent picture is when `Each Value` is selected, and as you can see, it does not have the desired effect.

When you set the property to `Prefix Characters`, you can then specify the number of characters that are to be used in the grouping. In the case of the Index letter example, it makes sense that the value of 1 is used. In Figure 11-14, the `Sorting and Grouping` box is displayed using these settings.

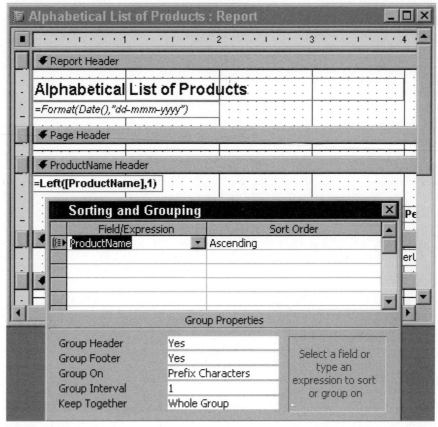

Figure 11-14

In this example of the `Sorting and Grouping` dialog box, the `Expression` is set to use a `Group Header` and `Footer` section in the report. The `Group On` property is set to `Prefix Characters` and the `Group Interval` is set to 1.

Summary

Using the right combination of report sections, controls, and properties, there are many forms tasks in Access that can be completed without VBA code. The key to learning the difference of when to use VBA, and when not to, lies in the examination of not only the properties of every object, section, and control, but also the settings of those properties.

12

Creating Classes in VBA

The ability to create self-contained software objects was first conceived in about 1970 with the development of *SIMULA 67* (SIMUlation LAnguage), an extension of the scientific ALGOL 60 computer language.

It took quite a while before the programming community realized the implications of the breakthrough that SIMULA represented. When they did, object-oriented programming (OOP) quickly became the new buzzword, relegating *structured programming* to the realm of the lesser informed code cutters.

With the release of languages like SmallTalk, C++, and later, Java, OOP earned its place in the software hall of fame as the new panacea to all our programming ills. When Visual Basic 4.0 was released in 1993, Basic developers were tantalized by a new toy: the class module.

Long snubbed by C++ developers who had been using class modules for years, Basic developers were finally able to hold their heads high with the new found ability to create fully self-contained and reusable objects.

In OOP parlance, an *object* is a unique *instance* of a data structure, called a *class*, that has both *properties*, which define its characteristics, and executable procedures called *methods*, which define its behavior in modifying those properties.

A class's properties are completely isolated from the outside world and can only be modified internally by its own methods. This doesn't mean that the programmer can't do anything to them, but that he or she can't do anything to them *directly*; he or she must use those methods that are exposed for that purpose. The properties and methods you create are termed its *implementation*, whereas the methods it exposes to the programming environment constitutes its *interface*. Thus an object is a completely self-contained programmatic entity, in that it contains both its own data and the program code necessary to implement its own behavior.

In this chapter, we will examine VBA classes and class objects. We'll first look at what a class actually is and the difference between it and a class object. We'll then jump straight in and create our first class module and figure out how it works. After that, I will discuss how to identify classes and then how to get them to communicate with the rest of your application, before diving into the more advanced topics, like building collection classes, and then finishing off with some object-oriented theory to round it all off.

Classes are not as daunting as you might first think, and we hope that after reading this chapter you will cast off any fears you may have had and happily find many uses for your newfound skills.

A Touch of Class

Classes have been likened to rubber stamps, cookie-cutters, and a raft of other everyday items in an attempt to make the concept more easily understandable. Since you are reading a book on software development, it is fairly safe to assume that you understand the concept of a template, like a Microsoft Word template. We like that analogy, because it succinctly describes the role of class modules and the distinction between them and class objects.

Just like a class module is equivalent to a Word template, a *class object* is equivalent to a Word document that is based on that template. Of course, with VBA class modules, you don't define styles or boilerplate text, but you do define a set of properties that includes their data types and read/write attributes. You also define the class's methods, the data types they return (if any), and the events the class exposes to the calling procedure. It is these properties and methods that constitute the object's interface to the programming environment.

Each unique class object will be exactly the same as the class module it was based on, except, of course, for the data it contains. In fact, the class module never gets instantiated and never contains any data because you don't actually work on it. You can, however, create as many *instances* of it as you like, in the form of class objects, each identified by a different name. To make a change to all the class objects, you need only change the class module. Probably the easiest way to describe a class is to compare it to a standard VBA module.

> Note: VBA modules can contain many procedures, such as subs and functions. Since we have already covered them in Chapter 2, I will assume you know the difference by now.

Let's say we have a VBA module called *modKennel* that contains procedures to implement a single property of a kennel, the number of dogs in residence.

```
Option Compare Database
Option Explicit

Private mintDogs As Integer

Public Sub AddDog()
    mintDogs = mintDogs + 1
End Sub

Public Function GetDogs() As Integer
    Dogs = mintDogs
End Function
```

Our property, the number of dogs, is stored in a module-level variable called `mintDogs`. To add a dog to the kennel, we call the `AddDog()` procedure, and to retrieve the current count we call the `GetDogs()` function.

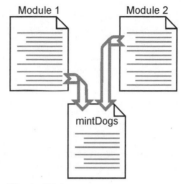

Figure 12-1

What if you had another module somewhere that also uses the `AddDog()` procedure? It would change the value of `mintDogs`. To ensure you can change the number of dog for different kennels, you would have to either create multiple `AddDog` procedures, or implement some other way of doing it, like arrays.

This is where class modules come in. Take a look at the following class module called `clsKennel`. Don't worry if you don't quite understand it; we'll explain everything as we go along.

```
Option Compare Database
Option Explicit

Private mintDogs As Integer

Public Sub AddDog()
    mintDogs = mintDogs + 1
End Sub

Public Property Get Dogs() As Integer
    Dogs = mintDogs
End Property
```

This class is exactly the same as `modKennel`. The nifty part about it is the fact that the code used to define the class is essentially a template than we can use to create as many kennel objects as we like. Further, if we had two different procedures that each called `AddDog()`, they would each operate on a different copy, or instance, of the `clsKennel` class.

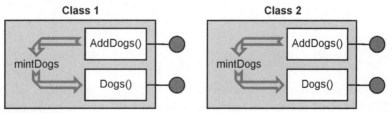

Figure 12-2

For example, the following VBA module contains two procedures, each of which creates a kennel object called myKennel. The first one, TestKennel1, adds one dog to the kennel and then calls TestKennel2, which creates a second kennel instance and adds two dogs.

```
Option Compare Database
Option Explicit

Public Sub TestKennel1()
    Dim MyKennel As clsKennel
    Set MyKennel = New clsKennel

    MyKennel.AddDog
    MsgBox "I have " & MyKennel.Dogs & " dog in my kennel."
    TestKennel2
    MsgBox "I still have only " & MyKennel.Dogs & " dog in my kennel."
End Sub

Public Sub TestKennel2()
    Dim MyKennel As clsKennel
    Set MyKennel = New clsKennel

    MyKennel.AddDog
    MyKennel.AddDog
    MsgBox "I have " & MyKennel.Dogs & " dogs in my kennel."
End Sub
```

Both instances of the cs1Kennel class are exactly the same in form and function, but are completely different entities. Thus the properties of each are completely distinct from each other.

Why Use Classes?

From a coding perspective, the only real difference between using the built-in Access or VBA objects and the ones you write yourself is that you have to *instantiate* your custom objects. Other than that, there's no difference at all.

There is a learning curve associated with creating you own class objects, but once learned, the major benefit is much simpler and more manageable code. Also, while you can instantiate the built-in objects, using the Dim construct, you don't always have to. For example, to expose the Name property of a Table object, either of the following examples will work.

Example 1

```
MsgBox DBEngine(0)(0).TableDefs(1).Name
```

Example 2

```
Set tdf = DBEngine(0)(0).TableDefs(1)
```

I must admit that I put off learning about classes for many years, as like so many others, I couldn't see a use for them in what I did. But during a particularly nasty project, I found working in standard modules far more complex than I felt it needed to be, so I created a few simple classes to encapsulate real world data entities and their associated functionality in a single object. I was amazed by how much simpler my programming task became. I ended up writing a complete object model for that project.

Now having just expounded the virtues of adopting modern OOP techniques, we certainly wouldn't recommend writing a collection class where a simple array would suffice. You should still apply the right tool to the right job. If a standard module is all you need, use one. In other words, don't overengineer a project, just so you can use the latest technology.

Creating a Class Module

We learn best by doing, so to learn the basic techniques used to create a class module, this section is devoted to creating one you may find useful in your own projects.

Adding a Class Module to the Project

To add a new class module to your project, press *Alt+F11* from the database window to open a new standard module. Then from the Visual Basic Designer window, select Class Module from the Insert menu. You can also right-click anywhere in the Project Explorer and select Insert|Class Module from the context menu.

VBA opens a new class module and adds a reference to it in the Project Explorer. Copy the clsKennel code into the module, as shown in Figure 12-3. That's it! You've created your first class module!

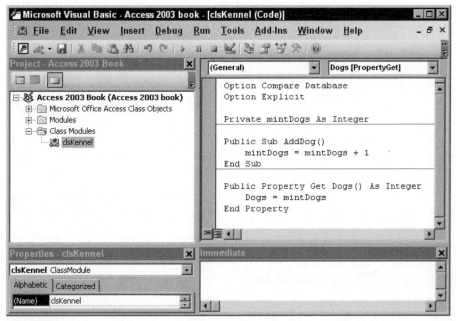

Figure 12-3

A Brief Word on Naming the Class

All things have names, and class modules are no different. The name you give a class module, however, is the name that is shown in both the `Project Explorer` and the `Object Browser`, so it should be something relevant and meaningful. For a more in-depth discussion on naming objects, refer to section on *Naming Objects*, later in this chapter.

To name your class, display the `Properties` window by selecting it from the `View` menu, or by pressing *F4*. Then enter a name in the `(Name)` property. You might like to review Appendix G for object-naming conventions and prefixes.

You will have undoubtedly noticed that there is another property in the `Properties` dialog box that we have not mentioned—`Instancing`. Since you need to understand several other concepts before we explain this one, and it would be inappropriate to do so now, we have left this topic until the very end of the chapter.

Figure 12-4 shows our `clsKennel` class in the `Object Browser`, which you can display by selecting `Object Browser` from the `View` menu, or by pressing *F2*.

Figure 12-4

Notice that details of the selected property or method are displayed under the `Classes` pane. You can filter the `Classes` pane by selecting a project or library from the `Project/Library` combo box, as shown in Figure 12-5.

A more detailed explanation of the `Object Browser` is given in Chapter 5, but since you can't do any damage by experimenting in the `Object Browser`, feel free to look around and click all the buttons.

Instantiating Class Objects

In Chapter 4, we saw how to declare and instantiate object variables, like the `Recordset` object, using the `Set` keyword. Class objects are brought into existence in exactly the same way. The following code

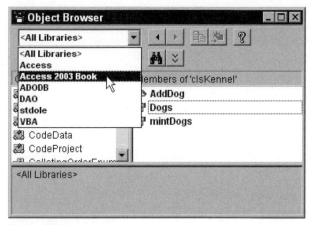

Figure 12-5

segment demonstrates how to declare and instantiate an object variable:

```
Dim myKennel As clsKennel
Set myKennel = New clsKennel
```

As mentioned earlier, once you instantiate a class, it is referred to as an object instance of that class.

If you were declaring a variable to hold an integer value, you would declare it as an `Integer` data type, using the `Dim intMyVariable As Integer` construct. But since we are declaring a variable to contain an instance of a class object, you declare it as an object, but more specifically as an object of the `clsSomeClass` type, where `clsSomeClass` is the name you gave to your class. Remember that when you save a named class module, Access understands that it is an object; that's why it appears in the `Object Browser`. So when you declare a variable of that type, Access allocates sufficient memory to hold a *pointer* to an instance of your object. That's right, when you instantiate the class object, the variable doesn't contain the object itself, just a pointer to it.

Of course, you could save a line of code by instantiating the object on one line using the `New` keyword, but it's not the recommended way of doing things. For example:

```
Dim myKennel As New clsKennel
```

The simple reason for this is that, although you might save a line of code, programmers often need to know exactly when an object is instantiated, particularly when debugging someone else's code. By using one line to declare the variable and one to instantiate the object, it is quite clear when things happen. The performance impact is negligible.

Creating Class Methods

In Chapter 4, we were introduced to the concept of *subs* and *functions*. Class modules have them as well, but just to give the impression that they're somewhat special, we refer to them as *methods*. It makes some sense when you consider that a class's procedures carry out actions on its properties and therefore constitute the method by which those actions are executed.

In the same way that methods are executed against objects in the Access object model, class methods are executed against class objects. For example, when we want to move a DAO recordset cursor to the next record, we are actually using method exposed by the Recordset object.

```
rst.MoveNext
```

There are three types of method: sub(program)s, functions, and properties. Subs and functions you know about, but properties, which I will introduce a little later, are a special type of method that can exhibit the characteristics of both.

To create an external interface for our class, we need to add subs, functions, and properties. Let's take a closer look at our friend, the Kennel class.

```
Option Compare Database
Option Explicit
Private mintDogs As Integer

Public Sub AddDogs(intHowMany As Integer)
    mintDogs = mintDogs + intHowMany
End Sub

Public Function FeedDogs() As Boolean
    'Code to implement the FeedDog action.
    If DogsNeedFood() = True Then
        'code to feed the dogs.
        FeedDogs = True
    End If
End Function

Private Function DogsNeedFood() As Boolean
    'Code to determine if the dogs are hungry.
    'For our example, we'll just return True.
    DogsNeedFood = True
End Function

Public Property Let Dogs(intNewValue As Integer)
    mintDogs = intNewValue
End Property

Public Property Get Dogs() As Integer
    Dogs = mintDogs
End Property
```

In this class module, we have a private integer variable called mintDogs, declared at module level, so all our procedures can access it. We also have a public subprocedure called AddDogs, a public function called FeedDogs(), a private function called DogsNeedFood(), and two *property procedures*, both called Dogs, which we'll explain later.

The AddDogs method takes a single integer argument that specifies the number of dogs to add to our kennel. Nothing special there! The FeedDogs method takes no arguments, but returns a Boolean value indicating success or failure. You might also notice that FeedDogs executes some code to actually feed the animals, but only if the DogsNeedsFood() function returns True. Once the dogs have had their dinner, FeedDogs returns True to the code that called it and everybody's happy.

Now, you've probably already noticed that we seem to have duplicate procedure names. We do, but property procedures are a special type of procedure for which duplicate names are allowed. But before we discuss property procedures, it's appropriate to first explain a term that is often used to describe the object properties and methods that are visible and accessible to the VBA code that instantiated the object—the *interface*.

So What's an Interface?

Having already mentioned the class interface, it may be worthwhile digressing a little to offer an explanation before we proceed with property procedures.

An *interface* is simply a set of properties and procedures that are exposed to the VBA environment so that code outside the class can access them. We do this by declaring them as `Public` or `Private`, much like you would do with any VBA procedure, and by defining their read/write attributes, as shown in Figure 12-6.

Figure 12-6

In the example shown in the preceding section, our interface is defined by those methods and procedures declared as `Public`. Code outside the class cannot see private members, and therefore, cannot execute them. Properties and methods declared as `Private` can only be executed from *inside* the class, and therefore, do not form part of our class's interface.

In the following example, the `PrintPayrise()` procedure is part of the object's interface, while `GivePayrise()` is not.

```
Public Sub PrintPayrise()
        'Public methods are part of the object's interface.
End Sub

Private Sub GivePayrise()
        'Private methods are not part of the object's interface.
End Sub
```

When creating classes, it is important that you maintain the integrity of its interface. That is, you should avoid changing the property or method names, the names of any arguments, the number of arguments, or their data types. Programmers take a great deal of trouble to write VBA code to instantiate and use a class object that has a specific interface; so if you change that interface, you *break* the very thing that VBA code needs to make it all work.

On large software projects, where there are many developers working on different parts of the system, a single changed interface can result in many weeks of lost time while everyone changes their code. Rarely does this make for a happy team.

The rule in most software development houses is "never break an interface!" If you need to make changes that will result in the need to change large sections of VBA code, either create a new class or add new methods to the existing one. Existing code will continue to use the existing interface, while newer code that needs to take advantage of any new or modified functionality can use the new ones.

Creating Property Procedures

A person's name, height, weight, age, and so on, can all be considered *properties* of the object known as *humans*. That is, they are the object's attributes or defining characteristics. In OOP, this definition also holds true of class properties.

In a programming environment, it is unwise to allow a user to change an object's properties without validating the value, a task that is best left in the object's capable hands. Additionally, there may be other actions that need to be taken when a property is changed. It is for these reasons that property procedures were invented.

Property procedures come in three flavors: `Property Get`, `Property Let`, and `Property Set`, and they provide a standardized way of setting and retrieving the object's properties.

> Note: Property procedures are the only procedures that can share the same name within the same module.

The `Property Get` procedure retrieves (or gets) the value of the class's property. Alternatively, the `Property Let` and `Property Set` procedures set (or change) their values. The difference between them is that `Property Let` procedures set scalar values (like integers, strings, and so on), whereas `Property Set` is used for objects.

In the `Kennel` class example, `mintDogs` is the actual property, and the two `Dogs` methods are its property procedures. The property itself is declared as `Private`, to ensure that VBA code must access the property through one of the defined property procedures. In this way, your class can always be assured of controlling how dogs are added to the kennel and knowing when a property changes.

Using Property Get

The `Property Get` procedure retrieves the value of a class property. Its declaration is much the same as a standard VBA function, but with the addition of the `Get` keyword. Like a function, you declare sits return data type to that of the class property it will return. Whatever receives the procedure's return value must be declared with the same data type.

For example, the following code is the `Dogs Property Get` procedure from our `Kennel` class example:

```
Public Property Get Dogs() As Integer
    Dogs = mintDogs
End Property
```

The name `Dogs` defines the name of the class's property as far as VBA code is concerned. Its return data type is declared as integer, and when VBA code calls the property like so:

```
intSomeVariable = myKennel.Dogs
```

VBA calls the procedure just like any standard function, and the code inside returns the privately declared property `mintDogs`. Property procedures can do anything a standard procedure can do, even accept arguments, but in practice, that is rarely done. Usually, since methods act on data in ways that often depend on other values or conditions, they tend to be used to accept arguments. Referring to an argument declared in a `Property Get` procedure is simple enough. For example, if we declare our procedure like so:

```
Public Property Get Dogs(strColor As String) As Integer
    ' Code that uses the strColor argument
    Dogs = mintDogs
End Property
```

We can refer to it like this:

```
intSomeVariable = myKennel.Dogs("black")
```

Using Property Let

While `Property Get` retrieves a value of a class property, the `Property Let` procedure sets the value. For example, the following code is the `Dogs Property Let` procedure from our `Kennel` class example. It is constructed in the same way as the `Property Get` procedure, but using the `Let` keyword.

```
Public Property Let Dogs(intNewValue As Integer)
    mintDogs = intNewValue
End Property
```

You can declare its arguments' data types according to your needs, and you can even rename the argument as you would with any other procedure argument. In fact, you can declare more than one argument if you need to—just like any other procedure.

`Property Let` procedures work differently to standard procedures, and it may take a little getting used to. When VBA code assigns a value to the property, like so:

```
myKennel.Dogs = intSomeVariable
```

The code inside passes the argument to the privately declared property `mintDogs`. Just like the `Property Get` procedure, you can declare more than one argument in `Property Let`. For example, if we declare our procedure like so:

```
Public Property Let Dogs(strColor As String, intNewValue As Integer)
    ' Code that uses the strColor argument
    mintDogs = intNewValue
End Property
```

We can refer to it like this:

```
myKennel.Dogs("black") = intSomeVariable
```

Notice that the property value being passed must be the last argument in the list.

Using Property Set

The `Property Set` procedure is very similar to `Property Let`, in that it sets the value of properties. But where `Property Let` populates scalar properties (integer, date, string, and so on), `Property Set` populates *object properties*; that is, properties that are actually pointers to other objects.

For example, in the following `clsKennel` class module, the `Property Set` procedure sets the value of the `Gate` property so that the `Property Get` procedure can return a new `Gate` object.

For clarity, we've removed the other properties and methods.

```
Option Compare Database
Option Explicit

'Private variable that will contain a reference
'to an instance of the clsGate object.
Private mobjGate As clsGate

Public Property Get Gate() As clsGate
    'Return an instance of the mobjGate object that
    'was instantiated by the Property Set procedure
    Set Gate = mobjGate
End Property

Public Property Set Gate(objGate As clsGate)
    'Instantiate the module-level object variable
    'using the object passed to the procedure
    Set mobjGate = objGate
End Property
```

To use this construct, external VBA code must pass the `clsGate` object to the `Property Set` procedure in a `Set` statement, after which it can access its properties and methods through `myKennel`'s Gate property.

```
Set myKennel.Gate = New clsGate
myKennel.Gate.Color = "Red"
myKennel.Gate.Paint
```

Although `Gate` is a property of the `myKennel` object, it has been instantiated as a `clsGate` object in its own right. Since `clsGate` has its own properties and methods, they can now be accessed through the object chain just created. This facility allows us the ability to create a basic relational object model.

Declaring Property Read/Write Attributes

To declare an object's property as readable (as far as external VBA code is concerned), you expose its associated `Property Get` procedure to the class's interface. This makes the procedure visible and accessible to VBA once the object is instantiated. You do this by declaring the property using the `Public` keyword.

To declare the property writable, you expose its `Property Let` or `Property Set` procedures to the interface in a similar fashion. If you want to make a property read-only, declare its `Property Let` or `Property Set` procedures as `Private`, or simply eliminate those procedures entirely. To make a property write-only, do the same thing to the `Property Get` procedure.

Using Enumerated Types with Properties and Methods

In VBA, we often need to create a set of related constants, and in Chapter 4 we discussed using enumerated types, or *enums* for that purpose. In class modules, we often use enumerated types in property procedures.

Recall that in the `clsKennel` class, we made provision for a `clsGate` class; after all, it wouldn't be much of a kennel if it didn't have a gate or two. Let's say that we want to color-code the kennel gates: red for big dangerous breeds, yellow for the less dangerous ones, and then blue and white for the least nasty breeds. To provide some measure of automation and consistency in the color selection process, let's set up some enumerated types for specifying the colors you may want to use on the kennel gates.

```
Public Enum GateColor
    gcRed
    gcYellow
    gcBlue
    gcWhite
End Enum
```

Notice that in the above example, we haven't specified a value for any of the constants. This is perfectly acceptable because VBA automatically assigns a `Long Integer` value to each of them starting at zero and incrementing by one for each member specified. Therefore, `gcRed` will have a value of `0`, `gcYellow` `1`, and so on. If you want to explicitly declare values, you can, like so:

```
Public Enum GateColor
    gcRed = 0
    gcYellow = 1
    gcBlue
    gcWhite = 3
End Enum
```

In the above example, the constants for which I specified a value will have that value, but notice that one of them (`gcBlue`) has no value specified. Its value is determined by the value of its preceding member, so in this case, `gcBlue` will have a value of `2`. Try changing the value of `gcYellow` to `123` and test it to see what `gcBlue`'s value will be.

Once you've defined the constants you need, just use the enum as you would any other data type. As you type your definition into the editor, Intellisense displays your enum as one of the data type options, as in Figure 12-7.

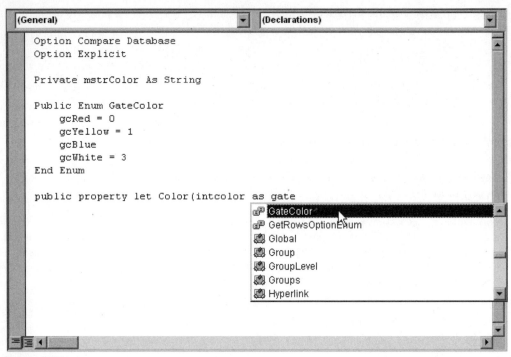

Figure 12-7

To use an enumerated value in your code, just begin typing the value assignment statement and Intellisense will do the rest, as shown in Figure 12-8.

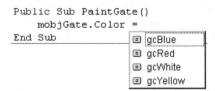

Figure 12-8

Keep in mind that VBA allows you to specify values other than those listed by Intellisense, so your code needs to account for that possibility, perhaps using If...Then, or Select Case...End Case constructs. For example:

```
Public Property Let Color(intColor As GateColor)
    Select Case intColor
        Case gcRed, gcYellow, gcBlue, gcWhite
            mstrColor = intColor
        Case Else
            ' Do something when the wrong color is selected
    End Select
End Property
```

Exiting Property Procedures

You might recall from Chapter 4 how you were able to exit a procedure using the `Exit Sub` and `Exit Function` constructs. Similarly, you can exit a `For...Next` loop or `Do...While` loop, using the `Exit For` and `Exit Do` constructs respectively. When your property procedure has done what it was supposed to do, there is no need to continue executing any more code. You can use the `Exit Property` construct to immediately stop processing any more code and exit the property procedure.

As with other procedures, it is always better to have a single point of exit, so I recommend using `Exit Property` sparingly.

Procedure Attributes

When declaring class properties and procedures, you can set a number of attributes that modify the procedure's behavior. These attributes are declared on the same line as the property or procedure declaration. The following examples demonstrate the possible declarations:

```
[Public | Private | Friend] [Static] Sub name [( arglist)]
[Public | Private | Friend] [Static] Function name [( arglist)] [As type]
[Public | Private | Friend] [Static] Property Get name [( arglist)] [As type]
[Public | Private | Friend] [Static] Property Let name ([ arglist,] value)
[Public | Private | Friend] [Static] Property Set name ([ arglist,] reference)
```

Since we can safely assume you know about `Public` and `Private` attributes by now, the following sections focus on describing the `Friend` and `Static` attributes.

Friendly Procedures

Let's say you wanted to create an animal management system that others will reference in their databases. Of course, you want your own database to be able to see and execute its own class properties and methods, but you don't want consumers of your database to execute them directly.

To protect your class's properties and methods, you can declare them using the `Friend` keyword. Procedures declared as `Friend` are public within the project in which they are defined, but invisible to other projects. The `Friend` keyword can only be used in form and class modules, and can't be late-bound.

For example, suppose you want to prevent other databases from changing the purchase price for your dogs; the following code illustrates the principle. The `mcurPrice` property is accessible to all consumers of the class; any procedure that instantiates the object can read the property's value, but only code within the project can assign a value to it.

```
Private mcurPrice As Currency

Public Property Get Price() As Currency
    Price = mcurPrice
End Property

Friend Property Let Price (curNewValue As Currency)
    mcurPrice = curNewValue
End Property
```

The Static Keyword

The `Static` keyword ensures that all the procedure-level variables retain their values between calls. Variables declared outside the procedure are unaffected. For more information on the `Static` keyword, refer to Chapter 4.

Naming Objects

In the early days of programming, we were limited in the number of characters we could use to name objects and variables. Thus we gave such meaningful names as *x*, *cbw*, or *A1*. Thanks to long filenames in 32-bit Windows, we are now able to identify objects using truly meaningful names, which in Access 2003 means 64 characters—plenty for most purposes. With such flexibility comes a dilemma: how do we name a class?

The name you assign to *any* database object will have an impact on its perceived purpose, and ultimately, its usability. It doesn't matter much whether it's a form, table, control, or class method; programmers will respond differently to it according to the name you give it. Ultimately it's up to you, but this section seeks to provide a few guidelines to help in the decision-making process.

What Does the Object Do?

I believe the most important aspect of object naming is to describe what it is or what it does. For example, Access has many built-in objects that are, in my opinion, aptly named. These include the `Database`, `TableDef`, `Collection`, `Error`, and so on. These names unambiguously describe the object to which they refer.

Other names describe the object's purpose, such as the `Add`, `Count`, and `Remove` methods; and let's not forget the `OpenRecordset` method. Fairly obvious what they do, wouldn't you say?

It is always good practice to keep the names as short as possible. The reason is that long names are really difficult to read and make for annoyingly laborious coding. The worst thing in my opinion is writing SQL against long table and field names.

```
SELECT tblTheDogsIBoughtFromUncleJoeLastSummer.TheDogsRegisteredName,
tblTheDogsIBoughtFromUncleJoeLastSummer.TheDogsBreed,
tblTheDogsIBoughtFromUncleJoeLastSummer.TheNameOfTheGuyIBoughtTheDogFrom,
tblTheDogsIBoughtFromUncleJoeLastSummer.ThePreviousOwnersAddress
FROM tblTheDogsIBoughtFromUncleJoeLastSummer
WHERE tblTheDogsIBoughtFromUncleJoeLastSummer. TheDogsRegisteredName
<> "Big Dog" AND tblTheDogsIBoughtFromUncleJoeLastSummer.
TheNameOfTheGuyIBoughtTheDogFrom <> "Fred J Nurk"@@@I could not get
this line to accept the correct style ☺ @@@
```

With just a little thought, this could have been simplified like so:

```
SELECT tblDogs.RegName, tblDogs.Breed, tblDogs.Seller, tblDogs.SellerAddr
FROM tblDogs WHERE tblDogs.RegName <> "Big Dog"
AND tblDogs.Seller <> "Fred J Nurk"
```

A great deal easier to read! You can make good use of abbreviations, acronyms, numbers, and so on, but ensure they are meaningful, rather than cryptic. What may be meaningful or obvious to you may not mean a thing to someone else.

Verbs, Nouns, and Adjectives

As mentioned above, using names that describe an object's purpose and function is arguably the best strategy, but the decision about whether to use verbs, nouns, or adjectives is equally important.

Most programmers use nouns and adjectives to describe properties, and use verbs to describe functions and methods. For example, typical properties might be called `Color`, `Name`, and `Width`, whereas functions and methods might have names like `Add`, `Calculate`, `Show`, and so on.

Naming variables is often a confusing decision, but these variables should follow the same naming strategy as for property names. An exception might be variables of the `Boolean` data type. Since they denote a true or false condition, you can use one of two stratagems. You can prefix them with "Is" (for example, `IsOpen`), or where they are used to indicate an authority to carry out some action, use verbs, for example, `ShowDialog`.

Events are often named in two ways: Firstly, by using verbs to denote the fact that some action has or is about to occur, for example, `BeforeUpdate` or `Finished`. Secondly, as is done in Web applications, by prefixing the name with "on," as in `onupdate` or `onopen` (Web projects often exclusively use lowercase for event names).

Whichever strategy you choose, try to be consistent throughout the application.

Case

The judicious use of case can be a highly effective means of naming an object. Traditionally, many objects are named with sentence case: that is, the first character of every word is uppercase. For example:

```
AddNewObject
```

Often to distinguish them from other objects, constants (described in Chapter 4) are named using all uppercase. For example:

```
ERR_NOT_FOUND
```

Hyphens and Underscores

Hyphens (-) and underscores (_) can also be used to great effect and clarity when naming objects. For example:

```
ERR_NOT_FOUND
```

A word of caution though: Access and other applications prefix many built-in objects with an underscore, so it's a good idea to treat objects with leading underscores as reserved keywords, and stay well away from them.

Prefixes and Suffixes

We have been using the *Reddick object-naming convention* throughout this book, which involves prefixing object names with acronyms that describe their type and attributes. Refer to Appendix G for a complete list.

Plurality

In code, and particularly with regard to classes, plural object names are best reserved for collections, such as the Access collection. Singular objects are therefore named in the singular, as with the `TableDef` object. This strategy unambiguously describes the *actual* state of the object.

Many people apply a plural naming convention to tables. Although this may make some sense in terms of the fact that tables can contain many records, my preference is to use the singular, for example, `tblAddress` and `tblPerson`. This is just personal preference; you can use plural if you like; just be consistent.

Except in the case of collections, applying plural names to some objects and singular to others of the same type is a definite no-no. Consistency is important, as object names are sometimes all a programmer has to determine the purpose and function of objects in the applications you create.

Using Class Events

Unlike standard modules, class modules can raise their own events. This is a very powerful feature of VBA, because it not only gives your code the ability to know what's going on inside the class instance, but also provides the opportunity to take whatever actions you deem necessary based on those events.

Another very important benefit of using class events is that you can keep User Interface (UI) functionality separate from the class implementation, making the class truly independent and reusable. You can then use your class in many places without worrying about specific UI implementation. This section focuses on getting your class to talk to the rest of your application, through events.

Initialize and Terminate Events

Every class module has two built-in events that fire automatically: `Initialize` and `Terminate`. The `Initialize` event fires when the class instance is first created. You can use the `Initialize` event to set default property values and create references to other objects. The `Terminate` event fires before the object is destroyed, and is normally used to clean up local object references.

To define code for these events, select `Class` from the `Object` drop-down list and then select the event from the `Procedure` drop-down list, as shown in Figure 12-9.

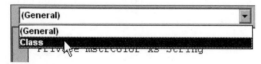

Figure 12-9

The following example shows what the `Initialize` and `Terminate` events might look like our friend the `Kennel` class.

```
Option Compare Database
Option Explicit

'Declare the Gate object
Private mobjGate As clsGate

'Declare the Dog object
Private mobjDog As clsDogs

'Declare the KennelID
Private mlngKennelID As Long

Private Sub Class_Initialize()
    mlngKennelID = 4

    Set mobjGate = New clsGate
    Set mobjDog = New clsDogs
End Sub

Private Sub Class_Terminate()
    Set mobjGate = Nothing
    Set mobjDog = Nothing
End Sub
```

Creating Custom Class Events

You can, of course, create your own events. Once you've decided on the specific events you want to expose, you declare them in the class's declarations section. Let's say we have a class that implements an animal purchase. You may want to provide events that notify your code before and after a purchase has been made.

```
Public Event BeforePurchase(Cancel As Integer)
Public Event AfterPurchase()
Public Event AmountInvalid()
```

Events are declared Public by default, but we always explicitly declare them for clarity. In any case, nothing outside the class would ever know about an event that was declared Private. Event names can be alphanumeric, but must begin with a nonnumeric character, and they can only be raised in the module that declared them.

To fire an event in your class, you issue the RaiseEvent command. For example, the following code demonstrates a typical use:

```
Public Sub Purchase_Dog(curAmount As Currency)
    If curAmount > 0 Then
        RaiseEvent Before_Purchase(Cancel As Integer)
    Else
        RaiseEvent Amount_Invalid()
    End If
End Sub
```

Just like VBA procedures, you can declare event arguments using the ByVal and ByRef keywords. By default, event arguments are passed ByRef, which means that the code that's listening for the event can change its value, and that change is passed back to the class procedure.

Responding to Events and the WithEvents Keyword

Now that you know how to create custom events in your object, you might want to know how to listen and respond to them in your code. It's actually quite simple. All you need to do is declare the object variable using the `WithEvents` keyword. Unfortunately however, you can only use `WithEvents` for object variables declared at module level and only in class modules.

Remember that the code behind forms are class modules too, so you can also use the `WithEvents` keyword in forms. The following declaration example demonstrates how easy it is:

```
Private WithEvents myKennel As clsKennel
```

Once you declare an object variable using the `WithEvents` keyword, select the object from the `Object` drop-down list, and the event becomes available from the `Procedure` drop-down list, as shown in Figure 12-10. VBA creates the procedure stub based on the arguments you supplied when you defined the event.

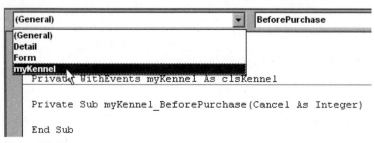

Figure 12-10

The only thing that might be considered a drawback to class events is that the object that raises the event must wait until the event code is responded to before it can continue processing.

Now let's see how we might be able to use the `WithEvents` keyword in a way that makes practical sense in your day-to-day application development. Let's say you have several text boxes on several different forms whose `BeforeUpdate` and `AfterUpdate` events contain exactly the same code. Normally, you would simply write the same code over and over in the event procedures for each control. But what if you were able to write the code once and have every control implement *that* code.

You're probably wondering, why not just write a public procedure in a standard module? That might work in many cases, but some built-in events have parameters, like the `BeforeUpdate` event's `Cancel` parameter. Access won't let you replicate that in a standard module.

We'll start by creating our class module, which we'll call `clsTBox`.

```
'Declare the class instance
Public WithEvents myTextbox As Textbox

Private Sub myTextbox_AfterUpdate()
    'Set the text to normal weight.
    Me.myTextbox.FontBold = False
End Sub
```

```
Public Sub myTextbox_BeforeUpdate(Cancel As Integer)
    'Test for the text box's value.
    Select Case Me.myTextbox.Value
        Case "Fred", "Mary"
            'The value is OK.
            'Change the text to black.
            Me.myTextbox.ForeColor = vbGreen
        Case Else
            'Wrong value! Undo the changes,
            'and change the text to bold red.
            Cancel = True

            Me.myTextbox.ForeColor = vbRed
            Me.myTextbox.FontBold = True
    End Select
End Sub
```

As you can see, this code implements the `BeforeUpdate` and `AfterUpdate` events for text boxes that can be anywhere in the project. The `BeforeUpdate` event checks the value of the text box and turns its text green if it equals `"Fred"` or `"Mary"`, otherwise it turns it bold red. The `AfterUpdate` event only fires (setting the text weight to normal) if the text is correct.

Now let's create the form, shown in Figure 12-11.

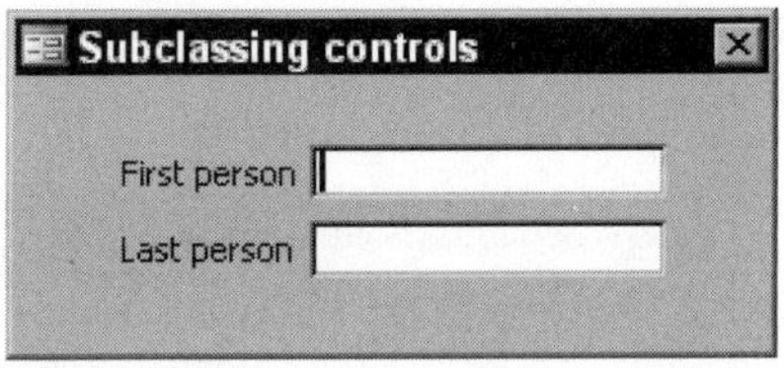

Figure 12-11

Add two text boxes named `txtFirst` and `txtLast` (it doesn't really matter what their captions read), and then add the following code to the form's module:

```
'Declare a reference to the class module
Public FirstTB As New clsTBox
Public LastTB As New clsTBox

Public Sub Form_Load()
    'Instantiate the class object for each control
    Set FirstTB.myTextbox = Me.txtFirst
    Set LastTB.myTextbox = Me.txtLast
End Sub

Private Sub Form_Unload(Cancel As Integer)
    'Clean up
    Set FirstTB = Nothing
    Set LastTB = Nothing
End Sub
```

```
Private Sub txtFirst_AfterUpdate()
    'This event exists solely to allow subclassing
End Sub

Private Sub txtFirst_BeforeUpdate(Cancel As Integer)
    'This event exists solely to allow subclassing
End Sub

Private Sub txtLast_AfterUpdate()
    'This event exists solely to allow subclassing
End Sub

Private Sub txtLast_BeforeUpdate(Cancel As Integer)
    'This event exists solely to allow subclassing
End Sub
```

You'll notice that the BeforeUpdate and AfterUpdate events exist, but contain no code. This is because they must exist in the form's class module for them to exist in our clsTBox class. All they need is the stub, but I always put a comment inside them to assist other programmers to understand what's going on.

The only other thing to mention here is that we have declared FirstTB and LastTB as Public. This is done so that clsTBox can see them.

Open the form and type "Fred" into the first text box. It turns green. Now enter "John" into the second text box, as shown in Figure 12-12.

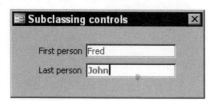

Figure 12-12

How It Works

1. A two-way "link" has been set up by declaring module-level object variables in both the form and clsTBox. In this way, when each is instantiated, they can "see" the other.

2. When the form class module is instantiated, clsTBox is immediately instantiated into FirstTB and LastTB (note that we used early binding). When the form loads, the two text box instances are created in clsTBox through the FirstTB.myTextBox object chain.

3. Once that happens, the linking is complete, and all the text box events that are exposed in the form are now available in clsTBox.

4. When the BeforeUpdate or AfterUpdate events occur for either text box, they actually fire in the instance of clsTBox created for it.

5. Try placing breakpoints in the form's Load event, and clsTBox's BeforeUpdate and AfterUpdate events to see what happens.

This is just a small example of how to subclass form controls using the `WithEvents` keyword. You can do the same thing with other controls and events, and also with forms and reports.

Handling Errors in Classes

A large part of developing software is trapping and handling errors, and all but the simplest procedure should include some form of error handling. We programmers can save some face by blaming many errors on the users of our brilliantly written software. Although we do have to account for our own mistakes (or those of other programmers), much of error handling is either responding to status conditions or protecting data from the users.

Status conditions are errors generated by conditions in other objects. For example, the following code shows one way to instantiate an Excel application object, using a status condition returned as an error:

```
Dim xlApp As Object
On Error Resume Next

'If Excel is already open, get a handle to
'the existing instance.
Set xlApp = GetObject(, "Excel.Application")

'Test for an error condition.
If Err <> 0 Then
    'Excel is not currently open, create an
    'instance.
    Set xlApp = CreateObject("Excel.Application")
End If

xlApp.Quit
Set xlApp = Nothing
```

In this example, a `GetObject` error indicates that an Excel instance is not currently running, in which case our code then creates an instance using `CreateObject`. You might say, "why not just create the instance with `CreateObject`?" The reason is that we often don't want two or more instances of the same object, so we try to use an existing instance where possible.

In any case, this kind of error is more an indication of the current status of the Excel object, rather than an actual error. It *should* be handled within the procedure in which it occurred, for obvious reasons.

Most other types of errors are unexpected, or at least undesirable. Not only do we have to trap and respond to them, but we need to understand how to work with them in class modules.

Trapping VBA Errors

In Chapter 9, we discussed trapping errors in standard modules. This included using the `On Error` and `If Err` constructs.

You might recall that when there is no error handler in the procedure in which the error occurs, VBA passes the error to the next highest procedure in the call chain. VBA continues passing the error up the call chain until it either finds an error handler or reaches the top level, in which case it then displays the standard runtime error dialog box. If you don't handle the errors, VBA will, but you may not like the idea that it resets all your variables when it does. Certainly the users of your application won't be too impressed either.

Error trapping in class modules is exactly the same; however, you also need to consider the runtime Error Trapping setting in the IDE's Options dialog box, as shown in Figure 12-13.

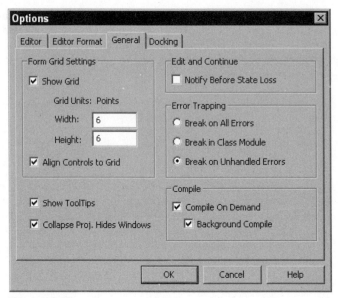

Figure 12-13

The Error Trapping settings control how Access handles runtime errors. The default setting, Break on Unhandled Errors, causes Access to display the standard Windows runtime error dialog box in the absence of any error handlers in the call chain. This is the desired behavior, because it lets your error handlers do their job.

Break on All Errors causes Access to override all your error handlers and display the runtime error dialog box whenever an error occurs in any module (including class modules). Finally, the Break in Class Module option overrides your class module error handlers, but not those in standard modules.

Raising Custom-Defined Errors

The descriptions for a great many error messages must have been written by programmers whose native language was something other than English. Some of them make for interesting reading, but there are quite a few that don't go too far toward educating you about the reason for the problem (or its resolution). Raising your own errors provides the flexibility of displaying more user-friendly or user-specific error messages.

The VBA Err object provides a Raise method, which lets you construct and fire your own custom errors. You must supply everything the Err object needs to return anything useful, which includes the error number, description, source, optional path to a help file, and the ContextID, which identifies a specific topic in the help file.

The syntax for the `Err.Raise` method is as follows:

```
Err.Raise number, source, description, helpfile, helpcontext
```

For example, the following procedure demonstrates the typical method for trapping errors and raising your own:

```
Const MyContextID = 1010407 ' Define a constant for ContextID

Private Sub ErrorTest()
    Dim xlApp As Object
    On Error Goto ErrorTest_Err

    'If Excel is already open, get a handle to
    'the existing instance.
    Set xlApp = GetObject(, "Excel.Application")

    ' Other code

ErrorTest_Exit:
    On Error Resume Next
    xlApp.Quit
    Set xlApp = Nothing
Exit Sub

ErrorTest_Err:
    Select Case Err.Number
        Case 429 'ActiveX component can't create object
            'Raise the error.
            strErrDescr = "Unable to open Excel. It may not be installed."
            Err.Raise vbObjectError + 513, TypeName(Me), _
                "Excel is not currently running", _
                "c:\MyProj\MyHelp.Hlp", MyContextID
        Case Else
            'Something else went wrong.
            Err.Raise Err.Number, Err.Source, Err.Description
    End Select
```

You might have noticed the `TypeName` function. `TypeName` returns information about a variable; for example:

`TypeName(strMyString)` returns `String`

`TypeName(intMyInteger)` returns `Integer`

`TypeName(db.TableDefs("Table1"))` returns `TableDef`

But when passed a class object, it returns the object's `Name` property.

Passing Errors in Class Modules

Although class objects can respond to errors that occur within them, they should not, because doing so forever binds the object to a specific implementation.

Class objects don't spontaneously leap into existence; they must be instantiated by other code. The code that creates the class is what implements the broader function, only calling the class for a smaller part of it, and so *it* should be the one to respond to errors that occur within the class object. By definition, any error in the class object is an error in the broader function. This is shown in Figure 12-14.

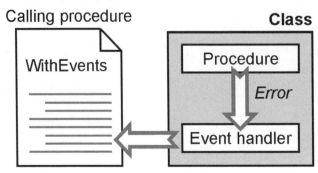

Figure 12-14

So what do we do? Our class must pass the error back to the calling code using the Err.Raise method. Whether it's a VBA error or a custom-defined error, our class procedures must trap the error and just pass it along. All that the calling code has to do is test for it. The following two examples demonstrate how you can do this.

Example 1

```
Public sub TestErrors()
    Dim obj As clsMyClass

    Set obj = New clsMyClass
    Obj.SomeMethod

    If Err <> 0 Then
        ' Handle the error
    End If
End Sub
```

Example 2

```
Public sub TestErrors()
    Dim obj As clsMyClass
    On Error Goto TestErrors_Err

    Set obj = New clsMyClass
    Obj.SomeMethod 'Error occurs in here

TestError_Exit:
    On Error Resume Next
    Set Obj = Nothing
    Exit Sub
```

```
TestErrors_Err:
    'Handle the error
    Resume TestErrors_Exit
End Sub
```

Forms as Objects

By now you should have a fair grasp on how to create classes and class objects in Access 2003. Something you might not be aware of is the fact that since form and report modules are also class modules, you can instantiate and use them in exactly the same way as any other class object. The greatest benefits of this are that you can create and operate on more than one instance of the object at any one time, and you can use its events by declaring their object variables using the WithEvents keyword.

Let's say we have a form called Form1. You would of course be familiar with the tried and true method of displaying a standard form.

```
DoCmd.OpenForm "Form1"

DoCmd.Close acForm, "Form1"
```

Copy the following code into a standard module and try stepping through it using the *F8* key:

```
Public Sub TestFormClass()
    Dim frm As Form_Form1
    Set frm = New Form_Form1

    Frm.Visible = True
    Set frm = Nothing
End Sub
```

Then try the same thing with a report.

```
Public Sub TestReportClass()
    Dim rpt As Report_Report1
    Set rpt = New Report_Report1

    rpt.Visible = True
    Set rpt = Nothing
End Sub
```

Many times you want to display a data selection dialog box while editing data in a form, and return the selected value from the dialog box to the original form. For example, in Microsoft Word, you select Date and Time... from the Insert menu. This displays the Date and Time dialog box, from which you select the format of the date you want to insert into your text. What I'm about to show you is a mechanism for returning the value selected by the user from the dialog box to the form whose code instantiates it. More often than not, the data selection dialog box must be used in different places throughout the application, so it must be completely independent of specific UI implementation. Past techniques for passing a value to another form included using the OpenForm method's OpenArgs argument.

```
DoCmd.OpenForm "Form1", , , , , strSomeValue
```

Passing multiple values involved stuffing `OpenArgs` with multiple values separated by some arbitrary character such as the vertical bar (|), and parsing `Me.OpenArgs` when the data selection dialog box opens, as shown in the following code:

```
Private Sub Form_Open()
    Dim varArgs As Variant

    'Extract all the values from OpenArgs that are separated
    'by the vertical bar character, and put them into varArgs.
    varArgs = Split(Me.OpenArgs, "|", -1, vbTextCompare)

    'Print out the resulting array.
    Debug.Print varArgs (0)
    Debug.Print varArgs (1)
    Debug.Print varArgs (2)
End Sub
```

Passing values back to the calling form usually involved either setting a global variable with the name of the calling form, or adding the form name to `OpenArgs` so that the dialog box can pass the value directly to the calling form, which meant hard-coding the value-passing code into the dialog box itself, none of which could be classified as a professional object-oriented approach.

In the following example, we'll create our own reusable data selection dialog box that is completely independent of all other forms. We'll use all the techniques we've discussed in this chapter, including form properties and events. Yes, that's right! Forms can have property procedures, and they can expose their events to the VBA environment.

It might be worth noting here that, unlike other classes, forms and reports don't have `Initialize` and `Terminate` events. Instead, forms and reports both have an `Open` event and a `Close` event, and forms have two additional events: `Load` and `Unload`. The form `Load` event fires before the `Open` event, and the `Unload` event fires after `Close`.

1. Create a new form, and set its properties as shown below.

Property	Value
Name	DlgMyDialog
Caption	My Dialog
BorderStyle	Dialog
Dialog	True
Modal	Yes

2. Add the following controls, and set their properties as shown below. Figure 12-15 shows how the form should look.

Control Type	Property	Value
Combo box	Name	CboCombo1
	RowSourceType	Value List
	RowSource	"Value 1"; "Value 2"; "Value 3"
	Enabled	No
Combo box	Name	cboCombo2
	RowSourceType	Value List
	RowSource	"Value 1"; "Value 2"; "Value 3"
	Enabled	No
Rectangle	Place as shown above	
Command button	Name	CmdOK
	Caption	OK
Command button	Name	CmdCancel
	Caption	Cancel

Figure 12-15

3. Copy the following code to the form's class module.

```
'Declare the event to notify the calling form
'that the dialog has finished
'We could also have used the dialog's Close or
'Unload events
Public Event Finished(varReturn As Variant)

'Declare the dialog properties
Private varValueSelected As Variant
Private intWhichOne As Integer

Private Sub cboCombo1_Change()
    varValueSelected = Me.cboCombo1
End Sub

Private Sub cboCombo2_Change()
    varValueSelected = Me.cboCombo2
End Sub
```

```
Private Sub cmdCancel_Click()
    varValueSelected = Null
    DoCmd.Close acForm, Me.Name
End Sub

Public Property Get WhichOne() As Integer
    WhichOne = intWhichOne
End Property

Public Property Let WhichOne(ByVal iNewValue As Integer)
    intWhichOne = iNewValue

    'Enable the appropriate combo
    Me.cboCombo1.Enabled = (intWhichOne = 1)
    Me.cboCombo2.Enabled = (intWhichOne = 2)
End Property

Private Sub cmdOK_Click()
    DoCmd.Close acForm, Me.Name
End Sub

Private Sub Form_Unload(Cancel As Integer)
    'Raise the Finished event so the calling
    'form knows what's happened
    RaiseEvent Finished(varValueSelected)
End Sub
```

4. Create a new form, and set its properties as shown below.

Property	Value
Name	FrmMyMainForm
Caption	My Main Form
BorderStyle	Sizable
Dialog	False
Modal	Yes

5. Add the following controls, and set their properties as shown below. Figure 12-16 shows how the form should look.

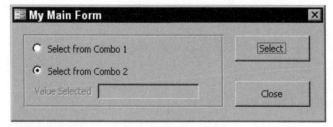

Figure 12-16

Control Type	Property	Value
Option group	Name	OptMyOptionGroup
Option button	Name	[Default]
	OptionValue	1
	Caption (of its label)	Select from Combo 1
Option button	Name	[Default]
	OptionValue	2
	Caption (of its label)	Select from Combo 2
Text box	Name	TxtMyTextBox
	Caption (of its label)	Value Selected
Command button	Name	CmdSelect
	Caption	Select
Command button	Name	CmdClose
	Caption	Close

6. Copy the following code to the form's class module.

```
'Declare the object variable using WithEvents
Private WithEvents dlg As Form_dlgMyDialog

Private Sub cmdClose_Click()
    DoCmd.Close acForm, Me.Name
End Sub

Private Sub cmdSelect_Click()
    'Instantiate the dialog
    Set dlg = New Form_dlgMyDialog

    'Enable the appropriate combo
    dlg.WhichOne = Me.optMyOptionGroup

    'If we had declared dialog properties, we
    'could pass their values here:
    'dlg.Property1 = 123
    'dlg.Property2 = "some value"
    'etc...

    'Show the dialog
    dlg.Visible = True
End Sub

Private Sub dlg_Finished(varReturn As Variant)
    Me.txtMyTextBox.Enabled = (Not IsNull(varReturn))

    If Not IsNull(varReturn) Then
        Me.txtMyTextBox = varReturn
    End If
End Sub
```

```
Private Sub Form_Unload(Cancel As Integer)
    'Clean up
    Set dlg = Nothing
End Sub
```

7.   Now open `frmMyMainForm`, select one of the options, and click `Select`. Pick a value from the combo box, and click `OK`.

Figure 12-17 shows the main form in action.

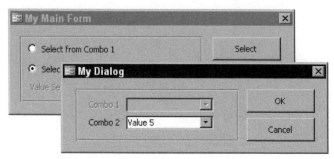

Figure 12-17

You can call this dialog box from anywhere in your application, without having to specify the name of the form that calls it, and you can also keep all the form-specific functionality in the main form where it belongs.

Variable Scope and Lifetime

Variables declared within class modules exhibit the same scope and lifetime as those declared within standard modules. For example, Private module-level variables are only available to procedures within the same module, and are destroyed when the class instance is destroyed. Public module-level variables are visible to any code that has access to the class instance.

Class variables declared at procedure level remain accessible only to code within that procedure and are destroyed when the procedure exits; unless of course the variable is declared using the `Static` keyword. In such a case, the variable is destroyed along with the module-level variables when the object is destroyed.

Although the variables used to hold pointers to objects obey the normal scope and lifetime rules as described above, they demand special consideration, as you will soon see.

To demonstrate how variable scope and lifetime works, create the following two class modules.

clsClass1

```
Private obj As clsClass2

Public Property Set Link(objMyObject As clsClass2)
    'Create a link from this object to the other one
```

```
        Set obj = objMyObject
        Debug.Print "Creating reference to clsClass2 from clsClass1"
End Property

Private Sub Class_Initialize()
    Debug.Print "Instantiating clsClass1"
End Sub

Private Sub Class_Terminate()
    Debug.Print "Terminating clsClass1 instance"
End Sub
```

clsClass2

```
Private obj As clsClass1

Public Property Set Link(objMyObject As clsClass1)
    'Create a link from this object to the other one
    Set obj = objMyObject
    Debug.Print "Creating reference to clsClass1 from clsClass2"
End Property

Private Sub Class_Initialize()
    Debug.Print "Instantiating clsClass2"
End Sub

Private Sub Class_Terminate()
    Debug.Print "Terminating clsClass2 instance"
End Sub
```

Then add the following procedure to a standard module:

```
Public Sub TestVariableLifetime()
    Dim objMyObject1 As clsClass1
    Dim objMyObject2 As clsClass2

     'Instantiate the two object variables
    Set objMyObject1 = New clsClass1
    Set objMyObject2 = New clsClass2

    'Create a link to one object from the other
    Set objMyObject2.Link = objMyObject1

     'Destroy the local object references
    Set objMyObject1 = Nothing
    Set objMyObject2 = Nothing
End Sub
```

Take a look at the TestClassLifetime procedure. If you step through the procedure line by line (by successively pressing *F8*), the debug window tells the real story.

The procedure begins by creating the two class objects: objMyObject1 and objMyObject2. The code then sets a second pointer to objMyObject1 in objMyObject2 (see Figure 12-18).

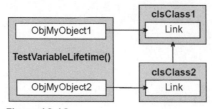

Figure 12-18

Despite the fact that the first local pointer to clsClass1 (objMyObject1) is then set to Nothing, you will see that the object itself is not destroyed until after objMyObject2 passes away. Why? Because the second pointer still exists after the demise of the first pointer, so the object itself remains alive.

When the pointer to clsClass2 is destroyed, its pointer to clsClass1 is also destroyed, thereby releasing the clsClass1 object. But that's not the worst that can happen. If we change TestClassLifetime() by setting a reference to clsClass2 from clsClass1, a circular reference is created.

```
'Create a link to one object from the other
Set objMyObject2.Link = objMyObject1
Set objMyObject1.Link = objMyObject2
```

Run the procedure to see what happens. Neither object is destroyed. Why? Because each object maintains a reference to the other. Once such code is executed, both objects remain in memory until the application is shut down; there is no way to programmatically terminate them (see Figure 12-19).

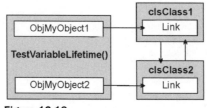

Figure 12-19

So how do we avoid such things from happening? Well, you must explicitly terminate each inner reference before destroying the outer reference. This is accomplished by adding the following method to each class:

```
Public Sub TerminateLink()
    'If the object exists, destroy it
    If Not obj Is Nothing Then
        Set obj = Nothing
    End If
End Sub
```

Then we add the following two lines to `TestClassLifetime()`:

```
objMyObject1.TerminateLink
objMyObject2.TerminateLink
```

The Me Property

The `Me` keyword behaves like an implicitly declared variable. It is automatically available to every procedure in a class module. When a class can have more than one instance, `Me` provides a way to refer to the specific instance of the class where the code is executing. Using `Me` is particularly useful for passing information about the currently executing instance of a class to a procedure in another module.

The `Me` keyword contains an object reference to the current class instance, and can be used by code written in forms, reports, and user-defined classes. It returns faster than a fully qualified object reference, and is useful when you have several instances of a class. For example, either of the following code fragments can be executed from the `Employees` form to refer to the value of the `LastName` text box on that form.

```
strLastName = Forms!Employees.LastName
```

```
strLastName = Me!LastName
```

You can also use `Me` to pass information about the current class instance to a procedure in another module or class.

Creating a Parent Property

Suppose you wanted to create a relationship between a parent class and a derived class. The parent class would have code like this:

```
Option Compare Database
Option Explicit

Private mobjDog As clsDog

Private Sub Class_Initialize()
    'Create a new instance of the derived class
    Set mobjDog = New clsDog

    'Create the relationship between the parent and child classes
    mobjDog.Parent = Me
End Sub
```

Of course, you would also need `Parent` property procedures in the derived class.

```
Option Compare Database
Option Explicit

Private mobjKennel As clsKennel
```

```
Public Property Set Parent(objKennel As clsKennel)
    'Check that the property hasn't already been set
    If objKennel Is Nothing Then
        Set mobjKennel = objKennel
    End If
End Property
```

In the above examples, the derived class has one property procedure, `Property Let`. This procedure accepts an object (of the type `clsKennel`) as its argument, and uses it to create a clone of the parent object.

Having a copy of the parent object stored locally (in `mobjKennel`), it can then act on the parent object by invoking its properties and methods through the clone.

The parent object instantiates the derived object and simply passes itself (`Me`) to the derived object's `Parent` property procedure.

Creating and Using Collection Classes

So far we've dealt with situations where the relationship between objects is one-to-one. Although that's often the case in real-world programming, it is also quite often the case where the relationship is one-to-many. A group of related objects is called a *collection*, and a `Collection` class is simply a class that contains a list, or collection of related classes. VBA provides us with a neat little object for creating and handling object collections, oddly enough called a `Collection` object.

The Collection Object

You would already be familiar with using object collections; VBA is full of them. The `TableDefs` and `QueryDefs` collections are examples we use almost every day. These collections maintain a list of pointers to the individual objects they control; in fact collection objects are also referred to as *Controllers*.

To access an individual object within an object collection, you refer to its collection name and either the name of one of the objects it contains, or its ordinal position within the collection. For example, to check the date a table was created, you could use either of the following constructs:

```
Debug.Print CurrentDb.TableDefs("Table1").DateCreated
Debug.Print CurrentDb.TableDefs(1).DateCreated
```

Most collection objects implement the `Add`, `Remove`, and `Item` methods, and the `Count` property. Unfortunately, the name given to the `Add` method can vary from application to application, and even from object to object, but they essentially do the same thing (see Figure 12-20).

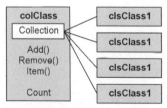

Figure 12-20

For example, to add a worksheet to an Excel workbook, you use the `Add` method of the `Worksheets` collection. By contrast, to add a table to the Access `TableDefs` collection, you create the new table object using `CreateTableDef()` and append it to the collection using the collection's `Append` method.

The VBA `Collection` object uses the `Add` method. Aren't standards a wonderful thing!

The Add Method

The `Add` method adds a member to the collection, and has the following syntax:

```
Collection object name.Add (Item, [Key], [Before], [After])
```

The method parameter arguments are:

❑ `Item`. As you can store almost anything in a collection, the `Item` parameter is an expression of any type that represents the member to add to the collection. In the case of object collections, this is where you supply a pointer to the object instance.

❑ `Key`. The `Key` parameter is an optional unique string expression that specifies a key that can be used to identify the collection member, instead of using its ordinal position in the collection. It must be a unique string, otherwise an error occurs.

❑ `Before`. The `Before` parameter allows you to optionally specify that the new member is to be added at the position immediately preceding an existing member in the collection. The parameter you supply can be either the ordinal numeric position of the existing member, or the `Key` that the existing member was saved with when it was added to the collection. If specifying a number, it must be in the range between 1 and the collection's `Count` property. You can specify a `Before` or `After` position, but not both.

❑ `After`. Similar to the `Before` parameter, the `After` parameter specifies that the new member is to be added at the position immediately following an existing collection member. The parameter you supply can be either the ordinal numeric position of the existing member, or the `Key` that the existing member was saved with when it was added to the collection. If specifying a number, it must be in the range between 1 and the collection's `Count` property. You can specify a `Before` or `After` position, but not both.

The Remove Method

The `Remove` method allows you to remove a member from the collection, and uses the following syntax:

```
object.Remove(index)
```

The `index` argument specifies the position of an existing collection member. The argument you supply can be either the ordinal numeric position of the existing member, or the `Key` that the existing member was saved with when it was added to the collection. If specifying a number, it must be in the range between 1 and the collection's `Count` property.

Note that this is in contrast to the built-in Access collections (like the `TableDefs` collection), which are zero-based (start at zero).

The Item Method

The Item method provides a way for you to specify an object by its ordinal position in the collection. It uses the following syntax:

```
object.Item(index)
```

The index argument specifies the position of an existing collection member. The argument you supply can be either the ordinal numeric position of the existing member, or the Key that the existing member was saved with when it was added to the collection. If specifying a number, it must be in the range between 1 and the collection's Count property.

Note that this is in contrast to the built-in Access collections (like the TableDefs collection), which are zero-based (start at zero).

As you add and remove members from the middle of the collection, the Item numbers of all the members around it are renumbered to maintain continuity. For example, if you remove item 2 from a four-member collection, item 3 is renumbered to 2, and item 4 is renumbered to 3. It is for this reason that you should not rely on an object's ordinal position in the collection.

The Count Property

The Count property returns a Long Integer containing the number of objects in a collection, and is read-only.

Collection Class Basics

To demonstrate the basic concepts and techniques used to create a class module, this section is devoted to creating a small class I recently used on an Access database application. The specifications required that the user interface take on the look and feel of an existing Web application. One of the features of this application was its navigation, which had to mimic the Back and Forward buttons found in Internet Explorer.

To implement this behavior, we could have created a string array that contained the names of each form visited, and simply increment or decrement a counter to move from form to form. Instead, we opted to create a collection class called clsDogs.

We have modified the following example class to make use of our clsDog class, as that's what we'll be storing in the collection. Take a while to look it over in order to understand how it works.

The Collection object is declared at module level and instantiated in the Initialize event. Following best practice, the Terminate event destroys the Collection instance and any objects it may still contain. The On Error statement in the Terminate event really isn't necessary, but I always add it just in case.

```
Option Compare Database
Option Explicit

Private col As Collection 'Declare the collection object

Private Sub Class_Initialize()
    'Instantiates the collection object.
    Set col = New Collection
End Sub
```

```
Private Sub Class_Terminate()
    'Destroys the collection object.
    On Error Resume Next
    Set col = Nothing
End Sub
```

The `Push` method adds a pointer to the new `Dog` object (already instantiated in the test code) to the collection, using the unique `Key` passed as one of the method's parameters. If an optional `Before` or `After` parameter is included in the call, the `Push` method inserts the object before or after the object that occupies the position specified by the `varBefore` or `varAfter` parameter.

```
Public Sub Push(objMember As clsDog, strKey As String, _
        Optional varBefore As Variant, Optional varAfter As Variant)
    'Adds a member to the collection.
    On Error Resume Next

    If Not IsMissing(varBefore) Then
        Col.Add objMember, strKey, varBefore
    ElseIf Not IsMissing(varAfter) Then
        Col.Add objMember, strKey, varAfter
    Else
        col.Add objMember, strKey
    End If

    If Err.Number <> 0 Then
        ThrowError Err.Number, Err.Description, Err.Source
    End If
End Sub
```

The following procedure removes the member specified by `strKey` from the collection, but does not return anything to the calling code:

```
Public Sub Remove(strKey As Variant)
    'Removes a member from the collection.
    On Error Resume Next

    col.Remove strKey

    If Err.Number <> 0 Then
        ThrowError Err.Number, Err.Description, Err.Source
    End If
End Sub
```

The `FirstMember` property returns a pointer to the object that occupies the first position in the collection, but it doesn't remove it from the collection as do the two `Pop` methods that will be discussed next. You can see that position 1 is specified in the object assignment statement:

```
Set FirstMember = col(1)
Public Property Get FirstMember() As clsDog
    'Returns the first member added to the collection,
    'but does NOT remove it from the collection.
```

```
    On Error Resume Next

    'Get the first member.
    Set FirstMember = col(1)

    If Err.Number <> 0 Then
        ThrowError Err.Number, Err.Description, Err.Source
    End If
End Property
```

Similarly, the `LastMember` property returns a pointer to the object that occupies the last position in the collection.

```
Public Property Get LastMember() As clsDog
    'Returns the last member added to the collection,
    'but does NOT remove it from the collection.

    On Error Resume Next

    'Get the last member.
    Set LastMember = col(col.Count)

    If Err.Number <> 0 Then
        ThrowError Err.Number, Err.Description, Err.Source
    End If
End Property
```

The `Pop` method returns a pointer to the object that occupies the last position in the collection, and then removes it from the collection, thus destroying it.

```
Public Function Pop() As clsDog
    'Pops the last member added to the collection,
    'and removes it from the collection.
    Dim objMember As clsDog

    On Error Resume Next

    'Pops the last member.
    Set objMember = col(col.Count)
    col.Remove col.Count

    If Err.Number <> 0 Then
        ThrowError Err.Number, Err.Description, Err.Source
    Else
        Set Pop = objMember
    End If

    Set objMember = Nothing
End Function
```

The `PopFirstMember` method returns a pointer to the object that occupies the first position in the collection, and then removes the object from the collection, destroying it.

```
Public Function PopFirstMember() As clsDog
    'Pops the first member added to the collection,
    'and removes it from the collection.
    Dim objMember As clsDog

    On Error Resume Next

    'Pop the first member
    Set objMember = col(1)
    col.Remove 1

    If Err.Number <> 0 Then
        ThrowError Err.Number, Err.Description, Err.Source
    Else
        Set PopFirstMember = objMember
    End If

    Set objMember = Nothing
End Function
```

The Item property is interesting and I will shortly explain why, but for the moment the explanation is that it returns a pointer to the object whose Key matches that supplied by the strKey parameter.

```
Public Property Get Item(strKey As String) As clsDog
    Set Item = col(strKey)
End Property
```

The following procedure simply returns a number that represents the number of objects contained in the collection:

```
Public Property Get Count() As Integer
    'Returns the collection count.
    Count = col.Count
End Property
```

The Clear method destroys the collection and thus all objects it contains, and then reinstantiates the collection. Although I could have iterated through the collection, removing and destroying objects as I went, destroying the Collection object is faster.

```
Public Sub Clear()
    'Clears the collection and destroys all its objects.
    'This is the fastest way.
    Set col = Nothing
    Set col = New Collection
End Sub
```

Finally, the ThrowError method takes all the errors that occur within the class and packages them up before passing them back up the error chain to the calling procedure.

```
Private Sub ThrowError(intError As Integer, strDescr As String,
strSource As String)
    'Procedure used to return errors
    Dim strMsg As String
```

```
        Select Case intError
            Case 5
                strMsg = "Member not found."
            Case 9
                strMsg = "Subscript out of range."
            Case 457
                strMsg = "Duplicate member."
            Case Else
                strMsg = "Error " & intError & vbCrLf & strDescr
        End Select

        Err.Raise vbObjectError + intError, strSource, strMsg
    End Sub
```

Setting Unique Object Keys

Before you get too carried away with testing the above class, the `Collection` object demands that each `Key` value be unique, so that's what we'll do now. Setting unique `Collection` object keys is not always easy. You can't easily use incrementing numbers, because the `Key` parameter requires a string data type, and once you set it, it can't be changed without removing the object and reinserting it.

The best method is to use a property of the object being added (if it has one), but that isn't hard to implement. Although we didn't show you the `Dog` class's implementation, the following is what we used during testing. Create a new class called `clsDog`, and copy the following code into its module:

```
Private lngID As Long

Private Sub Class_Initialize()
    'Generate the unique key for this object.
    lngID = CLng(Rnd * (2 ^ 31))
End Sub

Public Property Get ID() As Long
    'Return the object's unique key.
    ID = lngID
End Property
```

This calculation in the class's `Initialize` event returns a random number between 215 and 2,147,483,433. This is the largest number that will fit into a `Long Integer` data type, and offers sufficient range to minimize the risk of duplicates.

You can use whatever means you like to generate a key, but whichever method you choose, ensure the `Key` is unique in the collection.

Testing the Dogs Class

To test the functionality of the `Dogs` class, you can run the following code in a standard module. This test code adds four `Dog` objects to the `Dogs` object (the `Collection` class), and then starts removing them using three different methods: `PopFirstMember`, `Pop`, and `Remove`, all the while accessing the `Dog` object's `ID` property through the collection object. The first `Debug.Print` statement shows how to access the `Dog` object's `ID` property through the `Dogs` `Collection` class instance.

```
Option Compare Database
Option Explicit
```

```
Public Sub TestCollectionClass()
    Dim DOGS As clsDogs
    Dim obj As clsDog
    Dim strKey1 As String
    Dim strKey As String

    On Error Resume Next

    Set DOGS = New clsDogs
```

Now add code to add a dog to the collection using the Push method.

```
' Add a dog to the collection
Set obj = New clsDog
DOGS.Push obj, CStr(obj.ID)
strKey1 = obj.id
Set obj = Nothing
```

Do the same thing three more times, to add another three dogs.

```
' Add another dog to the collection
Set obj = New clsDog
DOGS.Push obj, CStr(obj.ID)
Set obj = Nothing

' And another one...
Set obj = New clsDog
DOGS.Push obj, CStr(obj.ID)
strKey = CStr(obj.id)
Set obj = Nothing

' And the final dog
Set obj = New clsDog
DOGS.Push obj, CStr(obj.ID)
Set obj = Nothing
```

Now print the ID of the dog that occupies the first position in the collection.

```
Debug.Print "The first collection Member ID = " & _
    DOGS.Item(strKey1).ID
```

Let's now start removing dogs from the collection. Firstly, let's use the PopFirst method.

```
'Start removing objects from the collection
Debug.Print "There are now " & DOGS.Count & " members."
Debug.Print "Just popped Dog " & DOGS.PopFirstMember.ID
Debug.Print "There are now " & DOGS.Count & " members."
Debug.Print "Just popped Dog " & DOGS.Pop.ID
Debug.Print "There are now " & DOGS.Count & " members."
```

Now we'll take advantage of the fact that we issued the `On Error Resume Next` line to trap an error.

```
    'Create an error
    DOGS.Remove strKey & "some text"
    If Err <> 0 Then Debug.Print "***ERROR " & Err.Number
```

Now, let's remove the remaining dogs from the collection, without causing any errors.

```
    'Now do it properly
    DOGS.Remove strKey
    Debug.Print "Just removed Dog " & strKey
    Debug.Print "There are now " & DOGS.Count & " members."

    Debug.Print "Just popped Dog " & DOGS.Pop.ID
    Debug.Print "There are now " & DOGS.Count & " members."
    Debug.Print "End test"

    Set DOGS = Nothing
End Sub
```

Specifying the Default Procedure

There are two major drawbacks to using custom `Collection` classes: one of them is that Access treats them as normal objects rather than true collections. As such, you do not have access to a default property or procedure. For example, using VBA, the following two statements are equivalent (to test it, ensure you have at least one form open):

```
Debug.Print Forms.Item(0).Name
Debug.Print Forms(0).Name
```

The default property of the `Forms` collection is the `Item` property, which means if you want to, you can omit the `Item` keyword.

Using a custom `Collection` class, you are forced to explicitly use the `Item` property, as we did in our example above. But all is not lost. There is a way to tell Access which procedure to use as the default, but, of course, things are never straightforward.

You have to export the procedure to a file, manually add a line of code to the procedure definition, and then import it back into Access. The procedure for doing so is as follows:

1. From the `Project Explorer` window in code view, right-click the module and select `Remove` from the context menu.

2. When asked if you want to export the module before removing it, click `Yes`. The `Export File` dialog box is displayed.

3. Browse to a convenient folder and rename it to `modulename.txt`, where `modulename` is the name of the module you're exporting.

4. Click `Save`. The class is removed from the `Project Explorer` and saved to disk as a text file.

5. Using Windows Explorer, browse to the appropriate folder and double-click the text file to open it in *Notepad*.

6. Locate the procedure in question (in this case the Item property), and add a single line of text like the one we've highlighted.

```
Public Property Get Item(strKey As String) As clsSpoke
Attribute Item.VB_UserMemId = 0
    Set Item = col(strKey)
End Property
```

7. Ensure that the procedure or property name appears in the attribute statement and that the attribute is set to zero.

8. Save the file and exit Notepad.

9. Back in Access code view, right-click anywhere in the Project Explorer and select Import File from the context menu. The Import File dialog box is displayed.

10. Browse to the appropriate folder, select the file you just edited, and click Open. The class is added to the Project Explorer.

You can check the Object Browser to see that a small blue ball is shown above the procedure's icon, indicating that it is now the default procedure (see Figure 12-21).

Figure 12-21

While our test code previously accessed the Dog object's ID through the Dogs object like this:

```
    DOGS.Item(strKey1).ID
```

it can now be accessed like this:

```
    DOGS(strKey1).ID
```

Enumerating Collection Classes

A second drawback to using custom `Collection` objects is that you can't enumerate through its members. For example, consider the following code:

```
Public Sub TestEnumeration()
    Dim tdf As TableDef

    For Each tdf In CurrentDb.TableDefs
        Debug.Print tdf.Name
    Next tdf
End Sub
```

This code allows us to enumerate, or iterate through the collection by declaring an enumeration type. To accomplish the same thing with our custom `Collection` class, we need to go back to Notepad as we did to specify the default procedure; only this time, we'll add an entire public procedure.

Export the class as before and open it in Notepad.

Now add the procedure *exactly* as it is shown below. The only change you can make is the name of the `Collection` object you're using (in this case, `col`).

```
Public Function NewEnum() As IUnknown
Attribute NewEnum.VB_UserMemId = -4
    Set NewEnum = col.[_NewEnum]
End Function
```

Save the file and reimport it into Access as you did before.

Now you can enumerate the collection objects as you can with other Access collections.

```
Dim mbr As Object 'or clsSpoke
For Each mbr In STACK
    Debug.Print mbr.ID
Next mbr
```

The Three Pillars

So far, we've talked about creating class modules that are complete with their own *properties* and *procedures*. We've talked about developing their *implementation code*, *instantiating* them as *objects*, linking them to other objects singly and in *collections*, and finally, using them in our application. For most cases, this is all you need to know.

But if you want to create a lot of related classes, and do it in the most efficient way, then you need to understand a few principles of OOP.

The three pillars of object-oriented theory are *encapsulation*, *inheritance*, and *polymorphism*. These things have different meanings to different people, and the extent to which they apply to an object-oriented language differs according to which language you happen to prefer. There are other factors like *operation overloading*, *parameterized constructors*, and *class-level attributes*, but their discussion is largely irrelevant because they are not implemented in the current version of Access—perhaps in a later version.

Encapsulation

A major advantage of OOP is the ability to *encapsulate,* or contain data and functionality within simple programmatic entities. That is, every instance of a class object contains exactly the same properties and methods as the class module it was based on. We've seen this in the classes we've been creating in this chapter.

Another way of describing encapsulation is *data hiding*. When you create a set of properties and methods to form a class's interface, external code can use this interface to implement its behavior without ever knowing what goes on inside. (You don't need to understand the physics of the internal combustion engine in order to drive to the corner store for milk.) This means you can package up data and functionality into a *black box* that represents some *thing*, and operate on that thing's interface using standard VBA code, without concerning yourself with how it implements its behavior.

The *interface* to objects of the same class is well defined, and allows the internal code implementing its methods to be changed as necessary, as long as the interface to the programmer's world remains unchanged.

This allows developers to execute long or complex operations using simple metaphors provided by the class's interface. For example, if your class implemented the mechanics of the human body, and included all the nerve–muscle–bone interactions, then a programmer using your class would need only issue commands like:

```
Person.Turn "right"
Person.Walk 10
Person.Stop
Person.Sit
```

Such reliable structure means that an organization can implement its business rules and processes in a class, and change those rules and processes at will without affecting any code that was written around it—provided, of course, that the class's interface remains unchanged.

A side benefit of this is that encapsulation also offers a way of hiding specific business rules and behavior from other developers. For example, suppose you have created a class that determines certain properties of a proprietary chemical formula. You wouldn't want your employees knowing the details of the formula, so you encapsulate it in a custom class and expose only the interface to it. What's an interface? Read on, all will be revealed.

Inheritance

In a nutshell, *inheritance* is the ability to create new classes from existing ones. A *derived class*, or *subclass*, inherits the properties and methods of the class that instantiated it (called the *base class*, or *superclass*), and may add new properties and methods. New methods can be defined with the same name as those in the superclass, in which case they override the original one.

There are two types of inheritance: interface and implementation inheritance. Interface inheritance has been available to Access since VBA 6.0 introduced the `Implements` keyword. Implementation inheritance is now available in Visual Basic .NET through the `Inherits` keyword, but unfortunately not in Access 2003.

The essential difference between the two forms of inheritance is that interface inheritance specifies only the interface. It doesn't actually provide any corresponding implementation code. For example, suppose we have a `Bike` object that wants to ask the `Wheel` object for its part number. The `Wheel` object wants to borrow the functionality from its superclass, `Parts`. The `Bike` object might implement the following functionality:

```
Private myWheel As Wheel

Private Function GetPartNo() As String
GetPartNo = myWheel.PartNo()
End Function
```

The implementation of this behavior is in `Parts'` `PartNo()` method. Because VBA 6.0 doesn't support implementation inheritance, you would need to put some code into the `Wheel` class.

```
Implements Part
Private MyPart As New Part

Private Function Part_PartNo() As String
Part_PartNo = myPart.PartNo()
End Function
```

VBA 6.0 allows the interface, in this case `Part`, to implement the actual behavior. `Wheel` retains an instance of `Part` (a behavior called *containment*), and then asks that reference to carry out some action for it (called *delegation*). This isn't true interface inheritance because it allows you to add code to `Wheel` to provide the actual behavior, but it's close enough.

Polymorphism

Polymorphism is not the ability for a cockatoo to magically change into a rabbit; it is in fact the ability for different object types to implement the same method, thereby allowing you to write VBA code without concerning yourself about what type of object you're using at the time. Another way of looking at it is that objects can be more than one type of *thing*.

There are two types of polymorphism: *ad-hoc* polymorphism (called *overloading* in Visual Basic .NET), and *parametric* polymorphism.

Parametric polymorphism is not implemented in Access 2003, and so will be ignored in this book.

Ad-hoc polymorphism provides the ability to use the same calling syntax for objects of different types. For example, suppose we have a `bikes` class and a `cars` class, each having its own methods to implement its own unique properties and behaviors, but since both need their tires pumped up occasionally, they would both have a `pump_tires` method. The actual code to implement this behavior would perhaps differ, but as long as their *interface* remained the same, our VBA code could simply call the `pump_tires` method for both, and be confident that each class knows how to pump up its own tires.

It's true that VBA doesn't demonstrate some of the characteristics of a true object-oriented language like C#, but it doesn't pretend to. Applications where you would need *polymorphism* or *inheritance* would not be written in VBA, so VBA doesn't need to implement them.

Inheriting Interfaces

Inheritance is an object-oriented concept that allows one class to *inherit* the public properties and methods (the interface) of another class. This section illustrates how you can implement that in your own Access object models.

The Implements Keyword

The `Implements` keyword in VBA allows you to implement *interface inheritance*, giving programmers access to a form of *polymorphism*.

For example, suppose we have two objects, `Object1` and `Object2`. If `Object1` inherits the interface exposed by `Object2`, we can say that `Object1` is a kind of `Object2`, which is polymorphism in a nutshell.

Often interfaces are referred to as a *Contract*. This is because there is an agreement between the creator of the object and its user that the object will provide all the properties and methods that form its interface. The internal implementation may vary, but the object's signature (its property and method names, parameters, and data types) may not.

You can use interfaces and polymorphism in any number of ways, but by way of explaining how it all works, let's examine the most common—categorizing objects on the basis of common traits. We like the example of dogs, where we implement different breeds, like German Shepherds, Poodles, and Huskies.

Each breed has its own physical attributes and behavioral patterns, such that they each merit their own class (at least for this example). All of them share common traits: they all belong to the canine family, all have height, weight, color, and so on. All bark, eat, and drop little presents on the lawn. If we put all the common traits into a single interface (`IDog`), we have a generic way of dealing with all breeds at once. For example, we can feed the entire kennel like so:

```
Dim Dog As clsIDog

For Each Dog In Kennel
    Dog.Eat
Next Dog
```

Although all dogs eat, they all perform the act of eating in very different (and sometimes bizarre) ways. Therefore, the code to implement each dog's unique eating habits must be in that dog's class, and will certainly differ from dog to dog.

Additionally, the members of an implemented interface do not automatically become part of the default interface for a class. That is, if the German Shepherd had only one public method, `Bite`, we would have to get at the `Bite` method like this:

```
Dim Dog As IDog

Set Dog = clsGShepherd
Dog.Bite
```

Traditionally, interface class names are distinguished from other types of class by prepending their name with an uppercase *I*.

We could copy the IDog interface into the default interface, and have both point to a common private procedure that contains the code that makes the dog bite, but we could also make it simple and just use the Implements keyword in each dog's class:

```
Implements IDog
```

By so doing, every dog whose class definition included the Implements keyword would *inherit* the public properties and methods exposed by the IDog interface.

So that you can begin to understand how interface inheritance works, let's start by turning our Dog class on its head and defining two Dog classes based on breed: one for German Shepherds and one for Poodles. But before we do that, we need to create an interface class that defines the traits that all dogs have in common. Naturally enough, we'll call it IDog.

```
Option Compare Database
Option Explicit

Public Property Let Color(strColor As String)
End Property

Public Property Get Color() As String
End Property

Public Sub Eat()
End Sub

Public Sub Bark()
End Sub

Public Sub Bite()
End Sub
```

The first thing you notice is that it doesn't have any code to implement a dog's attributes or behavior. That's because we're inheriting the *interface*, not the *implementation*. As we discussed at the beginning of the chapter, a class module is like a template. An implementation class is also like a template, but where the template provided by "standard" classes includes interface and implementation, an interface class only provides an interface template.

Now we can create our new Dog classes: the first being the Husky class. If we create a basic Dog class, with (for simplicity) only one method and two property procedures of its own, then:

```
Option Compare Database
Option Explicit

'Declare an object for the parent Collection class
Private mobjDogs As clsDogs

Public Property Set Parent(objDogs As clsDogs)
    'Check that the property hasn't already been set
    If objDogs Is Nothing Then
        Set mobjDogs = objDogs
```

```
        End If
End Property

Public Property Get Parent() As clsDogs
    'Return a pointer to the Customer instance
    Set Parent = mobjDogs
End Property

Public Sub PullSled()
    ' Code to implement pulling a sled
End Sub
```

Now we add the `Implements` keyword, after which you can select the `IDog` class from the `Object` drop-down list (see Figure 12-22).

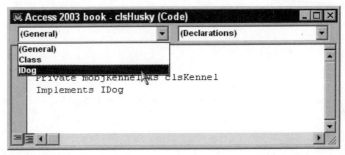

Figure 12-22

Selecting all the `IDog` class's interface procedures from the `Procedure` drop-down list, you can see that they've all been inherited as private members. This is because although all `IDog`'s public properties and procedures are inherited (in fact, an error will be generated if you don't inherit *all* of them), you may not want to expose all of them to consumers of the `Husky` class.

```
Private Sub IDog_Bark()
End Sub

Private Sub IDog_Bite()
End Sub

Private Property Let IDog_Color(RHS As String)
End Property

Private Sub IDog_Eat()
End Sub
```

We can now implement the unique behavior of this breed of dog, without affecting the implementation of any other breed of dog. Changing some of the procedures to `Public` and adding a local variable to store the dog's color, we end up with the following class definition.

First, we declare the objects and variables we'll need, and issue the `Implements` keyword.

```
Option Compare Database
Option Explicit
```

```
Private mobjDogs As clsDogs
Private strColor As String

Implements Idog
```

Next, we create the `Parent` property procedures, which will tell our class which dog it belongs to.

```
Public Property Set Parent(objDogs As clsDogs)
    'Check that the property hasn't already been set
    If objDogs Is Nothing Then
        Set mobjDogs = objDogs
    End If
End Property

Public Property Get Parent() As clsDogs
    'Return a pointer to the Customer instance
    Set Parent = mobjDogs
End Property
```

Now, we'll create some custom procedures to perform a range of breed-specific actions.

```
Public Sub PullSled()
    ' Code to implement pulling a sled
End Sub

Public Sub IDog_Bark()
    ' Code to implement a Husky's bark
End Sub

Public Sub IDog_Bite()
    ' Code to implement a Husky's bite
End Sub
```

Finally, let's add a property and a subprocedure to carry out what might be termed *Standard Operations* for all breeds.

```
Private Property Let IDog_Color(RHS As String)
    mstrColor = RHS
End Property

Public Sub IDog_Eat()
    ' Code to implement a Husky's eating habits
End Sub
```

We can then create any number of classes for any number of breeds, to which we can link an unlimited number of Dog classes, to track individual dogs.

Interface inheritance isn't terribly difficult; making sure it doesn't get out of hand is the hard part.

Instancing

You might recall from the section on *Naming the Class*, that I promised to explain the `Instancing` property. Well, now it's time.

A class's `Instancing` property defines whether the class is private or public (see Figure 12-23).

Figure 12-23

Setting a class's `Instancing` property to `Private` means that the class can only be used within the application in which it is defined.

Setting it to `PublicNotCreatable` means that although other applications can access type library information about the class, they can use it only after your application has created it first; they can't create instances of it.

Classes that have their `Instancing` property set to `PublicNotCreatable` are referred to as *dependent objects*, and typically form part of more complex objects. Using our Kennel/Dog example, you might want to allow an external application to create multiple `Kennel` objects, but only allow `Dog` objects to exist as a part of a `Kennel`. To do that, you make the `Dog` class `PublicNotCreatable` and let the user add new `Dogs` by adding a `Dogs` collection to the `Kennel` class. That way, they can only create new `Dogs` using the collection's `Add` method.

Summary

In this chapter, we gave you a whirlwind tour of the OOP techniques that are made available in Access 2003. If you had any trouble understanding the concepts presented, be consoled by the fact that it may just take a little practice. You should be confident in that before long, you'll be writing quite complex object-oriented code that will make your application development and maintenance a joy to behold.

Specifically in this chapter, we looked at class modules, how they differ from object instances, and when you would use object-oriented techniques in your applications. We created several classes of our own, designed their properties and methods, and instantiated the classes as objects to investigate how they work and how to use them.

We talked about the object-naming strategy, and then examined class events and errors, to understand how classes communicate with the outside world.

We practiced using forms and reports as objects, a technique which we hope you will find useful in the future. We next examined collection classes, which is the basis for building your own object models, and included an advanced technique for specifying an object's Item property.

Finally, we hopefully put this chapter into a wider context by introducing some basic object-oriented theory, and then demonstrating how to implement some of it in code. With that, along with the preceding chapters, we have now gone as far as standard VBA can take us. The next chapter, "Extending VBA with APIs," will start you on the next leg of your programming journey by introducing the Windows API and the many built-in functions that the Windows operating system can offer in terms of advanced programming functionality.

Extending VBA with APIs

Microsoft Visual Basic for Applications (VBA) is a full-featured software development language that offers a vast array of built-in functions, so much so that many Access developers never require anything else.

However, when you start developing more and more complex applications in Access, you may eventually find yourself needing to do things that VBA does not have a built-in function for. Moreover, you'll sometimes need to do things that VBA simply *can't* do. That's not to say that VBA is incomplete, but, like every other programming language, it does not include every function you're ever likely to need. A line has to be drawn somewhere, and Microsoft drew that line at the functions provided by the API.

The Windows operating system provides a large library of functions that you can access using VBA to extend what you're able to do in your applications. But since the API is inherently VBA-unfriendly, you must first understand *what* it is, and what special considerations you must take account of in order to use it from VBA.

This chapter explains what the Windows API is, and why you might want to use it. We'll describe the libraries that make up the API and how to link them in to your application. We'll then show you how to *declare* API functions to use them with VBA. Then we'll describe the differences between the data types used in APIs, those used in VBA, and provide the techniques and formulas to convert between them.

We'll finish off this chapter by briefly introducing two final topics: the VBA LastDLLError method for *dynamic-link library* (DLL) error handling and how to deploy and install applications that contain references to API or other libraries.

Introducing the Win32 API

API stands for *application programming interface*. It is simply a group of standard functions that are packaged together and made available to application programmers.

There are quite a few APIs, but the one that you've probably heard most about is the Windows API. The Windows API consists of many DLLs that make up the Windows operating system and ensure that every application that runs under Windows behaves in a consistent manner.

What this actually means is that standard Windows operations, such as saving files, opening forms, managing dialog boxes, and so on, are all handled by the Windows APIs. For example, the standard File Open dialog box is an API function called GetOpenFileName found in comdlg32.dll. Similarly, the GetTempPath function in Kern132.dll returns the name of the folder where temporary files are stored.

All Windows-based applications interact with the Windows APIs in some way, whether they are opening a file, displaying time, putting text on the screen, or managing computer memory while you play *Flight Simulator*.

When you program in Microsoft Access, you use the built-in VBA functions, which you could loosely refer to as an API. Similarly, when you use the Access Add-in Manager or References dialog box to link to an external DLL, OCX, MDB, and so on, you are linking to something that is essentially an API.

There's no need to feel intimidated by the API, despite the fact that it has the reputation of being highly complex. Because the Windows APIs were written in C++, there are rules that VB programmers must be aware of, but other than that, they can pretty much be used in the same way as any other function.

For example, enter the following example into a standard module and run it.

```
Private Declare Function GetUserName _
    Lib "advapi32.dll" Alias "GetUserNameA" _
    (ByVal lpBuffer As String, _
    nSize As Long) As Long

Private Const MAXLEN = 255

Function GetLoginName() As String
    Dim strUserName As String
    Dim lngSize As Long
    Dim lngReturn As Long

    lngSize = 256
    strUserName = Space(MAXLEN) & Chr(0)

    If GetUserName(strUserName, lngSize) <> 0 Then
        GetLoginName = left(strUserName, lngSize - 1)
    Else
        GetLoginName = ""
    End If
End Function
```

The above code returns the domain log-in name of the current Windows user (that'd be you). At this point, the Declare function part may be a bit of a mystery, but the rest is a standard VBA function. In Visual Basic, using most APIs is just that simple.

The following table lists just a few of the DLLs that contain APIs to use in VBA applications. For more information about the Windows API, refer to Appendix F.

API	Basic Description
KERNEL32.DLL	Low-level operating system functions, such as memory and task management, resource handling, and so on.
USER32.DLL	Window management functions, including messages, menus, cursors, carets, timers, communications, and most of the nondisplay functions.
GDI32.DLL	The Graphics Device Interface Library. Device output, including most drawing functions, display context, metafile, coordinate, and font functions.
COMDLG32.DLL	Common dialog boxes.
LZ32.DLL	File compression.
VERSION.DLL	Version control.
MAPI32.DLL	Electronic mail.
COMCTL32.DLL	Implements a new set of Windows controls and dialog boxes, including the tree view and rich text edit controls.
NETAPI32.DLL	Access and control of networks.
ODBC32.DLL	Implements ODBC (Open Database Connectivity), providing functions to work with databases.
WINMM.DLL	Multimedia.

32-bit Windows packs its APIs into function libraries called DLLs, but before we get too far into the details of how to use them, here is some historical background to help understand how they work.

Why Do You Need the API?

VBA is a very powerful language, but you can only control a small part of the operating system with its built-in functions. One of the best features of VBA is its extensibility; that is, you can extend its capabilities in a variety of ways—one of which is by using the API.

For example, VBA provides several built-in functions for manipulating the Windows Registry, but these functions only let you use one small part of the registry set aside for VBA. To access the remainder of the registry, you need to use the API.

Similarly, to retrieve and manipulate disk drive, printer, or system resource settings, you'll need the API. If you'd like your Access applications to do more than just beep, the `sndPlaySound` API function will let you play sound effects or music. You can even control the transparency of your Access forms using several API functions in conjunction.

The following example puts an icon in a form's title bar; something you can't do using standard VBA. Place the following code into a standard module.

```
Public Declare Function LoadImage Lib "user32" _
    Alias "LoadImageA" (ByVal hInst As Long, _
    ByVal lpsz As String, ByVal un1 As Long, _
    ByVal n1 As Long, ByVal n2 As Long, _
    ByVal un2 As Long) As Long

Public Declare Function SendMessage Lib "user32" _
    Alias "SendMessageA" (ByVal hWnd As Long, _
    ByVal wMsg As Long, ByVal wParam As Long, _
    LParam As Any) As Long

'Image type constants
Public Const IMAGE_BITMAP = 0
Public Const IMAGE_ICON = 1
Public Const IMAGE_CURSOR = 2
Public Const IMAGE_ENHMETAFILE = 3

'un2 Flags
Public Const LR_DEFAULTCOLOR = &H0
Public Const LR_MONOCHROME = &H1
Public Const LR_COLOR = &H2
Public Const LR_COPYRETURNORG = &H4
Public Const LR_COPYDELETEORG = &H8
Public Const LR_LOADFROMFILE = &H10
Public Const LR_LOADTRANSPARENT = &H20
Public Const LR_DEFAULTSIZE = &H40
Public Const LR_LOADMAP3DCOLORS = &H1000
Public Const LR_CREATEDIBHeader = &H2000
Public Const LR_COPYFROMRESOURCE = &H4000
Public Const LR_SHARED = &H8000

'Message params
Public Const WM_GETICON = &H7F
Public Const WM_SETICON = &H80
Public Const ICON_SMALL = 0
Public Const ICON_BIG = 1

'Default image size for the Access Titlebar
Public Const IMG_DEFAULT_HEIGHT = 16
Public Const IMG_DEFAULT_WIDTH = 16

Public Sub SetFormIcon(hWnd As Long, strIcon As String)
    Dim hIcon As Long
    Dim lngReturn As Long

    hIcon = LoadImage(0&, strIcon, IMAGE_ICON, IMG_DEFAULT_WIDTH, _
        IMG_DEFAULT_HEIGHT, LR_LOADFROMFILE)

    If hIcon <> 0 Then
        lngReturn = SendMessage(hWnd, WM_SETICON, ICON_SMALL, ByVal hIcon)
    End If
End Sub
```

Then create a new form and add the following code to the form's Load event, making sure to change the c:\myIcons\myIco.ico path to that of an icon file that exists on your computer.

```
Private Sub Form_Load()
    SetFormIcon Me.hWnd, "C:\myIcons\myIcon.ico"
End Sub
```

Now open the form to see the icon appear in the form's title bar.

With the APIs at your disposal, you can now control a significant portion of the Windows operating system and almost everything within it. Let's begin by discussing how the API works.

Introducing DLLs

We mentioned before that function libraries can be *linked* or incorporated into applications when required. There are two types of linking: *static* and *dynamic*. Static linking occurs at design time, when you create the application. Dynamic linking occurs at runtime.

Static Linking

Most programming languages provide the capability to access some operating system functions. They usually also allow you to create and store your own custom functions which you can compile into library (*.lib) files, and then merge into your applications.

When an executable program is compiled, a `Linker` scans the application for references to external functions and libraries, and then copies them into the final executable, thereby linking them to your application. This is called *static linking*, because the addresses your program uses to access these functions are fixed into the executable and remain unchanged (static) when the program runs. Figure 13-1 shows how static linking works.

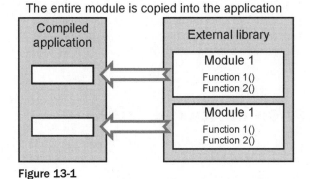

Figure 13-1

Although newer compilers allow you to copy individual functions, older ones typically copied the entire module to the application when linking each library. This meant that all the library's functions were merged into the executable, regardless of whether they were needed or not.

Of course, copying the entire module to the application increased the resulting file size. While the size increase was usually small, it started to actually mean something if there were 20 executables, each containing a copy of the same library. In a multitasking environment like Windows, all 20 programs could conceivably be running simultaneously, so it would use up a great deal of memory at any one time.

Dynamic Linking

Instead of grouping functions into libraries, later versions of Windows grouped these functions into a special type of executable called a DLL.

When you link a DLL, you specify which function you want to include in your application, and instead of copying in the entire contents of the DLL, the linker/compiler records the name of each externally referenced function along with the name of the DLL in which it resides.

When your application runs, Windows loads the required library so that all its functions are exposed, and it is then that the address of each function is resolved and dynamically linked to the application. That's why it's called *dynamic linking*. Figure 13-2 shows how dynamic linking works.

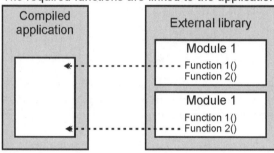

Figure 13-2

Only one copy of the library need be stored on disk. All the applications that need to use its functions access the same physical copy.

Dynamic linked libraries typically have the same file extension (*.dll), but this is not an absolute requirement. Custom controls, like those created in Visual Basic and C++, can have file extensions like *.ocx. Device drivers and some Windows system libraries sometimes use file extensions such as *.drv and *.exe.

Linking Libraries in Access 2003

There are two ways to link a library to an Access 2003 database; either *reference* the library, or *declare* it.

Referencing a Library

When you set a reference to an external library in Access 2003, you can use its functions as though they were built-in to Access. You can reference `type` libraries, `object libraries`, and `control` libraries.

For example, because the *Microsoft Excel Object Library* is itself a library of functions, you can reference (link to) it in Access and use its functions as though they were part of Access. To reference a library, launch the `References` dialog box, as shown in Figure 13-3, by selecting `References` from the `Tools` menu in the Visual Basic Editor.

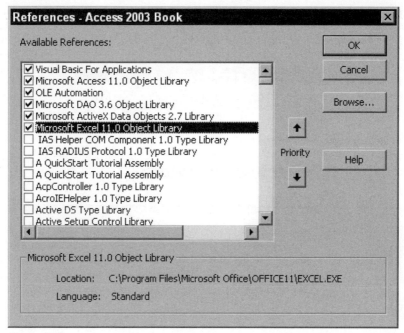

Figure 13-3

Browse the list to see a large range of libraries. Some typical libraries include:

- ❑ Microsoft Office 11 Object Library
- ❑ Microsoft Excel, Word, and the other members of the Office suite
- ❑ Microsoft ActiveX Data Objects 2.7 Library
- ❑ Microsoft DAO 3.6 Object Library
- ❑ Microsoft Scripting Runtime
- ❑ Microsoft SQLDMO Object Library

Of course, many of the libraries you'll find listed in the References dialog box are from suppliers other than Microsoft, and depend on the applications you have installed on your computer. You might find such things as

- ❑ Corel—CorelDraw 11.0 Library
- ❑ Symantec.Norton.AntiVirus.OfficeAntiVirus 1.0 Type Library

To reference a library, browse the list and check the box next to the library you want to use, then click OK. If you don't see anything you like, click Browse and locate the file.

It's worth noting here that not all the libraries can be used without purchasing a license from the supplier. Others are specifically written for C++ or Visual Basic and cannot be used in Access.

Reference object libraries by selecting `ActiveX Control` from the `Insert` menu in form `Design View`. The same thing can be accomplished by clicking `More Controls` on `Toolbox`. Figure 13-4 shows the `Insert ActiveX Control` dialog box.

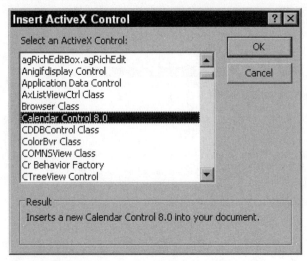

Figure 13-4

When you add a custom control (OCX) to a form in this way, Access adds a reference to it in the `References` dialog box. For example, adding the `Microsoft Calendar Control` adds a reference to C:\Windows\System32\mscal.ocx.

How Microsoft Access Resolves VBA References

When Access needs to use the file you've referenced, it does so in the following sequence.

1. The location indicated in the `References` dialog box is checked.

2. Access checks to see if the file is already loaded.

3. Access checks the `RefLibPaths` registry key for a value in the name of the referenced file.

4. If the `RefLibPaths` key does not exist, or doesn't contain the required value, Access checks the `Search Path` in the following order:

   ❑ `Application` folder (where msaccess.exe is located)

   ❑ `Current` folder

   ❑ `System` folder (System and System32 folders, located in the Windows or WinNT folder)

   ❑ `WinDir` system variable (the folder where the operating system is running, usually the Windows folder)

   ❑ `PATH` environment variable (contains a list of folders accessible by the system)

   ❑ `File` folder (the folder that contains the mdb, mde, adp, or ade file, and any subfolders

If, after doing all this, Access still can't find the referenced file, it generates an error. When you check the `References` dialog box, you may see a reference marked MISSING, as shown in Figure 13-5.

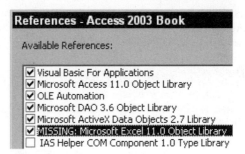

Figure 13-5

Although Access will warn you about broker references when you display the VBA editor, the following method call, issued in the Immediate window, will return `True` if a reference is broken, and `False` otherwise.

```
?Application.BrokenReference
```

Appendix B fully explains creating and managing references.

Once a library is linked, you can use its functions as easily as you would a built-in Access function. For example, after linking Excel, the following code demonstrates how to access Excel's `InchesToPoints()` function, which, as you would expect, converts inches to points.

```
Public Sub Linking2Excel()
    Debug.Print Excel.Application.InchesToPoints(1)
End Sub
```

Declaring APIs

The other way to link an external library is to *declare* it, naturally enough by using the `Declare` keyword. The `Declare` statement typically consists of eight parts, and supports both functions and subprograms (subs). You can only declare a procedure at module level (in the `Declarations Section`).

Here is Syntax 1:

```
[Public | Private] Declare Sub name Lib "libname" [Alias "aliasname"]
[([arglist])]
```

And here is Syntax 2:

```
[Public | Private] Declare Function name Lib "libname" [Alias
"aliasname"] [([arglist])] [As type]
```

The Declare Keyword

The `Declare` keyword alerts VBA that what follows is the interface definition for a procedure stored in a DLL. The `Declare` statement also defines the type of procedure being declared: `Function` or `Sub`.

As you've already discovered, you can specify that the procedure be either `Public` or `Private`, depending on whether you want the procedure to be available to the entire project or only to the module in which it appears. `Declare` statements made in class modules can only be `Private`.

Naming the Procedure

The name that follows the `Declare Function` or `Declare Sub` keyword is the name you'll use to call the procedure from VBA. There is a degree of flexibility here, because this name need not be the actual name of the procedure in the DLL.

As in the following example, you can rename the procedure to almost anything, provided you use the `Alias` keyword to specify the actual name of the API procedure.

```
Private Declare Function  MySillyProcedureName Lib "advapi32.dll" _
    Alias "GetUserNameA" (ByVal lpBuffer As String, _
    nSize As Long) As Long
```

The `Alias` keyword specifies the actual name of the procedure as it appears in the API. You cannot change this, but as we've seen, you can change the `Name` argument in the procedure declaration.

There are several reasons for renaming an API procedure:

❑ Some API procedures begin with an underscore character (_), which is illegal in VBA. To get around this, rename the procedure and use the `Alias` keyword.

❑ API procedure names are case sensitive, and terribly intolerant of programmers who forget that. VBA, on the other hand, doesn't care one way or the other, so by renaming the procedure, you build in a level of forgiveness.

❑ Several API procedures have arguments that can accept different data types. Supplying a wrong data type to such a procedure is a good way to get the API angry, because VBA does not check the data types of the arguments you supply. The kind of response you are likely to get by using a wrong data type can range from erroneous data, unexpected application behavior, application hang, or system crash. To avoid type problems, declare several versions of the same procedure, each with a different name and each using arguments of different data types.

❑ Some Windows APIs have names that are the same as the reserved keywords in Access, such as `SetFocus` and `GetObject`. Using these keywords will result in a compile error. So since you can't rename the Access keywords, the API gets to have a new name.

❑ Most API procedures that can take string arguments come in two flavors: one for *ANSI* and one for *Unicode*. The ANSI version is suffixed by an A, as in the `GetUserName` (or `MySillyProcedureName`) example. The Unicode flavor has a W suffix. VBA uses Unicode internally and converts all strings to ANSI before calling a DLL procedure, so you would usually use the ANSI version. But if you need to use both versions in the same project, renaming one or both of them would make sense.

What's Unicode? The Win32 API supports three different characters sets. The first two are the *single-byte* and *double-byte* character sets. The single-byte character set is 8-bits wide, and provides for 256 characters. The double-byte character set (DBCS) is also 8-bits wide, but some of its byte values are called *DBCS lead bytes*, which are combined with the byte that follows them to form a single character. DBCSs provide a sufficient number of characters for languages such as Japanese, which have hundreds of characters. The third type is the 16-bit character set called Unicode, which provides for up to 65,535 characters; enough to support all the characters in all the languages around the world. Lastly, you can create procedure names that conform to your object naming standards.

If you make a mistake when declaring the Alias, VBA won't be able to find the procedure in the DLL, will present a runtime error 453, *Can't find DLL entry point GetUserNameB in advapi32*, which your error handling code can trap.

Specifying the Lib(rary)

The Lib keyword specifies the filename of the library that contains the procedure you're declaring. You declare the filename as a string inside quotes. If VBA can't find the file, it generates a runtime error 53, *File not found*, which your error handler can also trap.

Specifying the Argument List

The API argument list is specified in much the same way as it is in standard VBA subs and functions. However, there are a few rules that you must understand and adhere to when calling API procedures.

Passing and Returning Values

Two things are worth noting at this point. First, even API subs can return values and second, the values returned by many API procedures can be quite different from those returned by VBA procedures. Let's deal first with those strange subs that return values.

Now we'll explain how the GetUserName arguments work.

```
Private Declare Function GetUserName _
    Lib "advapi32.dll" Alias "GetUserNameA" _
    (ByVal lpBuffer As String, _
    nSize As Long) As Long

Private Const MAXLEN = 255

Function GetLoginName() As String
    Dim strUserName As String
    Dim lngSize As Long
    Dim lngReturn As Long

    lngSize = 256
    strUserName = Space(MAXLEN) & Chr(0)

    If GetUserName(strUserName, lngSize) <> 0 Then
        GetLoginName = left(strUserName, lngSize - 1)
    Else
        GetLoginName = ""
    End If
End Function
```

You'll notice that two arguments are passed to the GetUserName procedure: lpBuffer and nSize. lpBuffer is a fixed-width string storage area that contains the value returned by the procedure. The declaration tells the API where to find the string in memory, and its width (nSize).

Now you might be thinking, "Hang on, ByRef passes a pointer, not ByVal." Normally we would agree, but VBA is somewhat inconsistent in the way it deals with strings.

By default, VBA passes variables ByRef, that is, it passes a pointer to the location in memory where the value can be found, thereby allowing the procedure to modify the actual value. To test this behavior in VBA, create the following two procedures in a standard module.

```
Public Sub TestByRef()
    Dim intMyValue As Integer

    intMyValue = 1

    Debug.Print "Initial value: " & intMyValue
    ChangeMyValue intMyValue
    Debug.Print "New value: " & intMyValue
End Sub

Private Sub ChangeMyValue(ByRef intSomeValue As Integer)
    intSomeValue = 3
End Sub
```

Run TestByRef() and you'll see that the value of intMyValue changes. If you modify the ChangeMyValue() procedure to pass intSomeValue ByVal, and re-run TestByRef(), the value doesn't change. In VBA, this is true of strings as well. But when you pass strings to an API, the reverse happens.

The reason is that since a string variable is itself a pointer, passing it to an API ByRef actually passes a pointer to an OLE 2.0 string (a BSTR data type). Generally the only APIs to use this type of string are those that are part of the OLE 2.0 API. Other APIs don't take too kindly to it. Windows API procedures expect strings to be passed as a pointer to a *Null-terminated string*, that is, the string ends with an *ASCII zero* character. This is a C language convention. When we pass a string ByVal, VBA converts the string to C language format by appending a Null-termination character. Because the value is a pointer, the DLL can modify the string even though the ByVal keyword is used.

If you fail to specify the ByVal or ByRef keyword, you run the risk of an error 49, Bad DLL calling convention. Also, if you pass a value ByRef when ByVal is expected, or vice versa, the procedure can overrun memory that it shouldn't, and the system can crash.

The other set of rules that must be followed when passing values to API procedures is that of data types, which are discussed in the next section.

Understanding C Parameters

Most APIs were written by C programmers, so most APIs are written specifically for the C language. Because of this, there are many APIs that are completely unusable by VBA, because VBA does not support some of the data types required by these APIs. Of those APIs that are accessible to VBA, most require consideration with regard to the data types used. Use a wrong data type and your computer will quickly let you know all about it.

The following sections describe the C data types often specified for API parameters, the VBA data types that should be used with them, the recommended calling conventions, and, where applicable, the technique that converts signed integer values from unsigned integer values and vice versa.

Signed and Unsigned Integers

The first thing to note at this point is that the C language uses something that is unknown to VBA: *signed numbers*. VBA only uses *unsigned numbers*. For example, Figure 13-6 shows an 8-bit byte. Notice that having a binary 1 in the most significant bit (the eighth bit) signifies that the number contained within the byte is a negative number. A 0 in the same position indicates that the number is positive.

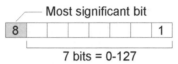

Figure 13-6

Although the total number of values that a single byte can hold (employing both positive and negative number ranges) increases, the number of possible positive numbers decreases by a factor of 2^7, 2^{15}, or 2^{31}, depending on the width of the byte.

Sometimes you'll run across parameters that require a signed value. There is a general algorithm to apply to supply this kind of value.

Convert the value to its next highest data type, subtract the maximum value that the data type can carry, and then convert it back to the original data type. The following table shows how to convert values from unsigned to signed, and vice versa, for the bit widths of values supported by VBA.

Type	Convert unsigned to signed	Convert signed to unsigned
8-bit	signed = Cbyte(unsigned – 255)	unsigned = (CInt(signed) And 255)
16-bit	signed = Cint(unsigned – 65535)	unsigned = (CLng(signed) And 65535)
32-bit	signed = CLng(unsigned – 1.79769313486232E308)	unsigned = (CDbl(signed) And 1.79769313486232E308)

8-Bit Numeric Parameters

There are three or four 8-bit (1-byte) parameter types: char, uchar, BYTE, and (if using the ANSI character set) 8-bit TCHAR. Although it is unlikely that you will run across them under Win32, they should be explained just in case.

Signed 8-bit values range between –128 and 127, whereas unsigned values range between 0 and 255. The reason for this is explained in the preceding section. VBA only supports unsigned Byte values, regardless of size.

If you do ever have to use unsigned 8-bit parameters, the VBA Byte data type works just fine. Supplying 8-bit signed values is not as straightforward and requires a small algorithm to produce the required value. This algorithm is shown in the previous section, "Signed and Unsigned Integers."

VBA parameter: `ByVal param As Byte`

Datatype	Prefix	Description
Char	Ch	8-bit signed integer
BYTE, uchar	Ch	8-bit unsigned integer
TCHAR	Ch	8-bit or 16-bit signed (depending on whether you're using ANSI or Unicode)

16-Bit Numeric Parameters

There are three or four 16-bit (2-byte) numeric parameter types: `short`, `unsigned short`, `WORD` and (if using the Unicode character set) 16-bit `TCHAR`. The VBA Integer data type can be used to supply values for the signed parameters (`short` and 16-bit `TCHAR`), because VBA Integer values range from –32,768 to 32,767.

To supply unsigned values to unsigned short and `WORD` parameters, you must first convert the value to something that the API will recognize as an unsigned value. Refer to the conversion formula shown in the section "Signed and Unsigned Integers."

VBA parameter: `ByVal param As Integer`

Datatype	Prefix	Description
Short	C	16-bit signed integer
unsigned short, WORD	W	16-bit unsigned integer
TCHAR	Ch	8-bit or 16-bit signed (depending on whether you're using ANSI or Unicode)

32-Bit Numeric Parameters

The six 32-bit (4-byte) numeric parameters include `int`, `unsigned int`, `long`, `unsigned long`, and `DWORD`.

The VBA `Long Integer` data type ranges between –2,147,483,648 and 2,147,483,647 and is equivalent to the signed C Integer types (`int` and `long`). As such, it can be used anywhere they appear. The unsigned type must be converted; see the conversion formula in the section "Signed and Unsigned Integers."

VBA parameter: `ByVal param As Long`

Datatype	Prefix	Description
Int	N	32-bit signed integer
Long	L	32-bit signed integer
Unsigned int, UINT	N	32-bit unsigned integer
Unsigned long, DWORD	Dw	32-bit unsigned integer (also referred to as a double-word)

Currency Parameters

The Win32 API does not use a `Currency` data type. There should be no conversion issues for any that do.

VBA parameter: None.

Floating-Point Parameters

There are very few APIs that use the `Single` (Float) or `Double` data types.

`Single` values are 32-bit (4-bytes) wide and range between –3.402823E38 and –1.401298E–45 for negative values, and from 1.401298E–45 to 3.402823E38 for positive values.

`Double` values are 64-bit (8-bytes) wide, and range from –1.79769313486231E308 to –4.94065645841247E–324 for negative values and from 4.94065645841247E–324 to 1.79769313486232E308 for positive values.

If you are supplying values to DLLs that use floating-point parameters, you must ensure that they are compatible with VBA, because not all are.

VBA parameter: Check DLL documentation.

Boolean Parameters

The VBA `Long Integer` data type can be used to supply a value for the `BOOL` parameter type. However, both C and VBA define the Boolean `False` as zero. By default, that means all nonzero values must not be `False`, thereby `True`.

The C language defines a Boolean `True` to be 1, whereas VBA defines `True` as –1.

Supplying a VBA `True` value can sometimes lead to problems when using some API functions, due to the way in which Boolean values are interpreted in the C language, because some APIs return any nonzero value as `True`.

The C language includes both logical and Boolean operations. The logical Not operation in C is distinguished by a tilde preceding the number or variable (~myvar). The Boolean Not operator is distinguished by an exclamation mark (!myvar).

If (in C) you perform a logical Not operation on the True value (~1), you get zero. If you do the same thing for the VBA True (~–1), you get zero. No problem, as long as both values are nonzero. Since VBA doesn't have a logical Not operator, performing a Not against both values returns –2 and 0, respectively.

To get around this problem, specify Abs(booMyVar), when supplying a Boolean parameter, and Not (booMyVar = False), when checking a return value.

Datatype	Prefix	Description
BOOL	B	32-bit Boolean value. Zero is False; one is True (although any nonzero VBA value will equate to True).

Handle Parameters

A Windows *handle* is a 32-bit (4-byte) number that identifies the memory location where the definition of a Windows object, such as a window, can be found. Handles come in different flavors, including HANDLE, hwnd, hDC, and so on.

For example, the hwnd of the Access application is a Windows handle that can be discovered using VBA code. The following table illustrates how to find the hwnd for familiar Access objects:

To find the hwnd of this Access object:	Do this:
The Access application	`Application.hWndAccessApp`
An Access form	`Me.hwnd`

A user control on a form	`Private Declare Function GetFocus Lib "user32" () As Long`
	`Function GetCtrlhWnd(ctrl As Control) As Long`
	`'Set the focus to the control`
	`ctrl.SetFocus`
	`'Get the hwnd from the API`
	`GetCtrlhWnd = GetFocus`
	`End Function`

Since handles are all 32-bits wide, the VBA Long data type suits this purpose nicely.

VBA parameter: ByVal param As Long

Datatype	Prefix	Description
HANDLE, hwnd,	H	32-bit unsigned integer. Handle to a Windows object.

Object Parameters

As far as the Windows API is concerned, the Object data type has no meaning. However, the OLE 2.0 API set does support parameters of this type, namely, LPUNKNOWN and LPDISPATCH, which are pointers to COM interfaces.

Therefore, if you ever have to specify an Object pointer, use the VBA Object data type.

VBA parameter: ByVal param As Object

Datatype	Prefix	Description
LPUNKNOWN, LPDISPATCH	Dw	32-bit pointer to an IUnknown OLE 2.0 interface.

String Parameters

Strings are represented in C by the LPSTR data type, which is a pointer to the memory location where the string begins. Most DLLs require Null-terminated strings, which VBA can pass ByVal. Some C-language DLLs might return LPSTR pointers that can be copied to VBA strings using API functions, but only those APIs that were specifically written for VB (like APIGID32.dll) actually accept or return VBA strings. Those that do so will declare its parameter using $ or As String.

A Null-terminated string is not the same as a null string or an empty string. A Null-terminated string is a string that ends in an ASCII Null character. To form such a string, you append an ASCII zero:

```
param = "abc" & Chr$(0)
```

A Null string (empty string), on the other hand, is an empty string, which is formed like this:

```
param = ""
```

A Null value string is formed by appending a Null character, or by using the vbNullString constant:

```
param = Chr(0), or
param = vbNullString
```

Special note: *DLLs do not always return strings directly. They do so by modifying strings that you pass as one of their parameters. When you pass a string parameter to an API that will modify that string, you must preinitialize the string with sufficient characters to take the value that will be returned. The API function will provide another parameter to accept a number that represents the length of the string. You can preinitialize the string using the VBA* Space() *function, and the* Len(strMyString)+1 *construct can be used to specify its length. Notice that we used +1; this is because you must account for the length of the string you expect to get back, plus the terminating Null character.*

For example, to find the Windows folder (the one that contains most of the Windows application and initialization files), use the following:

```
'Declare the function
Private Declare Function GetWindowsDirectory _
    Lib "kernel32" Alias "GetWindowsDirectoryA" ( _
     ByVal lpBuffer As String, _
     ByVal nSize As Long) As Long

Private Const MAXLEN = 255

Public Function WindowsDir() As String
    Dim strDirectory As String
    Dim lngSize As Long
    Dim lngReturn As Long

    'Pre-initialize the string
    strDirectory = Space(MAXLEN) & Chr(0)
    'Initialize the string length
    lngSize = MAXLEN + 1

    'Retrieve the length of the string returned by the function
    lngReturn = GetWindowsDirectory(strDirectory, lngSize)

    If lngReturn <> 0 Then
    'Return the string containing the Windows directory,
    'using lngReturn to specify how long the string is.
        WindowsDir = left(strDirectory, lngReturn)
    Else
        WindowsDir = ""
    End If
End Function
```

VBA parameter: `ByVal param As String`

Datatype	Prefix	Description
LPSTR, LPCSTR, LPTSTR	lpsz	32-bit (long) pointer to a C Null-terminated string

Variant Parameters

VBA `Variant` data types are not supported under the core Win32 APIs. The only ones to use it are those of the OLE 2.0 specification, in which case the VBA `Variant` data type can be used without conversion.

VBA parameter: `ByVal param As Variant`

Pointers to Numeric Values

There are a lot of pointers in the C language. Pointers to numeric values, such as `LPINT` and `LPSHORT`, can be passed by VBA simply by using the `ByRef` keyword (or just by omitting the `ByVal` keyword).

You must ensure, however, that the data type you pass matches what is required. For example, if a 32-bit data type is required, pass a Long Integer, not an Integer (16-bit). If you do pass an Integer when a Long Integer is required, the DLL will write not only into the 16 bits of the Integer, but also into the next 16 bits. This can cause all sorts of problems, from erroneous data to a system crash.

VBA parameters: `ByRef param As Integer`

```
param As Long
```

Datatype	Prefix	Description
LPSHORT	Lps	16-bit (short) pointer to a 16-bit signed integer
LPINT	Lpi	32-bit (long) pointer to a 32-bit signed integer

Pointers to C Structures

C-language structures are essentially the same as VBA *User-Defined Types* (UDTs), which were described in Chapter 5. You pass a UDT as a DLL parameter `ByRef`, specifying the name declared using the `Type` keyword, but you must also ensure that all the UDT's members consist of data types that are compatible with the API, as described in this section.

You cannot pass a UDT `ByVal`.

VBA parameter: `ByRef param As` *UDT name*

Datatype	Prefix	Description
Lpstructname	Lp	32-bit (long) pointer to a structure or other data item

Pointers to Arrays

Passing arrays to APIs not specifically written for VBA is accomplished by `ByRef`, because those APIs expect a pointer to the first array element. Such APIs also expect a parameter that indicates the number of elements in the array.

There are three issues to be aware of when passing arrays. First, you cannot pass entire string arrays. You can pass single array elements; just not the entire thing.

Second, when passing an entire array, you do so by specifying the first array element in the call.

```
myArray(0)
```

Third, when specifying the number of elements, you must specify UBound(strMyArray)+1, because UBound() only returns the maximum numeric bound of the array, not the actual count of its elements. Remember also that specifying Option Base 1 will affect the number returned by UBound(). You can, of course, just specify a number; just make sure it reflects the actual number of array elements.

C-style APIs don't care much whether you're telling the truth about the number of elements in the array. If you tell it you have ten elements when you only have five, C will happily write to the space required for ten, regardless of whether they actually exist or not. Naturally this is going to have interesting side effects, which you may not be too happy about.

VBA parameter: ByRef param(0) As Long

```
Param(0) As Long
```

You can also pass array elements either singly or as a subset of the array. For example, if you want to get the hwnd of the window within which a specific xy co-ordinate exists, and you have an array that contains a number of xy co-ordinates, call the WindowFromPoint API like this:

```
Myhwnd = WindowFromPoint(lngPtArray(2), lngPtArray(3))
```

Arrays that were written specifically with VBA in mind (and these are rare) expect an *OLE 2.0 SAFEARRAY* structure, and so expect a pointer that is itself a pointer to the array. Therefore, in this case, you simply pass the VBA array. This makes sense if you consider a string variable as a single-element array.

VBA parameter: ByRef param() As Long

```
Param() As Long
```

Pointers to Functions

FARPROC and *DLGPROC* are examples of pointers to functions. These pointers are supplied so the API can execute a function as part of its own functionality. These functions are referred to as Callback functions.

You specify the memory address of a callback function using the VBA AddressOf operator, but it is worth noting that the AddressOf operator has certain limitations:

❑ It can only be specified in a standard module—you can't use it in a class module.

❑ It must precede an argument in an argument list, and the argument it precedes must be the name of a procedure (sub, function, or property).

The procedure whose location it returns must exist in the same project, so it can't be used with external functions declared with the Declare keyword, or with functions referenced from type libraries.

You can pass a function pointer to an `As Any` parameter (discussed in the next section), and also create your own callback functions in DLLs compiled in Visual Basic or C++. To work with `AddressOf`, these functions must use the `_stdcall` calling convention.

VBA parameter: `AddressOf myFunc`

Datatype	Prefix	Description
FARPROC, DLGPROC	lpfn	32-bit (far) pointer to a function or procedure

The Any Datatype

Some DLL function parameters can accept different data types. Such parameters are declared using the `As Any` data type. Calling a DLL function with parameters declared `As Any` is inherently dangerous, because VBA doesn't perform any type checking on it. That is, VBA doesn't check that the data type you supply matches that which is required by the function. Therefore, you need to be absolutely certain that the data type you are supplying to the function is correct.

To avoid the hazards of passing such arguments, declare several versions of the same DLL function, giving each a different name (using the `Alias` keyword) and a different parameter data type.

VBA parameter: `ByVal param As data type`

`ByRef param As  data type`

Err.LastDLLError

Like the VBA procedures you write, API procedures can also generate errors. These can be the result of bad or missing data, invalid data type assignments, or a variety of other conditions or failures. This section describes how to trap and retrieve these API-generated errors, so you can take remedial or other action to shield the user from their adverse effects.

`LastDLLError` is a property of the VBA `Err` object. It returns the error code produced by a call to a DLL, and always contains zero on systems that don't have DLLs (like the Macintosh).

DLL functions usually return a code that indicates whether the call succeeded or failed. Your VBA code should check the value returned after a DLL function is called and, on detecting a failure code, should immediately check the `LastDLLError` property and take whatever action you deem necessary. The DLL's documentation will indicate which codes to check for.

Since no exception is raised when the `LastDLLError` property is set, you cannot use the `On Error Goto` construct; therefore, use `On Error Resume Next`.

Modify the `SetFormIcon` procedure to generate a DLL error by passing an empty string as the icon path. This shows the `LastDLLError` property in action.

```
Public Sub SetFormIcon(hWnd As Long, strIcon As String)
    Dim hIcon As Long
    Dim lngReturn As Long

    On Error Resume Next

    'Pass an empty string as the icon path
    hIcon = LoadImage(0&, "", IMAGE_ICON, IMG_DEFAULT_WIDTH, _
        IMG_DEFAULT_HEIGHT, LR_LOADFROMFILE)

    'Now check for an error
    If hIcon <> 0 Then
        lngReturn = SendMessage(hWnd, WM_SETICON, ICON_SMALL, ByVal hIcon)
    Else
        'Dsplay the error
        MsgBox "The last DLL error was: " & Err.LastDllError
    End If
End Sub
```

Since the error is a DLL-specific error, the Err object's Description property will be empty.

Distributing Applications That Reference Type Libraries and Custom DLLs

It is a bit trickier to deploy applications if they contain references to some Type libraries and DLLs. You can't always just drop a database file onto a disk and expect it to work, because the target system may not already contain the required Type libraries and DLLs.

To ensure the database functions correctly on every platform, you may have to include them in an installation package you create using the Package and Deployment Wizard that comes with the *Access Developer Extensions* (ADE).

The Package and Deployment Wizard scans the application for external references and includes them in the setup package it creates. When run on the target system, the setup program copies all the required files onto the hard disk, and usually registers the Type libraries and DLLs. For more information about the ADE, refer to Chapter 18.

Summary

In this chapter, we looked at what APIs and DLLs are, and why you might want to use them. We introduced the concept of *static* versus *dynamic linking* and how to reference APIs in Access projects. We then examined the anatomy of an API call, and went into great detail about how to use the correct data types when calling API functions.

We then looked at trapping errors generated by DLLs and the considerations in distributing an application that references Type libraries and custom DLLs.

Although this has been a whirlwind tour of the Windows APIs and their use in VBA, we hope any fear or apprehension you may have had toward using them has been allayed to the point where you are now willing to experiment and learn by doing.

14

SQL and VBA

You may be familiar with SQL; after all, it's in every query you create. SQL (Structured Query Language) is the language of queries and recordsets; it's how you retrieve, update, insert, and delete records in your database tables.

When you use the query `Design View` in Access, you are actually building a SQL statement under the covers. Most of the time you won't need to actually look at the SQL code, but you can see it using the `SQL View` if you're curious.

Conversely, you can take most SQL statements, paste them into the `SQL View` of a new query, and then switch over to `Design View` to see how they work. There are a few types of SQL statements where this won't work; Union queries and pass-through queries are a couple of examples that cannot be viewed using `Design View`.

Even if you're comfortable using SQL in queries, you may not be familiar with building SQL statements in VBA. If you're not, you're missing out! Using SQL in VBA is a powerful technique that can enable many great features in your Access applications. By using VBA you can build custom SQL statements for combo boxes, forms, and reports. For example, you'll be able to change the sorting and selecting of records on continuous forms, control the record selection on reports, and limit the drop-down lists of combo boxes based on other combo boxes.

First, we'll cover how to build SQL statements using string variables in VBA.

Working with SQL Strings in VBA

To build SQL statements in VBA, you should usually load them into string variables by concatenating various phrases together. Some of the phrases will be exact SQL text that you will supply, while others will be the contents of variables in VBA or controls on forms or reports. When the SQL statement is complete, you'll be able to use it in queries, in the recordsource of forms or reports, or in the rowsource of combo boxes or list boxes. This will allow you to deliver power and flexibility in your Access applications.

Building SQL Strings with Quotes

The first thing to learn about building SQL statements in VBA is handling concatenation and quotes. They may seem simple, but many programmers have stared at VBA strings with multiple nested quotes and struggled to make them work.

Consider a SQL string that selects a record for a particular business from a table of businesses:

```
Select * From tblBusiness Where BusinessKey = 17
```

In actual usage, we need to replace the 17 in the above statement with the BusinessKey that the user is currently working with. To build this SQL statement in VBA, using the BusinessKey from the current form, you would use something like this:

```
strSQL = "Select * From tblBusiness Where BusinessKey = " _
    & Me!BusinessKey
```

One reason this is so simple is that BusinessKey is a numeric value. In SQL, numeric values are just stated, without quotes around them. This is great for primary key values, which are often AutoNumbers (with Long Integer data types).

However, consider a SQL statement that selects businesses in a particular city:

```
Select * from tblBusiness Where BusinessCity = "Seattle"
```

This is where it starts to get complicated. As you can see, you need to wrap Seattle in quotes, because SQL expects them around text values. The VBA to create this statement, again assuming that BusinessCity is on the current form, is

```
strSQL = "Select * From tblBusiness Where BusinessCity = """ _
    & Me!BusinessCity & """"
```

At first glance, all those quotes seem a little extreme. But if we break them down, they make sense. The first thing to remember is that in order to have a quote (") inside a string, you need to type two quotes in a row. This lets VBA know that you aren't closing the string with a quote—you actually want a quote *inside* the string.

So, the string

```
"Select * From tblBusiness Where BusinessCity = """
```

results in a string that contains

```
Select * From tblBusiness Where BusinessCity = "
```

Notice that last quote? This is a result of the two quotes after the equal sign (=) "collapsing" into just one quote. This idea of *collapsing quotes* in the interior of your strings is crucial to understanding how to build complex SQL strings in VBA. You may even want to print out your VBA code and circle the interior quote pairs with a pen. Each of these circles represents a quote that will be included inside your string.

Now, let's look at the rest of this simple example. After the first phrase (the one that ends with a quote), we need to tack on the value of `BusinessCity` (Seattle) and then finish it off with a final quote. Concatenating the `BusinessCity` is easy:

```
& Me!BusinessCity
```

But what about that final quote? Here's how it is added:

```
& """"
```

Yes, that's four quotes in a row. Remember, the interior pairs of quotes are collapsed into a quote inside the string. In this case, the result is a string containing merely one quote mark, which is exactly what we need at the end of Seattle in our final SQL string.

```
Select * from tblBusiness Where BusinessCity = "Seattle"
```

To summarize the topic of quote collapsing, remember what is happening when you see three or four quotes in a row.

Whenever you see *three quotes in a row*, you can be sure that one quote mark is being included at the beginning or end of some other text, like this:

```
"Select * From tblBusiness Where BusinessCity = """
```

And whenever you see *four quotes in a row*, you are seeing just one quote mark being concatenated to the string, as in this example:

```
Me!BusinessCity & """"
```

Now that you know how to build SQL strings with text, values from variables and forms, and double quotes, there's one little side topic we need to cover: The use of single quotes (') instead of double quotes (").

Using Single Quotes Instead of Double Quotes

Some programmers use a mixture of single quotes (') and double quotes (") when they are building SQL strings. This can be a good technique, because you don't need to do any "quote collapsing" as described previously. However, to some people it can be confusing to see the different types of quotes mixed together. It's a style thing—there isn't a right or wrong way.

VBA remembers what kind of quote started a string, so if you use the other kind in the middle of the string, it won't get confused and try to close the string. Access Wizards often use this technique to build SQL strings. For example, here's how the Access Wizard generates the `WhereCondition` phrase when you ask to open a form filtered to a specific value:

```
stLinkCriteria = "[City]=" & "'" & Me![txtCity] & "'"
DoCmd.OpenForm stDocName, , , stLinkCriteria
```

Notice the mixture of single and double quotes in the string loaded into `stLinkCriteria`. The double quotes are used to indicate to VBA where the text phrases start and stop. The single quotes are built into the `stLinkCriteria` field itself. The reason the single quotes work is because the Access query processor recognizes either single or double quotes around text values. Therefore, the following two statements are identical to Access SQL:

```
Where City = 'Seattle'
Where City = "Seattle"
```

Also notice that the technique to build the string is a little more complicated than necessary. In order to generically handle either text or numeric values, the Access Wizard concatenates the first single quote separately. If you are building it yourself, you can tack the single quote right after the equals sign, like this:

```
stLinkCriteria = "[City]='" & Me![txtCity] & "'"
```

> **SQL Server Note: If you build SQL strings to use in SQL Server, remember that only single quotes are valid there—double quotes won't work. This won't be an issue if you are querying linked tables in Access, because Access will translate the syntax for you. But you must use SQL Server syntax if you are using a pass-through query or are opening a SQL Server recordset directly in code.**

For the rest of the examples in this chapter, we'll use the "collapsing quotes" method described previously. This method will work whether you use all single quotes (') or all double quotes (").

Concatenating Long SQL Strings

In order to keep your VBA readable, you should break your long statements onto multiple lines. While this is true any time, it's especially helpful when building long SQL strings. If you do not break them into multiple VBA lines, you would need to scroll far to the right to read it all. Breaking up these long statements can be done in two ways: By building up the string variable in multiple steps or by using the VBA line continuation character.

Many programmers still use the "build up" method for storing long SQL strings into a string variable. It might just be habit left over from the days when there wasn't a line continuation character, or maybe they just like the way it looks. This method looks like this:

```
strSQL = "Select * From tblBusiness"
strSQL = strSQL & " Where BusinessCity = """ & Me!BusinessCity & """"
strSQL = strSQL & " And BusinessActiveFlag = True"
```

Notice how the second and third lines concatenate more text to the same variable, which is why we call it "building up" the string. This method has a slight advantage during debugging since you can see you string's value step-by-step as it is being built.

Another way to do this is to use the VBA line continuation character, which is a space and underscore together:

```
strSQL = "Select * From tblBusiness" & _
" Where BusinessCity = """ & Me!BusinessCity & """" & _
" And BusinessActiveFlag = True"
```

Some developers indent the subsequent lines for clarity:

```
strSQL = "Select * From tblBusiness" & _
    " Where BusinessCity = """ & Me!BusinessCity & """" & _
    " And BusinessActiveFlag = True"
```

This method runs the entire concatenation as one line in VBA, even though it is visually spread across multiple lines in your code.

Breaking your VBA onto multiple lines is another area that's really a style choice—all these methods work just fine. However, whichever method you choose, you should break the statement where it makes sense, starting each new VBA line with a keyword like `Where`, `And`, `Or`, `Join`, and so on so that others can read along more easily.

Also, notice that you need to be careful to add the extra spaces around the keywords like `Where` and `And`. If you don't, your words will run together in the final string, and the syntax will be incorrect and the SQL statement won't run. Many programmers add them to the beginning of each section of text instead of the end, so that they really stand out. Also, remember that extra spaces between words aren't a problem in SQL; they're ignored by both Access and SQL Server.

Now that we've covered how to use quotes and build long SQL strings in VBA, let's use them to enhance Access forms and reports.

Using SQL When Opening Forms and Reports

Whenever you use the Access Wizard to build a command button to open a form or report with a filter to limit the records that are displayed, you are actually using SQL in VBA. This wizard will build VBA code to open the form with a `WhereCondition`, like this:

```
Private Sub cmdCityBusinesses_Click()
On Error GoTo Err_cmdCityBusinesses_Click

    Dim stDocName As String
    Dim stLinkCriteria As String

    stDocName = "frmBusiness"

    stLinkCriteria = "[City]=" & "'" & Me![txtCity] & "'"
    DoCmd.OpenForm stDocName, , , stLinkCriteria

Exit_cmdCityBusinesses_Click:
    Exit Sub

Err_cmdCityBusinesses_Click:
    MsgBox Err.Description
    Resume Exit_cmdCityBusinesses_Click

End Sub
```

The `WhereCondition` on the `OpenForm` command is used to filter the form being opened to a set of records that meet some criteria. Usually, it is used to drill down to a specific single record, so the criteria is merely the primary key value of the record. However, as in this example, it can be used to open a form to a set of multiple records that meet the specified criteria (in this case, the `City`).

> When you use the **WhereCondition**, you don't need to include the word **Where** at the beginning of the string. It's assumed.

This is a very simple example of using a fragment of SQL in your code; after all, the wizard will build it for you. The wizard to open a report works much the same way. However, there are many other more powerful ways to use SQL in your VBA code.

Using SQL to Enhance Forms

Using SQL, you can enhance your forms in many ways, including allowing quick and easy record sorting, narrowing a list of records by applying selections, and using combo box values to limit the drop-down lists for other combo boxes. These are all powerful tools that help your user get more value from your application. Let's study these techniques one at a time.

Sorting on Columns

Users often expect the ability to sort on columns, similar to other Windows applications like Outlook. For example, if you have an index form of businesses, your user may want to sort on either the `Business Name` or `Contact Name` column, as shown in Figure 14-1.

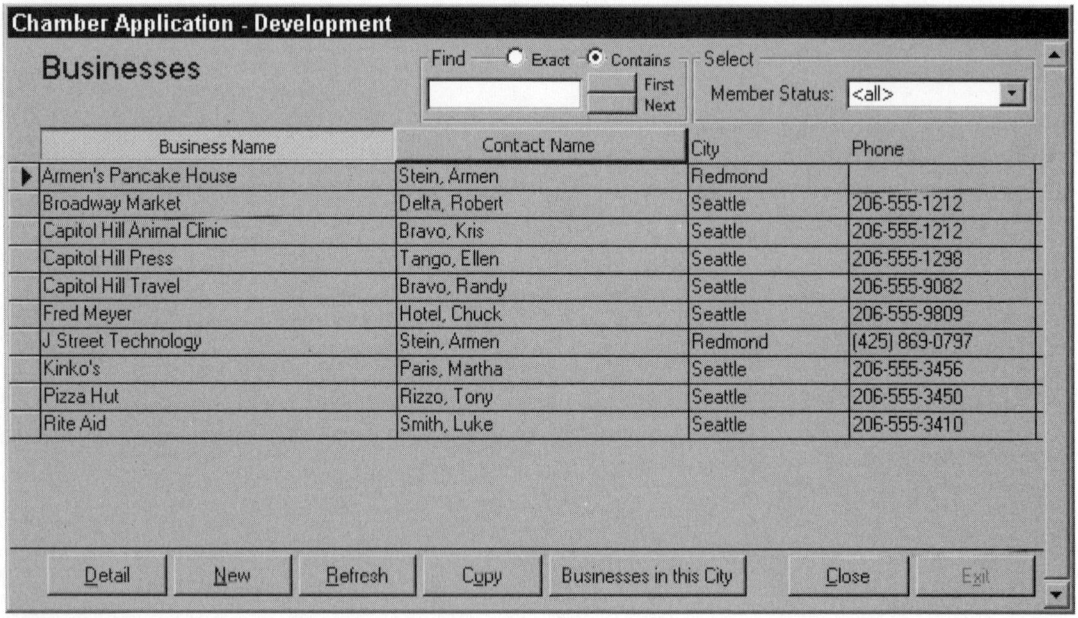

Figure 14-1

In this example, the user can click either the `Business Name` column heading or the `Contact Name` column heading. The two toggle buttons are in an option group called `optSort`. This control has an `After Update` event that contains the following code:

```
Private Sub optSort_AfterUpdate()
On Error GoTo Error_Handler

    Dim strOrderBy As Variant
    strOrderBy = Null

    Select Case Me!optSort
        Case 1 'Business Name
            strOrderBy = " tblBusiness.BusinessName, " & _
                "tblBusiness.LastName, tblBusiness.FirstName"
        Case 2 'Contact information
            strOrderBy = "tblBusiness.LastName, " & _
                "tblBusiness.FirstName, tblBusiness.BusinessName"
        Case Else
    End Select

    strOrderBy = " ORDER BY " + strOrderBy

    Me.RecordSource = ReplaceOrderByClause(Me.RecordSource, strOrderBy)
    Me.Requery

Exit_Procedure:
    On Error Resume Next
    Exit Sub
Error_Handler:
    MsgBox "An error has occurred in this application. " _
    & "Please contact your technical support person " _
    & "and tell them this information:" _
    & vbCrLf & vbCrLf & "Error Number " & Err.Number & ", " & _
Err.Description, _
    Buttons:=vbCritical, title:="My Application"
    Resume Exit_Procedure
    Resume

End Sub
```

This technique takes advantage of the fact that you can change the recordsource of a form while it is already open, and then requery the form. When you do, the form is reloaded with the records from the new recordsource, including their sort order.

We build a new `Order By` clause based on the button that is clicked. To swap the new `Order By` clause into the RecordSource, we use a function called `ReplaceOrderByClause`. The codes for this function and its cousin `ReplaceWhereClause` are at the end of this chapter. For now, just assume that the `Order By` clause will be magically "cut and pasted" into the SQL string in the `RecordSource` property of the form.

421

> A SQL string RecordSource: In order to replace part of the SQL string in a `Record-`
> `Source` property, you need to start with a SQL string! That means to use this technique,
> you can't have just the name of a query or table in the RecordSource. It needs to be
> a real SQL statement. To make one, just take the query name, say `qryBusinesses`,
> and turn it into a SQL string like `"Select * From qryBusinesses"`. Then you'll
> be able to manipulate it with new **Where** and `Order By` clauses.

So, when your user clicks a column heading, the records are instantly resorted by that column. This is
much more intuitive and Windows-standard than right-clicking or selecting menu options. Your user will
appreciate how easy it is to sort records this way.

Sorting isn't the end of the story. Let's examine how you can also provide instant record selection also.

Selections on Index Forms

One of the most powerful features you can offer your user is the ability to narrow a set of records so that
they can more easily find the information they are looking for. By adding selection criteria to your index
forms, you add a lot of power to your application with only a little work.

Easy Selection Criteria on an Index Form

The simple selections are the most common. Your user would like to be able to narrow the recordset by
selecting a criterion for a particular field. However, you also need to provide the ability to open the
selection up again to include all records, as shown in Figure 14-2.

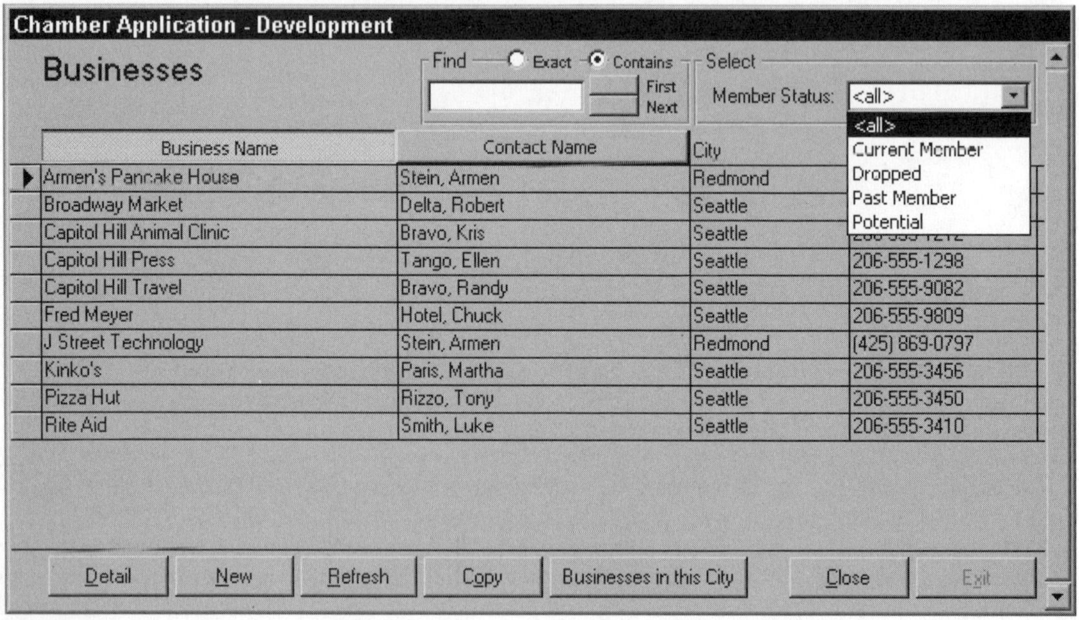

Figure 14-2

First of all, the default selection criterion for a field is <all>. To include this in the drop-down list for your criteria combo box, you must use a Union query. An easy way to understand a Union query is to think of it joining tables vertically instead of horizontally; a Union query adds records to the result instead of columns. In this case, we just want to add one additional record: the <all> value.

A Union query cannot be built using the Query Designer, but fortunately it isn't difficult to build using SQL. In this case, the RowSource for the Combo box looks like this:

```
SELECT tblMemberStatus.MemberStatusKey, tblMemberStatus.MemberStatusName
FROM tblMemberStatus
UNION
SELECT "<all>", "<all>" FROM tblMemberStatus
ORDER BY tblMemberStatus.MemberStatusName;
```

Note that the Union is really just patching together two Select statements. The first one returns the actual member statuses from tblMemberStatus. The second one is "fake"; it just returns the values "<all>" and "<all>".

> *Sometimes cheaters do prosper: To more easily build your Union query, build the first part (that retrieves records from a table) using the Query Designer. Then, switch over to SQL View and add the Union and second Select parts.*

Since the Order By clause specifies that the records should be sorted in an ascending order by MemberStatusName, the <all> value appears at the top of the list since "<" is a lower value than any alphabet letter. The code to process the user's criteria selection is in the After Update event of the Combo box:

```
Private Sub cboMemberStatusKey_AfterUpdate()
On Error GoTo Error_Handler

    SelectRecords
    cboMemberStatusKey.Requery

Exit_Procedure:
    On Error Resume Next
    Exit Sub
Error_Handler:
    MsgBox "An error has occurred in this application. " _
    & "Please contact your technical support person " _
    & "and tell them this information:" _
    & vbCrLf & vbCrLf & "Error Number " & Err.Number & ", " &
Err.Description, _
    Buttons:=vbCritical, title:="My Application"
    Resume Exit_Procedure
    Resume

End Sub
```

This code calls another procedure in this form called SelectRecords. We don't want to actually rebuild the SQL statement here, because we may add other selection criteria fields later. By rebuilding the Where clause in a central procedure, we can easily add the new criteria fields with a simple procedure just like this one.

> **Why the extra Requery?** You'll notice that there is a `Requery` of the combo box after `SelectRecords` runs. This is there to handle a little bug that has been in the last several versions of Access, including Access 2003. The bug causes the text in an unbound combo box to become invisible if the recordset of the form contains no records. Requerying the combo box (just the control itself, not the whole form) causes the mysterious invisible text to appear again.

The `SelectRecords` procedure is where the SQL statement is rebuilt and the form requeried:

```
Public Sub SelectRecords()
On Error GoTo Error_Handler

    Dim varWhereClause As Variant
    Dim strAND As String

    varWhereClause = Null
    strAND = " AND "

    If cboMemberStatusKey & "" <> "<all>" Then
        varWhereClause = (varWhereClause + strAND) & _
            "tblBusiness.MemberStatusKey = """ & _
            cboMemberStatusKey & """"
    End If

    varWhereClause = " WHERE " + varWhereClause

    Me.RecordSource = ReplaceWhereClause(Me.RecordSource,
varWhereClause)
    Me.Requery

    EnableDisableControls

Exit_Procedure:
    On Error Resume Next
    Exit Sub
Error_Handler:
    MsgBox "An error has occurred in this application. " _
    & "Please contact your technical support person " _
    & "and tell them this information:" _
    & vbCrLf & vbCrLf & "Error Number " & Err.Number & ", " &
Err.Description, _
    Buttons:=vbCritical, title:="My Application"
    Resume Exit_Procedure
    Resume

End Sub
```

Note that if the combo box contains "`<all>`", no `Where` clause is built at all. The `ReplaceWhereClause` function is designed to just remove the `Where` clause (and return all records) if a Null is passed in for the `WhereClause` parameter.

All this code runs immediately when the user chooses a different criterion in the drop-down list, and the records meeting the criteria are displayed. If there are any records that match the selection criteria, they are displayed and the command buttons are enabled, as shown in Figure 14-3.

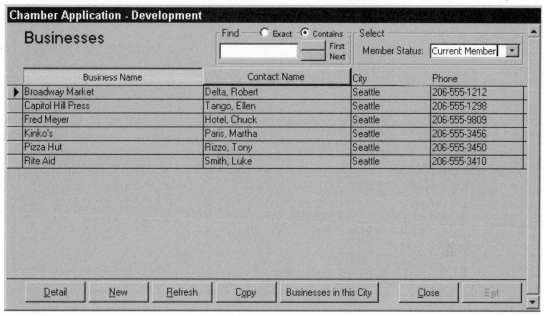

Figure 14-3

Now that we've seen how the selection looks to the user, let's examine the VBA code more closely. Using some simple techniques, we can handle multiple selections of different types on the same form.

The Amazing Expandable SelectRecords Procedure

The code in `SelectRecords` to build the `Where` clause may seem overly complex, but there are good reasons: expandability and flexibility. It is all ready for you to add more criteria fields. For example, if you wanted to add another selection for District, you would just need to add:

```
If cboDistrictKey & "" <> "<all>" Then
    varWhereClause = (varWhereClause + strAND) & _
        "tblBusiness.DistrictKey = """ & _
        cboDistrictKey & """"
End If
```

The key to this expandability is the concatenation of `varWhereClause` and `strAND`. When the procedure starts `varWhereClause` is null. And it continues like that until the code discovers a specified selection criterion.

When it does, the phrase

```
(varWhereClause + strAND)
```

425

performs its magic. The first time it runs, `varWhereClause` is still null, so the null-propagating "+" operator (see Chapter 8, "Executing VBA") does NOT add the word "AND".

However, the second time it runs (because the user has specified another selection criterion), things are different. Now, `varWhereClause` has a value in it, so the "+" operator successfully concatenates the "AND" onto the string before the next part of the `Where` clause is added.

When all the pieces have been built, the final step is to add the word "Where" onto the front of the newly built `Where` clause. However, we don't need it if there are no selection criteria, so it's "+" to the rescue again. If `varWhereClause` is still Null, then we have the following statement:

```
varWhereClause = " WHERE " + varWhereClause
```

This will append "WHERE" to the front of `varWhereClause`, but only if `varWhereClause` has a value. If it doesn't, it will remain Null. Regardless of the order in which you build the parts of the `Where` clause, this logic will work. It makes the `SelectRecords` procedure very easy to change and expand.

Now that we have seen how to build `Where` clauses with multiple fields, let's look at a couple of other selection scenarios you might encounter.

Selection Criteria Using Numeric Keys

The previous selection examples assumed that you were using text fields. If your combo box contains a numeric value (such as an `AutoNumber` key), the Union query looks a little different. Let's say the `DistrictKey` is an `AutoNumber` primary key:

```
SELECT tblDistrict.DistrictKey, tblDistrict.DistrictName
FROM tblDistrict
UNION
SELECT  0, "<all>" FROM tblDistrict
ORDER BY tblDistrict.DistrictName;
```

Note that the first "<all>" value has been replaced with a 0, to match type with the other numeric key values. Since 0 isn't used by Access as an `AutoNumber` key, it won't be confused with a real record from the District table.

The code in the `SelectRecords` procedure will be a little different too:

```
If cboDistrictKey <> 0 Then
    varWhereClause = (varWhereClause + strAND) & _
        "tblBusiness.DistrictKey = " & cboDistrictKey
End If
```

Note that we are now checking to see if the combo box value is 0 instead of <all>. Also, with a numeric value you don't need all the nested quotes—you can just concatenate that number right after the equals sign.

Selection Criteria in Child Records

Sometimes, your user wants to be able to search for records that contain a value not in those records, but in their child records. In our example, they might want to find all Businesses that made one or more Payments of a certain amount, as shown in Figure 14-4.

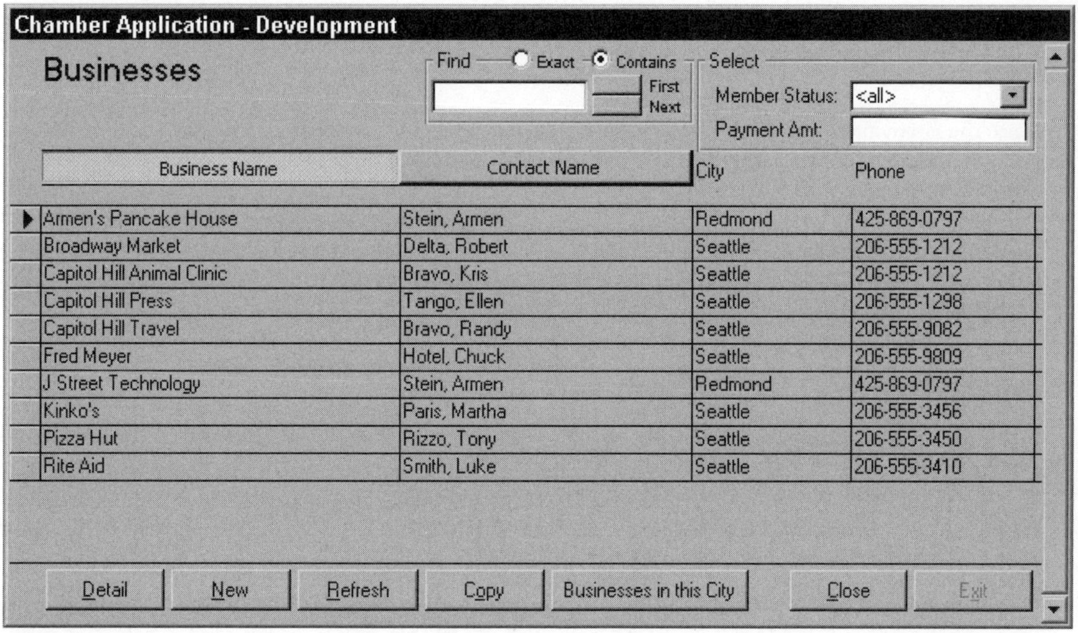

Figure 14-4

In this case, we do not want to apply selection criteria to the Business records themselves. Instead, we want to display all Businesses that have one or more records in the Payment table that are for the desired dollar amount.

To perform this kind of selection, we use a *subquery*. A subquery is a query inside another query, and in this example it is used to select Businesses that appear in another query: A list of payments of a certain dollar amount. Just as with Union queries, subqueries cannot be represented directly in the graphical Design View. However, they are easy to build using SQL View.

In this case, where we want the Businesses that have made one or more payments of $150, the desired Where clause would be

```
WHERE tblBusiness.BusinessKey IN (Select BusinessKey
From tblPayment Where PaymentAmount = 150)
```

The key thing here is the SQL operator IN. Using IN allows you to determine if a value appears anywhere in a recordset from another Select statement. In this case, we want all Businesses whose BusinessKeys appear in a list of Payments that equal $150.

The code in the `SelectRecords` procedure looks like this:

```
If Not IsNull(txtPaymentAmt) Then
    varWhereClause = (varWhereClause + strAND) & _
        "tblBusiness.BusinessKey IN (" & _
        "Select BusinessKey From tblPayment Where" & _
        " PaymentAmount = " & Me!txtPaymentAmt & ")"
End If
```

Since the Payment Amount is a numeric value, we don't need the nested quotes. However, we do need to build the inner subquery with its own `Select` statement and wrap in its own set of parentheses `"()"`.

Now we know how to apply different kinds of selections to a continuous index form. However, with all these selections going on, we need to take a look at what happens if the user specifies criteria that omit all of the records.

Disabling Buttons if No Records Are Displayed

When you give your user the ability to narrow a list of records, they might figure out a way to omit all of them! The subroutine `EnableDisableControls` is called just in case there are no records meeting the criteria. In this case, the user would get an error if they clicked the `Detail` button, because there wouldn't be a key to open the detail record with. To prevent this, the `Detail` button is disabled so that the user won't be able to click it, as shown in Figure 14-5.

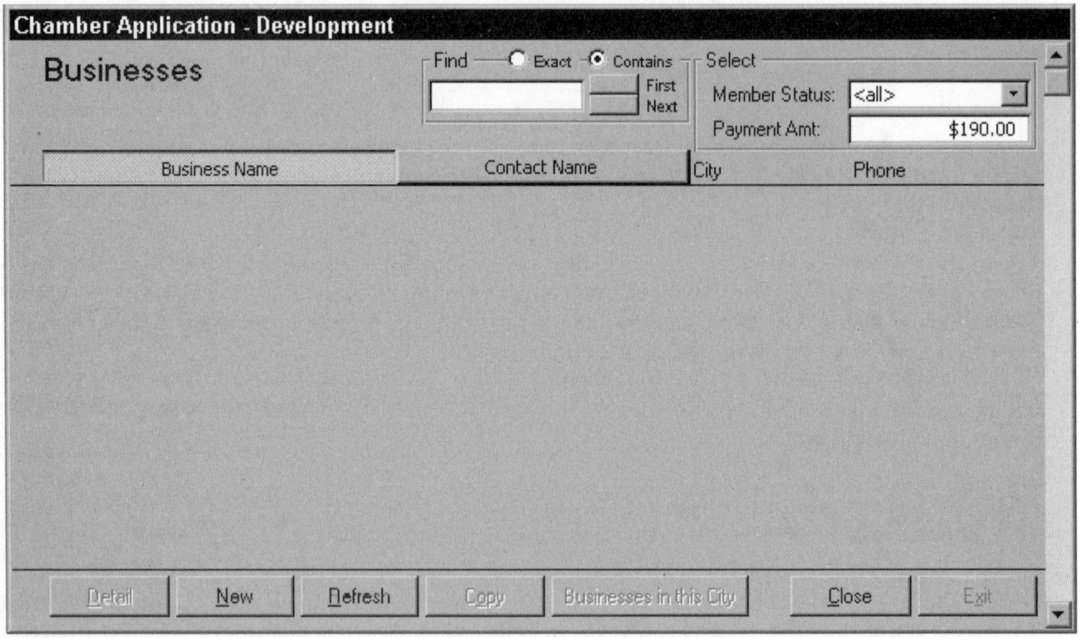

Figure 14-5

The code to disable or enable the appropriate buttons looks like this:

```
Public Sub EnableDisableControls()
On Error GoTo Error_Handler

    If Me.RecordsetClone.RecordCount = 0 Then
        Me!cmdDetail.Enabled = False
        Me!cmdCityBusinesses.Enabled = False
        Me!cmdCopy.Enabled = False
    Else
        Me!cmdDetail.Enabled = True
        Me!cmdCityBusinesses.Enabled = True
        Me!cmdCopy.Enabled = True
    End If

Exit_Procedure:
    On Error Resume Next
    Exit Sub
Error_Handler:
    MsgBox "An error has occurred in this application. " _
    & "Please contact your technical support person " _
    & "and tell them this information:" _
    & vbCrLf & vbCrLf & "Error Number " & Err.Number & ", " &
Err.Description, _
    Buttons:=vbCritical, title:="My Application"
    Resume Exit_Procedure
    Resume

End Sub
```

Now that we've handled how to sort and select records on a continuous form, and to prevent errors when the selection omits all the records, let's examine how to enhance forms with cascading combo boxes.

Cascading Combo Boxes

Sometimes, you would like your user to choose a value of a combo box, and then use that value to limit the selections in another combo box. Since the upper combo box affects the lower, this is sometimes called "cascading" the combo boxes.

To accomplish this, you need the SQL statement building techniques described earlier in this chapter. Let's say we have two combo boxes: one for County and one for City. Each County can have many Cities and each City is in one County. The table design would look something like this:

tblCounty	
CountyKey	AutoNumber
CountyName	Text 255

tblCity	
CityKey	AutoNumber
CityName	Text 255
CountyKey	Long Integer

When we present the selection form, we want the County to be selected first, then limit the City to those found in that County.

The control cboCounty will start off enabled in Design View, but cboCity will be disabled. In the After Update event for cboCounty, we'll include the following code:

```
Me!cboCity = Null

If IsNull(cboCounty) Then
    Me!cboCity.Enabled = False
Else
    Me!cboCity.Enabled = True
    Me!cboCity.Rowsource = ReplaceWhereClause(Me!cboCity.Rowsource, _
        "Where CountyCode = " & Me!cboCounty)
    Me!cboCity.Requery
End If
```

Let's take this code section by section.

```
Me!cboCity = Null
```

First, we clear out the City combo box by setting it to Null. We do this because we are in the After Update event of the County combo box, so we know it's been changed. If the whole County has been changed, then any value that was in the City combo box is no longer valid, so we just wipe it out.

```
If IsNull(cboCounty) Then
    Me!cboCounty.SetFocus
```

We are about to disable the City combo box, which won't be possible if it has the focus. Just in case it does, we set the focus back to cboCounty.

```
Me!cboCity.Enabled = False
```

Now, if the user just deleted the value for County (setting it to Null), we need to disable the City combo box, since they must choose a County before they can select a City.

```
Else
    Me!cboCity.Enabled = True
```

Alternatively, if the user changed the County to another value, the City combo box can be enabled so they can select a City.

```
Me!cboCity.Rowsource = ReplaceWhereClause(Me!cboCity.Rowsource, _
    "Where CountyCode = " & Me!cboCounty)
```

But now we need to limit the Cities in the drop-down list to those that are in the selected County. To do this, we modify the `Rowsource` property for the City combo box using our old friend `ReplaceWhereClause`.

```
    Me!cboCity.Requery
End If
```

Although we have changed the `Rowsource` property of the City combo box, it won't take effect until we requery it. At this point, the user can go down and select from a list of Cities that are in the selected County. Our cascading selection is complete!

Using SQL for Report Selection Criteria

Many developers build Access reports so that their users can quickly view and print out their data. Consider a report to list businesses from the database, as shown in Figure 14-6.

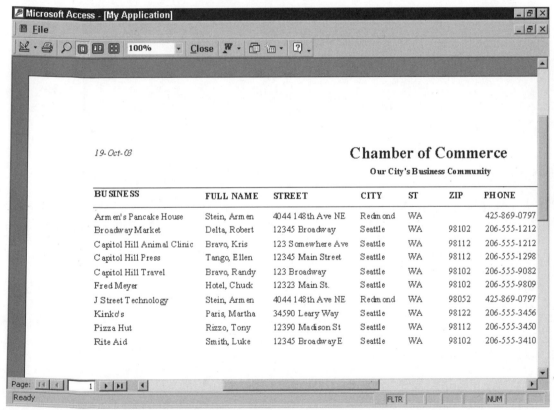

Figure 14-6

However, your user will often want to print only some of the records, based on selection criteria. You can create a different report for each selection criteria, but that approach will result in duplication of report code and difficulty in handling combinations of selection criteria.

Chapter 14

When novice Access developers want to allow their users to specify the selection criteria for reports, they often use parameter queries. Unfortunately, parameter queries have a few problems:

❑ They prompt the user with a separate dialog box for each value

❑ They don't allow any formatting or validation of the values

❑ They often require the user to know key values instead of descriptions

❑ They are awkward in handling Null or <all> values

A better way to prompt for report selection criteria is to display a form to gather them in easy to use fields and combo boxes. This way, you can handle null values, multiple criteria simultaneously, and validation checking.

For the business list report, your user wants to select whether to see all the businesses in the table, or just those with a particular Member Status, as in Figure 14-7.

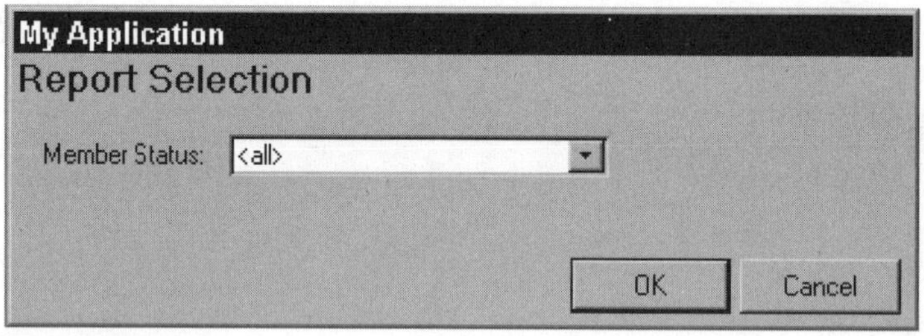

My Application
Report Selection

Member Status: <all>

OK   Cancel

Figure 14-7

After they make their selection and click OK, the report is displayed (Figure 14-8).

The first thing to note here is that the order of events might be different than you expect. Many programmers would think that the selection form opens the report when the OK button is clicked. In fact, it's the opposite. First, the report is opened. During its On Open event, the report calls the selection form in Dialog mode, which halts the report code until the selection form is hidden. Given below is the code in the On Open event of the report.

```
Private Sub Report_Open(Cancel As Integer)
On Error GoTo Error_Handler

    Me.Caption = "My Application"

    DoCmd.OpenForm FormName:="frmReportSelector_MemberList", _
        Windowmode:=acDialog

    'Cancel the report if "cancel" was selected on the dialog form.
    If Forms!frmReportSelector_MemberList!txtContinue = "no" Then
        Cancel = True
        GoTo Exit_Procedure
    End If
```

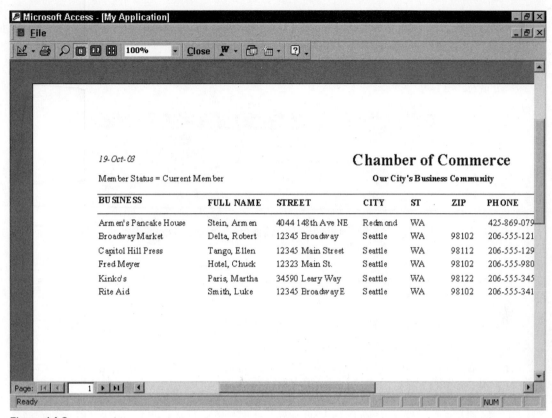

Figure 14-8

```
    Me.RecordSource = ReplaceWhereClause(Me.RecordSource, _
        Forms!frmReportSelector_MemberList!txtWhereClause)

Exit_Procedure:
    Exit Sub

Error_Handler:
    MsgBox "An error has occurred in this application. " _
    & "Please contact your technical support person " _
    & "and tell them this information:" _
    & vbCrLf & vbCrLf & "Error Number " & Err.Number & ", " &
Err.Description, _
    Buttons:=vbCritical, title:="My Application"

    Resume Exit_Procedure
    Resume

End Sub
```

The important thing to note here is that during the report's Open event, its recordset has not been evaluated yet, so you still have a chance to change it. When you open the selection form in Dialog mode, the report code waits until that form is hidden.

Now it's time to see what the selection form really does. It has a few fields that are normally hidden, as shown in Figure 14-9.

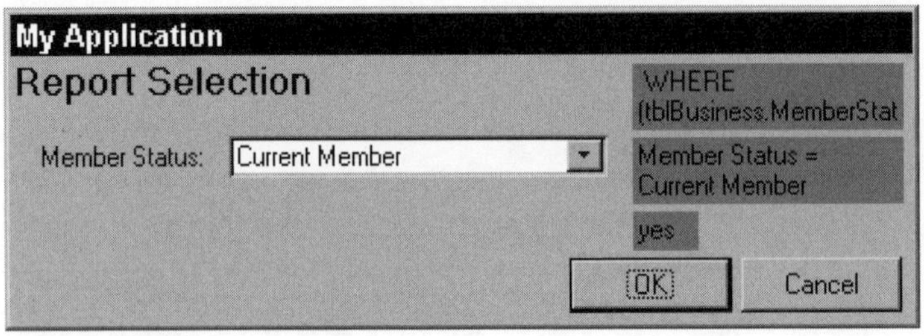

Figure 14-9

The extra fields above the OK button are normally set to Visible = No. They hold three pieces of information:

❑ The Where clause to use in the report's recordsource

❑ A selection title to use in the report's heading

❑ A field to indicate whether the report should continue (OK was clicked) or not (Cancel was clicked)

Red for Danger: It's a good idea to mark normally invisible fields in some special way, so that you can easily see them if you forget to hide them. A good technique is to make the background color of a hidden field red (BackColor = 255). That way you'll notice it if you forget to hide it!

Here's the code in the form that builds the Where clause and the selection title, both stored in the hidden fields:

```
Sub RebuildWhereClause()
On Error GoTo Err_RebuildWhereClause

'This subroutine builds an SQL WHERE clause based on the choices
'made by the user on the form. It can be used as the WHERE parameter
'in the OpenReport command. The invisible text box Me![txtWhereClause]
'displays the completed WHERE clause.
'
'SelectionTitle    string that contains a title to place at the top
'                  of the report, which specifies the selection made.
'                  Stored on form in invisible text box
Me![txtSelectionTitle].


Dim varWhereClause As Variant
Dim strWhereAnd As String
Dim strSelectionTitle As String
Dim strComma As String
```

```
    varWhereClause = Null
    strWhereAnd = ""
    strSelectionTitle = ""
    strComma = ""

    'Member Status Combo Box
    If Not (Me!cboMemberStatus & "" = "") And Not _
    (Me!cboMemberStatus = 0) Then
        varWhereClause = (varWhereClause + strWhereAnd) _
        & " (tblBusiness.MemberStatusKey = """ & _
        Me!cboMemberStatus.Column(0) & """) "
        strWhereAnd = " AND "
        strSelectionTitle = strSelectionTitle & strComma _
        & "Member Status = " & Me!cboMemberStatus.Column(1)
        strComma = ", "
    End If

    If strWhereAnd = "" Then
        varWhereClause = Null
    Else
        varWhereClause = " WHERE " + varWhereClause
    End If

    Me![txtWhereClause] = varWhereClause
    Me![txtSelectionTitle] = strSelectionTitle

Exit_RebuildWhereClause:
    Exit Sub
Err_RebuildWhereClause:
    MsgBox Err.Number & ", " & Err.Description
    Resume Exit_RebuildWhereClause
    Resume
End Sub
```

Notice that to build the Where clause, Column(0) of the combo box is used, because it contains the key value. However, to build the selection title, we use Column(1), since it contains the more friendly description of the Member Status record.

This code runs when the OK button is clicked. It rebuilds the Where clause and tells the report to proceed:

```
Sub cmdOK_Click()
On Error GoTo Err_cmdOK_Click

    RebuildWhereClause
    Me!txtContinue = "yes"
    Me.Visible = False

Exit_cmdOK_Click:
    Exit Sub
Err_cmdOK_Click:
    MsgBox Err.Number & ", " & Err.Description
    Resume Exit_cmdOK_Click
End Sub
```

After the `RebuildWhereClause` procedure builds the first two hidden fields, just two more things need to happen. First, the third hidden field, `txtContinue`, is set to `Yes`. This is the field that the report will check to see if it should continue to open or just cancel.

Lastly, the current form's Visible property is set to `False`. Remember, this form was opened in Dialog mode, so hiding it causes the report code to continue running.

> *A Nice Side Effect: Because the selection form is always hidden, not closed, the selection criteria will be retained each time the form is used during an Access session. This makes it easier for your user to re-run reports with the same selection criteria or to adjust the criteria slightly instead of typing it all again each time.*

If the user clicks `Cancel`, this code runs instead. It tells the report to stop opening:

```
Sub cmdCancel_Click()
On Error GoTo Err_cmdCancel_Click

    Me!txtContinue = "no"
    Me.Visible = False

Exit_cmdCancel_Click:
    Exit Sub
Err_cmdCancel_Click:
    MsgBox Err.Number & ", " & Err.Description
    Resume Exit_cmdCancel_Click
    Resume
End Sub
```

The only difference between this code and the `OK` code is that we don't bother to rebuild the `Where` clause, because the user is canceling anyway, and we set `txtContinue` to `No` so that the report will cancel itself before it even gets a chance to display anything.

When the report is cancelled it generates `Error 2501`, which you should handle so that your user doesn't see an ugly error message. See Chapter 9, "VBA Error Handling," for a description of how to do this.

By adding more fields to your selection form and building the `Where` clause to apply them to the report's recordset, you can deliver a report to your user that is very flexible and easy to use.

Altering the SQL Inside Queries

Sometimes it can be advantageous to alter the SQL inside a saved query. This is especially common when you are using pass-through queries to another database like SQL Server, but it can also come in handy when you need to nest Access queries several layers deep. Since the queries a few layers down can't be modified directly in a report or form's recordsource you may need to change them directly.

> **Use the right syntax:** Remember, if you use this technique for a pass-through query, you must use the SQL syntax of the back-end database, not Access syntax. For example, the wildcard in SQL Server is %, not *. Also, SQL Server expects string values to be surrounded by single quotes ('), whereas Access doesn't care whether you use single quotes (') or double quotes (").

First, you need to realize that this technique will work only if your user is using the front-end application database exclusively. Since we are changing an actual query in the application, you need to make sure that you aren't causing problems for other users. Most developers recommend that each user run a copy of the front-end application on their local computer, not share it on the network. If you follow this recommendation, altering saved queries in your front-end application will work just fine.

To change the `Where` clause in a saved query, use code like the following one:

```
Dim qdf as QueryDef
Dim db as Database

Set db = CurrentDB
Set qdf = db.QueryDefs("YourQueryName")

qdf.SQL = ReplaceWhereClause(qdf.SQL, strYourNewWhereClause)

set qdf = Nothing
set db = Nothing
```

The SQL property of the query definition contains the actual SQL statement of the query; it's the same SQL statement that you see in the `SQL View` in the Query Designer. Note that you don't have to do anything else to change it; the SQL is replaced instantly.

> **But won't this bloat my database?** Database bloating is a problem caused by the fact that Access doesn't reclaim unused space until the database is compacted, so the database size can increase dramatically if developers create and delete objects in the front-end database. However, replacing the SQL inside an existing query doesn't cause significant bloating.

The ReplaceOrderByClause and ReplaceWhereClause Functions

It is often necessary to "cut and replace" the `Where` and `Order By` clauses of a SQL string using VBA. Throughout this chapter, we used the `ReplaceWhereClause` and `ReplaceOrderByClause` functions to do this. Finally, here is the code that was doing all that hard work!

This first procedure `ParseSQL` does the "heavy lifting" of the SQL handling functions. It breaks up the original SQL string into components, so that individual pieces can be replaced. Although `ParseSQL` is Public, it will rarely be called from anywhere other than the `ReplaceWhereClause` and `ReplaceOrderByClause` functions that follow it.

```
Option Compare Database
Option Explicit

Public Sub ParseSQL(strSQL As Variant, strSELECT As Variant, strWhere As
Variant, strOrderBy As Variant, strGROUPBY As Variant, strHAVING As Variant)
```

```
On Error GoTo Error_Handler
'
'This subroutine accepts a valid SQL string and passes back separated
SELECT, WHERE, ORDER BY and GROUP BY clauses.
'
'INPUT:
'    strSQL       valid SQL string to parse
'OUTPUT:
'    strSELECT  SELECT portion of SQL (includes JOIN info)
'    strWHERE   WHERE portion of SQL
'    strORDERBY ORDER BY portion of SQL
'    strGROUPBY GROUP BY portion of SQL
'    strHAVING  HAVING portion of SQL
'
'Note: While the subroutine will accept the ';' character in strSQL,
'      there is no ';' character passed back at any time.
'
```

Note that this Sub takes in only one parameter (the original SQL string), but modifies and outputs five parameters; one for each portion of the parsed SQL string.

```
    Dim intStartSELECT As Integer
    Dim intStartWHERE As Integer
    Dim intStartORDERBY As Integer
    Dim intStartGROUPBY As Integer
    Dim intStartHAVING As Integer

    Dim intLenSELECT As Integer
    Dim intLenWHERE As Integer
    Dim intLenORDERBY As Integer
    Dim intLenGROUPBY As Integer
    Dim intLenHAVING As Integer

    Dim intLenSQL As Integer
```

This next code determines the starting location of each clause in the SQL statement by finding the position in the string of the corresponding keywords.

```
    intStartSELECT = InStr(strSQL, "SELECT ")
    intStartWHERE = InStr(strSQL, "WHERE ")
    intStartORDERBY = InStr(strSQL, "ORDER BY ")
    intStartGROUPBY = InStr(strSQL, "GROUP BY ")
    intStartHAVING = InStr(strSQL, "HAVING ")

    'if there's no GROUP BY, there can't be a HAVING
    If intStartGROUPBY = 0 Then
        intStartHAVING = 0
    End If

    If InStr(strSQL, ";") Then      'if it exists, trim off the ';'
        strSQL = Left(strSQL, InStr(strSQL, ";") - 1)
    End If

    intLenSQL = Len(strSQL)
```

The following section of code calculates the length of the Select clause of the SQL statement. Basically, it starts by assuming that the Select clause is the entire remaining length of the SQL statement and then tries shorter and shorter lengths by testing against the starting positions of the other SQL clauses.

```
    ' find length of Select portion
If intStartSELECT > 0 Then
    ' start with longest it could be
    intLenSELECT = intLenSQL - intStartSELECT + 1
    If intStartWHERE > 0 And intStartWHERE > intStartSELECT _
    And intStartWHERE < intStartSELECT + intLenSELECT Then
        'we found a new portion closer to this one
        intLenSELECT = intStartWHERE - intStartSELECT
    End If
    If intStartORDERBY > 0 And intStartORDERBY > intStartSELECT _
    And intStartORDERBY < intStartSELECT + intLenSELECT Then
        'we found a new portion closer to this one
        intLenSELECT = intStartORDERBY - intStartSELECT
    End If
    If intStartGROUPBY > 0 And intStartGROUPBY > intStartSELECT _
    And intStartGROUPBY < intStartSELECT + intLenSELECT Then
        'we found a new portion closer to this one
        intLenSELECT = intStartGROUPBY - intStartSELECT
    End If
    If intStartHAVING > 0 And intStartHAVING > intStartSELECT _
    And intStartHAVING < intStartSELECT + intLenSELECT Then
        'we found a new portion closer to this one
        intLenSELECT = intStartHAVING - intStartSELECT
    End If
End If
```

This next section of code does the same thing for the Group By clause. It determines the length of the Group By clause finding the beginning of the next clause.

```
    ' find length of GROUPBY portion
If intStartGROUPBY > 0 Then
    ' start with longest it could be
    intLenGROUPBY = intLenSQL - intStartGROUPBY + 1
    If intStartWHERE > 0 And intStartWHERE > intStartGROUPBY _
    And intStartWHERE < intStartGROUPBY + intLenGROUPBY Then
        'we found a new portion closer to this one
        intLenGROUPBY = intStartWHERE - intStartGROUPBY
    End If
    If intStartORDERBY > 0 And intStartORDERBY > intStartGROUPBY _
    And intStartORDERBY < intStartGROUPBY + intLenGROUPBY Then
        'we found a new portion closer to this one
        intLenGROUPBY = intStartORDERBY - intStartGROUPBY
    End If
    If intStartHAVING > 0 And intStartHAVING > intStartGROUPBY _
    And intStartHAVING < intStartGROUPBY + intLenGROUPBY Then
        'we found a new portion closer to this one
        intLenGROUPBY = intStartHAVING - intStartGROUPBY
    End If
End If
```

The following one does the same thing for the Having clause:

```
' find length of HAVING portion
If intStartHAVING > 0 Then
    ' start with longest it could be
    intLenHAVING = intLenSQL - intStartHAVING + 1
    If intStartWHERE > 0 And intStartWHERE > intStartHAVING _
    And intStartWHERE < intStartHAVING + intLenHAVING Then
        'we found a new portion closer to this one
        intLenHAVING = intStartWHERE - intStartHAVING
    End If
    If intStartORDERBY > 0 And intStartORDERBY > intStartHAVING _
    And intStartORDERBY < intStartHAVING + intLenHAVING Then
        'we found a new portion closer to this one
        intLenHAVING = intStartORDERBY - intStartHAVING
    End If
    If intStartGROUPBY > 0 And intStartGROUPBY > intStartHAVING _
    And intStartGROUPBY < intStartHAVING + intLenHAVING Then
        'we found a new portion closer to this one
        intLenHAVING = intStartGROUPBY - intStartHAVING
    End If
End If
```

This does the same thing for the Order By clause:

```
' find length of ORDERBY portion
If intStartORDERBY > 0 Then
    ' start with longest it could be
    intLenORDERBY = intLenSQL - intStartORDERBY + 1
    If intStartWHERE > 0 And intStartWHERE > intStartORDERBY _
    And intStartWHERE < intStartORDERBY + intLenORDERBY Then
        'we found a new portion closer to this one
        intLenORDERBY = intStartWHERE - intStartORDERBY
    End If
    If intStartGROUPBY > 0 And intStartGROUPBY > intStartORDERBY _
    And intStartGROUPBY < intStartORDERBY + intLenORDERBY Then
        'we found a new portion closer to this one
        intLenORDERBY = intStartGROUPBY - intStartORDERBY
    End If
    If intStartHAVING > 0 And intStartHAVING > intStartORDERBY _
    And intStartHAVING < intStartORDERBY + intLenORDERBY Then
        'we found a new portion closer to this one
        intLenORDERBY = intStartHAVING - intStartORDERBY
    End If
End If
```

Finally, the length of the Where clause is determined.

```
' find length of WHERE portion
If intStartWHERE > 0 Then
    ' start with longest it could be
    intLenWHERE = intLenSQL - intStartWHERE + 1
```

```
            If intStartGROUPBY > 0 And intStartGROUPBY > intStartWHERE _
            And intStartGROUPBY < intStartWHERE + intLenWHERE Then
                'we found a new portion closer to this one
                intLenWHERE = intStartGROUPBY - intStartWHERE
            End If
            If intStartORDERBY > 0 And intStartORDERBY > intStartWHERE _
            And intStartORDERBY < intStartWHERE + intLenWHERE Then
                'we found a new portion closer to this one
                intLenWHERE = intStartORDERBY - intStartWHERE
            End If
            If intStartHAVING > 0 And intStartHAVING > intStartWHERE _
            And intStartHAVING < intStartWHERE + intLenWHERE Then
                'we found a new portion closer to this one
                intLenWHERE = intStartHAVING - intStartWHERE
            End If
        End If
    End If
```

Now that all the starting positions and lengths of the five SQL clauses have been determined, the output parameters can be set:

```
    ' set each output portion
    If intStartSELECT > 0 Then
        strSELECT = Mid$(strSQL, intStartSELECT, intLenSELECT)
    End If
    If intStartGROUPBY > 0 Then
        strGROUPBY = Mid$(strSQL, intStartGROUPBY, intLenGROUPBY)
    End If
    If intStartHAVING > 0 Then
        strHAVING = Mid$(strSQL, intStartHAVING, intLenHAVING)
    End If
    If intStartORDERBY > 0 Then
        strOrderBy = Mid$(strSQL, intStartORDERBY, intLenORDERBY)
    End If
    If intStartWHERE > 0 Then
        strWhere = Mid$(strSQL, intStartWHERE, intLenWHERE)
    End If

Exit_Procedure:
    Exit Sub

Error_Handler:
    MsgBox Error.Number & ": " & Error.Description
    Resume Exit_Procedure
End Sub
```

The next two functions merely use the `ParseSQL` procedure to break up the SQL statement into its five clauses, and then they replace the appropriate clause with the new clause that was passed in.

```
Public Function ReplaceWhereClause(strSQL As Variant, strNewWHERE As
Variant)
On Error GoTo Error_Handler
```

```
'This subroutine accepts a valid SQL string and Where clause, and
'returns the same SQL statement with the original Where clause (if any)
'replaced by the passed in Where clause.
'
'INPUT:
'    strSQL       valid SQL string to change
'OUTPUT:
'    strNewWHERE New WHERE clause to insert into SQL statement
'
Dim strSELECT As String, strWhere As String
Dim strOrderBy As String, strGROUPBY As String, strHAVING As String

Call ParseSQL(strSQL, strSELECT, strWhere, strOrderBy, _
strGROUPBY, strHAVING)

ReplaceWhereClause = strSELECT & " " & strNewWHERE & " " _
& strGROUPBY & " " & strHAVING & " " & strOrderBy

Exit_Procedure:
    Exit Function
Error_Handler:
    MsgBox Err.Number & ", " & Err.Description
    Resume Exit_Procedure
End Function

Public Function ReplaceOrderByClause(strSQL As Variant, strNewOrderBy As
Variant)
On Error GoTo Error_Handler
'
'This subroutine accepts a valid SQL string and Where clause, and
'returns the same SQL statement with the original Where clause (if any)
'replaced by the passed in Where clause.
'
'INPUT:
'    strSQL       valid SQL string to change
'OUTPUT:
'    strNewOrderBy New OrderBy clause to insert into SQL statement
'
Dim strSELECT As String, strWhere As String
Dim strOrderBy As String, strGROUPBY As String, strHAVING As String

Call ParseSQL(strSQL, strSELECT, strWhere, strOrderBy, _
strGROUPBY, strHAVING)

ReplaceOrderByClause = strSELECT & " " & strWhere & " " & strNewOrderBy

Exit_Procedure:
    Exit Function
Error_Handler:
    MsgBox Err.Number & ", " & Err.Description
    Resume Exit_Procedure
End Function
```

These SQL handling procedures can be added to all of your Access applications in their own module, such as basSQLTools. By using `ReplaceWhereClause` and `ReplaceOrderByClause` you can take a lot of the hassle out of manipulating SQL strings in your VBA code.

Summary

VBA and SQL are both powerful tools for you to use in your Access applications, and they work very well together. By using the techniques explained in this chapter you should now be able to add instant sorting to column headings, provide easy record selection on continuous forms, build smart combo boxes that change their drop-down lists based on other selections, prompt your user for report selection criteria without using parameter queries, and change the SQL statement inside saved queries. With these features, your Access applications will be more flexible and easy to use.

Working with Office Applications

You can design complete applications within Microsoft Access and never have the need for another Microsoft Office program. After all, you can use Access forms to enter data, Access reports to print data, and the `SendObject` method to send Access information via e-mail. However, it's also possible that you'll want to utilize some of the other Office programs to enhance your applications. For example, you might want to use Outlook to generate a custom form with information from an Access table. If you allow users to export some data to Excel, they can further manipulate the data without causing any unwanted interaction with your application. Exporting information to Microsoft Word gives users the ability to add their own text, perform mail merges, and e-mail information to others in an easy-to-use format.

We'll cover all of these examples and more in this chapter. There aren't many new concepts introduced in this chapter, just examples and code. Along the way we'll try to provide as many real-world situations as we can so you can truly understand how the interaction with other Office programs can enhance your application.

Sharing Information Is a Two-Way Street

When sharing information between multiple Microsoft Office programs, you can write code two ways. The first way is to write the code within Access to *push* the data into the other Office programs. The second way is to write code within those other programs to *pull* code from Access into the other program. This two-way street works for Word, Excel, Outlook, and PowerPoint. Because this is an Access 2003 VBA book, we'll spend more time covering the push direction, but don't worry, we'll provide examples of the pull direction as well. Many of the examples in this chapter are based on an Inventory Control application for pallets of material from a manufacturing plant. The sample database with a large amount of the code discussed here is available. Our Inventory Control application launches with the switchboard shown in Figure 15-1.

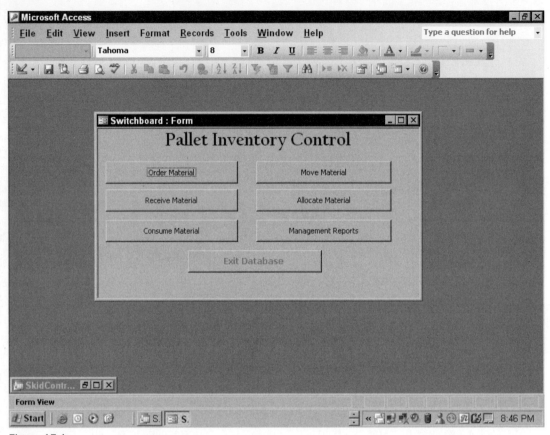

Figure 15-1

The application allows users to receive new material into a particular location, move material from one location to another, allocate material to a particular order, and consume material against a particular order. All of these tasks are easily performed with Access. A series of forms, reports, and queries allow users to accomplish all of these tasks quickly, without leaving the application. However, there are a number of advanced tasks that require other components of Microsoft Office. Outlook, Word, and Excel are all used to enhance this Inventory Control application.

Access and Outlook—Sharing Data with Others

Within our Inventory Control application, users often need to communicate information between departments about inventory that has been ordered, allocated, or consumed. If the Planning department receives a rush order, it might not have enough material in stock to completely cover the job. It might need to communicate with the Order Entry department about possible delays with the order. The easiest way to handle this communication is to write some simple VBA code to send a formatted e-mail message to the Order Entry department. The Planning department can accomplish this directly from the Material Ordering form of the database, shown in Figure 15-2.

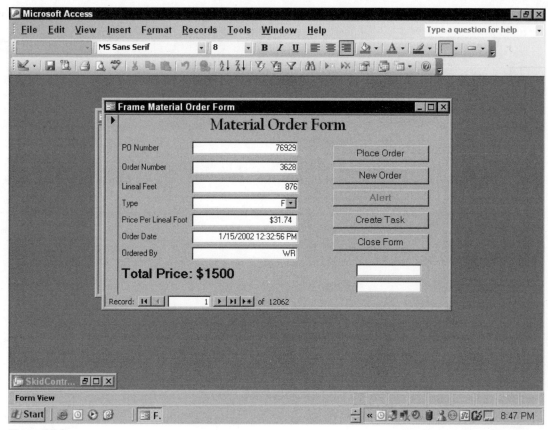

Figure 15-2

In order to communicate back to the Order Entry department that the order is going to be delayed, all the planner needs to do is click the Alert button to display the e-mail message as shown in Figure 15-3.

The e-mail to the Order Entry department contains the order number, the original order due date, and the expected material receipt date. There is enough information in the e-mail for the Order Entry department to contact the customers and inform them of the delay. Because the e-mail message is delivered directly to the Order Entry department inbox with Outlook 2003 desktop alert, the customers are immediately informed of any delays without having to open the Access application, a significant savings in time and resources.

To write VBA code to export the information from Access to Outlook, invoke the Code Builder from the Click event of the cmdAlert command button on the Frame Order Form.

In order to manipulate the Outlook object model, choose References from the Tools menu and select the Microsoft Outlook 11 Object Model. You can now manipulate the objects, properties, and methods available within Microsoft Outlook.

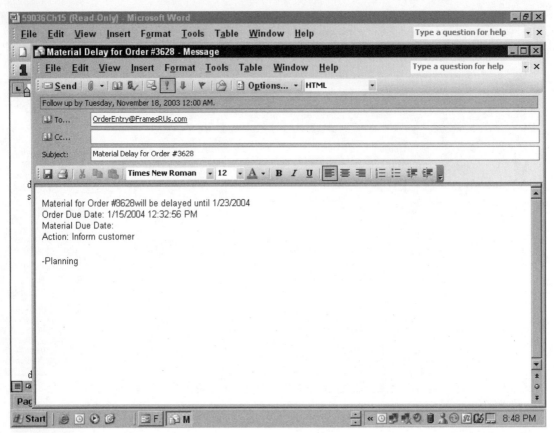

Figure 15-3

First, declare the various object variables you'll need to work with the Outlook application and e-mail objects.

```
'First reference the Outlook Application
Dim olApp As Outlook.Application
'The NameSpace object allows you to reference folders
Dim olApp as Outlook.NameSpace
Dim olFolder as Outlook.MAPIFolder

'Create a reference to the e-mail item you will use to send your e-mail
Dim olMailItem As Outlook.MailItem
```

Once you've created the object variables, you can start writing code to use these objects. First, create the Outlook Application object. You can only have one instance of an Outlook Application running at once and so you don't have to worry about using the `GetObject` method. The `CreateObject` method works fine for our purposes. Now that you have the Application object, continue by referencing the `NameSpace` object, setting a reference to the Inbox folder, and adding a new e-mail message (`IPM.Note`).

```
Set olApp = CreateObject("Outlook.Application")
Set olNS = olApp.GetNamespace("MAPI")
Set olFolder = olNS.GetDefaultFolder(olFolderInbox)
Set olMailItem = olFolder.Items.Add("IPM.Note")
```

If you want to display the e-mail message on the screen as you're creating it, add the following line to your code. However, unless your users need to manipulate the e-mail message, it's better to keep the message hidden.

```
olMailItem.Display
```

The Outlook Mail item has several properties you'll manipulate. Our example changes the Subject, To, Priority, and Body properties as shown in the following code.

```
Private Sub cmdAlert_Click()
Dim olApp As Outlook.Application
Dim olNS As Outlook.NameSpace
Dim olFolder As Outlook.MAPIFolder
Dim olMailItem As Outlook.MailItem
Dim strBodyText As String
Set olApp = CreateObject("Outlook.Application")
Set olNS = olApp.GetNamespace("MAPI")
Set olFolder = olNS.GetDefaultFolder(olFolderInbox)
Set olMailItem = olFolder.Items.Add("IPM.Note")
strBodyText = "Material for Order #" & Me.OrderNumber & _
" will be delayed until " & Me.DueDate & vbCrLf & _
"Order Due Date: " & Me.OrderDate & vbCrLf & _
"Material Due Date: " & Me.MaterialDueDate & vbCrLf & _
"Action: Inform customer" & vbCrLf & vbCrLf & "-Planning"
With olMailItem
    .Subject = "Material Delay for Order #" & Me.OrderNumber
    .To = "OrderEntry@FramesRUs.com"
    .Body = strBodyText
    .Send
End With
'Release all of your object variables
Set olMailItem = Nothing
Set olFolder = Nothing
Set olNS = Nothing
Set olApp = Nothing
End Sub
```

The preceding code creates the e-mail message previously shown in Figure 15-3. While that message contains all of the basic information you need to communicate to the Order Entry department, you might want to enhance your code just a bit to add a follow-up flag and a high-priority distinction to your message. Simply add the following lines of code immediately before the .Send line.

```
    .Importance = olImportanceHigh
    .FlagStatus = olFlagMarked
    'Set the flag reminder date for two days in advance
    .FlagDueBy = Date + 2
```

You now have working code to create and send an alert e-mail message from the Planning department to the Order Entry department.

Working with Outlook's Security Features

If you've implemented code similar to the preceding example, you've probably noticed a dialog box that pops up when the .Send line is called. This dialog box appears because of new security features introduced within Outlook after the Melissa and ILoveYou viruses. These security measures include two warning dialog boxes. The first appears when you try to manipulate the addresses in your Contacts folder. The second, which is the one you'll run into with the previous code, displays a dialog box warning you that a program is trying to send an e-mail message programmatically. To send the e-mail, you'll need to wait 10 seconds before you can choose to allow the e-mail to be sent. This can be quite annoying for your users and might even make it virtually impossible for your application to work properly. There are a couple of methods you can use to work around this problem.

Using an Exchange Server to Configure Security

First, if you're in an Exchange environment (or you know your application will be used with an Exchange Server), you can configure the Administrative Options Package for Exchange Server. This package allows you to allow programmatic sending of e-mail through configuration of a public folder and custom form stored on the Exchange Server. The advantage of this system is that you don't need to touch the client machines at all. Once you install the form within the public folder on the Exchange Server, all you need to do is decide which types of programmatic access you need to allow. You can allow access to the address book, to the Send method, as well as to a variety of other types of settings (such as attachment blocking). The major disadvantage to this method is that unless you're writing code within a COM add-in for Outlook, allowing programmatic sending is an all or nothing proposition. If you ease the restriction for your application, you're also easing the restriction for viruses that use the Outlook object model to propagate. The one saving grace to this problem is that the majority of viruses prevalent these days do not use the Outlook object model, they use their own SMTP (Simple Mail Transfer Protocol) engines to send copies of themselves to others. If you do choose to use the Administrative Options package, make sure that your users have an up-to-date virus scanner both on the desktops and on the Exchange Server.

Using Redemption to Save Your Application

The second option you can utilize to prevent the security dialogs involves downloading a third party .dll called Redemption. The Redemption.dll serves as a wrapper for Extended MAPI (messaging application programming interface), another method of creating and sending e-mail messages. Extended MAPI isn't affected by the Outlook security features. The advantage to Redemption is that you can use it only for one application. So merely having the Redemption.dll present on your system poses no security risk. You can use Redemption only when you need it within your code. The major disadvantage to Redemption is that it must be registered on all machines using your application (using Regsvr32.exe). For single users, Redemption is free. If you want a redistributable license for Redemption, it will cost you $99. You can find Redemption at www.dimastr.com/Redemption.

Redemption is very easy to use. Once you've registered it on your system, set a reference to the "Safe Outlook Library". Then make just a few key changes to your code. The following code sample takes the previous listing and rewrites it to use Redemption.

```
Private Sub cmdAlert_Click()
Dim olApp As Outlook.Application
Dim olNS As Outlook.NameSpace
```

```
    Dim olFolder As Outlook.MAPIFolder
    Dim olMailItem As Outlook.MailItem
    Dim strBodyText As String

    'Add a reference to the Redemption Safe Mail Item
    Dim objSafeMail as Redemption.SafeMailItem

    Set olApp = CreateObject("Outlook.Application")
    Set olNS = olApp.GetNamespace("MAPI")
    Set olFolder = olNS.GetDefaultFolder(olFolderInbox)
    Set olMailItem = olFolder.Items.Add("IPM.Note")

    strBodyText = "Material for Order #" & Me.OrderNumber & _
    " will be delayed until " & Me.DueDate & vbCrLf & _
    "Order Due Date: " & Me.OrderDate & vbCrLf & _
    "Material Due Date: " & Me.MaterialDueDate & vbCrLf & _
    "Action: Inform customer" & vbCrLf & vbCrLf & "-Planning"
    With olMailItem
        'Set all properties of mail item here
        .Subject = "Material Delay for Order #" & Me.OrderNumber
        .To = "OrderEntry@FramesRUs.com"
        .Body = strBodyText
        'Remove the .Send method of the olMailItem to avoid
        'security dialogs
    End With

    Set objSafeMail = New Redemption.SafeMailItem

    'Do not need the Set statement here
    objSafeMail.Item = olMailItem
    objSafeMail.Send

    'Release all of your object variables
    Set objSafeMail = Nothing
    Set olMailItem = Nothing
    Set olFolder = Nothing
    Set olNS = Nothing
    Set olApp = Nothing
    End Sub
```

With only a handful of additional lines, you've just bypassed all of those annoying security dialogs.

Creating Other Types of Outlook Items from Access

Creating e-mail messages in Outlook isn't the only way you can use VBA and Outlook to enhance your application. You can create meetings, appointments, tasks, and journal items within Outlook using VBA. The Planning department can create an Outlook task directly from the Access application. This task will remind them to check with the receiving department on the appointed day to ensure the frame material has arrived. If the material hasn't arrived within several days, the Planning department knows that it needs to contact the supplier.

Once you've added another button to your Material Order form, add the following code to the Click event of the command button.

The initial portion of the code is very similar to the code used to create an e-mail message. However, instead of referencing the Inbox folder, set a reference to the Task folder, as shown in the following code.

```
Private Sub cmdCreateTask_Click()
Dim olApp As Outlook.Application
Dim olNS As Outlook.NameSpace
Dim olfolder As Outlook.MAPIFolder
Dim olTaskItem As Outlook.TaskItem
Dim strBodyText As String
Set olApp = CreateObject("Outlook.Application")
Set olNS = olApp.GetNamespace("MAPI")
Set olfolder = olNS.GetDefaultFolder(olFolderTasks)
Set olTaskItem = olfolder.Items.Add("IPM.Task")
With olTaskItem
    .DueDate = Date + 2
    .Subject = "Confirm Material Receipt for Order #: " & Me.OrderNumber
    .ReminderTime = Date + 2
    .ReminderSet = True
    .Categories = "Material Order"
    .Save
End With
Set olTaskItem = Nothing
Set olfolder = Nothing
Set olNS = Nothing
Set olApp = Nothing
End Sub
```

Executing this code creates a task item like the one shown in Figure 15-4.

Sending Information from Access to Excel

Within your Access database, you can create detailed reports including graphs and tables. However, it's impossible to design enough reports to please all of your users, all the time. Sometimes it's better to simply allow your users to export some of the data to Excel where they can manipulate the data in a variety of different ways. In addition to exporting data from Access to Excel, you can even create charts in Excel directly from Access.

First, add a reference to the Excel 11 object model from the References dialog box. Now you can manipulate not only the Excel application, but worksheets, cells, and graphs.

Provide Management with Flexible Data Access

Within any company, you typically have a variety of managers. Some are quite technically savvy while others are not. Some love to fiddle and massage data, creating their own reports and graphs. By allowing management to export a variety of queries directly to Excel, you don't have to worry about designing a new report every time they want to view the data in a slightly different manner. Our first example utilizes a form (shown in Figure 15-5) with a list box that a manager can use to choose the query he or she wants to export.

When you create your form and list box, make sure to set the Row Source for the list box to Value List. The default Row Source value of a list box is Table/Query. You can fill your list box in two

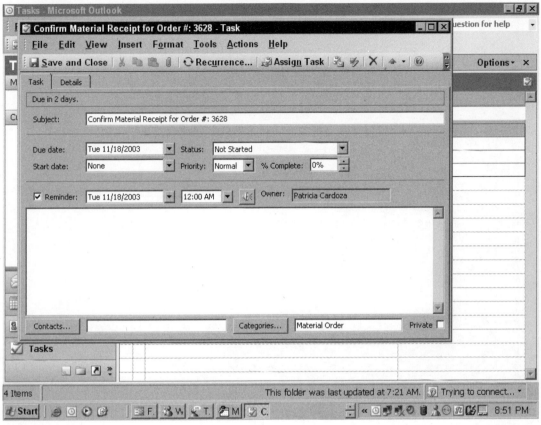

Figure 15-4

different ways. If you want the managers to be able to choose any report to export, consider using the following code to populate the list box. This code loops through each query in your database and adds its name to the list box.

```
Private Sub Form_Open(Cancel As Integer)
Dim strQryName As String
Dim itmQuery As QueryDef
For Each itmQuery In Application.CurrentDb.QueryDefs
    strQryName = itmQuery.Name
    Me.lstQuery.AddItem strQryName
Next
End Sub
```

If you don't want management to be able to choose from every report in your database, you can always hard-code the query names into the data source for your list box. Now that you have a list of queries in your list box, you can write code to export the results of one of those queries to Excel. You can perform the export in several ways. We'll cover two of those methods here. The first method we'll cover involves opening Excel, creating a new workbook with a new worksheet, and transferring the data into the worksheet. The second method utilizes the Save As method of the RunCommand method to automate

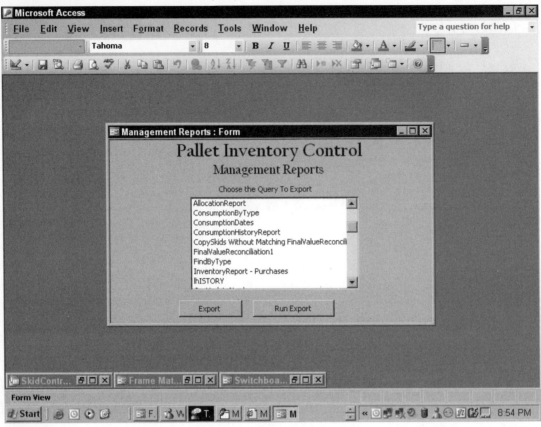

Figure 15-5

this process. After we've walked through both of these steps we'll cover why you might want to use each of those steps.

Opening Excel and Creating a New Worksheet with Code

We'll build the code in a few steps. First, we need to create a reference to an Excel application and create a new worksheet, as shown in the following code.

```
Private Sub cmdExport_Click()
Dim xlApp As Excel.Application
Dim xlSheet As Excel.Worksheet
Dim xlWorkbook As Excel.Workbook
Set xlApp = CreateObject("Excel.Application")
xlApp.Visible = True
Set xlWorkbook = xlApp.Workbooks.Add
Set xlWorkbook = Nothing
Set xlApp = Nothing
End Sub
```

Once you verify that Excel opens with a new worksheet, it's time to fill that worksheet with data. There are several ways of accomplishing this task. You can use a recordset object (from DAO) and set that recordset to the result set from your query. Once you have the recordset object, you can use Excel's `CopyFromRecordset` method of the `Cells` object to send the results to your spreadsheet. This method is accomplished by the following code.

```
Private Sub cmdExport_Click()
Dim xlApp As Excel.Application
Dim xlSheet As Excel.Worksheet
Dim xlWorkbook As Excel.Workbook
Dim acQuery As QueryDef
Dim objRST As Recordset
Dim strQueryName As String
Dim strSheetName as String
strQueryName = Me.lstQuery
strSheetName = Left(strQueryName, 31)
strSheetName = Trim(strSheetName)
Set xlApp = CreateObject("Excel.Application")
xlApp.Visible = True
Set xlWorkbook = xlApp.Workbooks.Add
Set objRST = Application.CurrentDb.OpenRecordset(strQueryName)

Set xlSheet = xlWorkbook.Sheets(1)
With xlSheet
    .Cells.CopyFromRecordset objRST
    .Name = strSheetName
End With
Set objRST = Nothing
Set xlSheet = Nothing
Set xlWorkbook = Nothing
Set xlApp = Nothing
End Sub
```

> The name of your Excel worksheet can only be of 31 characters. If your query name is longer than 31 characters, the line `.Name = strQueryName` will produce an error. Instead, use the `Left` function to choose the leftmost 31 characters from the name of your query. If the name of your query is less than 31 characters, you'll also need the `Trim` function to prevent the `strSheetName` variable from being padded with extra spaces.

The preceding code creates a fairly plain Excel spreadsheet, as shown in Figure 15-6, and displays it on the screen. However, let's add a little pizzazz to our spreadsheet. We can add just a few lines of code and add column headings, shade those column headings, and save the spreadsheet with a filename and location the user specifies.

We're using a DAO recordset object so we can use the properties and methods of this object within our code. To add column headings, we'll need to loop through the `Fields` collection of the recordset and add a heading for each field. You can accomplish this with the following lines of code.

```
For lvlColumn = 0 To objRST.Fields.Count - 1
   xlSheet.Cells(1, lvlColumn + 1).Value = _
   objRST.Fields(lvlColumn).Name
Next
```

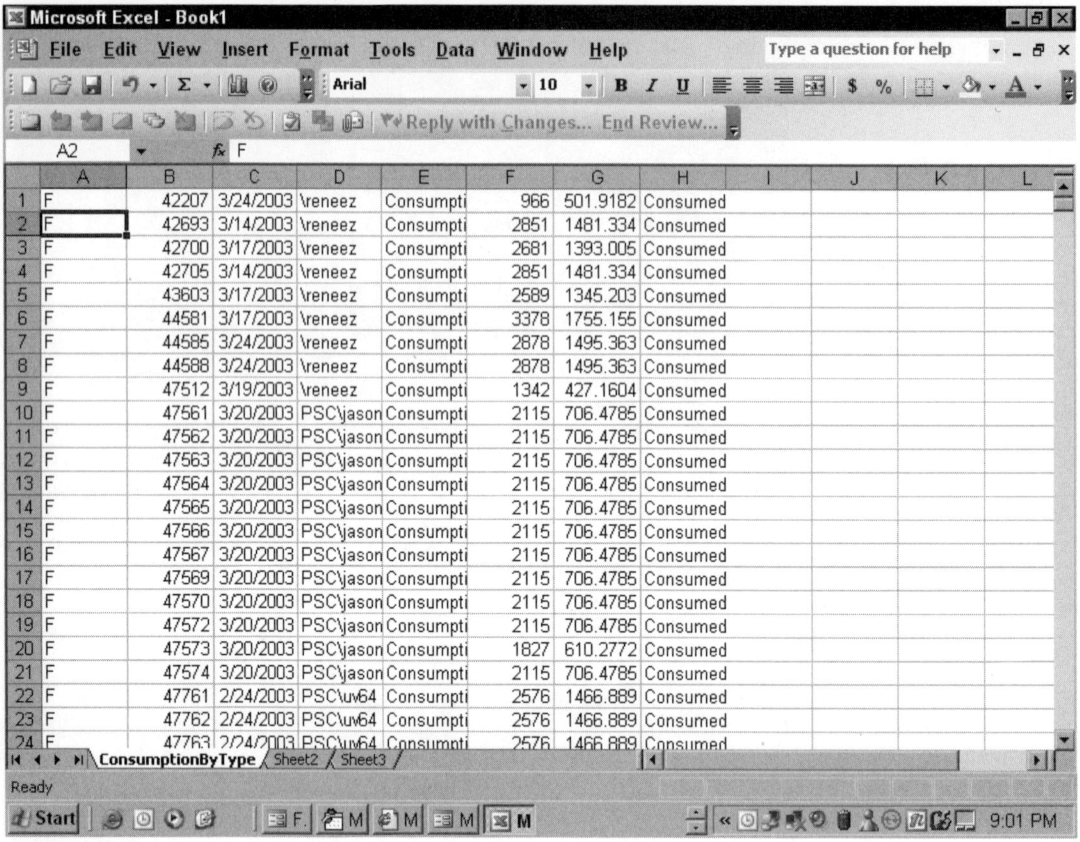

Figure 15-6

This code loops through every column in the worksheet and places the appropriate field name within that column. But, just placing field names in the appropriate column isn't very exciting. Why not add some color? Column headings are typically colored gray. For some added pizzazz let's also add a cell border and a bolded font. You can accomplish these tasks with the following code (don't worry, we'll put all the code together at the end of the section):

```
'Change the font to bold for the header row
xlSheet.Range(xlSheet.Cells(1, 1), _
xlSheet.Cells(1, objRST.Fields.Count)).Font.Bold = True
'Add a border to header row cells
With xlSheet.Range(xlSheet.Cells(1, 1), _
xlSheet.Cells(1, objRST.Fields.Count)).Borders(xlEdgeLeft)
    .LineStyle = xlContinuous
    .Weight = xlThin
    .ColorIndex = xlAutomatic
End With
With xlSheet.Range(xlSheet.Cells(1, 1), _
xlSheet.Cells(1, objRST.Fields.Count)).Borders(xlEdgeTop)
    .LineStyle = xlContinuous
```

```
            .Weight = xlThin
            .ColorIndex = xlAutomatic
        End With
        With xlSheet.Range(xlSheet.Cells(1, 1), _
        xlSheet.Cells(1, objRST.Fields.Count)).Borders(xlEdgeBottom)
            .LineStyle = xlContinuous
            .Weight = xlThin
            .ColorIndex = xlAutomatic
        End With
        With xlSheet.Range(xlSheet.Cells(1, 1), _
        xlSheet.Cells(1, objRST.Fields.Count)).Borders(xlEdgeRight)
            .LineStyle = xlContinuous
            .Weight = xlThin
            .ColorIndex = xlAutomatic
        End With
```

Now that's a lot of code. But it's pretty simple code. All you're doing is setting each border (top, bottom, left, and right) to a thin line. Now, you're ready to return to the code to fill the sheet with data. You'll need to make one simple alteration to the previously listed code. If you add the code to fill and format the column headings and then try to execute the previously listed code as is, you'll end up with no header row and the first row of data formatted with bold font and borders. In order to start the actual data in the second row of the spreadsheet, change the code

```
With xlSheet
    .Cells.CopyFromRecordset objRST
    .Name = strSheetName
End With
```

to the following code:

```
With xlSheet
    .Range("A2").CopyFromRecordset objRST
    .Name = strSheetName
End With
```

That's a pretty simple change. Your worksheet should now look like the one shown in Figure 15-7.

In order to create the spreadsheet as shown in Figure 15-7, you can use the following procedure.

```
Private Sub cmdExport_Click()
Dim xlApp As Excel.Application
Dim xlSheet As Excel.Worksheet
Dim xlWorkbook As Excel.Workbook
Dim acQuery As QueryDef
Dim objRST As Recordset
Dim strQueryName As String
strQueryName = Me.lstQuery
Set xlApp = CreateObject("Excel.Application")
xlApp.Visible = True
Set xlWorkbook = xlApp.Workbooks.Add
Set objRST = Application.CurrentDb.OpenRecordset(strQueryName)
```

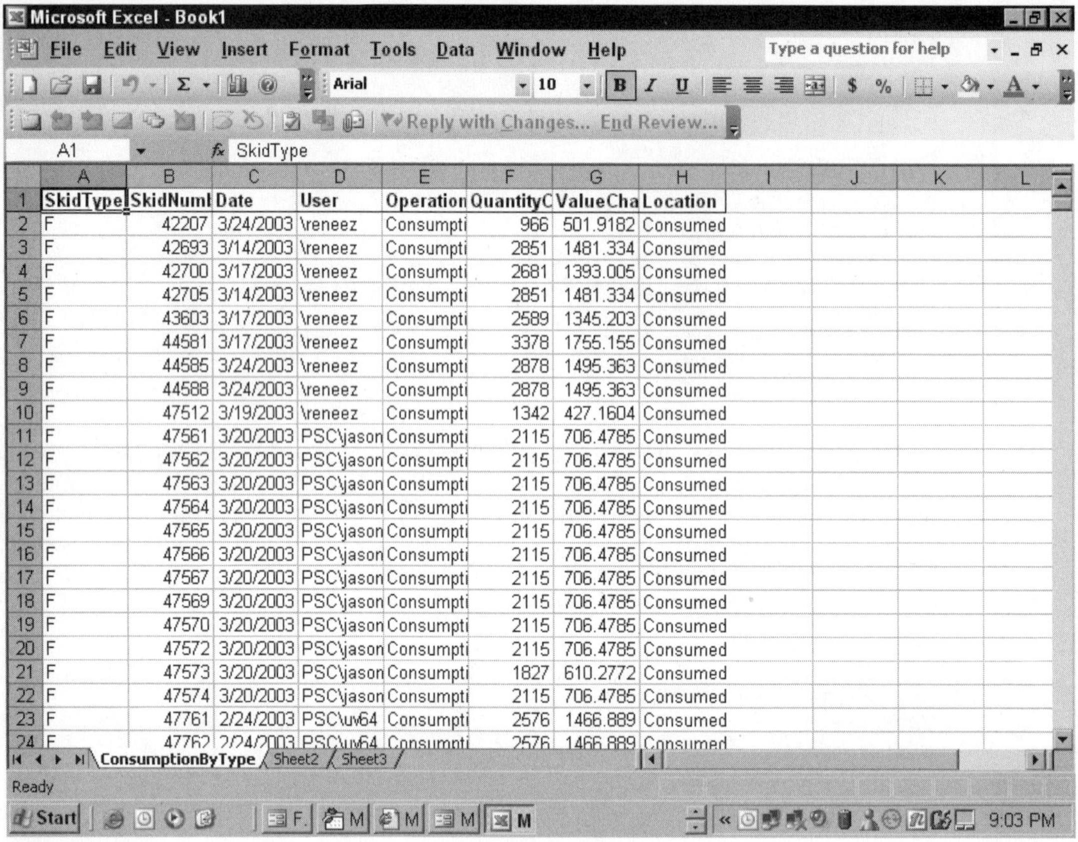

Figure 15-7

```
Set xlSheet = xlWorkbook.Sheets(1)
    For lvlColumn = 0 To objRST.Fields.Count - 1
      xlSheet.Cells(1, lvlColumn + 1).Value = _
      objRST.Fields(lvlColumn).Name
    Next
    'Change the font to bold for the header row
    xlSheet.Range(xlSheet.Cells(1, 1), _
    xlSheet.Cells(1, objRST.Fields.Count)).Font.Bold = True
    'Add a border to header row cells
    With xlSheet.Range(xlSheet.Cells(1, 1), _
    xlSheet.Cells(1, objRST.Fields.Count)).Borders(xlEdgeLeft)
        .LineStyle = xlContinuous
        .Weight = xlThin
        .ColorIndex = xlAutomatic
    End With
    With xlSheet.Range(xlSheet.Cells(1, 1), _
    xlSheet.Cells(1, objRST.Fields.Count)).Borders(xlEdgeTop)
        .LineStyle = xlContinuous
        .Weight = xlThin
```

```
            .ColorIndex = xlAutomatic
        End With
        With xlSheet.Range(xlSheet.Cells(1, 1), _
        xlSheet.Cells(1, objRST.Fields.Count)).Borders(xlEdgeBottom)
            .LineStyle = xlContinuous
            .Weight = xlThin
            .ColorIndex = xlAutomatic
        End With
        With xlSheet.Range(xlSheet.Cells(1, 1), _
        xlSheet.Cells(1, objRST.Fields.Count)).Borders(xlEdgeRight)
            .LineStyle = xlContinuous
            .Weight = xlThin
            .ColorIndex = xlAutomatic
        End With
    With xlSheet
        .Range("A2").CopyFromRecordset objRST
        .Name = Left(strQueryName, 31)
    End With
    Set xlSheet = Nothing
    Set xlWorkbook = Nothing
    Set xlApp = Nothing
    End Sub
```

> There's one circumstance in which the previous code will fail. If your query requires
> the user to enter parameters, you'll have problems with your code. If your query re-
> quires parameters, you should probably use an alternate method of opening a query.
> You can use the `OpenRecordset` method of the `QueryDef` object to open a parameter
> query.

If you prefer not to use the `CopyFromRecordset` method, you can use a slightly older method, the
`TransferSpreadsheet` method, from the `DoCmd` object. You might remember that the `DoCmd` object is
more of a legacy object left over from previous versions of Access and it's now been replaced by the
`Application.RunCommand` method. Well, unfortunately there are still a few instances where you need
the `DoCmd` object as opposed to the `Application.RunCommand` method. There are a few distinct
advantages to the `TransferSpreadsheet` method. First of all, you can export an entire table to a
spreadsheet with one line of code. For example,

```
DoCmd.TransferSpreadsheet acExport, acSpreadsheetTypeExcel9, "Samples",
"c:\ samples.xls"
```

The previous line of code is all you need to export the Samples table to a spreadsheet called
`Samples.xls` on the C drive. This method allows you to export either tables or queries stored in your
database. The next advantage to this method is that you don't actually invoke the Excel object model.
Why is this an advantage? Well, it's not so much an advantage as it is simpler.

There are a couple of disadvantages to this method, however. First of all, if you already have a file called
`Samples.xls` stored in the location you've specified, this code will fail without error. The code runs, but
the existing spreadsheet isn't replaced by the new spreadsheet. So you could wind up with outdated
spreadsheets. You could work around this error by checking for the existence of a file of that name before
this line of code runs. You can do this with the following code.

```
Dim intFileLength As Integer
Dim strFilePath As String
strFilePath = "C:\samples.xls"
intFileLength = Len(Dir$(strFilePath))
If Err Or intFileLength = 0 Then
'Run Transfer Spreadsheet code - file does not exist
Else
'Do something else, file already exists
End If
```

Here's the entire procedure as we've used it in the past with a `CommonDialog` control from the Windows Common Controls. This control isn't available in the default installation of Microsoft Access 2003, but it's installed when you install Visual Basic 6.0 or Visual Studio .NET. If you have access to this control, you can use it to prompt your users to select a folder and file to open. Prompt the user to choose a filename and location. Because you can never trust users to always follow instructions, check to make sure the filename doesn't exist in the location they've chosen. If the file already exists, prompt them to enter another filename. If the file doesn't yet exist, run the `TransferSpreadsheet` method.

```
Private Sub cmdTransferSpreadsheet_Click()
Dim intFileLength As Integer
Dim strFilePath As String
Dim strFileName As String
Me.cmdlg.DialogTitle = "Choose File Name and Location"
Me.cmdlg.ShowOpen
strFilePath = Me.cmdlg.FileName

intFileLength = Len(Dir$(strFilePath))
While Not (Err Or intFileLength = 0)
MsgBox "You entered a file that already exists. Please choose another file
name or location.", _
vbOKOnly, "Duplicate File"
Me.cmdlg.DialogTitle = "Choose File Name and Location"
Me.cmdlg.ShowOpen
strFilePath = Me.cmdlg.FileName
intFileLength = Len(Dir$(strFilePath))
Wend
DoCmd.TransferSpreadsheet acExport, acSpreadsheetTypeExcel9, "Samples",
strFilePath
End Sub
```

The second disadvantage is that you can't control the look and feel of the spreadsheet. Your spreadsheet will look similar to Figure 15-8. You can't manipulate the column headings, fonts, or shading.

You'll need to decide whether your project requires the formatting and flexibility of the first method or the ease of use of the second method. Both work equally well for their basic task, transferring data between Access and Excel.

Exchanging Information with Microsoft Word

Access has some wonderful reporting features. You can sort, group, filter, and even perform sophisticated combinations of those operations using VBA. If you can create such sophisticated reports in Access would you even need Word? Well, the simple answer is yes. There are a number of tasks you can't

	A	B	C	D	E	F	G	H	I	J	K	L
1	SkidNumb	PONumbe	OrderNum	Location	Quantity	SkidType	Type	ReceivedD	Width	Grain	PriceMSF	InitialV
2	35276	76929	3628	L4H	876	F	.018 SUS	1/15/2002	34.375	39.1875	$31.74	$555
3	39451	81693	1232	L4F	620	F	.024 CCKB	6/5/2002	54.375	40.4375	$42.49	$402
4	42500	83622	1713	L4F	2112	S	.017 KP	8/30/2002	41.0625	58.6875	$25.84	$1,017
5	42642	Orphan	ORPHAN	L4G	476	S	.016 SUS	9/5/2002	40.375	34.125	$25.67	$11F
6	42753	84689	2062	L4G	1411	S	.012 SBS	9/9/2002	24.4375	48.375	$23.25	$742
7	44791	86567	3351	L4A	1500	F	.018 SUS	11/6/2002	30.25	45.9375	$28.17	$770
8	44902	87028	4820	L4A	1508	S	.014 SBS	11/9/2002	41.8125	28.0625	$24.70	$303
9	44928	86814	4965	L4G	600	S	.014 SBS	11/9/2002	23.625	50.25	$24.70	$122
10	45258	87399	5727	L4H	500	F	.024 SUS	11/22/2002	61.0625	27	$34.91	$319
11	46302	88381	68300200	L4H	923	F	.014 SBS	12/26/2002	41.8125	28.0625	$24.70	$460
12	47187	89287	8071	L4A	833	S	.028 SUS	1/27/2003	36.25	56.5	$40.17	$475
13	48227	90563	8991	L4G	1338	F	.016 SBS	3/5/2003	28.5625	23.625	$27.58	$226
14	48307	90625	2873	L4A	581	S	.012 CCKB	3/10/2003	25.5	48.75	$16.32	$430
15	48697	90415	9156	L4H	700	F	18SB87	3/24/2003	29.8125	31.5625	$30.16	$415
16	49197	91598	1328	L4G	913	F	16SB87	4/8/2003	46	29.375	$27.58	$475
17	49399	91837	1534	L4F	2300	F	.022 SUS	4/14/2003	33.5	27.0625	$30.47	$441
18	49387	91779	1	L4F	301	S	.012 SBS	4/14/2003	35.625	50.6875	$23.25	$479
19	49498	91945	1582	L4F	2572	F	.020 SBS	4/16/2003	27.125	53.0625	$32.13	$825
20	49705	91926	1509	L4G	1180	S	.011 USBS	4/22/2003	24.875	45.375	$23.05	$349
21	50046	91525	2629	L4G	588	F	.024 SBS N	5/5/2003	30.4375	27.25	$101.01	$1,047
22	50047	91525	2629	L4H	1070	F	.024 SBS N	5/5/2003	30.4375	27.25	$101.01	$622
23	50184	92679	2074	L4G	1010	F	18SB87	5/7/2003	26.375	33.875	$30.16	$526
24	51268	93768	2374	L4F	1245	S	.012 CBF	6/5/2003	33.125	28	$38.84	$375

Figure 15-8

perform in Access and still others that you might simply want to transfer into Microsoft Word. For example, the first code sample we'll build starts a mail merge within Word from your Access data. While you can create a letter within Access, it must be done by someone with adequate permissions on your database. You probably don't want to give every user of your application permissions to create and modify reports. Many users probably have no desire to ever modify a report. Working around this limitation is pretty simple. Provide your users with a boilerplate mail merge document in Word and allow them to customize the mail merge document to suit their needs. Then they can simply initiate the mail merge from within Access.

You can write the mail merge code in two ways. The first, and simplest way, is to use Access VBA to simply define your data source and open the merge document. The second way is to use VBA to perform every step of the mail merge process. We'll examine both methods in this section.

The Easy Way—Use Access VBA to Start Your Merge

If your users are fairly technically savvy with Microsoft Word, you can rely on them to perform most of the steps of the mail merge. In this case, use Access VBA to define the data source and initiate the merge. The following short code segment assumes the user has already created a mail merge template and saved it to his or her hard disk. The code allows the user to select the created template and initiate the merge. Like the previous example, this code utilizes the `CommonDialog` control from the Windows Common Controls to allow the user to select the filename and location.

```
Private Sub cmdMailMerge_Click()
Dim strFilePath as String
Dim objWord As Word.Document
Me.cmdlg.DialogTitle = "Choose File Name and Location"
Me.cmdlg.ShowOpen
strFilePath = Me.cmdlg.FileName

Set objWord = GetObject(strFilePath, "Word.Document")
' Make Word visible.
objWord.Application.Visible = True

objWord.MailMerge.OpenDataSource _
Name:="C:\Program Files\Microsoft " & _
"Office\Office11\Samples\Northwind.mdb", _
LinkToSource:=True, _
Connection:="TABLE Customers", _
SQLStatement:="Select * from [Customers]"

' Execute the mail merge.
objWord.MailMerge.Execute
End Sub
```

This code creates a new document, opens the data source, and executes the mail merge. However, there's one key component missing. There are no merge fields. If you have a standard merge document already set up with merge fields and you're only attempting to requery the data source and fill the document with data, this code will work just fine. However, what if you want to start with a blank document? Now we'll examine how you'd set up the merge document with content and merge fields.

The Hard Way—Using VBA to Set Up Your Merge Document

This method really isn't difficult, it merely requires you to write more code. It's actually easier for your users, as they really don't have to do anything other than click the big button. The following code sample will create the merge document from a blank document, add the merge fields, and merge the data.

```
Private Sub cmdMailMerge_Click()
Dim objWordApp As Word.Application
Dim objWord As Word.Document
Dim oSel As Word.Selection
Set objWordApp = CreateObject("Word.Application")
Set objWord = objWordApp.Documents.Add

' Make Word visible.
objWord.Application.Visible = True

objWord.MailMerge.OpenDataSource _
Name:="C:\Program Files\Microsoft " & _
"Office\Office11\Samples\Northwind.mdb", _
LinkToSource:=True, _
```

```
            Connection:="TABLE Customers", _
            SQLStatement:="Select * from [Customers]"
            'Add fields
            With objWord.MailMerge.Fields
                Set oSel = objWord.Application.Selection

                .Add oSel.Range, "CompanyName"
                oSel.TypeParagraph
                .Add oSel.Range, "Address"
                oSel.TypeParagraph
                .Add oSel.Range, "City"
                oSel.TypeText ", "
                .Add oSel.Range, "Country"
                oSel.TypeParagraph
                oSel.TypeParagraph
                oSel.TypeText "Dear "
                .Add oSel.Range, "ContactName"
                oSel.TypeText ","
                oSel.TypeParagraph
                oSel.TypeParagraph
                oSel.TypeText " Replace with your pithy text."
                oSel.TypeParagraph
                oSel.TypeParagraph
                oSel.TypeText "Sincerely, [Your Name Here]"
            End With
                ' Execute the mail merge.
                objWord.MailMerge.Execute
                objWord.Close (0)
            Set oSel = Nothing
            Set objWord = Nothing
            Set objWordApp = Nothing
            End Sub
```

When populating the Word document with the message text, it's important to know that the TypeParagraph method of the selection object inserts a carriage return in the document. The TypeText method pretty simply types the specified text on the screen. You can build your entire letter this way line by line. If you want to give your users the ultimate flexibility, put a text box on your form and allow the users to type their text right on the form. Then set a string variable to the text box's text property and then use that same variable to populate the letter within your VBA code. When you're done executing the previous code, you'll wind up with a letter similar to the one shown in Figure 15-9.

Non-Mail Merge Operations—Sending Access Data to Word

In addition to using VBA within Access to create a mail merge, you can also export just about any information within Access to Word using VBA and the Word object model. As a short example, the following code uses the CommonDialog control to allow a user to export an Access report to a specific Word document. You might want to do this if you have users who need to modify the report or need to perform other operations such as sending an external document to the report or e-mailing the report to others in an editable format.

```
    Dim objWordApp As Word.Application
    Dim objWord As Word.Document
```

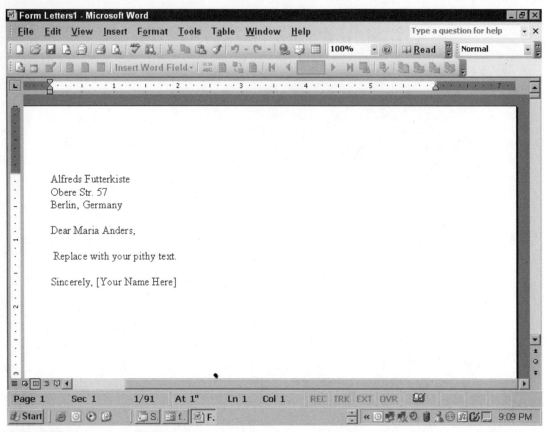

Figure 15-9

```
Dim strFilePath As String
Me.cmdlg.DialogTitle = "Choose File Name and Location"
Me.cmdlg.ShowOpen
strFilePath = Me.cmdlg.FileName
DoCmd.OutputTo acOutputReport, "Samples", acFormatRTF, strFilePath
Set objWordApp = CreateObject("Word.Application")
Set objWord = objWordApp.Documents.Open(strfilePath)

' Make Word visible.
objWord.Application.Visible = True
Set objWord = Nothing
Set objWordApp = Nothing
```

An Advanced Example—Creating a Graph in Access and Inserting It into PowerPoint

There aren't many applications for using VBA to send data from Access to PowerPoint. However, one application that's often requested but a little tricky to accomplish is exporting a graph from Access to

PowerPoint. You could take advantage of the following example to update your presentation with the most current graph from your Access report.

This procedure is a bit complicated so we'll cover it in several steps. First of all, there's no easy method of copying a chart from within Access. Some developers have had success copying the actual MS Graph object, but we've found that method to be buggy at best and completely unreliable at worst. So, we've come up with another method that produces fairly accurate and reliable results. The first part of the procedure involves exporting the recordset you're interested in to an intermediate Excel file. You can easily use VBA code to create the graph within Excel. Once you have the graph created within Excel, you can reliably copy the graph object within Excel. The next step is to use VBA to create your PowerPoint presentation and add a slide. Once you've done that, you can paste the chart object into your slide and you get an instant updated presentation.

> It's worth noting that you could also use VBA code to open an existing PowerPoint presentation, find a specific slide within the presentation, and place your graph there.

To perform these tasks, you'll need to declare the following Excel and PowerPoint object variables in your procedure.

```
Dim objExcelApp As Excel.Application
Dim objExWkb As Excel.Workbook
Dim objExSheet As Excel.Worksheet
Dim objPPTApp As PowerPoint.Application
Dim objPPTPresen As PowerPoint.Presentation
Dim objPPTSlide As PowerPoint.Slide
```

The first portion of the code is rather simple. All you're doing is exporting a recordset object to Excel much like you did earlier in this chapter. In order to create your chart within Excel, use the following code.

```
With objExSheet
    .Range("A2").CopyFromRecordset objRST
    .Name = "Chart"
    objExcelApp.Charts.Add
    objExcelApp.ActiveChart.ChartType = xlColumnClustered
    objExcelApp.ActiveChart.SetSourceData
Source:=Sheets("Chart").Range("A2:C13"), PlotBy:=xlColumns
    objExcelApp.ActiveChart.Location Where:=xlLocationAsObject,
Name:="Chart"

    With objExcelApp.ActiveChart
        .HasTitle = False
        .Axes(xlCategory, xlPrimary).HasTitle = False
        .Axes(xlValue, xlPrimary).HasTitle = False
        .CopyPicture
    End With

End With
```

Once you've copied the object, you can close Excel and start the PowerPoint portion of the code. You need to create a new presentation, add a slide, and paste your copied chart on to the slide. The following code accomplishes this for you.

```
Set objPPTApp = CreateObject("Powerpoint.Application")
Set objPPTPresen = objPPTApp.Presentations.Add(msoTrue)
objPPTApp.Visible = True
Set objPPTSlide = objPPTPresen.Slides.Add(Index:=1, Layout:=ppLayoutBlank)
objPPTSlide.Shapes.Paste
```

Finally, you need to release all of your object variables and clean up your code. The following procedure can be run from a command button (cmdChart) and will accomplish all of the previously described steps to create the slide shown in Figure 15-10.

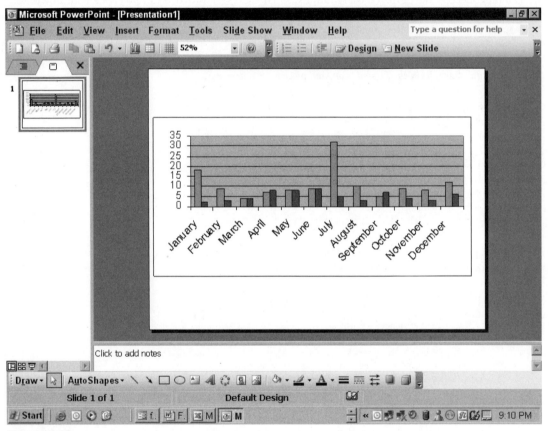

Figure 15-10

```
Private Sub cmdChart_Click()
Dim objRST As Recordset
Dim objExcelApp As Excel.Application
Dim objExWkb As Excel.Workbook
Dim objExSheet As Excel.Worksheet
Dim objPPTApp As PowerPoint.Application
Dim objPPTPresen As PowerPoint.Presentation
Dim objPPTSlide As PowerPoint.Slide
Set objRST = Application.CurrentDb.OpenRecordset("Samples")
```

```
Set objExcelApp = CreateObject("Excel.Application")
Set objExWkb = objExcelApp.Workbooks.Add
Set objExSheet = objExWkb.Worksheets.Add
objExcelApp.Visible = True
With objExSheet
    .Range("A2").CopyFromRecordset objRST
    .Name = "Chart"
    objExcelApp.Charts.Add
    objExcelApp.ActiveChart.ChartType = xlColumnClustered
    objExcelApp.ActiveChart.SetSourceData _
Source:=Sheets("Chart").Range("A2:C13"), PlotBy:=xlColumns
    objExcelApp.ActiveChart.Location Where:=xlLocationAsObject, _
Name:="Chart"
    'Configure properties of the chart
    With objExcelApp.ActiveChart
        .HasTitle = False
        .Axes(xlCategory, xlPrimary).HasTitle = False
        .Axes(xlValue, xlPrimary).HasTitle = False
        .CopyPicture
    End With

End With
'Do not forget to close Excel
objExcelWkb.Close(0)
objExcelApp.Quit
Set objPPTApp = CreateObject("Powerpoint.Application")
Set objPPTPresen = objPPTApp.Presentations.Add(msoTrue)
objPPTApp.Visible = True
Set objPPTSlide = objPPTPresen.Slides.Add(Index:=1, Layout:=ppLayoutBlank)
objPPTSlide.Shapes.Paste
Set rptSamples = Nothing
Set objExSheet = Nothing
Set objExWkb = Nothing
Set objExcelApp = Nothing
Set objPPTSlide = Nothing
Set objPPTPresen = Nothing
Set objPPTApp = Nothing
End Sub
```

Once you've run the preceding code, you'll have a slide in a new presentation with an image of your Excel chart, as shown in Figure 15-10.

Using the Access Object Model to Pull Data from Access to Other Applications

The following sections don't use any VBA within Access, but if you're going to use Access to control other applications, chances are you'll eventually need to use VBA or VBScript within other applications to manipulate Microsoft Access. We'll only spend a very brief couple of pages on these concepts. You can utilize the Access object model from Visual Basic to enhance your Visual Basic applications with Access reports. Before you can write code utilizing the Access object model from your Visual Basic applications, you need to first add a reference to the Access 11 object model in your project's References dialog box.

The following code opens an Access report based on prompted criteria and prints it from within your Visual Basic application.

```
Private Sub mnuConsumptionReport_Click()
Dim objAccess As Access.Application
Set objAccess = CreateObject("Access.Application")
If Not (objAccess Is Nothing) Then
    objAccess.OpenCurrentDatabase _
"\\server\f\SkidControl\SkidControlBE.mdb", False _
    objAccess.DoCmd.OpenReport "AllocationReport", acViewNormal
    objAccess.CloseCurrentDatabase
    Set objAccess = Nothing
Else
    MsgBox "Report not printed. Please contact Tech Support", _
vbOKOnly, "Report failure"
End If
If Err <> 0 Then
    Err.Clear
End If
End Sub
```

You can even utilize Visual Basic to export information from Access into Excel. The following code performs that export and allows the user to either create a new spreadsheet or add a worksheet to an existing spreadsheet. This method utilizes an ADO Recordset that pulls data from an Access database. You could just as easily alter your code to utilize the Access object model to execute a query to gather this data to export to Excel.

```
Private Sub mnuSheeter_Click()
Dim strSQL As String
Dim xlapp As Object
Dim xlwkb As Object
Dim xlwks As Object
Dim objRST As ADODB.Recordset
Dim Response As String
Dim lvlColumn As Long
Dim NewFile As String
Dim flname As String

'Always have a way to handle errors
On Error GoTo errhandler
'Establish your ADO connection
Set objConn = CreateObject("ADODB.Connection")
objConn.Provider = "Microsoft.Jet.OLEDB.4.0"
g_objDBPath = "\\server\f\FrameControl\FrameControlBE.mdb"
objConn.Open g_objDBPath
'Allow the user to enter the filter parameter for the report
Response = InputBox("Please enter the date for the inventory report." _
, "Enter Date")
'dt will be the name of the worksheet
dt = DatePart("m", Response) & DatePart("d", Response) _
 & DatePart("yyyy", Response)
strSQL = "SELECT SkidNumber, PONumber, ReceivedBy, PriceMSF, " _
```

```
            & "Width, Grain, Type, SkidType, InitialQuantity, " _
            & "InitialValue, Format([ReceivedDate], 'Short Date') " _
            & "AS [Date] From Skids WHERE " _
            & "(((Format([ReceivedDate],'Short Date')) " _
            & "= #" & Response & "#) AND Location <> 'Deleted');"
    'Create and open your recordset
    Set objRST = CreateObject("ADODB.Recordset")
    objRST.Open strSQL, objConn, adOpenStatic, adLockReadOnly
    'Create your Excel spreadsheet
    Set xlapp = CreateObject("Excel.Application")
    blnNewFile = MsgBox("Do you want to create a new file?", vbYesNo, _
    "Create File?")
    If blnNewFile = vbYes Then
    Set xlwkb = xlapp.Workbooks.Add
    Else
        'Allow the user to select an existing spreadsheet
        Me.CommonDialog1.ShowOpen
        flname = Me.CommonDialog1.FileName
        Set xlwkb = xlapp.Workbooks.Open(flname)
    End If
    xlapp.Visible = True
    With xlwkb
        Set xlwks = .Worksheets.Add
        xlwks.Name = dt
        For lvlColumn = 0 To objRST.Fields.Count - 1
          xlwks.cells(1, lvlColumn + 1).Value = _
    objRST.Fields(lvlColumn).Name
        Next
        xlwks.Range(xlwks.cells(1, 1), _
        xlwks.cells(1, objRST.Fields.Count)).Font.Bold = True


        With xlwks
            xlwks.Range("A2").CopyFromRecordset objRST
        End With
    End With
    xlapp.Visible = True
    objRST.Close
    Set objRST = Nothing
    Set objConn = Nothing
    Set xlwks = Nothing
    Set xlwkb = Nothing
    Set xlapp = Nothing
    Exit Sub
    errhandler:
        If Err.Number = 3021 Then
            MsgBox "There are no records for today. Please enter another
    date.", vbOKOnly, "Error"
            objRST.Close
            Set objRST = Nothing
        Else
            basErrorLogger.LogAddInErr Err, "Sheeter Report", _
    "Export to Excel", "error line"
            basErrorLogger.LogAddInErr Err, Err.Number, _
```

```
Err.Description, "error specifics"
    End If
Exit Sub
End Sub
```

No matter how you choose to utilize other Office Applications within your VBA code, you're sure to dazzle your coworkers with the rich content you can provide from your Access database.

Summary

We've covered a variety of examples that use VBA to transfer information between Microsoft Access and other Office applications. We've covered sending information to Outlook, creating a mail merge in Word, exporting a query to an Excel spreadsheet, and even creating a PowerPoint slide with data sent from Access and then to Excel. You might not perform these exact operations within your application, but the methods and code samples included within this chapter should give you a starting point for further development.

These code samples make extensive use of the object models of each Office Application. If you don't understand the various objects and methods you need in your target application, you'll probably run into problems in your code. Viewing the Help files for the various Office applications will help you understand the objects you want to manipulate.

Next we'll move on to covering the important topic of Security within Access. These days, you can't develop any application without taking into account the various methods of securing your code and access to the data within your application. Chapter 16 should help you cope with this critical task.

16

Database Security

Security is receiving an increasing amount of focus. With everything from privacy issues, government regulations, and computer crimes, security requires a fair amount of attention and dedication. Your Microsoft Access databases are not exempt from this need for attention.

This chapter discusses the various security methods available to secure your Access databases, including the data contained in them and the custom forms, reports, and code you've developed in your databases. Whether you need to set up security to meet regulations regarding the privacy of information about people stored in your database or to meet your organization's security standards over confidential company information or to protect intellectual property rights, this chapter will help you choose which security methods to use.

You should also be aware that Access 2003 also has some new security features that enhance its ability to protect your computer from an Access database with malicious code designed to attack your computer. Those security enhancements are covered in Chapter 20—*"Macro Security"—Digital Signatures and Sandboxes*.

This chapter will cover shared-level security, user-level security, encoding a database, making an MDE file, and using VBA to manipulate security. This chapter also covers some aspects of the Access security model, which require a deeper level of thought. This especially includes a discussion about user-level security and the detachment between the MDW file and the database that is user-level secured.

Since there are many ways to achieve security in Access, you should review every section in this chapter completely to understand some of the pitfalls of using one type of security over another, as well as to determine when it is appropriate to combine security methods for optimum security. After you have finished this chapter, be sure to review Chapter 20 as well.

Access Security Model Overview

With so many methods to set up security in Access, you can easily become overwhelmed deciding which method to choose. This section provides a synopsis of Access security methods, with suggestions for when to use one method over another and when to combine methods. This section also covers the relative difficulty of using these methods.

There are two common scenarios used when setting up Access databases:

❑ Standalone databases which contain all of the objects necessary to maintain the desired data, including tables, forms, reports, modules, and so on.

❑ Linked databases in which one database typically contains all user-interface components, such as forms, reports, and modules, with links to tables in another database, which contains all of the tables and data. The database containing the user-interface components and links is called the *Front end*. The database containing the tables and the data is called the *Back end*.

There are seven security methods that can be used in Access. You may apply any or all of these security methods to a single database. Additionally, all of the security methods can be applied to a standalone, a front-end, or a back-end database.

❑ *Encoding*: Encoding a database encrypts the data in the file such that the data cannot easily be read using a file explorer/browser tool (for example, Windows Notepad). This type of security is useful when the folder that contains the database file can be opened by anyone with access to the system but you need to restrict reviewing the data contained in the database to authorized users only. This method does not require a password to view the data using Access and is very easy to implement. You should probably combine this method with shared-level security or user-level security.

❑ *Shared-level security*: Shared-level security is established by setting a password on a database. When a database has a password, the user is required to enter the password before they can open it. This type of security works well in small workgroups where it is not necessary to know who opened the database or restrict users from altering any objects in the database. If your users are not allowed to share a common password, this method will not be satisfactory. You can combine this method with encoding and user-level security.

❑ *User-level security*: User-level security is established when you attach a workgroup information file (MDW) file to the database. User-level security permits you to set permissions for each object in the database at a single user or at a user group level. This method can be useful when you have a number of users using the database and each user needs different types of access (permission) to the database. Types of access include data deleting, updating, or inserting, each of which can be authorized or not independently depending on the user. Additionally, queries, forms, and reports can be made available to specific users depending on their needs. This method can be combined with encoding and shared-level security, and requires more maintenance and planning than other methods and is therefore more time consuming to implement and maintain.

❑ *Compile*: Compiling the database produces an Access compiled database (type MDE) file. When a database is compiled, the code is compiled and compacted and the user readable code is removed from the database. Additionally, forms, reports, pages, or modules cannot be modified, nor can they be exported to another database.This method can be used to protect your intellectual property rights as well as prevent users from changing forms, reports, pages, or modules. This does not secure the data in database tables. This method does not secure the data in an Access database. You can set up shared-level security or user-level security to require a password. This method is most commonly used on a front-end database.

> **If your database has shared-level security or user-level security when you make an MDE, you will not be able to remove the security from the MDE.**

❑   *Set project password*: If you have written code that you do want others to be able to view or change, you can set a password on the project for your database using the Visual Basic Editor. This will only prevent users from viewing or changing code. It does not prevent them from changing form, report, or page layouts. This method does not secure the data in an Access database. You can set up shared-level security or user-level security to require a password. This is most commonly used on a front-end database.

Figure 16-1 shows the shared-level security and user-level security methods as they apply to the linked database scenario. The encoding and compile methods, shown in Figure 16-1, could be applied to these databases—though you will probably not compile a back-end database because it usually has no code.

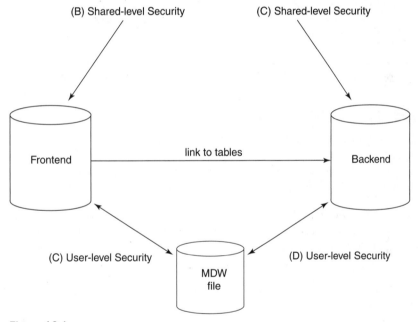

Figure 16-1

Options (B) and (C) in Figure 16-1 are the same as when they are applied to a single database as described above. Options (F) and (G) are described here because of the difference in the way the methods apply to a back-end database.

❑   *Shared-level security*: Like the single database scenario, you set shared-level security by setting a password on the database. Setting a password on a back-end database will require that a password be entered before the database can be opened. The password for the front-end database does not have to be the same as the password for the back-end database. In order to establish a link to a table in a back-end database that has a password, the password must be entered at the time the link is created.

This method is fairly easy to implement, but has some problems. The main problem is that the password to the back-end database is stored in one of the Access database system tables in the front-end database. An experienced user can determine the password to the backend database. For this reason, you should also have a password for the front-end database. Of course, having a password on the front-end will not prevent users who know that password from determining the password to the back-end database. However, it will prevent persons who are not authorized to use either the front-end or the back-end from easily obtaining the passwords.

> If you change the password on the back-end database, you must recreate the links in a front-end database. The linked table manager will not be able to relink the tables.

❑   *User-level security*: Using this method is also like the single database scenario. It has the same level of difficulty as setting user-level security on a single database. You should keep in mind that if you are going to use a workgroup information file (MDW) on the back end, it must be the same file used on the front end. This is because Access can only use one MDW file at a time. Also, when you set up permissions to secure data, you will apply those permissions to the back-end database, not the front-end one.

The rest of this chapter covers each of these security methods in more detail. You will see how to set up security on your database as well as some other problems you might encounter.

Shared-Level Security

Shared-level security involves setting a password on a database. Setting a database password is a simple solution to protect a database for a small group of people. This can be effective in situations where anyone who can access the database is permitted to insert, delete, or update the data and update any of the objects (for example, forms, reports, and so on) in the database.

When shared-level security is applied to a database, the user is prompted for a password each time that database is opened. Shared-level security only protects the MDB file on which the password is set. When the correct password is entered, the user gains full access to that database including all data and all objects contained in that database.

Be aware that setting a database password only affects attempts to access the database using the Microsoft Jet Engine. *See Encoding a Database* for more discussion.

> User-level security (discussed later) does not override the database password. User-level security will require the user to log on to use a database in Access. However, if the database the user opens is also password protected, the user will have to enter the shared-level password after entering their own username and password.

Shared-Level Secured Back-End Databases

Be careful while linking to tables in a shared-level protected database. When your front end links to tables in the protected back-end database, you will be required to specify its password. After the tables are linked, the link and the password are recorded. This is true whether you link from another Access database or create an ODC linking file [(through Open Database Connectivity (ODBC)] to access the protected database from Excel or Word. After the link has been established, anyone can then open the protected database without entering the password.Note: ODC is an Office Data Connection. These connections use HTML and XML to store the connection information. Users can view and edit the data in a database through the ODC using Word, Excel, and other text editors.

As mentioned in the *Overview*, if the link is from another Access database, the password is recorded in the front-end database without encoding in one of the system tables. A user with a moderate level of experience can determine where to find this password and could begin accessing the remote database without the benefit of the front end you have written for them.

Since user-level security does not expose its passwords in this way, user-level security is preferred for databases that utilize linked tables. At the very least, any front-end database that accesses a shared-level secured back-end database should also have shared-level security applied.

> **If you change the password on the protected database, linked tables must be deleted and linked again. The `Linked Table Manager` will not fix the link.**

Setting Up Shared-Level Security Using the Access Interface

Shared-level security is added to a database from the `Tools | Security` menu. The option `Set Database Password` will be visible if the database does not have a shared-level password. The option `Unset Database Password` will be visible if the database has a shared-level password.

Adding a Database Password

To set a database password, the database must be opened in Exclusive mode. Figure 16-2 shows how to select `Open Exclusive` to open the file in Exclusive mode.

Select `Tools | Security | Set Database Password...` from the menu as shown in Figure 16-3.

This displays the `Set Database Password` dialog box as shown in Figure 16-4.

Enter a valid password in the `Password` text box and reenter the password in the `Verify` text box. Click `OK` to apply the password.

> **There are no restrictions for a valid database password. You should follow good practices for establishing a password.**

Removing a Database Password

After a password has been set on a database, the menu option changes to `Tools | Security | Unset Database Password`.

To unset a database password, the database must be opened in Exclusive mode.

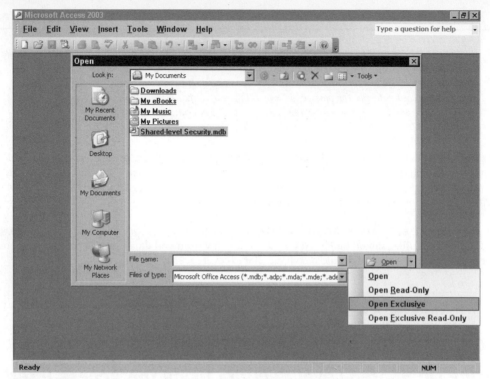

Figure 16-2

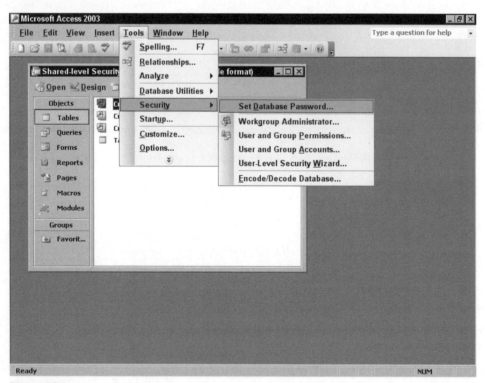

Figure 16-3

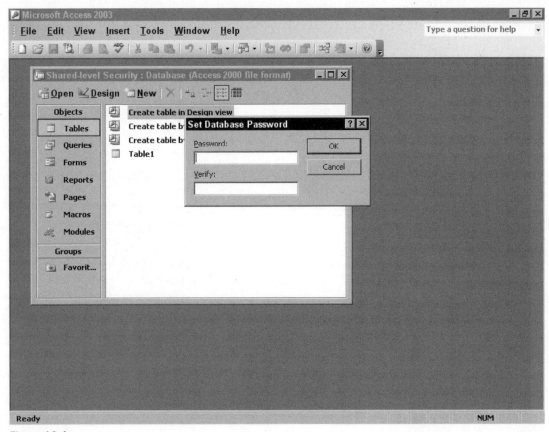

Figure 16-4

Select Tools | Security | Unset Database Password... from the menu to display the Unset Database Password dialog box shown in Figure 16-5.

Enter the current password for the database and click OK to unset the password.

Using Jet and ADO to Set a Database Password

You can use Visual Basic code to set or change a database password. To change the password, open the database in Exclusive mode and use the SQL statement ALTER DATABASE PASSWORD newpassword oldpassword. The password is case sensitive and must be specified within square brackets ([]). When setting a password on a database that does not currently have a password, use NULL without the brackets as the old password. When removing a password from a database use, NULL without the brackets as the new password.

The procedure SetDatabasePassword provides functionality to add, update, or remove a database password. Notice that if either the new or the old password is not specified (IsMissing) when calling SetDatabasePassword, the word NULL is substituted for the password. If the password is specified, SetDatabasePassword encloses the value in square brackets ([]). Also notice that if the old password is specified, the ADODB Connection properties uses the password without square brackets.

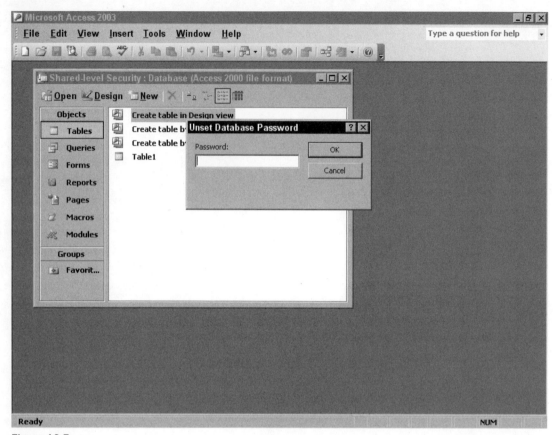

Figure 16-5

Error traps are provided in the code to show errors that can occur. You will likely wish to move the error traps to the procedure that calls `SetDatabasePassword` and enhance the error messages to provide friendly feedback to the user.

```
Public Function SetDatabasePassword _
(pDBName As String, _
 Optional pNewPassword As Variant, _
 Optional pOldPassword As Variant) As String
On Error GoTo report_error
Const cProvider = "Microsoft.Jet.OLEDB.4.0"
Dim cnn As ADODB.Connection
Dim strNewPassword As String
Dim strOldPassword As String
Dim strCommand As String
Dim strResult As String
' if a password is not specified (IsMissing),
' the string is "NULL" WITHOUT the brackets
If IsMissing(pNewPassword) Then
    strNewPassword = "NULL"
Else
```

```
        strNewPassword = "[" & pNewPassword & "]"
    End If
    If IsMissing(pOldPassword) Then
        strOldPassword = "NULL"
    Else
        strOldPassword = "[" & pOldPassword & "]"
    End If
    ' define the string to change the password
    strCommand = "ALTER DATABASE PASSWORD " _
    & strNewPassword & " " & strOldPassword & ";"
    ' Open a connection to the database
    Set cnn = New ADODB.Connection
    With cnn
        .Mode = adModeShareExclusive
        .Provider = cProvider
        If Not IsMissing(pOldPassword) Then
            .Properties("Jet OLEDB:Database Password") = pOldPassword
        End If
        .Open "Data Source=" & pDBName & ";"
        .Execute strCommand
    End With
    strResult = "Password Set"
exit_SetDatabasePassword:
    On Error Resume Next
    cnn.Close
    Set cnn = Nothing
    SetDatabasePassword = strResult
    Exit Function
report_error:
    If Err.Number = -2147467259 Then
        strResult = "Specified an old password when one was not set"
    ElseIf Err.Number = -2147217843 Then
        strResult = "Invalid password for database"
    Else
        strResult = Err.Number & " " & Err.Description
    End If
    Resume exit_SetDatabasePassword

End Function
```

The procedure `ShowSamplePasswordSetting` shows how to use `SetDatabasePassword` to set a new password, change a password, and remove a password from the database. The resulting SQL ALTER DATABASE PASSWORD statement is documented for each call.

```
Public Sub ShowSamplePasswordSetting()
Const cDBName = "C:\Access\Security Samples\DatabasePassword.mdb"
' give the database a password
' the statement becomes: ALTER DATABASE PASSWORD [newpass] NULL;
Debug.Print "New password result: " _
& SetDatabasePassword(cDBName, "newpass")
' change the password from "newpass" to "NEWPASS" (all caps)
' the statement becomes: ALTER DATABASE PASSWORD [NEWPASS] [newpass];
Debug.Print "Change password result: " _
& SetDatabasePassword(cDBName, "NEWPASS", "newpass")
```

```
' remove the password from the database
' the statement becomes: ALTER DATABASE PASSWORD NULL [NEWPASS];
Debug.Print "Remove password result: " _
& SetDatabasePassword(cDBName, , "NEWPASS")
End Sub
```

Encoding a Database

When a database is secured as described in *Shared-Level Security*, the security only applies to attempts to access the database using the Microsoft Jet Engine. Any attempt to open the database using ODBC, for example, from Excel will request the database password. However, if the MDB file is opened using a non-Jet access method, such as through Windows Notepad, the data can be viewed.

If it is necessary to prevent anyone from analyzing the information in a database using a non-Jet access method, you should encode the database. This will encrypt the information contained in the database to prevent unauthorized access to the data through other means.

When you encode a database, you encode to a new database and the original database is saved without encoding.

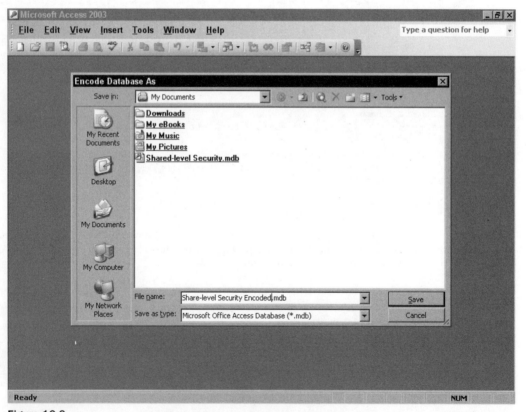

Figure 16-6

Creating an Encoded Database

To encode a database, the database must be opened in Exclusive mode as described earlier and depicted in Figure 16-3.

Select `Tools | Security | Encode/Decode Database...` from the menu to display the `Encode Database As` dialog box shown in Figure 16-6.

Then select a location to store the encoded database and enter a name for it. Click `Save` to create the encoded database.

After you have encoded the database, either delete the original database or move it to a secured location where it has adequate protection from unauthorized users and from being unintentionally changed or deleted.

Decoding an Encoded Database

To decode a database that has been previously encoded, the database must be opened in Exclusive mode as described earlier. Select `Tools | Security | Encode/Decode Database...` from the menu to display the `Decode Database As` dialog box shown in Figure 16-7.

Select a location to store the decoded database and enter a name for it. Click `Save` to create the decoded database.

Secure VBA Code

There are many reasons to protect your Microsoft Visual Basic for Application (VBA) code. You may wish to prevent persons who are not experienced with the design of the code from introducing errors. You may also wish to conceal your intellectual property by preventing anyone from viewing the code. Or, you may want to ensure consistent application of business rules by preventing unauthorized changes. And, of course, there is the concern about hackers. Access provides two primary methods for protecting the code: securing a project and making an MDE file.

Securing Modules by Securing the Project

You can secure Visual Basic code from viewing or editing by locking the project from viewing and setting a password on your project. You set the project password while viewing the project in the Visual Basic Editor (VBE). When a project has a password and is locked for viewing, the password must be entered in the VBE before the Visual Basic code can be opened. The password is requested only once for each time that database is opened, and it is only requested if there is an attempt to access the code using the VBE.

Setting a password and locking the project from viewing also prevents changing the `HAS Module` property on forms and reports until the password has not been entered in the VBE. This is because Access needs to open the code before it can delete it, or add to it.

Setting a password and locking the project from viewing does not prevent users from changing event properties on forms or reports. Specifically, a user can remove the [Event procedure] setting from an

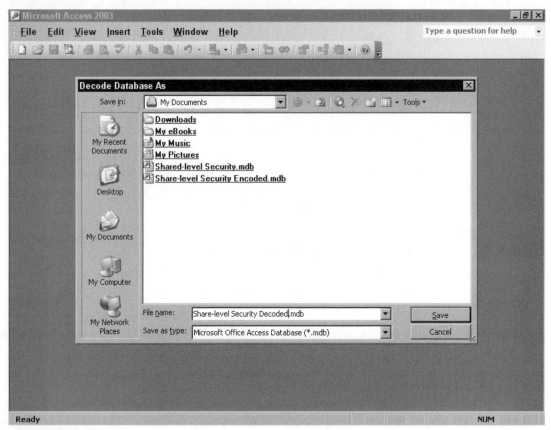

Figure 16-7

event, causing the code to not be executed. Obviously, this could be disastrous if the code executes a critical action when that event occurs. Although users clear the [Event procedure] setting, they cannot add a new [Event procedure] to an event. However they can specify [Event procedure], and if a procedure already exists for the event, it will be called.

To prevent users from making form or report layout changes or changing the properties on events, you can generate an MDE file from your database and distribute an MDE file instead of an MDB file. Another way to prevent changes is to institute user-level security and not grant modify permissions to selected users or user groups. Both of these methods are discussed later.

Lock Project from Viewing

To prevent unauthorized access to the VBA code, lock the project from viewing and set the module password to open your project in the VBE. In the VBE, select the project in the Project Explorer. Then select Tool | *project* Properties. (*project* is the name of your project, that is, your database). This displays the Project Properties dialog box for your project, as shown in Figure 16-8.

Select the Protection tab as shown in Figure 16-9.

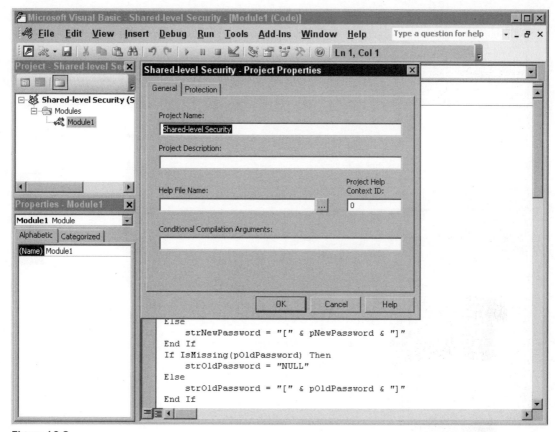

Figure 16-8

On the `Protection` tab, check the box next to `Lock project for viewing`. If this option is selected, you are required to enter a password. Specify a password in the `Password` text box and reenter the password in the `Confirm Password` text box. Click `OK` to save the password.

To test the module password, return to Microsoft Access and close the database. Reopen the database, then open the VBE, and select the project. The *project* `Password` dialog box displays requesting the password.

Removing a Module Password

To remove the lock on the module, open your project and select your project in the `Project Explorer`. Then select `Tool | project Properties`. (*project* is the name of your project, that is, your database). This displays the `Project Properties` dialog box for your project.

Then select the `Protection` tab. Uncheck the box next to `Lock project for viewing`.

Note: You do not have to clear the password. If you do not clear the password, the next time the database is closed and opened you will be prompted to enter the password to set properties for the project, but will not be prompted for the password to display the code.

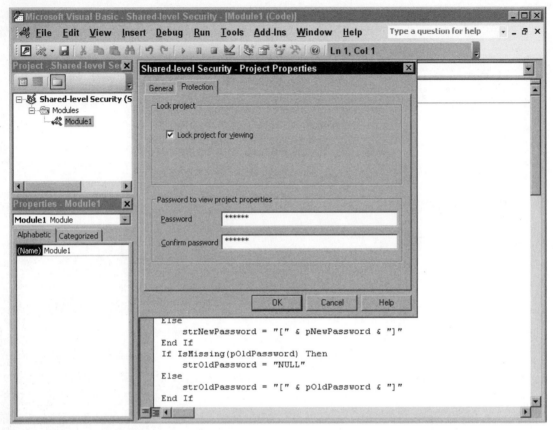

Figure 16-9

Be sure you store the password information so that you can retrieve it later. If you do not have the correct password, you will not be able to access the VBA code. Many developers choose to create a backup of the file before securing the code. This is also inexpensive insurance just in case the file becomes corrupted or the password fails. What? Did we really mean that a valid password might someday fail to allow access to the code. You bet. And, that can be incredibly frustrating and time consuming if there isn't a current backup of the file.

Compiling to Make an MDE File

If your database has a user interface where you control the user's experience, you may wish to prevent the user from making any kind of changes to code or other objects. An MDE file can accomplish this.

When you make an MDE file, all of your code is compiled and removed from viewing. The compile process also compacts the database, which makes the database much smaller. Compiling also optimizes the code and provides faster execution.

Before you can make an MDE file using Access 2003, you must open the database exclusively. You must also convert older databases to Access 2002 format. Access 2002 and 2003 share the same database format.

A few words of caution: If your project has references to other databases, you must make MDE files of those other databases and update the references to them in your project before you make an MDE of your project. Ah, you may be noticing a bit of a snowball effect here.

Converting a Database to 2002 Format

The title bar of the Database window indicates the database file format. Notice the *Access 2000 file format* in Figure 16-10.

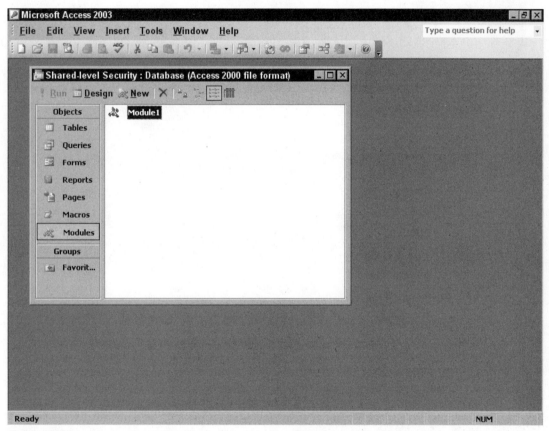

Figure 16-10

If your database is the 2000 format, convert it to the 2002–2003 format before making the MDE.

Tip: If you wish to always create databases in the 2002–2003 format, you can change the default file format through the Advanced tab of the Tools | Options dialog box.

To convert your database to the 2002 format, select `Tools | Database Utilities | Convert Database | To Access 2002-2003 File Format...` as shown in Figure 16-11.

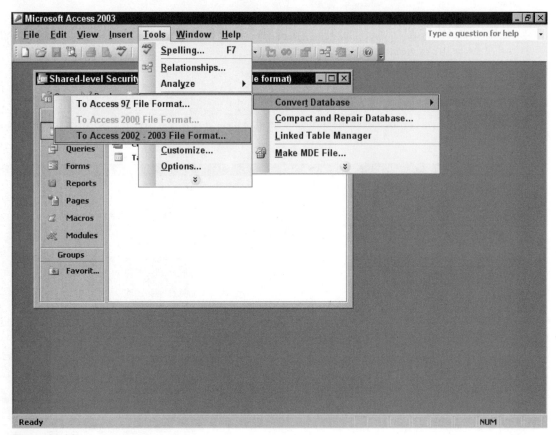

Figure 16-11

The `Convert Database Into` dialog box displays options for you to specify the destination file for the new format. Enter the name of the destination file and click `Save`. The conversion begins immediately.

> *After you have converted the database (to the 2002–2003 format), it can no longer be shared with Access 2000 or Access 97 users.*

With the database in the 2002–2003 format, you can now build an MDE file. Be aware that when you create an MDE, you will not be able to import, export, create, modify, or rename any forms, reports, pages, or modules in the MDE file itself. Therefore, you should retain the original MDB file in the event changes need to be made in the future. Obviously, at that time, you will need to make the changes to the MDB, and then create a new MDE to distribute.

To begin the `Make MDE file process`, select `Tools | Database Utilities | Make MDE file...` as seen in Figure 16-12.

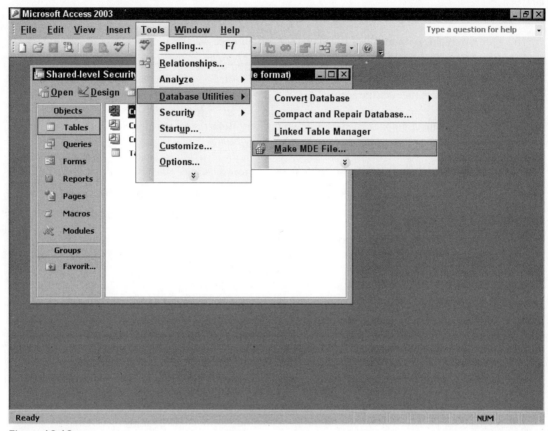

Figure 16-12

The Save MDE As dialog box displays for you to specify the destination file for the MDE. Enter the name of the file you wish to create and click Save. The MDE file will be created.

User-Level Security

The most advanced security provided in Access 2003 is the user-level security. This method permits you to grant permissions to groups of users and/or to specific users for each object in a database. Objects include tables, queries, forms, reports, and macros, as well as the database itself.

Since user-level security is the most advanced form of security, it requires additional explanation. Thorough planning and documentation will be invaluable to set up and maintain user-level security.

User-level security does not override shared-level security. User-level security will require the user to log on to use a database in Access. However, if the user opens a shared-level protected database, the user will also have to know the password to that database. Also, as with shared-level security, user-level security does not prevent the data from being viewed using tools other than Access. So again, one option is that the database can be encoded to prevent viewing the data from other tools such as Windows Notepad.

Main Components of User-Level Security

There are two main components of user-level security in Access 2003:

❏ The MDW file, commonly referred to as the WIF.

❏ The database that is to be secured.

With these two main components, there are two primary steps necessary to secure a database with user-level security:

❏ Create or update the MDW file to define user groups and users.

❏ Set up the database to grant user groups or individual users of the MDW file specific permissions to objects in the database.

The distinction, detachment, and dependency between the MDW file and the secured database will be clarified by the following discussion.

The MDW File

The MDW file is used to uniquely identify an individual Access user and the user groups to which that user belongs. The MDW file does not contain any information about the database that is being secured. Conversely, the database that will be secured knows nothing about the user groups or users defined in the MDW file until you begin to set permissions to objects in the secured database using the MDW file.

Because of the distinction between the MDW file and the secured database, it is important to consider the structure of the business that will be using database(s), as well as the purpose of the database(s).

When setting up the MDW file, you will define user groups and users. User groups should be designed around the roles people have in an organization. For example, one group might handle accounting activities while another group might maintain customer contacts.

A business or a single computer can have multiple MDW files. An Access user can choose the MDW file they want to use. Therefore, by taking the organizational structure into account, you can create an MDW file that can be shared by multiple databases across an organization.

Users can be assigned to one or more user groups. So if a user only handles accounting activities, they can be assigned to the accounting group. Later if the user becomes involved with customer contacts (changes or additions to their responsibilities), they can be assigned to the customer contacts group in addition to the accounting group. It is important to realize that permissions are cumulative, meaning that the user will have the maximum permissions allowed by combining the permissions rather than restrictions of each group that the user belongs to. There will be more discussion on the cumulative effect a bit later.

Later you will learn that granting permissions to a database is best done through user groups rather than by granting permissions to individual users. As just mentioned, users can change groups or roles. By granting permissions in a database to groups instead of users, you can change the permissions a user has simply by changing the group(s) that they belong to in the MDW file. The security changes will then be picked up the next time the user signs into that MDW file. On the other hand, if you had granted permissions to the user for a specific database, you would have to change the permissions that user has to that database (or any database where you have granted that user specific permissions).

When an MDW file is created, you specify an internal name (not a file name), an organization, and a workgroup ID. Since there can be more than one MDW file, the unique combination of these values authenticates the file.

Within the MDW file, each user is assigned their own Personal ID (PID). A user can belong to one or more user groups. Each user group is assigned its own Group ID (GID). The authentication information of the MDW file, together with the username and PID, uniquely identifies an Access user.

> *Usernames in the MDW file are not associated with the names in the Windows user login.*

When Access users have identified themselves using an MDW file, they receive a set of identifications. You can view this set of identifications as a set of pass codes or keys. Each pass code has a unique characteristic based on the authentication information of the MDW file plus the username and PID, or the authentication information of the MDW file plus the group name and GID.

The user-level secured database (not the MDW file) will use these pass codes to determine what permissions to grant a user when accessing the objects in that database. The factors for determining what user groups and users should be defined will become clearer with the discussion about setting permissions in a database that is to be secured. That's next!

Note: Before beginning to manipulate the information in an MDW file, it is highly recommend that you make a backup copy of the file. The default MDW file name is SYSTEM.MDW. The default location is `C:\Documents and Settings\[username]\Application Data\Microsoft\Access` *folder.*

The Database to be Secured

The second component of user-level security is the database that is secured at the user level by granting permissions to each object in that database. Permissions authorize the actions that can be performed on an object. Those permissions are granted to Access users based on the pass codes in the MDW file that is in use when user-level security is set up.

An Access user does not use the MDW file until they open a database. The MDW file that is used is chosen by the user by joining *the MDW file or is automatically chosen if the* / wkgrp *is used on the command line when Access is started. These techniques are discussed later.*

The object types that can have permissions set include the database, tables, queries, forms, reports, and macros. Each object, regardless of type, has its own set of permissions. That is, each table in a database has a set of permissions distinct from other tables in the database. Therefore it is possible to permit a particular user group to have read-only access to some tables while allowing them to update data in other tables. For example, you could have database administrators be able to set values in lookup tables but not be able to change records that refer to those lookup tables.

When granting permissions to a user group or an individual user, the permissions are granted based on the pass codes previously mentioned. Remember that the pass code consists of the MDW file authentication information plus the group name and Group ID or the MDW file authentication information plus the username and Personal ID. Therefore, if a user has selected the wrong MDW file, even if the user is defined in the MDW file that they have selected, the user will not be granted the intended permissions because the pass codes will not be the same. This is another reason why it is important to maintain backups of your MDW file.

Microsoft Support provides additional information regarding Access Security and the MDW file. For an alternative explanation of security visit http://support.microsoft.com/default.aspx?scid= kb;EN-US;305542. You can search the Microsoft Knowledge base for more answers at http://support.microsoft.com/default.aspx?pr=kbhowto.

Permissions are granted to the user cumulatively. If permissions are granted to a user group, then all users who belong to that group receive those permissions as well as their own permissions. If a user is granted permissions that exceed any of the permissions of the groups that user belongs to, that user receives the additional individual permissions as well as the most permissive authority from each group that they belong.

To put this cumulative effect another way, when users identify themselves to Access through an MDW file, they receive pass codes as follows: one for their username and one for each group that they belong to. Those pass codes then grant that user all of the permissions that have been granted to each of those pass codes.

This cumulative effect shows why it is important to define the appropriate user groups when setting up the MDW file. This cumulative effect is also the reason to design your security around user groups rather than users. Since a user gets all of the permissions for each group that they belong to, if the user changes groups, you need only change the group that user belongs to rather than analyze and update the user's individual permissions for each object. Also, if another user starts working under a role you have defined in the MDW file, you need only set up that user and assign them to the group(s) that has the correct permissions for the database(s) that user will be using. This also means you do not have to change the permissions on each database the user will need to use.

As previously mentioned, permissions are assigned to each object in a database. Permissions are granted to specific user groups or users. If a database consists of lots of objects, lots of user groups, and lots of users, setting up user-level security can be a time-consuming process. Clearly, if you maintain permissions at the group level and not the user level, you reduce the amount of effort needed to set up and maintain user-level security.

Note: The Owner of the database or of an object in a database always has all permissions to that database or object in the database.

Permission	Objects	Actions
Open/Run	Database, Form, Report, Macro	Open a database, form, or report, or run a macro in a database.
Open Exclusive	Database	Open a database with exclusive access.

Continues

Permission	Objects	Actions
Read Design	Table, Query, Form, Report, Macro	View tables, queries, forms, reports, or macros in design view.
Modify Design	Table, Query, Form, Report, Macro	View and change the design of tables, queries, forms, reports, or macros; or delete them.
Administer	Database, Table, Query, Form, Report, Macro	For databases, set a database password, replicate a database, and change startup properties. For tables, queries, forms, reports, and macros, have full access to these objects and data, including ability to assign permissions.
Read Data	Table, Query	View data in tables and queries.
Update Data	Table, Query	View and modify, but not insert or delete, data in tables and queries.
Insert Data	Table, Query	View and insert, but not modify or delete, data in tables and queries.
Delete Data	Table, Query	View and delete, but not modify or insert, data in tables and queries.

A Comment About User-Level Security

While working with an MDW file, we evaluated how effective Access user-level security is. We have heard that Access Security isn't really secure. This was in reference to Access's inability to provide true data security. Macro security is a different matter and is discussed in Chapter 20.

One concern came from one of the things we expected while opening and closing the forms to work with the MDW file. We discovered that the authentication information (name, organization, and workgroup ID) in the MDW file was not retained and displayed each time we displayed the Workgroup Administrator (Tools | Security | Workgroup Administrator...). The name and organization actually came from the machine we were using rather than from what we entered. We expected that all pieces of the authentication information would be used to make the MDW file unique and secure. Since the name and organization didn't display from what we entered, we wonder how secure the authentication information is. That is, could our MDW file be recreated more easily than you would expect since some of the authentication information may not have to be correct. This is particularly frustrating, because things like this might lead to complaints that "there is no security in Access."

Another issue comes from the fact that the owner of the database has full permissions to the database. (This is discussed later.) Since the default owner of a database is Admin and Admin is also a default user in any MDW file, this leaves situations where an Access developer can accidentally leave their database open for security breach (by simply forgetting to change the owner away from Admin).

In our opinion, Access could be much more reliable if the secured database is more aware of the authentication information of the MDW file that must be used to access it and simply not allow Jet Engine access to the database unless the MDW file is truly authentic. I'm sure there is a tradeoff between making Access an open tool useful for more common users and making it the reliable application development tool it can be. But as a member of the Pacific Northwest Access Developers Group (PNWADG.org) I am aware of a significant number of developers who have developed sophisticated applications using Access with no other tools. We would like rock-solid reliable security without having to turn to SQL Server and Access Database Projects (ADP files).

This is not to say Access security is completely unreliable. For applications that are maintained behind the security of a good, secure operating system, where only authorized users can access files, the Access security model can provide adequate protection. This protection can be set at the user level by authorizing users to the data they are *supposed to be* authorized to access. And with the additional features available in Access 2003 and Jet SP7 or greater, Access has very good security for applications you will build and deliver to clients.

The point is, don't give up on Access user-level security as totally ineffective. But do be aware that the Access security model is not hacker proof and choose your security measures wisely.

Methods to Create User-Level Security

There are essentially three effective methods to secure a database at the user level.

❑ Use the User-level Security Wizard.

❑ Use the Access user interface to maintain the MDW file and set database permissions.

❑ Use Visual Basic for Applications to maintain the MDW file and database permissions. This includes using DAO, ADO, ADOX, or some combination thereof.

The User-level Security Wizard is perhaps the easiest, since the wizard takes you through all the steps necessary to secure the database. From the previous sections you should have a good understanding of the MDW file and how permissions are set. So, using the User-level Security Wizard can produce sufficient and effective results. The wizard can also be a good method to set up the initial security for a database.

> Note: The User-level Security Wizard cannot be used while a database has shared-level security or if the project has been locked from viewing (both discussed earlier). You will have to disable those options while you run the wizard. These options can be added back after the wizard has completed its processes.

The wizard is very self-explanatory and quite useful for initial user-level security setup. However, after user-level security has been established and if it becomes necessary to modify the security settings for a database, the multistep process of the wizard can be cumbersome. Nevertheless, the wizard provides useful tools for making changes to security. For example, the wizard has the ability to set passwords for users and provides a random personal ID. Other Access user-interface options do not support this.

Additionally, the wizard has a set of default user groups that include a set of default permissions. These groups can be useful if the permissions fit the roles of users in the business that will be using your database. But before relying on these groups, it is important that you design your own groups consistent with the organizational structure.

The following section walks you through setting up and maintaining user-level security using the Access user interface. First it will show you the User and Group Accounts menu option. Then it will walk you through using the User-level Security Wizard. Later sections show you how you can maintain user-level security using VBA with DAO and ADO.

User-Level Security Using the Access User Interface

There are many steps involved with creating and using user-level security using the Access user interface. Fortunately, Microsoft provides the User-level Security Wizard to help with the initial setup as well as continued maintenance. In order to help you fully understand all of the components of user-level security, this section covers all of the options available to maintain security using the user interface.

Creating an MDW

Your first step in creating user-level security is to select or create the MDW file that will contain the user groups and users you will define. As mentioned earlier, this can be a new file or the default file provided when Access is first used.

The recommended approach is to create a new MDW file. The User-level Security Wizard will not permit you to use the default SYSTEM.MDW file. Also, if you corrupt the default MDW file, you will have to manually recover that file from another source.

Many developers prefer to create application-specific MDW files with names that indicate the underlying application. This makes it easy to keep track of the MDW associations. It also makes creating (or reading) shortcuts and target paths a bit more obvious.

> TIP: Before beginning to manipulate the information in an MDW file, it is highly recommend that you make a backup copy of the file, even if you are creating a new MDW file. The default MDW file name is SYSTEM.MDW. The default location is the C:\Documents and Settings\[username]\ Application Data\Microsoft\Access folder.

To create or select the MDW file, select Security | Workgroup Administrator... from the Tools menu as shown in Figure 16-13.

The Workgroup Administrator dialog box displays information about the MDW file that is currently selected, as shown in Figure 16-14.

To create a new MDW file, select the Create... button. This displays the Workgroup Owner Information dialog box, as shown in Figure 16-15.

The Workgroup Owner Information dialog box requests the Name, Organization, and Workgroup ID. This information uniquely identifies the authenticity of the MDW file. The workgroup ID can be from 4 to 20 characters. This value should be treated much the same as a password to prevent anyone from guessing the value.

Select OK to display the Workgroup Information File dialog box shown in Figure 16-16.

Note that the default location is the C:\Documents and Settings\[username]\Application Data\Microsoft\Access folder with the default name of SYSTEMx.MDW. Then enter the location for the workgroup file and click OK. The Confirm Workgroup Information displays all the settings for the MDW file as shown in Figure 16-17. Be sure to keep a record of the information displayed on this form.

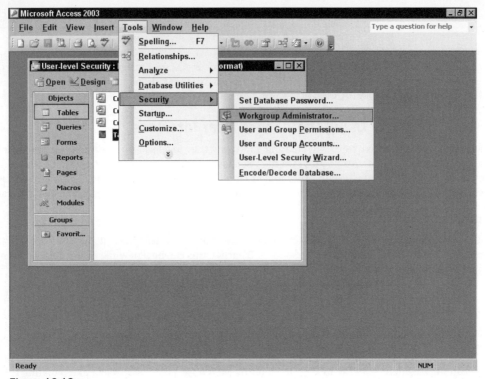

Figure 16-13

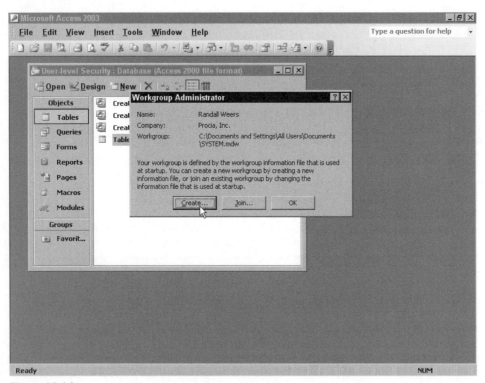

Figure 16-14

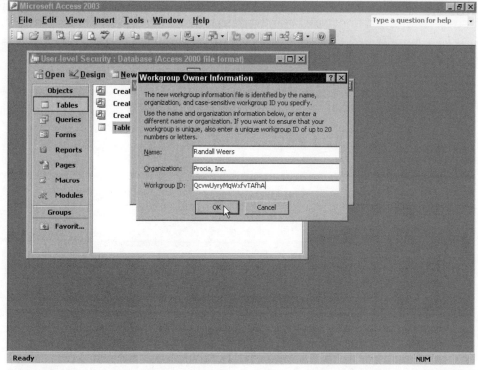

Figure 16-15

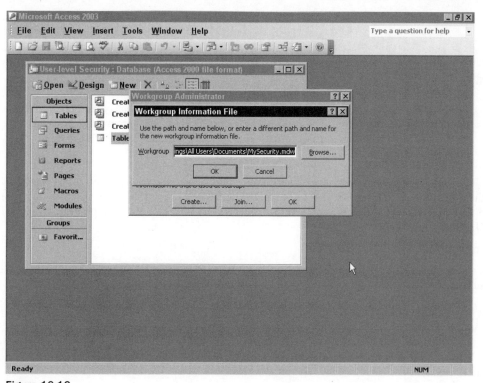

Figure 16-16

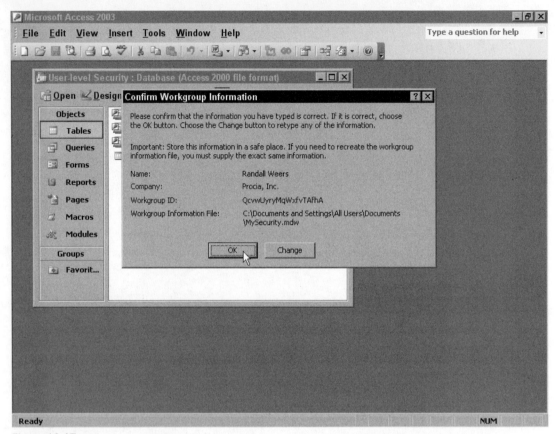

Figure 16-17

TIP: You may wish to print an image or otherwise document the information on this form in the event you need to manually recover the MDW file. Alt+PrtScn is a handy tool for capturing the window so that it can be pasted into Word and printed or saved. Then click OK to create the MDW file or Change to alter the information.

When you create an MDW file, you will automatically be joined to that file. The MDW file that you last joined is automatically selected the next time you use Access under the same Windows user profile on the computer. Others who need to use the same MDW file should use the Join option to join an existing MDW file.

Joining an MDW

Users will join an MDW file to get access to the correct set of pass codes for the database they will use. Refer to *The MDW file* previously discussed for more information about pass codes.

To join an existing MDW file, select Security | Workgroup Administrator... from the Tools menu. The Workgroup Administrator dialog box displays, as show in Figure 16-14. Then click the Join... button to display the Workgroup Information File dialog box, as shown in Figure 16-17. Enter the file name of the desired MDW file in the Workgroup text box or click Browse ... to select the file from the file system. Click OK to join that MDW file.

TIP: To have the MDW file automatically selected for a user when they start Access, add the /wrkgrp startup command-line option. To help your users, you may wish to create a shortcut that opens your database and applies this command-line option.

> **If the user has access to the** Workgroup Administrator **menu option, this startup parameter does not prevent them from selecting another MDW file. However, the file specified in the command line is sill used to authenticate a user.**

Updating the MDW File

By default, the MDW file contains one user (Admin) and two groups (Admins and Users). The Admin user is initially assigned to both groups. An MDW file must have at least one user that belongs to the Admins group. All users must belong to the Users group.

The first recommended action for an MDW file is to create a new user that you will use to administer the MDW file. Later you will remove the Admin user from the Admins group and change the ownership of the database to your new administrator. This is necessary because all MDW files have the Admin user and Admins group. If you do not make these changes, a default MDW file could be used to gain access to your database. (Learn more about this in the *Setting Permissions on Objects* section below.)

To create a new user as the administrator, select Tools | Security | User and Group Accounts... to display the User and Group Accounts dialog box as shown in Figure 16-18.

Then select the Users tab and click the New ... button to display the New User/Group dialog box as shown in Figure 16-19.

Enter the name for the user you will use as an administrator and a personal ID number. The personal ID must be 4 to 20 characters or digits in length. The same general rules as for specifying a password should be followed. You may wish to record the personal ID, especially for this new administrator user. This information is critical in the event that you need to recover the MDW file.

> *Tip: Later you will see how to use the User-level Security Wizard to set up user-level security. Since the wizard permits you to assign passwords and provides a random personal ID when you are setting up a new user, you may wish to wait until using the wizard to define the rest of the users.*

Click OK to save the user. In the User and Group Accounts dialog box, shown in Figure 16-20, be sure the user you created is selected in the Name field.

In the Group Membership section of the form, in the Available Groups list, select the Admins group and click Add>> to add the Admins group to the new user.

To remove the Admin user from the Admins group, select the Admin user in the Name field. In the Member Of list, select the Admins group and click <<Remove.

Activating the MDW File

The MDW file does not become active until the Admin user in that MDW file is assigned a password. Meaning, that until the Admin password is set, Access does not require any user using that MDW file to

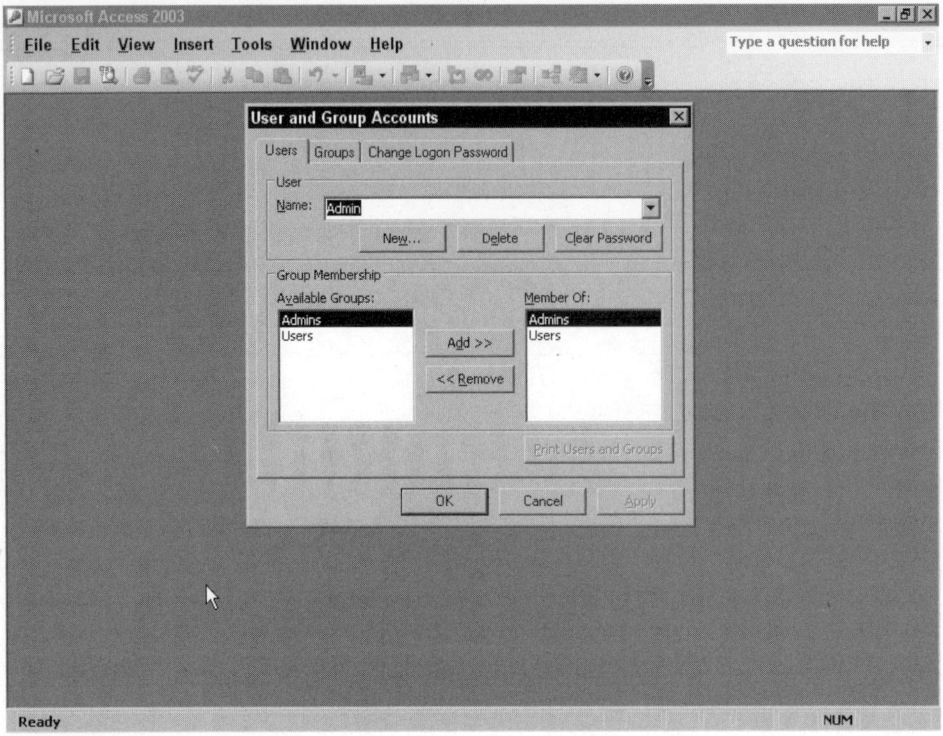

Figure 16-18

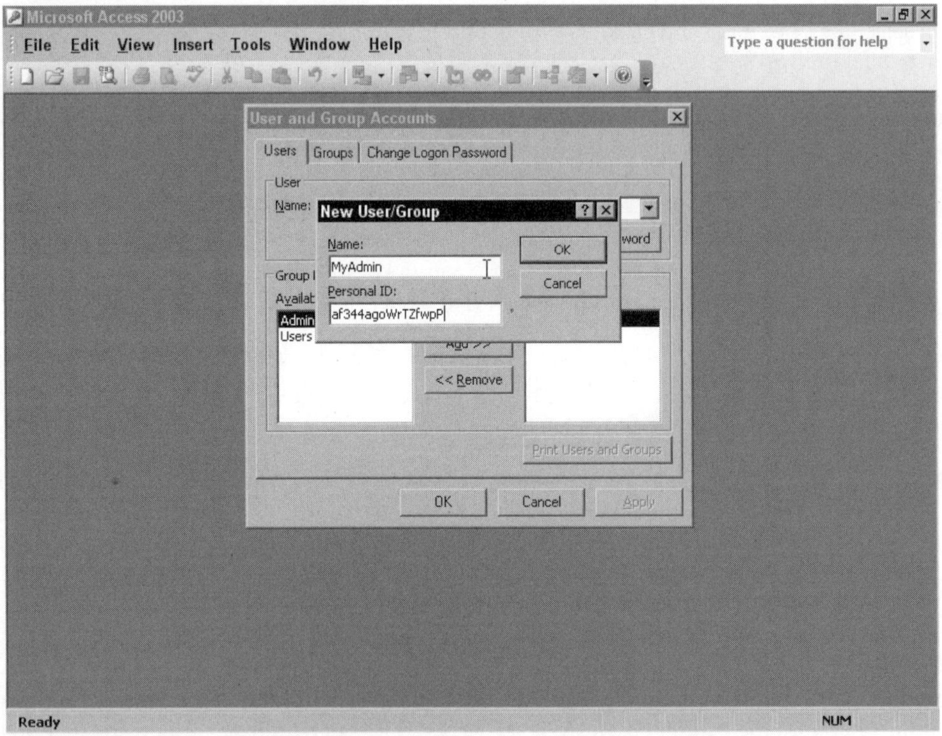

Figure 16-19

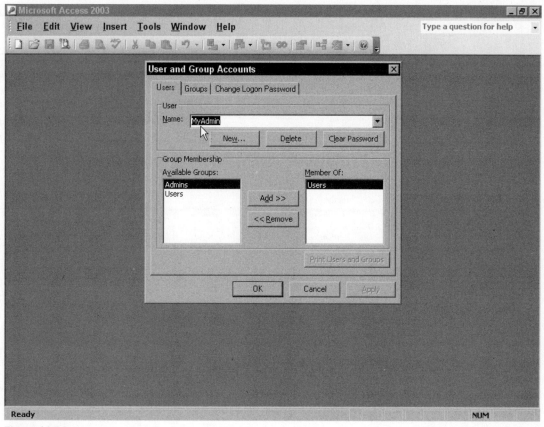

Figure 16-20

enter their username and password. A user using a different MDW file will not be impacted by whether or not your MDW file is activated.

After the MDW file is activated, the prompt to enter a username is not displayed until the first-time user has performed certain operations in Access. These operations include opening a database or attempting to change information in the MDW file. The log-on prompt occurs only once per session or if the user joins another (or rejoins the current) MDW file.

> *Note: You can inactivate the MDW file by removing the password from the Admin user. This may be useful if you find problems while testing your security setup. This is another good reason to make a note of the password and keep it in a secure place.*

To activate the MDW file, select the Change Log-on Password tab of the User and Group Accounts dialog box as shown in Figure 16-21. See previous section to learn how to display this dialog box.

Leave the Old Password field empty and enter a new password in the New Password field and the Verify field. Click Apply to apply the changes.

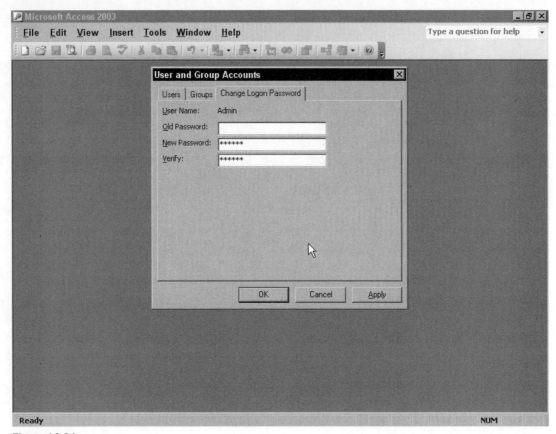

Figure 16-21

Since you effectively logged on as the Admin user when you created the MDW file, you must either close Access or rejoin the MDW file to have your new setting take effect. It is recommended that you activate the MDW file now and log on as the new administrator to be sure that you have a user that can perform further setup.

A shortcut to picking up the changed MDW file is to rejoin the MDW file. To do this, select Tools | Security | Workgroup Administrator. Click Join.... The MDW file that is currently in use will be displayed as the file name. Click OK to select that file. This logs the current user off. The next action that opens a database, including attempting to administrate the MDW file, will prompt for a username and password.

When you have logged on under the new administrator user, you may wish to give that user a password. Follow the same steps used to assign a password for the Admin user. Now you can define the user groups and users for the MDW file. Repeat the same steps you just used to define the new administrator user to define user groups and users.

> *To assign passwords to new users you must log on as that user or use Visual Basic and Jet to set passwords. Later you will see how to use the User-level Security Wizard to set up user-level security. Since the wizard*

permits you to assign passwords when you are setting up a new user, you may (yet again) wish to wait until using the wizard to define the rest of your users.

Setting Permissions on Objects

User-level security permissions are assigned to the database that needs security opened. As explained previously, permissions are granted to objects in the database for user groups or users. There is one caveat to this: the owner of the database or any object in the database *always* has full permissions.

This presents a bit of a problem. The first problem is that the user Admin owns a database if that database was created where the default MDW file was in use. Which means that database *can be* accessed through the Admin user of any MDW file, even after removing all permissions from the Admin user, even if the MDW file is not the one you use to set up user-level security.

The second problem is that the Access user interface only allows you to change ownership using the User-level Security Wizard. The upside to this is that the wizard also adjusts other permission settings very quickly. Since this is the case, the following leads you through the User-level Security Wizard.

> *Note: If you do not want to use the wizard to change database ownership, you can use your MDW file to log on to Access as the user you want to have ownership, and then create a new database and import all the objects.*

Using the User-Level Security Wizard

This wizard is a great way to start setting up security on a database. By using the wizard you will secure the database so that:

- ❑   Your new administrator user will own the database and each object in the database.
- ❑   Your new administrator user will have full access to the database.
- ❑   The Admins group will have full access to the database.
- ❑   The default Admin user will have no access to the database.
- ❑   The Users group will have no access to the database.
- ❑   The database itself is encoded (see the section *Encoding a Database*).

To start the User-level Security Wizard, select Tools | Security | User-level Security Wizard.... If you start the security with the database open exclusively, you are prompted to reopen the database in shared mode. With the database open in shared mode, the Security Wizard dialog box shown in Figure 16-22 displays.

If you have followed the steps above to create an MDW file, you should already be joined to your new MDW file. This will enable the option Modify my current workgroup information file. If that option is not enabled, cancel the wizard and join your MDW file as described above.

Select the option to modify your current workgroup information file and click Next>. This displays the objects contained in the database as shown in Figure 16-23.

The wizard sets permission for the objects that are selected, but only for the predefined groups provided by the wizard. It also sets ownership for the selected objects. On the next panel of the wizard, you can

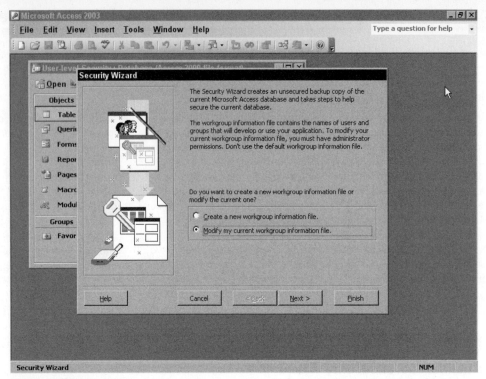

Figure 16-22

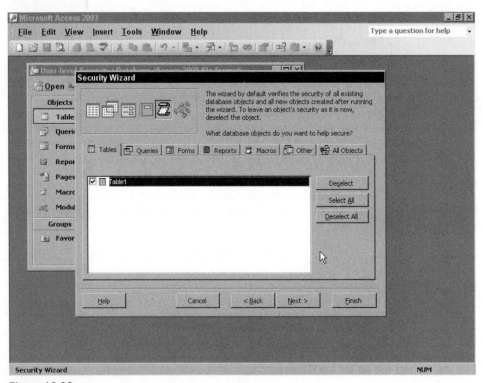

Figure 16-23

select groups to receive permissions on the selected object. Since this is the first time through the wizard, select all objects using the `All Objects` tab and the `Select All` button. Click `Next>` to see the `Groups` panel shown in Figure 16-24.

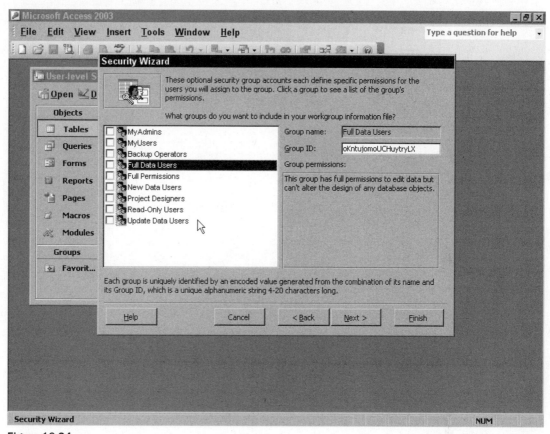

Figure 16-24

Since you have defined your own set of groups, they are displayed in the list. Also, the wizard provides a set of default groups to choose from. A description of the permissions that will be set is displayed at that right when you click `Group`. The advantage to using the default groups is that when they are selected, default permissions will be set up for the groups. A disadvantage is that any user signed in through Access (2003) will have the same default groups and permissions. You will notice the bright yellow caution notice posted by Access.

The wizard does not remove any groups from the MDW file. The wizard also doesn't know how to set up permissions for your groups. So you do not need to select your own groups. Click `Next>` to see the `All users` panel, as shown in Figure 16-25.

This panel permits you to adjust the permissions that will be set for the group `Users`. Recall that every user must belong to the `Users` group. Which means, anyone who logs on will receive the permissions assigned to the `Users` group. Therefore, it is strongly recommended that you select the `No, the Users group should not have any permissions` option to prevent unwanted access to your database.

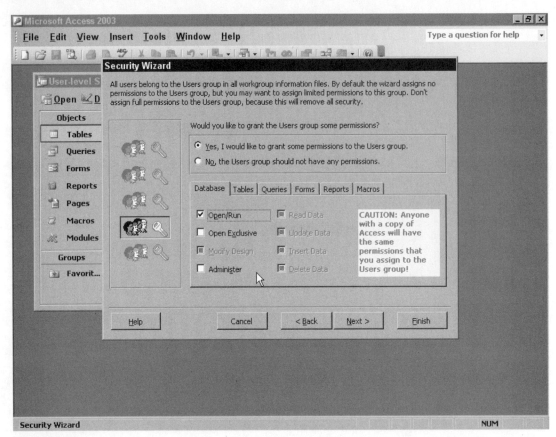

Figure 16-25

TIP: Since all users are members of the Users"group, you may wish to grant the Open/Run permission of the Database object to this group. If you do so, you will not have to remember to set it for any new groups you create. You do provide better security if you use the No, the Users group should not have any permissions. And, since there may be some objects that you do not want all users to have Open/Run permission, the only way to provide that flexibility is to select No, the Users group should not have any permissions at this point.

After selecting No option, click Next> to display the New users panel as shown in Figure 16-26.

On this panel you can create new users and assign them a password. If you created your users when you set up the MDW file, you can skip this. If you didn't create your users earlier, you can add them now. If you do add users, be sure to record the PID (personal ID) in case you need to recreate the MDW file later.

Tip: Sometimes it is effective to use the same PID for all users. Since the PID cannot be changed by the user, having a standard PID for the database can make it possible to recreate a MDW file if necessary.

Click Next> to display the User/group assignment panel as shown in Figure 16-27.

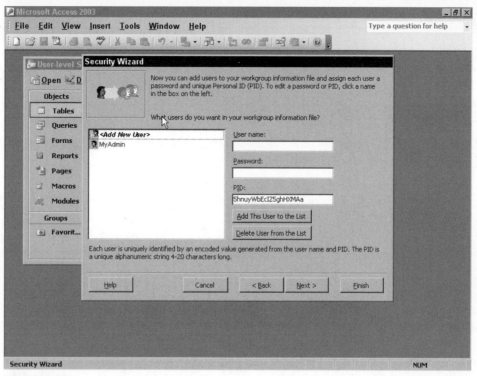

Figure 16-26

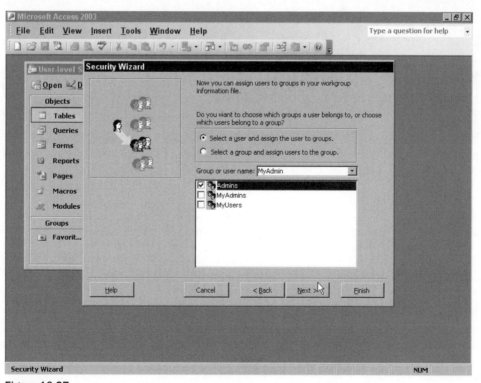

Figure 16-27

This panel permits you to assign groups to users or users to groups depending on which option is selected. If you created new users on the previous panel, be sure to assign them to the appropriate group or groups.

Click Next> to display the Backup file specification panel as shown in Figure 16-28.

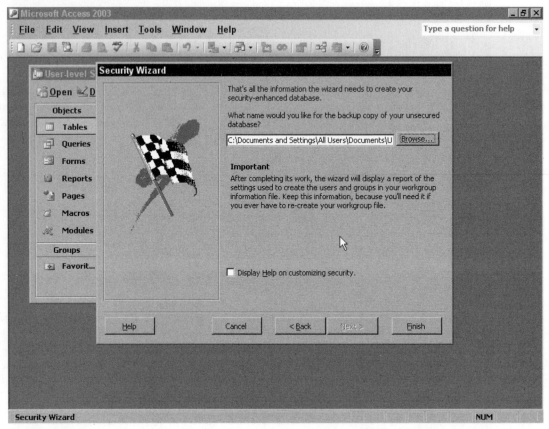

Figure 16-28

This panel asks you for the name of the file you want to use to store your unsecured database. This file will contain the database *without* the user-level security applied. You should keep this file until you have validated the security setup.

Click Finish to complete the User-level Security Wizard.

Adjusting Permissions

After you have used the User-level Security Wizard to establish some initial settings for security, you are likely to need to adjust those settings. The following describes how to adjust permissions for users and groups.

The steps described here can be accomplished through the wizard. They are presented to reinforce the reason for selecting the options described when using the wizard.

One of the first steps in setting up user-level security should be to remove all permissions from the group Users and from the user Admin. Recall that all users in an MDW file must belong to the Users group. Also recall that each user gets a set of pass codes from each group they belong to. Removing all security from the Users group ensures that no user will be granted permissions that you didn't intend to grant.

> Note: The database owner and the owner of an object in the database always have full permissions to the database or object no matter how other permissions are set.

If the database was created prior to using your new MDW file, you may have to log on as user Admin to set permissions using your new MDW file. This happens because the default owner of a database created under the default MDW file is Admin. If you have not yet given your new administrative user ownership of the database, it will not have permissions to administer the database.

By now, you should have joined the MDW file that contains the user groups and users for which you will set permissions. If the database has previously been secured using user-level security, be sure that you are logged on as a user that has administrative permissions for that database.

> Note: Since administrative permissions are granted by the database, not by the MDW file, a user that belongs to the Admins group of the MDW file may not be able to administer the database. The user will only be able to administer the database if the group the user belongs to or the user has been given administrative permissions or if the user is the database owner. Some permissions can only be set by the owner of the database.

To begin setting permissions, select Tools | Security | User and Group Permissions.... This displays the dialog box shown in Figure 16-29.

To remove the permissions for the user group Users, click the Groups option below the User/Group Name list. Highlight the group named Users. The form shows a list of all of the objects under the Object Name list for the type of the object selected in the Object type field. You can select multiple objects from the Object Name list using the *click-and-drag-over, Ctrl-click,* or *Shift-click* methods. To revoke all permissions from the selected objects, remove the check from the box for each permission.

> Tip: Removing the check from the Read Design permission removes all other permissions except the Open/Run permission.

When the desired permissions are set or unset, be sure to click Apply before selecting another Object type or User or Group. Continue to remove permissions from the user group Users by selecting each of the other object types: Database, Query, Form, Report, and Macro. Permissions do not change until a user has logged into the database after the updated settings have been saved.

> Note: In some instances, removing the permissions from <New Tables/Queries> does not prevent a user from creating a new table. You should verify these security settings for each user. (Using the User-level Security Wizard for the initial setup can prevent this problem.) If removing permissions using the user interface doesn't work, you can use Visual Basic to change permissions. This is described later.

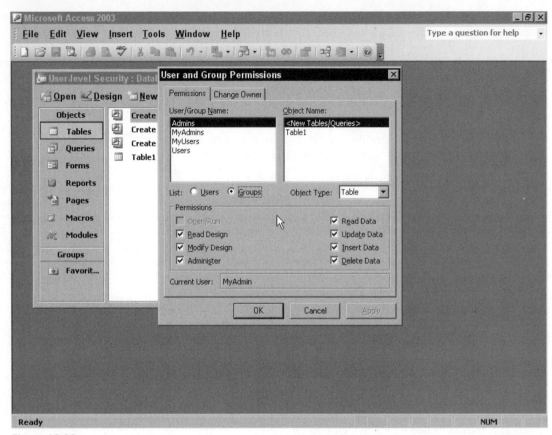

Figure 16-29

Additionally, removing permissions from <New Form>, <New Report>, and <New Macros> objects does not always prevent a user from attempting to create a new object. However, if the user does not have permission to open the database exclusively, they will not be able to save the object.

As noted earlier, the owner of the database and the owner of each object in the database *always* have administrative permissions. Permissions cannot be revoked from these owners even if the permission settings are changed. For this reason you should use the User-level Security Wizard to perform initial setup of security. The wizard changes ownership of all of the selected objects to the user that is logged on when the wizard is run.

To change the owner of objects other than the database itself, select the Change Owner tab of the User and Group Permission form as shown in Figure 16-30.

Select the objects for which you wish to set permissions using the *click-and-drag-over, Ctrl-click*, or *Shift-click* methods. You may choose to assign ownership to a user group or a user. Since any user who belongs to the Admins group probably needs full access no matter what permission are set, setting the owner to Admins is desirable. Select the Groups option from the New Owner drop-down list. Select the Admins group. Then click Change Owner. Like setting permissions, each object type can have a different user. Be sure to set the ownership for each object type.

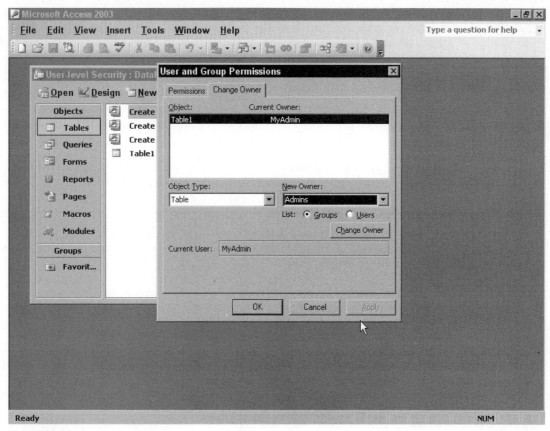

Figure 16-30

> New groups will not be granted any permissions. When you create a new group, be
> sure to grant *Open/Run* permission for the Database object type to that group, other-
> wise users that belong to that group and on other groups will not be able to open the
> database.

*TIP: Since all users are members of the Users group, you may wish to grant the Open/Run permission of
the Database object to this group. If you do so, you will not have to remember to set it for any new groups
you create. However, you should also remember that since Users is a default group created by Access, this
allows all users Open/Run permission of the Database object.*

Finishing Up User-Level Security

If you have followed the steps up to this point, the new administrative user you created in the MDW file
will be the only user with access to the database. And because you have used the User-level
Security Wizard, you have given ownership of the database and all objects to your new administrator
user. Therefore, you cannot accidentally remove permission from your administrator user.

Now you can begin to grant permissions for the objects in the database. In the *MDW File* section earlier, it was recommended that you grant permissions to user groups rather than to users. Recall that the reason for this is that a user's role may change. If that happens and you have granted permissions for that user, you will have to revoke them from each database where you have individually granted them permissions.

Encoding a User-Level Secured Database

Securing a database with user-level security does not prevent anyone from exploring the database using a tool other than Access. For instance, Windows Notepad could be used to look at the data contained in the database.

As with shared-level security, if your data needs to be more secure, you should encode the database. Fortunately, if you use the `User-level Security Wizard`, the database is encoded.

Linking to a User-Level Secured Database

Unlike shared-level security, linking to tables in a user-level secured database will not store security information. In fact, you must be joined to the MDW file associated with the database you are linking to before opening a database that links to it.

Recall that the username and password prompt only appear once per Access session. This happens when you take certain actions such as opening a database or attempting to maintain security. This establishes your identity to the MDW file you are joined to at that time.

If you use the wrong MDW file when you identify yourself to Access, you may not be prompted for a username and password. If you are not prompted, the `Admin` user password has not been set to activate the MDW file, so you become the `Admin` user by default. If you are prompted, the identity you establish will not be the same. Recall that your identity gets you access to a set of pass codes. These pass codes are a combination of the MDW file authentication information plus the username and PID or the MDW file authentication information plus the group name and GID. With the wrong pass codes, you will not be able to get the permissions the remote database has granted you.

User-Level Security Using DAO

User-level security can be maintained using VBA and DAO. This section demonstrates sample procedures for setting user-level security using DAO.

`Users` and `Groups` are collections of the Database Engine Workspace. The procedures defined here work with users and groups on the `open a workspace` in the current database engine. Therefore you must be joined to the correct MDW file to use these procedures.

Additionally, these sample procedures set permissions in the database that is open (`CurrentDB`). The sample ADO procedures, discussed later in this chapter, do not expect the database to be open.

The `DAO.PermissionsEnum` enumeration defines the appropriate numeric values for setting a permission. The `ShowSampleDAO` procedure, discussed later in this section, demonstrates how to use this enumeration.

The following declarations are used in the procedures that show how to use DAO to set up user-level security.

```
Const cAdminUser = "MyAdmin"
Const cAdminPW = ""
```

Maintaining Groups with DAO

The `AddGroupDAO` procedure adds groups to the MDW file. The `DropGroupDAO` procedure drops groups from the MDW file.

To add a group, the procedure creates an object of type `Group` and sets the properties for it. It then appends the group to the `Groups` collection of the `Workspace`.

```
Public Sub AddGroupDAO(pGroupName As String, pGID As String)
On Error Resume Next
Dim ws As Workspace
Dim grp As Group
' connect to the engine with a workspace
Set ws = DBEngine.CreateWorkspace("DAOWS", cAdminUser, cAdminPW)
' create a new group object
Set grp = New Group
' set the objects properties
grp.Name = pGroupName
grp.PID = pGID
' append the group to the collection of groups
ws.Groups.Append grp
If Err.Number = 0 Then
    Debug.Print pGroupName & " added"
Else
    Debug.Print Err.Number, Err.Description
    Stop
End If
ws.Close
Set ws = Nothing
End Sub
```

To drop a group, the procedure simply deletes it from the `Groups` collection of the `Workspace`.

```
Public Sub DropGroupDAO(pGroupName As String)
On Error Resume Next
Dim ws As Workspace
' connect to the engine with a workspace
Set ws = DBEngine.CreateWorkspace("DAOWS", cAdminUser, cAdminPW)
' delete the group from the collection of groups
ws.Groups.Delete (pGroupName)
If Err.Number = 0 Then
    Debug.Print pGroupName & " deleted"
Else
    Debug.Print Err.Number, Err.Description
    Stop
End If
ws.Close
Set ws = Nothing
End Sub
```

Maintaining Users with DAO

The `AddUserDAO` procedure adds users to the MDW file. The `DropUserDAO` procedure drops users from the MDW file. Notice that the `AddUserDAO` procedure also calls the `AddUserToGroupDAO` procedure. This is to keep the data in the MDW file consistent with the Access rule that all users must belong to the `Users` group.

To add a user, create an object of type `User` and set the properties for it. Then append the user to the `Users` collection of the `Workspace`.

```
Public Sub AddUserDAO(pUserName As String, _
    pPassword As String, pPID As String)
On Error Resume Next
Dim ws As Workspace
Dim usr As User
' connect to the engine with a workspace
Set ws = DBEngine.CreateWorkspace("DAOWS", cAdminUser, cAdminPW)
' create a user object
Set usr = New User
' assign the properties to the user
usr.Name = pUserName
usr.Password = pPassword
usr.PID = pPID
' append the user object to the collection of users
ws.Users.Append usr
If Err.Number = 0 Then
    Debug.Print pUserName & " added"
    Call AddUserToGroupDAO(pUserName, "Users")
Else
    Debug.Print Err.Number, Err.Description
    Stop
End If
ws.Close
Set ws = Nothing
Set usr = Nothing
End Sub
```

To drop a user, simply delete it from the `Users` collection of the `Workspace`.

```
Public Sub DropUserDAO(pUserName As String)
On Error Resume Next
Dim ws As Workspace
' connect to the engine with a workspace
Set ws = DBEngine.CreateWorkspace("DAOWS", cAdminUser, cAdminPW)
' delete the user from the set of users
ws.Users.Delete (pUserName)
If Err.Number = 0 Then
    Debug.Print pUserName & " deleted"
Else
    Debug.Print Err.Number, Err.Description
    Stop
End If
ws.Close
Set ws = Nothing
End Sub
```

The procedure that adds a user to a group first establishes a connection with the user that has already been added to the Users collection of the Workspace. Then it creates a group object to contain the group and appends it to the Groups collection for the user.

```
Public Sub AddUserToGroupDAO(pUserName As String, pGroupName As String)
On Error Resume Next
Dim ws As Workspace
Dim grp As Group
Dim usr As New User
' connect to the engine with a workspace
Set ws = DBEngine.CreateWorkspace("DAOWS", cAdminUser, cAdminPW)
' point to the user
Set usr = ws.Users(pUserName)
' create a connection to the group
Set grp = usr.CreateGroup(pGroupName)
' append the group connection back to the groups collection
usr.Groups.Append grp
If Err.Number = 0 Then
    Debug.Print pUserName & " added to " & pGroupName
Else
    Debug.Print Err.Number, Err.Description
        Stop
End If
Set usr = Nothing
Set grp = Nothing
ws.Close
Set ws = Nothing
End Sub
```

To drop a user from a group, delete it from Users collection of the group.

```
Public Sub DropUserFromGroupDAO(pUserName As String, pGroupName As String)
On Error Resume Next
Dim ws As Workspace
Dim usr As User
' connect to the engine with a workspace
Set ws = DBEngine.CreateWorkspace("DAOWS", cAdminUser, cAdminPW)
' delete the user from the groups collection
ws.Groups(pGroupName).Users.Delete pUserName
If Err.Number = 0 Then
    Debug.Print pUserName & " removed from " & pGroupName
Else
    Debug.Print Err.Number, Err.Description
    Stop
End If
ws.Close
Set ws = Nothing
End Sub
```

Maintaining Permissions with DAO

With your understanding of the detachment between the MDW file and the file that is being secured (see the first section under *User-Level Security*) you recognize that unlike users and groups that are maintained through the DB Engine Workspace, permissions are set against the current database.

The following procedures demonstrate setting permissions for `Containers` (`SetPermissionsOnContainerDAO`) and `Objects` (`SetPermissionsOnObjectDAO`).

Setting permissions for `Containers` (`Tables`, `Queries`, `Forms`, `Macros`) sets the permissions for the `New` object, for example, `<New Table/Query>`.

```
Public Sub SetPermissionsOnContainerDAO(pContainer As String, _
        pName As String, _
        pPermissions As Long)
On Error Resume Next
Dim db As Database
Dim con As Container
' connect to the current database
Set db = CurrentDb()
' point to the container
Set con = db.Containers(pContainer)
' point to the user within the container
con.UserName = pName
If Err.Number <> 0 Then
    Debug.Print Err.Number, Err.Description
    Stop
End If
' set the user's permissions for the container
con.Permissions = pPermissions
If Err.Number = 0 Then
    Debug.Print "Permissions set for " & pName
Else
    Debug.Print Err.Number, Err.Description
End If
Set con = Nothing
db.Close
Set db = Nothing
End Sub
```

Setting permissions on objects sets them for one object. Notice that SetPermissionsOnObjectDAO requires that you specify the container of the object. This is because a form and a table, for instance, could have the same name.

```
Public Sub SetPermissionsOnObjectDAO(pContainer As String, _
        pDocument As String, _
        pName As String, _
        pPermissions As Long)
On Error Resume Next
Dim db As Database
Dim doc As Document
' connect to the current database
Set db = CurrentDb()
' point to the document within the correct container
Set doc = db.Containers(pContainer).Documents(pDocument)
If Err.Number <> 0 Then
    Debug.Print Err.Number, Err.Description
    Stop
End If
```

```
' point to the user name of that document
doc.UserName = pName
If Err.Number <> 0 Then
    Debug.Print Err.Number, Err.Description
    Stop
End If
' set the permissions for that user
doc.Permissions = pPermissions
If Err.Number = 0 Then
    Debug.Print "Permissions set for " & pName
Else
    Debug.Print Err.Number, Err.Description
End If
Set doc = Nothing
db.Close
Set db = Nothing
End Sub
```

This text does not include sample procedures for revoking permissions using DAO. Samples are included for ADO. In these DAO examples, permissions are set by determining which will be granted and by using AND operation on those values. However, you could write procedures to revoke permissions. The following code snippet shows you a method that could be used to set up a procedure to revoke specific permissions. (This code has not been tested.)

```
Public Sub RevokePermissionsFromObjectDAO(pContainer As String, _
        pDocument As String, _
        pName As String, _
        pPermissions As Long)
...
' revoke the permissions for that user
doc.Permissions = doc.Permissions and Not pPermissions
...
End Sub
```

The ChangeOwnerDAO procedure is included with the permissions section because owners always have full permissions. Notice that you can only change ownership on documents (that is, Tables, Forms, Reports, Pages, and Macros), not on the database or the containers.

```
Function ChangeOwnerDAO(pContainer As String, _
        pDocumentName As String, _
        pOwner As String, _
        pPassword As String)
Dim db As Database
Dim con As Container
Dim doc As Document
' connect to the current database
Set db = CurrentDb()
' access the desired container
Set con = db.Containers(pContainer)
' access the correct document
Set doc = con.Documents(pDocumentName)
' change the owner of that document
doc.Owner = pOwner
```

```
If Err.Number = 0 Then
    Debug.Print "Owner changed to " _
        & pOwner & " on " & pDocumentName & " in " & pContainer
Else
    Debug.Print Err.Number, Err.Description
End If
Set doc = Nothing
Set con = Nothing
db.Close
Set db = Nothing
End Function
```

Sample Setup Using DAO

The following sample shows various calls to the above DAO procedures.

```
Public Sub ShowSamplesDAO()
Debug.Print "Start sample...."
' start with a drop - this will error
' since "Fred Derf" isn't defined yet
Call DropUserDAO("Fred derf")
' add the user with no password and PID=1234
Call AddUserDAO("Fred Derf", "", "1234")
' set the permissions on the container
' this sets the permissions for things like <New Table/Query>
' use the Permissions Enum from DAO
' for multiple permissions, use "AND" between each
Call SetPermissionsOnContainerDAO("Tables", "Fred Derf", _
    DAO.PermissionEnum.dbSecReadDef And _
    DAO.PermissionEnum.dbSecRetrieveData)

' set permissions on a specific object
' in this case the object type is a Table and its name is "Table2"
Call SetPermissionsOnObjectDAO("Tables", "Table2", "Fred Derf", _
    dbSecFullAccess)
' add a groupd
Call DropGroupDAO("mygroup1")
Call AddGroupDAO("MyGroup1", "sdfxefhr3wqerf")
' add a user to the group
' notice that user names are not case sensitive
Call AddUserToGroupDAO("fred derf", "MyGroup1")
Call DropUserFromGroupDAO("Fred Derf", "MyGroup1")
' add another user and give him ownership over "Table2"
Call DropUserDAO("Mike Ekim")
' give Mike a password, NOTE: passwords are case sensitive
Call AddUserDAO("Mike Ekim", "mike", "2342355")
Call ChangeOwnerDAO("Tables", "Table2", "Mike Ekim", "")
Debug.Print "End samples"
End Sub
```

The ListUsersDAO procedure prints a list of the users and the groups they belong to and a list of groups and the users that belong to them. This procedure can be useful when you need to validate your users and groups setup.

```
Public Sub ListUsersDAO()
On Error Resume Next
Dim ws As Workspace
Dim usr As User
Dim grp As Group
' connect to the engine with a workspace
Set ws = DBEngine.CreateWorkspace("DAOWS", cAdminUser, cAdminPW)
Debug.Print "---- Users and their groups ---"
For Each usr In ws.Users
    Debug.Print usr.Name
    For Each grp In usr.Groups
        Debug.Print , grp.Name
    Next grp
Next usr
Debug.Print "---- Groups and their users ---"
For Each grp In ws.Groups
    Debug.Print grp.Name
    For Each usr In grp.Users
        Debug.Print , usr.Name
    Next usr
Next grp
ws.Close
Set ws = Nothing
End Sub
```

User-Level Security Using ADO

The Microsoft Jet Engine and ADO can be used to set up groups and users and permissions for user-level security.

Groups and users are set up using the SQL statements CREATE, ALTER, and DROP. As suggested by their names, these statements permit creating, altering (or modifying), and dropping (or deleting) user groups and users. The GROUP and USER keywords are used to indicate whether the action is for a user group or a user. The ADD and DROP statements are used to add users to a group or remove them from a group.

Permissions are set up using the GRANT and REVOKE statements. As suggested by the names, these statements are used to grant permissions to or remove permissions from an object for a user group or user. The SELECT, INSERT, UPDATE, and DELETE keywords are used to indicate which permissions are granted or revoked. (The table later in this chapter lists the meaning of these keywords and additional keyword options.)

These routines have some basic error trapping. You will of course want to improve the traps to suit your needs. The examples also include several Debug.Print statements to show the SQL statements to be executed for each operation. The following declarations are used in the procedures that show how to use ADO to set up user-level security:

```
Const cProvider = "Microsoft.Jet.OLEDB.4.0"
Const cDBName = "C:\MyDatabase.mdb"
Const cMDWfile = "C:\MySystem.mdw"
Const cAdminUser = "MyAdmin"
Const cAdminPW = ""
```

```
Enum eObjectTypes
    Database = 1
    Container = 2
    Table = 3
    Other = 4
End Enum
```

All procedures establish a connection to the database using the ADODB.Connection object. The provider for the connection is Microsoft.Jet.OLEDB.4.0. Indicate the MDW file by setting a value for the connection property `Properties(Jet OLEDB:System database)`. Open the connection using the `Data Source=` your database. You only need to specify the database that will be secured when you set permissions using the GRANT and REVOKE options. Otherwise the data source can be any database. Be sure to include the User ID and Password parameters for the Open method.

The Execute method executes the SQL statement. After the SQL statement has executed, the connection is closed and the object destroyed.

Note: The SQL statements in these examples cannot be executed from an Access Query.

Maintaining Groups with ADO

The first two procedures demonstrate techniques for adding a group (`AddGroupADO`) and dropping a group (`DropGroupADO`).

Notice that when a group is added, you can specify the Group ID. A group must be added before a user can be added to the group. If you wish to add a group name that contains an embedded space, enclose the name within square brackets ([]). You may wish to change the code to always add the brackets.

```
Sub AddGroupADO(pGroupName As String, pGID As String)
On Error Resume Next
Dim cnn As ADODB.Connection
Dim strCommand As String
' Open a connection to the database
Set cnn = New ADODB.Connection
With cnn
    .Provider = cProvider
    .Properties("Jet OLEDB:System database") = cMDWfile
    .Open "Data Source=" & cDBName _
        & ";User ID=" & cAdminUser _
        & ";Password=" & cAdminPW
    If Err.Number <> 0 Then Debug.Print Err.Number, Err.Description

    ' build the command to create the Group
    strCommand = "CREATE GROUP " & pGroupName & " " & pGID & ";"
    Debug.Print strCommand
    ' execute the command to create the Group
    .Execute strCommand
    If Err.Number = 0 Then
        ' nop
    ElseIf Err.Number = -2147467259 Then
        Debug.Print "Group name already exists."
```

```
        Else
            Debug.Print Err.Number, Err.Description
        End If
    End With

    cnn.Close
    Set cnn = Nothing
End Sub
```

When a group is dropped, users are dropped from the group but are not dropped from the security database.

```
Sub DropGroupADO(pGroupName As String)
On Error Resume Next
Dim cnn As ADODB.Connection
Dim strCommand As String
' Open a connection to the database
Set cnn = New ADODB.Connection
With cnn
    .Provider = cProvider
    .Properties("Jet OLEDB:System database") = cMDWfile
    .Open "Data Source=" & cDBName _
        & ";User ID=" & cAdminUser _
        & ";Password=" & cAdminPW
    If Err.Number <> 0 Then Debug.Print Err.Number, Err.Description

    ' build the command to create the Group
    strCommand = "DROP GROUP " & pGroupName & ";"
    Debug.Print strCommand
    ' execute the command to create the Group
    .Execute strCommand
    If Err.Number = 0 Then
        ' nop
    ElseIf Err.Number = -2147467259 Then
        Debug.Print "Group name does not exist."
    Else
        Debug.Print Err.Number, Err.Description
    End If
End With

cnn.Close
Set cnn = Nothing
End Sub
```

Maintaining Users and User Passwords with ADO

The next three procedures demonstrate techniques for adding a user (AddUserADO), dropping a user (DropUserADO), and setting a user password (AlterUserPasswordADO).

Notice that when a user is added, you can specify the personal ID. Also notice that the AddUserADO procedure automatically adds the user to the group Users with a call to AddUserToGroup. This is done to keep the MDW file consistent with the Access rule that requires that all users belong to the Users group.

> If you wish to add a username that contains an embedded space, enclose the name within square brackets ([]). You may wish to change the code to always add the brackets.

```
Sub AddUserADO(pUserName As String, pPID As String, pPassword As String)
On Error Resume Next
Dim cnn As ADODB.Connection
Dim strCommand As String
' Open a connection to the database
Set cnn = New ADODB.Connection
With cnn
    .Provider = cProvider
    .Properties("Jet OLEDB:System database") = cMDWfile
    .Open "Data Source=" & cDBName _
        & ";User ID=" & cAdminUser _
        & ";Password=" & cAdminPW
    If Err.Number <> 0 Then Debug.Print Err.Number, Err.Description

    ' build the command to create the user
    strCommand = "CREATE USER " & pUserName _
            & " [" & pPassword & "] " & pPID & ";"
    Debug.Print strCommand
    ' execute the command to create the user
    .Execute strCommand
    If Err.Number = 0 Then

        ' MS Access prefers to have all users assigned to the "Users"
        ' group. Since using SQL to add the user doesn't add the user
        ' to the group "Users", add this user to the group
        Call AddUserToGroupADO(pUserName, "Users")
    ElseIf Err.Number = -2147467259 Then
        Debug.Print "Account name already exists."
    Else
        Debug.Print Err.Number, Err.Description
    End If
End With

cnn.Close
Set cnn = Nothing
End Sub
```

Dropping a user from a group removes only that user without impacting the group or permission settings for the group that user belonged to.

```
Sub DropUserADO(pUserName As String)
On Error Resume Next
Dim cnn As ADODB.Connection
Dim strCommand As String
' Open a connection to the database
Set cnn = New ADODB.Connection
With cnn
```

```
            .Provider = cProvider
            .Properties("Jet OLEDB:System database") = cMDWfile
            .Open "Data Source=" & cDBName _
                & ";User ID=" & cAdminUser _
                & ";Password=" & cAdminPW
            If Err.Number <> 0 Then Debug.Print Err.Number, Err.Description

            ' build the command to create the user
            strCommand = "DROP USER " & pUserName & ";"
            Debug.Print strCommand
            ' execute the command to create the user
            .Execute strCommand
            If Err.Number = 0 Then
                ' nop
            ElseIf Err.Number = -2147467259 Then
                Debug.Print "Account name does not exist."
            Else
                Debug.Print Err.Number, Err.Description
            End If
        End With

        cnn.Close
        Set cnn = Nothing
        End Sub
```

The `AlterUserPasswordADO` procedure and the ALTER USER PASSWORD SQL statement seem to suggest that you need to know the password to alter a user password. However, if the password is not known, you can specify a null password. To do this, use empty square brackets ("[]") or the SQL reserved word NULL for the password.

> You can also use empty square brackets or NULL to set the new password to nothing (that is, to clear the password).

```
Sub AlterUserPasswordADO(pUserName As String, _
                    pPassword As String, _
                    pOldPassword As String)
On Error Resume Next
Dim cnn As ADODB.Connection
Dim strCommand As String
' Open a connection to the database
Set cnn = New ADODB.Connection
With cnn
    .Provider = cProvider
    .Properties("Jet OLEDB:System database") = cMDWfile
    .Open "Data Source=" & cDBName _
        & ";User ID=" & cAdminUser _
        & ";Password=" & cAdminPW
    If Err.Number <> 0 Then Debug.Print Err.Number, Err.Description

    ' To specify and empty password, you can use either the NULL keyword
```

```
        ' or empty square brackets "[]" as parameters to this routine
        ' Alternatively, you could make this function like AddUserADO by
        ' surrounding each password with square brackets.
        '    e.g. " [" & pPassword & "] ".
        ' This will permit using the null string ("") to set the password.
        strCommand = "ALTER USER " & pUserName _
                & " PASSWORD " & pPassword & " " & pOldPassword & ";"
        Debug.Print strCommand
        ' execute the command to create the user
        .Execute strCommand
        If Err.Number = 0 Then
            ' nop
        Else
            Debug.Print Err.Number, Err.Description
        End If
    End With

    cnn.Close
    Set cnn = Nothing
End Sub
```

Maintaining Users and Groups with ADO

The next two procedures demonstrate how to add users to a group (AddUserToGroupADO) and drop users from a group (DropUserFromGroupADO).

> If a group name or a username has embedded spaces, enclose the name within square brackets ([]). You may wish to change the code to always add the brackets.

```
Sub AddUserToGroupADO(pUserName As String, pGroupName As String)
On Error Resume Next
Dim cnn As ADODB.Connection
Dim strCommand As String
' Open a connection to the database
Set cnn = New ADODB.Connection
With cnn
    .Provider = cProvider
    .Properties("Jet OLEDB:System database") = cMDWfile
    .Open "Data Source=" & cDBName _
        & ";User ID=" & cAdminUser _
        & ";Password=" & cAdminPW
    If Err.Number <> 0 Then Debug.Print Err.Number, Err.Description

    ' build the command to create the user
    strCommand = "ADD USER " & pUserName & " TO " & pGroupName & ";"
    Debug.Print strCommand
    ' execute the command to create the user
    .Execute strCommand
    If Err.Number = 0 Then
        ' nop
```

```
        Else
            Debug.Print Err.Number, Err.Description
        End If
    End With

    cnn.Close
    Set cnn = Nothing
    End Sub
```

Dropping a user from a group does not remove the user. The user can be assigned to another group, or you can drop the user using the DropUserADO procedure.

```
Sub DropUserFromGroupADO(pUserName As String, pGroupName As String)
On Error Resume Next
Dim cnn As ADODB.Connection
Dim strCommand As String
' Open a connection to the database
Set cnn = New ADODB.Connection
With cnn
    .Provider = cProvider
    .Properties("Jet OLEDB:System database") = cMDWfile
    .Open "Data Source=" & cDBName _
        & ";User ID=" & cAdminUser _
        & ";Password=" & cAdminPW
    If Err.Number <> 0 Then Debug.Print Err.Number, Err.Description

    ' build the command to create the user
    strCommand = "DROP USER " & pUserName & " FROM " & pGroupName & ";"
    Debug.Print strCommand
    ' execute the command to create the user
    .Execute strCommand
    If Err.Number = 0 Then
        ' nop
    Else
        Debug.Print Err.Number, Err.Description
    End If
End With

cnn.Close
Set cnn = Nothing
End Sub
```

Maintaining Database Permissions with ADO

The next four procedures demonstrate techniques for granting permissions to users or groups (GrantPermissionsOnTableADO and GrantPermissionsToObjectADO) and revoking permissions from users or groups (RevokePermissionsFromTableADO and RevokePermissionsFromObjectADO).

Permissions can be granted to either user groups or individual users. (The name of the parameter pUserName is not meant to imply that it must be a user.) This is fortunate, since the ideal setup is to grant permissions to groups and then add users to groups so they can have the permissions they need.

Unlike the procedures that update the user group and user information, the correct database must be specified in the Data Source to grant permissions to the correct objects. (The discussion about the MDW file explains the *detachment* between the MDW file and the database being secured.)

For these procedures, the pPermissions parameter can be one privilege (see the table later in this chapter) or many privileges separated by commas. If the username has embedded spaces, enclose the name within square brackets ([]). You may wish to change the code to always add the brackets.

While not generally recommended, using PUBLIC for the group/username (pUserName) will set permissions for the default users group account so that everyone will get the assigned privileges. The best use for this would be to grant CONNECT permission to the database since this will permit all users access to the database but not necessarily to all objects in the database.

```
Sub GrantPermissionsOnTableADO(pUserName As String, _
                pTableName As String, pPermissions As String)
On Error Resume Next
Dim cnn As ADODB.Connection
Dim strCommand As String
' Open a connection to the database
Set cnn = New ADODB.Connection
With cnn
    .Provider = cProvider
    .Properties("Jet OLEDB:System database") = cMDWfile
    .Open "Data Source=" & cDBName _
        & ";User ID=" & cAdminUser _
        & ";Password=" & cAdminPW
    If Err.Number <> 0 Then Debug.Print Err.Number, Err.Description

    ' build the command to create the user
    strCommand = "GRANT " & pPermissions _
            & " ON TABLE " & pTableName _
            & " TO " & pUserName & ";"
    Debug.Print strCommand
    ' execute the command to create the user
    .Execute strCommand
    If Err.Number = 0 Then
        ' nop
    Else
        Debug.Print Err.Number, Err.Description
    End If
End With

cnn.Close
Set cnn = Nothing
End Sub
```

Permissions are revoked from the user or the group depending on the value of pUserName, if revoking permissions from a user does not affect the permissions of the group to which that user belongs.

```
Sub RevokePermissionsFromTableADO(pUserName As String, _
                pTableName As String, pPermissions As String)
On Error Resume Next
```

```
Dim cnn As ADODB.Connection
Dim strCommand As String
' Open a connection to the database
Set cnn = New ADODB.Connection
With cnn
    .Provider = cProvider
    .Properties("Jet OLEDB:System database") = cMDWfile
    .Open "Data Source=" & cDBName _
        & ";User ID=" & cAdminUser _
        & ";Password=" & cAdminPW
    If Err.Number <> 0 Then Debug.Print Err.Number, Err.Description

    ' build the command to create the user
    strCommand = "REVOKE " & pPermissions _
            & " ON TABLE " & pTableName _
            & " FROM " & pUserName & ";"
    Debug.Print strCommand
    ' execute the command to create the user
    .Execute strCommand
    If Err.Number = 0 Then
        ' nop
    Else
        Debug.Print Err.Number, Err.Description
    End If
End With

cnn.Close
Set cnn = Nothing
End Sub
```

GrantPermissionsToObjectADO is a more generic form of the GrantPermissionsToTableADO
procedure. This procedure is used for object types other than tables and can easily replace the
table-specific procedure.

```
Sub GrantPermissionsToObjectADO(pUserName As String, _
        pObjType As eObjectTypes, _
        pObjectName As String, _
        pPermissions As String)
On Error Resume Next
Dim cnn As ADODB.Connection
Dim strCommand As String
' Open a connection to the database
Set cnn = New ADODB.Connection
With cnn
    .Provider = cProvider
    .Properties("Jet OLEDB:System database") = cMDWfile
    .Open "Data Source=" & cDBName _
        & ";User ID=" & cAdminUser _
        & ";Password=" & cAdminPW
    If Err.Number <> 0 Then Debug.Print Err.Number, Err.Description

    ' build the command to create the user
    strCommand = "GRANT " & pPermissions & " ON "
    Select Case pObjType
```

```
            Case eObjectTypes.Database:
                strCommand = strCommand
            Case eObjectTypes.Container:
                strCommand = strCommand & "CONTAINER"
            Case eObjectTypes.Table:
                strCommand = strCommand & "TABLE"
            Case eObjectTypes.Other:
                strCommand = strCommand & "OBJECT"
            Case Else
                Debug.Print "Object type incorrect"
        End Select
        strCommand = strCommand & " " _
                & pObjectName _
                & " TO " & pUserName & ";"
        Debug.Print strCommand
        ' execute the command to create the user
        .Execute strCommand
        If Err.Number = 0 Then
            ' nop
        Else
            Debug.Print Err.Number, Err.Description
        End If
    End With

    cnn.Close
    Set cnn = Nothing
End Sub
```

RevokePermissionsFromObjectADO is a more generic form of the
RevokePermissionsFromTableADO procedure. This procedure is used for object types other than
tables, and can easily replace the table-specific procedure.

```
Sub RevokePermissionsFromObjectADO(pUserName As String,
            pObjType As eObjectTypes, _
            pObjectName As String, _
            pPermissions As String)
On Error Resume Next
Dim cnn As ADODB.Connection
Dim strCommand As String
' Open a connection to the database
Set cnn = New ADODB.Connection
With cnn
    .Provider = cProvider
    .Properties("Jet OLEDB:System database") = cMDWfile
    .Open "Data Source=" & cDBName _
        & ";User ID=" & cAdminUser _
        & ";Password=" & cAdminPW
    If Err.Number <> 0 Then Debug.Print Err.Number, Err.Description

    ' build the command to create the user
    strCommand = "REVOKE " & pPermissions & " ON "
    Select Case pObjType
        Case eObjectTypes.Database:
            strCommand = strCommand
```

```
            Case eObjectTypes.Container:
                strCommand = strCommand & "CONTAINER"
            Case eObjectTypes.Table:
                strCommand = strCommand & "TABLE"
            Case eObjectTypes.Other:
                strCommand = strCommand & "OBJECT"
            Case Else
                Debug.Print "Object type incorrect"
        End Select
        strCommand = strCommand & " " _
                    & pObjectName _
                    & " FROM " & pUserName & ";"
        Debug.Print strCommand
        ' execute the command to create the user
        .Execute strCommand
        If Err.Number = 0 Then
            ' nop
        Else
            Debug.Print Err.Number, Err.Description
        End If
    End With

    cnn.Close
    Set cnn = Nothing
    End Sub
```

Sample Set Up Using ADO

The following procedure (ShowSampleADO) shows various ways to call the previous ADO procedures. Embedded comments explain how things work.

```
Sub ShowSampleADO()
Debug.Print "Start Samples..."
' add a user with a Personal ID and Password
Call AddUserADO("DerfFred", "34434ox94f21", "DerfFred")
' if you do not know the old password,
' specifying the "NULL" keyword will work.
' See the AlterUserPasswordADO procedure for more information
Call AlterUserPasswordADO("DerfFred", "NULL", "NULL")
' To embed a space in the user name,
' enclose the username in square brackets
Call AddUserADO("[Mike Ekim]", "2120s95mr2foarw", "")
' notice user names are not case sensitive
Call DropUserADO("[mike ekim]")
' Give the user the usual permissions but don't allow INSERT
' (Prefer not to do this. But show as a sample anyway.)
Call GrantPermissionsOnTableADO _
    ("DerfFred", "WebBasedList", "SELECT, DELETE, UPDATE")
' Add a group
Call AddGroupADO("Group1", "325dao42")
' give permissions to the group
Call GrantPermissionsOnTableADO _
    ("Group1", "WebBasedList", "SELECT, DELETE, UPDATE")
```

```
' add a user to the group
Call AddUserToGroupADO("DerfFred", "Group1")
' since the user has the same permissions as the group,
' revoke permissions from the user
' Notice this is using the more generic "Revoke.." procedure
Call RevokePermissionsFromObjectADO _
    ("DerfFred", Table, "WebBasedList", "SELECT, DELETE, UPDATE")
' More samples setting permissions
Call GrantPermissionsToObjectADO _
    ("PUBLIC", Database, "Database", "CONNECT")
Call GrantPermissionsToObjectADO _
    ("DerfFred", Container, "Tables", "SELECT")
Call GrantPermissionsToObjectADO _
    ("DerfFred", Container, "Forms", "SELECT")
Call GrantPermissionsToObjectADO("DerfFred", Other, "Query1", "DROP")
' these next three calls show that when the group is dropped,
' users are automatically dropped from the group
' (an error will be displayed on DropUserFromGroupADO)
Call DropGroupADO("Group1")
Call AddGroupADO("Group1", "325dao42")
Call DropUserFromGroupADO("DerfFred", "Group1")
Debug.Print "End samples"
End Sub
```

The following table details the privileges and their descriptions.

Privilege	Applies To	Description
SELECT	Tables, Objects, Containers	Allows a user to read the data and read the design of a specified table, object, or container.
DELETE	Tables, Objects, Containers	Allows a user to delete data from a specified table, object, or container.
INSERT	Tables, Objects, Containers	Allows a user to insert data into a specified table, object, or container.
UPDATE	Tables, Objects, Containers	Allows a user to update data in a specified table, object, or container.
DROP	Tables, Objects, Containers	Allows a user to remove a specified table, object, or container.
SELECTSECURITY	Tables, Objects, Containers	Allows a user to view the permissions for a specified table, object, or container.
UPDATESECURITY	Tables, Objects, Containers	Allows a user to change the permissions for a specified table, object, or container.
UPDATEIDENTITY	Tables	Allows a user to change the values in autoincrement columns.

Continues

Privilege	Applies To	Description
CREATE	Tables, Objects, Containers	Allows a user to create a new table, object, or container.
SELECTSCHEMA	Tables, Objects, Containers	Allows a user to view the design of a specified table, object, or container.
SCHEMA	Tables, Objects, Containers	Allows a user to modify the design of a specified table, object, or container.
UPDATEOWNER	Tables, Objects, Containers	Allows a user to change the owner of a specified table, object, or container.
ALL PRIVILEGES	All	Allows a user all permissions, including administrative, on a specified table, object, container, or database.
CREATEDB	Database	Allows a user to create a new database.
EXCLUSIVECONNECT	Database	Allows a user to open a database in Exclusive mode.
CONNECT	Database	Allows a user to open a database.
ADMINDB	Database	Allows a user to administer a database.

User-Level Security Using ADOX

The previous section has shown you how to maintain user-level security programmatically using ADO and the Jet engine. Another method to maintain security through programming is to use *Microsoft ADO Ext. for DDL and Security* (ADOX).

ADOX uses an object model that supports the Catalog, Group, and User objects. Using these objects you can perform most of the tasks described in the ADO above. Because of the object model, developing VBA procedures to maintain security can be easier. That is, rather than having to learn all of the correct SQL syntax, you can utilize Intellisense in the Visual Basic Editor to help build the right VBA statements in your code.

ADOX also attempts to do some of the work for you. For example, ADOX will provide the personal ID for you. You may like it to do this. On the other hand, since you won't know what the PID is, this can make it difficult to recreate an MDW file, if necessary.

For more information about ADOX, you can visit the Microsoft Developers Network library. See the article http://msdn.microsoft.com/library/default.asp?url=/library/en-us/ado270/htm/pg_adox_fundamentals_1.asp.

Summary

In most business environments, it is good practice and may even be essential to institute some level of security for an Access database. There are several factors that help determine what is appropriate for the situation. Typically it is a combination of methods that will provide the most cost-effective solution. And, implementing Access security alone is typically not sufficient. If the risks are sufficient, firewalls, network security, and strong business rules are critical compliments to what Access can provide.

For the most part, an MDE will protect the code and prevent users from intentionally or inadvertently making changes to the database application itself. However, just having an MDE file does not protect the data. Encoding data will prevent (or at least provide a serious challenge to) unauthorized users from viewing or manipulating the data. Instituting user-level security can help enforce business rules and regulate which users and groups can do what with specific database objects. User-level security can be complicated to set up and to maintain. However, it is worth the effort. Network security is critical to protecting the file itself. In many cases, without the proper network security, a user that could not open a database can merely copy or even delete it.

In addition to determining the types of security to implement for each application, there are several options for how to work with security. Many developers may want to use a combination of the wizard and code. The wizard is excellent for establishing group and user-level security. However, many developers may want to use code to make changes after the initial permissions have been set. It is certainly handy to use code to generate custom documentation about user-level security.

The Access help files, knowledge base articles, and MSDN all provide useful instructions and guidance about various aspects of Access security and how to secure data and code. Chapter 20—*"Macro Security"—Signatures and Sandboxes* covers more about how Access has been enhanced to protect your computer system from malicious attacks that use code in a database.

17

Understanding Client/Server Development with VBA

Access makes it very easy to create applications that interact with other desktop database formats and enterprise-level database servers. However, the easiest methods are not always the best, and wrong choices can have serious unintended effects in the long run. A thorough understanding of how Access interacts with other databases and the various alternatives available for developers is critically necessary to make the best design choices for a specific application.

In a typical business environment, Access MDB applications tend to sprout up from nowhere because some individual or small group wanted functionality that the IT department just wasn't providing. After the file is created, other people notice the application's usefulness and ask to use it themselves. Before long, the application is shared on a file server and becomes an unintended but nonetheless critical piece of company's business processes. Perhaps at some point, someone had even split the data tables into a file of its own and added links from the existing application so that users could store a front-end application on their local machines and connect to the tables stored on a central server.

However, merely storing your data on a server does not make your Access file a client/server application. At minimum, client/server development implies that the processing is separated between at least two processes, one on the client and one on the server. This is an architectural difference in the structure of an application. A traditional Access MDB application with no linked ODBC (Open Database Connectivity) tables is a file-server application, where all processing occurs on the local client machine regardless of where the data files are physically stored. Just as storing a Microsoft Word document on a server share does not make Word a client/server application, neither does storing MDB files on a server make Access client/server.

Although it's tempting to think that moving your data tables to a server database such as Microsoft SQL Server will make your application "client/server," in reality this is only the beginning. It's more accurate to say that moving your data to SQL Server gives you the *potential* for a client/server application. Your application needs to take advantage of that potential for any benefits to be realized. For reasons that will be explained later in this chapter, it is not uncommon for an application to be slower immediately after migrating data from an MDB file to SQL Server (or a similar server database) and relinking the tables in your front-end MDB application. Regardless of the client format you choose, significant performance and other benefits can be realized by utilizing good design practices.

ADP Versus MDB: Choosing the Right Client Format

Many misconceptions exist regarding the differences between an Access project (ADP) and regular Access database (MDB). Even before ADP files were available starting with Access 2000, many developers did not fully understand how MDB files worked or how to optimize their usage in a client/server environment. While even serious design mistakes can still provide acceptable performance with only a few simultaneous users, as applications grow the effects of inefficient application design can have serious detrimental effects on performance and reliability.

What Is an MDB File?

Although it is quite common to refer to MDB files as Access databases, it is more accurate to call them Jet (Joint Engine Technology) databases. Microsoft Access uses the Jet database engine to create and manage MDB files. Although Access is the most common application used for creating and managing them, you can create Jet databases without ever installing or using Access itself (by using Microsoft Visual Basic, for example).

A traditional Access database uses the Jet database engine to store all data, forms, code, and properties associated with your application. Starting with Access 2000, all nondata objects are stored in a single record of a database system table used by Access. When Access goes to open an MDB file, it searches for this record and loads the VBA project and any objects that are needed by your application.

Linking to External Data

To create a link to an external data source from an Access MDB file, select `Get External Data` from the `File` menu, and click `Link Tables`. A Link dialog box that looks similar to the one shown in Figure 17-1 should then appear.

Although the dialog box defaults to Access databases, you can click the `Files of Type` drop-down box and select from various indexed sequential access method (ISAM) and Open Database Connectivity (ODBC) data sources.

ISAM drivers are typically, but not always, used for connecting to other desktop or file-based data sources, such as Excel, text, and HTML. ODBC data sources are usually supplied by a database vendor for use with their product. In most cases, you will need to purchase and install the relevant client utilities for a specific database before you are able to connect to it from within Access. For example, even though Access ships with an ODBC driver for Oracle, the Oracle client utilities still need to be installed for the ODBC driver to be of any use.

To create a link to an ODBC data source, select the `ODBC Databases()` option from the list, which will then cause the `Select Data Source` dialog box to appear, as shown in Figure 17-2.

From this dialog box, you can select a preexisting data source name (DSN) or create a new one. For now, click `Machine Data Source`, and then click `New`. The dialog box shown in Figure 17-3 should appear.

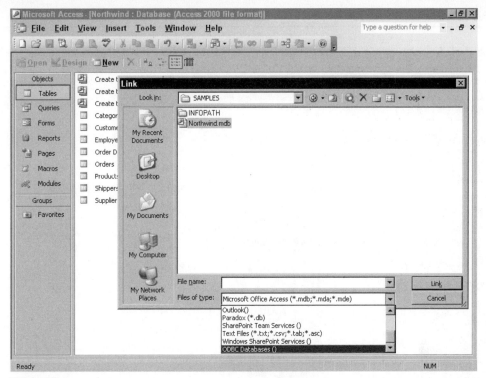

Figure 17-1

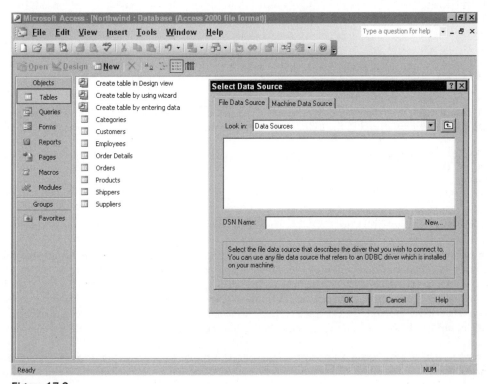

Figure 17-2

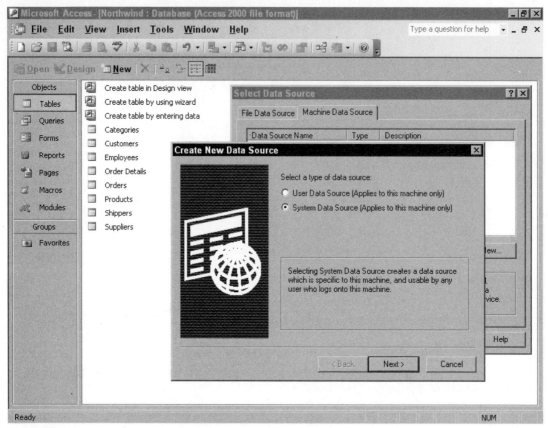

Figure 17-3

The choice made here determines where in the registry the connection information will be stored. User data sources will be stored to the following registry key and will only be available to the current user:

```
HKEY_CURRENT_USER\Software\ODBC\ODBC.INI
```

Machine data sources will be available for all users and will be stored to the following registry location:

```
HKEY_LOCAL_MACHINE\SOFTWARE\ODBC\ODBC.INI
```

For now, choose System Data Source, and click Next. You should then be presented with the Create New Data Source dialog box, as shown in Figure 17-4.

From this point, the screens and options presented will vary depending on what driver you choose, and even what driver version. For now, select SQL Server from the list, click Next, and then click Finish to bring up the dialog information specific to SQL Server, as shown in Figure 17-5.

Enter "TestDSN" for a name, an optional description, and select your SQL Server from the list of available servers. If you are running Microsoft SQL Server (MSDE) on the local machine, then you can enter

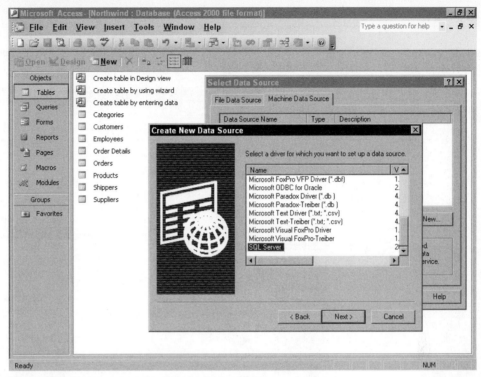

Figure 17-4

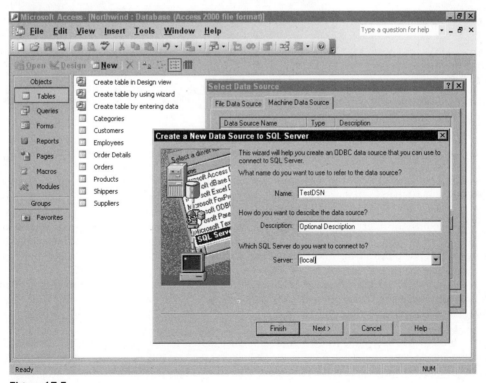

Figure 17-5

"(local)" to reference a default instance of SQL Server on the local machine. Click Next to continue and the dialog box shown in Figure 17-6 should then appear.

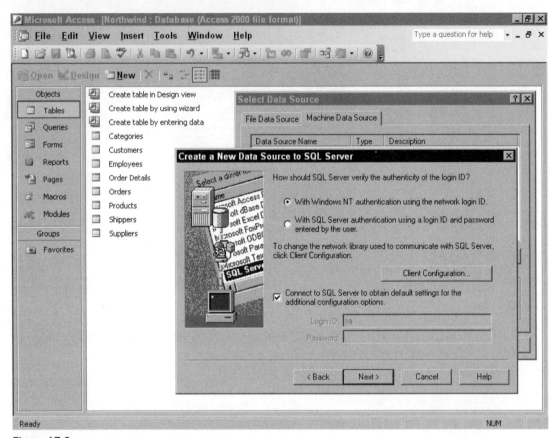

Figure 17-6

Enter the necessary security credentials to log into the server, and click Next again, as shown in Figure 17-7.

The last setting you should need to change is the default database. The default database selection determines the database context in which commands are issued against the server. For example, if code is issued to select records from a table and the default database specified is the master database used by SQL Server, then the query will execute against the master database and an error may result if the table does not exist in the master database. A default database other than the master database should always be specified to help prevent any accidental modification of the master database.

Select NorthwindCS from the list, and choose Next. The remaining default options should be fine, so click Finish on the next screen, check your configuration options, and click OK on the final screen shown in Figure 17-8 to have your new DSN created.

If new links are needed in the future to the same data source, the new DSN can be used instead of creating another one from scratch. After the DSN is created, it can then be selected from the Select Data Source dialog box, as shown in Figure 17-9.

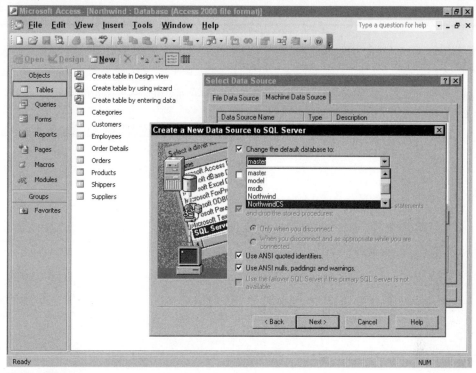

Figure 17-7

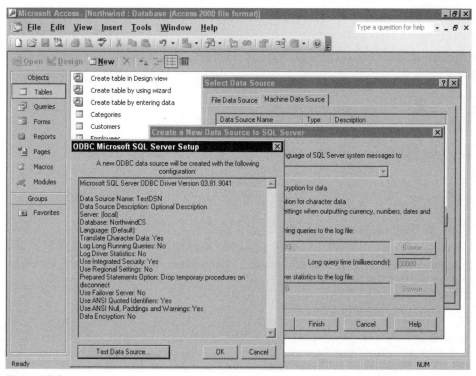

Figure 17-8

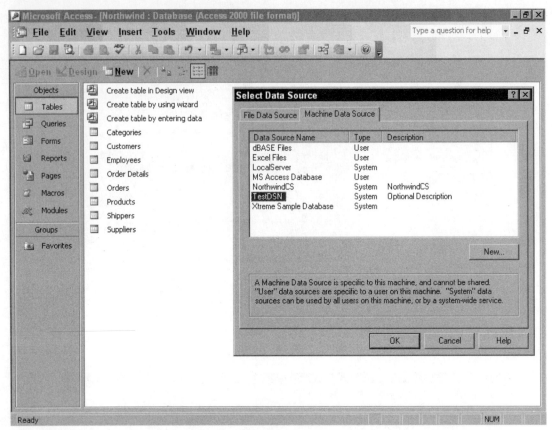

Figure 17-9

Select the TestDSN listing and click OK. Access will then present you with a list of available tables and views that can be linked, as shown in Figure 17-10.

The type of objects listed will depend on the data source. Select the Orders table from the list and click OK. Access will then add a link to the NorthwindCS Orders table to the Tables tab of the Database window. The table link is now available for viewing or binding to a form or report, as shown in Figure 17-11.

What Type of DSN Should Be Used?

There are two primary DSN types to be aware of: File and Machine. A file DSN is a text file that contains the relevant connectivity information for the link and can be easily moved around from machine to machine or deployed with an installation package. A machine DSN stores the connectivity information in the registry.

Access handles links differently depending on which type is chosen. With a file DSN, Access will store the connectivity information in the MDB file and will not need to requery the DSN each time the table is opened. With a machine DSN, Access will need to query the registry to retrieve the connectivity information with each new connection to the DSN.

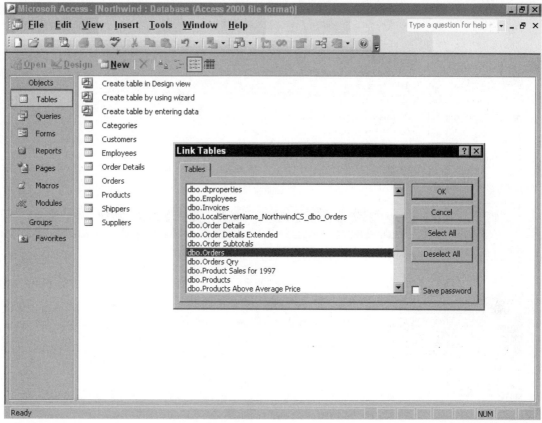

Figure 17-10

How Jet Interacts with ODBC Data Sources

When you double-click a linked table to open it, Access retrieves the primary key information for the table and then retrieves records from the table a few at a time. For example, after double-clicking a link to the Orders table in the NorthwindCS database on SQL Server, Access would first send the following query:

```
SELECT "dbo"."Orders"."OrderID" FROM "dbo"."Orders"
```

This gives Access a full list of the unique record identifiers for the data source. Once Access has this information, it can then retrieve the full record data for display or processing. In this case, the next query sent would look similar to the following:

```
declare @P1 int
set @P1=3
exec sp_prepexec @P1 output, N'@P1 int,@P2 int,@P3 int,@P4 int,@P5
int,@P6 int,@P7 int,@P8 int,@P9 int,@P10 int', N'SELECT
"OrderID","CustomerID","EmployeeID","OrderDate","RequiredDate","ShippedD
ate","ShipVia","Freight","ShipName","ShipAddress","ShipCity","ShipRegion
","ShipPostalCode","ShipCountry"
FROM "dbo"."Orders"
```

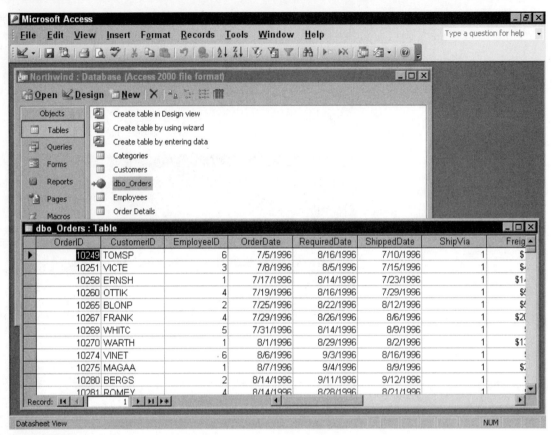

Figure 17-11

```
WHERE "OrderID" = @P1 OR "OrderID" = @P2 OR "OrderID" = @P3 OR "OrderID"
= @P4 OR "OrderID" = @P5 OR "OrderID" = @P6 OR "OrderID" = @P7 OR
"OrderID" = @P8 OR "OrderID" = @P9 OR "OrderID" = @P10', 10249, 10251,
10258, 10260, 10265, 10267, 10269, 10270, 10274, 10275
select @P1
```

The sp_prepexec stored procedure prepares a SQL statement for use by subsequent queries as well as accepts parameter input to retrieve the first few rows (those with OrderID 10249–10275). After this statement is run, Access can then just use the sp_execute procedure to retrieve small batches of rows at a time.

```
exec sp_execute 3, 10280, 10281, 10282, 10284, 10288, 10290, 10296,
10309, 10317, 10323
```

> The exact query text used is specific to the back-end database server and is handled by the ODBC driver for the DSN. Although the specifics are different, Access (Jet) uses the same overall process of getting the primary key information first and then retrieving batches of rows based on the key information.

When you open a query instead of a table, the behavior is typically multiplied for each table in the query and Access will usually do the following:

1. Request primary key data for each table separately

2. Join the key data locally on the client machine

3. Request all needed field data from each table separately based on the key field

4. Join the requested data together in a local recordset and display to the user

The end result is that if you have large compound primary keys defined for each table, Access can pull down a lot of data that needs to be joined locally before it even begins to retrieve data that will eventually be displayed to the user. If you have a table with 13 fields but 12 fields comprise a compound primary key, Access will end up bringing down the 12 primary key fields twice, once to get the primary key data by itself and a second time to get data for display to the user.

Under certain circumstances, Access will have the primary key joining done on the server. Unlike the above example where Access retrieved all the primary key data for each table and then joined it locally, if *all* the tables in a particular query are based on the same DSN, Access can sometimes pass a WHERE clause to join the data on the server. For example, if you created a local query in an MDB file that was based on linked `Products`, `Suppliers`, and `Categories` tables from the `NorthwindCS` database on SQL Server, and all three tables were based on the same DSN, a query similar to the following may be executed in step 1, above:

```
SELECT "dbo"."Products"."ProductID","dbo"."Categories"."CategoryID",
"dbo"."Suppliers"."SupplierID"
FROM "dbo"."Categories","dbo"."Products","dbo"."Suppliers"
WHERE(("dbo"."Products"."CategoryID" = "dbo"."Categories"."CategoryID")
AND ("dbo"."Products"."SupplierID" = "dbo"."Suppliers"."SupplierID"))
```

This effectively causes step 2, mentioned above, to be executed on the server. The benefit here is that only the primary key data that is necessary for the join will be passed over the network and brought down to Access. Although this is not as ideal as having all query processing happen on the server, it can dramatically improve performance depending on how your tables are structured.

> The most important element here is that *all* tables must be based on the same DSN. If two tables are from the same SQL Server database but one table uses a file DSN and the other uses a system DSN, the less efficient process will be used. The more efficient processing is not guaranteed and will depend on other factors but it won't happen at all if there is more than one DSN. *Always* base linked tables from the same database using the same DSN if at all possible.

As you can see, although a robust server database is being used, most of the processing still happens locally when working with linked tables. The benefit with this design is that Jet makes it very easy to create queries that can join multiple remote data sources. This ease of use, however, comes with the price of inefficiency in many cases, and the increased network traffic that can result.

How Can Performance Be Improved?

When dealing in a client/server environment, the most important factor to remember is to not bring any data across a network unless needed. The best way to accomplish this depends on what the application is designed to do and where the performance problem lies. There are three main contributors to performance problems in a client/server environment:

- ❑ The time taken in processing a query on the server
- ❑ The time taken in processing a query on the client
- ❑ The time taken in moving records over a network

All three areas need to be examined closely to see if it might be a bottleneck in the process.

Insufficient server resources are rarely the cause of a problem for a specific Access application. It is far more likely that performance will increase by shifting more processing to the server. If the query processing time on the server seems longer than expected, then make sure that indexes are properly set and optimized. If locking issues are occurring, then changing to optimistic locking may improve performance.

Unlike with servers, insufficient client resources are a frequent source of performance issues. Because of the join work that Access performs locally, queries that cause Access to bring down a lot of records for joining will tend to be slow if there are insufficient resources on the machine. All things being equal, the more RAM on the client machine, the better your query is likely to run.

Networks tend to be a bottleneck because of the amount of data Access will retrieve for local joining. It is not uncommon for Access to process tens or even hundreds of megabytes of data before displaying results to a user that may consist of only a few records. This can especially be an issue in WAN or dial-up environments, where network bandwidth can be very low.

Pass-Through Queries

Pass-through queries are often the quickest way to improve performance of an MDB application. Unfortunately, they are usually underutilized. Pass-through queries are processed entirely on the server and, as such, are a very good technique for transferring data processing to the server. However, there is no graphical interface for creating the SQL statements of a pass-through query and the data they return is read-only.

Because pass-through data is not updatable, they are not always appropriate for forms. However, they are perfect for list boxes, combo boxes, and reports. Since report data does not need to be updatable, and they tend to be based on multiple tables that require a lot of local join work, report record sources that have been converted from local queries to pass-though queries can benefit dramatically.

To create a pass-through query, simply create a new query in Design View and select SQL Specific->Pass-Through from the Query menu. Because there is no graphical interface, the SQL text specific to the ODBC data source the query will run against needs to be used. Access does not parse or validate the SQL text of a pass-through query in any way. Instead, the SQL text will be sent (passed-through) to the specified ODBC data source as-is and Access will attempt to create a recordset from whatever is sent back.

Pass-through queries should be used whenever practical because they shift processing to the server and result in less data brought over the network. The combination results in a far more efficient query-processing environment when using MDB files.

What Is an ADP?

Unlike a traditional Access MDB file, Access project (ADP) files are client/server by design. Tables and queries are stored on a SQL Server, and the ADP file only contains the forms, reports, and other nondata objects like the VBA project. Instead of opening a database and then retrieving the VBA project stored within the database, the VBA project is opened directly and then Access connects to the desired SQL Server based on connection properties stored within the ADP file.

Access projects neither use nor depend on the Jet database engine. MSDE is used as the database engine and all table and query objects are stored on SQL Server. After opening an ADP and connecting to the relevant SQL Server, Access retrieves a list of server objects that the user has permission to view or execute and then displays the names in the `Tables` or `Queries` tabs in the `Database` window.

When you double-click a table or query in an ADP, Access sends a simple SQL statement to retrieve all the records from the object. All data processing happens on the server and Access only handles presentation processing on the client side. If a SQL statement is specified as the recordsource for a form, report, or control, the SQL statement is sent "as is" to the server.

Although ADP files make it easier to shift processing to the server, this won't help performance much if an application is repeatedly bringing down whole tables of data from the server. Care still needs to be taken to bring down only necessary data.

Understanding Query Options in SQL Server

There are three types of query objects in SQL Server that can be used from an ADP: views, stored procedures, and functions. All three types have strengths that can be leveraged.

Views

Views can be thought of as virtual tables. They can be used in the same way as regular tables in other query objects. The benefit of views is that they can be based on more than one source table and can be limited to just include the fields needed for a particular action.

Although you can generally update, delete, and insert records into a view, if the view is based on multiple tables then there may be limitations on the type of actions a view can be used for. For example, if a SQL statement attempts to insert a record into a view based on multiple tables, the SQL statement will generate an error because SQL Server doesn't always know what needs to be done to add a record to a view with multiple underlying tables.

This behavior can be modified on the SQL Server side by adding what are called *triggers*. A trigger is conceptually similar to having a VBA event procedure for a table or other SQL Server objects. Instead of running VBA code, triggers are written in SQL Server specific Transact-SQL (T-SQL). As an example, it is possible to define a trigger for a view so that the actual inserts are handled by the trigger and don't generate a SQL Server error. Although the creation of SQL Server triggers is outside the scope of this book, developers should be aware of their existence.

Access projects, however, have a built-in mechanism for adding records to views based on two tables by adding the new records to the source tables directly and bypassing the view. This can sometimes have unexpected side effects for developers who are used to the regular SQL Server behavior. Even if a view is updatable directly (perhaps because a trigger has been added), Access will attempt to update the view's source tables. If a user has permissions to a view but not its source tables, then a permissions error will be generated when Access attempts to update the underlying table.

However, this behavior can be modified by changing a property of the view. While in Design View of a view, right-click the background in the upper half of the design area and select Properties. To tell Access to update the view directly, instead of attempting to update source tables, check the box next to Update using view rules, as shown in Figure 17-12.

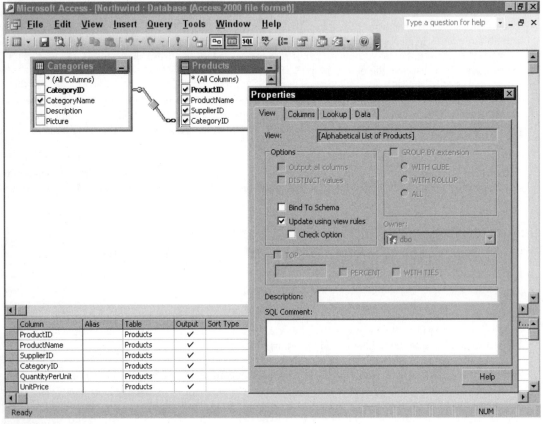

Figure 17-12

Stored Procedures

Unlike views, stored procedures are not updatable directly and can't be used as a data source by other query objects. However, stored procedures can be used to run updated queries and can contain somewhat complicated logic that regular views cannot. Although the data returned from stored procedure objects is read-only, it can appear to be updatable from the user interface of an ADP. Access gets around the read-only restriction by updating the source tables directly. Unlike a view, there is no method for having Access update the stored procedure directly.

Functions

Functions are a sort of cross between views and stored procedures. Unlike stored procedures, you can use a function as a data source in another query object like you can with a view. Unlike a view, however, the data returned by a function is not updatable. When opening a function from the user interface, Access is able to update the data, if possible, by updating the source tables directly, similar to the method used to update a stored procedure. Functions tend to be useful in situations that call for returning a single value or a read-only recordset as part of another query.

How Access Projects Link to External Data Sources

ADP files cannot be bound directly to any other data source besides SQL Server. They are tightly bound with and optimized for use with SQL Server. Fortunately, SQL Server has strong capabilities that allow linking to many other data sources.

Access projects rely on the *linked server* capability of SQL Server. Although structured differently than linked ODBC tables in an MDB file, similar functionality is obtained. Similar to how a machine DSN stores connection information in the registry that can be referenced by using the DSN name, SQL Server can store connection information (linked servers) in a system table in the SQL Server Master database. Once created, a linked server's connection details can be referenced by using an alias defined when creating the linked server. This alias can be used from other SQL Server objects such as views, functions, and stored procedures.

Views based on linked servers can be created programmatically or through the user interface in an ADP. If you have the personal, standard, developer, or enterprise version of SQL Server, then a linked server can also be created through one of the SQL Server client tools, such as Enterprise Manager.

To create a new view based on a linked server, select `Get External Data` from the `File` menu and click `Linked Tables`. A dialog box similar to the one shown in Figure 17-13 should then appear.

The `Linked Server` option should be selected by default. The transact SQL option stores the connection information in the query instead of creating a linked server. This option is useful when a developer does not have permissions to create a linked server or when the resulting view is run on an infrequent basis. To continue, select the `Linked Server` option and click `Next` to view the `Select Data Source` dialog box, as shown in Figure 17-14.

From this point the screens vary depending on which data source is chosen. To create a new link to another SQL Server, choose the `+New SQL Server Connection.odc` listing and click `Open`. A dialog box similar to the one shown in Figure 17-15 should then appear.

Enter the server name of the SQL Server to be linked, and then enter the necessary security credentials and click `Next` to continue. A dialog box similar to the one shown in Figure 17-16 should then appear.

Select the `NorthwindCS` database from the list and choose `Next`. A dialog box similar to the one shown in Figure 17-17 should then appear.

Change the name of the file to save the connection information, enter any desired description, and click `Finish`.

Access will then prompt you to select objects to create views against, as shown in Figure 17-18. Select `Table:Orders` from the left list, click the > character to move it to the right list, and click `Finish`. A

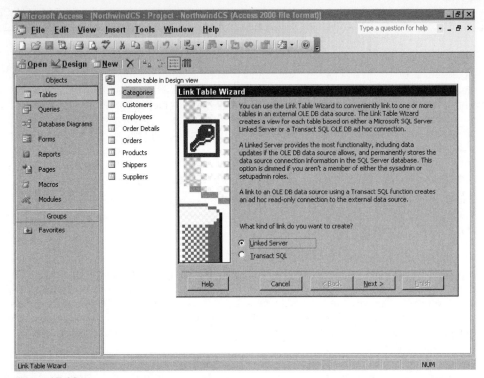

Figure 17-13

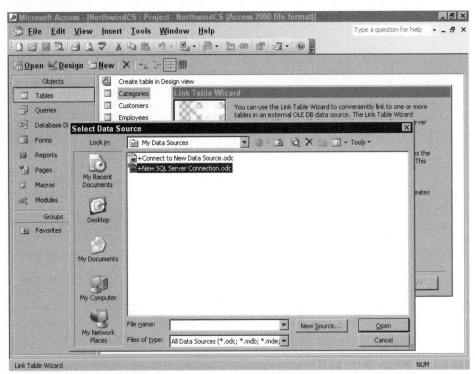

Figure 17-14

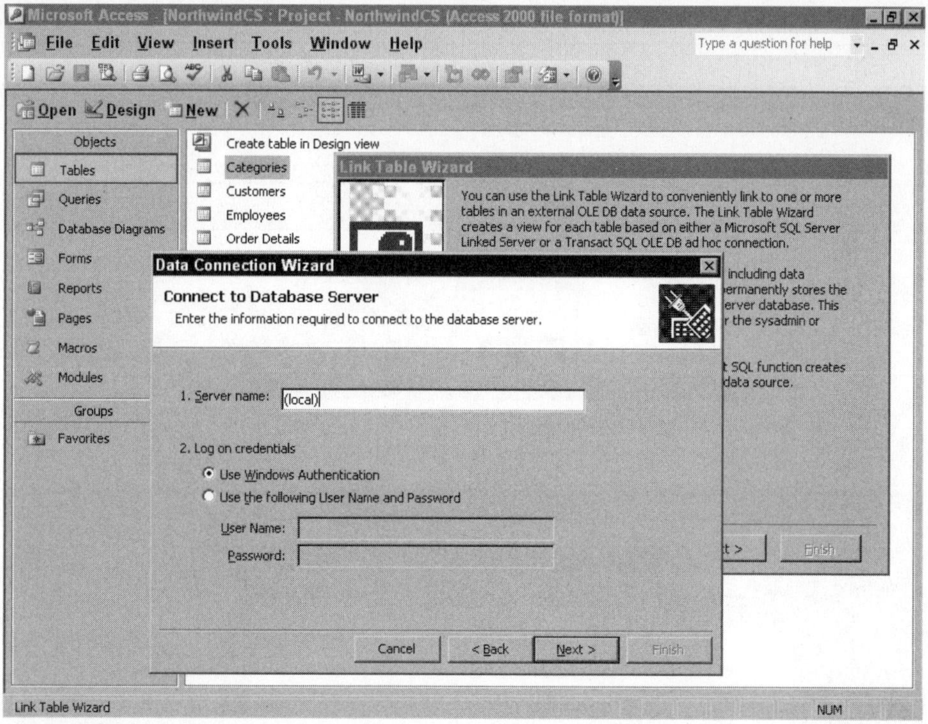

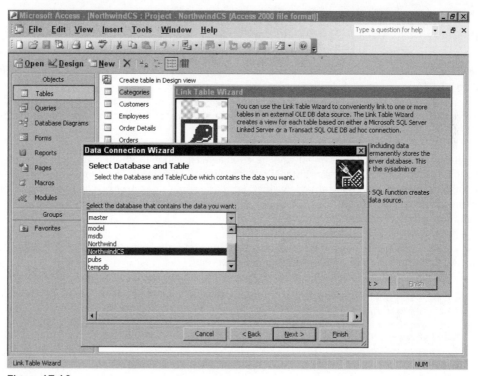

Figure 17-15

Figure 17-16

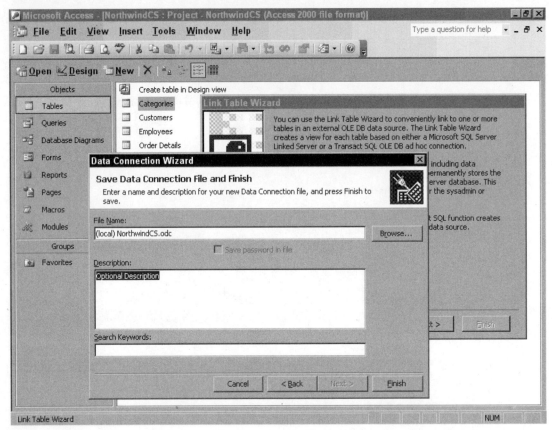

Figure 17-17

new view should then be listed in the `Views` tab of the ADP that will display data from the `Orders` table, as shown in Figure 17-19.

Unfortunately, the wizard does not always function as well as one might like. It's generally very good for creating links to other SQL Servers but less reliable with other data sources. Sometimes Access will create the linked server but not create any views that use it and sometimes Access won't even be able to create the linked server. Fortunately, it's not too complicated to create the linked servers and views programmatically, if needed.

First, a linked server will need to be created by running code similar to the following in the code module of an ADP (in this example, a link to another SQL Server):

```
Public Sub pAddLinkedServer()
  Dim strCommand As String
  strCommand = "EXEC sp_AddLinkedServer " & _
    "@server='RemoteServerAlias', " & _
    "@srvproduct='', " & _
    "@provider='SQLOLEDB', " & _
```

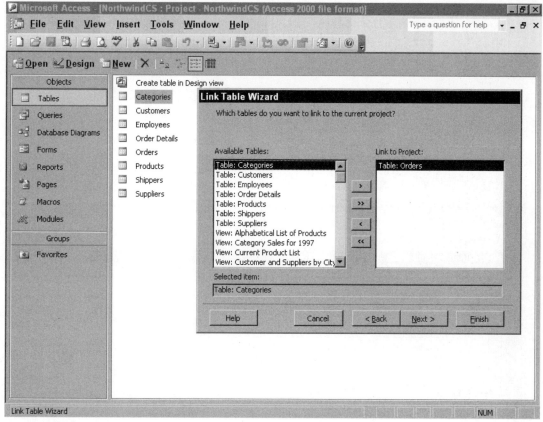

Figure 17-18

```
    "@datasrc='RemoteServerName'"
  CurrentProject.Connection.Execute strCommand
End Sub
```

The RemoteServerAlias is the name you want to use when referencing the linked server in queries. The RemoteServerName is the actual name of the remote network server. If this was a SQL Server named instance then the RemoteServerName would be Servername\InstanceName. After creating the linked server, you can then create other database objects that reference it by using code similar to the following:

```
Public Sub pCreateView()
  Dim strCommand As String
  strCommand = "Create View ViewName as " & _
    "Select ShipperID, CompanyName, Phone " & _
      "From RemoteServerAlias.NorthwindCS.DBO.Shippers"
CurrentProject.Connection.Execute strCommand
End Sub
```

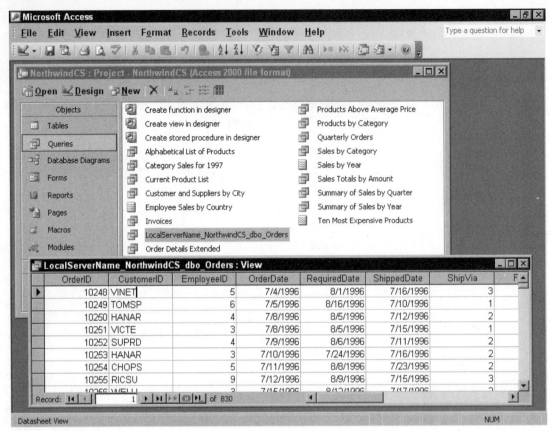

Figure 17-19

Which Format Is Right for You?

Both MDB and ADP formats have benefits and tradeoffs when connecting to SQL Server or other data sources. The following topics are just a small sampling of what should be considered before choosing one format or the other.

Recordset Differences

MDB files use a Dynaset recordset by default. Dynaset-type recordsets have the ability to see changes by other users in near real time. However, it's a very expensive recordset to maintain in terms of resource and network usage. If a user moves to the first record in a given table, then to the last record, and then back to the first, Access will requery the first record from the back-end database for updated values. In effect, Jet maintains a "rolling" recordset that contains just the records you are viewing and a small buffer of records outside the current viewable set.

With an ADP, Access maintains what is called an updatable "snapshot" recordset. You can scroll through the records and make changes but you will not see changes by other users until you rerun the query. The main benefit is that there is much less network traffic and once the records are brought down, you can very quickly scroll through the records without having to requery the back-end database. However, if an application is required to have many records in a datasheet type mode and needs to see continuous changes by other users, then MDB files may be preferred. Although there are ways to see streaming changes by other users in an ADP, it does require more custom code.

The other main recordset difference is that MDB files use Jet and Jet is tightly bound with DAO but ADP files work more naturally with ADO. Although DAO can be used in an ADP and ADO in an MDB, much of Access's built-in timesaving capabilities are lost this way. Some developers have a personal preference for using one object library over the other (usually because they are more familiar with one than the other) and will base their format choice on this preference.

Security Differences

With MDB files, Access developers are able to enforce user-level security using the Jet database engine on almost all database objects, including forms and reports. However, this is not the case with Access projects.

Once tables and queries are moved to SQL Server, SQL Server becomes the primary enforcer of security for those objects. With an Access project, almost all security relies on SQL Server. There is no user-level security at the ADP level for controlling access to forms or reports. Instead, data access is controlled at the server level. The primary security mechanism at the client level is to add a VBA project password or to convert the file to an ADE, which strips away the source code. Usually this is all that is needed.

Local Data Storage

The inability to store tables and query objects in an ADP file is probably the biggest complaint developers have when moving from MDB files to the ADP environment. However, this is not as big of a limitation as it may seem at first. There are three primary ways to utilize local storage in an Access project:

❑ Use MSDE on the local machine and have MSDE link to the remote data source

❑ Use a separate MDB file to store local data and connect to it programmatically

❑ Store data locally in XML files

Each of the three primary options above involves tradeoffs but each is also a very suitable solution for various scenarios. The best option for a given scenario usually depends on how you want to use the locally stored data. For serious local number crunching, using MSDE for the local store gives you the power of SQL server at each client, but at the expense of more resource usage requirements. Alternatively, XML files consume very few resources but are more difficult to update and manipulate. Using MDB files to store local data for an ADP uses less resources than MSDE and can be easier to update than XML, but involves more code than with MSDE.

Ability to Share from a File Server

Although the recommended practice when using MDB files in a multiuser scenario is to install the front-end MDB file onto each user's machine, in practice many times it is shared from a central network location and opened over the network. This functionality was made possible through use of the Jet database engine. Since ADP files don't use the Jet database engine, the same copy can't be opened by multiple users over a network. Although it is possible to work around this limitation by flagging the ADP file as read-only, it is neither recommended nor supported by Microsoft and can potentially corrupt your ADP file.

> **ADP files should always be installed to each user's local client machine!**

Controlling the Logon Process

The only way to deftly handle logon errors when your application starts is by controlling the logon process to the back-end database. Sometimes the database server is down or there are network connectivity issues. If you don't control the connection process upon startup, then users may get a very unpleasant and confusing error message. Additionally, if you control the logon process then you can store the supplied username and password information for connecting to the same data store subsequently without having to re-ask the user for security credentials. The process and code needed will vary depending on whether you are using an ADP or MDB file.

Using Linked Tables with MDB Files

If you don't have a custom startup form with an MDB file when using linked tables, then you can't control the logon process. If your application uses SQL Security, then your users may get prompted for passwords at random points in the application when Access first tries to use a given linked table. It is easy to create a custom startup login form that looks similar to the one shown in Figure 17-20 and prompts for username and password.

Using this simple form, you can then run code for the Next button to refresh the table links, save the username and password to global variables, or whatever your specific application needs to do. In the case of linked tables, you will likely need code at some point to create a DSN to store connection information for the tables. The following code illustrates how to programmatically create a DSN:

```
Public Sub pCreateNewDSN()
    Dim strDSNName As String
    Dim strDriverName As String
    Dim strDescription As String
    Dim strServer As String
    Dim strDatabase As String

    'This is the DSN name you want to use when
    'referencing this DSN in your code
    strDSNName = "MyDSN"

    'The name of the ODBC Driver used for the connection
    strDriverName = "SQL Server"

    ' This is for any optional description you might want to
    ' view in the ODBC Driver Manager program
    strDescription = "Test DSN Description"

    ' In the case of SQL Server, the following line if for the
    ' network name of the server you want to connect to
    strServer = "(local)"

    '   Then name of the Default database on the server you want
    '   used for this DSN. If you don't specify, then SQL
```

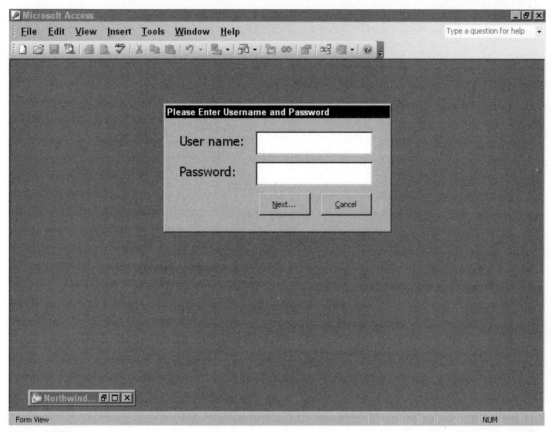

Figure 17-20

```
     '  Statements may end up getting executed in the wrong database
     strDatabase = "NorthwindCS"

     DBEngine.RegisterDatabase strDSNName, strDriverName, _
       True, "Description=" & strDescription & _
       Chr(13) & "Server=" & strServer & _
       Chr(13) & "Database=" & strDatabase
End Sub
```

Once the DSN has been created you can then reference that DSN in code to create and refresh linked tables. The following code demonstrates how to create linked tables based on the DSN created above:

```
Public Sub pCreateLinkedTable()
' NOTE: This code required the DAO object library to function
' If you are using the Northwind.mdb sample file then this
' reference should already be present.  If you are not sure,
' you should check your references under Tools->references
' in the VBA environment and make the sure the reference to
' Microsoft DAO 3.6 Object library is checked
```

```
Dim strDSNName As String
Dim strAppName As String
Dim strDatabase As String
Dim strUID As String
Dim strPW As String
Dim strRemoteTableName As String
Dim strLocalTableName As String
Dim strConnection As String
Dim daoTableDef As DAO.TableDef

' This must reference an existing DSN
strDSNName = "MyDSN"

' The application name can be used for tracing and
' troubleshooting the source of problems on the server.
' This can be anything you want but usually the more
' specific the better.
strAppName = "Microsoft Access 2003"

' The database where the table resides on SQL Server
strDatabase = "NorthwindCS"

' User name for logging into the database server.
' This could captured by a logon form and stored in a global
' variable.
strUID = "SA"

' Password for logging in to the database server
' This could captured by a logon form and stored in a global
' variable.
strPW = "password"

' Then name of the table on the remote server
strRemoteTableName = "Customers"

' The name of the table we want create in the local file
' that links to strRemotetableName
strLocalTableName = "NewTable"

' This will build the ODBC connection string for our new table
strConnection = "ODBC:" & _
        "DSN=" & strDSN & ";" & _
        "APP=" & strAppName & ";" & _
        "DATABASE=" & strDatabase & ";" & _
        "UID=" & strUID & ";" & _
        "PWD=" & strPW & ";" & _
        "TABLE=" & strRemoteTableName

' This creates a new table object and adds it to the local
' database.  If your tables already exist, then you would
' skip this code and use code to refresh the links, instead
Set daoTableDef = CurrentDb.CreateTableDef(strLocalTableName _
    , dbAttachSavePWD, strRemoteTableName, strConnection)
CurrentDb.TableDefs.Append daoTableDef
```

```
    ' Clean up
    Set daoTableDef = Nothing
End Sub
```

Alternatively, if your tables already exist in the database and you just need to refresh the links, then the following code would be substituted at the end of the above procedure:

```
' This code assumes that the tables have already been created.
' If not, then you would need to run code to create the
' tables instead
Set daoTableDef = CurrentDb.TableDefs(daoTableDef)
daoTableDef.Connect = strConnection
daoTableDef.RefreshLink
```

Using Access Projects

Since Access projects don't store tables in the ADP file, you just need to reconnect the ADP to the SQL Server database used by the application. You can use a similar startup form as suggested for an MDB to collect a username and password or you can just run code automatically if you only allow integrated security. Whether or not you use a login form, code to reconnect the ADP would be similar to the following:

```
Public Sub pConnectADP()
    Dim strServerName As String
    Dim strDatabase As String
    Dim strUN As String
    Dim strPW As String
    Dim boolUseIntegratedSecurity As Boolean
    Dim strConnect As String

    ' Required.  This is the network name of the SQL Server.
    ' "(local)" can be used to reference a default SQL Server
    ' installation on the local machine
    strServerName = "(local)"

    ' Required.  This is the database you want the ADP to be based on.
    strDBName = "NorthwindCS"

    ' Optional.  The SQL Server username
    ' Not needed if using integrated security
    strUN = "SA"

    ' Optional.  The password for the username above.
    ' Not needed if using integrated security
    strPW = "Password"

    ' Use this flag to signify whether the connection string should
    ' contain a username and password or use integrated security
    boolUseIntegratedSecurity = True

    ' This is the full connection string for the ADP.
    ' The Provider, Data Source, and Initial Catalog arguments are
```

```
   ' required.
   strConnect = "Provider=SQLOLEDB.1" & _
     ";Data Source=" & strServerName & _
     ";Initial Catalog=" & strDBName

   'Add the necessary argument if using integrated security
   If boolUseIntegratedSecurity Then
      strConnect = strConnect & ";integrated security=SSPI"
   ' Add the username and password arguments if using SQL Server Security
   Else
      strConnect = strConnect & ";user id=" & strUN & _
         ";password=" & strPW
   End If


   ' Open the connection.
   ' If there is already an existing connection open then this will
   ' change it.
   Application.CurrentProject.OpenConnection strConnect
End Sub
```

Unfortunately, one of the limitations of the `CurrentProject.OpenConnection` method is that you can't specify the *advanced* connection properties programmatically, such as `Application Name` or `Connect Timeout`. In addition, since Access does not expose these properties programmatically, there is no convenient method for changing them after the connection is made, either. The properties that can't be specified are the ones displayed on the `Advanced` and `All` tabs of the `Connection Properties` dialog box for the ADP. To view these properties and change them manually, select `Connection` from the `File` menu, as shown in Figure 17-21.

If the normal server happens to be down and your code generates an error, it would be useful to have a convenient way to specify an alternate server, which may not be known when the application was developed. One way of accomplishing this is to use a UDL file to store the connection information for your SQL Server. However, the `CurrentProject.OpenConnection` method does not accept UDL files as a parameter directly, so code will be needed to retrieve the connection information by using a regular ADO connection and then passing the information to the ADP.

```
Dim cnnTest As ADODB.Connection
Set cnnTest = New ADODB.Connection

' Change the following path to your actual path to Test.udl
' This could also be stored as a property of the ADP so it
' could be configured by an administrator instead of being
' hardcoded.
cnnTest.Open "File Name=\\Server\Share\Test.udl;"

' Now pass the connection string of the ADO connection to the ADP.
Application.CurrentProject.OpenConnection cnnTest.ConnectionString

' Test the connection
If CurrentProject.IsConnected = False Then
   'It didn't work. Handle accordingly
End If
```

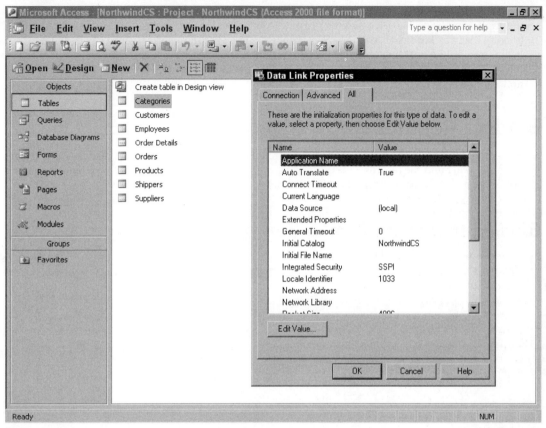

Figure 17-21

```
' Clean up
cnnTest.Close
Set cnnTest = Nothing
```

One more step needs to be taken for this to work seamlessly. If you just close the ADP in a normal fashion, the connection information will be stored and Access will attempt to reconnect the next time the ADP is opened. Since Access does this before your own code has a chance to run, you won't be able to trap any errors that occur. To prevent this from occurring (as best you can), run the following line of code from the Close event of the last form to be closed:

```
CurrentProject.OpenConnection ""
```

This not only closes the connection but clears the connection information from the file so that the ADP will open in a disconnected state the next time around. This will allow your code to run and reconnect the ADP as you wish. A good place to run the code is from the Close event of the initial logon form. If you hide the logon form instead of closing it, this will guarantee that the code will run no matter how the ADP was closed.

The only exception to this is when a power or abnormal close of the application occurs, perhaps because the application froze. In such cases, the previous connection information will still be present in the ADP because that was not a chance to remove it. However, this exception normally just causes there to be two logon prompts the next time the ADP is open: the default Access prompt and then the one presented by the application's code. If the application is using integrated security then the users will likely not even notice any difference.

Binding Recordsets to Objects

Sometimes built-in links do not provide the desired flexibility for controlling the recordset and it can be very useful to build the recordset in code and bind it to an object. Recordsets can be bound to combo boxes, list boxes, forms, and reports (ADP files only).

Binding to a Form, Combo Box, or List Box

The code and methods used for binding forms, combo boxes, and list boxes are basically the same. They all have a `Recordset` property that can be assigned an active ADO recordset object.

```
Private Sub Form_Open(Cancel As Integer)
Dim RS As ADODB.Recordset
Dim CN As ADODB.Connection
Dim STRConnect As String
Set RS = New ADODB.Recordset
Set CN = New ADODB.Connection
STRConnect = "Provider=SQLOLEDB.1" & _
    ";Data Source=(local)" & _
    ";Initial Catalog=NorthwindCS" & _
    ";user id=sa" & _
    ";password=password"

CN.Open STRConnect
RS.Open "Products", CN, adOpenKeyset, adLockOptimistic
Set Me.Recordset = RS
RS.Close
CN.Close
Set RS = Nothing
Set CN = Nothing
End Sub
```

Binding to a Report

Unlike with forms, list boxes, and combo boxes, reports are not nearly as easy to dynamically bind to an active recordset. In addition, it's not possible at all with MDB files. The key difference is that the recordset has to be a shaped recordset, using the Microsoft Data Shaping services for OLEDB (MSDataShape) provider or the Microsoft Client Data Manager (Microsoft.Access.OLEDB.10.0) provider.

For example, the Invoice report in the NorthwindCS.adp sample file is based on the invoices view stored on SQL Server. However, if you try to bind a simple ADO recordset based on the invoices view to the Invoice report like you might do for a form, you would get an error or see unpredictable behavior.

```
Private Sub Report_Open(Cancel As Integer)
'Dim RS As ADODB.Recordset
'Dim CN As ADODB.Connection
'Dim STRConnect As String
'
'Set RS = New ADODB.Recordset
'Set CN = New ADODB.Connection
'STRConnect = "Provider=SQLOLEDB.1" & _
'    ";Data Source=(local)" & _
'    ";Initial Catalog=NorthwindCS" & _
'    ";user id=sa" & _
'    ";password=password"
'
'CN.Open STRConnect
'RS.Open "customers", CN, adOpenKeyset ', adLockReadOnly
'Set Me.Recordset = RS
'Set RS = Nothing
'Set CN = Nothing
End Sub
```

To get a starter shape:

```
?reports![products by category].shape
result:
SHAPE (SHAPE {SELECT CategoryName, ProductName, UnitsInStock
FROM dbo.[Products by Category]} AS rsLevel0
COMPUTE rsLevel0, Count(rsLevel0.[ProductName])
AS __Agg0 BY CategoryName AS __COLRef0) AS RS_148
```

You can then use the above SQL to bind the shaped recordset to the *Products* by *Category* report by clearing the report's `Recordsource` property and adding the following code to the report's `Open` event procedure:

```
Private Sub Report_Open(Cancel As Integer)
  Dim RS As ADODB.Recordset
  Dim CN As ADODB.Connection
  Dim strConnect As String
  Dim strSQL As String
  Set RS = New ADODB.Recordset
  Set CN = New ADODB.Connection
  strConnect = "Provider=Microsoft.Access.OLEDB.10.0" & _
    ";Data Provider=SQLOLEDB.1" & _
    ";Data Source=(local)" & _
    ";Initial Catalog=NorthwindCS" & _
    ";user id=sa" & _
    ";password=password"
  CN.Open strConnect
  strSQL = "SHAPE (SHAPE {SELECT CategoryName, " & _
    "ProductName, UnitsInStock FROM [Products by Category]} " & _
    "AS rsLevel0 COMPUTE rsLevel0, Count(rsLevel0.[ProductName]) " & _
    "AS __Agg0 BY CategoryName AS __COLRef0) AS RS_230"
```

```
      RS.Open strSQL, CN, adOpenKeyset ', adLockReadOnly
      Set Me.Recordset = RS
      Set RS = Nothing
      Set CN = Nothing
   End Sub
```

However, there is still one more step that must be done before the report will render correctly. Although the above SQL is valid, if you use the above code to bind a shaped recordset to the *Products by Category* report, the report will generate the error shown in Figure 17-22 and the `Categories` will be displayed as "#Name?"

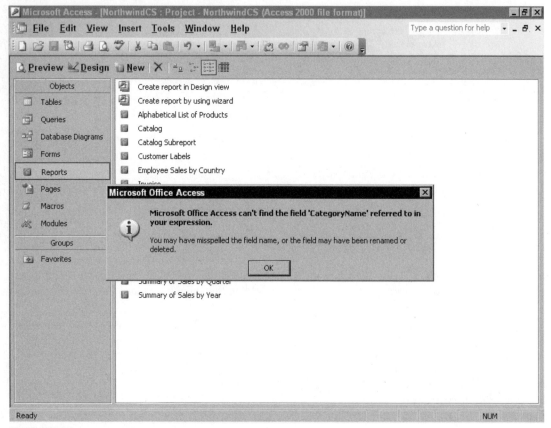

Figure 17-22

After clicking OK, the report would then look similar to the report shown in Figure 17-23.

The reason for the error is that the `CategoryName` field is aliased as `__COLRef0` in the SQL statement but the text box bound to `CategoryName` is still expecting `CategoryName`. Since `CategoryName` is not defined in the SQL, an error is generated. Why this doesn't work since we are using the same SQL given to us by Access for the same report is a good question. Under the hood, Access must be accounting for this discrepancy in some way and coordinating the two values dynamically. However, there are two ways to fix the problem:

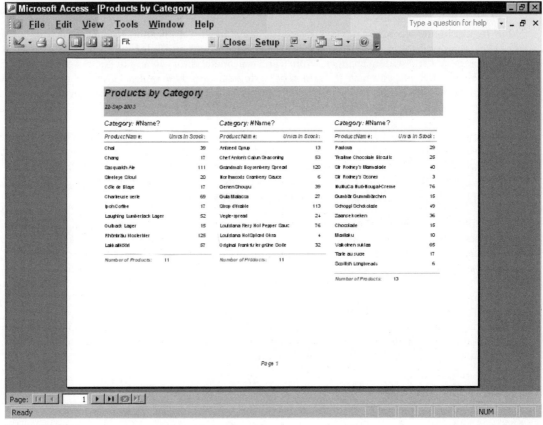

Figure 17-23

❑ Change the `Control Source` property of the `CategoryName` text box to `__COLRef0`. This fixes the problem by using the alias defined in the SQL statement.

❑ Change the `__COLRef0` alias in the SQL to `CategoryName`, as follows:

```
SHAPE (SHAPE {SELECT CategoryName, ProductName, UnitsInStock
FROM dbo.[Products by Category]} AS rsLevel0
COMPUTE rsLevel0, Count(rsLevel0.[ProductName])
AS __Agg0 BY CategoryName AS CategoryName) AS RS_148
```

Now if you run code to bind the SQL statement, the names will match and the report will display as expected.

As you have probably figured out by now, binding recordsets to reports is usually more trouble than it is worth. If you have a lot of reports then we normally suggest using the `Recordsource` property and letting Access do the shaping for you. For forms and combo or list boxes, however, binding recordsets can be a very effective means of quickly connecting to remote data sources on the fly without relying on linked tables or queries.

Using Persisted Recordsets

While regular bound recordsets can be very useful, sometimes an application will need the same recordset in multiple forms or controls and the data gets retrieved multiple times. In cases where the data usage is read-only and seldom changes, a quick and easy method for caching the data locally can be very useful. With an MDB file, you have the option of storing data locally in tables. However, although local tables are easy to populate by appending data from a linked ODBC table, it is not as convenient when the data has been retrieved via an ADO recordset.

Fortunately, the ADO object model allows for a very simple method of saving data to a local XML file and quickly recreating it as an ADO recordset when needed. This often overlooked and underutilized feature of ADO can dramatically reduce network traffic and increase application performance when used correctly. The best scenarios for using local persisted recordsets are when data is read-only, seldom changes, and is used in multiple locations throughout an application.

For example, you may have a "states" table for an order entry application. This is a good candidate because states rarely change, there is no need to modify a state's name, and the data is likely used in several places: the Customers form when adding the customer, the Vendors form when adding vendors, and the Orders form when entering shipping addresses. With persisted recordsets, once the data is brought down locally and cached, you can then use it in all your forms without retrieving the data again from the server.

Creating a persisted recordset is fairly straightforward: just create an ADO recordset (using ADO 2.6 or later) and use the Save method to persist the data to an XML file. The following steps use the Products form from the NorthwindCS.adp sample file as an example.

Persisting the Data to XML

Add a command button named cmdSaveXML to the header section of the Products form in NorthwindCS.adp. Add the following code to the Click event of the newly added command button:

```
Private Sub cmdSaveXML_Click()
  Dim adoRS As ADODB.Recordset

  ' Create the recordset. You can create a separate ADO connection
object
  ' but the following code uses the current ADP connection for
simplicity
  ' MAke sure to use a keyset cursor and adLockBatchOptimistic locking
  Set adoRS = New ADODB.Recordset
  adoRS.Open "products", CurrentProject.Connection, adOpenKeyset,
adLockBatchOptimistic

  ' The following single line of code saves the data to an XML file
  adoRS.Save "D:\test\products.xml", adPersistXML
  adoRS.Close
  Set adoRS = Nothing
End Sub
```

Once saved, the XML file can be opened in Notepad or a Web browser like Microsoft Internet Explorer, and should look similar to Figure 17.24.

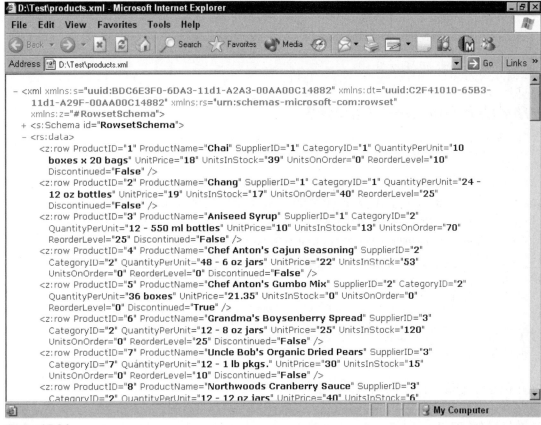

Figure 17-24

Loading the XML Data

Clear the Recordsource property of the form (but not the controls) and add the following code to the Open event of the form:

```vba
Private Sub Form_Open(Cancel As Integer)
  Dim adoRS As ADODB.Recordset

  ' Create the recordset against the existing XML file
  Set adoRS = New ADODB.Recordset
  adoRS.Open "D:\test\products.xml"

  ' Bind the new recordset to the form
  Set Me.Recordset = adoRS
  adoRS.Close
  Set adoRS = Nothing

End Sub
```

At this point, the form should be functional and a user should be able to scroll through records in the XML file.

Using Unbound Forms

Sometimes, the only way to get the form data to behave the way you want is to use what's called an "unbound" form, which is a form where any data display and manipulation is handled by the programmer instead of by Access.

Why Use Unbound Forms?

There are a lot of reasons to use unbound forms in Access. Sometimes there is just no other way to do what you want. Typical scenarios include the following:

❑ The ADO recordset is updatable directly but becomes read-only when bound to a form

❑ You have a trigger on a multitable SQL server view to allow insertion of new records but Access gives an error when bound to a form

❑ You want to use SQL Server application role security for data access

❑ You want to use DAO recordsets in an ADP or updatable ADO recordsets in an MDB

❑ You want to use server-side recordsets

❑ You want finer control over the recordset behavior

For example, you may have an ADO recordset that is completely updatable when using the recordset directly but it becomes read-only when bound to a form. Or you may have a trigger for a multitable view to handle insertions but you get errors trying to insert a new record from a form. In such cases, using an unbound form can allow the needed flexibility.

The primary drawback to using unbound forms is that there is no built-in method for displaying data in *datasheet* or *continuous form* view. Although it is possible to add ActiveX controls to an Access form that will allow for datasheet-type functionality, it may be more efficient to use another development environment like Visual Studio.NET. For forms that display single records at a time, however, unbound forms can be very effective.

Although it does take more lines of code to have an unbound form than a bound one, the code itself is not that complicated. Once a basic unbound form is written, you can also save it as a template for easy reuse in the future. As a general rule, DAO would normally be used in an MDB file and ADO would be used for an ADP file.

Creating Unbound Forms

It is normally easier to create a normal form and then convert it to an unbound form than it is to create an unbound form from scratch. When your form is bound, you are able to use the built-in form design tools to drag and drop fields onto the form and minimize the chance for misspelling a field name. Once you have your data fields added to the form, you can then convert it to an unbound form relatively easily.

To keep things simple, the Shippers table in the NorthwindCS SQL Server database will be used as an example. Since these forms are unbound, an ADO recordset can be used and the code will be the same for both an ADP and MDB file. If you want to have an unbound form that uses a DAO recordset, the steps would be similar but the DAO code would be slightly different. The following steps demonstrate how to create a simple regular Access form in an ADP and then convert it to an unbound form connected to a SQL Server table.

Create a Regular Form as a Template

If your ADP is connected to the `NorthwindCS` database, the quickest method to create a regular form is to click `New` from the `Forms` tab of the `Database` window. A dialog box similar to the one shown in Figure 17-25 will then appear.

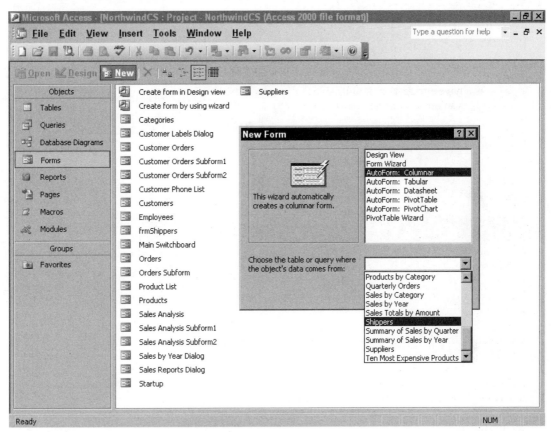

Figure 17-25

Specify `AutoForm:Columnar` and then select the `Shippers` table from the list. Access will then create an autogenerated form, as shown in Figure 17-26, that we can use as the basis for an unbound form. When finished, save the form as `frmShippers`.

Modify the Design of the Form

Because the record selectors and navigation buttons won't be usable when the form is unbound, those properties should be set to `No` on the `Format` tab of the `Form Properties` dialog box. Also, the `Recordsource` property on the `Data` tab of the form and the `Control Source` properties of the three text boxes will need to be cleared.

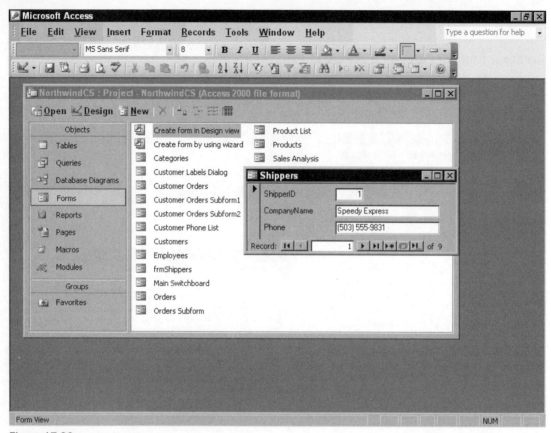

Figure 17-26

Additionally, add nine command buttons to the form with the following names and captions:

Name	Caption
cmdEdit	Edit
cmdSave	Save
cmdCancel	Cancel
cmdNewRecord	Add New
cmdMoveFirst	First
cmdPrevious	Previous
cmdNext	Next
cmdMoveLast	Last
cmdExit	Exit

When finished, the form should look similar to Figure 17-27 while in Form view:

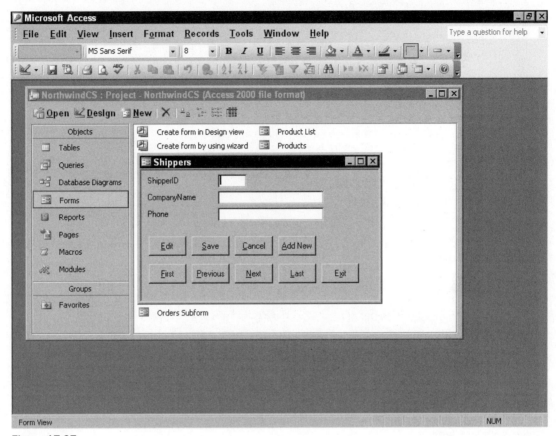

Figure 17-27

Note that the text boxes are blank because there is no record source defined for the form.

Creating theRecordset

Now that the basic form is created, code can be added to give it functionality. This section will discuss modifications that will allow the form to display custom data specified by the developer. Add the following code to the General Declarations section of the form's code module:

```
Dim rsTest As ADODB.Recordset
Dim cnTest As ADODB.Connection
Dim boolAddNewMode As Boolean

Private Sub pPopulateFields()
  ' Check to be sure the recordset is not in a BOF or EOF state.
  ' If it is then do nothing
  If Not rsTest.BOF And Not rsTest.EOF Then
    ' rsTest.Resync adAffectCurrent
    Me.ShipperID = rsTest.Fields("ShipperID")
```

```
      Me.CompanyName = rsTest.Fields("CompanyName")
      Me.Phone = rsTest.Fields("Phone")
   End If

   ' Set focus to the Exit control
   Me.cmdExit.SetFocus

   ' Reset the text boxes and save/cancel buttons to a
   ' locked or disabled state.
   Me.ShipperID.Locked = True
   Me.CompanyName.Locked = True
   Me.Phone.Locked = True
   Me.cmdCancel.Enabled = False
   Me.cmdSave.Enabled = False

   ' Reset the boolAddNewMode flag
   boolAddNewMode = False
End Sub
```

The pPopulateFields() procedure will be used in several other events. Next, add the following to the Open event of the Form:

```
Private Sub Form_Open(Cancel As Integer)
   ' For simplicity, we will use the built-in connection of the ADP.
   ' If we were creating an MDB or connecting to a different SQL Server,
   ' then the full connection string would need to be supplied
   Set cnTest = New ADODB.Connection
   cnTest.ConnectionString = CurrentProject.BaseConnectionString
   cnTest.Open

   ' Create the recordset and move to the first record
   Set rsTest = New ADODB.Recordset
   rsTest.Open "shippers", cnTest, adOpenDynamic, adLockOptimistic
   rsTest.MoveFirst

   ' Populate the text boxes on the form with data
   pPopulateFields
End Sub
```

When the form is opened now, data as shown in Figure 17-28 should appear.

Adding Code to Scroll the Recordset

Although the form can now display our custom data, it does not yet have much functionality because we have no method to scroll through records or to change any data. This section will go over adding code to some of the buttons created earlier to allow for browsing records. Add the following code to the cmdMoveFirst button:

```
Private Sub cmdMoveFirst_Click()
   rsTest.MoveFirst
   pPopulateFields
End Sub
```

Add the following code to the cmdPrevious button:

```
Private Sub cmdPrevious_Click()
    ' Code is needed to check to see if the recordset is
    ' already before the beginning of the recordset.
    ' If it is, then do nothing
  If rsTest.BOF Then
    Exit Sub
  End If
  rsTest.MovePrevious

    ' Test for BOF again after moving the recordset
    ' If it is, then reverse the move and do nothing
  If rsTest.BOF Then
    rsTest.MoveNext
    Exit Sub
  End If

    ' If everything is fine, then repopulate the controls
    ' with data from the new record
  pPopulateFields
End Sub
```

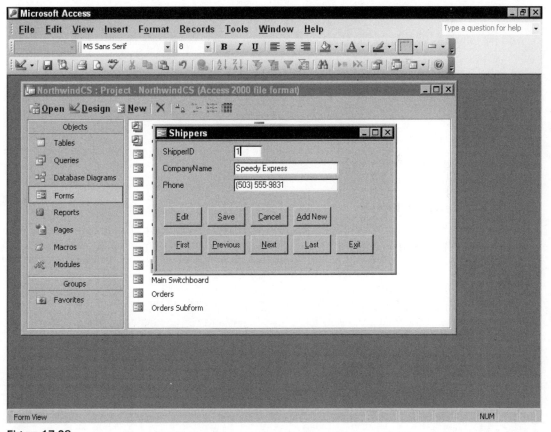

Figure 17-28

Add the following code to the cmdNext button:

```
Private Sub cmdNext_Click()
    ' Code is needed to check if the recordset is
    ' already beyond the end of the recordset.
    ' If it is, then do nothing
    If rsTest.EOF Then
        Exit Sub
    End If
    rsTest.MoveNext

    ' Test for EOF again after moving the recordset
    ' If it is, then reverse the move and do nothing
    If rsTest.EOF Then
        rsTest.MovePrevious
        Exit Sub
    End If

    ' If everything is fine, then repopulate the controls
    ' with data from the new record
    pPopulateFields
End Sub
```

Add the following code to the cmdMoveLast button:

```
Private Sub cmdMoveLast_Click()
    rsTest.MoveLast
    pPopulateFields
End Sub
```

After adding the above code, you should now be able to click the next, previous, first, and last buttons to scroll through the records without generating any errors. However, the text boxes are locked so the user can't make any changes at this point.

Enable Records To Be Edited

Although an edit-type button is not absolutely necessary, it simplifies the coding necessary to keep track of changes. Otherwise, code would be needed each time the recordset is moved to compare values and see if anything needs to be updated. With this method, nothing is updated until the user clicks the Save button.

To enable modifications, add the following code to the Click event of the Edit button:

```
Private Sub cmdEdit_Click()
    ' Only allow edits if there is a current record.
    ' Note that the ShipperID Fiield does not get unlocked
    ' Because it is a Primary Key Field.
    If Not rsTest.BOF And Not rsTest.EOF Then
        Me.CompanyName.Locked = False
        Me.Phone.Locked = False
    End If
```

```
    ' Sets focus to the Company Name field
    Me.CompanyName.SetFocus

    ' Enable the save/cancel buttons
    Me.cmdSave.Enabled = True
    Me.cmdCancel.Enabled = True
End Sub
```

To enable saving the modifications, add the following code to the cmdSave button:

```
Private Sub cmdSave_Click()

    ' Check if this is for new Record or change to existing
    If boolAddNewMode = True Then
        rsTest.AddNew
    End If

    ' Update the recordset
    ' Be prepared to handle any errors that may occur
    rsTest.Fields("CompanyName") = Me.CompanyName
    rsTest.Fields("Phone") = Me.Phone
    rsTest.Update

    ' This command refreshes the newly added record
    If boolAddNewMode = True Then
        rsTest.MoveLast
    End If

    pPopulateFields
End Sub
```

To allow for cancelling a pending modification without saving it, add the following code to the cmdCancel button:

```
Private Sub cmdCancel_Click()

    ' Check if the recordset is in an add new state.
    ' Clear any data present, if needed
    If boolAddNewMode Then
        Me.ShipperID = ""
        Me.CompanyName = ""
        Me.Phone = ""
    End If

    pPopulateFields
End Sub
```

You should now be able to modify existing records and have them updated. To enable adding new records, add the following code to the Click event of the cmdNewRecord command button:

```
Private Sub cmdNewRecord_Click()

    ' Set the boolAddNewMode flag to true
    boolAddNewMode = True
```

```
    ' Clear data from the controls and unlock
    ' In this case the SHipperID is autogenerated
    ' so there is no need to unlock the shipperid field
    Me.ShipperID = ""
    Me.CompanyName = ""
    Me.Phone = ""
    Me.CompanyName.Locked = False
    Me.Phone.Locked = False

    ' Set focus to a field
    Me.CompanyName.SetFocus

    ' Enable the save/cancel buttons
    Me.cmdSave.Enabled = True
    Me.cmdCancel.Enabled = True
End Sub
```

Add some code to the cmdExit button to close the form:

```
Private Sub cmdExit_Click()
    DoCmd.Close
End Sub
```

At this point, the form should be fully functional when run and you should not generate any errors when testing it out. None of the code above is overly complex and could be modified to behave differently depending on your needs. This form could also be saved as a template and reused when needed to speed development of future unbound forms.

Summary

Although there is certainly far more to client/server development with Access than we can print in one chapter, one of the key issues we hope you take from this is that client/server development is more than just moving your data tables from Access to SQL Server. Designing an efficient client/server application takes a little more effort and planning, but the end result can be well worth it.

18

Working with the Win32 Registry

The Registry is the heart and soul of the 32-bit Windows operating system. It maintains information about the hardware and software installed on a computer, configuration settings, user settings, and information that the operating system needs to function. In fact, 32-bit Windows cannot operate without it.

The ability to access and edit the information contained in the Registry is essential to all but the most basic software developer, and, if you plan to do any serious programming, understanding the Registry is essential.

As you'll see, VBA only supports four native Registry functions, which allow you to store, retrieve, and delete values from one specific area of the Registry. To do anything more advanced, you'll need to use the Windows Registry APIs. If you don't feel confident with API programming, you should first peruse Chapter 13, "*Extending VBA with APIs,*" which will give you the background you'll need to understand the more advanced topics in this chapter.

Although it's true that you can't damage anything by poking about in the Registry, it's also true that making changes to Registry entries when you don't know what you're doing is like randomly pressing buttons in the control room of your local nuclear power station; press the wrong button and everything will melt down to a bubbling fluorescent ooze at your feet.

This chapter is not intended to provide highly detailed information about every *key*, *subkey*, and *value* in the Registry; to do so would require a book far larger than you could carry. Instead, our aim is to provide you with enough information so you can confidently find your way around the Registry and can write basic VBA code to create, retrieve, edit, and delete Registry values. We'll start by taking a basic look at what the Registry is, what's in it, how it is structured, how it works, and, finally, how programmers can make best use of it.

About the Registry

The Registry first appeared in Windows 3.1, in a file called *Reg.dat* and was mainly used to store information about OLE objects. At that time, several files, namely, Win.ini, System.ini, and other .ini files that were application-specific, carried out the bulk of what is handled by today's Registry.

System.ini maintained information and settings for the hardware (disk drives, memory, mice, and so on). Win.ini controlled the desktop and the applications that were installed. Changes to device drivers, fonts, system settings, and user preferences would all be recorded in the .ini files, and new applications added their information to the .ini files too.

This all worked pretty well until the number of applications grew and their complexity increased, because each installed application added a raft of information to the Registry to the point where it was obvious its 64kB file size limit would be reached. Additionally, everyone made additions to the .ini files, but no one ever deleted anything, even if the application was upgraded or uninstalled. So System.ini and Win.ini grew and grew, and as they grew, performance degraded.

To counter this problem, software vendors started supplying .ini files of their own, and instead of the Windows .ini files containing application-specific information and settings, they contained only pointers to the custom .ini files. This seemed like a good idea at the time; however, good ideas sometimes create problems of their own. In this case, it was the fact that a large number of .ini files began appearing throughout the system, and since an application's .ini settings could override those of Win.ini, there was no systemwide setting that had priority. Anything could happen!

In 32-bit Windows, Registry's role was expanded to include all the operating system and application settings and preferences, doing away with the necessity for .ini files.

As it is today, the Registry is a set of files, called *hives*, which control all aspects of the operating system and how it interacts with the hardware and software that operate within it. It brings together all the information previously held in Reg.dat and all the .ini files. It was designed to work exclusively with 32-bit applications, and its file size has been increased to about 30MB. With the exception of the hive that controls hardware (which is re-created every time you log on), you can find a list of the hive files in the following Registry key.

```
HKEY_LOCAL_MACHINE\System\CurrentControlSet\Control\hivelist
```

What the Registry Does

Without the Registry, Windows will not have enough information to run. It certainly will not have enough information to control devices, to run, and to control applications, or to respond to user input. The Registry essentially performs the following functions.

❑ *Hardware and device driver information*: In order for the operating system to access a hardware device, it gets the location and settings of the driver from the Registry, even if the device is a basic input/output system (BIOS)-supported device. Drivers are independent of the operating system, but Windows still needs to know where to find them and how to use them. So information such as their filename, location, version, and configuration details must be accessed, otherwise they would be unusable.

❑ *Application information*: When you launch an application, the Registry supplies all the information the operating system needs in order to run it and manage it.

The Registry also contains information like file locations, menus and toolbars, window status, and other details. The operating system also stores file information in the Registry, such as installation date, the user who installed it, version number, add-ins, and so on.

Often, applications store temporary or runtime information in the Registry, such as the current position of a window, the last document opened by a user, or the value of a `Don't display this` check box.

What the Registry Controls

The Registry doesn't *control* anything, but it does contain information that is used by the operating system and applications to control almost everything. The type of information that the Registry stores is about users and machines (computers). That's why there are only two persistent Registry hives: `HKEY_LOCAL_MACHINE` and `HKEY_USERS`.

Every Registry entry controls either a user function or a computer function. User functions include customizable options, while computer functions include those items that are common to all users, such as the printers and the software installed on a computer.

Some other examples of user functions controlled by the Registry include:

❑ Control panel functions

❑ Desktop appearance

❑ Network preferences

❑ Explorer functionality and features

Some of these functions are the same regardless of the user, while others are user-specific.

Computer-related items are based on the computer name, without regard to the specific user, for example, installing an application. Availability and access to the application are constant, regardless of the user; however, icons to launch the application are dependent on the user. Network protocol availability and priority are based on the computer, but current connections are based on user information.

Some examples of computer-based control items in the Registry include:

❑ Access control

❑ Log-in validation

❑ File and print sharing

❑ Network card settings and protocols

❑ System performance and virtual memory settings

The Windows Registry is much more complex than the older .ini files, but then 32-bit Windows is also far too complex for them now. It is time, then, to acquire an understanding of how the Registry works, what it does, and how to work with it. The remainder of this chapter is devoted to just that.

Accessing the Registry

You can access the Registry with a built-in Windows utility called the *Registry Editor*. There are two flavors of Registry Editor: RegEdit.exe and Regedt32.exe.

RegEdit.exe

Prior to Windows NT, *Regedit.exe* was a 16-bit application for editing the Registry on 16-bit Windows platforms. It was included in Windows NT and 2000 for backward compatibility, but due to its limited functionality under the 32-bit environment, Microsoft recommends that you use Regedit.exe only for its search capabilities on Windows NT 4.0 and Windows 2000.

> Note: Microsoft rewrote RegEdit.exe as a 32-bit application for Windows XP and Windows Server 2003, so, on those platforms, RegEdit.exe is the preferred 32-bit Registry Editor.

Regedt32.exe

Prior to Windows XP and Windows Server 2003, *Regedt32.exe* was the preferred 32-bit Registry Editor for Windows NT and 2000. But, of course, nothing is perfect, and Regedt32.exe had limitations, for example, it could not import or export Registry entries (.reg) files.

Now, under Windows XP and Windows Server 2003, Regedt32.exe is a simple wrapper program that runs Regedit.exe. On Windows NT and 2000, you should use Regedt32.exe; whereas on Windows XP and Windows Server 2003, you can use either Regedt32.exe or RegEdit.exe.

Launching and Using the Registry Editor

You won't find the Registry Editor on the Start menu. As it's not something that Microsoft wants the average user to fool around with, the only way to launch it is via the Run dialog box.

1. Click the Start button, and then click Run. The Run dialog box is displayed.

2. Type regedit or regedt32, then click OK. The Registry Editor is displayed.

Figure 18-1 shows the Registry Editor with the HKEY_CURRENT_USER hive (the purpose of which is explained in *Registry Organization*, below) expanded to show some of its keys, subkeys, and values. You can think of keys and subkeys as being like the hierarchy of folders and subfolders in the Windows file system. As its name suggests, a *value* is a named container for a single piece of information, such as the width of a menu. The Registry Editor's right-hand pane shows the values contained within the subkey selected in the left pane. With the exception of a default value that is present in every subkey, each value has its own unique name. The icon to the left of each value indicates its data type.

Registry Organization

The Registry *tree* is divided into the following six sections (five in Windows NT). These major sections are called *Root Keys*, much like c:\ is the *root directory* of your hard disk. Since the Registry can differ greatly from one operating system version to another, we have shown the most common keys, and for the

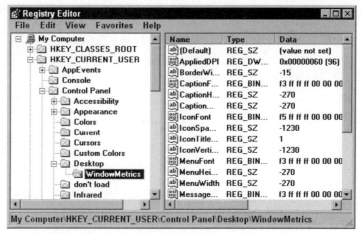

Figure 18-1

sake of simplicity, we have listed them in the order in which they appear in the Registry Editor (see Figure 18-2).

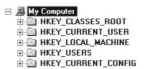

Figure 18-2

HKEY_CLASSES_ROOT

This branch of the Registry tree is actually an alias for HKEY_LOCAL_MACHINE\Software\Classes, and contains information about file associations, documents, and OLE objects. It is a very large branch, containing several thousand entries at the first level alone.

The first group contains subkeys that look like file associations, and they are. Each of these subkeys contains a reference to the second group that makes up the remainder of the first-level subkeys. These are the class definitions associated with the relevant document. The class definitions contain information that includes the following:

❑ A descriptive name for the document type (as you might see in the Windows Explorer type column). See Figure 18-3.

❑ A pointer to the default icon.

❑ Information about how the application handles the documents as OLE objects.

❑ Information about how the documents are manipulated from the Windows shell (what context menu actions can be taken). See Figure 18-4.

HKEY_CLASSES_ROOT is updated every time an application is installed or removed.

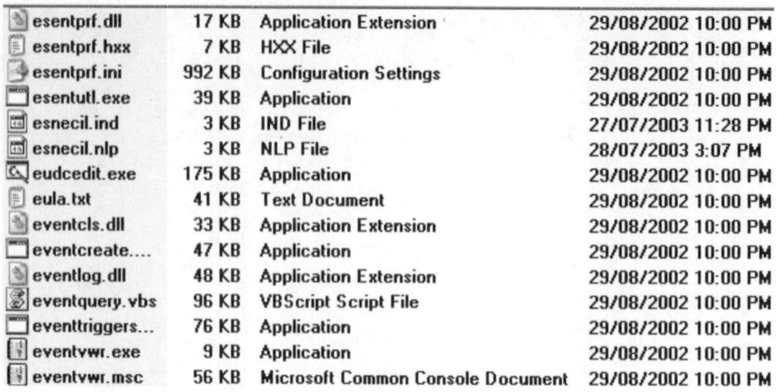

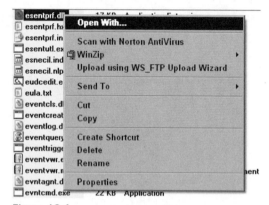

esentprf.dll 17 KB Application Extension 29/08/2002 10:00 PM
esentprf.hxx 7 KB HXX File 29/08/2002 10:00 PM
esentprf.ini 992 KB Configuration Settings 29/08/2002 10:00 PM
esentutl.exe 39 KB Application 29/08/2002 10:00 PM
esnecil.ind 3 KB IND File 27/07/2003 11:28 PM
esnecil.nlp 3 KB NLP File 28/07/2003 3:07 PM
eudcedit.exe 175 KB Application 29/08/2002 10:00 PM
eula.txt 41 KB Text Document 29/08/2002 10:00 PM
eventcls.dll 33 KB Application Extension 29/08/2002 10:00 PM
eventcreate.... 47 KB Application 29/08/2002 10:00 PM
eventlog.dll 48 KB Application Extension 29/08/2002 10:00 PM
eventquery.vbs 96 KB VBScript Script File 29/08/2002 10:00 PM
eventtriggers... 76 KB Application 29/08/2002 10:00 PM
eventvwr.exe 9 KB Application 29/08/2002 10:00 PM
eventvwr.msc 56 KB Microsoft Common Console Document 29/08/2002 10:00 PM
Figure 18-3

eula.txt
esnecil.ind
esnecil.nlp
Open With...
Scan with Norton AntiVirus
WinZip
Upload using WS_FTP Upload Wizard
Send To
Cut
Copy
Create Shortcut
Delete
Rename
Properties
Figure 18-4

HKEY_CURRENT_USER

This branch is built during logon and is an alias for the current user's subkey in the `HKEY_USERS` branch (see below), and contains user-specific information. There are seven major subkeys in this branch, but depending on how your system is set up and what's installed, you might find some extra ones.

AppEvents

This subkey contains information about the sound files that are specified for individual system and application events, for example, the Windows `Logon` sound and the `MailBeep` sound. The `AppEvents` subkey contains two subkeys of its own: `Event Labels`, which contains the event names, and `Schemes`, which contains references to the actual sound files organized by the application.

Console

This subkey contains all the user options for the MS-DOS Windows, including layout, screen color, and font settings.

Control Panel

This subkey contains many other subkeys for all the `Control Panel` settings, such as color schemes, screen savers, keyboard repeat rate, mouse speed, and so on.

Environment

This key contains the environment settings, specifically the temporary file locations. The `Environment` subkey contains the environment variables that you would see in DOS when you typed `SET` at the command line. Much of the information contained in this key is connected to the `System` applet in the `Control Panel`.

Identities

If Outlook Express 5.*x* (or later) is installed, there will also be an Identities key. This key contains other subkeys for Outlook Express account, e-mail, and newsgroup settings, and the MSN Messenger, if installed.

InstallLocationsMRU

This subkey contains a historical list of the locations from which programs were most recently installed. The acronym *MRU* stands for *most recently used*.

Keyboard Layout

This subkey contains three other subkeys that contain information about the current keyboard layout, which you can set using the Control Panel's `Keyboard` properties. The `Preload` subkey contains a value for each installed keyboard layout. These values point to keys in `HKEY_LOCAL_MACHINE\System\CurrentControlSet\Control\Keyboard Layouts`, which contains references to the keyboard drivers.

Network

This subkey contains two other subkeys that describe the mapped network drives, including persistent connections and recent connections. These subkeys contain values for the connection type and the provider name of each connection.

Printers

This subkey contains information about the current user's installed printers. There may also be a subkey for each remote printer, if installed.

RemoteAccess

This subkey contains address and profile subkeys for the user's dial-up and networking connections. The subkey itself contains global connection details, such as the area code and the number of redial attempts, whereas the `Address` and `Profile` subkeys contain settings for specific connection.

Software

This subkey is easily the largest key in the Registry, and is one of the two Registry keys that are intended to be used for applications; the other being `HKEY_LOCAL_MACHINE\Software`, which is discussed below.

The `Software` subkey contains vendor-specific subkeys that describe the current user's software settings and a raft of application-specific information that were previously stored in the Win.ini or custom vendor .ini files under Windows 3.*x*. Each vendor subkey contains a separate subkey for each software application supplied by that vendor. The subkeys and values below them are completely determined by the vendor, but typically contain user preferences, histories, and so on.

Of particular interest to VB and VBA programmers is the `HKEY_CURRENT_USER\Software\VB and VBA Program Settings` key, which has been set aside specifically for us. Naturally, you will find this key mirrored in HKEY_USERS\current user subkey\Software\VB and VBA Program Settings.

UNICODE Program Groups

This key contains information about the installed applications that use Unicode.

HKEY_LOCAL_MACHINE

The HKEY_LOCAL_MACHINE branch contains all the computer-specific settings, including hardware configuration and any computer-specific settings for installed software. In Windows XP, there are five major subkeys in this branch.

Hardware

This subkey contains profiles for all the hardware that has been installed on the computer, for example, device drivers, resources (like IRQ assignments), and other details.All the information contained in this subkey is built during startup and deleted again during shutdown. That being the case, you should only use this subkey for viewing, not writing.

SAM

This subkey contains all the user and group account information for the Security Account Manager (SAM). The information in its subkeys is maintained in User Manager. The information contained in this subkey is also mapped to HKEY_LOCAL_MACHINE\Security, so changes to either are immediately reflected in the other.

You should not attempt to change anything in here unless you want to reformat your hard disk afterwards. Since all the data is binary, you would probably need C3PO to decipher it anyway.

Security

This subkey contains all the security information for the computer, such as password policies, user rights and permissions, and the groups to which each user belongs. The information in its subkeys is maintained in User Manager. You should not attempt to change anything in here either.

Software

As mentioned earlier (in HKEY_CURRENT_USER\Software), this subkey contains specific configuration information about the software installed on the computer. The entries under this subkey apply to all users, not just the current user, and contain information about what software is installed, and also define file associations and OLE information.

You will also notice under this key, a subkey called Classes, which is an alias for HKEY_CLASSES_ROOT.

System

This subkey contains other subkeys that contain the persistent information about devices and parameters that the system needs in order to start up. This includes control sets that contain information like the computer name, subsystems that need to be started, hardware configuration for devices and drivers that the operating system loads, specific hardware profile information when multiple hardware profiles are configured, file system services, and so on.

HKEY_USERS

This branch contains all the settings for the current user and the default user. Depending on the number of users registered on the system, there can be a variable number of subkeys.

.DEFAULT

The settings in this key constitute the default template that is applied when new users are added to the system, and includes user profiles, environment, screen, sound, and other user-related settings. If you change any of the settings in this subkey, all new users will inherit the same settings. Existing users will retain their existing settings, though.

The information for the current user changes according to who is logged on. The user information is represented by subkeys whose names represent each user's security ID (SID).

```
S-1-5-21-1475383443-718524000-196120627-1006
```

There may be several subkeys such as this, each representing a user who has logged on to the system. The number is the user's SID. Every user on the network is assigned an SID by User Manager for domains, and each SID is unique. The information will change, therefore, depending on who is currently logged on.

The information for this key is gleaned from the NTUSER.DAT file, found in the user's profile directory (c:\Documents and Settings\username). This subkey carries the same data as HKEY_CURRENT_USER:

```
S-1-5-21-1475383443-718524000-196120627-1006_Classes
```

For every user key, there will be a _Classes key, like this one. This is where HKEY_CURRENT_USER gets its Network and Software subkey information.

HKEY_CURRENT_CONFIG

This branch contains all of the details for the profiles that are current in the system, and is taken from HKEY_LOCAL_MACHINE at system startup.

Using the Built-In VBA Registry Functions

Many programmers use global variables to hold values that are used throughout the application. There are two problems associated with this approach. First, if an unhandled error occurs, all your global variables are reset. Second, you have to reassign their values every time the application is launched. An alternative is to store this type of value in the database, but if you're storing the connection string to the remote data store, you might find it a little difficult to get at if your application doesn't know where to look.

Another alternative, one that is used in most professional applications, is to store such information in the Registry. You can store all sorts of information in the Registry, from simple values that your applications use from time to time, to connection strings, to user preferences, such as the position and color of forms, and so on.

VBA provides four native functions for manipulating the Registry within VB and VBA. The sole drawback to these functions (if you want to call it a drawback) is that they operate on only one part of the Registry; one that has been specifically allocated to VB and VBA.

The HKEY_CURRENT_USER\Software\VB and VBA Program Settings key has been set aside for our exclusive use. As mentioned earlier in this chapter, this key is mirrored in HKEY_USERS\current user subkey\Software.

As application-specific Registry entries are stored using the *application-name, section, key* construct, it makes sense that VBA should do the same. The remainder of this section describes the native VBA Registry functions and how to use them.

SaveSetting

SaveSetting() allows you to store a single value in the HKEY_CURRENT_USER\Software\VB and VBA Program Settings hive. Its syntax is as follows:

```
SaveSetting appname, section, key, setting
```

The arguments are described in the following table:

Argument	Description
appname	This argument is a required string expression that contains the name of the application or project whose key is being set.
section	This is a required string expression that contains the name of the section under which the key is to be set.
key	This is a required string expression that contains the name of the key you are setting.
setting	This is a required expression of any data type that defines the value to which the key will be set.

You can store as many values as you like, in as many keys and subkeys as you like. All VB/VBA applications will have access to the values you store, as long as they know the correct appname, section, and key names.

To standardize your Registry entries, you would normally use the CurrentProject.Name property as the appname argument, although you are free to use any expression you like. We typically use the Application Title property.

The following two calls to SaveSetting() are equivalent:

```
SaveSetting CurrentDb.Properties("AppTitle"), "Settings", "myKey",
"123"

SaveSetting appname := CurrentDb.Properties("AppTitle"), section :=
"Settings", key := "myKey", setting := 123
```

Notice we used a string value "123" in the first example, and a numeric example in the second. This is acceptable; however, you must remember that `GetSetting` always returns a string and `GetAllSettings` always returns a variant.

Note: You can set the `Application Title` *property through the* `Tools, Startup` *menu option.*

GetSetting

You can use the `GetSetting()` function to retrieve a string value from a single Registry key that you have previously saved. It returns the value specified by the *default* argument if the *key* is empty or doesn't exist. `GetSetting()` has the following syntax:

```
GetSetting(appname, section, key[,default])
```

The function arguments are explained in the following table.

Argument	Description
appname	This argument is a required string expression that contains the name of the application or project whose key is being sought.
section	This is a required string expression that contains the name of the section under which the key is found.
key	This is a required string expression that contains the name of the requested key.
default	This argument is the optional default expression to be returned if the key is empty. If you omit this argument, it is assumed to be a zero-length string (" ").

The following two calls to `GetSetting()` are the same:

```
?GetSetting(CurrentDb.Properties("AppTitle"), "Settings", "SomeSetting",
"myDefault")

?GetSetting(appname := CurrentDb.Properties("AppTitle"), section :=
"Settings", key := "myKey", default := "myDefault")
```

Note: You can set the `Application Title` *property through the* `Tools, Startup` *menu option.*

GetAllSettings

The `GetAllSettings()` function retrieves all the key values that exist under the specified section, as a two-dimensional variant array. It has the following syntax:

```
GetAllSettings(appname, section)
```

The `GetAllSettings()` function returns an uninitialized (empty) variant if either `appname` or `section` does not exist. The arguments are described in the following table.

Argument	Description
Appname	This argument is a required string expression that contains the name of the application or project whose key is being sought.
Section	This is a required string expression that contains the name of the section under which the key is found.

The following two calls to `GetAllSettings()` are equivalent:

```
?GetSetting(CurrentDb.Properties("AppTitle"), "Settings", "myKey")

?GetSetting(appname := CurrentDb.Properties("AppTitle"), section :=
"Settings")
```

To use this function, you must declare a standard variant that will hold the return values. That's right, a standard variable—not an array. If there are values to return, the function redimensions the variable as an array.

For example, the following code segment saves several values to the Registry using `SaveSetting` and retrieves them into a variant using `GetAllSettings()`.

```
Dim varMySettings As Variant
Dim intCtr As Integer

SaveSetting "myapp", "mysection", "mykey1", "my first setting"
SaveSetting "myapp", "mysection", "mykey2", "my second setting"
SaveSetting "myapp", "mysection", "mykey3", "my third setting"
varMySettings = GetAllSettings("myapp", "mysection")

For intCtr = LBound(varMySettings, 1) To UBound(varMySettings, 1)
    Debug.Print varMySettings(intCtr, 0) & " - " &
varMySettings(intCtr, 1)
Next intCtr

DeleteSetting "myapp", "mysection"
```

Notice that the first dimension contains the key name, whereas the second dimension contains the actual value.

DeleteSetting

The last of the native VBA Registry functions is `DeleteSetting()`. As its name suggests, `DeleteSetting` deletes a section or key, depending on whether the optional key is supplied. It has the following syntax:

```
DeleteSetting appname, section[, key]
```

The DeleteSetting() arguments are described in the following table.

Argument	Description
Appname	This argument is a required string expression that contains the name of the application or project whose key is being sought.
Section	This is a required string expression that contains the name of the section where the key is being deleted. If only appname and section are provided, the specified section is deleted, along with all its keys.
Key	This is an optional string expression that contains the name of the key to be deleted.

The following two calls to DeleteSetting() are equivalent in that they both delete the specified key:

```
DeleteSetting CurrentDb.Properties("AppTitle"), "Settings",
"myKey"
DeleteSetting appname := CurrentDb.Properties("AppTitle"), section
:= "Settings", key :="myKey"
```

Similarly, the following DeleteSetting() calls both delete the entire specified section and all its keys:

```
DeleteSetting CurrentDb.Properties("AppTitle"), "Settings"
DeleteSetting appname := CurrentDb.Properties("AppTitle"), section
:= "Settings"
```

Typical Uses for the Built-In VBA Registry Functions

Now that you have a fundamental understanding of the Registry, you might still be wondering how you would use it and what values you would want to store there. In short, why bother? We remember asking that very same question!

It all comes down to functionality. As programmers, we are already disciplined enough to know not to use a particular technology, function, or facility unless it is necessary. For example, you wouldn't build a complex procedure where a native one exists. But by the same token, we should employ things that allow us to provide the functionality our application requirements demand.

Implementing a Daily Reminders Screen

A typical example might be the humble Daily Reminders screen, which is implemented in many applications. This screen usually pops up when the application starts up, to remind the user of overdue accounts, tasks they need to perform that day, or any number of things that the user needs to be made aware of.

Having such a facility can be of great benefit to both the organization and the user, but some users prefer to display this screen when *they* choose to display it. Having the screen pop up every time they start the application can be a real nuisance, particularly if it takes some time to process and sort the information that's displayed. The resolution here is to offer the user the ability to have the screen pop up, or not.

To do this, you would need to store a Boolean value somewhere. You can store it in a table, but if your database is built on a client/server model, with the tables stored on a server share, the setting would affect all users. Storing the value in a local table would mean all users of that particular computer would similarly share the same setting. The answer is to store the value in the Registry so each user can set their own preferences. Let's look at how you would implement this behavior.

Start by creating an `Overdue Accounts` form, containing a list box, command button, and check box. For this example, we simply added the company names and amounts to the list box's `RowSource` property, but a real form would probably populate it using a recordset.

Figure 18-5

To implement the behavior we want, add the following code to the check box's `Click()` event.

```
Private Sub chkShowAtStartup_Click()
    Dim strApp As String

    'Assuming you have set the Application Title property in Tools,
Startup.
    strApp = DBEngine(0)(0).Properties("AppTitle")

    'Save the new checkbox setting.
    SaveSetting strApp, "Settings", "Show at Startup", _
Me.chkShowAtStartup
End Sub
```

In the above code, it doesn't matter if the user doesn't click the check box, because the form will display whether the setting exists or not. But if they do click it, the appropriate setting will be immediately saved to the Registry.

Of course, you need to set the initial value of the check box when the form displays, so add the following code to the form's `Load` event.

```
Private Sub Form_Load()
    Dim strApp As String

    'Assuming you have set the Application Title property in Tools,
Startup.
    strApp = DBEngine(0)(0).Properties("AppTitle")

    'Set the checkbox value.
    'If the setting doesn't exist, assume a default True.
    Me.chkShowAtStartup = GetSetting(strApp, "Settings","Show at
Startup", True)
End Sub
```

Then all you have to do is modify your startup code to decide whether to show this form or not.

```
Dim strApp As String
Dim booShowForm As Boolean

'Assuming you have set the Application Title property in Tools, Startup.
strApp = DBEngine(0)(0).Properties("AppTitle")

booShowForm = GetSetting(strApp, "Settings","Show at Startup", True)
'If the setting doesn't exist, it is probably the
'first time the user has launched the application,
'so show the form.
If booShowForm = True Then
    DoCmd.OpenForm "frmOverDueAccts"
End If
```

Storing and Retrieving Connection Strings

Where several temporary databases, spreadsheets, and files are frequently connected, you can store their connection strings in the Registry to save time and memory. For example, the following function retrieves the connection string for one of several external data sources:

```
Public Function GetConnString(strSourceName As String) As String
    Dim strApp As String
    Dim strCon As String

    strApp = DBEngine(0)(0).Properties("AppTitle")

    strCon = GetSetting(strApp, "Settings", strSourceName, "")
    GetConnString = strCon
End Function
```

Storing User Preferences

We often use the VBA Registry functions to store user preferences, such as the following:

❑   Control default values, for example, the default date to enter into a text box.

❑   List sort orders, for example, whether to display the delinquent customers list by value or by due date.

❑   Menus and toolbars that the user wants displayed.

❑   Form colors.

❑   Sound effects on/off.

❑   Language settings, and so on.

Storing a Last Used List

Like the Documents list on the Windows Start menu (stored in HKEY_CURRENT_USER\Software\ Microsoft\Windows\CurrentVersion\Explorer\RecentDocs), you can store your own lists in the Registry. For example, a list of the last 10 forms that a user visited, the last six files opened, or the last one that the user changed.

Using the Win32 Registry APIs

This section describes the Win32 Registry API functions you can use to access and manipulate a wider range of Registry keys than you can with the inbuilt VBA functions. Before attempting this section, however, we strongly advise that you read Chapter 14, "*Extending VBA with APIs."*

The Win32 API provides all the functions you'll need to access the Registry. Of course, the scope of some functions is restricted for purely common-sense reasons; after all, there is little point in making changes to the temporary areas.

But, of course, this begs the question: Where do I find information about all these constants and functions? Welcome to the wonderful world of programming! Unfortunately, Microsoft has not published a definitive text on the Registry, or indeed the Win32 API, so you need to rely on the various books, web pages, and third-party software utilities that deal with these topics.

With regard to using the Registry, this section provides a real-world example of how to use the Registry API functions. In Appendix L, you will find a complete list of all the Registry functions, along with declarations of the Registry-related constants and user-defined types. Also, at the end of this chapter, we have listed the few resources that we believe are worth a look. The *Resources* section at the end of Chapter 13 also indicates where to source information about the Win32 API, which will also provide details about the many functions, constants, and user-defined types you'll need.

Putting It All together

To make sense of all the information presented in the preceding sections, we need to see how the Registry APIs are used. To do that, we have created a module to perform the five most widely used functions: create a key, set a key value, read that value, delete the value, and, of course, delete the key itself.

Create a new standard module and add the following declarations to it (you can find a complete list in Appendix J). Note the addition of two enums: w32Key and w32ValueType. These enums are useful when actually writing the procedures, so you don't have to remember all the constant declarations.

Notice also that all the declarations are now Public. This allows them to be accessed from anywhere in our application. If you were to create a class to wrap all your Registry functions, the declarations would still need to be in a standard module, and they would still need to be declared Public.

```
'Key declarations
Public Const HKEY_CLASSES_ROOT As Long = &H80000000
Public Const HKEY_CURRENT_CONFIG As Long = &H80000005
Public Const HKEY_CURRENT_USER As Long = &H80000001
Public Const HKEY_DYN_DATA As Long = &H80000006
Public Const HKEY_LOCAL_MACHINE As Long = &H80000002
Public Const HKEY_PERF_ROOT As Long = HKEY_LOCAL_MACHINE
Public Const HKEY_PERFORMANCE_DATA As Long = &H80000004
Public Const HKEY_USERS As Long = &H80000003
```

```
'Root key Enum
Public Enum w32Key
    w32CLASSES_ROOT = HKEY_CLASSES_ROOT
    w32CURRENT_CONFIG = HKEY_CURRENT_CONFIG
    w32CURRENT_USER = HKEY_CURRENT_USER
    w32DYN_DATA = HKEY_DYN_DATA
    w32LOCAL_MACHINE = HKEY_LOCAL_MACHINE
    w32PERF_ROOT = HKEY_PERF_ROOT
    w32PERF_DATA = HKEY_PERFORMANCE_DATA
    w32USERS = HKEY_USERS
End Enum

'Parameter declarations
Public Const REG_NOTIFY_CHANGE_ATTRIBUTES As Long = &H2
Public Const REG_NOTIFY_CHANGE_LAST_SET As Long = &H4
Public Const REG_NOTIFY_CHANGE_NAME As Long = &H1
Public Const REG_NOTIFY_CHANGE_SECURITY As Long = &H8
Public Const REG_CREATED_NEW_KEY As Long = &H1
Public Const REG_OPENED_EXISTING_KEY As Long = &H2
Public Const REG_OPTION_BACKUP_RESTORE As Long - 4
Public Const REG_OPTION_VOLATILE As Long = 1
Public Const REG_OPTION_NON_VOLATILE As Long = 0
Public Const STANDARD_RIGHTS_ALL As Long = &H1F0000
Public Const SYNCHRONIZE As Long = &H100000
Public Const READ_CONTROL As Long = &H20000
Public Const STANDARD_RIGHTS_READ As Long = (READ_CONTROL)
Public Const STANDARD_RIGHTS_WRITE As Long = (READ_CONTROL)
Public Const KEY_CREATE_LINK As Long = &H20
Public Const KEY_CREATE_SUB_KEY As Long = &H4
Public Const KEY_ENUMERATE_SUB_KEYS As Long = &H8
Public Const KEY_NOTIFY As Long = &H10
Public Const KEY_QUERY_VALUE As Long = &H1
Public Const KEY_SET_VALUE As Long = &H2

'Key value types
Public Const REG_BINARY As Long = 3
Public Const REG_DWORD As Long = 4
Public Const REG_DWORD_BIG_ENDIAN As Long = 5
Public Const REG_DWORD_LITTLE_ENDIAN As Long = 4
Public Const REG_EXPAND_SZ As Long = 2
Public Const REG_LINK As Long = 6
Public Const REG_MULTI_SZ As Long = 7
Public Const REG_NONE As Long = 0
Public Const REG_RESOURCE_LIST As Long = 8
Public Const REG_SZ As Long = 1

'Key value type Enum
Public Enum w32ValueType
    w32BINARY = REG_BINARY
    w32DWORD = REG_DWORD
    w32DWORD_BIG = REG_DWORD_BIG_ENDIAN
    w32DWORD_LITTLE = REG_DWORD_LITTLE_ENDIAN
    w32EXPANDSz = REG_EXPAND_SZ
    w32LINK = REG_LINK
```

```
    w32MULTISz = REG_MULTI_SZ
    w32NONE = REG_NONE
    w32RESLIST = REG_RESOURCE_LIST
    w32REGSz = REG_SZ
End Enum

Public Const KEY_READ As Long = (( _
    STANDARD_RIGHTS_READ _
    Or KEY_QUERY_VALUE _
    Or KEY_ENUMERATE_SUB_KEYS _
    Or KEY_NOTIFY) _
    And (Not SYNCHRONIZE))

Public Const KEY_WRITE As Long = (( _
    STANDARD_RIGHTS_WRITE _
    Or KEY_SET_VALUE _
    Or KEY_CREATE_SUB_KEY) _
    And (Not SYNCHRONIZE))

Public Const KEY_EXECUTE As Long = (KEY_READ)

Public Const KEY_ALL_ACCESS As Long = (( _
    STANDARD_RIGHTS_ALL _
    Or KEY_QUERY_VALUE _
    Or KEY_SET_VALUE _
    Or KEY_CREATE_SUB_KEY _
    Or KEY_ENUMERATE_SUB_KEYS _
    Or KEY_NOTIFY _
    Or KEY_CREATE_LINK) _
    And (Not SYNCHRONIZE))
```

Then add the following constant which is used to test success or failure of each API function. In your applications, you can test for any of the other return codes for specific errors and conditions, but in our example, we'll just test for success or failure.

```
'API return codes
Public Const ERROR_SUCCESS As Long = 0&
```

Next, add the following API declarations. Note that this is not the complete list; it includes only those that are needed by the procedures that will follow.

```
Private Declare Function RegCloseKey Lib "advapi32.dll" _
    (ByVal hKey As Long) As Long

Private Declare Function RegCreateKeyEx Lib "advapi32.dll" _
    Alias "RegCreateKeyExA" ( _
    ByVal hKey As Long, _
    ByVal lpSubKey As String, _
    ByVal Reserved As Long, _
    ByVal lpClass As String, _
    ByVal dwOptions As Long, _
    ByVal samDesired As Long, _
    ByVal lpSecurityAttributes As Long, _
```

```
        phkResult As Long, _
        lpdwDisposition As Long) As Long

    Private Declare Function RegDeleteKey Lib "advapi32.dll" _
      Alias "RegDeleteKeyA" ( _
      ByVal hKey As Long, _
      ByVal lpSubKey As String) As Long

    Private Declare Function RegDeleteValue Lib "advapi32.dll" _
      Alias "RegDeleteValueA" ( _
      ByVal hKey As Long, _
      ByVal lpValueName As String) As Long

    Private Declare Function RegOpenKeyEx Lib "advapi32.dll" _
      Alias "RegOpenKeyExA" ( _
      ByVal hKey As Long, _
      ByVal lpSubKey As String, _
      ByVal ulOptions As Long, _
      ByVal samDesired As Long, _
      phkResult As Long) As Long

    Private Declare Function RegQueryValueEx Lib "advapi32.dll" _
      Alias "RegQueryValueExA" ( _
      ByVal hKey As Long, _
      ByVal lpValueName As String, _
      ByVal lpReserved As Long, _
      lpType As Long, _
      lpData As Any, _
      lpcbData As Long) As Long

    Private Declare Function RegSetValueEx Lib "advapi32.dll" _
      Alias "RegSetValueExA" ( _
      ByVal hKey As Long, _
      ByVal lpValueName As String, _
      ByVal Reserved As Long, _
      ByVal dwType As Long, _
      lpData As Any, _
      ByVal cbData As Long) As Long
```

Now add the following variable declaration, which is used to store the result of the API function calls. You could declare this variable in each procedure that uses it, but for the purpose of a convenient example, we have declared it at module level.

```
'Return value for most procedures
Private lngReturn As Long
```

Next, add the following procedures to the same module as the declarations above. Some of them may look a bit complicated, but if you were to strip out the error handling, you would see that they are actually quite simple.

The first procedure, CreateKey(), wraps the RegCreateKeyEx function to create a new subkey. After the call, it checks that the call completed successfully, and if not, raises a custom error. If the call is successful, it returns the name of the newly created subkey.

```vb
Public Function CreateKey(lngRootKey As w32Key, _
        strSubKey As String, _
        lngValueType As w32ValueType) _
        As String

    Dim hKey As Long
    Dim hSubKey As Long
    Dim strClass As String
    Dim lngSize As Long
    Dim lngDisposition As Long

    On Error GoTo CreateKey_Err

    'Create the key
    lngReturn = RegCreateKeyEx(lngRootKey, _
                               strSubKey, _
                               0&, _
                               vbNullString, _
                               0&, _
                               KEY_WRITE, _
                               0&, _
                               hSubKey, _
                               lngDisposition)

    'Check that the call succeeded
    If lngReturn <> ERROR_SUCCESS Then
        Err.Raise vbObjectError + 1, , "Could not create key."
    End If

    'If successful, return the name of the new subkey
    CreateKey = strSubKey

CreateKey_Exit:
    On Error Resume Next
    'Close the key
    lngReturn = RegCloseKey(hKey)
    Exit Function

CreateKey_Err:
    CreateKey = ""
    DoCmd.Beep
    MsgBox "Error " & Err.Number & vbCrLf & _
        Err.Description, vbOKOnly + vbExclamation, _
        "Could not save the key value"

    Resume CreateKey_Exit
End Function
```

The next procedure, SetKeyValue(), wraps both RegOpenKeyEx and RegSetValueEx functions to open the subkey and set its value, respectively. After each function call, it checks that the call completed successfully, and if not, raises a custom error and returns a Boolean False. If the call completes successfully, it returns a Boolean True.

```
    Public Function SetKeyValue(lngRootKey As w32Key, _
            strSubKey As String, _
            strValueName As String, _
            strNewValue As String) _
            As Boolean

        Dim hKey As Long
        Dim lngSize As Long

        On Error GoTo SetKeyValue_Err

        'Open the key and get its handle
        lngReturn = RegOpenKeyEx(lngRootKey, strSubKey, _
                0&, KEY_WRITE, hKey)

        'Check that the call succeeded
        If lngReturn <> ERROR_SUCCESS Then
            Err.Raise vbObjectError + 1, , "Could not open key."
        End If

        'Initialize the size variable
        lngSize = Len(strNewValue)

        'Set the key value
        lngReturn = RegSetValueEx(hKey, _
                                  strValueName, _
                                  0&, _
                                  REG_SZ, _
                                  ByVal strNewValue, _
                                  lngSize)

        'Check that the call succeeded
        If lngReturn <> ERROR_SUCCESS Then
            Err.Raise vbObjectError + 1, , "Could not save value."
        End If

SetKeyValue_Exit:
        On Error Resume Next

        'Return success or failure
        SetKeyValue = (lngReturn = ERROR_SUCCESS)

        'Close the key
        lngReturn = RegCloseKey(hKey)
        Exit Function

SetKeyValue_Err:
        DoCmd.Beep
        MsgBox "Error " & Err.Number & vbCrLf & _
            Err.Description, vbOKOnly + vbExclamation, _
            "Could not save the key value"

        Resume SetKeyValue_Exit
    End Function
```

The `GetKeyValue()` procedure wraps both `RegOpenKeyEx` and `RegQueryValueEx` functions, which open the subkey and retrieve its value, respectively. Again, after each function call, it checks if the call completed successfully, and if not, raises a custom error and returns a `Null` value. If the call does complete successfully, it returns the current value.

```
Public Function GetKeyValue(lngRootKey As w32Key, _
        strSubKey As String, _
        strValueName As String) _
        As Variant

    Dim hKey As Long
    Dim strBuffer As String
    Dim lngSize As Long

    On Error GoTo GetKeyValue_Err

    'Open the key and get its handle
    lngReturn = RegOpenKeyEx(lngRootKey, strSubKey, _
            0&, KEY_READ, hKey)

    'Check that the call succeeded
    If lngReturn <> ERROR_SUCCESS Then
        Err.Raise vbObjectError + 1, , "Could not open key."
    End If

    'Initialize the variables
    strBuffer = Space(255)
    lngSize = Len(strBuffer)

    'Read the key value
    lngReturn = RegQueryValueEx(hKey, _
                                strValueName, _
                                0&, _
                                REG_SZ, _
                                ByVal strBuffer, _
                                lngSize)

    'Check that the call succeeded
    If lngReturn <> ERROR_SUCCESS Then
        Err.Raise vbObjectError + 1, , "Could not read value."
    End If

    'Return the key value
    GetKeyValue = Left(strBuffer, lngSize - 1)

GetKeyValue_Exit:
    On Error Resume Next
    'Close the key
    lngReturn = RegCloseKey(hKey)
    Exit Function

GetKeyValue_Err:
    GetKeyValue = Null
    DoCmd.Beep
```

```
        MsgBox "Error " & Err.Number & vbCrLf & _
            Err.Description, vbOKOnly + vbExclamation, _
            "Could not retrieve the key"

        Resume GetKeyValue_Exit
    End Function
```

The `DeleteValue()` function wraps both `RegOpenKeyEx` and `RegDeleteValue` functions to open the subkey and set its value, respectively. If both calls complete successfully, a Boolean `True` is returned, otherwise a Boolean `False` is returned.

```
    Public Function DeleteValue(lngRootKey As w32Key, _
            strSubKey As String, strValueName As String) _
            As Boolean

        Dim hKey As Long

        On Error GoTo DeleteValue_Err

        'Open the key and get its handle
        lngReturn = RegOpenKeyEx(lngRootKey, strSubKey, _
            0&, KEY_ALL_ACCESS, hKey)

        'Check that the call succeeded
        If lngReturn <> ERROR_SUCCESS Then
            Err.Raise vbObjectError + 1, , "Could not open key."
        End If

        'Delete the key value
        lngReturn = RegDeleteValue(hKey, strValueName)

    DeleteValue_Exit:
        On Error Resume Next

        'Return success or failure
        DeleteValue = (lngReturn = ERROR_SUCCESS)

        'Close the key
        lngReturn = RegCloseKey(hKey)
        Exit Function

    DeleteValue_Err:
        DoCmd.Beep
        MsgBox "Error " & Err.Number & vbCrLf & _
            Err.Description, vbOKOnly + vbExclamation, _
            "Could not retrieve the key"

        Resume DeleteValue_Exit
    End Function
```

The `DeleteKey()` function is the last of our action procedures. This function wraps both `RegOpenKeyEx` and `RegDeleteKey` functions to open the subkey and delete it. If both calls complete successfully, a Boolean `True` is returned, otherwise a Boolean `False` is returned.

```
Public Function DeleteKey(lngRootKey As w32Key, strSubKey As String, _
strKillKey As String) As Boolean
    Dim hKey As Long

    On Error GoTo DeleteKey_Err

    'Open the key and get its handle
    lngReturn = RegOpenKeyEx(lngRootKey, strSubKey, _
            0&, KEY_ALL_ACCESS, hKey)

    'Check that the call succeeded
    If lngReturn <> ERROR_SUCCESS Then
        Err.Raise vbObjectError + 1, , "Could not open key."
    End If

    'Delete the subkey
    lngReturn = RegDeleteKey(hKey, strKillKey)

DeleteKey_Exit:
    On Error Resume Next

    'Return success or failure
    DeleteKey = (lngReturn = ERROR_SUCCESS)

    'Close the key
    lngReturn = RegCloseKey(hKey)
    Exit Function

DeleteKey_Err:
    DoCmd.Beep
    MsgBox "Error " & Err.Number & vbCrLf & _
        Err.Description, vbOKOnly + vbExclamation, _
        "Could not retrieve the key"

    Resume DeleteKey_Exit
End Function
```

Finally, the following procedure is the one you can use to test the above API function wrappers. Copy this to a standard module and step through it using the F8 key.

```
Public Sub TestReg()
    Dim strBaseKey As String
    Dim strSubKey As String
    Dim strMsg As String
    Dim varReturn As Variant

    'For convenience only, initialize variables with the subkey
names.
    strBaseKey = "Software\VB and VBA Program
Settings\myapp\Settings"
    strSubKey = "Software\VB and VBA Program
Settings\myapp\Settings\myNewKey"
```

```
        '=== Create a new subkey.
     varReturn = CreateKey(w32CURRENT_USER, strSubKey, w32REGSz)

     'Check for success or failure.
     'If success, continue with the remaining procedures.
     If Not IsNull(varReturn) Then

         strMsg = "Created a new key '" & varReturn & "'."
         MsgBox strMsg, vbOKOnly + vbInformation, "Test Registry
functions"

         '=== Set a new subkey value.
         varReturn = SetKeyValue(w32CURRENT_USER, strSubKey,
"myValue", "11123")

         'Check success or failure.
         If varReturn = True Then
             strMsg = "Set a new key value to '11123'."
         Else
             strMsg = "Failed to set new key value."
         End If

         MsgBox strMsg, vbOKOnly + vbInformation, "Test Registry
functions"

         '=== Retrieve the value we just set.
         varReturn = GetKeyValue(w32CURRENT_USER, strSubKey,
"myValue")

         'Check success or failure.
         If Len(varReturn) > 0 Then
             strMsg = "The current value of key '" & strSubKey & _
                 "' is '" & varReturn & "'"
         Else
             strMsg = "Failed to read key value."
         End If

         MsgBox strMsg, vbOKOnly + vbInformation, "Test Registry
functions"

         '=== Now delete the key value
         varReturn = DeleteValue(w32CURRENT_USER, strSubKey,
"myValue")

         'Check success or failure.
         If varReturn = True Then
             strMsg = "Deleted the key value."
         Else
             strMsg = "Failed to delete the key value."
         End If

         MsgBox strMsg, vbOKOnly + vbInformation, "Test Registry
functions"
```

```
        '=== Lastly, delete the subkey itself
        varReturn = DeleteKey(w32CURRENT_USER, strBaseKey,
"myNewKey")

        'Check success or failure.
        If varReturn = True Then
            strMsg = "Deleted the key."
        Else
            strMsg = "Failed to delete the key."
        End If

        MsgBox strMsg, vbOKOnly + vbInformation, "Test Registry
functions"
    Else
        strMsg = "Failed to create the new key."
        MsgBox strMsg, vbOKOnly + vbInformation, "Test Registry
functions"
    End If
End Sub
```

Summary

In this chapter, we began by looking at the evolution of the Win32 Registry, what it does, how it works, and how it is used. We also briefly looked at the tools you can use to examine and modify the Registry.

We then examined the Win32 Registry structure and perused the built-in VBA functions you can use to manipulate that portion of the Registry specifically set aside for VBA programmers. Finally, we rounded off by building our own modest Registry module.

Having reached the end of this chapter, you should now have acquired enough information and experience to develop some fairly sophisticated database applications. All you have left to do then is to package it all up, so you can distribute it to your many users. Chapter 19 focuses on using the Access Developer Extensions to help you on your way.

19

Using the ADE Tools

Access Developer Extensions (ADE) is a set of great tools for the serious, and possibly not-so-serious, Access application developer. The ADE package includes tools that enhance your ability to design, develop, and deploy Access-based applications.

The ADE package includes a tool designed to improve your application development capabilities: the *Property Scanner*. The Property Scanner makes it easy to search collections, objects, and properties of a database for the occurrence of a particular term or value right from the Access user interface. This add-in allows you to target searches precisely and to save the search criteria for future use. This tool makes it easier to perform impact analysis, which means you can provide a better estimate of effort for change requests as well as develop a better strategy to test the application if change requests are approved.

The ADE package also includes the Custom Startup Wizard. Have you ever been locked out of a database because you set startup properties to lock the user out of changing the application but forgot to make a backup so you could get back in to change the application yourself? Or, maybe you have written code to control the startup so you didn't accidentally lock yourself out. No matter which route you took, you've had some overhead during application development. The Custom Startup Wizard can be used to quickly define startup properties for your application. The startup properties are used to compile the database to create an MDE. But these startup properties are not applied to your MDB in the same way as they would be if you set them yourself. So the wizard does its task without you accidentally getting locked out of the database yourself.

Having gone through all the trouble to set custom start properties and create a compiled database, you'll wish for an easy way to create some kind of installation package for the application. Well, with this release of Access, Microsoft has granted your wish. The ADE package includes the Package Wizard: A tool that provides a straightforward way to generate a standard Windows Installer Package (an MSI file) from an Access-based application. And since the output of the wizard is an MSI file, you can even use an MSI Editor, such as Orca (free from Microsoft), to customize the installation package.

One of the frustrations you may have faced in preparing to deploy an Access-based application, and a question that is often asked on the Access Newsgroups, is how to determine whether or not it is legal to deliver the Access runtime engine with the application to users who do not have Access on their machine. The ADE clearly defines the distribution licensing requirements (unlimited distribution) and even includes a redistributable, standalone Access runtime engine. In fact, the Package Wizard includes an option to include the runtime engine in the MSI.

One thing that you need to know before attempting to use the tools in the ADE package is that the ADE is *not* included with Microsoft Office 2003 or Microsoft Access 2003. In order to get the ADE you'll need to acquire Visual Studio Tools for the Microsoft Office System (VSTO). In addition to getting the ADE package to use with your Access applications, VSTO provides significant advances in the areas of language choice and innovation, security, deployment, and the integrated development environment (IDE). For more information, visit `http://msdn.microsoft.com/vstudio/office/officetools.aspx`.

Redistributable Access Runtime

A computer with the full version of Microsoft Access installed on it can run an Access-based application no matter where that application was developed. Just copy the MDB or MDE files to that computer and away you go.

But what if you want to deploy your application on a computer that doesn't have a full version of Access? And what if you don't want to buy a full version of Access because that computer won't ever use Access's features, except where those features are needed to run your application? That's where the Access Runtime comes into the picture.

Let's take a step back for a minute. Why would you want to deploy your application on another computer? Well, when you started developing your Access-based application maybe you hadn't considered where it might be deployed. That's a typical situation for many Access-based applications. You create an ad hoc database to help one person solve his or her problem. Before you know it, 30 people are using the application and requesting enhancements. When you realize that more than one user might want to use the application, you start trying to determine what would be required to run your application on other computers.

The least common denominator necessary to run an Access-based application on a computer is the Access Runtime. Prior to Access 2003, the runtime could only be distributed if you purchased the "developer" edition of Microsoft Office. Since Microsoft Office 2003 doesn't have the developer edition you'll need to acquire the ADE to get rights to redistribute the Access Runtime. With the ADE you get unlimited rights to redistribute the runtime.

> **Be aware that installing the Access Runtime on a computer that already has a different version of either a full copy of Microsoft Access or the Access Runtime installed can cause problems with other databases used on that computer. When installing the 2003 Runtime, be sure that all databases or Access-based applications used on that computer are compatible with Access 2003.**

Property Scanner

The ADE package includes an add-in for Access called the Property Scanner. As an add-in it is accessed from within Access while you have your database open. As the name suggests, the ADE Property Scanner scans collections, objects, and properties of a database for the occurrence of a particular term or value. This includes pretty much every type of object your application can have: the project, the current DB, documents, containers, tables, references, queries, forms, reports, macros, modules, and command bars.

So what is the purpose of the Property Scanner? Have you ever wanted to change the name of a field in a table and wondered how the heck you were going to figure out where that field is used throughout your entire application? Have you ever decided to "go for it" only to find out that the change impacts everything and trying to test every part of your application is a monumental task? Ever decided *not* to change the name for fear of breaking your application? We have deliberated and succumbed to all three. With the Property Scanner you can perform an impact analysis before you make any final decision. So this tool will help with your impact analysis as well as help you get through all of the changes you need to make if you decide to make such a change.

Property Scanner Search Specification

As indicated earlier, you use the Property Scanner from within Access with your database open. Select `Tools | Add-ins | Property Scanner` to display the Property Scanner search specification dialog box. Figure 19-1 shows the dialog after the `Advanced>>` button has been clicked.

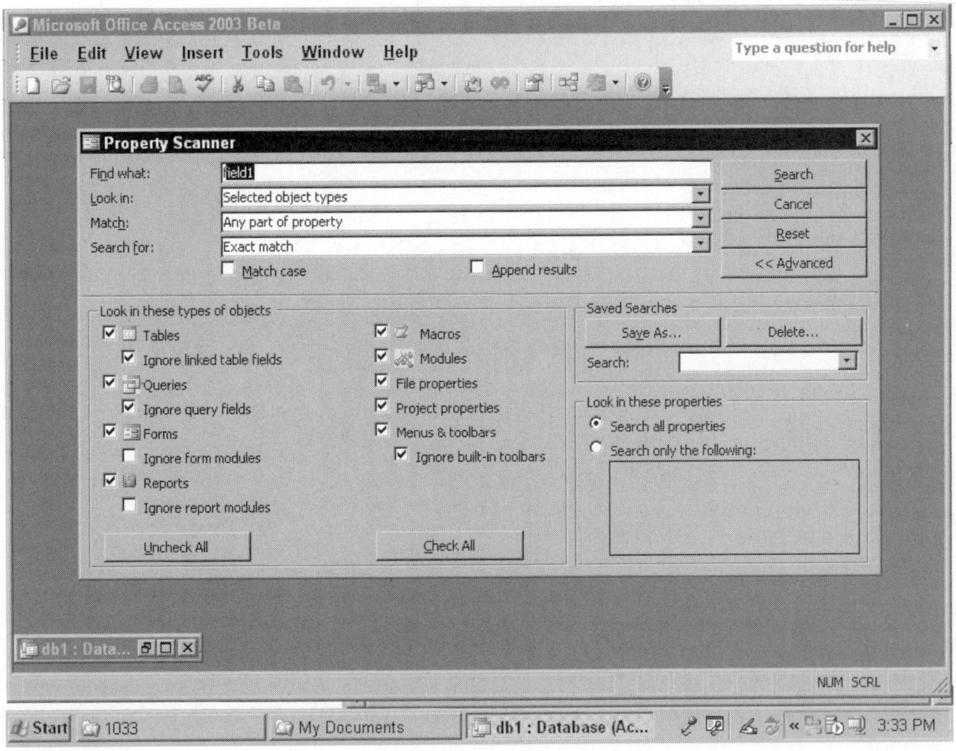

Figure 19-1

In the `Property Scanner` dialog box you'll specify your search criteria. Obviously you specify the thing you're looking for in the `Find what` text box.

The `Look in` drop-down list always lets you to specify where to search—no need to waste time searching inappropriate places. As you read through and use this, it will look very familiar. Isn't that nice—another use for the search tool that we've been comfortable with for years. The choices start with the object that was selected when you started the Property Scanner. One choice is `All objects`. The last choice is `Selected object types` (which automatically puts you in Advanced mode). The object types are specified with checks in the list at the bottom left.

The `Match` drop-down list allows you to specify what part of the property you want to match: `Any Part of`, `Whole`, or `Start of`. The `Search for` drop-down list allows you to specify how the match should occur: `Exact`, `Match any words`, or `Match all words`. And of course you can select the box to `Match case` as well. The ability to `Append results` will come in handy if you have a cascading change to make.

If you only want to look at certain properties, you can specify `Search only the following`. So, for instance, if your search includes the word `Exit`, you may only want to look at the `Name` and `Caption` properties. As mentioned you can save the search criteria with the `Save as...` button.

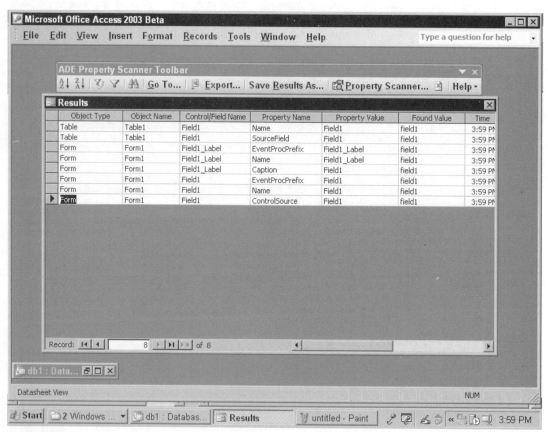

Figure 19-2

Search Results

The Property Scanner provides useful tools to deal with the results from the search. Figure 19-2 show the ADE Property Scanner Toolbar that automatically opens when the search is finished, and the result of the search.

Of course the results display in an Access table. Well, at least it's a temporary table, but you can save it for later use by clicking the Save Results As... button on the toolbar.

In the meantime, one of the great things that you can do with the information is use Go To... to actually go to the instance. Select one of the records in the table, and you can open that object for editing. It's a little disappointing that if the value occurs on a control of a form, for example, the specific control is not selected. On the other hand, if the object is a module, including the code behind a form, the Go To... button will take you to the exact line in the VBE.

Custom Startup Wizard

The ADE package includes the Custom Startup Wizard to help you set the startup properties of the database just before you create a compiled version of the database. The startup properties determine how the database will display when the user opens it. For example, it controls whether the database window display or not. So, the Custom Startup Wizard helps adjust the startup properties so that when a user opens your database, the display is presented exactly the way you want the user to see it.

So when do you use the Custom Startup Wizard? You use the wizard when you're ready to compile your database. Since your application has a really cool user interface with all the features your users will ever need, you only want the users to have access to what you developed for them.

Why do you need the Custom Startup Wizard? There are really several reasons:

First of all, you've spent a lot of time developing your application. (You are calling your database an application by this point, aren't you? Microsoft Access Team may finally have acknowledged that Access developers do this—create applications rather than databases, that is. And, having heard our pain (needs), they created these tools for us.)

Your application has a really cool user interface that contains all of the tools you want your users to have and only the tools that you want them to have. You don't want users to be able to mass delete a bunch of data without your code having the opportunity to verify what they're doing. Nor do you want users to be able to redesign your forms. Most of us have heard, "All I did was change this and now it doesn't work anymore."

So you need to adjust all the startup properties to protect your application and preserve your sanity. The wizard will help you do that. Plus it has options to include your cool splash screen and make sure that users can't bypass all of the great stuff you wrote by holding down the *Shift* key when they start your application.

The second reason to use the Custom Startup Wizard is to simplify your development. You could keep writing code to handle this stuff yourself. And typically that task has always been put off until you had proven that the database, make that *application*, would perform the desired tasks. By the time you're ready to wrap up the package you could have an entire page of things that you'd need to remember to do to setup the proper startup properties . . . consistently . . . every time! If this process can be automated, more of your time can be spent on development.

The last and perhaps most important reason to use the Custom Startup Wizard is to simplify creating the compiled database (the MDE). Since the wizard doesn't adjust the startup properties of the original MDB, you don't have to be sure that you saved a copy of the database without all the startup control so you could get back in to edit it later. Plus the wizard allows you to save the settings that you define for your application; so you can use the same settings the next time you're ready to create the MDE. We can't tell you how much time has been wasted tweaking and retweaking start-up settings, just to get them consistent from one roll-out to the next.

The Custom Startup Wizard is a four-step process that starts at the Windows `Start` menu. Start the wizard from the menu option you created when you installed the ADE. This will be something like `Start | Microsoft Office | Microsoft Office Access 2003 Developer Extensions | Custom Startup Wizard`.

The wizard starts with a welcome screen explaining all the wonderful things you can do with it. Figure 19-3 shows the welcome screen. Of course you can skip this screen in the future.

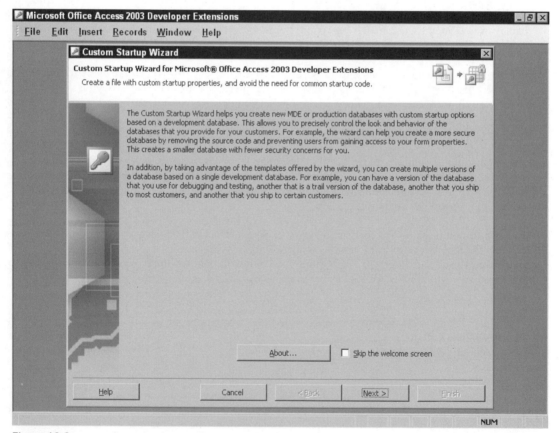

Figure 19-3

Step 1: Identify the Template

The first step in the wizard is to identify whether you want to create a new template or use an existing template. Figure 19-4 shows the template selection form.

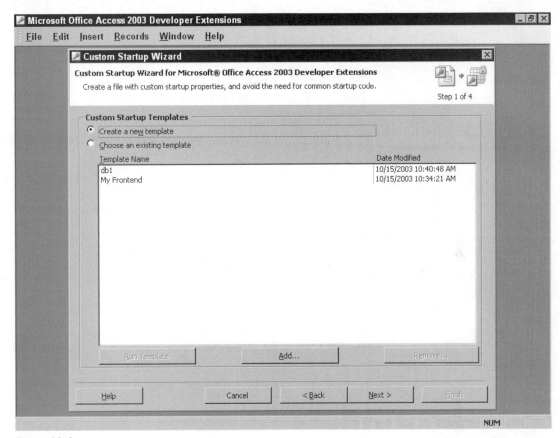

Figure 19-4

If you select an existing template, you can run it without modification. Which means, by selecting the template and clicking `Finish` on this dialog box you can very easily and quickly create an MDE after you've made a simple modification to an application you have previously generated. How great is that?

Since the template output from the wizard is an XML file, you can inherit an application *as well as* the template used for building that application. The `Add...` button allows you to add the template for that application from the XML file. It just keeps getting better. You're probably already thinking, "I could acquire a template, modify it, and *voila* have a new custom template of my own."

Step 2: Describe the Database and Set Startup Options

In the second step in the wizard you start to specify the details about the application (database) and the startup (custom) options. Figure 19-5 is the form that shows for the second step. The following explains the purpose of each startup option:

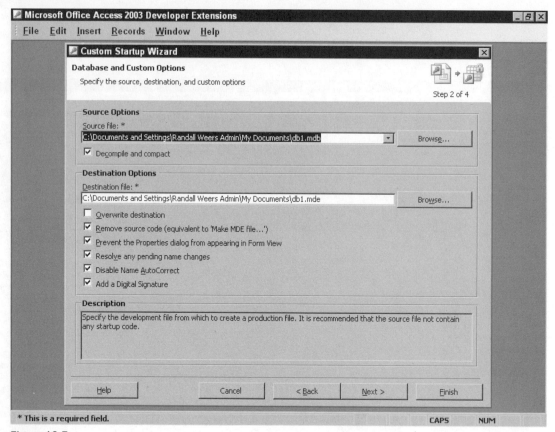

Figure 19-5

The `Source file` specifies the MDB file that you want to use for input. You can browse to select the file.

As you read the explanation about `Decompile and compact`, you may agree that it can be a bit confusing. The description of that field indicates that it "removes the code and compacts the database," which means that the MDB file would no longer contain code. This is not the case. The purpose is to make the MDB as small as possible. Obviously it does not permanently remove the code from the project, otherwise the application would not work the same as it does with your code.

The `Destination file` is the output for the application (not the template). You can overwrite an existing destination file. So, as a typical safety check, if the destination file name already exists and you don't select `Overwrite destination` you will be prompted to explicitly specify whether to overwrite it or not.

If `Remove source code` is selected, the wizard will make the destination the equivalent of an MDE (from an MDB) or ADE (from an ADP). If the destination file includes a file type, the file type selection will take precedence and the wizard will generate the appropriate file type.

Did you ever forget to change the `Allow Design Changes` on a form to `Design View Only`? If you have, you know that every time the user displays a form that isn't set to allow changes `Design View Only`, the `Properties` page displays. Checking `Prevent the Properties dialog from appearing in Form View` will set the value to `Design View Only`.

`Resolve any pending name changes` clears the name map. The name map is used in conjunction with the `Name AutoCorrect` feature to automatically propagate name changes for tables, forms, reports, and fields throughout your Access databases. If you change the name of a query, for example, that change is automatically propagated to any forms or reports that use the query. This option will clean up any problems you have been having due to renaming objects.

Name `AutoCorrect` is used to propagate object name changes within the database. This feature generally isn't necessary in an application intended for distribution. `Disable Name AutoCorrect` will disable that feature. Even if you haven't run into this, take our advice on this one. No need to cause frustration for the users.

`Add a Digital Signature` allows you to add a digital signature to the downloaded file. A digital signature is an electronic, cryptographic-based, secure stamp of authentication that can be used to both verify the source of a file and to ensure that the file has not been altered. See Chapter 20, "Macro Security," for more details on digital signatures.

At this point you can finish the wizard. If you have made changes to the template, you will be prompted to save them to the existing template or to a new template. Alternatively, you can go to step 3 to set startup options.

Step 3: Define the Startup Options in the Database

The `Startup Options` dialog box is shown in Figure 19-6.

Without the ADE, you can adjust the startup properties for your application while the database is open in Access. Of course, doing so impacts the database every time you open it. If you want the startup options adjusted just before you build the MDE, you can select `Set Startup Properties` at this time. To set the properties you want the wizard to use, click `Open Startup Dialog`. Your database will appear to open with the `Startup` dialog box showing. However, when you adjust the settings in this dialog box, they *do not* impact your MDB file. This one feature alone alleviates the worry that you might forget to save a copy of the database without the startup options.

By now, you've either found the code to disable the *Shift* key on startup or at least considered looking for it. Or perhaps, you've just allowed the *Shift* key override hoping your application users wouldn't bother with it. The wizard automatically disables the key for you. If you don't want it disabled, you should select `Allow Bypass Key`.

For some applications, you may have used the `AutoExec macro` to start some action as soon as the application starts. If you have written a macro that you want to start automatically, you can select it in the `AutoExec macro` drop-down list. Be aware that this will replace the existing `AutoExec macro`, if there is one.

Note: you can also have the macro start from a command line parameter. This can be set in the Package Wizard. We'll cover that in a bit.

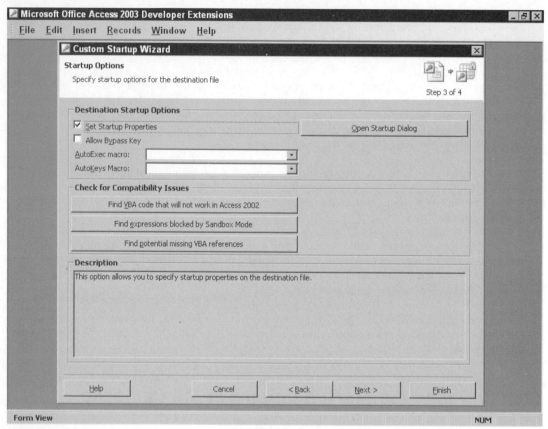

Figure 19-6

The AutoKeys macro is used to provide a set of custom hot keys for your database application, which will augment or replace existing Access hot keys. If you have a macro for creating AutoKeys, you can specify it in the AutoKeys macro drop-down list.

So, what about all those databases in Access 2000 file format? Since the output of the template is generally an MDE, and since you cannot compile an Access 2000 database with Access 2003, the wizard will essentially convert the database to 2002–2003 format. To verify that your database is compatible with this conversion, click the Find VBA code that will not work in Access 2002. This is a cool method of "prescreening." We really love the screening checks provided by this wizard.

> Note: The wizard does not convert the source database to 2002–2003 format. Instead the database is converted to a temporary database that is used to make the MDE. The temporary database is not preserved by Access. If you really want to convert your database to 2002–2003 format, use the Access user interface and select Tools | Database utilities | convert database. You can read more about converting in Appendix A.

Since the new Jet Engine Expression Service blocks certain expressions when it is in Sandbox mode, you may want to check to see if your code uses any of those expressions. Click Find expression blocked by Sandbox Mode to learn what will be blocked.

See Chapter 20 "Macro Security," for more information about the Jet Expression Service Sandbox.

If you've ever deployed an application and then had trouble with missing references, you may want to (that is, really ought to) search for them now. This will check for references that might not be included with a Microsoft Office 2003 installation. Click `Find potential missing VBA references` to do this.

If you do get reference warnings, you need to plan to remove the reference(s) from your application, have a prerequisite for your application that requires the user to install software that contains your references or, if you have a license to distribute the files that are referenced, package those files with your application, which you can do with the Package Wizard.

Step 4: Save the Template/Create a Batch File

As with other steps, you can finish now or proceed to the fourth and final step: `Completing Your Custom Startup File`, as show in Figure 19-7.

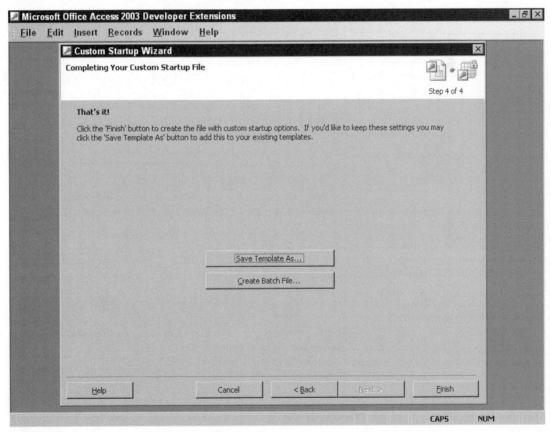

Figure 19-7

In this last step you can save your template to a file to use next time you use the Custom Startup Wizard. Not only that, but you can create a batch file (BAT) that you can use to run the template through the

Custom Startup Wizard without even opening the wizard. We're sure that you'll be as impressed with the Startup Wizard as we are. But, the ADE offers so much more. This is just the tip of the iceberg.

Package Wizard

By now you've tried out the Property Scanner—a great little tool. It helps you feel more confident that you didn't miss some tiny thing during a big change that you made. And, you've used the Custom Startup Wizard to develop a cool startup to your equally cool user interface for your MDE. Now it's time to put the application in front of someone else . . . perhaps a lot of someone else's. Enter the Package Wizard.

The Package Wizard creates a Microsoft Windows Installation Package (MSI). It builds the cabinet files (CAB). It will include Windows System Register keys; it will even allow you to add your own keys to the register and to include your digital certificate if you created one. (See Chapter 20 for more information about digital certificates.) And, since it is an MSI file, you can manipulate the package with MSI Editors, such as Orca, allowing for even more customization.

You will see a similar look-and-feel between the Custom Startup Wizard and the Package Wizard. Like the Custom Startup Wizard, the Package Wizard is started from the Windows `Start` menu. Although the Package Wizard is a seven-step process, like the Custom Startup Wizard, after you've set up the template for a package you can rebuild the package without executing all seven steps. Again, like the Custom Startup Wizard you can also create a BAT file to build the installation package without going through the wizard.

Start the wizard from the menu option that was created when you installed the ADE. This will be something like `Start | Microsoft Office | Microsoft Office Access 2003 Developer Extensions | Package Wizard`.

> *Reminder Note: Unless you have adjusted your Macro security in Access, the wizard will not start. You will receive an error from the security check indicating the problem. (Note: Microsoft may have a digital signature with the final release that will allow you to start the wizard if you accept the digital certificate. See Chapter 20 for more information.)*

The wizard starts with a welcome screen explaining all of the wonderful things that you can do with it (see Figure 19-8). Of course, you can skip this screen in the future.

You will probably notice that the screen says, "`You will want to verify [the target system]`." That's just another way of saying that the target system must have Microsoft Windows Installer 2.0 or later. It is also saying that the target system must be able to run the Access 2003 runtime. In other words, if the system can't run Access 2003, don't bother trying to install your application on it. You can review what these requirements mean in the Access 2003 install package.

Step 1: Identify the Template

Of course no matter what the target system, you can still run the wizard on your system. So the first step in the wizard is to identify whether you want to create a new template or to use an existing template. Figure 19-9 shows the template selection form.

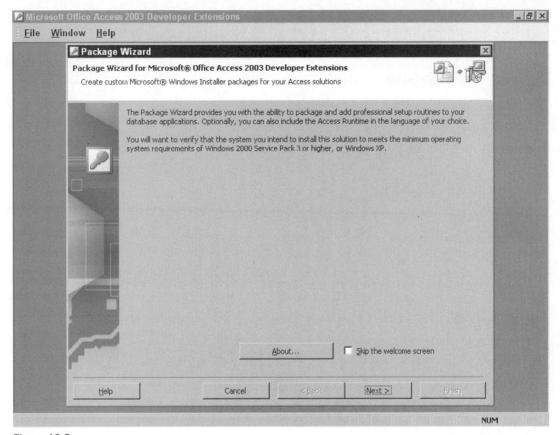

Figure 19-8

If you select an existing template, you can run it without modification. Which means, by selecting the template and clicking Finish on this dialog box you can (again) very easily (re)create a package after you've changed the MDE, using the equally quick and easy steps given in the Custom Startup Wizard.

Since the template output of the wizard is an XML file, you can inherit an application *as well as* the template used for building it *and* the template used for packaging it (sounds like a combo meal). The Add... button allows you to add the inherited template for the (inherited) application from the XML file. Wow, if you kept all those references to templates straight, you have some pretty impressive focus!

Step 2: Define the Package to Create

In the second step in the wizard you start to specify the details about the package that you want to build. Figure 19-10 shows the second step, specifying the packaging options. The following describes the fields on the Package Wizard dialog box and how to use them.

The File to package will generally be the MDE you built using the Custom Package Wizard. You will have an opportunity to bundle additional components (files) in a later step (start thinking supersize).

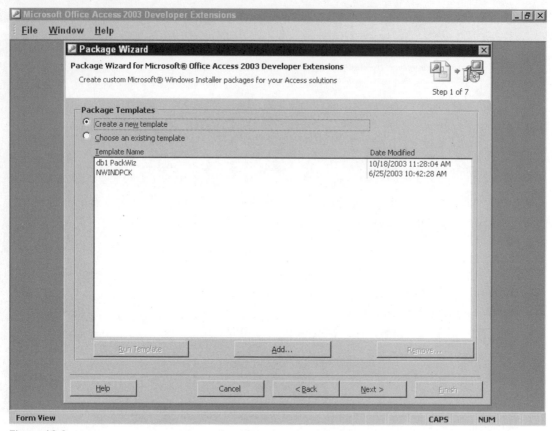

Figure 19-9

The `Root installation folder` sets up the MSI to default the installation to that folder. As with all MSIs the user can specify the target folder. You can target the installation for all users of the target system by selecting "`Program Files`," "`Common AppData`," or "`Common Files`." Or, you can target to a user specific folder using "`My Documents`," "`Desktop`," or "`User AppData`."

> *Tip: If you target to one of the `AppData` folders, the default setting in Windows Explorer won't display the folder. The user must adjust their Windows Explorer settings to show hidden folders. This may be useful in situations where you don't want the user to browse to the file and run it from Windows Explorer. This might be the case if you have built a shortcut that includes some parameters needed when users start your application.*

> *Note: You can adjust the target folder by editing the MSI file after the wizard is complete.*

The `Installation subfolder` allows you to specify a folder that will hold the application.

The `Example installation location` will show where the application will be installed based on the information that is entered.

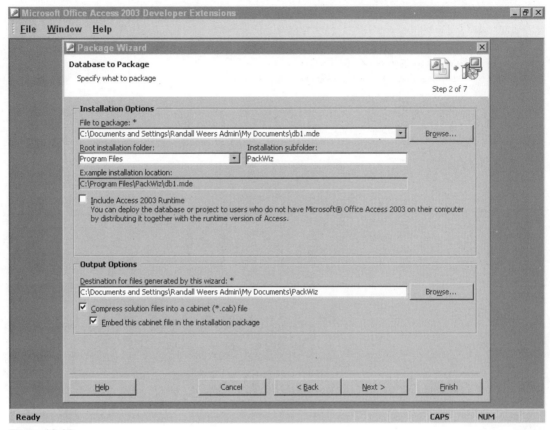

Figure 19-10

`Include Access 2003 Runtime` should be selected if you think that the target system will not have Microsoft Office Access 2003 installed.

The `Destination for files generated by this wizard` is a folder that will contain the installation package. Within that folder, the wizard will create a subfolder each time you build a package. To prepare your package for distribution, you will copy the contents of that subfolder to your install media, such as a floppy or CD.

You can compress the cabinet files (CAB). Of course this means a smaller package to deliver but a bit longer installation process. Additionally, you can embed the CAB within the SETUP.EXE file rather than making it a separate file in your install package. You're probably starting to see a pattern here—plenty of wizardy, but the ultimate control and decisions are left to the developer.

Step 3: Define the Application Startup Options

In step 3 you will tell the wizard how to build the shortcut to your application and where to put the shortcut. Figure 19-11 shows the various shortcut options. The following explains the command line parameters that can be included in the shortcut.

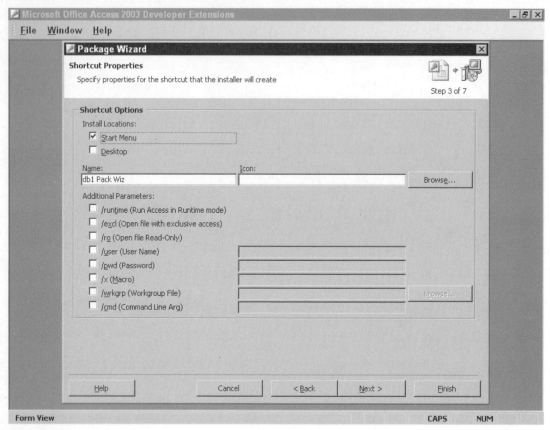

Figure 19-11

You may have the shortcut to your application added to the Start Menu or to the user's Desktop.

Name is the name you want for the shortcut and you can include a special Icon to display for the shortcut. The icon file will be included in the installation package.

Hopefully by now you know that Access has a number of startup or command line parameters you can use when starting Access. The following table lists the parameters you can employ here along with the purpose of the parameter. To see additional parameters or more details about these parameters, type **command line** in Access help.

Parameter	Purpose
/runtime	Runs Access in runtime modewithout displaying the Access user interface.
/excl	Opens your database for exclusive access. (The default is shared.)

Continues

Parameter	Purpose
/ro	Opens your database for read-only access.
/user	Starts Access by using the specified user name.
/pwd	Starts Access by using the specified password.
/x	Starts Access and runs the specified macro. Another way to run a macro when you open a database is to use an AutoExec macro, which you can set up using the Custom Startup Wizard.
/wrkgrp	Starts Access by using the specified workgroup information file. See Chapter 16, "Database Security," for more information.
/cmd	Specifies that what follows on the command line is the value that will be returned by the Command function in your VBA code.

Step 4: Add Files and Registry Keys

In step 4 you can add more files to the installation package, and you can specify information for the Windows System Registry. Additional files can be installed in the root folder you specified in step 2 or in a subfolder of that folder. Figure 19-12 shows the dialog box.

If you are using a workgroup file and have selected the /wrkgrp parameter to be added to your shortcut path in step 3, you can add a windows Help File (.hlp or .chm) to your package.

Now here's a little-known fact—you have to be someone who likes to tinker with startup options to have found this one: If you create a BMP file with the same name as your database or application and put it in the same folder as your database, your BMP will display instead of the MS Access splash screen. Since you could just include the file in the list above, we suppose Microsoft included the Splash Screen option to let people know that this capability exists.

> Tip: The BMP will only display for a short time. If you want it to appear that the splash screen is holding constant while your application starts, create a form in your database as your splash screen, then create the BMP from the screen capture of that splash screen form.

If your application uses the Windows Registry to control execution (for example, you store screen colors in the Registry), you can set the defaults by adding Registry Keys here. The advantage of adding them here as opposed to when your program first runs is that (heaven forbid the user decides to uninstall your application) the uninstall will remove those keys.

Step 5: The Installer's Experience

In step 5, you set up some parameters that control how the Microsoft Windows Installer will perform. Figure 19-13 shows the Installer Experience dialog box. The following explains the options.

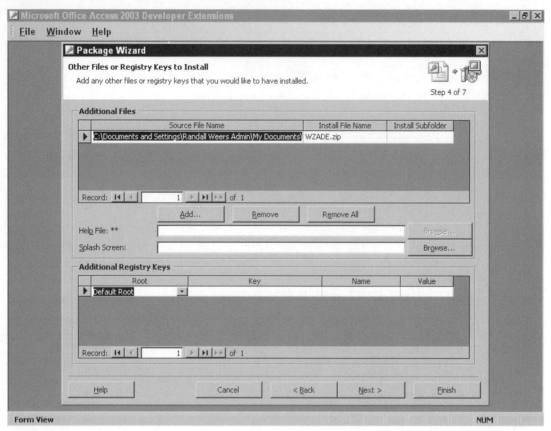

Figure 19-12

This dialog box is about setting up how the Windows Installer will look—not about changing your application. That is, when you run the SETUP.EXE program the information entered here will tell the setup program how to run and what information to display.

The `Product Name` is strictly for the Windows installer so it will not change the product name within your application. The `Product Name` displays while your application is being installed. It is also the name that displays in the `Add or Remove Programs` list.

The `Install Language` indicates which language will display during the installation. This language must be included somewhere in the files that will be installed. So, when you specify a language you have to cache the language with your install. Notice in Figure 19-14 that `Dutch` has been selected for the `Install Language`.

To cache the language, you need to tell the wizard where to find that language. To find the language, you will likely need to go back to the install disk where the `AccessRT.MSI` can be found.

The `Product Code` and `Upgrade Code` could pretty much have their own chapter in this book. Essentially they amount to a unique identifier for your product. These permit your application to be

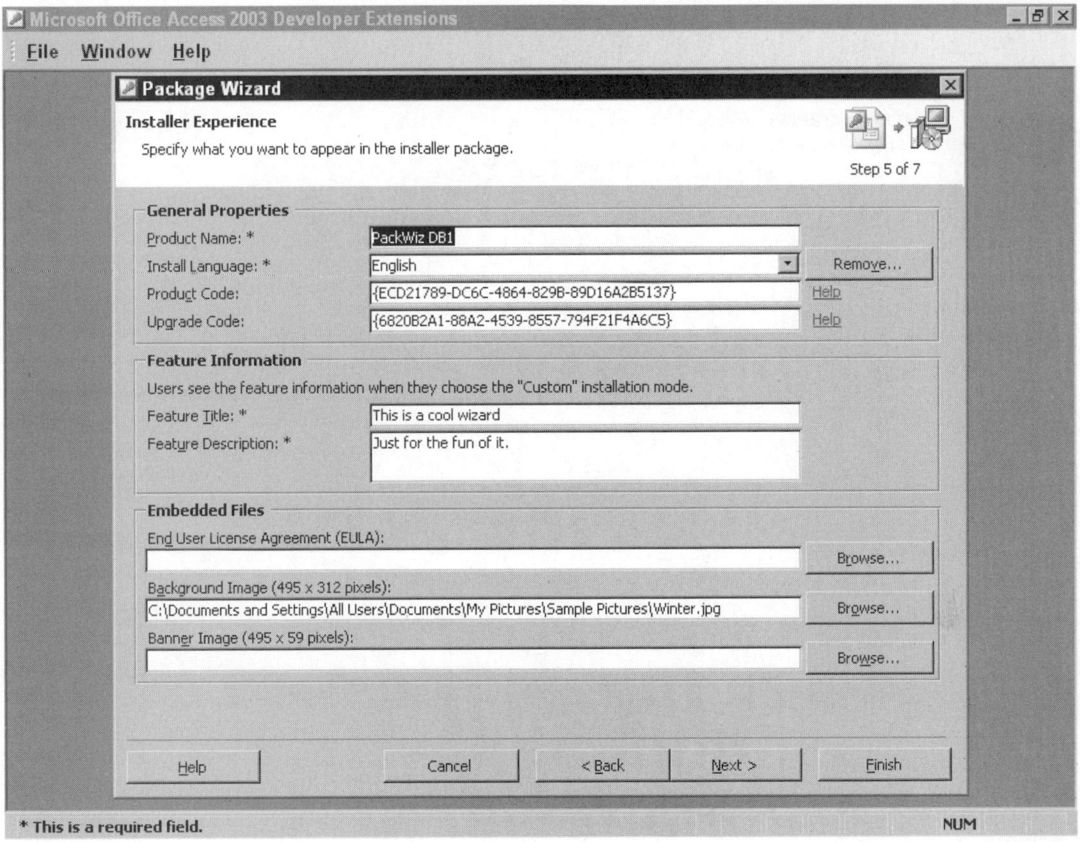

Figure 19-13

unique in the Windows Registry. For a complete description of these, connect to the Internet and select the Help links on the form. These links take you the MSDN library Web site to articles contained in the "Windows Installer" section.

> Note: The Readme.htm file included in the Whitepapers subfolder of ADE contains more information about the Product Code and the Upgrade Code.

The Feature Information section sets up information that the user sees when they select Custom install. Figure 19-15 shows how the information that is entered in Figure 19-13 will display during the install.

Obviously, you can see that the wizard allows only setting up one feature in your package. If you have many features you can modify the MSI using a MSI Editor. (Again, more control to the developer.)

Embedded Files are added to the package. These control the operation of the installer. For example, if you specify an End User License Agreement (EULA) the installer will prompt the user to accept the agreement before they can proceed with the install. If you don't specify the EULA, the user is not prompted.

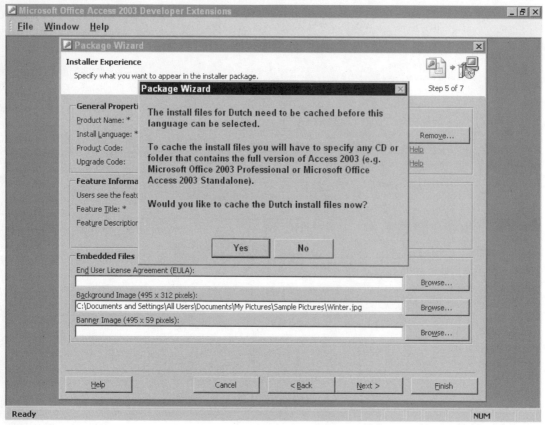

Figure 19-14

The Background Image displays in the background of the installer dialog boxes when the only controls on the screen are buttons at the bottom of the screen. This is generally the first and last screen of the install. (Note: The image selected in Figure 19-15 is not the correct size. Thankfully, the Windows installer crops it to display appropriately when the application is installed.)

The Banner Image displays at the top of the installer dialog boxes when the installation dialog box has several options that the user can choose from. This provides a nice, polished touch.

Step 6: Set Installer Package Properties

In step 6, you identify more of the properties for information that will appear in the Add or Remove Programs feature in Windows and you set the properties that display in Windows Explorer for the MSI file of your package. Figure 19-16 shows the properties you can set.

The Add/Remove Programs Information displays when you select the Click here for support information link for your application in the Add or Remove Programs dialog box of Windows XP.

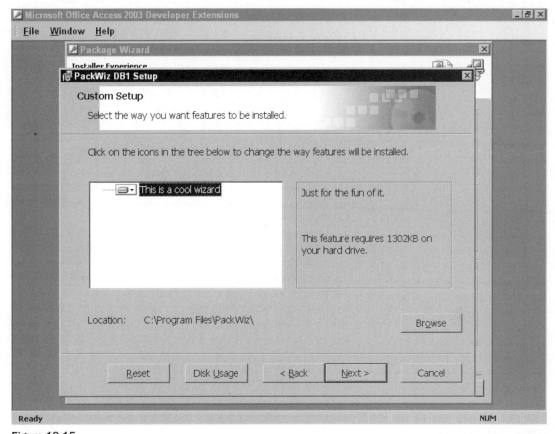

Figure 19-15

To have a better appreciation of this feature, think back. Have you ever downloaded software, installed it, and saved the install package in case you need it later? Or, have you ever gone back and looked at all the stuff you downloaded and wondered what the heck is in it? Have you ever started to install whatever it is (again) so that you could just find out what it is for?

The Windows Explorer "Properties" Information specifies what you and your user will see if you select your MSI file then display the properties of the file. This is the perfect place to enhance your professional image by entering relevant, meaningful information. Do your users the favor that you would like others to do for you.

Step 7: Save the Template/Create a Batch File

You have probably noticed that each of the dialog boxes have a Finish button. Clicking the Finish button on any of the dialog boxes causes the wizard to check if there are any changes to the template, prompts to save the template if there are changes, and executes the process to generate the installer package.

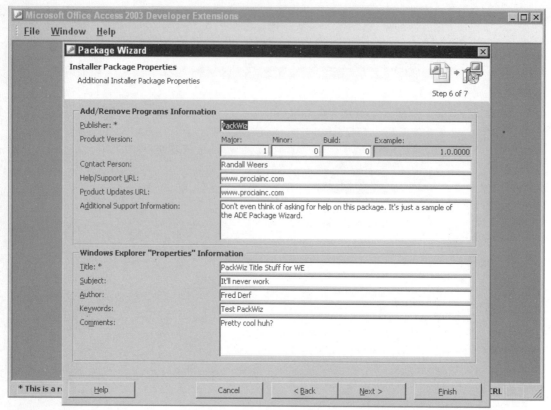

Figure 19-16

When you get to this step you will see the `Completing Your Installer Package` dialog box, as shown in Figure 19-17.

Just like the Custom Startup Wizard, in this last step you can save your template to a file that you can use the next time you use the Package Wizard. Not only that, but you can create a batch file (BAT) that you can use to run the template through the Package Wizard without even opening the wizard.

Step 8: (Optional) Modify Your Install Package (MSI)

The truth is, we hate to start writing about this step. Having walked you through the Package Wizard to write this chapter, we found that the wizard produced highly satisfactory results. So, why mess with success? On the other hand, we like to tinker. We don't think that we have ever bought anything that works exactly the way we want it to right off the shelf. And, knowing that many developers share that character flaw—err, trait—it is worth exploring how to make modifications to the MSI.

The example that we walked you through didn't show how to handle situations where you might have your front end (the user interface portion of your application) installed on all the clients' PCs with the back end (the tables and data) installed on a "server" computer. Of course, one way to cover that

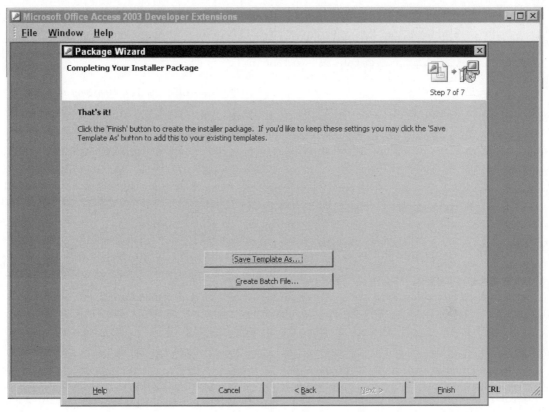

Figure 19-17

situation would be to create two install packages. The "Client" package would be installed on every computer. The "Server" package would be installed only once. But wouldn't it be nice to be able to give out one install package that leads the installer through the correct steps without requiring yet another piece of paper containing additional instructions?

And so, we have already found a reason to modifying the MSI. One way to handle this front-end/back-end situation is to add the back end as a file during *Step 4: Add Files and Registry Keys*. The trouble is *Step 5: The Installer's Experience* allows you to describe the feature information for only one feature (probably your front end). Plus, adding the back end during step 4 creates the problem of how to make the user understand that when they are running the install program, they have to install the back end first and that it must be on a "server" computer. At the very least, they need to know not to run (open) the front-end file until the back end has been properly installed.

As you can see, it would require a lot of information to adequately explain everything needed to understand how to modify the MSI. And, in fact, the ADE and related topics could be another entire book. So rather than trying to write a whole Microsoft Windows Installer package tutorial, this will get you started in the right direction in the event you decide you want to tweak your application's install package.

Tools for Tweaking

If you're going to tweak the MSI file, you'll need an MSI Editor. Microsoft provides a free one. You can get it by downloading the Windows Installer SDK from `http://www.microsoft.com/msdownload/platformsdk/sdkupdate/default.htm?&gssnb=1`.

> *Note: The Windows Installer SDK requires some Core SDK components. If you don't already have other components, the download could be as much as 1GB.*

Before mentioning other places that you could go to for installer help, maybe we should start with a few tips about how to get help from Microsoft. That way if any of these links change, you will still be able to search and find the information.

You can go the Microsoft support route by telephone. Or, you can do as we have done for years: visit support on the web at: `http://support.microsoft.com/default.aspx`. Or, simply go to `www.microsoft.com` and click the Support link at the top right of the page.

When you're on the support page, at the top of the column on the left side of the page has a text box to `Search the Knowledge Base`—long time users refer to this as "Microsoft KB" or "MSKB" or simply "KB." Obviously, page layouts are subject to change. But, again, this gives you a good idea of where and how to find information. Type in a word or a couple of words and click the green arrow next to the text box. Provided that you've entered a word that has some meaning to MS products, you'll get plenty of information. And don't miss the `Advance Search and Help` option under the text box.

We typed `orca` in the text box and found that the second MSKB article titled "How to: Use the Orca Database Editor to Edit Windows Installer Files" led to `http://support.microsoft.com/default.aspx?scid=kb;en-us;255905`. Unfortunately, the article only tells you what you can do with the Orca user interface. You could figure that out on your own. On the other hand, the page contains a link to the Platform SDK. And that link is the first link that we specified above. The moral of this story is: Follow the leads. Dig, drill down, however you want to phrase it. There is typically plenty of valid, useful information available when you need it.

Tips for Tweaking

The links provided above are good places to go for information. Fortunately, the Microsoft Access Team was considerate enough to realize that we might want to tweak things or even to build our own packages. So, they included the `SetupPak.mht` file in the Whitepapers subfolder of the ADE. That is a good place to start to build an understanding of the components of the MSI database. But truthfully, it only barely scratches the surface. Here are a few more tips.

Here may be a reason why the MSI Editor shares its name with a type of whale (Orca). Maintaining an MSI database is a little like trying to develop a user interface by building all of the forms with VBA code. Imagine not having the Access user interface to layout your forms!

Figure 19-18 shows the MSI file generated from the steps laid out in this chapter in Orca. (`db1 Backend .mdb` was added after the screen shot taken in step 4.) The figure shows only one simple section of the MSI file—the files that are in the CAB file; the files that will be installed.

The left column lists the tables that control the Windows installer process. Some of them will not need to change when you customize the install. And, those that will change typically require changes to multiple tables. For example, let's say that you decide to change the setup so that it will install a front-end

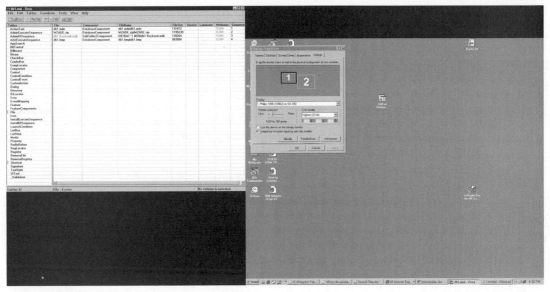

Figure 19-18

application and a back-end data file. There are many ways to do this. One way might be to set up the package so that the back end is installed only if the user goes through the Custom install.

To accomplish this you will have to add a Feature. Recall that you described one feature in step 5 and it was quite easy because the wizard added that feature to the MSI file. When you add the second feature things get a little more complicated. For one thing, you need to identify the feature in the Feature table. You'll enter a title and description the same as you did in step 5. But while using Orca you'll also record additional values, including Display and Level.

Display specifies the order of features in the interface and specifies if the features are displayed expanded or collapsed. Level specifies the initial installation levels of features. You can visit http://msdn .microsoft.com/library/default.asp?url=/library/en-us/msi/setup/controlling _feature_selection_states.asp for more information.

Eventually you will discover that you can customize the install package any way that you want. But to do that, you will have to modify the following:

❑ The Control table to define a control the user can select

❑ The ControlEvent table to set the install level

❑ The Feature table to define the feature

❑ The Property table to define the install levels

This just listed a few of the changes. There are always trade-offs to be able to deliver what you want to deliver. There will always be some price to pay to have more options and more power to customize your applications. Maybe this is why there are a number of vendors who have written user interfaces to help with the installation process. Wise Solutions and InstallShield are among the better known providers of installation solution software.

The point of all this is, it would be foolish to imagine that it will be easy to customize the MSI file without using a tool designed to help you understand the components of the MSI file. So if you are going to start tweaking, here are two recommendations.

❑   Budget some time for it.

❑   Use the Package Wizard to add all the files needed in the package. The wizard will set up all the details needed in the `File` table (shown in Figure 19-18).

Install Chaining

One more thing you can do with the installation package is called *Install Chaining*. Install chaining is part of the "Office Setup Bootstrap." Does the term "Upsize" come to mind? We think that was affectionately tossed around at least during the development of the ADE tools.

Install chaining is the ability to cause additional installation packages to run at the completion of the installation of an application. You could chain to your application installation to install service packs to updated components. Or, you could use it to install the ActiveX controls or auxiliary programs (for example, DLLs) that your application needs.

Another way to use this capability is to modify the Microsoft Office installation to include installing your application. So, if you are partnering with Microsoft to resell Microsoft Office, you can use this to add on an application as a Value Added Reseller. For more information about this functionality visit `http://www.microsoft.com/office/ork/2003/two/ch5/DepD02.htm`.

Summary

Access developers have started developing "real" applications using Microsoft Access. The Developer's Edition of previous versions of Microsoft Office has given Access developers permission to distribute the Access Runtime with their applications. This is no longer true with Microsoft Office 2003 because it does not offer a developer's version. Instead, the VSTO package includes these tools and the permission to distribute Runtimes.

But Microsoft has included much more than just permission to distribute the runtime in the VSTO. They created the Access Developers Extensions, specifically for Access developers who develop these "real" applications. All of these tools are intended to enhance our productivity and the professionalism of the applications.

With the ADE we can perform impact analysis using the Property Scanner. This can help justify level of effort for a change request. It can also improve our productivity and our ability to deliver well-tested solutions by helping us discover which objects must be changed to fulfill a request.

With the ADE we can also easily create a compiled database with custom startup properties using the Custom Startup Wizard. This helps save valuable time that was lost because the Startup properties got set on our only development database (that is, because we forgot to make a backup before we started changing the properties). And because we can save the settings from the wizard, we can consistently reproduce compiled databases with the same startup properties.

And, with the ADE, we can package our solutions into real Microsoft Windows Installer packages. This provides professional-looking installations for the professional applications we've been developing. Not only do the installations look more professional, but also, because we can save installation package settings from the wizard, they are more consistent and take less time to build.

Before you go off to use these great tools to build and deploy your Access-based applications, you'll need to know about another (new) security development in Access 2003. The next chapter will help you understand the changes to "Macro Security" and how they impact Access 2003. These are important changes that help to ensure that users are protected from malicious code in databases. But these changes can make your deployment task a little more complicated; complicated enough to demand your attention, but not so complicated that you can't justify the effort to help ensure you have the type of security you need on your users' computers.

20

Macro Security

Now more than ever, we have to concern ourselves with the security of our computer systems. One form of security addresses securing the information contained in our databases as well as the intellectual property built into our databases. This form of security was discussed in Chapter 16, "Database Security."

Another form of security has to do with preventing malicious attacks on our computers—attacks that can delete files, spread viruses, or otherwise disrupt our work. This chapter discusses the security enhancements built into Access 2003, which help us protect our computer systems and our users' computer systems.

In Microsoft's efforts to make sure everything is secure, they had to deal with the fact that an Access database has a lot of power (something Access developers have known all along). And because of this power, someone who chooses to use Access maliciously can make an Access database perform destructive operations.

Unfortunately, curbing this power led Microsoft to make changes to Access 2003 that will cause us to do a little more work to make databases as easy to use as they have been with prior versions of Access. But let's face it, if our users used Access to open a database from someone else and that database then attacked their computer, they could easily blame Access, rather than the database they opened, for the attack. Their confidence level for using Access in the way we would like them to use it would be right out the window. So, really, these security changes aren't all bad. We just have to learn a few new techniques to keep our databases as easy to use as they were prior to Access 2003.

This chapter explains more about why Access 2003 has the new security features and what they are. (Some might not consider these as features since they just create more work.) But more important than why the features are there, we'll cover the things you can do to make and keep it easy for your users to use your databases in Access 2003. Some of the ways you can get around the macro security feature include: adjusting the Macro Security settings, using Visual Basic scripts, and creating a digital signature to sign your database. These are not difficult solutions. And once you learn them, they will become second nature.

Of course the macro security enhancements aren't the only security enhancements for Access 2003. You'll find it difficult to use the wizards in Access to create forms, reports, and the like, until you update your Jet Engine to Service Pack 8. We'll also explain why this is and talk about the new Jet Expression Services' "Sandbox mode" and its implications for using certain built-in functions in Access.

Macro Security

Macro Security may not be the first thing you want to deal with now that you're working with Access 2003. In fact, most references regarding the new security features in Access 2003 start talking about the Jet Expression Service before macros. The truth is you'll probably want to download Jet SP8 so you can use wizards and the like before you move onto this macro security stuff. But this Macro Security Warning will probably be the first thing you encounter. So we'll describe the ins and outs of it and get to SP8 later.

Let's start with what the new macro security is and then move onto why it is there.

What Is Macro Security?

The first big change you'll find in Access 2003 can be quite annoying: If you attempt open a database that isn't digitally signed using Access 2003 and you have not adjusted Access's macro security settings, you will not be able to open that database, even if it contains no objects—no tables, no queries, no forms or reports, no macros, no modules, no anything.

This is referred to as *macro security*—even though the fact that this security check occurs in an empty database makes the term macro security seem a bit misleading.

So macro security is a check that is performed by Access before the database is opened. The check performs different operations depending on the security level setting for Access and whether or not the database has a digital signature. The concepts of security level and digital signatures are discussed later. For now, just know that a database will not be opened until it has gone through these security checks.

Why Have Macro Security?

Why all this concern over opening a database, even an empty one? Well, with all the capabilities in Access, add-ins and wizards and whatnot, there must be a way for someone to choose to give you a malicious MDB file. And if there is a way, someone will find it and exploit it.

Take the following lines of code for example.

```
docmd.SetWarnings false
docmd.RunSQL "update msysaccessobjects " _
    & "set data = shell(""c:\windows\system32\notepad.exe"");"
```

We entered these commands in the VBE Immediate window using Access 2000. The result? Since the RunSQL command has to execute the VBA Shell function to determine what the value of the field data should be, the Windows Notepad (c:\windows\system32\notepad.exe) started.

Of course the Notepad is not likely to cause problems that would result in destroying my computer. But there are a lot of other destructive programs on your computer, for example `format.com`, as well as destructive commands like `DEL`, which could be run using such a technique.

The two code lines above could have been written in an Access macro. That macro could have been named `AutoExec`, which automatically runs when a database is opened. If the `Shell` function had called a destructive program, instead of Notepad, or the SQL had contained a destructive command like `DEL`, data could be destroyed on the computer that opened the database, or worse yet, data could be destroyed on other computers networked to the computer that opened the database. So if you're not paying attention to the databases you open, or worse yet, your users aren't paying attention, well, you have heard about the countless hours spent recovering from viruses. That is nothing compared to the value of data that can be deleted if a hard disk drive is reformatted. And, malicious code can do just that.

Security Checks Done before Opening a Database

The first thing you might see when you start Access 2003 and open one of your databases from a previous version of Access is the message shown in Figure 20-1. This message is the first sign that Access 2003

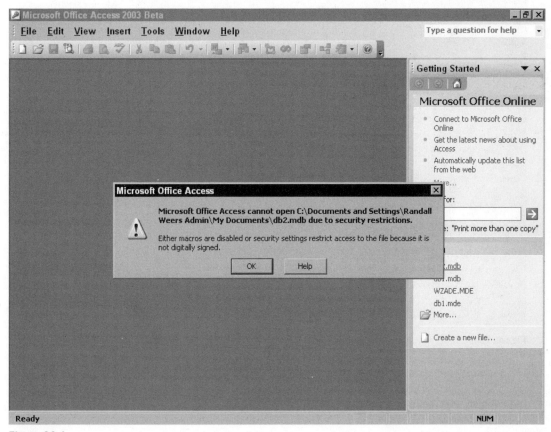

Figure 20-1

macro security is working properly. So, don't panic—you can set the macro security level with one quick adjustment and you'll be able to start working with your database.

The message shown in Figure 20-1 appears when the macro security level setting for Access is set to *High*. At this security level, the database won't open unless it has a digital signature. We'll get to digital signatures in a moment. For now, to adjust Access so that it will open a database without a digital signature, you can set the macro security level to Medium or Low as described below.

Setting Macro Security Level

If you've worked with Word or Excel documents that have macros (VBA code) in them, you've probably seen the `Security Warning` message like the one showing in Figure 20-2.

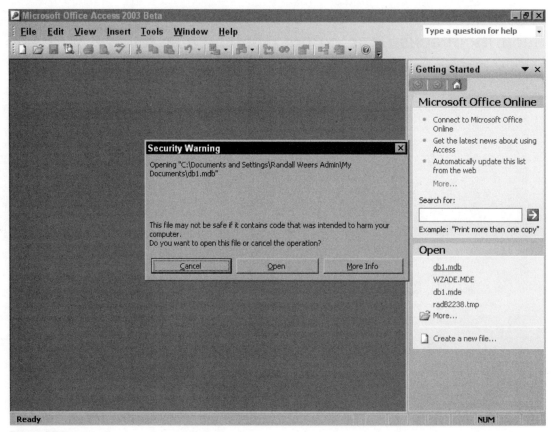

Figure 20-2

If you have seen that warning, you probably already have an idea about how to adjust the security settings in Access so that you can open your database. The instructions are pretty basic but have some implications that you should consider.

To set up Access so that you can open your database, select `Tools | Macro | Security`. You will see the `Security` setting dialog box like the one shown in Figure 20-3.

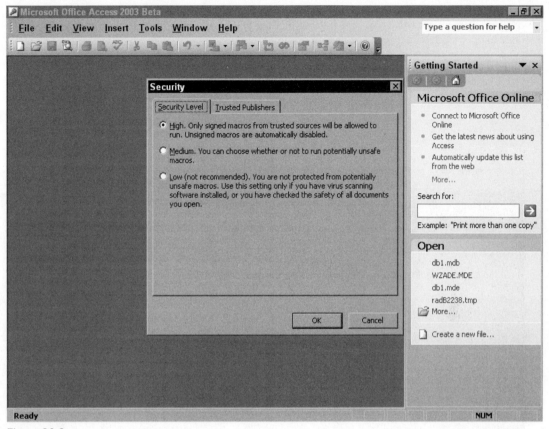

Figure 20-3

For right now you'll probably want to start with the *Medium* security level setting. Using this setting will show the `Security Warning` shown in Figure 20-2 whenever you open a database. To proceed with opening your database all you have to do is click the `Open` button.

This isn't necessarily the optimal solution. After all, when you put your database in front of users, you don't particularly want them to have to respond to this warning every time they open your database. We'll describe a few options to get around this, including digital signatures and how to sign your database. But first we'll explain the implications of setting the macro security level and the various security levels shown in Figure 20-3.

Setting the macro security level in Access affects the way almost all databases are opened by Access. The exception is a digitally signed database. A digitally signed database can be opened regardless of the macro security level.

> **The macro security level for Access is independent of the macro security level setting for other Office applications.**

In the High setting you can only open databases that have been digitally signed and that you have confirmed are from a trusted source. If you are going to sign all your databases and your users will only need to open signed database, you should use this setting.

In the Medium setting you get the warning message shown in Figure 20-2 whenever the database is not signed or the warning show in Figure 20-4 if the database is signed but is from a source that is not on your list of trusted sources.

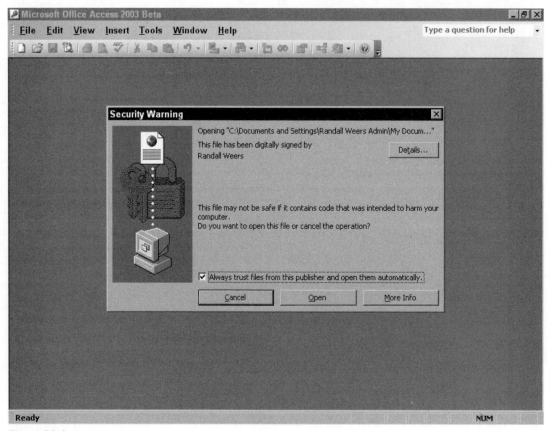

Figure 20-4

In either case, you can choose whether to open the database depending on whether or not you think you can trust the source of the database.

If the database is signed, you can view the details of the source by clicking the Details button as seen in Figure 20-4. Additionally, if the database is signed, you can select *Always trust files from this publisher and open them automatically*. Obviously, whenever you open that database, or any other database from the same publisher, it will automatically open without prompting. So signing your database is one option to avoid making your users respond to the prompt.

If the database is not signed, you will receive the prompt shown in Figure 20-1 every time you open the database. This is the down side to using the Medium setting. It would be nice if you didn't have to respond to this prompt every time you open your database.

In the Low (not recommended) setting, the database will open without a prompt. If you are sure that all the files and add-ins you open are safe, you can select this option. It turns off macro protection (except functions that are disabled by the Jet Expression Service Sandbox mode, which we'll discuss later).

I earnestly recommend *against* using the Low setting. I consider myself a pretty savvy computer user. I have firewalls and virus software. I have a pretty good idea of what to download and whether or not to open a file that has been downloaded for me. But I won't use this setting myself. I guess I would rather have just made the decision to open something that hosed my computer than have it be the result of some setting I chose months ago and then forgot about.

There is one other setting, Very High. As you can see in Figure 20-3, this setting is not available in the Security setting dialog. The setting can be set using system policies. When this setting is chosen, Access cannot open any databases or projects. This setting is intended more for system administrators than for developers or Access users.

Opening Remote Databases Programmatically

The macro security warnings and working around them can be annoying. For one thing, as mentioned before, it would be nice if you users didn't have to deal with the security warning when you're opening a database. For another, if you work in an environment where you are opening remote databases from VBA code, you'll want (and essentially need) those remote databases to open without the warning.

To solve the first annoyance, you could create a Visual Basic Script file (type VBS) to open a database without getting the security prompt. The following code will temporarily disable security (actually, it will set the security level to low) while the database is being opened. When the script ends, control is turned over to Access and the AcApp object is released. Since the security setting is only persistent while the AcApp object exists, the security level in Access will return to whatever setting was chosen using Tools | Macro | Security as described earlier.

```
Const cDatabaseToOpen = "C:\ <FileToOpen>.mdb"
On Error Resume Next
Dim AcApp
Set AcApp = CreateObject("Access.Application")
If AcApp.Version >= 10 Then
    AcApp.AutomationSecurity = 1
End If
AcApp.Visible = True
AcApp.OpenCurrentDatabase cDatabaseToOpen
If AcApp.CurrentProject.FullName <> "" Then
    AcApp.UserControl = True
Else
    AcApp.Quit
    MsgBox "Failed to open '" & cDatabaseToOpen & "'."
End If
```

Similar code can be used in VBA to open and access a remote database. That is, depending on the reason you are opening the remote database you may or may not want to switch control to the user (AcApp.UserControl = True).

Of course, if you use this Visual Basic Script for databases that your users open, you cannot specify command line parameters (for example, /wrkgrp to specify a Workgroup Information file (mdw). If you don't need to specify parameters, this gets around the security warnings quite easily. But there is another way to get around the security warnings: Sign your database with a digital signature.

Signing a database isn't as difficult as it might seem and is something worth looking into. The next section discusses digital signatures, digital certificates, and how to sign your database.

Digital Signatures and Certificates

Up to this point we've been talking about how databases with digital signatures are exceptions to the macro security checks. That is, if a database is digitally signed, it can be opened regardless of the macro security level setting.

So what is a digital signature and how do you create one?

You have probably seen various forms of digital signatures or digitally signed programs while browsing the Internet or installing software. Typically you'll see a security warning dialog box. The dialog box contains information that describes the purpose of the digital certificate used to sign the program, the date and time the certificate was published, and who published it. Some certificates permit you to obtain more information about the program and/or the publisher. After reviewing the information about the certificate, you can accept the certificate or reject it. If desired, you can choose to have that certificate accepted automatically by selecting the `Always trust content from this publisher` check box.

So a digital certificate is an electronic attachment applied to a program, database, or other electronic document. The digital certificate identifies the person or entity that published it and the date and time that it was published. The certificate can also identify the purpose of the certificate and/or the purpose of the program, database, or electronic document to which it applies.

Therefore, a digital signature is a means to apply a digital certificate to programs, databases, or other electronic documents so that a user of that program, database, or document can confirm that the document came from the signer and that it has not been altered since it was signed. If the program, database, or document is altered after it has been digitally signed, the signature is invalidated (removed). This feature means that you can be assured that nobody can introduce viruses after the signature is applied.

What all of this means is that you will have to obtain a digital certificate in order to give your database a digital signature. In a moment, we'll explain more about how to obtain a digital certificate. And a bit later, we'll describe how to sign your database with the digital certificate. But first a bit more explanation about how digital certificates and digital signatures work with Access.

Microsoft Office 2003 uses Microsoft Authenticode technology to enable you to digitally sign your Access database by using a digital certificate. A person using your signed database can then confirm that you are the signer and that your database has not been altered since you signed it. If that person then trusts you, they can open your database without regard to their Access macro security level setting.

You're probably thinking that your database *will* be altered. After all, that's what a user does when they insert or delete data. Since a database is likely to be altered in anticipated ways, a digital signature for an Access database applies to specific aspects of the database rather than to the entire database. Therefore, a database can be updated in the ways you would expect without the signature being invalidated.

More specifically, a digital signature on an Access database covers only objects that could be modified to do malicious things. These objects include modules, macros, and certain types of queries, for example, action queries, SQL pass-through queries, and data definition queries. The signature also applies to the ODBC connection string in queries and properties of ActiveX controls. If any of these types of objects are modified after you sign your database, the digital signature will be invalidated (removed).

Types of Digital Signatures

There are two types of digital certificates: *commercial* and *internal*. Commercial certificates are obtained through a commercial certification authority such as Verisign, Inc. Internal certificates are intended for use on a single computer or within a single organization and can be obtained from your organization's security administrator or created using the `Selfcert.exe` program, which we'll describe later.

Commercial Certificates

To obtain a commercial certificate, you must request (and usually purchase) one from an authorized commercial certificate authority vendor. When the vendor sends you one of these certificates, you will receive instructions about how to install the certificate on your computer and how to use it with your Access application.

> **The certificate you will need for your Access databases is called a "coding signing certificate." Also look for certificates that are suitable for "Microsoft Authenticode" technology.**

The commercial certificate provides full protection of your database for authenticity. Since the digital certificate is removed if the file or VBA project is modified, you can be sure that your database will not be authenticated if anyone tampers with it.

Likewise, commercial certificates provide protection for users. In the event someone obtains a certificate and then uses that certificate for malicious purposes, the commercial authority will revoke the certificate. Then anyone who uses software that is signed with that certificate will be informed of its revocation.

> **The computer opening a digitally signed program, database, or other electronic document must have access to the Internet to verify the authenticity and status of a commercial certificate.**

Internal Certificates

An internal certificate is intended for use on a single computer or within a single organization. An internal certificate provides similar protections as the commercial certificate in that if the file or VBA project is changed, the certificate is removed, and the database will not automatically open under High or Medium security.

Internal certificates can be created and managed by a certificate authority within your organization using tools such as `Microsoft Certificate Server`. You can create a certificate for your own computer using the `Selfcert.exe` tool.

Obtaining a Digital Certificate

As mentioned earlier, you can obtain a certificate from a commercial authority such as Verisign, Inc. For internal certificates you can turn to your security administrator or Digital Certificate group, or you can create your own certificate using the `Selfcert.exe` tool.

You need to be aware that if you create your own certificate, Access will still generate the macro security warning when your signed database is opened on a computer other than the one where the certificate was created (High or Medium security). This happens because Microsoft considers this to be a self-signed database.

The trouble with self-certification is that the certificate isn't trusted because it is not in the Trusted Root Certification Authorities store. This means that if your certificate isn't registered so that Microsoft Authenticode technology can determine its authenticity, the certificate will get a crosswise look. And the reason for this is that a digital certificate you create can be imitated. Which means that someone can mimic your certificate and sign a database with it. Then if you have trusted a digital certificate that has been mimicked, a database signed with that certificate will open. So, if that database contains malicious code, it could execute that code. This brings up two important issues:

❑   If a certificate you create can be imitated, what kind of security do you really get?

❑   If your certificate won't be trusted on another computer, why bother creating your own certificate?

We'll discuss how you can use self-certification in the next section. Let's take the imitation question now.

A certificate is nothing more than a digital document. As with any digital document it can be copied, replicated, or otherwise imitated. However, Microsoft's Authenticode technology is able to determine authenticity of the certificate if, and only if, it is in a Trusted Root Certification Authorities store.

Therefore, using self-certification is a solution that should only be considered if your databases will only be used behind the security of a firewall, with virus software, for protection. If your database, and therefore your certificate, will be made publicly available, such as through the Internet, you will be putting your certificate out where someone could copy it. They could then attach the copy to a database with malicious code and send that database back to you, or worse yet on to other users who could think the database is from you. If the certificate has been on the computer that is opening the database, that database will be trusted. The database will open and the malicious code will be executed.

If you are interested in acquiring a commercial certificate, the Microsoft Developer's Network has list of root certificate program vendors at: http://msdn.microsoft.com/library/default.asp?url=/library/en-us/dnsecure/html/rootcertprog.asp. When you are looking for a vendor to supply a certificate, you need one that provides a certificate for *code signing* or that works with *Microsoft Authenticode technology*.

Using Self-Certification

Having sufficiently warned you in the previous section of the pitfalls of self-certifying, this section will explain how you can self-certify in situations that you believe are secure from hacker attacks.

The question asked in the previous section was: If your certificate isn't going to be trusted on another computer, why bother creating one? The precise statement is that the certificate isn't trusted unless it is installed on the computer that is opening the signed database. Therefore, the solution is to install your certificate on that computer so that it will be trusted.

Next we'll take you through all the steps necessary to self-certify and use the certificate for your database as well as how to use that database on any computer. There are a few steps, but they're not difficult. Some of the steps will only have to be done once. Some will have to be repeated for each computer that will use your certificate to open your database. First you need to run Selfcert.exe to create a certificate on your computer.

With the certificate created, there are two requirements to use your database on another computer:

1. Sign your database.

2. Create a file from your certificate and install it on the target computer.

Signing your database is done through the Visual Basic Editor. Creating a file from your certificate can be accomplished many ways. Mainly this task is accomplished while viewing the certificate details. Installing the certificate on the target computer can be accomplished from Windows Explorer.

Keep in mind these steps only apply to self-certification. For example, if you use a commercial certificate you won't have to install your certificate on each computer.

Creating a Self-Certification Certificate

To create a certificate for yourself, simply run the SelfCert.exe program. For example, mine is located in C:\Program Files\Microsoft Office\OFFICE11\SELFCERT.EXE.

> If **SelfCert.exe** is not installed on your computer, use the Microsoft Office 2003 installation disk to install it.

When Selfcert.exe starts you will see the screen as shown in Figure 20-5.

To complete the process, enter a name for your certificate and click OK. This will create a certificate and add it to the list of certificates for this computer only.

Adding a Certificate to Your Database

To digitally sign your database you add a certificate to it using the Visual Basic Editor. In the Visual Basic Editor select Tools | Digital Signature, as shown in Figure 20-6.

This menu option will open the Digital Signature dialog seen in Figure 20-7.

> Note: This database has been previously signed with the certificate named Randall Weers. If the database is not previously signed, the Sign As Certificate Name will be [No certificate].

To pick a digital signature to sign your database, click Choose... This will display the dialog box show in Figure 20-8, which shows all the digital certificates on this computer.

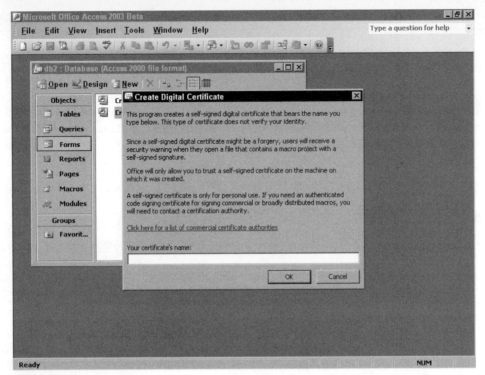

Figure 20-5

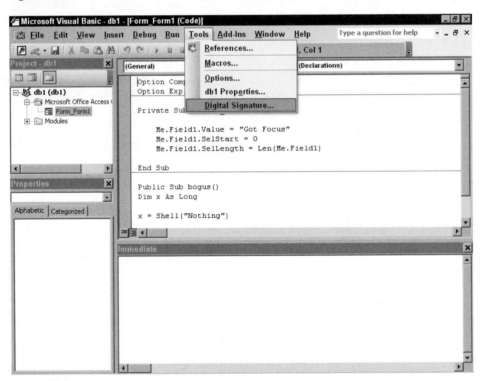

Figure 20-6

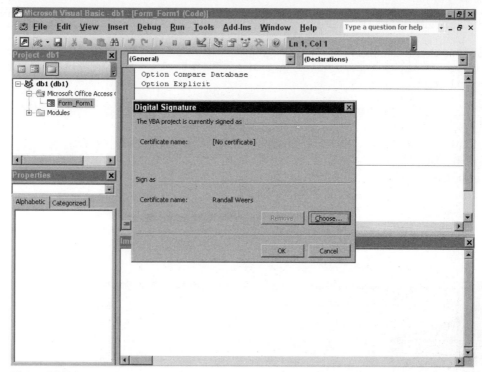

Figure 20-7

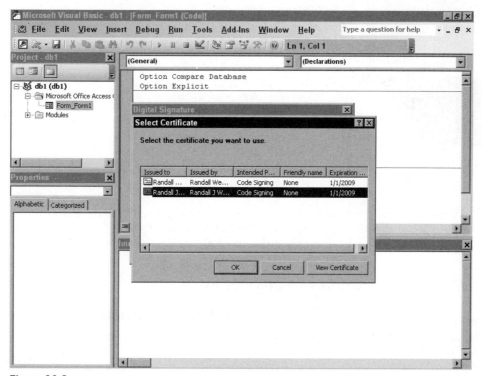

Figure 20-8

Click on the certificate you want to use to sign this database and click OK. The name of the selected certificate will display on the Digital Signature dialog box and a Detail... button will show, as it does in Figure 20-9.

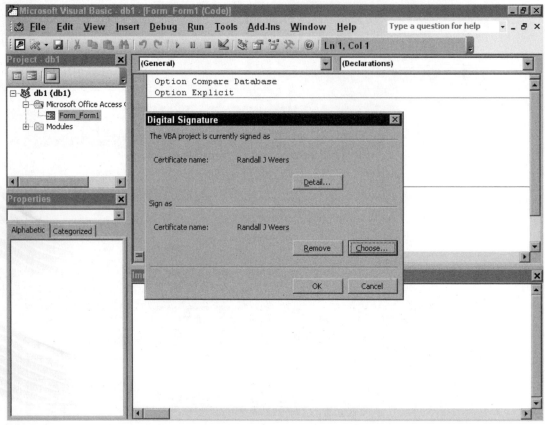

Figure 20-9

You will use the Detail... button to get access to an option to create a file from your certificate so you can copy that certificate to another computer. To sign your database now, click OK.

If you sign your database and then make code changes on the computer that has the certificate, the digital certificate is removed and the database is automatically resigned. If you make code changes on a computer that does not have the certificate, the signature is removed without resigning the database.

> Note: If you are using Access Developer Extensions, the Custom Startup Wizard has an option to add the certificate to your database just before creating the MDE.

Using a Self-Certification Certificate on Another Computer

Since self-certified databases won't be trusted on another computer, you need to add your self-certification certificate to other computers that will be accessing your databases. To do this you need to create a file from your certificate, copy the file to the other computer, and add the certificate to that computer.

One way to create the Certificate (CER) file is to view the details of the certificate from the Visual Basic Editor. To get to the details of the certificate, select `Tools | Digital Signature`. This displays the `Digital Signature` dialog box like the one shown in Figure 20-9. On that dialog, click the `Detail...` button. This will display the `Certificate Information`, as shown in Figure 20-10.

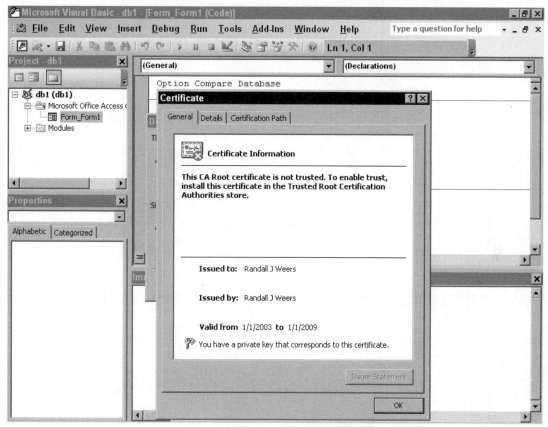

Figure 20-10

Notice that the bottom of the form shows `You have a private key that corresponds to this certificate`. This message will be missing from other computers that have trusted the signature when they opened your database and will prevent your certificate from being trusted. After you copy the certificate and install it on those other computers, they will show the message.

To get to the option that will permit you to save the certificate to a file, click the `Details` tab. This will show the certificate details as seen in Figure 20-11.

Note: the `Value` column has been hidden in Figure 20-11 so as not to show the details of my certificate.

Notice the button `Copy to File...` on the form. Click this button to start the `Certificate Export Wizard` as shown in Figure 20-12. The Wizard will lead you through a process to create a file that you can copy to another computer.

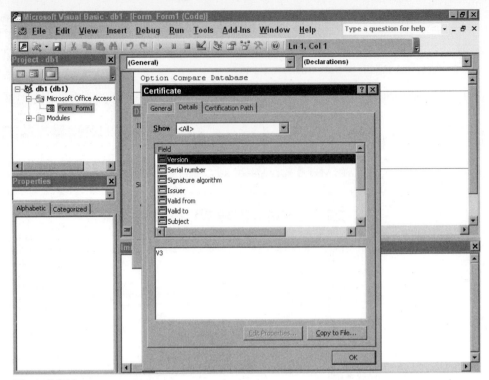

Figure 20-11

Figure 20-12

After you create the file, you may take the file to another computer and open it. A file of type CER is known to Windows and will show the certificate details as shown in Figure 20-13.

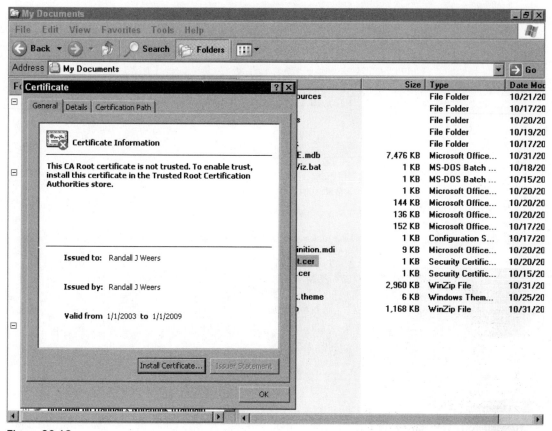

Figure 20-13

To install the Certificate, click `Install Certificate...` That will start the Certificate Import Wizard.

After the certificate is installed on the computer, the first time you open a database signed with that certificate, you will be prompted to approve the certificate as seen in Figure 20-4. If you select the option to always trust the publisher, databases that are signed with that certificate will be opened without a prompt.

Keep in mind that signing the database will only handle issues related to macro security. You may need to update the Jet Engine to Service Pack 8 to avoid other issues around the new security protections in Access 2003. The next section describes the changes in Jet Expression Services, Sandbox mode and Jet Engine SP 8.

Microsoft Jet Expression Services and Sandboxes

After you have been working along in your database, at some point you may get a message that looks something like the one shown in Figure 20-14.

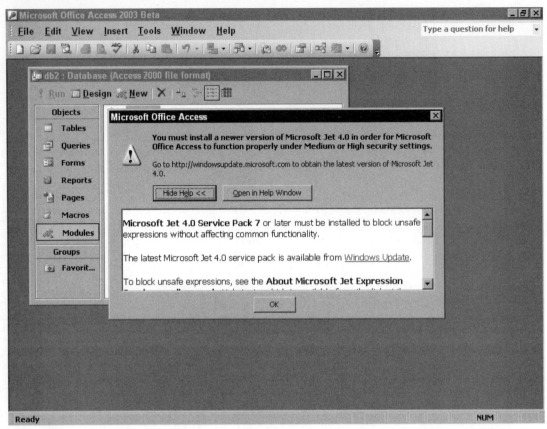

Figure 20-14

Why do you get this message and what do you do about it? As you know by now, Microsoft is taking security very seriously. As a result, they are looking at their software for anything that provides an opportunity that someone could exploit to maliciously attack your computer.

As mentioned previously in this chapter (see section *Why Have Macro Security?*), Access has many ways to execute functions that could be exploited maliciously on your computer. So, in addition to providing macro security enhancements, Microsoft has enhanced the Jet Engine to include checking for potentially unsafe VBA functions.

This isn't a new concept for Access or for the Jet Engine. But with Access 2003, the default is to block unsafe VBA functions. This is called the "Sandbox mode." In Sandbox mode, certain expressions cannot be executed from SQL queries.

More about Errors and How to Fix Them

In addition to the warning message seen in Figure 20-14, you may run into the error message showing in Figure 20-15. The error occurs if you have not installed Service Pack 8 and attempt to use one of the wizards in Access.

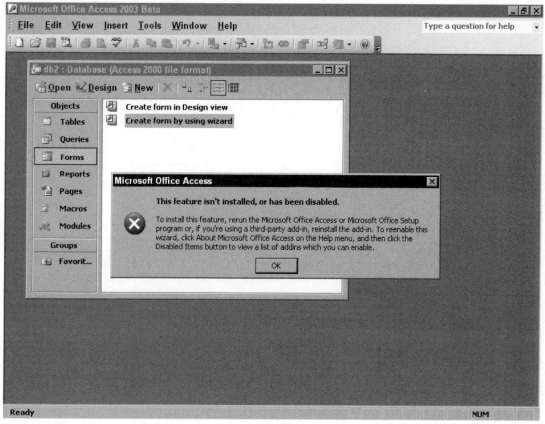

Figure 20-15

Some features will not work properly until you install Jet 4.0 SP 8. They include the following:

- ❑ Wizards may not start.
- ❑ Switchboards created by Switchboard Manager won't function properly.
- ❑ You can't use the RunCode macro action to call a VBA procedure.
- ❑ Event handlers that call VBA procedures won't function.
- ❑ VBA procedures that are called from a property sheet or used in an SQL statement won't function.
- ❑ The following VBA functions won't work when called from a property sheet or used in an SQL statement: FormatCurrency, FormatDateTime, FormatNumber, FormatPercent, InStrB, InStrRev, MonthName, Replace, StrReverse, and WeekDayName.

Obviously, to stop getting the warning message as well as to enable all wizards and other functionality in Access, you need to download the service pack. Follow the link provided in the warning message and install the service pack.

645

Sandbox Mode Limitations

The Sandbox Mode blocks VBA functions or commands that could be harmful to a computer. These functions or commands are blocked by the Jet Engine when they are executed from a SQL query. The table below contains a list of functions that are blocked when the Sandbox mode is enabled:

AppActivate	Beep	Calendar	CallByName	ChDir
ChDrive	Command	Command$	CreateObject	CurDir
CurDir$	DeleteSetting	DoEvents	Environ	Environ$
EOF	Err	FileAttr	FileCopy	FileDateTime
FileLen	FreeFile	GetAllSettings	GetAttr	GetObject
GetSetting	Input	Input$	InputB	InputB$
Kill	Load	Loc	LOF	Randomize
Reset	SaveSetting	Seek	SendKeys	SetAttr
Shell	Spc	Tab	Unload	UserForms
Width				

The Microsoft Knowledge Base has an excellent article that describes the Sandbox mode as well as expressions that are blocked when the Sandbox is enabled at http://support.microsoft.com/default.aspx?scid=kb;en-us;294698. The article also describes how to adjust the Sandbox mode by changing a setting in the Windows Registry. If you decide to adjust the Sandbox mode, be aware that the Jet Engine is used by services other than Access, for example, the Windows error reporting mechanism.

In addition to the functions listed in the table, some of the properties of Microsoft ActiveX controls are also blocked. Standard properties, such as Name, Value, and Tag are not blocked. But custom properties specific to the control may be blocked, for example, Day and Month on the Calendar control.

Workarounds

After you update to Jet Engine 4.0 SP 8 and enable Sandbox Mode (SandBox mode is enabled be default), you can get around some of the limitations of Sandbox Mode.

Blocked Functions

If you attempt to call one of the functions listed in the table from an SQL query, you will receive a runtime error indicating that you have used an "Unknown Function Name".

The functions listed the table are not blocked when executed from your VBA code. So if it is necessary for you to execute one of these functions, you can define a Public function in your VBA code to call from your query.

For example, if you use the CurDir function as shown in this SQL statement:

```
Select curdir() as src from Customers;
```

you can write a Public function like this:

```
Public Function CurDir ()
CurDir = VBA.CurDir()
End Function
```

Blocked Custom Properties of ActiveX Controls

If you need to access custom properties of an ActiveX control through Jet, you can create a function as described above. Alternatively, you can add the ActiveX control to a list of safe controls when your database is loaded or at any time before accessing the property of the control.

To register the control, call `SYSCMD 14, <ActiveX Control GUID>`. Be careful to only register ActiveX controls that you are certain cannot do anything malicious.

Summary

Microsoft has taken security seriously. As a result they've created some nuisances for us to deal with; however, the nuisances aren't that difficult. Jet 4.0 Service Pack 8 helps protect us from malicious attacks on our computer by blocking some functions from SQL queries. Since the Sandbox mode doesn't affect VBA, you can get around these protections by defining Public functions to execute from queries where necessary. You can also use Public functions or register ActiveX controls if the properties of those controls are blocked.

We can set our macro security level to protect us from malicious databases. While the macro security warning is kind of a misnomer—since the warnings can come from an empty database—it gives us the ability to protect our users and ourselves. And because of the power of Access and its increasing widespread usage, this added protection is a good thing.

And there are a variety of ways we can get around the security warnings, including using Visual Basic scripts to start our databases or digitally signing the databases we publish. Yes, all this means more effort. But what price do you put on security? Or, think of this as a small price to pay for some very effective insurance.

Appendices

Upgrading to Access 2003

With all of the exciting new features, controls, and interfaces, there is no doubt that anyone starting fresh should use Access 2003. But, what about those of us with older applications? What should people do if they have to deal with mixed environments where there are applications developed using various versions of Access? And, we can sense the trepidation of developers who are faced with having multiple versions of Access sharing the same database in a networked environment. If you have applications that were created in previous formats, you will need to decide whether to convert or to enable.

This appendix highlights some of the key factors that need to be considered in making those decisions. And, of course, it also provides some steps that you may want to follow, as well as a couple of cautions, before starting any conversion process. We will address special circumstances, such as dealing with MDWs and replication, and also touch on some of the issues faced when converting from 2003 to an earlier format.

Although this appendix discusses converting an application into multiple versions of Access, it does not cover working with multiple versions of Access on the same computer.

To Convert or To Enable—The Age-Old Question

There are several things to consider when deciding to convert or to enable an application to run with Access 2003. This appendix will describe some of the scenarios and some of the options. But first, it would probably be good to make sure that we are all interpreting the words in the same way. Terms like *upgrade*, *migrate*, *convert*, and *enable* sometimes seem to be used interchangeably. So, for the purposes of this appendix, we'd like to clarify how they are intended to be used.

❑ *Upgrade*: You wisely choose to purchase and begin using Access (Office) 2003. Upgrade does not specify that you have changed the file format of your applications. Upgrade is so often associated with getting a discount when purchasing the application that we'll just leave it at that.

❏   *Migrate*: You have some Access applications created in previous versions that you will now convert or enable so that they can be used with Access 2003.

❏   *Convert*: The specific process that Access runs to change the database format from one version to another. Obviously, we are going to focus on converting *to* Access 2003. Converting allows you to work with the database objects and to utilize the features of the specified version of Access.

❏   *Enable*: Enabling allows a newer version of Access to open a database created by a previous version of Access, but it does not change the file format. In some situations, the need to have older versions of Access using the database makes enabling the practical choice. This allows Access 2003 to open the database. The user can view and update data, but they will not be able to modify objects, create new database objects, and so on.

Key Decision Factors

Having established some common terminology, we can focus on the key factors for making the decision to enable or to convert. A pivotal factor is dealing with multiple versions of Access that need to utilize the same data file or application. Other key issues include: Will any new features from Access 2003 be incorporated into the application? Is an MDE file required? What version is the original application in, and of course, what would the time and resources or cost/benefit be?

For the most part, it is very straightforward to either enable or convert a database to 2003. User-level security will require extra steps, but if the situation warrants a secured database, the effort is well worth it. And, as always, replication proves to be a special case. However, an evaluation of the trade-offs typically supports the effort to convert. If you are considering some of the costs and time associated with rolling out a new version over a vast network, it is very handy to have several options that are a mix of status quo, enabling and converting. And, if you are responsible for making the decision about upgrading or staying with earlier versions of Access, we strongly recommend that you focus on how Access 2003's new features can pay for themselves and provide a significant return on investment. Before converting, you will definitely want to spend some time getting familiar with the various security features incorporated in Access 2003. Again, special consideration needs to be taken to address secured applications and replication. Although this appendix refers to various security features, the focus is on factors dealing with upgrading. For help with security issues when upgrading, you should review the new security features that are highlighted in Chapter 20, "Macro Security," as well as Chapter 16, "Database Security." There is also additional information available online, such as through MSDN and Microsoft Access Online Help.

Networks with Only One Version of Access

Obviously, in a controlled environment where everyone will be using Access 2003, it would be a shame to not convert and take advantage of the new features in Access 2003. Well, except (yes, the exception will prove the rule), if the application in question is 2000 or 2002, it does everything that you want it do, it is working fine, and you don't want to incorporate any of the Access 2003 features. In that case, you may choose to enable rather than to convert.

Moving from Access 2002 to Access 2003 is almost a freebie. Yes, it is really that easy. 2002 databases do not need to be converted because the file format is the same for 2002 and 2003. So, you can just open the 2002 database with Access 2003 and start working. This is essentially the case for MDEs, MDBs with or without code, and for DAPs (data access pages).

Note: Pay me now or Pay me later – Just because the program was Access 2002, it does not mean that the file was 2002 format. Remember that Access 2002 was often set up to use Access 2000 as the default file format. Thankfully, the price for "later" is pretty low.

Access 2003 can convert a database from Access 2.0, 95, 97, and 2000 to Access 2003 (2002–2003 file format). It can also convert an Access 2003 file format to 2000 or 97 file formats, but not to 95 or 2.0. Figure A-1 shows the display for selecting the conversion path. Keep in mind that merely converting the file does not ensure that the application will function properly. The guidelines, cautions, and tips in this appendix will help to ensure a smooth transition. But you may also need to work with some of the code, special toolbars, and other features after converting a file to or from a different version of Access.

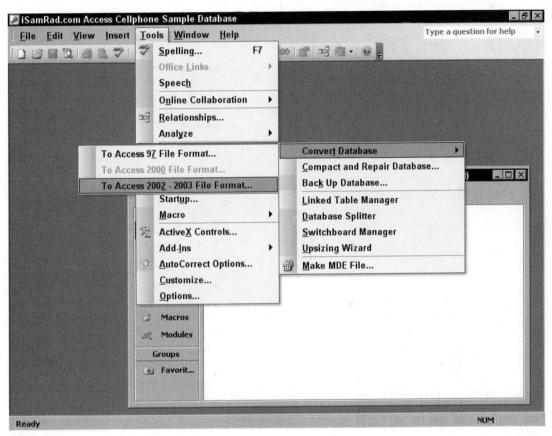

Figure A-1

Networks Having Multiple Versions of Access

In the real world, companies often have multiple versions of Access (preferably installed on different computers). Although not ideal, it is often better to allow some of the people to upgrade than it is to hold everyone back pending a complete network roll-out. There are a few options for working with multiple versions of Access. Let's identify some options and benefits.

This is really where it is appropriate to thoroughly review the trade-offs associated with enabling or converting. Upgrading often requires an investment of time and resources into both the purchase and the deployment of the new program. Then, if you decide to convert (now we're talking about changing the file format) an application, there may be additional time required to update the code, work with the MDW (the workgroup information file), and deal the new 2003 security features. In addition to time and costs, it is important to remember that once a file has been converted, it cannot be opened by older versions of Access. Again there is an exception: 2002 can open a 2003 database. These factors could all be considered as part of the cost of converting.

> The cost of upgrading each workstation might be minimized if it is practical to create and install runtime versions of the applications.

At the top of the list of benefits from converting is the opportunity to enjoy the new features. And, Access 2003 has some pretty awesome (read that as powerful) timesaving tools, wizards, and functionality. As a developer, you definitely want to benefit from the ADE (Access Developer Extensions), which is discussed in Chapter 19. As you know, you need to use the "original" version of Access to create an MDE, so you'll need to convert to 2003 if you want to use 2003 to create your MDE files. Another key reason to convert is the peace of mind associated with having everyone using the same file format. Why introduce the potential for unnecessary (and often hidden) complications?

As with many things, converting does not have to be an either–or decision. It is likely that a combination of original, converted, and enabled applications could be appropriate. With the scenario of a multiuser environment with the back end and the application in Access 97, it is possible for an Access 2003 application to share the data. In fact, you can both keep the application in a 97 format and convert (create a copy of) the application in Access 2003. So, people with Access 97 can continue to use their original files and a new application file could be created by converting the 97 file to Access 2003. Then, it is possible to add functionality to the new file by incorporating Access 2003 features. You could also provide an enabled file for users who have 2000, 2002, or 2003 and who don't need the new features. The key is that users would need to open the file associated with their version of Access. All versions would connect to the same data file, which would be maintained in the original (or oldest version maintained) file format.

> When multiple versions of Access are sharing one data file, the data file needs to be in the file format of the oldest version of Access that is linked to it. This is because databases are backward compatible but not forward compatible. So an Access 97 application cannot link to an Access 2003 data file.

Instead of converting an entire database, there is an option of importing database objects into an Access 2003 file. This is particularly handy if you only want to retain or convert some of the objects. This process does not automatically import references to libraries, so the references may need to be set in the new Access file.

Another item to consider is that when converting an Access 2000 file with DAPs, the pages are not automatically converted to the Microsoft Office 2002 Web Components format. This is the format shared by Access 2002 and 2003. However, when a DAP is opened in Design view, Access will convert it to the most recent version of Web Components and make a backup of the original page.

Splitting a Database

There may be a situation where multiple users actually share one database file that contains both the user interface (UI) and the data. Let's hope that this is a very rare situation, because it is a scenario that is prone to database corruption. But, having the data in the same file as the forms and reports becomes a significant limitation if users want to use different versions of Access. This situation has plenty of other limitations, particularly those related to performance and corruption. One reasonably straightforward solution is to spilt the database and have multiple front ends sharing one back-end data file.

> **Actually, we strongly recommend splitting your databases under all but the most simplistic single-user situations.**

Here's how to split the a single database into front-end (UI) and back-end (data) files:

1.   Start by making a copy of the database.

2.   Then, if the all users will be converting to a newer file format, the next step would be to convert the database. However, if some users will continue using the original (older) version of Access, split the database before converting it.

3.   To split the database, open it in its current version of Access. Click `Tools` on the menu bar and select `Database Utilities`. Then select `Database Splitter` and let the wizard walk you through splitting the database.

4.   After the database has been converted, confirm that the tables are correctly linked by using the `Linked Table Manager`, which is found by clicking `Tools` and then selecting `Database Utilities`.

Now, if you want to create multiple versions of the database, you will only be converting the front end. You can convert the front-end file to whatever versions of Access that users will need. All of the front-end files can be linked to the back-end (data) file that was just created.

> **You will want to keep the back-end (data) file in the oldest version of Access that will be used to link to the data.**

Converting to Access 2003

You can convert a Microsoft Access database from 2.0 or later to the Access 2000 or Access 2003 file format. You can also convert an Access Project (connected to SQL Server) from Access 2000 to the Access 2003 file format. Keep in mind that converting a database affects only the file that is being converted; it does not affect linked tables.

Before you convert any database, always make a backup. OK, you probably already planned on doing that, but it can't be overemphasized. A handy way to make a backup is to put all associated files into a clearly named zip file. Using a zip file or putting the backup in a different folder provides just a little extra insurance in case something goes awry during a conversion process. With a split database, it is important that all linked tables are in the locations specified in the path in the Linked Table properties. And, if at all possible, compile the database before converting it. This extra step is certainly worth the time because it reduces the possibility of errors during conversion. Fortunately, Access 2003 will open and compile an Access 2000 file. However, databases created in Access 97 or before must be opened by their "original" version of Access to be compiled.

> When converting a database that contains linked tables, be sure that the linked tables are still in the location specified in the **Table** properties. After the database has been converted, the tables can be moved and the **Linked Table Manger** can be used to relink to the tables in their new location.

The steps to compile a database depend on the version of Access. First, open a module in Design view (note: if there is not a module, create and save one) then:

❑ For Access 2002 or 2003, click Debug on the menu bar and then click Compile<ProjectName>. Notice that the ProjectName is listed.

❑ For Access 95 or 97, click Debug on the menu bar and then click Compile All Modules.

❑ For Access 2.0, click Run on the menu bar and then click Compile Loaded Modules.

This seems so self-explanatory that we'll skip including a screen shot.

> The project name in the IDE window may not be the same as the database file name. This is often the case if a database has been renamed, because renaming the database does not rename the VBA project. You can change the name of the project by clicking **Tools** on the menu bar and then clicking **<ProjectName>Properties**. This will open the **Project Properties** window, as displayed in Figure A-2.

To convert a database, it must be closed, meaning that no users can be accessing the database, and you essentially need to have the equivalent of Administrator permissions for the database. Handily, the default mode for an unsecured database to open gives the user these permissions. There will be more about permissions in the section on converting a secured database, which is discussed later in this appendix.

The following steps walk you through converting an Access 2.0, 95, or 97 databases to Access 2003:

❑ Open Access 2003 without specifying a database.

❑ On the File menu, click Open, (or select the Open Folder icon on the toolbar) and browse to the folder containing the database file to be converted.

❑ Click (or double-click) File to open the database. The Convert/Open Database window, as shown in Figure A-3, will appear.

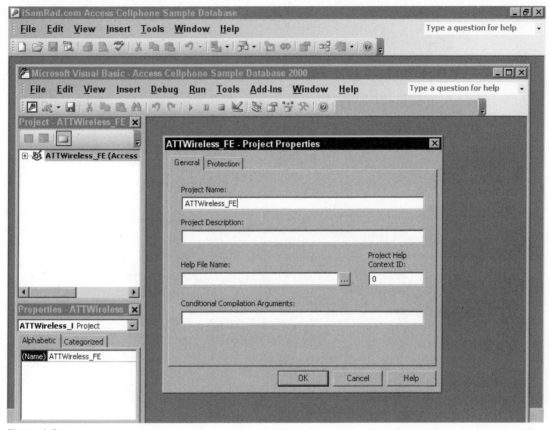

Figure A-2

- ❑ Select `Convert Database` and click `OK`. This will open the `Convert Database Into` explorer window, which will require the database name and location. Access will not allow the converted database to be saved with the same name in the same location. Figure A-4 shows the error message from attempting to give the database the same name in the original folder. Again, this is a handy insurance that the original file is not inadvertently overwritten.

- ❑ Finally, click `Save`. Voila! Access will do the work.

The conversion process may produce some error messages about compile errors. This could likely be due to some of the Visual Basic commands no longer being valid. The code can be corrected after the database is converted. This book has several chapters that may help resolve the errors, such as "VBA Basics," "Executing VBA," and "VBA Error Handling."

It is worth noting that converting Access 2.0 and Access 95 to 2003 automatically converts the built-in and custom toolbars to the new toolbar styles. However, Access 95 custom menu bars are interpreted but not automatically converted, so they cannot be modified in the `Customize` dialog box. The underlying macros can be used to create new menus, toolbars, and shortcut menus. Click `Tools` on the menu bar, then click `Macro`, and then select the desired action: Create a menu, toolbar, or shortcut menu from a macro.

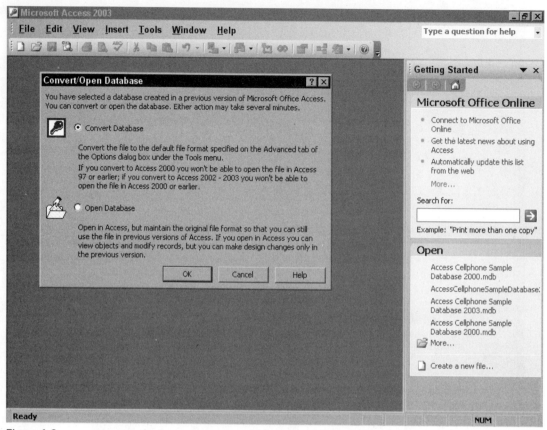

Figure A-3

Figure A-4

Converting a Secured Database

This section will cover issues associated with converting a secured database to Access 2003. To really delve into security issues please read Chapter 16, which provides detailed information about creating and working with workgroup information files (WIFs).

As previously mentioned, converting a secured database entails a few extra steps and considerations. For one thing, you will need to have the necessary permissions to convert the database. Plus, there is a WIF to deal with. Ideally, if all users have converted to 2000, 2002, or 2003, the WIF should be recreated to take advantage of the new security and performance features. Do not create a new WIF if some users still have pre-2000 versions of the application. You do not need to recreate an Access 2000 MDW. And, you don't need to worry about security with an Access project, because its security is maintained in the associated 11.

When upgrading a secured database from Access 95 or 97 to 2003, recreating the WIF in the new format is beneficial but it is not mandatory. However, the MDW should at least be compacted after the database is converted. After the MDW is compacted, users will need to use the Workgroup Administrator to join that MDW before opening the converted database.

Converting a Secured Database from Access 95 or Later to Access 2003

When Access 2003 is installed, it creates a new WIF. This becomes the default WIF for Access 2003. However, to convert a secured database, you will need to join the WIF (or MDW) associated with the database that you want to convert. To ensure that you have the necessary permissions to convert a database, it is best to log on as Admin or as a member of the Admins group. If for some reason that approach is not feasible, then you will need to ensure that you are logged on with at least the following permissions:

❑   Open/Run and Open Exclusive permissions for the database

❑   Administer permissions for the MSysACEs and MSysObjects system tables

❑   Modify Design permissions for all of the tables—the Owner automatically has those permissions

❑   Read Design permissions for all of the objects in the database

Once you have joined the WIF with the necessary permissions, follow the steps previously detailed in section *Converting to Access 2003*. When you have saved the converted database, open it in Access 2003 and compact it by clicking `Tools` on the menu, then select `Database Utilities`, and click `Compact and Repair Database`.

Close the database and use the Workgroup Administrator to temporarily join a different WIF (.MDW) (one other than the one used for that secured database). You need to join a different WIF in order to recreate the one for the converted database. Access Help and Chapter 16 both provide instructions on how to join work groups.

To recreate the MDW use the following steps:

❑   Create a new WIF, using the exact, name, company name, and workgroup ID (WID) that were used to create the original file. The entries are case sensitive and must be entered exactly as in the original file or it will not create a valid Admins group for the new database.

❑   Create the group accounts as they were in the original MDW. Again, the group name and personal ID (PID) is case sensitive.

❑   Create each user account by entering the exact user name and PID for each user.

❑   Compact the new MDW.

❑   Finally, have the users use the Workgroup Administrator to join the newly created and compacted MDW.

Converting a Secured Database from Access 2.0 to Access 2003

Converting a secured Access 2.0 database to Access 2003 starts out very much like converting other versions of a secured database to Access 2003. However, you will need to convert the security files (WIF), which then had an extension of MDA. And, it is prudent to take extra precautions and to allow plenty of time for updating any code.

As always, start by making a backup of the original database. Then, follow the steps previously detailed in the section *Converting to Access 2003*. This will convert the database itself.

Next, convert the associated WIF. For an Access 2.0 database the WIF is typically named `system.mda`. Follow the steps previously detailed in section *Converting a Secured Database from Access 95 or Later to Access 2003*.

Since a lot has changed since Access 2.0 (talk about a world-class understatement), it is likely that there will be several compile errors to be addressed after the database has been converted. In some cases, it may be more efficient to build a new form or report utilizing current wizards than it would be to patch old code.

Converting a Database with Password-Protected VBA

If you have implemented the security features of the Microsoft Visual Basic for Applications (VBA) code (that is, put a password on the IDE), you must supply the password before you convert the file. Figure A-5 shows message box that you will see if you attempt to convert a database that has a password to protect the code.

Figure A-5

> There are mixed opinions about using a password to protect the code. Since many developers think that this is more prone to corruption or being locked out of the code, they often prefer to use an MDE.

To provide the password, open the IDE, (a couple of quick ways include using *Alt+F11* or by clicking `Code` on the `Database` toolbar) and then enter the password in the `<databasename> Password` dialog box. Figure A-6 shows where to input the VBA password.

Since the password will be remembered as long as the database is open, the conversion process will be able to open and work with the underlying project.

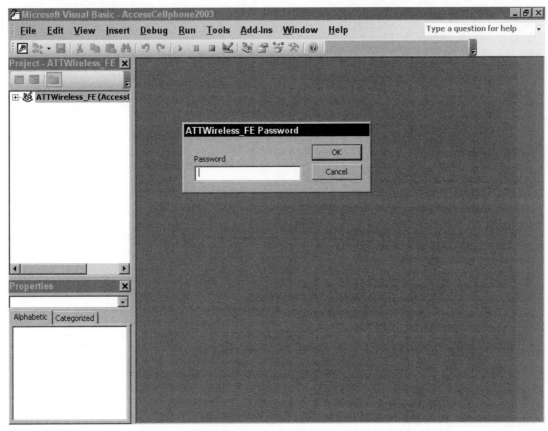

Figure A-6

Converting a Replicated Database

First and foremost, start testing the process by using *copies* of the Design Master and replicas. Do *not* work with the real files until you have successfully completed the complete conversion process on the copies. Incorrectly converting and synchronizing the real files could compromise both the real data and the structure of the replica set. OK, it may not have been necessary to use that much emphasis to get the point across, because if you are working with replicas, you probably already know to use extreme caution. That being said, this section is going to focus on the steps to convert a replicated database with the premise that anyone attempting this will already be somewhat familiar with replications.

Let's get the other cautionary notes out of the way.

❑   When the Design Master is converted from Access 2000 to Access 2003 file format and then synchronized with other replicas, Access will convert the other replicas to the 2003 file format. At that point, Access 2000 will not be able to open them.

❑   Replica sets that contain partial replicas (databases with subsets of the full record set) should be synchronized before converting the files. Then, after converting the files, recreate the partial replicas. Synchronizing a 2003 Design Master with Access 2000 partial replicas might delete some database objects in the VBA project.

❑ When converting to 2003, all users of the replica set must have Access 2002 or 2003.

❑ When converting from Access 97 or earlier, it is necessary to convert all of the original replicas after converting the Design Master.

❑ Preserve a copy of the current Design Master in its original file format. Heck, this is an excellent time to burn a CD and preserve all the related files while you are at it.

❑ If the database is password protected, it may be helpful to remove the password before starting the process to convert the database.

Steps for Converting a Replicated Database

After ensuring that the original files and data are adequately (safely) preserved, and having thoroughly and successfully tested the conversion process on some remote computer, it is finally time to do this for real.

Make a copy of the Design Master and save it where it can be worked on without affecting any of the existing replica set. A separate computer would be ideal.

In the "original" version of Access, make the copy of the Design Master into a Design Master. To do that, open the appropriate version of Access, click on `Tools` on the menu bar and click on `Replication`. Then click on `Recover Design Master`. Access will provide informative error messages if you select the wrong options when attempting to create a Design Master or replicas. Many of the messages are informative and provide options. They may even indicate the consequences of an option, as shown in Figure A-7.

❑ Create a few replicas based on the new design master. Again, this is done by clicking `Tools` on the menu bar, then click on `Replication` and select `Create Replica`.

❑ Next, convert the new Design Master to Access 2003. To do this, click `Tools` on the menu bar and click on `Database Utilities`, then `Convert Database`. Select `Access 2003`.

❑ Now, it is time to synchronize the converted Design Master with the new replicas.

❑ Test, test, test. Be sure that this sample set works as intended. It is better to spend your time testing now than lamenting later.

❑ Once you are satisfied and confident that this sample replica set is working the way it should, Delete It and all of the replicas. *What?* Yes, delete it, because you are now ready to convert the real thing.

❑ Convert the original Design Master to Access 2003. Heck, disk space is cheap, so why not create a current backup of the data before converting the files. It's likely that some of the data has changed, and again, this is cheap insurance. *Reminder*: If the original file was pre-2000, convert the Design Master and then each replica. Do not use the converted Design Master to attempt to automatically convert the replicas.

❑ And at last, synchronize the replicas.

Well, one more step—as a conservative soul, I would make a copy of the new replication set. This might be a good time to burn another CD.

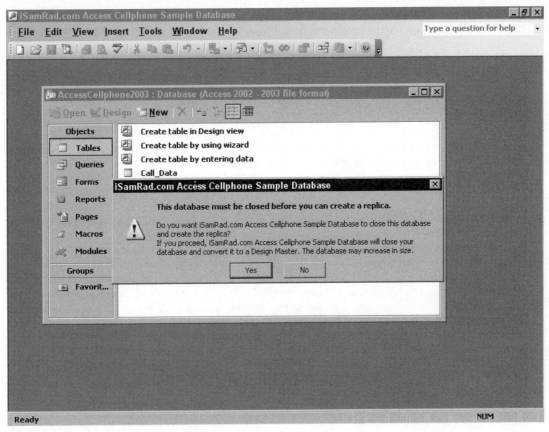

Figure A-7

Enabling a Database

As mentioned at the beginning of this appendix, Access 2003 can open databases in prior versions of Access by either enabling or converting the database. If the database created in Access 97 or earlier is opened by Access 2003, the `Convert/Open Database` window will appear, see Figure A-3. This window clearly states the effects of each option. The `Convert/Open Database` dialog box appears each time an earlier version database is opened. So, if down the road, converting becomes the desired avenue, it is only a click away.

Enabling allows a user with Access 2003 to open a database created in an earlier version of Access without converting the file to the Access 2003 file format. The 2003 user will be able to add, delete, and modify records and to view database objects, but they will not be able to modify database objects or add new objects. Enabling is quite beneficial if there are users who have still not upgraded to Access 2003. It allows the same application file to be shared by multiple versions of Access.

There are some logical limitations when working with an enabled database. Considering that databases are not forward compatible, it makes sense that you cannot link or import an Access 2003 table to an enabled database. (Obviously the enabled database is in an earlier format or it wouldn't need to be enabled.) However, you can open a 2003 database and export the tables to a prior-version database. You can also move or copy data from a 2003 table and paste it directly into a table in a prior-version database.

For ease and consistency, when a database is enabled in 2003, the custom toolbars and menu bars are temporarily converted to the new style of menu and toolbars. In this case, "temporarily" means that the conversion is not preserved when the file is closed. And, although menu bar macros are not converted, they are still supported. So, although they can be used, they cannot be modified.

Yet again, security requires special treatment, or at least special acknowledgment. When a database with user-level security is enabled in 2003, it is recommended that the WIF is recreated in 2003. This ensures that proper security is retained. However, if recreating the WIF (MDW file) is not practical, then it will be necessary to join the original WIF in order to sign into the database.

Converting from Access 2003 to Prior Versions

Although this appendix focuses on converting to Access 2003, it is important to know that it is also possible to convert from Access 2003 to 2000 and 97. It is pretty logical that converting to a prior version will forfeit use of any features that were not yet available in the older version. Access provides a message to that effect during the conversions process. Figure A-8 is an example of such a message. And again, replication and security pose special problems for converting databases. In fact, it is better to create a new replica set in 97 than to try to convert. Similarly, it is better to remove user-level security, convert the database, and then create a new WIF in 97 than to convert a database with user-level security from 2003 to 97.

Figure A-8

Other concerns deal with the file format, mostly because features of the new file formats were not available or supported in Access 97. For example, data that relied on Unicode compression may not convert correctly. And, since Access 97 had a 256 character set, some of the characters in the new format may not have equivalent characters in 97. Also, the `Decimal FieldSize` property for `Number` fields was not available in 97. This property must be changed prior to conversion. Typical alternatives include `Single` or `Double` or change the datatype to `Currency`.

Steps for Converting from Access 2003 to Access 97

To convert an Access 2003 database to Access 97, start by following the typical preparatory steps described in converting to Access 2003. Obviously, make a copy of the file and make sure that no other users have the file open. If there is user-level security, remove it and then follow these steps:

❑ Log on to the database with `Open/Run` and `Open Exclusive` permission for the database and `Read Design` permission for all of the database objects.

❑ If the code is password protected, open the IDE and enter the password. To enter the password, in the VBE window, click on `Tools` on the menu, then `Properties`, and enter the password in the `Project Properties` dialog box, see Figure A-2.

❑ Return to the Access window and click on `Tools` on the menu. Click `Database Utilities`, then `Convert Database`, and then select `To Access 97 File Format`.

❑ In the `Convert Database Into` dialog box, enter a new name for the converted (97) database and then click `Save`.

This will convert the database to Access 97. It would be prudent to test the application and correct problems created by the conversion process.

B

References for Projects

Throughout this book you have seen type libraries or object libraries, such as those described in the Automation chapter, used to enhance functionality through VBA code. You have seen how libraries can provide access to functions that manipulate the Windows System Registry or retrieve and send data to other applications.

In addition to libraries supplied with Microsoft Office, you can acquire type libraries to help simplify a variety of programming tasks. Like Microsoft Office libraries, other vendors' libraries provide classes to manipulate objects. An example would be the QuickBooks libraries provided in the QuickBooks Software Development Kit (SDK). These libraries provide classes you can use to create objects that contain data that is returned from a QuickBooks data file through an XML access method.

Acquiring libraries can be a cost-effective way to get more work done in less time. Of course there is always the trade off between what you pay for a library and writing your own functions. Not to mention the effort that may be required to learn how to use the library. And because of that trade off, you shouldn't neglect the effort you have already put into writing your own code. After all of the "bold, test, and swears" you put into your routines, you really must consider creating code libraries from your code.

This appendix describes techniques for using references to libraries in your projects, including how to reference libraries provided by others and why the order of your reference list can be important. It also discusses the types of libraries available (for example, DLLs and ActiveX Controls).

This appendix also discusses techniques for referring to the References class and why you would want to. It describes some correct techniques for writing code that will go into your own code libraries. And it suggests ways to avoid getting MISSING libraries and what to do when they go missing.

Types of References

You can add references to many types of libraries from your Access projects. Library types include the following: type or object libraries (OLB, TLB, and DLL), ActiveX controls (OCX) and references to other Access databases (MDB and MDE), Access add-ins (MDA), and Access projects (ADP and ADE).

An object library or type library generally provides functionality for access to other applications or adds functionality to use in your Visual Basic code. For example, Microsoft Office exposes its Component Object Model (COM) through the Microsoft Office DLLs. These include the Microsoft Access 11.0 Object Library, Microsoft Excel 11.0 Object Library, Microsoft Word 11.0 Object Library, to name just a few.

ActiveX Controls generally include controls that you can add to your user interface. These controls can display data on forms or provide an access method to data through a form with little or no extra programming. For example, DBi Grid Tools control displays a grid of data, a two-dimensional table that looks similar to Access's datasheet view. The tool has properties to indicate which data to display, adjust colors of cells, and add icons and much more, all without programming. The Grid Tool also enables more functionality through Visual Basic when a reference is made to the Grid Tool DLL.

Access add-ins provide enhanced functionality to Access as a whole. For example, the "New Form" wizard provided with Access is an add-in. By now you know the form wizard leads you through a process to design an initial form that you can then modify to suit you needs. By creating an MDA from Access, you can create your own add-ins for Access.

References to Access databases and projects permit you to access routines from your own code library. These routines can then be used with all of your applications. This is discussed more in the section *Building Code Libraries* later in this appendix.

Adding References to Your Projects

As noted above, adding references to libraries from your Access project can allow you to quickly enhance the functionality of your application with less coding effort. The types of type or object libraries that Access can reference include:

❑   Type libraries: OLB, TLB, and DLL

❑   ActiveX Controls: OCX

You have seen that you can automate Office applications by adding a reference to one of the libraries that comes with Microsoft Office, for example, Microsoft Office 11.0 Object Library. Here are the steps necessary to add a reference, as well as what it means when you do.

Open the Visual Basic Editor and select `Tools | References`. This will display the `References` dialog box as shown in Figure B-1.

The items listed in the `Available References` list include items that have been registered to the Windows System Registry. To add one of these libraries to references for your project, check the box to the left of the library. When you close and reopen the `References` dialog box, any libraries you have checked will move above all unselected libraries.

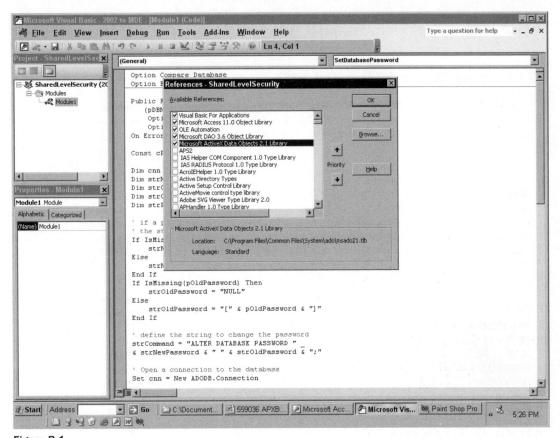

Figure B-1

> The order of the libraries you have selected is important. See section *Order of References Is Important* later in this appendix.

Many application installation packages will handle registering libraries for you. If the application you install does register the library you want, there are two ways to use the library in your references.

One method to get to an unregistered library is to use the Browse... button. Click the Browse... button to open a file selection dialog box. Select the type of library you want from the drop-down list for Files of type. Browse to the folder that contains that library and select the library.

Another method to get to an unregistered library is to register the library yourself. If the library is a 32-bit library (most are), use REGSVR32 to register it. To run REGSVR32 select Run... from the Windows Start menu. In the Open box of the Run dialog box enter REGSVR32 followed by the full file specification of the library you want to register. For example:

```
REGSVR32 "C:\Program Files\Common Files\Microsoft\Office11\MSOCFU.DLL"
```

After you register a library, you will need to close and reopen the `References` dialog box to get the library to display in the `Available References` list.

Reference Order Is Important

One of the reasons for adding references to your project is to make additional classes available so you can declare variables in your code and manipulate objects of those classes. But you should be aware that the name of a class in one library does not have to be unique from the names of classes in other libraries.

A classic example of this occurs when you include references to both DAO and ADO. Both libraries have a `Recordset` class. (You can use the `Object Browser` to see when a class occurs in more than one library. The `Object Browser` is discussed below.)

In situations where there is a duplication of class names, Access determines which class to use by searching sequentially down the list of libraries listed in the `Available Libraries` list. Unfortunately, the compiler won't always tell you that you have the wrong reference. If you refer to a property or method that is not available for the class you have used in your variable declaration, the compiler will report the problem. Otherwise, you'll discover the problem only when you test your code.

If you have libraries that have classes with the same names, you can get Access to choose the class you want by changing the Priority of the library in the list. The up arrow and down arrow buttons, above and below the `Priority` on the `References` dialog box (refer to Figure B-1), will move the library selected in the `Available Libraries` list up or down in the list. Move the library containing the class you want higher than libraries containing the same class name.

You can also avoid problems with duplicate class names by making a specific reference to the library that contains the class you want to use. For example, if you reference both the ADO and DAO libraries, and you want to declare a variable for the `Recordset` class of ADO, you can declare your variable using the following syntax.

```
Dim rsADO as ADODB.Recordset
```

If you want to declare a variable for the DAO `Recordset` class, you can use the following syntax.

```
Dim rsDAO as DAO.Recordset
```

Using this syntax does not eliminate the need to have the reference to the library in your `Reference` list. But it will prevent any confusion about which library you are referring to in your variable declaration.

The Object Browser

After you have added a reference to a library, the classes contained in that library are available for viewing in the `Object Browser`. To see the `Object Browser` in the Visual Basic Editor, press *F2* or select `View | Object Browser` from the menu. The Visual Basic Editor will display the `Object Browser` as shown in Figure B-2.

Notice that when you select an item in the `Classes` list, the properties and methods of that class display in the right-hand list. Select an item in the right-hand list to display more specific information about the

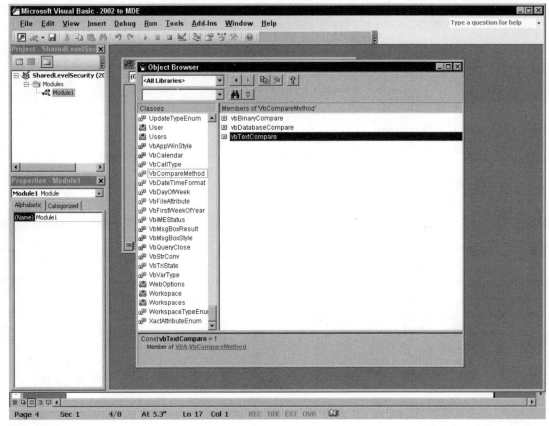

Figure B-2

item. For example, Figure B-2 shows that vbTextCompare is a constant with a value of 1 and is a member of VBA.VBCompareMethod.

You can specify which of the referenced library you want to browse by choosing it from the library selection drop-down list. Notice the list starting with <All Libraries> in Figure B-3.

If you are looking for a particular class, property, method, or declared constant, you can specify a portion of the string to search for and click the Search button (the binoculars) to find it. Figure B-4 shows the results of searching for recordset. Notice that since <All Libraries> is selected the class recordset is listed twice.

Building Code Libraries

Aside from the four types of reference libraries listed above (OLB, TLB, DLL, and OCX), there is a set of "library" types that are often overlooked. These are library types you can use to link to Access projects you have created. They include:

❑   MS Access Databases: MDB and MDE

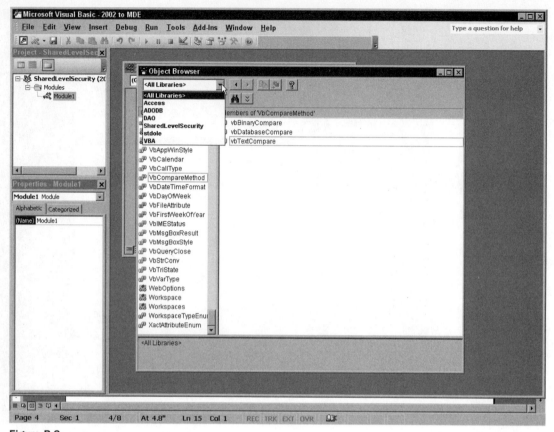

Figure B-3

❏   MS Access Add-ins: MDA

❏   MS Access Projects: ADP and ADE

With these types of references you can develop your own Code Libraries that contain routines to share in all of your applications. An example might be something like a common Error Handling routine.

Since you can reuse these routines over and over, you can justify putting a little more effort into them. Take error handling for example. Commonly, we develop code to display a message to the user and request that the user report the error to us. Have you ever been watching a user use your application and expose an error you hadn't found in testing? They click OK on the message without giving it a second thought. You ask why they didn't wait to review the message and they say, "Oh, that happens all the time. I was told to just ignore it."

Suppose that instead of just depending on the users to call to report errors, you write routines to track the errors in a table. Then you could investigate what is happening. Perhaps your tables could even maintain some trace data to help find out what causes the problem. Suppose you also realize that the main reason the errors don't get reported is that it is too difficult for the user to report them. So you add some functionality that builds an e-mail message for the user to send through Outlook.

Figure B-4

Of course there are always so many things to do when building the current application, we don't have time for tasks like these. But if you could find time to write these routines on time and reuse them in all of your applications with all your customers, would that make it worthwhile? That's what Code Libraries are for.

> **If you are going to make an MDE from a database that uses a reference to your Code Library databases, your code library databases must be made into MDEs as well.**

Note: If you have a particular piece of code that you do not want people to be able to read easily you can make an MDE from it. This removes all the editable code and compresses the database. See the "Chapter 16, Database Security," for more information.

Office XP Developer edition included a component call Code Librarian to help manage these code libraries. However, Office 2003 does *not* include that component. For those who have not previously enjoyed using Code Librarian from Office XP, the bad news is that the Code Librarian can only be installed if you install the full Office XP package. So unless you want to buy Office XP, you won't be able to try it. For those who have Code Librarian installed on their machines, the good news is that it is still compatible with Office 2003. So don't remove it.

Visual Basic and References

There are a few techniques that make working with Access References easier. And there are a few techniques that you should be aware of to avoid problems when using references to your own code libraries. These techniques are listed in this section.

The Reference Object

The Access Application object includes the `References` collection. The References collection can be easily used for a number of purposes. You can determine the number of references in the project using

```
Application.References.Count
```

You can walk through the references to be sure that all the references are found using something like this:

```
For Each ref in Application.References
     If ref.IsBroken then
          Debug.Print ref.name & " is broken."
     End if
Next Ref
```

You can add references using the `AddFromFile` or `AddFromGUID`. For `AddFromFile`, you simply specify the file specification. For `AddFromGUID`, the reference library must be registered in the Windows System Registry and you must know the exact GUID for that library.

Using CurrentDB versus CodeDB

One thing to consider when developing Code Libraries is that `CurrentDB` refers to the database that is open in the Access user interface. So, if you want your Code Library project to refer to objects that are in its own database, you need to use `CodeDB`. Likewise, there are the `CurrentProject` and `CodeProject` properties so be sure that you are setting a reference to the correct objects.

Running a Procedure from a Library Database

If you need to call routines in your Code Library from the database referencing the code database, you can call the routine using the `Call` statement in Visual Basic. You can also use the `Application.Run` method. For example say you have an `Errors.MDB` that contains the `HandleError` procedure. You may call that procedure with code that looks like this (depending on the parameters needed in the routine, of course):

```
Call Errors.HandleError _
          (Err. .Number, Err.Description, Err.Source)
Application.Run("Errors.HandleError", _
     Err.Number, Err.Description, Err.Source)
```

Note: The qualifier does not have to be the same as the name of the MDB. In the above example, Errors. was used to qualify where the HandleError procedure is located. You can change the name of the qualifier by changing the Name property of the project.

Compiling to Validate References

An easy way to be sure that the References in your project are not broken is to use the `Debug | Compile` menu option. This quickly finds declarations that use classes that are not available to your project.

> For best results with this technique, *always* use `Option Explicit` for every module to be sure that you are declaring all variables. The compiler will tell you if you have not declared a variable even before you attempt to run the code. And, since all variables must be declared, if any variables reference classes or object types from a library that has gone missing, the compiler will let you know.

Be aware that since Access uses late binding, types are not checked until the code is executed. That means that until a procedure is run, you may not know that a variable has been defined using a class from a missing library. You can avoid having the users find these problems later by checking the IsBroken property of the References in your application during start up. This would be a good routine to write and put into your code library so that you can use it with all of your applications.

Fixing Broken References

If your code suddenly stops working after you have installed your database on another computer, it's a good idea to check the References. One of the first things to check for is the MISSING referenced type library. As you can see in Figure B-5, MISSING stands out at the left of any missing type library.

To fix the missing references, open the `References` dialog box from the Visual Basic Editor and update the References.

Note: There are two problems you typically run into here. One, if you have delivered the database as an MDE, you cannot modify references. Two, if the library you are referencing doesn't exist on the computer. In either case, the most likely solution is to get the library into the right place on the computer. For that, see section Avoiding Broken References.

When you have fixed missing references, it's a good idea to compile the module using `Debug | Compile`, that is if you're not working with an MDE. Compiling will help make sure that the library on the new computer matches the one on the computer where you did your testing. Meaning, it will indicate if the library has the same classes and type definitions you used in your code.

If you have a broken or missing reference, compiling may report an error incorrectly. In particular, you may find that Visual Basic functions (for example, Right or Ucase) are reported as undefined. If this occurs, fix the missing references first, then proceed with other fixes.

Avoiding Broken References

Can you claim that you've never had a problem delivering an application to one of your users? Then we're betting that you've never used references. Either that or you are one of the fortunate developers who get to develop on a machine with a configuration that is identical to your users. But even if the machine is

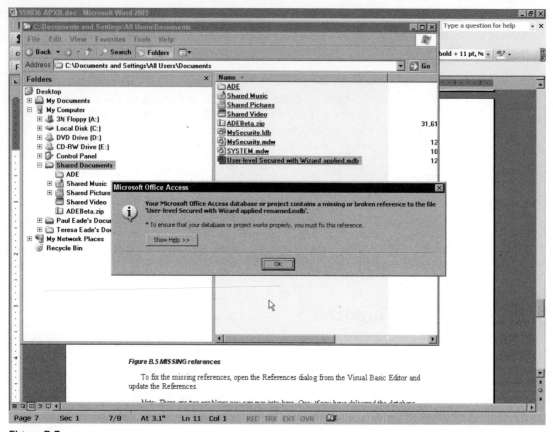

Figure B-5

identical, you probably haven't taken the opportunity to develop a Code Library. You know what we mean—the one you forgot to take with you when you went to the user's machine to install your database.

Of course the first thing to do to avoid broken references is to be sure that you are delivering all of the components that go with your application. And don't forget those DLLs that you acquired from a vendor to improve the features in your application. And just delivering them isn't all that there is to it, you need to be sure you've installed those DLLs in the right folder.

So how do you know what the right folder is? When Access searches for referenced libraries, it first searches based on the file specification provided when the library was added. If the library is not found, it then searches as follows:

1. First, Access searches for a RefLibPaths key in the following location in the Microsoft Windows Registry: HKEY_LOCAL_MACHINE\Software\Microsoft\Office\11.0\Access

2. If the key exists, Access checks for the existence of a value name that matches the name of the referenced file. If it finds a matching value name, Access loads the reference from the path specified in the corresponding value data.

3.   If Access doesn't find a `RefLibPaths` key, it searches for the referenced file in the locations listed below in the following order:

      ❑   Application folder containing the application (the folder where `Msaccess.exe` is located).

      ❑   Current folder.

      ❑   System folders (the System and System32 folders located in the Windows or WINNT folder).

      ❑   Windows or WINNT folder.

      ❑   PATH environment variable. For more information about environment variables, see Windows Help.

      ❑   The folder that contains the Access file, and any subfolders located in that folder.

If Access still can't find the reference after performing this search, you must fix the reference manually.

> When running your code, classes from referenced libraries are not checked until the procedure that declares a variable using one of those classes. In your `StartUp` procedure, you can walk through the References using the technique previously mentioned and use the `IsBroken` property to find broken references. If you find a broken reference you can inform your user with a meaningful message instead of letting an error pop up from Visual Basic.

Resources

There are a number of commercially available products that provide libraries for you to reference from your Access projects. You can also find many libraries through sharing. Here are a few resources to get you started. We have not tried all of the controls and libraries found. So we cannot endorse all of them.

You should also be aware that many libraries and ActiveX controls that are designed for Visual Basic programming languages can be used by Access. Contact the vendor to find out.

Access Advisor Search for "ActiveX Control" or search for "DLL." This is a great site for other information too.	http://accessadvisor.net
The Access Web With many resources including ActiveX controls and beyond.	http://www.mvps.org/access/resources/products.htm

Continues

DBi Technologies Inc.
Solutions::PIM and Solutions::   http://www.dbi-tech.com
Schedule and many more, tested with
Microsoft Access

FMS Inc.
Quite a number of ActiveX controls   http://www.fmsinc.com/products/
and add-ins for Microsoft Access.

ID Automation
Barcode ActiveX Control & DLL   http://www.idautomation.com/activex/
designed for Office Programs

Intuit Developer Network
Software Development Kit (SDK) to   http://www.developer.intuit.com/
work with data in QuickBooks

Acctsync Technologies, Inc.
A front end to the Intuit QuickBooks   http://www.acctsync.com/acctsync/
SDK

C

DAO Object Method and Property Descriptions

In this appendix you will find diagrams for the two DAO object models discussed in Chapter 6: Microsoft Jet and ODBCDirect. This is followed by a detailed alphabetical list of all the objects that DAO supports, including descriptions of their methods, properties, and collections. As the Microsoft Jet and ODBCDirect models both share many objects in common, they have been included in the same list.

These descriptions are for reference purposes only, and you should consult the online Help for more in-depth descriptions.

Diagrams
DAO Object Model for Microsoft Jet Workspaces

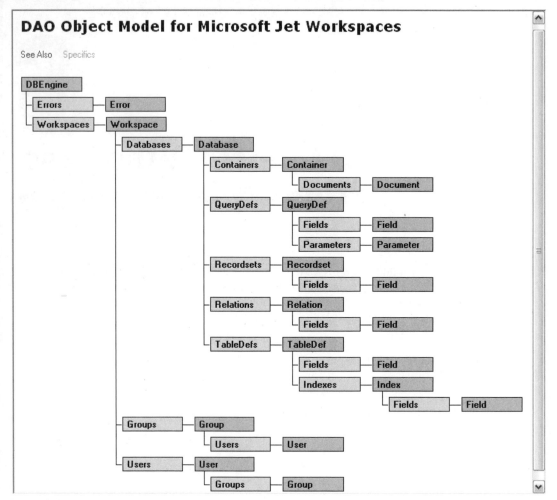

Figure C-1

DAO Object Model for ODBCDirect Workspaces

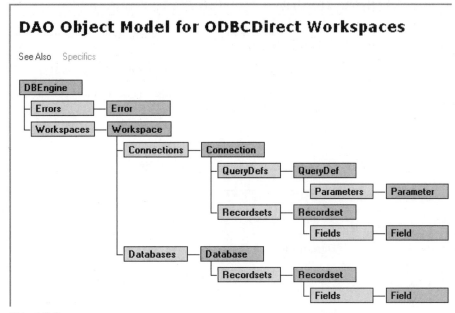

Figure C-2

DAO-Supported Objects
Connections Collection

The Connections collection contains the current Connection objects of a Workspace object (ODBCDirect workspaces only).

Methods

Method	Description
Refresh	Refreshes the collection

Properties

Property	Description
Count	Returns a count of Connection objects in the collection (ODBCDirect workspaces only)

Connection Object

The Connection object is a connection to an ODBC database (ODBCDirect workspaces only).

Methods

Method	Description
Cancel	Cancels execution of a pending asynchronous method call (ODBCDirect workspaces only)
Close	Closes an open Connection object (ODBCDirect workspaces only)
CreateQueryDef	Creates a new QueryDef object in an ODBCDirect Connection (ODBCDirect workspaces only)
Execute	Runs an action query on an ODBCDirect Connection (ODBCDirect workspaces only)
OpenRecordset	Creates a new Recordset object (ODBCDirect workspaces only)

Properties

Property	Description
Connect	Sets/returns a value that indicates the source of an open connection (ODBCDirect workspaces only)
Database	Returns the Database object that corresponds to this connection (ODBCDirect workspaces only)
Name	Sets/returns the connection name. Read-only if the connection has already been added to the collection (ODBCDirect workspaces only)
QueryTimeout	Sets/returns a value that specifies the number of seconds to wait before a time-out error occurs when a query is executed on an ODBC data source (ODBCDirect workspaces only)
RecordsAffected	Returns the number of records affected by the most recently invoked Execute method (ODBCDirect workspaces only)
StillExecuting	Indicates whether or not an asynchronous operation (that is, a method called with the dbRunAsync option) has finished executing (ODBCDirect workspaces only)
Transactions	Returns a flag that indicates whether an object supports transactions (ODBCDirect workspaces only)
Updatable	Returns a flag that indicates whether you can change the connection's definition (ODBCDirect workspaces only)

Collections

- ❑ Properties
- ❑ QueryDefs
- ❑ Recordsets

Containers Collection

The `Containers` collection contains all of the `Container` objects that are defined in a database (Microsoft Jet databases only).

Methods

Method	Description
Refresh	Refreshes the collection

Properties

Property	Description
Count	Returns a count of `Container` objects in the collection

Container Object

The `Container` object contains similar types of `Document` object.

Methods

None

Properties

Method	Description
AllPermissions	Returns a bit field that contains all the permissions that apply to the current user (as identified by the `UserName` property) of the `Container` object, including user-specific and inherited (from group membership) permissions (Microsoft Jet workspaces only)
Inherit	Sets/returns a flag that specifies whether new `Document` objects will inherit the default permissions (Microsoft Jet workspaces only)
Name	Sets/returns a user-defined name for a DAO object. For an object not appended to a collection, this property is read/write
Owner	Sets/returns the `Container`'s name (Microsoft Jet workspaces only)
Permissions	Returns a bit field that contains the permissions that specifically apply to the current user (or group) of the `Container` object, as identified by the `UserName` property (Microsoft Jet workspaces only)
UserName	Sets/returns the name of the user, group, or the owner of the `Workspace` object

Collections

- ❑ Documents
- ❑ Properties

DBEngine

The DBEngine object is the top-level object in the DAO object model.

Methods

Method	Description
BeginTrans	Begins a new transaction
CommitTrans	Ends the current transaction and saves the changes to disk
CompactDatabase	Copies and compacts a closed Access database
CreateDatabase	Creates a new Database object, and saves it to disk
CreateWorkspace	Creates a new Workspace object
Idle	Suspends data processing to allow Jet to complete any pending tasks, such as memory optimization or page timeouts
ISAMStats	(Hidden) Returns disk statistics (refer to Chapter 6)
OpenConnection	Opens a Connection to an ODBC data source (ODBCDirect workspaces only)
OpenDatabase	Opens an existing database
RegisterDatabase	Enters ODBC data source connection information in the registry
RepairDatabase	(Hidden) This method is no longer implemented
Rollback	Ends the current transaction and cancels any changes made to DAO objects in the workspace
SetOption	Temporarily overrides Jet engine values in the registry

Properties

Property	Description
DefaultPassword	Sets the password used to create the default workspace, when it is initialized. Write-only
DefaultType	Sets/returns a value that defines the type of workspace (Microsoft Jet or ODBCDirect) that will be used by the next Workspace object to be created

Continues

Property	Description
DefaultUser	Sets the user name that is used to create the default workspace when it is initialized
IniPath	Sets/returns information about the registry key that contains values for the Jet engine (Microsoft Jet workspaces only)
LoginTimeout	Sets/returns the number of seconds before an error occurs when you attempt to log on to an ODBC database
SystemDB	Sets/returns the path to the Workgroup Information File (Microsoft Jet workspaces only)
Version	Returns the current DAO version in use

Collections

- ❑ Errors
- ❑ Properties
- ❑ Workspaces

Databases Collection

The Databases collection contains all open Database objects opened or created within a Workspace object.

Methods

Method	Description
Refresh	Refreshes the collection

Properties

Property	Description
Count	Returns a count of Database objects in the collection

Database Object

The Database object is an open database.

Methods

Method	Description
Close	Closes the database
CreateProperty	Creates a new user-defined Property object (Microsoft Jet workspaces only)
CreateQueryDef	Creates a new QueryDef object
CreateRelation	Creates a new Relation object (Microsoft Jet workspaces only)
CreateTableDef	Creates a new TableDef object (Microsoft Jet workspaces only)
Execute	Runs an action query
MakeReplica	Creates a new database replica from another replica (Microsoft Jet workspaces only)
NewPassword	Changes the password of an existing database (Microsoft Jet workspaces only)
OpenRecordset	Creates a new Recordset object
PopulatePartial	Synchronizes changes between a full and partial replica
Synchronize	Synchronizes two replicas (Microsoft Jet databases only)

Properties

Property	Description
CollatingOrder	Returns the text sort order for string comparisons and sorts (Microsoft Jet workspaces only)
Connect	Sets/returns a value for the source of an open database or a database used in a pass-through query
Connection	Returns a Connection object for the database (ODBCDirect workspaces only)
DesignMasterID	Returns a 16-byte value that uniquely identifies the database as being the design master in a replica set (Microsoft Jet workspaces only)
Name	Sets/returns the database's name
QueryTimeOut	Sets/returns the number of seconds before an error occurs when a query is executed against an ODBC data source
RecordsAffected	Returns the number of records affected by the most recent Execute method
Replicable	Sets/returns a value that defines whether a database can be replicated (Microsoft Jet workspaces only)
ReplicaID	Returns a 16-byte value that uniquely identifies a database replica (Microsoft Jet workspaces only)

Continues

Property	Description
Transactions	Returns a value that indicates whether the database supports transactions
Updatable	Returns a value that indicates whether you can change the Database object
V1xNullBehaviour	Indicates whether zero-length strings (" ") used in code to fill Text or Memo fields are converted to Null
Version	Returns the version of the ODBC driver currently in use

Collections

- ❑ Containers
- ❑ Properties
- ❑ QueryDefs
- ❑ Recordsets
- ❑ Relations
- ❑ TableDefs
- ❑ Transactions

Documents Collection

The Documents collection contains all of the Document objects for a specific type of object (Microsoft Jet databases only).

Methods

Method	Description
Refresh	Refreshes the collection

Properties

Property	Description
Count	Returns a count of Document objects in the collection

Document Object

The Document object contains information about an instance of an object. The object can be a database, saved table, query, or relationship (Microsoft Jet databases only).

Methods

Method	Description
CreateProperty	Creates a new user-defined Property object (Microsoft Jet workspaces only)

Properties

Method	Description
AllPermissions	Returns a bit field that contains all the permissions that apply to the current user (as identified by the UserName property) of the Document object, including user-specific and inherited (from group membership) permissions (Microsoft Jet workspaces only)
Container	Returns the name of the Document object's parent Container (Microsoft Jet workspaces only)
DateCreated	Returns the date and time that the Document object was created (Microsoft Jet workspaces only)
LastUpdated	Returns the date and time of the most recent change that was made to the document (Microsoft Jet workspaces only)
Name	Returns the document's name. This property is read-only
Owner	Sets/returns a value that specifies the document's owner (Microsoft Jet workspaces only)
Permissions	Returns a bit field that contains the permissions that specifically apply to the current user (or group) of the Document object, as identified by the UserName property (Microsoft Jet workspaces only)
Replicable	Sets/returns a flag that specifies whether the document can be replicated (Microsoft Jet workspaces only).
UserName	Sets/returns the name of the user, group, or the owner of the Document object

Collections

Properties

Errors Collection

The Errors collection contains all stored Error objects.

Methods

Method	Description
Refresh	Refreshes the collection

Properties

Property	Description
Count	Returns a count of the current Error objects

Error Object

The Error object contains details about data access errors. Each Error object relates to a single DAO operation.

Methods

None

Properties

Property	Description
Description	Default. Returns a descriptive string associated with an error
Help Context	(Hidden) Returns a context ID for a topic in a Help file
Help File	(Hidden) Returns a fully qualified path to the Help file
Number	Returns an error number
Source	Returns the name of the object that generated the error

Collections

None

Fields Collection

The Fields collection contains all stored Field objects of an Index, QueryDef (Microsoft Jet workspaces only), Recordset, Relation, or TableDef.

Methods

Method	Description
Append	Appends a new Field object to the collection
Delete	Deletes a Field from the collection
Refresh	Refreshes the collection

Properties

Property	Description
Count	Returns a count of `Field` objects in the collection

Field Object

The `Field` object is a column of data.

Methods

Method	Description
AppendChunk	Appends data from a string expression to a Memo or Long Binary `Field` object in a `Recordset`
CreateProperty	Creates a new user-defined `Property` object (Microsoft Jet workspaces only)
GetChunk	Returns all or some of the contents of a Memo or Long Binary `Field` object in the `Fields` collection of a `Recordset` object

Properties

Property	Description
AllowZeroLength	Sets/returns a flag that indicates whether you can enter a zero-length string (" ") in a Text or Memo field object (Microsoft Jet workspaces only)
Attributes	Sets/returns a value that indicates a Field's characteristics
CollatingOrder	Returns a value that specifies the sort order for string comparison and sorting (Microsoft Jet workspaces only)
DataUpdatable	Returns a flag that specifies whether the data in the field can be updated
DefaultValue	Sets/returns the default value of a `Field` object. Read-only for `Field` object in the `Fields` collection (Microsoft Jet workspaces only)
FieldSize	Returns the number of bytes actually stored in a Memo or Long Binary `Field` object in a `Recordset` object's `Fields` collection
ForeignName	Sets/returns the name of the foreign table involved in a relationship with the field (Microsoft Jet workspaces only)
Name	Sets/returns a `Field` object's name. Read-only for `Field` objects in the `Fields` collection
OrdinalPosition	Sets/returns the relative position of a `Field` object within the `Fields` collection. Read-only for `Field` objects in the `Fields` collection

Continues

Property	Description
OriginalValue	Returns the value of the Field that existed prior to the last batch update (ODBCDirect workspaces only)
Required	Sets/returns a flag that indicates whether data in the Field must be non-Null
Size	Sets/returns a value that indicates the maximum size, in bytes, of the data a Field
SourceField	Returns the name of the field that is the original source of the data for a Field object
SourceTable	Returns the name of the table that is the original source of the data for a Field object.
Type	Sets/returns a value that indicates the field's data type
ValidateOnSet	Sets/returns a flag that specifies whether the value of a Field is immediately validated when data is entered (Microsoft Jet workspaces only)
ValidationRule	Sets/returns an expression that validates the data in a field as it is changed or added to the table (Microsoft Jet workspaces only)
ValidateText	Sets/returns a value that specifies the text of the message that displays if the data entered in a Field doesn't satisfy the validation rule (Microsoft Jet workspaces only)
Value	Default. Sets/returns the field's actual value
VisibleValue	Returns the field value that is newer than the OriginalValue property, as determined by a batch update conflict (ODBCDirect workspaces only)

Collections

Properties

Groups Collection

The Groups collection contains all stored Group objects of a Workspace or User object (Microsoft Jet workspaces only).

Methods

Method	Description
Append	Appends a new Group object to the collection
Delete	Deletes a Group from the collection
Refresh	Refreshes the collection

Properties

Property	Description
Count	Returns a count of Group objects in the collection

Group Object

The Group object is a group of User objects that have common access permissions when a workspace operates in a secure workgroup.

Methods

Property	Description
CreateUser	Creates a new User object (Microsoft Jet workspaces only)

Properties

Method	Description
Name	Sets/returns the group's name. Read-only if the group has already been added to the collection
PID	Sets the group's personal identifier (PID) (Microsoft Jet workspaces only)

Collections

❑ Properties

❑ Users

Indexes Collection

The Indexes collection contains all stored Index objects of a TableDef object.

Methods

Method	Description
Append	Appends a new Index object to the collection
Delete	Deletes an Index from the collection
Refresh	Refreshes the collection

Properties

Property	Description
Count	Returns a count of Index objects in the collection

Index Object

The Index object specifies the order in which records are accessed from a table and whether duplicate records are allowed.

Methods

Property	Description
CreateField	Creates a new Field object (Microsoft Jet workspaces only)
CreateProperty	Creates a new Property object (Microsoft Jet workspaces only)

Properties

Method	Description
Clustered	Sets/returns a flag that specifies whether the index is clustered. The Microsoft Jet database does not support clustered indexes, so this property is ignored. ODBC data sources always return False, because it does not detect if ODBC data sources have clustered indexes.
DistinctCount	Returns the number of unique values (keys) that exist in the table for the index (Microsoft Jet workspaces only)
Foreign	Returns a flag that specifies whether the index is a foreign key in another table (Microsoft Jet workspaces only)
IgnoreNulls	Sets/returns a flag that specifies whether records that have Null values also have indexes
Name	Sets/returns the index's name
Primary	Sets/returns a flag that specifies whether the index is the primary key
Required	Sets/returns a flag that specifies whether a Field object (or the entire index) can accept Null values. Read-only if the index has been appended to the collection
Unique	Sets/returns a flag that specifies whether the index keys must be unique

Collections

Fields

Parameters

The Parameters collection contains all the Parameter objects of a QueryDef object.

Methods

Method	Description
Refresh	Refreshes the collection

Properties

Property	Description
Count	Returns a count of Parameters objects in the collection

Parameter Object

The Parameter object is a defined value supplied to a query.

Methods

None

Properties

Property	Description
Direction	Sets/returns a flag that specifies whether a Parameter object is an input parameter, output parameter, input/output parameter, or the return value from a procedure (ODBCDirect workspaces only)
Name	Returns the parameter's name. Read-only
Type	Sets/returns a value that indicates the parameter type
Value	Default. Sets/returns the parameter value

Collections

Properties

Recordsets Collection

The Recordsets collection contains all open Recordset objects in a Connection or Database.

Methods

Method	Description
Refresh	Refreshes the collection

Properties

Property	Description
Count	Returns a count of Recordset objects in the collection

Recordset Object

The Recordset object represents the records in a base table, or those that result from executing a query.

Methods

Method	Description
AddNew	Begins a recordset editing session that creates a new record for an updatable Recordset object
Cancel	Cancels the execution of a pending asynchronous method call (ODBCDirect workspaces only)
CancelUpdate	Cancels any pending updates for a Recordset object.
Clone	Creates a new Recordset object that is a duplicate of the original Recordset object
Close	Closes an open Recordset object
CopyQueryDef	Creates a new QueryDef object that is a copy of the original QueryDef that was used to create the Recordset object (Microsoft Jet workspaces only)
Delete	Deletes the current record in an updatable Recordset object
Edit	Begins a recordset editing session
FillCache	Fills all or a part of a local cache for a Recordset object that contains data from a Microsoft Jet-connected ODBC data source (Microsoft Jet-connected ODBC databases only)
FindFirst	Locates the first record in a dynaset- or snapshot-type Recordset object that matches the specified criteria and makes that row the current row (Microsoft Jet workspaces only)

Continues

Method	Description
FindLast	Locates the last record in a dynaset- or snapshot-type Recordset object that matches the specified criteria and makes that row the current row (Microsoft Jet workspaces only)
FindNext	Locates the next record in a dynaset- or snapshot-type Recordset object that matches the specified criteria and makes that row the current row (Microsoft Jet workspaces only)
FindPrevious	Locates the previous record in a dynaset- or snapshot-type Recordset object that matches the specified criteria and makes that row the current row (Microsoft Jet workspaces only)
GetRows	Retrieves the specified number of rows from a Recordset object
Move	Moves the recordset's current cursor position to the specified row
MoveFirst	Moves the Recordset's current cursor position to the next row in the recordset and makes that row the current row
MoveLast	Moves the Recordset's current cursor position to the last row in the recordset and makes that row the current row
MovePrevious	Moves the Recordset's current cursor position to the previous row in the recordset and makes that row the current row
NextRecordset	Gets the next set of records (if any) returned by a compound select query in an OpenRecordset call and returns a Boolean value indicating whether one or more additional records are pending (ODBCDirect workspaces only)
OpenRecordset	Creates a new Recordset object
Requery	Refreshes the data in a Recordset object by requerying its data source
Seek	Locates the record in an indexed table-type recordset that matches the specified criteria for the current index and makes that row the current row (Microsoft Jet workspaces only)
Update	Saves all data changes made via a recordset during an editing session

Properties

Property	Description
AbsolutePosition	Sets/returns a recordset's relative row number
BatchCollisionCount	Returns the number of records that failed to complete during the last batch update (ODBCDirect workspaces only)
BatchCollisions	Returns an array of bookmarks that specify the rows that generated collisions during the last batch update (ODBCDirect workspaces only)

Continues

Property	Description
BatchSize	Sets/returns the number of statements returned to the server during each batch (ODBCDirect workspaces only)
BOF	Returns a flag that indicates whether the current record position is before the first record in a Recordset object
Bookmark	Sets/returns a bookmark that uniquely identifies the current record in a recordset
Bookmarkable	Returns a flag that indicates whether a Recordset object supports bookmarks
CacheSize	Sets/returns the number of ODBC data source records will be locally cached
CacheStart	Sets/returns a value that specifies the bookmark of the first record in a dynaset-type Recordset object that contains data to be locally cached from an ODBC data source (Microsoft Jet workspaces only)
Collect	(Hidden) Returns a field's actual value
Connection	Returns a Connection object for the recordset (ODBCDirect workspaces only)
DateCreated	Returns the date and time that the Recordset object was created (Microsoft Jet workspaces only)
EditMode	Returns a value that indicates the current recordset editing state for the current record
EOF	Returns a flag that indicates whether the current record position is after the last record in a Recordset object
Filter	Sets/returns a value that specifies the records that will be included in a recordset that is created from the current Recordset object (Microsoft Jet workspaces only)
Index	Sets/returns the name of the current Index object in a table-type Recordset object (Microsoft Jet workspaces only)
LastModified	Returns a bookmark that specifies the most recently added or changed record
LastUpdated	Returns the date and time of the most recent change that was made to the recordset or to a base table on a table-type recordset (Microsoft Jet workspaces only)
LockEdits	Sets/returns a value indicating the type of locking that is in effect while editing the recordset
Name	Returns the first 256 characters of the recordset's SQL statement
NoMatch	Returns a flag that indicates whether one of the find methods (FindFirst, FindPrevious FindNext, FindLast, or Seek) found the record it was looking for (Microsoft Jet workspaces only)

Continues

Property	Description
ODBCFetchCount	Hidden
ODBCFetchDelay	Hidden
Parent	Hidden. Returns a Database object against which the recordset was created
PercentPosition	Sets/returns a value that indicates the current row's approximate position, based on a percentage of the records in the recordset
RecordCount	Returns the number of records accessed (so far) in a recordset or the total number of records in a table-type recordset
RecordStatus	Returns a value that indicates the current record's update status if it is part of a batch update (ODBCDirect workspaces only)
Restartable	Returns a flag that indicates whether a Recordset object supports the Requery method
Sort	Sets/returns the sort order for records in a recordset (Microsoft Jet workspaces only)
StillExecuting	Returns a flag that indicates whether an asynchronous operation (that is, a method called with the dbRunAsync option) is still executing (ODBCDirect workspaces only)
Transactions	Returns a flag that indicates whether the recordset supports transactions
Type	Sets/returns a value that indicates the recordset type
Updatable	Returns a flag that indicates whether you can change the recordset's definition
UpdateOptions	Sets/returns a value that indicates how the WHERE clause is constructed for each record during a batch update, and whether the batch update should use an UPDATE statement or a DELETE followed by an INSERT (ODBCDirect workspaces only)
ValidationRule	Sets/returns an expression that validates the data in a field as it is changed or added to the table (Microsoft Jet workspaces only)
ValidationText	Sets/returns a value that specifies the text of the message that displays if the data entered in a Field doesn't satisfy the validation rule (Microsoft Jet workspaces only)

Collections

- ❑ Fields
- ❑ Properties

Properties Collection

The `Properties` collection contains all of the `Property` objects associated with a DAO object.

Methods

Method	Description
Append	Appends a new user-defined `Property` object to the collection
Delete	Deletes a user-defined `Property` object from the collection
Refresh	Refreshes the collection

Properties

- ❏ Count
- ❏ Item

Property Object

The `Property` object is an attribute that defines an object's characteristics or behavior.

Methods

None

Properties

Property	Description
Inherited	Returns a flag that specifies whether a `Property` object is inherited from an underlying object
Name	Sets/returns a property's name. Read-only for built-in properties
Type	Sets/returns a value that indicates the propety's data type
Value	Default. Sets/returns the property's actual value

Collections

Properties

QueryDefs Collection

The `QueryDefs` collection contains all `QueryDef` objects of a Database (Microsoft Jet workspaces), and all `QueryDef` objects of a Connection (ODBCDirect workspaces).

Methods

Method	Description
Append	Appends a new QueryDef object to the collection
Delete	Deletes a QueryDef from the collection
Refresh	Refreshes the collection

Properties

Property	Description
Count	Returns a count of QueryDef objects in the collection

QueryDef Object

The QueryDef object is a stored definition of a query in a Microsoft Jet database, or a temporary definition of a query in an ODBCDirect workspace.

Methods

Method	Description
Cancel	Cancels execution of a pending asynchronous method call (ODBCDirect workspaces only)
Close	Closes an open QueryDef object.
CreateProperty	Creates a new user-defined Property object (Microsoft Jet workspaces only)
Execute	Runs an action query
OpenRecordset	Creates a new Recordset object

Properties

Method	Description
CacheSize	Sets/returns the number of records retrieved from an ODBC data source that will be cached locally
Connect	Sets/returns a value that indicates the source of an open database used in a pass-through query or a linked table. Read-only

Continues

Method	Description
DateCreated	Returns the date and time that the QueryDef object was created (Microsoft Jet workspaces only)
KeepLocal	Sets/returns a flag that specifies whether you want to replicate the query when the database is replicated (Microsoft Jet workspaces only)
LastUpdated	Returns the date and time of the most recent change that was made to the QueryDef (Microsoft Jet workspaces only)
LogMessages	Sets/returns a flag that specifies whether the messages returned from a Microsoft Jet-connected ODBC data source are recorded (Microsoft Jet workspaces only)
MaxRecords	Sets/returns the maximum number of records to return from a query against an ODBC data source
Name	Sets/returns the QueryDef name. Read-only
ODBCTimeout	Returns the number of seconds to wait before a time-out error occurs when a QueryDef is executed against an ODBC data source
Prepare	Sets/returns a flag that specifies whether the query should be prepared on the server as a temporary stored procedure prior to execution (ODBCDirect workspaces only)
RecordsAffected	Returns the number of records affected by the most recent Execute method
Replicable	Sets/returns a value that defines whether a query can be replicated (Microsoft Jet workspaces only)
ReturnsRecords	Sets/returns a flag that specifies whether an SQL pass-through query to an external database returns records (Microsoft Jet workspaces only)
SQL	Sets/returns the SQL statement that defines the query
StillExecuting	Flag that indicates whether an asynchronous operation (that is, a method called with the dbRunAsync option) has finished executing (ODBCDirect workspaces only)
Type	Sets/returns a value that indicates the type of QueryDef
Updatable	Returns a value that indicates whether you can change the QueryDef object

Collections

- ❑ Fields
- ❑ Parameters
- ❑ Properties

Relations Collection

The Relations collection contains stored Relation objects of a Database object (Microsoft Jet databases only).

Methods

Method	Description
Append	Appends a new Relation object to the collection
Delete	Deletes a Relation from the collection.
Refresh	Refreshes the collection

Properties

Property	Description
Count	Returns a count of Relation objects in the collection

Relation Object

The Relation object is a defined relationship between fields in tables or queries (Microsoft Jet databases only).

Methods

Method	Description
CreateField	Creates a new Field object (Microsoft Jet workspaces only)

Properties

Property	Description
Attributes	Sets/returns a value that defines the relation's characteristics
ForeignTable	Sets/returns the name of the foreign table in a relationship (Microsoft Jet workspaces only)
Name	Sets/returns the relation's name. Read-only if the relation has already been added to the collection

Continues

Property	Description
PartialReplica	Sets/returns a flag that indicates whether that relation should be considered when populating a partial replica from a full replica (Microsoft Jet databases only)
Table	Sets/returns the name of a Relation object's primary table (TableDef name or QueryDef name). Read-only if the relation has already been added to the collection (Microsoft Jet workspaces only)

Collections

- ❑ Fields
- ❑ Properties

TableDefs Collection

The TableDefs collection contains all stored TableDef objects in a database (Microsoft Jet workspaces only).

Methods

Method	Description
Append	Adds a TableDef object to the collection
Delete	Deletes a TableDef object from the collection
Refresh	Refreshes the objects in the collection

Properties

Property	Description
Count	Returns a count of TableDef objects in the collection

TableDef Object

The TableDef object is the stored definition of a table (linked or otherwise) (Microsoft Jet workspaces only).

Methods

Method	Description
CreateField	Creates a new Field object (Microsoft Jet workspaces only)
CreateIndex	Creates a new Index object (Microsoft Jet workspaces only)
CreateProperty	Creates a new user-defined Property object (Microsoft Jet workspaces only)
OpenRecordset	Creates a new Recordset object
RefreshLink	Refreshes the connection for a linked table (Microsoft Jet workspaces only)

Properties

Property	Description
Attributes	Sets/returns a value that defines the TableDef's characteristics
ConflictTable	Returns the name of the conflict table that contains details about the records that conflicted during synchronization (Microsoft Jet workspaces only)
Connect	Sets/returns a value that indicates the source of a linked table. This setting is read-only on base tables
DateCreated	Returns the date and time that the TableDef object was created (Microsoft Jet workspaces only)
KeepLocal	Sets/returns a flag that specifies whether you want to replicate the table when the database is replicated (Microsoft Jet workspaces only)
LastUpdated	Returns the date and time of the most recent change that was made to the table (Microsoft Jet workspaces only)
Name	Sets/returns the table's name. This property is read-only on linked tables
RecordCount	Returns the number of records in the table
Replicable	Sets/returns a flag that specifies whether the table can be replicated (Microsoft Jet workspaces only)
ReplicaFilter	Sets/returns a value within a partial replica that specifies which subset of records will be replicated to the table from a full replica (Microsoft Jet databases only)
SourceTableName	For linked tables sets/returns the name of the remote table to which the table is connected (Microsoft Jet workspaces only). This property is read-only for base tables.
Updatable	Returns a flag that indicates whether you can change the table definition

Continues

Property	Description
ValidationRule	Sets/returns an expression that validates the data in a field as it is changed or added to the table (Microsoft Jet workspaces only)
ValidationText	Sets/returns a value that specifies the text of the message that displays if the data entered in a Field doesn't satisfy the validation rule (Microsoft Jet workspaces only)

Collections

❑   Fields

❑   Indexes

❑   Properties

Users Collection

The Users collection contains all stored User objects of a Workspace or Group object (Microsoft Jet workspaces only).

Methods

Method	Description
Append	Appends a new User object to the collection
Delete	Deletes a User from the collection
Refresh	Refreshes the collection

Properties

Property	Description
Count	Returns a count of User objects in the collection

User Object

The User object is a user that has access permissions when a workspace operates in a secure workgroup (Microsoft Jet workspaces only).

Methods

Method	Description
CreateGroup	Creates a new User object (Microsoft Jet workspaces only)
NewPassword	Changes the password of an existing User object (Microsoft Jet workspaces only)

Properties

Property	Description
Name	Sets/returns the user's name. Read-only if the user has already been added to the collection
Password	Sets the password for a User object (Microsoft Jet workspaces only)
PID	Sets the personal identifier (PID) for a User object (Microsoft Jet workspaces only)

Collections

- ❑ Groups
- ❑ Properties

Workspaces Collection

The Workspaces collection contains all active, unhidden Workspace objects of the DBEngine object.

Methods

Method	Description
Append	Appends a new Workspace object to the collection
Delete	Deletes a persistent object from the collection
Refresh	Refreshes the collection

Properties

Property	Description
Count	Returns a count of Workspace objects in the collection

Workspace Object

The Workspace object defines a named user session.

Methods

Method	Description
BeginTrans	Begins a new transaction
Close	Closes a workspace
CommitTrans	Ends the current transaction and saves the changes to disk
CreateDatabase	Creates a new Database object and saves it to disk
CreateGroup	Creates a new Group object (Microsoft Jet workspaces only)
CreateUser	Creates a new User object (Microsoft Jet workspaces only)
OpenConnection	Opens an ODBC data source connection (ODBCDirect workspaces only)
OpenDatabase	Opens a specific database in a Workspace
Rollback	Ends the current transaction and cancels any changes made to DAO objects in the workspace

Properties

Property	Description
DefaultCursorDriver	Sets/returns the type of cursor driver used on a connection that is created using the OpenConnection or OpenDatabase methods (ODBCDirect workspaces only)
IsolateODBCTrans	Sets/returns a value that specifies if multiple transactions involving the same Jet-connected ODBC data source are isolated (Microsoft Jet workspaces only)
LoginTimeOut	Sets/returns the number of seconds before an error occurs when you attempt to log on to an ODBC database
Name	Sets/returns the workspace name
Type	Sets/returns a value that specifies the type of workspace being used (dbUseJet or dbUseODBC)
UserName	Sets/returns the name of a user, group, or the owner of a Workspace object

Collections

- ❏ Connections
- ❏ Databases

- ❑ Groups
- ❑ Properties
- ❑ Users

Undocumented Tools and Resources

There are several Jet-specific utilities and object methods that are shipped with Microsoft Access 2003. These utilities and methods are either not very well documented by Microsoft or not documented at all. Notwithstanding, you can use them to help you develop and maintain your DAO applications.

Utilities

ISAMStats

Microsoft Jet 4.0 contains an undocumented DBEngine method called ISAMStats, which returns various internal statistics. You use ISAMStats to get statistics about different operations. For example, if you want to determine which of several queries will run faster, you can use ISAMStats to return the number of disk reads performed by each query.

Each of the ISAMStats options maintains a separate statistics counter that records the number of times its metric occurs. To reset the counter, set the Reset argument to True. The syntax is as follows:

```
lngReturn = DBEngine.ISAMStats(StatNum [, Reset])
```

Where StatNum is one of the following values:

StatNum	Description
0	Number of disk reads
1	Number of disk writes
3	Number of reads from cache
4	Number of reads from read-ahead cache
5	Number of locks placed
6	Number of locks released

You must call ISAMStats twice: once to get a baseline statistic and once (after the operation to be analyzed) to get the final statistic. You then subtract the baseline statistic from the final one, to arrive at the statistic for the operation under test. The following example demonstrates two ways to use ISAMStats:

Method 1

```
Call DBEngine.IsamStats(0, True)
Set rs = db.OpenRecordset("qryGetOverdueAccts", dbOpenSnapshot)
Debug.Print "Total reads: " & DBEngine.IsamStats(0)
```

```
In the above example, the first call resets the ISAMStats counter. The code
then opens a recordset using a query you want to test. The last line retakes
the statistics and prints it.
Method 2:
lngBaseline = DBEngine.IsamStats(0)
Set rs = db.OpenRecordset("qryGetOverdueAccts", dbOpenSnapshot)
lngStatistic = DBEngine.IsamStats(0)
Debug.Print "Total reads: " & lngStatistic - lngBaseline
```

Method 2

In Method 2, ISAMStats is not reset, but its return value is stored in a variable. The code then opens the recordset. The third line retakes the statistic after the operation, while the fourth and final line calculates the actual statistic.

ShowPlan

Microsoft Jet implements a cost-based query optimizer in its query engine. Jet determines the most effective way to execute a query while it's compiling it. You can view this plan using the ShowPlan Registry setting. To use ShowPlan, add the following key to the registry:

```
\\ HKEY_LOCAL_MACHINE\SOFTWARE\MICROSOFT\Jet\4.0\Engines\Debug
```

Then add a String data type entry called "JETSHOWPLAN" (in uppercase). Turn ShowPlan on or off by setting its value to "ON" or "OFF", respectively.

When the feature is on, and when you restart Access and open a database, Jet begins to log query optimization plans into a text file called SHOWPLAN.OUT, which is created in the current directory (or the My Documents folder in Windows XP). If this file already exists, subsequent query plans will be appended to the file. You need only to open a query in Design view, modify it, and save it in order to force Jet to recreate the plan for the query.

ShowPlan is completely undocumented and unsupported by Microsoft, and as such, you would be wise to treat its use with care. Some of the known issues with ShowPlan are as follows:

❑ Closing one database and opening another without exiting and restarting Access will result in query plans for the new database not being logged.

❑ Some internal Access queries will likely appear in the log file.

❑ Plan logging may adversely affect application performance.

❑ As the log file will grow over time, you should delete it (or delete its contents) periodically.

❑ Parameter queries and subqueries are not logged.

❑ ShowPlan has been known to incorrectly log information for other queries.

Methods
DAO.privDBEngine

The unsupported privDBEngine object allows you to connect to an external database that uses a different Workgroup Information File to the one currently being used. You can open an Access database without having to create another instance of Access. `privDBEngine` only allows access to DAO objects, such as `TableDefs` and `QueryDefs`, and so on.

```
Dim dbX As PrivDBEngine
Dim wsX As Workspace
Dim dbe As Database
'Return a reference to a new instance of the PrivDBEngine object
Set dbe = New PrivDBEngine
'Set the SystemDB property to specify the workgroup file
dbe.SystemDB = strWIFPath
`Specify the username (this could be any valid username)
dbe.DefaultUser = strUserName
`Specify the password
dbe.DefaultPassword = strPassword
`Set the workspace
Set wsX = dbe.Workspaces(0)
'Open the secured database
Set dbe = ws.OpenDatabase(strDBPath)
```

The `PrivDBEngine` object does nothing more than create a new instance of the Jet engine. You can get the same functionality by doing the following:

```
Dim dbe As DAO.DBEngine
Set dbe = CreateObject("DAO.DBEngine")
```

Note: The following table lists the `CreateObject` argument for different versions of the Jet engine.

Jet version	Argument	Example
3.0	DAO.DBEngine	**Set** dbe = CreateObject("DAO.DBEngine")
3.5	DAO.DBEngine.35	**Set** dbe = CreateObject("DAO.DBEngine.35")
3.6	DAO.DBEngine.36	**Set** dbe = CreateObject("DAO.DBEngine36")

Recordset.Collect

The DAO `Recordset` object exposes a hidden, undocumented property; `Collect`. Although `Collect` is a property, it behaves like the `Recordset` object's `Fields` collection, but it's faster because it doesn't need a reference to the `Field` object. `Collect` only returns a field's value; it doesn't expose any other properties. You can use this property by passing it a numeric item number, or a field name, just like the `Fields` collection. For example:

```
Set rs = db.OpenRecordset("tblCustomers")
Debug.Print "CustID: " & rs.Collect(0)
Debug.Print "CustomerNo: " & rs.Collect("CustomerNo")
```

Figure C-3 shows the comparative speed of the `Collect` property versus the other well-known ways of returning field values.

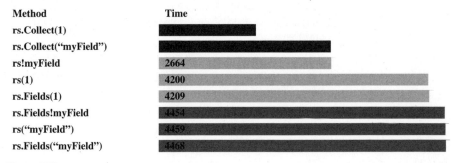

Method	Time
rs.Collect(1)	
rs.Collect("myField")	
rs!myField	2664
rs(1)	4200
rs.Fields(1)	4209
rs.Fields!myField	4454
rs("myField")	4459
rs.Fields("myField")	4468

Figure C-3

Recordset.Parent

The undocumented recordset `Parent` property is an object reference to the database to which the recordset belongs. This may be especially useful in situations where you have several `Database` objects in the same application.

OpenRecordset Constants

There are a variety of constants you'll use when writing VBA code. The following tables list just a few of the constants you might use when opening a DAO recordset.

> A runtime error occurs if you attempt to use **dbOpenTable** in the following Microsoft Jet workspace situations:
>
> ❑   When the recordset is based on a **QueryDef**.
>
> ❑   When the **Type** argument is set to **dbOpenSnapshot**.
>
> ❑   When the **Source** argument refers to an SQL statement or **TableDef** that refers to a linked-table.
>
> The following table lists the constants that can be specified for the **Type** argument.

Constant	Description
DbOpenTable	Returns an editable dataset consisting of records from a single local table only. Cannot be used with linked tables (Microsoft Jet workspaces only)

Continues

Constant	Description
dbOpenDynamic	Returns an editable dataset consisting of pointers to records in a table or query. Can be used on multiple remote tables (ODBCDirect workspaces only)
dbOpenDynaset	Returns an editable dataset consisting of pointers to records in a table or query. Can be used on multiple local and linked tables (Microsoft Jet workspaces only)
dbOpenSnapshot	Returns a read-only dataset consisting of a copy of records in a table or query. Can be used on multiple local and linked tables (Microsoft Jet workspaces only)
dbOpenForwardOnly	Returns an editable dataset consisting of records in a table. Use this option when you only need to move through the dataset in one pass and in one direction—forward (Microsoft Jet workspaces only)

The following table lists the constants that can be specified for the Options argument.

The **dbInconsistent** and **dbConsistent** constants are mutually exclusive. Similarly you cannot supply a **LockEdits** argument on a recordset whose **Options** argument is set to **dbReadOnly**. If you attempt to do so, a runtime error occurs.

Constant	Description
dbAppendOnly	Signifies that you can add new records, but not edit or delete them (Microsoft Jet dynaset recordsets only)
dbSQLPassThrough	Signifies that the SQL statement will be passed directly to a Microsoft Jet-connected ODBC data source for processing (Microsoft Jet snapshot recordsets only)
dbSeeChanges	Triggers a runtime error if another user attempts to change data that you're currently editing (Microsoft Jet dynaset recordsets only)
dbDenyWrite	Locks all the underlying tables so other users can only view the data. They cannot add, edit, or delete records while the lock is in place (Microsoft Jet recordsets only).
DbDenyRead	Completely locks all the underlying tables so other users cannot even view the data (Microsoft Jet table recordsets only).
dbForwardOnly	Creates a forward-only recordset (Microsoft Jet snapshot recordsets only). This option is provided for backward compatibility only, and you should use the dbOpenForwardOnly constant in the Type argument instead of this option.

Continues

Constant	Description
DbReadOnly	Creates a read-only recordset, preventing users from making changes to the data (Microsoft Jet only). You can use dbReadOnly in either the Options argument or the LockEdits argument, but not both. If you attempt to do so, a runtime error occurs. This option is provided for backward compatibility only, and you should use the dbReadOnly constant in the LockEdits argument instead of this option.
dbRunAsync	Runs an asynchronous query (ODBCDirect workspaces only). This allows your code to keep running while the query is loading. You can use the StillExecuting property to determine if the query has completed.
dbExecDirect	Executes the query without first calling the SQLPrepare ODBC API function (ODBCDirect workspaces only). Only use this option when not opening a recordset based on a parameter query.
dbInconsistent	Allows inconsistent updates (Microsoft Jet dynaset and snapshot recordsets only). An inconsistent update is one in which you can update all the columns in a multi-table recordset unless referential integrity rules prevent it.
dbConsistent	Allows only consistent updates (Microsoft Jet dynaset-type and snapshot-type Recordset objects only). A consistent update is one in which you can only perform updates that result in a consistent view of the data. For example, you cannot update the many side of a relationship unless a matching record exists in the one side.

The following table lists the constants that can be specified for the LockEdits argument.

> You cannot supply a **LockEdits** argument on a recordset whose **Options** argument is set to **dbReadOnly**. If you attempt to do so, a runtime error occurs.

Constant	Description
DbReadOnly	Creates a read-only recordset, preventing users from making changes to the data (This is the default setting for ODBCDirect workspaces). You can use dbReadOnly in either the Options argument or the LockEdits argument, but not both. If you attempt to do so, a runtime error occurs. Setting dbReadOnly in the Options argument is provided for backward compatibility only. You should use it in the LockEdits argument instead.

Continues

Constant	Description
dbPessimistic	Uses pessimistic locking for changes made to the recordset in a multi-user environment. Pessimistic locking is where the entire data page that contains the record you're editing is locked (made unavailable to other users) as soon as you issue the Edit method, and remains locked until you issue the Update method (this is the default setting for Microsoft Jet workspaces).
DbOptimistic	Uses optimistic locking for changes made to the recordset in a multi-user environment. Optimistic locking is where the entire data page that contains the record you're editing is locked (made unavailable to other users) as soon as you issue the Update method, and remains locked until the data is written to the table (this is the default setting for Microsoft Jet workspaces). You use optimistic locking when manipulating ODBC databases or when the LockEdits property is set to False.
dbOptimisticValue	Uses optimistic concurrency based on row values (ODBCDirect workspaces only)
dbOptimisticBatch	Enables batch optimistic updating (ODBCDirect workspaces only)

ADO Object Model Reference

When using VBA to access data in ODBC compliant databases, you can choose from DAO or ADO. In order to use either technique, you'll need to understand the object model for the appropriate technology. The ADO object model isn't overly complicated, but understanding the details of all the various ADO objects can help you use the proper object for the proper task.

This appendix lists all of the major objects you'll use when using ADO to access data within VBA. For each of the major objects, properties, methods, events, and associated collections are provided. Keep this appendix handy when programming ADO and refer to it when you have questions about the specific property, method, or event to use in your code.

The Connection Object

The Connection object represents a unique session with a data source. The Connection object has collections, methods, and properties associated with it. The availability of these collections, methods, and properties are dependent on the functionality supported by the provider.

Properties of the Connection Object

The following table lists the properties of the Connection object and a brief description of their use.

Property	Data Type	Description
ConnectionString (default property)	String	Use the ConnectionString property to specify a data source by passing a detailed connection string containing a series of *argument = value* statements separated by semicolons

Continues

Property	Data Type	Description
ConnectionTimeout	Long	Indicates how long to wait while establishing a connection before terminating the attempt and generating an error
Mode	Long	Indicates the level of permissions available for modifying data in a connection, record, or stream object
State	Long	Describes whether the connection is open or closed
CursorLocation	Long	Allows you to choose between various cursor locations (usually either client or server)
DefaultDatabase	String	Sets or returns a string that resolves to the name of a database available from the provider
IsolationLevel	Long	Sets or returns an IsolationLevelEnum value. The default is adXactReadCommitted
Provider	String	Sets or returns a string value representing the provider name. If no provider is specified, the property will default to MSDASQL (Microsoft OLE DB Provider for ODBC)
Attributes	Long	Generic property indicating one or more characteristics of the Connection object
Version	String	Reads the version from the ADO implementation
CommandTimeout	Long	Configures the timeout value for the execute method on the Connection object

Methods of the Connection Object

The Connection object also has several methods you'll use. Those methods are explained in the following table.

Method	Description
Open	Establishes the physical connection to the data source
Cancel	Cancels the execution of a pending Open or Execute method
Close	Breaks the physical connection to the data source
Execute	Executes a command on the connection. This method can pass a query string to the execute method to use without a Command object

Continues

Method	Description
	or use a Command object to persist the command text and re-execute it. A Command object is also required to use query parameters
BeginTrans	Begins a new transaction
CommitTrans	Saves any changes and ends the current transaction
RollbackTrans	Cancels any changes made in the current transaction and ends the transaction
OpenSchema	Obtains database schema information from the provider

Collections of the Connection Object

Collection	Description
Errors	Contains all of the error objects related to the current connection object
Properties	Contains all the property objects for the current connection

The Errors Collection and Error Object

The Errors collection contains all Error objects created by a response to a provider-related failure. The Error object contains the details about the error. The Error object also has properties and methods you can use within your code. Any operation that involves an ADO object can generate errors. Every time another error occurs for the same object, an additional Error object is added to the Errors collection. One caveat of error processing is that when a new ADO operation generates an error, the Errors collection is cleared and a new set of Error objects can be added to the Errors collection. You can use your error handling routine to examine that the Error objects in the Errors collection provide specific reactions to each of your errors. This allows you to display helpful error messages in plain language rather than relying on the system to generate errors for you that your users can understand.

Properties of the Errors Collection

The various properties of the Errors collection are summarized in the following table.

Property	Data Type	Description
Count	Long	Returns the number of error objects stored in the Errors collection
Item		References a specific member of the Errors collection by name or ordinal number

Methods of the Errors Collection

The following table lists the methods available for the `Errors` collection.

Method	Description
Clear	Removes all `Error` objects from the `Errors` collection
Refresh	Updates the `Errors` collection to encompass all current error objects

Properties of the Error Object

The following table lists the properties of the `Error` object.

Property	Data Type	Description
Description (default property)	String	Contains the text of the error
HelpFile	String	Name and location of the `Help` file
HelpContext	Long	Context ID of a topic in the `Help` file
Number	Long	Long integer value of the error constant
Source	String	Identifies the object that raised the error
SQLState	Variant	Returns a five-character error code from the provider when an error occurs during the processing of an SQL statement
NativeError	Long	Returns a long value used to retrieve the database specific error information for an `Error` object

There are no methods for the `Error` object.

The Properties Collection and Property Object

The `Properties` collection contains all of the property objects for a specific instance of an object. That's a confusing statement, but what it really means is that every object contains properties. All of those properties are stored in a `Properties` collection for that object. The `Properties` collection for the `Error` object contains the `Description`, `Number`, `Source`, `SQLState`, and `NativeError` properties. There are two types of properties: dynamic and built-in. You cannot delete either type of property.

Properties of the Property Object

All property objects have four properties of their own. Those properties are detailed in the following table.

Property	Data Type	Description
Name	String	String that identifies the property
Type	Integer	Integer that specifies the property data type
Value (default value)	Variant	A variant that contains the property setting
Attributes	Long	Long value that indicates characteristics of the property that are provider specific

There are no methods associated with the Property object.

The Command Object

The Command object allows you to do several things. You can query a database and return records in a recordset, execute a bulk operation, or manipulate the database structure. The flexibility of the Command object depends on the provider used. Depending on the provider, some properties or methods might generate errors when referenced.

Properties of the Command Object

The following table lists the various properties of the Command object.

Property	Data Type	Description
ActiveConnection	String or Connection	Indicates which Connection object the Command object uses
CommandText	String	Indicates the text of the Command being executed
CommandTimeout	Long	Sets the number of seconds a provider will wait for a command to execute
CommandType	CommandTypeEnum	Specifies the type of command executed, values include: adCmdUnspecified, adCmdText, adCmdTable, adCmdStoredProc, adCmdUnknown, adCmdFile, adCmdTableDirect

Continues

Property	Data Type	Description
CommandStream	Stream object	Stream used as the input for the Command object
Dialect	GUID	Contains a GUID that represents the dialect of the command text or stream
Name	String	Identifies the Command object as a method on the associated Connection object
Prepared	Boolean	True if the provider should save a compiled version of a Command before execution
State	Long	Value that represents if the Command object is open, closed, or in the process of connecting, executing, or retrieving information
NamedParameters	Boolean	Indicates whether parameter names are passed to the provider

You don't call methods on the Command object like you would on other objects. To execute a Command object, just call it by its Name property on the associated Connection object.

Collections of the Command Object

Collection	Description
Parameters	Contains all the parameter objects used for stored queries and stored procedures
Properties	Contains all the property objects for the current command object

The Parameters Collection

The Command object has a Parameters collection associated with it that contains all of the Parameter objects of the Command object. The actual Parameters collection does not contain any properties.

Methods of the Parameters Collection

Method	Arguments	Description
Append	Parameter object	Used to add a Parameter object to the collection
Refresh	None	Updates all of the Parameter objects in the collection with the latest information from the provider

Continues

Method	Arguments	Description
Delete	Index	Deletes a `Parameter` object from the collection. The `Index` value is either the name or ordinal position of the `Parameter` in the collection

Properties of the Parameter Object

The following table lists the various properties of the `Parameter` objects in the `Parameter` collection.

Property	Data Type	Description
Name	String	Sets or returns the name of the `Parameter`
Value (default property)	Variant	Sets or returns the value of the `Parameter`
Attributes	Long	A read/write property that is the sum of any one or more `ParameterAttributesEnum` values. The default value is `adParamSigned`
Direction	ParameterDirectionEnum	Indicates if the `Parameter` represents an input parameter, an output parameter, an input and an output parameter, or if the parameter is the return value from a stored procedure
Precision	Byte	Indicates the degree of precision for a `Parameter` object. This sets or returns a byte field to represent the maximum number of digits used to represent values
NumericScale	Byte	Sets or returns a byte value that indicates the number of decimal places to which numeric values are resolved
Size	Long	Indicates the maximum size in either bytes or characters of the `Parameter` object
Type	DataTypeEnum	Indicates the data type of the `Parameter`

The only method you need to be concerned with for the `Parameter` object is the `AppendChunk` method. This method simply appends data to the `Parameter` object.

You can use the `CreateParameter` method of the `Parameters` collection to create a `Parameter` with a specific name and properties. Then use the `Append` method to add the newly created `Parameter` to the `Parameters` collection.

Collections of the Parameter Object

Collection	Description
Properties	Contains all the property objects for the current Parameter object

The Recordset Object

Whenever you're using ADO to access data in an external data source, you'll likely use the Recordset object. This object represents the set of records from a table or the results of an executed command. When you use ADO, you manipulate data almost completely using Recordsets. All Recordsets consist of records (rows) and fields (columns). Depending on the functionality supported by the provider, some Recordset methods or properties may not be available.

Properties of the Recordset Object

The Recordset object has a variety of properties and methods you'll use in your programming. The following table lists the properties of the Recordset object you'll use.

Property	Data Type	Description
AbsolutePage	Long	Identifies the page the current record of the Recordset is on
AbsolutePosition	Long	Identifies the position of the current record in the Recordset
ActiveCommand	Variant	Pointer to the Command object that created the Recordset
ActiveConnection	String or Connection	Specifies the Connection object used to retrieve the Recordset
BOF	Boolean	True if you're currently at the beginning of file, the position before the first record
Bookmark	Variant	Allows you to return to a specific record in the Recordset
CacheSize	Long	The number of records ADO caches from the server
CursorLocation	Long	Lists whether the cursor service that maintain the results of the query is client-side or server-side

Continues

Property	Data Type	Description
CursorType	CursorTypeEnum	Specifies the type of cursor used to access the query results (dynamic, keyset, status, forwardonly)
DataMember	String	Specifies which Recordset in the data source you're referring to
DataSource	Object	Allows you to associate the Recordset with a data source
EditMode	EditModeEnum	Specifies the editing status for the current record
EOF	Boolean	True if you're currently at the end of file, the position after the last record in your Recordset
Filter	Variant	Allows you to filter your Recordset for particular values
Index	String	Controls the index currently applied in your Recordset
LockType	LockTypeEnum	Controls how the contents of the Recordset are locked and updated
MarshalOptions	MarshalOptionEnum	Specifies which records are transfered back to the server
MaxRecords	Long	Long value representing the maximum number of records returned by the query
PageCount	Long	The number of pages in your Recordset
PageSize	Long	Specifies the number of records per page in the Recordset
RecordCount	Long	Long value representing the number of records in the Recordset
Sort	String	Allows you to specify a sort order in your Recordset
Source	String or Command	String value or Command object that contains the query string used for the Recordset
StayInSync	Boolean	True if the child record needs to be kept updated
State	Long	Returns the current state of the Recordset
Status	RecordStatusEnum	Stores the update status of the current record

There are two properties you'll use when using a `Recordset` object. The first, and probably most important, is the `Fields` collection. This collection stores all of the fields that contain the results of your query. The second collection you'll use is the `Properties` collection. This is a collection of dynamic properties associated with your recordset.

Methods of the Recordset Object

There are a number of methods you'll use when manipulating your `Record` object as well. Those methods are listed in the following table.

Method	Description
AddNew	Adds a new record to the Recordset
Cancel	Cancels an asynchronous query
CancelBatch	Cancels pending changes in a Recordset that uses batch optimistic updates
CancelUpdate	Cancels pending changes currently being edited
Clone	Creates a new reference to your Recordset that allows you to navigate independently from the original Recordset
Close	Closes the `Recordset` object and releases its contents
CompareBookmarks	Compares two bookmarks in the same Recordset
Delete	Deletes the current record in your Recordset
Find	Searches a Recordset for a record based on a string criteria
GetRows	Returns data in a two-dimensional Variant array
GetString	Returns data in a string format
Move	Moves the position of the current record
MoveFirst	Moves to the first record in your Recordset
MoveLast	Moves to the last record in your Recordset
MoveNext	Moves to the next record in your Recordset
MovePrevious	Moves to the previous record in your Recordset
Open	Opens the Recordset
Requery	Re-executes the query that generated the Recordset
Resync	Retrieves the current data for the records in the recordset
Save	Writes the Recordset contents to a file
Seek	Searches the Recordset for a specific string

Continues

Method	Description
Supports	Returns a Boolean value indicating whether the Recordset supports a particular type of functionality
Update	Writes pending changes to the Recordset
UpdateBatch	Submits pending changes in a Recordset that uses batch optimistic updating

Collections of the Recordset Object

Collection	Description
Properties	Contains all the property objects for the current command object

The Fields Collection

The collection contains all the field objects of a Recordset or Record object. The Fields collection has only two properties you'll use: the Count property, which returns the number of Field objects in the collection; and the Item property, which returns a specific field in the collection.

Methods of the Fields Collection

Methods for the Fields collection are listed in the following table.

Method	Description
Append	Creates and adds a field object to the Fields collection
Update	Finalizes any additions or deletions to the Fields collection
CancelUpdate	Cancels any pending changes for a record
Delete	Deletes a field from the collection
Refresh	Refreshes the Fields collection
Resync	Resynchronizes the current record

The Field Object

The Fields collection contains Field objects. Each object represents an individual field within an ADO Recordset.

Properties of the Field Object

The properties for the Field object are listed in the following table.

Property	Data Type	Description
ActualSize	Long	Returns the actual size of the value of the field
Attributes	Long	Describes certain characteristics of the field
DataFormat	Object	Can be used to format your data
DefinedSize	Long	Describes the defined size for the field
Name	String	Contains the name of the field
NumericScale	Byte	Number of digits allowed to the right of the decimal point for a numeric field
OriginalValue	Variant	Stores the original value for the field
Precision	Byte	Indicates the precision for numeric data
Status	FieldStatusEnum	Determines whether the field has been successfully added to the collection
Type	Byte	Lists the data type for the field
UnderlyingValue	Variant	Lists the most recently retrieved value for the field
Value	Variant	Contains the field's current value

There are two methods available for the Field object. AppendChunk allows you to append data to a large string or binary field. GetChunk allows you to retrieve data from a large string or binary field.

Collections for the Field Object	Description
Properties	Contains all the property objects for the current command object

Record Object

The Record object represents a row from a Recordset or any object returned by a data provider.

Properties of the Record Object

The following table lists the properties associated with a Record object.

Property	Data Type	Description
ActiveConnection	Variant	The Connection object used to retrieve the data for the Record object
Fields	Collection of Field objects	Pointer to the collection of Field objects that contain data
Mode	ConnectModeEnum	Specifies the permissions for modifying the Record object
ParentURL	String	The parent URL for the Record object
RecordType	RecordTypeEnum	Specifies the type of the Record object
Source	Variant	Specifies the source of the data contained in the Record object
State	ObjectStateEnum	Indicates the state of the Record object

Methods of the Record object

The Record object has seven methods, listed in the following table.

Method	Description
Cancel	Cancels an asynchronous action on the Record object
Close	Closes an open Record object
CopyRecord	Copies the Record object to another location
DeleteRecord	Deletes the Record
GetChildren	Retrieves the child data associated with the Record object
MoveRecord	Moves the Record to another location
Open	Opens an existing Record or creates a new Record

Collections of the Record Object

Collection	Description
Properties	Contains all the property objects for the current command object

The Stream Object

The Stream object in ADO represents a stream of binary data or text.

Properties of the Stream Object

The following table lists the various properties of the Stream object.

Property	Data Type	Description
Charset	String	Specifies the character set for the stream
EOS	Boolean	True if the current position is at the end of stream (EOS)
LineSeparator	LineSeparatorEnum	Specifies the character or combination of characters used as the line separator in the stream
Mode	ConnectModeEnum	Specifies the permissions for modifying data in the Stream object
Position	Long	The current position in the stream
Size	Long	Specifies the current size of the stream of data
State	ObjectStateEnum	Specifies the current state of the Stream object
Type	StreamTypeEnum	Specifies the type of data stored in the Stream object

Methods of the Stream Object

The methods you can use with the Stream object can be found in the following table.

Method	Description
Cancel	Cancels a pending asynchronous call to a Stream object
Close	Closes an open Stream object
CopyTo	Copies data from the Stream object to another Stream object
Flush	Flushes the contents stored in the stream's buffer
LoadFromFile	Loads the contents of a file into the Stream object
Open	Opens the Stream object

Continues

Method	Description
Read	Reads binary data from the stream
ReadText	Reads text data from the stream
SaveToFile	Writes data from the Stream object to a file
SetEOS	Sets the current position as the end of the Stream object
SkipLine	Moves to the beginning of the next line of data in the text stream
Write	Appends binary data to the stream
WriteText	Appends text data to the stream

The Access Object Model

By now you've probably read at least a few of the chapters in this book and have realized that there are a lot of tasks you can accomplish by programming in VBA. One concept that should be abundantly clear is that in order to use VBA to manipulate Access, you'll need to have some knowledge about the Access object model. We talked very briefly about object models in Chapter 5, but as a refresher, an object model is a set of objects and collections that programmers use to manipulate a program. Microsoft Access has a very rich object model. You'll use the Access object model to manipulate forms, reports, queries, macros, and other components of the Access interface.

As just about every component of the Access object model is related in some way to at least one other component, the following tables will also include information about related objects (both parent objects and child objects). For a graphical representation of the Access object model, you can search your hard drive for the file VBAAC10.hlp (the Microsoft Access Visual Basic Reference help file). As soon as you open that file, you'll see a graphical representation of the entire Access object model.

Much of the information within this appendix can be found in some form within the Access Visual Basic Reference Help file.

The Application Object

All of the Access objects you'll manipulate within code are derived from the Application object. This is the parent object for all other objects and collections within the Access object model. All objects and collections are related to the Application object, either through a direct parent/child relationship or through multiple parent/child relationships. Figure E-1 lists the objects and collections that are the direct children of the Application object.

The Application object refers to the currently active Access application. This object contains all Microsoft Access objects and collections. You can use the Application object to apply methods or set properties for the entire Access application. For example, you can use the SetOptions method

Application

Code Data	**CurrentProject**
Code Project	**DataAccessPages**
CurrentData	**DefaultWebOptions**
	DoCmd
	Forms
	Modules
	Printers
	References
	Reports
	Screen

Figure E-1

of the `Application` object to control just about all the settings visible on the `Tools | Options` dialog box. The various settings you can use with the `SetOptions` method are listed a little later in this appendix. The following code displays hidden objects in the database window.

```
Application.SetOption "Show Hidden Objects", True
```

Just about all code you write within Access utilizes the `Application` object somewhere within the code.

Properties of the Application Object

The following table lists the various properties of the `Application` object. Please note that this table contains not only string and Boolean properties, but also properties that refer to other objects within the Access object model. Those objects are discussed later in this appendix.

Property	Data Type	Description
AnswerWizard	AnswerWizard	Used to reference the current AnswerWizard object
Application	Application object	Used to reference the current Application object (for example, Me.Application on a form)
Assistant	Assistant object	References the Office Assistant object

Continues

Property	Data Type	Description
AutoCorrect	AutoCorrect object	Returns an AutoCorrect object that represents the AutoCorrect settings for the specified control
AutomationSecurity		Returns or sets an MsoAutomationSecurity constant that represents the security mode Access uses when opening files
BrokenReference	Boolean	True if the current database has any broken references to databases or type libraries
Build	Long	Build number of the currently installed copy of Access
CodeContextObject	Object	Used to determine the object in which a macro or VBA code is executing
CodeData	CodeData	Use this property to access the CodeData object
CodeProject	CodeProject	Use this property to access the CodeProject object
COMAddIns	COMAddIns collection	References the current COMAddIns collection object
CommandBars	CommandBars collection	References the CommandBars collection
CurrentData	CurrentData object	Used to access the CurrentData object
CurrentObjectName	String	The name of the active database object
CurrentObjectType	Intrinsic constant (acTable, acQuery, acForm, acReport, acMacro, acModule, acDataAccessPage, acServerView, acDiagram, acStoredProcedure)	Used to determine the type of the active database object (table, query, form, report, macro, module, data access page, server view, database diagram, or stored procedure)
CurrentProject	CurrentProject object	Used to access the CurrentProject object
DataAccessPages	DataAccessPages collection	Used to reference the current DataAccessPages collection
DBEngine	DBEngine object	Used to reference the current DBEngine object and its related properties

Continues

Property	Data Type	Description
DefaultWebOptions	DefaultWebOptions object	Used to reference the DefaultWebOptions object and its properties
DoCmd	DoCmd object	Used to access the DoCmd object
FeatureInstall	MsoFeatureInstall	Determines or specifies how Access handles calls to methods or properties not yet installed
FileDialog	FileDialog object	Returns a FileDialog object (represents a single instance of a FileDialog box)
FileSearch	FileSearch object	Returns a read only reference to the FileSearch object
Forms	Forms collection	Returns a read-only reference to the Forms collection
IsCompiled	Boolean	True if the current Visual Basic project is in a compiled state
LanguageSettings	LanguageSettings object	Returns a read-only reference to the current LanguageSettings object
MenuBar	String	Specifies the MenuBar to use for an Access database, Access project, form, or report
Modules	Modules collection	Used to access the Modules collection and its related properties
Name	String	String expression that identifies the application name
NewFileTaskPane	NewFile object	Returns a NewFile object listed in the NewFile task pane
Parent	AccessObject	Returns an AccessObject for the Application object
Printer	Printer object	Returns or sets a Printer object representing the default printer on the current computer
Printers	Printers collection	Returns the Printers collection on the current computer
ProductCode	String	Returns the globally unique identifier (GUID) for the Access application
References	References collection	Used to access the References collection for the current database
Reports	Reports collection	Returns the Reports collection for the current database

Continues

Property	Data Type	Description
Screen	Screen object	Returns a reference to the current Screen object
ShortcutMenuBar	String	Used to specify the shortcut menu that appears when you right-click a form, report, or control
UserControl	Boolean (True if started by the user, False if started by Automation)	Used to determine whether the current Access application was started by a user or by another application
VBE	VBE object	References the current VBA object
Version	String	Indicates the current version of Access
Visible	Boolean (True if minimized, False if not)	Used to determine whether the current application is minimized

Methods of the Application Object

The following table lists all of the methods available from the Application object. If any arguments for the methods are present, those are also listed in the following table. For example, you can use the CompactRepair method of the Application object with the following code.

```
Application.CompactRepair("c:\DB\Samples.mdb", _
  "c:\DB\SamplesSm.mdb", "c:\DB\log.txt"
```

Method Name	Arguments	Description
AccessError	ErrorNumber (variant)	Return a string associated with an Access or DAO error
AddToFavorites	None	Adds a hyperlink address to the Favorites folder (name of the current database)
BuildCriteria	Field, FieldType, Expression	Returns a parsed criteria string as it would appear in the query design grid, in Filter By Form or Server Filter By Form mode
CloseCurrentDatabase	None	Closes the current database (either an MDB or ADP)
CodeDb	None	Used to determine the name of database object within which the code is currently running

Continues

Method Name	Arguments	Description
CompactRepair	SourceFile, DestinationFile, LogFile	Compacts and repairs the specified database (either an MDB or ADP), returns a Boolean if the process was successful
ConvertAccessProject	SourceFileName, DestinationFileName, DestinationFileFormat,	Converts the specified Access database from one version to another
CreateAccessProject	FilePath, Connect	Used to create a new Access Data Project (ADP)
CreateAdditionalData	None	Creates an AdditionalData object that can be used to add additional tables and queries to a parent table
CreateControl	FormName, ControlType [Section, Parent, ColumnName, Left, Top, Width, Height]	Creates a control on a currently open form
CreateForm	Database, FormTemplate	Creates a form and returns a Form object
CreateGroupLevel	ReportName, Expression, Header, Footer	Specifies a field or expression to be used for grouping
CreateNewWorkgroupFile	Path, Name, Company, WorkgroupID, Replace	Creates a new Workgroup file for secure access to a database
CreateReport	Database, ReportTemplate	Creates a new report and returns a report object
CreateReportControl	ReportName, ControlType [Section, Parent, ColumnName, Left, Top, Width, Height]	Creates a control on a currently open report
CurrentDb	None	Returns a database object that represents the currently opened database
CurrentUser	None	Returns the current user of the database
DAvg	Expr, Domain, Criteria	Use this function to calculate the average of a set of values in a specified set of records

Continues

Method Name	Arguments	Description
DCount	Expr, Domain, Criteria	Used to determine the number of records within a set of records
DDEExecute	ChanNum, Command	Can be used to send a command from a client application to a server application
DDEInitiate	Application, topic	Opens a DDE (Dynamic Data Exchange) channel between two applications
DDEPoke	ChanNum, Item, Data	Can be used to supply text data from a client application to a server application over an open DDE channel
DDERequest	ChanNum, Item	Used to request information over a DDE channel
DDETerminate	ChanNum	Can be used to close a specified DDE channel
DDETerminateAll	None	Closes all open DDE channels
DefaultWorkspaceClone	None	Creates a new Workspace object without requiring the user to log on again
DeleteControl	FormName, ControlName	Deletes a control on a specified form
DeleteReportControl	ReportName, ControlName	Deletes a control on a specific report
DFirst	Expr, Domain, Criteria	Used to return a random record from a particular field in a table or query
DLast	Expr, Domain, Criteria	Used to return a random record from a particular field in a table or query
DLookup	Expr, Domain, Criteria	Used to get the value from a particular field from a specified set of records
DMax	Expr, Domain, Criteria	Used to determine the maximum value in a specified set of records
DMin	Expr, Domain, Criteria	Used to determine the minimum value in a specified set of records
DStDev	Expr, Domain, Criteria	Used to estimate the standard deviation across a set of values in a set of records
DStDevP	Expr, Domain, Criteria	Used to estimate the standard deviation across a set of values in a set of records
DSum	Expr, Domain, Criteria	Used to calculate the sum of a set of values in a set of records

Continues

Method Name	Arguments	Description
DVar	Expr, Domain, Criteria	Used to estimate the variance across a set of values in a set of records
DVarP	Expr, Domain, Criteria	Used to estimate variance across a set of values in a set of records
Echo	EchoOn, bstrStatusBarText	Specifies whether Access repaints the display screen
EuroConvert	Number, SourceCurrency, TargetCurrency, fullprecision, triangulationprecision	Can be used to convert a number to euro or from euro to a participating currency. You can also use it to convert a number from one participating currency to another by using the euro as an intermediary (triangulation)
Eval	StringExpr	Used to evaluate an expression that results in a text string or numeric value
ExportXML	ObjectType, DataSource, DataTarget, SchemaTarget, PresentationTarget, ImageTarget, Encoding, OtherFlags, FilterCriteria, AdditionalData	Allows for export of XML data, schemas, and presentation information from Microsoft SQL Server 2000 Desktop Engine (MSDE 2000), Microsoft SQL Server 6.5 or later, or the Microsoft Jet database engine
FollowHyperlink	Address, SubAddress, NewWindow, AddHistory, ExtraInfo, Method, HeaderInfo	Opens the document or Web page specified by a hyperlink
GetHiddenAttribute	Objecttype, objectname	Returns the value of a hidden attribute
GetOption	OptionName	Returns the current value of an option in the Options dialog box.
GUIDFromString	String	Converts a string to a GUID
hWndAccessApp	None	Determines the handle assigned to the main Access window by Microsoft Windows
HyperlinkPart	Hyperlink, part	Returns information about data stored as a hyperlink data type

Continues

Method Name	Arguments	Description
ImportXML	DataSource, ImportOptions	Allows import of XML data and/or schema information into Microsoft SQL Server 2000 Desktop Engine (MSDE 2000), Microsoft SQL Server 7.0 or later, or the Microsoft Jet database engine
LoadPicture	FileName	Loads a graphic into the ActiveX control
NewAccessProject	Filepath, Connect	Used to create and set a new ADP as the active data project
NewCurrentDatabase	Filepath	Creates a new Access database (mdb) in the Access window
Nz	Value, ValueIfNull	Used to return zero, a zero-length string, or another value when a value is null
OpenAccessProject	FilePath, Exclusive	Opens an ADP as the current Access project
OpenCurrentDatabase	FilePath, Exclusive, bstrPassword	Can be used to open an MDB file as the current database
Quit	Option (acQuitPrompt, acQuitSaveAll, acQuitSaveNone)	Quits Microsoft Access
RefreshDatabaseWindow	None	Updates the database window after an object has been created
RefreshTitleBar	None	Refreshes the Access title bar after the AppTitle or AppIcon has been changed via code
Run	Procedure (optional arguments can also follow)	Can be used to carry out a sub or function
RunCommand	Command	Runs a built-in menu or toolbar command
SetDefaultWorkgroupFile	Path	Sets the default Workgroup file to the file specified in the Path agrument
SetHiddenAttribute	ObjectType, ObjectName, fHidden	Sets the hidden attribute of the Access application

Continues

Method Name	Arguments	Description
SetOption	OptionName, Setting	Sets the current value of an option in the Options dialog box. The various OptionName arguments are detailed at the end of this appendix
StringFromGUID	GUID	Converts a GUID to a string
SysCmd	Action, Argument2, Argument3	Can (1) display a progress meter or specified text in the status bar, (2) return information about Access and its associated files, or (3) return the state of a current database object
TransformXML	DataSource, TransformSource, OutputTarget, WellFormedXMLOutput, ScriptOption	Applies an Extensible Stylesheet Language (XSL) stylesheet to an XML data file and writes the XML to an XML data file

The CodeData Object

The CodeData object is used to refer to objects stored within the code database by the source application (Jet or SQL). The CodeData object has a variety of properties you can manipulate as well as several collections of its own.

Properties of the CodeData Object

The following table lists the various properties of the CodeData object.

Property	Data Type	Description
AllDatabaseDiagrams	AllDatabaseDiagrams collection	Used to reference the AllDatabaseDiagrams collection
AllFunctions	AllFunctions collection	Represents all the user-defined functions in the SQL Server database
AllQueries	AllQueries collection	Used to represent all of the queries defined in the database
AllStoredProcedures	AllStoredProcedures collection	Used to reference all of the stored procedures in the database
AllTables	AllTables collection	Used to reference all the tables in the database
AllViews	AllViews collection	Used to reference all views in the database

AllDatabaseDiagrams Collection

The `AllDatabaseDiagrams` collection contains an Access object for every database diagram in the `CurrentData` or `CodeData` object. As it's a collection, it doesn't have properties and methods of its own that we'll cover here. The `AllDatabaseDiagrams` collection contains one object, the `AccessObject`.

AccessObject

The `AccessObject` refers to a particular Access object within any of the following collections: `AllDataAccessPages`, `AllDatabaseDiagrams`, `AllForms`, `AllFunctions`, `AllMacros`, `AllModules`, `AllQueries`, `AllReports`, `AllStoredProcedures`, `AllTables`, and `AllViews`.

Properties of the AccessObject

The `AccessObject` has its own properties and methods you can implement within your code. The following table lists the various properties of the `AccessObject`.

Property	Data Type	Description
CurrentView	acCurrentView (acCurrentViewDatasheet, acCurrentViewDesign, acCurrentViewFormBrowse, acCurrentViewPivotChart, acCurrentViewPivotTable, acCurrentViewPreview)	Returns the current view for the specified Access object
DateCreated	Date	Returns the date the `AccessObject` was created
DateModified	Date	Returns the date the `AccessObject` was last modified
FullName	String	Sets or returns the full path (including name) of the object
IsLoaded	Boolean	Boolean value that specifies whether the current object is loaded
Name	String	String that contains the name of the currently loaded object
Parent	AccessObject	Returns an `AccessObject` for any currently loaded `AccessObject`
Properties	AccessObject Properties collection	Returns a reference to the `AccessObject` `Properties` collection

Continues

Property	Data Type	Description
Type	acObjectType (acDataAccessPage, acDefault, acDiagram, acForm, acFunction, acMacro, acModule, acQuery, acReport, acServer View, acStoredProcedure, acTable)	Returns the type of the AccessObject

Methods of the AccessObject

The AccessObject has two methods you can use. Those methods are detailed in the following table.

Method	Arguments	Description
GetDependencyInto	N/A	Returns a DependencyInfo object that represents the database objects that are dependent upon the specified object
IsDependentUpon	ObjectType, ObjectName	Returns a Boolean value that indicates whether the specified object is dependent upon the database object specified in the ObjectName argument

The AllFunctions Collection

As its name implies, the AllFunctions collection contains an Access object for each function in the CurrentData or CodeData object.

Properties of the AllFunctions Collection

The AllFunctions collection contains the typical collection properties of Application, Count, Item, and Parent. Many of the other collections listed in this appendix have the same set of properties. The properties are listed in the following table.

Property	Data Type	Description
Application	Application object	Returns the Application object associated with the current collection

Continues

Property	Data Type	Description
Count	Long	Returns the number of items in the specified collection
Item	Various	Returns a specific member of a collection (by position or index)
Parent	Various	Returns the parent object of the current collection

Other Similar Collections

The rest of the collections previously described (AllDatabaseDiagrams, AllQueries, AllStoredProcedures, AllTables, and AllViews) have the same child object, the AccessObject.

❑ The AllQueries collection contains an AccessObject for every query in the CodeData or CurrentData object.

❑ The AllStoredProcedures collection contains an AccessObject for every stored procedure in the CodeData or CurrentData object.

❑ The AllTables collection contains an AccessObject for every table in the CodeData or CurrentData object.

❑ The AllViews collection contains an AccessObject for every view in the CodeData or CurrentData object.

The CurrentData Object

The CurrentData object is used to refer to all of the objects stored in the current database by the server application (either Jet or SQL). The properties associated with the CurrentData object are the same as those for the CodeData object. So what's the difference? Well, it's just one word. If you re-read the definitions of both you'll notice one key difference. The CurrentData object allows you to manage the objects in the current database. The CodeData object takes care of the objects in the code database. The code database is a database used as a reference for the current database. For example, if you have a database called Samples.mdb, and that database contains a reference to a database called VBASamples.mdb, the current database would be Samples.mdb and the code database would be VBASamples.mdb. The properties and methods of the CurrentData object are the same as the CodeData object, so we won't cover them separately here.

The CodeProject Object

The CodeProject object allows you to manipulate the set of all code modules (including both standard and class modules) in the code database of an Access Project (adp) or Access Database (mdb). The CodeProject object has several collections and a number of properties you can use within your application.

Properties of the CodeProject Object

The various properties of the CodeProject object are listed in the following table.

Property	Data Type	Description
AccessConnection	Connection	Used to return a reference to the currently active ADO Connection object
AllDataAccessPages	AllDataAccessPages collection	Used to return a reference to the AllDataAccessPages collection and its associated properties
AllForms	AllForms collection	Used to return a reference to the AllForms collection and its associated properties
AllMacros	AllMacros collection	Used to return a reference to the AllMacros collection and its associated properties
AllModules	AllModules collection	Used to return a reference to the AllModules collection and its associated properties
AllReports	AllReports collection	Used to return a reference to the AllReports collection and its associated properties
Application	Application object	Used to return a reference to the current Application object
BaseConnectionString	String	Used to return the base Connection String for the CurrentProject or CodeProject object
Connection	Connection object	Used to return the currently active ADO Connection object
FileFormat	acFileFormat (acFileFormatAccess2, acFileFormatAccess2000, acFileFormatAccess2002, acFileFormatAccess95, acFileFormatAccess97)	Returns a constant representing the Microsoft Access version of the specified project
FullName	String	Returns the full path and name for the CodeProject object
IsConnected	Boolean	Used to determine if the CodeProject is currently connected

Continues

Property	Data Type	Description
Name	String	Returns the name of the current `CodeProject`
Parent	Application object	For the `CodeProject` object, the `Parent` property returns the associated `Application` object
Path	String	Returns the path to the data location for the Access database (mdb) or Access Project (adp)
ProjectType	acProjectType (acADP, acMDB, acNull)	Used to determine the type of project currently open through the `CodeProject` object
Properties	Properties collection	Returns a reference to the entire `Properties` collection for the `CodeProject` object
RemovePersonalInformation	Boolean	True if user information is removed from the specified project, False if user information is stored within the project

Properties of the CodeProject Object

The `CodeProject` object also contains several methods. These methods are listed in the following table.

Method	Arguments	Description
CloseConnection	None	Closes the current connection between the `CodeProject` object and the database specified in the project's base connection string
OpenConnection	BaseConnectionString, UserID, Password	Opens an ADO Connection to an existing Access Project (adp) or Access Database (mdb) as the current Access Project or Database
UpdateDependencyInfo	None	Updates the dependency information for the database

The `CodeProject` object contains several collections that contain `AccessObjects`. Those collections are `AllForms`, `AllReports`, `AllMacros`, `AllModules`, and `AllDataAccessPages`. These collections have the same properties as the `AllFunctions` collection, listed previously.

The CurrentProject Object

The CurrentProject object is very similar to the CodeProject object. It contains the set of all code modules (class modules and standard modules) for the current Access Database (mdb) or Access Project (adp). The properties and methods of the CurrentProject are the same as those for the CodeProject.

The DataAccessPages Collection

Another child object of the Application object is the DataAccessPages collection. This collection, as the name implies, contains all of the DataAccessPages currently open within an Access Project (adp) or an Access Database (mdb). The DataAccessPage object is found within the DataAccessPages collection.

The DataAccessPage Object

As its name implies, this object refers to a DataAccessPage.

Properties of the DataAccessPage Object

The properties of a DataAccessPage are listed in the following table.

Property	Data Type	Description
Application	Application object	Used to access the currently active Application object
ConnectionString	String	Returns the base ConnectionString for the DataAccessPage
CurrentView	Integer (Design View = 0, Page View = 1)	Determines how a DataAccessPage is displayed
Document	Document object	Used to access the Internet Explorer Dynamic HTML document object for HTML pages
MailEnvelope	msoMailEnvelope object	Represents the e-mail header for a data access page
MSODSC	DataSourceControl object	Returns a DataSourceControl object for the current DataAccessPage
Name	String	Specifies the name of the DataAccessPage object

Continues

Property	Data Type	Description
Parent	Object	Returns the parent object of the DataAccessPage (the Application object)
RemovePersonalInformation	Boolean	True if personal information about the user is not stored in the DataAccessPage object, false if personal information is stored in the DataAccessPage object
Visible	Boolean	False if the DataAccessPage object is minimized
WebOptions	WebOptions object	Used to represent the WebOptions object
WindowHeight	Long	Returns or sets the height of the DataAccessPage object in twips
WindowWidth	Long	Returns or sets the width of the DataAccessPage object in twips

The DataAccessPage object has one method, the ApplyTheme method. This method takes one argument, the ThemeName. This allows you to specify a Microsoft Office Theme for your data access page.

The DefaultWebOptions Object

This object contains application-level attributes used globally by Microsoft Access when you save a data access page as a Web page or open a Web page. You can return or set attributes either at the application (global) level or at the data access page level.

Properties of the DefaultWebOptions Object

The properties of the DefaultWebOptions object are listed in the following table. The DefaultWebOptions object doesn't have any methods or events exposed.

Property	Data Type	Relationship
AlwaysSaveInDefaultEncoding	Boolean	Used to determine if the Web browser opens a data access page with its default encoding or the original encoding
Application	Application object	Returns the currently active Application object

Continues

Property	Data Type	Relationship
CheckIfOfficeIsHTMLEditor	Boolean	Used to determine the default HTML Editor for the system (either Office or another type of HTML editor such as Visual InterDev)
DownloadComponents	Boolean	True if the Office Tools are automatically downloaded with the Web page
Encoding	msoEncoding	Used to determine the encoding used by the Web browser when viewing the saved data access page
FolderSuffix	String	Used to determine the suffix used when you save a data access page as a Web page (both OrganizeInFolder and UseLongFileNames must also be set to True)
FollowedHyperlinkColor	Color constant	Sets the color for all followed hyperlinks
HyperlinkColor	Color constant	Sets the color for all hyperlinks (not followed)
LocationOfComponents	String	Used to determine a central URL or path for Office controls to be downloaded by users viewing the saved database
OrganizeInFolder	Boolean	True if all associated files (such as image files) are stored in their own folder, false if they are stored in the folder with the data access page
Parent	Object	Returns the Application object
TargetBrowser	msoTargetBrowser (msoTargetBrowserIE4, msoTargetBrowserIE5, msoTargetBrowserIE6, msoTargetBrowserV3, msoTargetBrowserV4)	Returns or sets a constant indicating which Web browser the data access page uses as its intended target

Continues

Property	Data Type	Relationship
UnderlineHyperlinks	Boolean	Used to determine whether hyperlinks are underlined when displayed
UseLongFileNames	Boolean	Used to determine whether long file names are used when saving a data access page

The DoCmd Object

As its name implies, this object allows you to do things within Microsoft Access. There are no properties of the DoCmd object, but there are a variety of methods you can utilize within your Access application.

Methods of the DoCmd Object

The methods of the DoCmd object are listed in the following table. All of the methods here actually carry out an action with the same name as the method. We've included the description of the action, rather than the description of the method (which merely calls the action).

Method	Arguments	Description
AddMenu	MenuName, MacroName, StatusBarText	Creates a custom menu bar, shortcut bar, or shortcut menu
ApplyFilter	FilterName, WhereCondition	Used to apply a filter, a query, or a SQL WHERE clause to a table, form, or report
Beep	None	Causes the system to beep
CancelEvent	None	Used to cancel the event that caused Access to run the macro or module containing this action
Close	ObjectType, ObjectName, Save	Closes the object specified in the ObjectName argument
CopyDatabaseFile	DatabaseFileName, OverwriteExistingFile, DisconnectAllUsers	Copies the database connected to the current project to a SQL Server database for export
CopyObject	DestinationDatabase, NewName, SourceObjectType, SourceObjectName	Copies the specified object to another database (mdb) or Access project (adp)
DeleteObject	ObjectType, ObjectName	Deletes the specified object

Continues

Method	Arguments	Description
DoMenuItem	MenuBar, MenuName, Command, SubCommand, Version	Executes the specified menu item (*Note:* This is a legacy method from Access 97. In later versions of Access this method was replaced by the RunCommand method. It is only included for backwards compatibility)
Echo	EchoOn, StatusBarText	Turns Echo on or off
FindNext	None	Finds the next record that meets the criteria specified in the FindRecord action
FindRecord	FindWhat, Match, MatchCase, Search, SearchAsFormatted, OnlyCurrentField, FindFirst	Finds the first instance of a record that meets the criteria specified by the FindWhat argument
GoToControl	ControlName	Moves focus to the specified control
GoToPage	PageNumber, Right, Down	Moves the focus in a form to the first control on the specified page
GoToRecord	ObjectType, ObjectName, Record, Offset	Makes the specified record the current record in a table, form, or result set
Hourglass	HourglassOn	Changes the mouse pointer to an hourglass while the macro or code is running
Maximize	None	Maximizes the entire Access Application window
Minimize	None	Minimizes the entire Access Application window
MoveSize	Right, Down, Width, Height	Moves or resizes the active window
OpenDataAccessPage	DataAccessPageName, View	Opens the specified data access page in the specified view
OpenDiagram	DiagramName	Opens the specified database diagram in design view
OpenForm	FormName, View, FilterName, WhereCondition, DataMode, WindowMode, OpenArgs	Opens the specified form in the specified view. Can also be used to filter the data displayed on the form

Continues

Method	Arguments	Description
OpenFunction	FunctionName, View, DataMode	Opens a user-defined function in SQL Server for viewing in Access
OpenModule	ModuleName, ProcedureName	Opens the specified module at the specified procedure
OpenQuery	QueryName, View, DataMode	Opens the specified query with the specified type of view
OpenReport	ReportName, View, FilterName, WhereCondition, WindowMode, OpenArgs	Opens the specified report in the specified view. Can also be used to filter the data displayed on the report
OpenStoredProcedure	ProcedureName, View, DataMode	Used to open the specified stored procedure
OpenTable	TableName, View, DataMode	Used to open the specified table in the specified view
OpenView	ViewName, View, DataMode	Opens the specified view in datasheet view, design view, or print preview
OutputTo	ObjectType, ObjectName, OutputFormat, OutputFile, AutoStart, TemplateFile, Encoding	Outputs the specified object in the specified file format
PrintOut	PrintRange, PageFrom, PageTo, PrintQuality, Copies, CollateCopies	Prints the active object
Quit	Options	Quits the active Access application
Rename	NewName, ObjectType, OldName	Renames the specified object
RepaintObject	ObjectType, ObjectName	Completes any pending screen updates for the specified object
Requery	ControlName	Updates the data in the specified control by requerying the source of the control
Restore	None	Restores a maximized or minimized window to its previous state
RunCommand	Command	Runs a built-in menu or toolbar command (see *RunCommand Method Arguments* later in this appendix for command options)

Continues

Method	Arguments	Description
RunMacro	MacroName, RepeatCount, RepeatExpression	Used to run the specified macro
RunSQL	SQLStatement, UseTransaction	Runs an Access action query by using the corresponding SQL statement
Save	ObjectType, ObjectName	Saves the specified object
SelectObject	ObjectType, ObjectName, InDatabaseWindow	Selects the specified database object
SendObject	ObjectType, ObjectName, OutputFormat, To, Cc, Bcc, Subject, MessageText, EditMessage, TemplateFile	Sends the specified Access datasheet, form, report, module, or data access page via e-mail
SetMenuItem	MenuIndex, CommandIndex, SubCommandIndex, Flag	Enable, disable, check, or uncheck the specified menu item
SetWarnings	WarningsOn	Turns system messages on or off
ShowAllRecords	None	Removes any applied filter for the table, query, or form
ShowToolbar	ToolbarName, Show	Display or hide a built-in toolbar
TransferDatabase	TransferType, DatabaseType, DatabaseName, ObjectType, Source, Destination, StructureOnly, StoreLogin	Used to import or export data between the current database (mdb) or Access project (adp) and another database
TransferSpreadsheet	TransferType, SpreadsheetType, TableName, FileName, HasFieldNames, Range, UseOA	Used to import or export data between the current database (mdb) or Access project (adp) and a spreadsheet
TransferSQLDatabase	Server, Database, UsedTrustedConnection, Login, Password, TransferCopyData	Transfers the entire SQL Server database to another SQL Server database
TransferText	TransferType, SpecificationName, TableName, FileName, HasFieldNames, HTMLTableName, CodePage	Used to import or export data between a database (mdb) or Access project (adp) and a text file

The Forms Collection

The `Forms` collection contains all of the forms associated with the current database.

Properties of the Form Object

The `Form` object contains a variety of properties, methods, and events that are listed in the following tables.

Property	Data Type	Description
ActiveControl	Control object	Used with the `Screen` object to determine the control that has the focus
AfterDelConfirm	String	Indicates which macro, event procedure, or user-defined function runs when the `AfterDelConfirm` event occurs
AfterFinalRender	String	Indicates which macro, event procedure, or user-defined function runs when the `AfterFinalRender` event occurs
AfterInsert	String	Indicates which macro, event procedure, or user-defined function runs when the `AfterInsert` event occurs
AfterLayout	String	Indicates which macro, event procedure, or user-defined function runs when the `AfterLayout` event occurs
AfterRender	String	Indicates which macro, event procedure, or user-defined function runs when the `AfterRender` event occurs
AfterUpdate	String	Indicates which macro, event procedure, or user-defined function runs when the event `AfterUpdate` event occurs
AllowAdditions	Boolean	Determines whether a user can add a record when using a form
AllowDataSheetView	Boolean	Determines whether the form can be switched to datasheet view
AllowDeletions	Boolean	Determines whether a user can delete a record when using a form
AllowDesignChanges	Boolean	Determines whether a user can make changes to the design of a form in design mode only (`False`) or in all views (`True`)

Continues

Property	Data Type	Description
AllowEdits	Boolean	Determines whether a user can edit save records when using a form
AllowFilters	Boolean	Determines whether a user can filter the records when using a form
AllowFormView	Boolean	Determines whether a form can be viewed in Form view
AllowPivotChartView	Boolean	Determines whether a form can be viewed in PivotChart view
AllowPivotTableView	Boolean	Determines whether a form can be viewed in PivotTable view
Application	Application object	Returns the currently active application object
AutoCenter	Boolean	Determines whether the form will be automatically centered within the Application window
AutoResize	Boolean	Determines whether the form will be automatically resized to display complete records
BeforeDelConfirm	String	Indicates which macro, event procedure, or user-defined function runs when the BeforeDelConfirm event occurs
BeforeInsert	String	Indicates which macro, event procedure, or user-defined function runs when the BeforeInsert event occurs
BeforeQuery	String	Indicates which macro, event procedure, or user-defined function runs when the BeforeQuery event occurs
BeforeRender	String	Indicates which macro, event procedure, or user-defined function runs when the BeforeRender event occurs
BeforeScreenTip	String	Indicates which macro, event procedure, or user-defined function runs when the BeforeScreenTip event occurs
BeforeUpdate	String	Indicates which macro, event procedure, or user-defined function runs when the BeforeUpdate event occurs
Bookmark	Variant	Used to set a bookmark that identifies a particular record in the form's underlying table'

Continues

Property	Data Type	Description
BorderStyle	Byte	Specifies the type of border and border elements for the form
Caption	String	Specifies text that appears in the Form's title bar
ChartSpace	ChartSpace object	Returns a ChartSpace object
CloseButton	Boolean	Specifies whether the Close button on a form is enabled
CommandBeforeExecute	String	Indicates which macro, event procedure, or user-defined function runs when the CommandBeforeExecute event occurs
CommandChecked	String	Indicates which macro, event procedure, or user-defined function runs when the CommndChecked event occurs
CommandEnabled	String	Indicates which macro, event procedure, or user-defined function runs when the CommandEnabled event occurs
CommandExecute	String	Indicates which macro, event procedure, or user-defined function runs when the CommandExecute event occurs
ControlBox	Boolean	Specifies whether the form has a control menu (in form and datasheet view only)
Controls	Controls collection	Returns the collection of all controls on the form
Count	Integer	Determines the number of items in a collection
CurrentRecord	Long	Used to identify the current record being viewed on a form
CurrentSectionLeft	Integer	The distance in twips from the left side of the current section to the left side of the form
CurrentSectionTop	Integer	The distance in twips from the top of the current section to the top of the form
CurrentView	Integer	Determines how a form is displayed (design view, form view, or datasheet view)
Cycle	Byte	Specifies what happens when you press the *Tab* key while the last control on the form has the focus

Continues

Property	Data Type	Description
DataChange	String	Indicates which macro, event procedure, or user-defined function runs when the DataChange event occurs
DataEntry	Boolean	Specifies whether a bound form only allows data entry (if true the form opens showing only a blank record)
DataSetChange	String	Indicates which macro, event procedure, or user-defined function runs when the DataSetChange event occurs
DataSheetBackColor	Long	Specifies the background color of a table, query, or form in datasheet view
DataSheetBorderLineStyle	Byte	Indicates the style used for the border of the datasheet
DataSheetCellsEffect	Byte	Indicates whether special effects are applied to cells in a datasheet
DatasheetColumnHeader-UnderlineStyle	Byte	Indicates the style to use for the bottom edge of the column headers on the datasheet
DatasheetFontHeight	Integer	Indicates the font point size used to display and print field names and data on the form's datasheet
DatasheetFontItalic	Boolean	Indicates whether the font used on the form's datasheet is italicized
DatasheetFontName	String	Specifies the font used in the datasheet of the form
DatasheetFontUnderline	Boolean	Indicates whether the font used on the form's datasheet is underlined
DatasheetFontWeight	Integer	Used to indicate the line width for the font used in the form's datasheet view
DatasheetForeColor	Long	Used to indicate the default font color for a form's datasheet view
DatasheetGridlinesBehavior	Byte	Used to specify which gridlines appear in a form's datasheet view
DatasheetGridlinesColor	Long	Used to determine the color of gridlines in a form's datasheet view
DefaultControl	Control object	Can be used to specify the properties of a particular type of control on a form

Continues

Property	Data Type	Description
DefaultView	Integer	Used to specify the opening view for a form
Dirty	Boolean	True if data has been entered but not saved on a form
DividingLines	Boolean	Specifies whether dividing lines separate sections on a form
FastLaserPrinting	Boolean	Specifies whether lines and rectangles are replaced by text character lines to speed printing
FetchDefaults	Boolean	Indicates whether Access shows default values for new rows on the form before the row is saved
Filter	String	Used to specify a subset of records to be displayed when a filter is applied to a form
FilterOn	Boolean	Specifies whether the Filter property of a form is applied
Form	Form object	Used to refer to the form
FrozenColumns	Integer	Determines how many columns in a datasheet are frozen
GridX	Integer	Specifies the horizontal divisions of the alignment grid in the form's design view
GridY	Integer	Specifies the vertical divisions of the alignment grid in the form's design view
HasModule	Boolean	Determines whether the form has a class module
HelpContextID	Long	Specifies the context ID of a topic in the custom help file
HelpFile	String	Returns the name of the help file associated with the form
HorizontalDatasheet-GridlineStyle	Byte	Indicates the horizontal gridline style for a form's datasheet
Hwind	Long	Used to determine the handle of the current window
InputParameters	String	Can be used to specify the input parameters passed to a SQL statement in the RecordSource property of a form
InsideHeight	Long	Height in twips of the window containing the form
InsideWidth	Long	Width in twips of the window containing the form

Continues

Property	Data Type	Description
KeyPreview	Boolean	Specifies whether the form level keyboard event procedures are invoked before a control's keyboard event procedures
LayoutForPrint	Boolean	Specifies whether the form uses printer (True) or screen (False) fonts
MaxRecButton	Boolean	Determines if the maximum record limit button is available on the navigation bar of a form
MaxRecords	Long	Specifies the maximum number of records returned
MenuBar	String	Specifies the menu bar to use for a form
MinMaxButtons	Byte	Specifies whether the Maximize and Minimize buttons are visible on the form
Modal	Boolean	Specifies whether a form opens as a modal window
Module	Module object	Used to specify a form module
MouseWheel	String	Indicates which macro, event procedure, or user-defined function runs when the MouseWheel event occurs
Movable	Boolean	True if a form can be moved by the user
Name	String	Name of the current form
NavigationButtons	Boolean	Indicates whether navigation buttons and the record number box are displayed on a form
NewRecord	Integer	Determines whether the current record is a new record
OnActivate	String	Indicates which macro, event procedure, or user-defined function runs when the OnActivate event occurs
OnApplyFilter	String	Indicates which macro, event procedure, or user-defined function runs when the OnApplyFilter event occurs
OnClick	String	Indicates which macro, event procedure, or user-defined function runs when the OnClick event occurs
OnClose	String	Indicates which macro, event procedure, or user-defined function runs when the OnClose event occurs

Continues

Property	Data Type	Description
OnConnect	String	Indicates which macro, event procedure, or user-defined function runs when the OnConnect event occurs
OnCurrent	String	Indicates which macro, event procedure, or user-defined function runs when the OnCurrent event occurs
OnDblClick	String	Indicates which macro, event procedure, or user-defined function runs when the OnDblClick event occurs
OnDeactivate	String	Indicates which macro, event procedure, or user-defined function runs when the OnDeactivate event occurs
OnDelete	String	Indicates which macro, event procedure, or user-defined function runs when the OnDelete event occurs
OnDirty	String	Indicates which macro, event procedure, or user-defined function runs when the OnDirty event occurs
OnDisconnect	String	Indicates which macro, event procedure, or user-defined function runs when the OnDisconnect event occurs
OnError	String	Indicates which macro, event procedure, or user-defined function runs when the OnError event occurs
OnFilter	String	Indicates which macro, event procedure, or user-defined function runs when the OnFilter event occurs
OnGotFocus	String	Indicates which macro, event procedure, or user-defined function runs when the OnGotFocus event occurs
OnInsert	String	Indicates which macro, event procedure, or user-defined function runs when the OnInsert event occurs
OnKeyDown	String	Indicates which macro, event procedure, or user-defined function runs when the OnKeyDown event occurs
OnKeyPress	String	Indicates which macro, event procedure, or user-defined function runs when the OnKeyPress event occurs
OnKeyUp	String	Indicates which macro, event procedure, or user-defined function runs when the OnKeyUp event occurs
OnLoad	String	Indicates which macro, event procedure, or user-defined function runs when the OnLoad event occurs
OnLostFocus	String	Indicates which macro, event procedure, or user-defined function runs when the OnLostFocus event occurs
OnMenu	String	Indicates which macro, event procedure, or user-defined function runs when the OnMenu event occurs
OnMouseDown	String	Indicates which macro, event procedure, or user-defined function runs when the OnMouseDown event occurs

Continues

Property	Data Type	Description
OnMouseMove	String	Indicates which macro, event procedure, or user-defined function runs when the OnMouseMove event occurs
OnMouseUp	String	Indicates which macro, event procedure, or user-defined function runs when the OnMouseUp event occurs
OnOpen	String	Indicates which macro, event procedure, or user-defined function runs when the OnOpen event occurs
OnResize	String	Indicates which macro, event procedure, or user-defined function runs when the OnResize event occurs
OnTimer	String	Indicates which macro, event procedure, or user-defined function runs when the OnTimer event occurs
OnUndo	String	Indicates which macro, event procedure, or user-defined function runs when the OnUndo event occurs
OnUnload	String	Indicates which macro, event procedure, or user-defined function runs when the OnUnload event occurs
OpenArgs	Variant	Determines the string expression specified by the OpenArgs method of the OpenForm method
OrderBy	String	Specifies how records on a form should be shortened
OrderByOn	Boolean	Specifies whether a form's OrderBy property is applied
Orientation	Byte	Specifies the form's orientation (left to right or right to left)
Page	Long	Specifies the current page number when a form is being printed
Pages	Integer	Returns information needed to print page numbers on a form
Painting	Boolean	Specifies whether forms are repainted
PaintPalette	Variant	Specifies the palette used by a form
PaletteSource	String	Used to specify the palette for the form
Parent	Application object	The Application object is the parent of the form

Continues

Property	Data Type	Description
Picture	String	Can be used to specify a bitmap on a form
PicturePalette	String	Contains the palette information
PictureType	Byte	Used to specify if the picture is stored as a linked (1) or embedded (0) object
PictureAlignment	Byte	Specifies where a background picture appears in an image control on a form
PictureData	Variant	Can be used to copy the picture in a form to another object
PictureSizeMode	Integer	Specifies how a picture on a form is sized
PictureTiling	Boolean	Specifies whether a background picture is tiled across the entire form
PivotTable	PivotTable object	Returns a specific PivotTable on the form
PivotTableChange	String	Indicates which macro, event procedure, or user-defined function runs when the PivotTableChange event occurs
PopUp	Boolean	Specifies whether a form opens in a pop-up window
Printer	Printer object	Represents the default printer on the current system
Properties	Properties collection	Collection of all properties of the form
PrtDevMode	Variant	Sets or returns the printing device mode information for the form in the Print dialog box
PrtDevNames	Variant	Sets or returns information about the printer selected in the Print dialog box
PrtMip	Variant	Sets or returns the printing device mode information for the form in the Print dialog
Query	String	Indicates which macro, event procedure, or user-defined function runs when the Query event occurs
RecordLocks	Integer	Determines how records are locked and what happens when two users try to edit the same record at the same time
RecordSelectors	Boolean	Determines whether a form displays record selectors in form view

Continues

Property	Data Type	Description
Recordset	Recordset object	Returns the recordset object for the form
RecordsetClone	Recordset object	Can be used to refer to a form's recordset specified by the form's RecordSource property
RecordsetType	Integer	Specifies the type of recordset is used within the form
RecordSource	String	Used to specify the source of the data for the form
RecordSourceQualifier	String	Returns or sets a string indicating the SQL Server owner name of the record source for the form
ResyncCommand	String	Used to specify the SQL statement or stored procedure used in an update snapshot of a table
RowHeight	Integer	Specifies the height of rows in a form's datasheet view
ScrollBars	Byte	Specifies whether scrollbars appear on a form
Section	Section object	Used to identify a section of a form
SelectionChange	String	Indicates which macro, event procedure, or user-defined function runs when the SelectionChange event occurs
SelHeight	Long	Specifies the number of selected rows or records in the current selection rectangle in a form's datasheet
SelLeft	Long	Specifies which column is leftmost in the current selection rectangle in the form's datasheet
SelTop	Long	Specifies which row is topmost in the current selection rectangle in the form's datasheet
SelWidth	Long	Specifies the number of selected columns in the current selection rectangle in the form's datasheet
ServerFilter	String	Used to specify a subset of records displayed when a server filter is applied
ServerFilterByForm	Boolean	Specifies whether a form is opened in the Server Filter By Form window

Continues

Property	Data Type	Description
ShortcutMenu	Boolean	Specifies whether a shortcut menu is displayed when you right-click an object on a form
ShortcutMenuBar	String	Specifies the shortcut menu that appears when you right-click a form
SubdatasheetExpanded	Boolean	Specifies the saved state of all subdatasheets within a form
SubdatasheetHeight	Integer	Determines the display height of a subdatasheet when expanded
Tag	String	Stores extra information about a form
TimerInterval	Long	Specifies the interval (in milliseconds) between Timer events on a form
Toolbar	String	Specifies the toolbar used for a form
UniqueTable	String	Identifies the "most many" table of a join of a data source of a form
UseDefaultPrinter	Boolean	Determines whether the form uses the system's default printer
VerticalDatasheet-GridlineStyle	Byte	Specifies the line style to use for vertical gridlines within the form's datasheet
ViewChange	String	Indicates which macro, event procedure, or user-defined function runs when the ViewChange event occurs
ViewsAllowed	Byte	Specifies whether users can switch between form and datasheet views
Visible	Boolean	True when the form isn't minimized
WhatsThisButton	Boolean	Specifies whether a What's This button is displayed on a toolbar
Width	Integer	Width of the form in twips
WindowHeight	Integer	Specifies the height of a form in twips
WindowLeft	Integer	Indicates the screen position in twips of the left edge of the form relative to the left edge of the Access window
WindowTop	Integer	Specifies the screen position in twips of the top edge of the form relative to the top edge of the Access window
WindowWidth	Integer	Sets the width of the form in twips

Methods of the Form Object

The Form object also has a number of methods you can use within your code. Those methods are listed in the following table.

Method	Arguments	Description
GoToPage	PageNumber, Right, Down	Moves the focus to the first control on a specified page in the current form
Move	Left, Top, Width, Height	Moves the form to the specified coordinates
Recalc	None	Immediately updates the calculated controls on a form
Refresh	None	Immediately updates the records in the underlying record source for a form
Repaint	None	Completes any pending screen updates for the current form
Requery	None	Updates the data in the form from the underlying recordset
SetFocus	None	Sets the focus to the current form
Undo	None	Used to reset the value of a form when it has been changed

Events of the Form Object

There are a large number of events you'll use within your code behind forms. You probably will only use a handful of these events, but they are all available for you when writing code. A Form's events are summarized in the following table.

Event	Description
Activate	Occurs when the form receives focus and becomes the active window
AfterDelConfirm	Occurs after the user confirms the delete and the records are actually deleted
AfterFinalRender	Occurs after all elements in the PivotChart have been rendered
AfterInsert	Occurs after a new record is added
AfterLayout	Occurs after all charts in the PivotChart have been laid out but before they have been rendered
AfterRender	Occurs after an object represented by the ChartObject has been rendered
AfterUpdate	Occurs after changed data in a control or record is updated

Continues

Event	Description
ApplyFilter	Occurs when a filter is applied to a form
BeforeDelConfirm	Occurs after the user deletes records but before the delete confirmation dialog is displayed
BeforeInsert	Occurs when the user types the first character in a new record
BeforeQuery	Occurs when the specified PivotTable queries its data source
BeforeRender	Occurs before any object in the specified PivotChart has been rendered
BeforeScreenTip	Occurs before a screen tip is displayed for an element in a PivotChart or PivotTable view
BeforeUpdate	Occurs before changed data in a control is updated
Click	Occurs when a user presses and releases the mouse button over an object
Close	Occurs when a form is closed and removed from the screen
CommandBeforeExecute	Occurs before a specified command is executed
CommandChecked	Occurs when the specified Microsoft Office Web Component determines whether the specified command is checked
CommandEnabled	Occurs when the specified Microsoft Office Web Component determines whether the specified command is enabled
CommandExecute	Occurs after the specified command is executed
Current	Occurs when the focus moves to a record or when the form is refreshed or requeried
DataChange	Occurs when certain properties are changed or when certain methods are executed
DataSetChange	Occurs whenever the specified PivotTable view is data-bound and the dataset changes
DblClick	Occurs when a user presses and releases the mouse button twice in rapid succession over an object
Deactivate	Occurs when a form loses focus to another object
Delete	Occurs when the user presses the *Delete* key, but before the record is actually deleted
Dirty	Occurs when data has changed on the form, but the current record hasn't been saved
Error	Occurs when a runtime error occurs when the form has the focus

Continues

Event	Description
Filter	Occurs when a user chooses the `Filter By Form` option from the `Filter` menu or clicks the `Filter By Form` button on the toolbar
GotFocus	Occurs when the form receives the focus
KeyDown	Occurs when a key is depressed
KeyPress	Occurs when a key is pressed and released
KeyUp	Occurs when a key is released
Load	Occurs when a form is opened and records are displayed
LostFocus	Occurs when the form loses focus to another object
MouseDown	Occurs when the mouse button is depressed
MouseMove	Occurs when the user moves the mouse
MouseUp	Occurs when the mouse button is released
MouseWheel	Occurs when the mouse wheel is moved
OnConnect	Occurs when the `PivotTable` view connects to a data source
OnDisconnect	Occurs when a `PivotTable` view disconnects from a data source
Open	Occurs when a form is opened but before the first record is displayed
PivotTableChange	Occurs whenever the specified `PivotTable` view field, field set, or total is added or deleted
Query	Occurs whenever the specified `PivotTable` view query becomes necessary
Resize	Occurs when a form opens and any time it is resized
SelectionChange	Occurs whenever a user makes a new selection in a `PivotChart` or `PivotTable` view
Timer	Occurs at regular intervals controlled by the form's `TimerInterval` property
Undo	Occurs when the user undoes a change to a control on a form
Unload	Occurs after a form is closed but before it's removed from the screen
ViewChange	Occurs whenever the specified `PivotChart` view or `PivotTable` view is redrawn

The Control Object

Within a form, you can have a variety of different controls. You use the controls to display data from tables, queries, and other data sources such as ADO recordsets.

Control Properties

The Control object has a variety of properties found in the following table.

Property	Data Type	Description
Application	Application object	Returns the currently active Application object
Column	Variant	Used to refer to a specific column in a combo box or list box
Controls	Controls collection	Used to refer to the collection of all the controls on the form
Form	Form object	Refers to the current form object
Hyperlink	Hyperlink object	Used to access the properties and methods of a hyperlink object associated with a control
ItemData	Variant	Returns the data in the bound column for the specified row in a combo box or list box
ItemsSelected	ItemsSelected collection	Returns a reference to the ItemsSelected collection
Object	ActiveX object	Returns a reference to the ActiveX object associated with a linked or embedded OLE object in a control
ObjectVerbs	String	Used to determine the list of verbs an OLE object supports
OldValue	Variant	Used to determine the unedited value of a bound control
Pages	Integer	Returns the number of pages in a control that supports tabbed pages
Parent	Various	For controls, usually a form object
Properties	Properties collection	Returns a reference to the entire collection of properties for the object
Report	Report object	Refers to a report or the report associated with a subreport control
Selected	Long	Determines if an item in a list box is selected
SmartTags	SmartTags collection	Returns the collection of SmartTags that have been added to a control

Control Methods

The methods you can use with a control object are found in the following table. For all of the following methods, the specified object is the control whose method is being called.

Method	Arguments	Description
Dropdown	None	Forces the list in the specified combo box to drop down
Move	Left, Top, Width, Height	Moves the specified object to the coordinates specified
Requery	None	Updates the data behind a control by requerying the source data for the control
SetFocus	None	Moves the focus to the specified control
SizeToFit	None	Sizes the control to fit the text or image it contains
Undo	None	Resets a control whose value has been changed

The Module Object

The Module object refers to either a standard module or a class module within your database.

Module Properties

The properties of the Module object are listed in the following table.

Property	Data Type	Description
Application	Application object	Returns the currently active Application object
CountOfDeclaration-Lines	Long	Count of the number of lines in the General Declarations section of a standard or class module
CountOfLines	Long	Count of lines of code in a standard or class module
Lines	String	Contains the contents of a specified line or lines in a standard or class module
Name	String	Returns the name of the standard or class module
Parent	Various	Usually the Application object
ProcBodyLine	Long	Contains the number of the line at which the body of the specified procedure begins
ProcCountLines	Long	Contains the number of lines in a specified procedure of a standard of class module
ProcOfLine	String	Contains the name of the procedure that contains the specified line in a standard or class module

Continues

Property	Data Type	Description
ProcStartLine	Long	Identifies the line at which a specified procedure begins in a standard or class module
Type	acModuleType (acClassModule, acStandardModule)	Indicates whether a module is a standard or a class module

Module Methods

The methods for the Module object are listed in the following table.

Method	Arguments	Description
AddFromFile	FileName	Adds the contents of the text file to a module
AddFromString	String	Adds the contents of the string to a module
CreateEventProc	EventName, ObjectName	Creates an event procedure in a class module
DeleteLines	StartLine, Count	Deletes lines from a module
Find	Target, StartLine, StartColumn, EndLine, EndColumn, WholeWord, MatchCase, PatternSearch	Finds the specified text in a class module
InsertLines	Line, String	Inserts a line or group of lines of code in a module
InsertText	Text	Inserts a string of text into a module
ReplaceLine	Line, String	Replaces the specified line with a string value

The Section Object

Every form has several sections including the header, footer, and detail sections. Each section has a number of properties and methods you can use within your code.

Properties of the Section Object

The properties of the Section object are listed in the following table.

Property	Data Type	Description
Application	Application object	Returns the currently active application
BackColor	Long	Specifies the color for the interior of a section
CanGrow	Boolean	True if you want the section to automatically grow to print or preview all data within the section
CanShrink	Boolean	True if you want the section to automatically shrink to print or preview only the data within the section (with no extra space)
Controls	Controls collection	References all of the controls within the section
DisplayWhen	Byte	Controls which sections you want displayed on screen and in print
EventProcPrefix	String	Used to get the prefix portion of an event procedure name
ForceNewPage	Byte	Specifies when sections print on a separate page
HasContinued	Boolean	Determines if part of the current section begins on the previous page
Height	Integer	Height (in twips) of the current section
InSelection	Boolean	Determines if a control on a form is selected
KeepTogether	Boolean	True if the entire section should print on one page
Name	String	Name of the current section
NewRowOrCol	Byte	Specifies whether a section is printed within a new row or column within a multicolumn report or form
OnClick	String	Sets or returns the value of the OnClick box in the Properties window
OnDblClick	String	Sets or returns the value of the OnDblClick box in the Properties window
OnFormat	String	Sets or returns the value of the OnFormat box in the Properties window
OnMouseDown	String	Sets or returns the value of the OnMouseDown box in the Properties window
OnMouseMove	String	Sets or returns the value of the OnMouseMove box in the Properties window
OnMouseUp	String	Sets or returns the value of the OnMouseUp box in the Properties window

Continues

Property	Data Type	Description
OnPrint	String	Sets or returns the value of the OnPrint box in the Properties window
OnRetreat	String	Sets or returns the value of the OnRetreat box in the Properties window
Parent	Various	Refers to the parent of the section (usually either a form, report, or data access page)
Properties	Properties collection	Refers to the entire collection of properties for the section
RepeatSection	Boolean	Specifies whether the group header is repeated on the next page of column (when the group spans more than one page or column)
SpecialEffect	Byte	Specifies whether any special formatting applies to a section (such as shadow, sunken lines, or highlight)
Tag	String	Stores extra information about a section
Visible	Boolean	Specifies whether a section is visible on a form or report
WillContinue	Boolean	Specifies if the current section continues on the next page

Events of the Section Object

There are five events you can use in your code for the Section object. Those events are listed in the following table.

Event	Description
Click	Occurs when the user presses and releases the mouse button
DblClick	Occurs when the user presses and releases the mouse button twice in rapid succession
MouseDown	Occurs when the user depresses the mouse button
MouseMove	Occurs when the user moves the mouse
MouseUp	Occurs when the user releases the mouse button

The Printer Object

Access VBA allows you to manipulate the printers available on your system through code. All available printers are members of the Printers collection. You can access an individual printer through the Printer object.

Printer Object Properties

The properties of the `Printer` object are listed in the following table.

Properties	Data Type	Description
BottomMargin	Long	Specifies the bottom margin for the printed page
ColorMode	acPrintColor (acPRCMColor, acPRCMMonochrome)	Specifies whether the printer should output in color or monochrome mode
ColumnSpacing	Long	Specifies the vertical space between detail sections (in twips)
Copies	Long	Indicates the number of copies to be printed
Dataonly	Boolean	True if Access only prints the data and not the labels, borders, gridlines, and graphics
DefaultSize	Boolean	True when the size of the detail section in design view is used for printing. False if the `ItemSizeHeight` and `ItemSizeWidth` properties are used
DeviceName	String	Name of the printer
DriverName	String	Name of the driver used by the specified printer
Duplex	acPrintDuplex (acPRDPHorizontal, acPRDPSimplex, acPRDPVertical)	Specifies how the printer handles duplex printing
ItemLayout	acPrintItemLayout (acPRHorizontalColumnLayout, acPRVerticalColumnLayout)	Specifies whether the printer lays out columns across, then down, or down, then across
ItemsAcross	Long	Indicates the number of columns to print across a page
ItemSizeHeight	Long	Specifies the height of the detail section in twips
ItemSizeWidth	Long	Specifies the width of the detail section in twips
LeftMargin	Long	Specifies the left margin for the printed page

Continues

Properties	Data Type	Description
Orientation	acPrintOrientation (acPRORLandscape, acPRORPortrait)	Specifies the print orientation
PaperBin	acPrinterBin (acPRBNAuto, acPRBNCassette, acPRBNEnvelope, acPRBNEnvManual, acPRBNFormSource, acPRBNLargeCapacity, acPRBNLargeFmt, acPRBNLower, acPRBNManual, acPRBNMiddle, acPRBNSmallFmt, acPRBNTractor, acPRBNUpper	Specifies which paper bin the printer should use
PaperSize	acPrintPaperSize (various)	Specifies the paper size to use when printing
Port	String	Specifies the port name for the specified printer
PrintQuality	acPrintObjQuality (acPRPQDraft, acPRPQHigh, acPRPQLow, acPRPQMedium)	Specifies the resolution the printer uses to print jobs
RightMargin	Long	Specifies the right margin for the printed page
RowSpacing	Long	Specifies the horizontal space between detail sections (in twips)
TopMargin	Long	Specifies the top margin for the printed page

The References Collection and Reference Object

When programming in Access you can use not only the various Access objects detailed in this appendix, but also objects from other applications, such as Excel, Word, Outlook, or non-Microsoft programs like AutoCad and Peachtree Accounting. In order to use these other object models, you need to set a reference to their type libraries. The References collection contains a reference for every external type library you add to the References dialog box within your code.

Reference Object Properties

The properties of the Reference object are listed in the following table.

Property	Data Type	Description
BuiltIn	Boolean	Specifies whether a reference points to a default Reference necessary for Access to function properly
Collection	References object	Returns a reference to the collection that contains an object
FullPath	String	Specifies the path and file name of the referenced type library
Guid	String	Returns a GUID that identifies the type library in the registry
IsBroken	Boolean	Specifies whether a Reference object points to a valid reference in the registry
Kind	Vbext_RefKind (vbext_rk_Project, vbext_rk_TypeLib)	Specifies the type of reference that a Reference object represents
Major	Long	Specifies the major version number of an application you're referencing
Minor	Long	Specifies the minor version of the application you're referencing
Name	String	The name of the Reference object

The Reports Collection and Report Object

Microsoft Access contains a Reports collection that contains a Report object for every report within your database.

Properties of the Report Object

The properties of the Report object are listed in the following table.

Property	Data Type	Description
ActiveControl	Control object	Used with the Screen object to determine the control that has the focus
Application	Application object	Returns the currently active application object
AutoCenter	Boolean	Determines whether the report will be automatically centered within the Application window

Continues

Property	Data Type	Description
AutoResize	Boolean	Determines whether the report will be automatically resized to display complete records
BorderStyle	Byte	Specifies the type of border and border elements for the report
Caption	String	Specifies the caption in the title bar for the report
CloseButton	Boolean	Specifies whether the Close button on a report is enabled
ControlBox	Boolean	Specifies whether the form has a control menu (in form and datasheet view only)
Controls	Controls collection	Specifies the collection of all controls on the report
Count	Integer	Specifies the number of items within the Reports collection
CurrentRecord	Long	Used to identify the current record being viewed on a report
CurrentX	Single	Used to specify the horizontal coordinates for the starting position of the next printing and drawing method on a report
CurrentY	Single	Used to specify the vertical coordinates for the starting position of the next printing and drawing method on a report
DateGrouping	Byte	Specifies how you want to group dates on a report
DefaultControl	Control object	Can be used to specify the properties of a particular type of control on a report
Dirty	Boolean	True if data has been entered but not saved on a form
DrawMode	Integer	Specifies how the pen interacts with existing background colors on a report when the Line, Circle, or Pset method is used when printing
DrawStyle	Integer	Specifies the line style when using the Line and Circle methods to print lines on reports
DrawWidth	Integer	Specifies the line width for the Line, Circle, and Pset methods to print lines on reports

Continues

Property	Data Type	Description
FastLaserPrinting	Boolean	Specifies whether lines and rectangles are replaced by text character lines to speed printing
FillColor	Long	Specifies the color that fills in boxes and circles drawn on reports with the Line and Circle methods
FillStyle	Integer	Specifies whether circles and lines are transparent, opaque, or filled with a pattern
Filter	String	Used to specify a subset of records to be displayed when a filter is applied to a report
FilterOn	Boolean	Specifies whether the Filter property of a report is applied
FontBold	Boolean	Specifies whether a font appears in bold on a form or report
FontItalic	Boolean	Specifies whether a font appears in italics on a form or report
FontName	String	Specifies the font for printing controls on reports
FontSize	Integer	Specifies the font size for printing controls on reports
FontUnderline	Boolean	Specifies whether a font appears underlined on a form or report
ForeColor	Long	Specifies the color for text in a control
FormatCount	Integer	Specifies the number of times the OnFormat property has been evaluated for the current section on a report
GridX	Integer	Specifies the horizontal divisions of the alignment grid in report design view
GridY	Integer	Specifies the vertical divisions of the alignment grid in report design view
GroupLevel	GroupLevel object	Refers to a particular group level you're grouping or sorting in a report
GrpKeepTogether	Byte	Specifies whether groups in a multiple column report that have the KeepTogether property set to Whole Group or With First Detail will be kept together by page or by column
HasData	Long	Specifies if a report is bound to an empty recordset

Continues

Property	Data Type	Description
HasModule	Boolean	Specifies whether a report has a class module associated with it
Height	Integer	Specifies the height of the report in twips
HelpContextID	Long	Specifies the context ID of a topic in the custom help file
HelpFile	String	Returns the name of the help file associated with the report
Hwind	Long	Used to determine the handle of the current window
InputParameters	String	Can be used to specify the input parameters passed to a SQL statement in the RecordSource property of a report
LayoutForPrint	Boolean	Specifies whether the report uses printer (True) or screen (False) fonts
Left	Integer	Specifies the object's location on a report
MenuBar	String	Specifies the menu bar to use for a report
MinMaxButtons	Byte	Specifies whether the Maximize and Minimize buttons are visible on the report
Modal	Boolean	Specifies whether a report opens as a modal window
Module	Module object	Used to specify a module for the report
Moveable	Boolean	True if a report can be moved by the user
MoveLayout	Boolean	Specifies if Access should move to the next printing location on the page
Name	String	Specifies the name of the report
NextRecord	Boolean	Specifies whether a section should advance to the next record
ObjectPalette	String	String property containing the palette information
OnActivate	String	Indicates which macro, event procedure, or user-defined function runs when the OnActivate event occurs
OnClose	String	Indicates which macro, event procedure, or user-defined function runs when the OnClose event occurs
OnDeactivate	String	Indicates which macro, event procedure, or user-defined function runs when the OnDeactivate event occurs

Continues

Property	Data Type	Description
OnError	String	Indicates which macro, event procedure, or user-defined function runs when the OnError event occurs
OnMenu	String	Indicates which macro, event procedure, or user defined function runs when the OnMenu event occurs
OnNoData	String	Indicates which macro, event procedure, or user-defined function runs when the OnNoData event occurs
OnOpen	String	Indicates which macro, event procedure, or user-defined function runs when the OnOpen event occurs
OnPage	String	Indicates which macro, event procedure, or user-defined function runs when the OnPage event occurs
OpenArgs	Variant	Determines the string expression specified by the OpenArgs method of the OpenReport method
OrderBy	String	Specifies how records on a report should be shortened
OrderByOn	Boolean	Specifies whether the OrderBy property is applied.
Orientation	Byte	Specifies the report's orientation (left to right or right to left)
Page	Long	Specifies the current page number when a report is printed
PageFooter	Byte	Specifies whether a report's page footer is printed on the same page as the report footer
PageHeader	Byte	Specifies whether a report's page header is printed on the same page as the report header
Pages	Integer	Returns information needed to print page numbers on a report
Painting	Boolean	Specifies whether reports are repainted
PaintPalette	Variant	Specifies the palette used by a report
PaletteSource	String	Used to specify the palette for the report
Parent	Application object	The Application object is the parent of the report

Continues

Property	Data Type	Description
Picture	String	Can be used to specify a bitmap on a report
PictureAlighment	Byte	Specifies where a background picture appears in an image control on a report
PictureData	Variant	Can be used to copy the picture in a report to another object
PicturePages	Byte	Specifies on which page or pages of a report a picture is displayed
PicturePalette	String	Contains information about the palette for the object
PictureSizeMode	Integer	Specifies how a picture on a report is sized
PictureTiling	Boolean	Specifies whether a background picture is tiled across the entire report
PictureType	Byte	Specifies whether Access stores a report's picture as a linked or embedded object
PopUp	Boolean	Specifies whether a report opens in a pop-up window
PrintCount	Integer	Specifies the number of times the OnPrint property has been evaluated for the current section of the report
Printer	Printer object	Represents the default printer on the current system
PrintSection	Boolean	Specifies whether a section of a report should be printed
Properties	Properties collection	Represents the collection of all properties for the report
PrtDevMode	Variant	Sets or returns the printing device mode information for the report in the Print dialog
PrtDevNames	Variant	Sets or returns information about the printer selected in the Print dialog
PrtMip	Variant	Sets or returns the printing device mode information for the report in the Print dialog
RecordLocks	Integer	Determines how records are locked and what happens when two users try to edit the same record at the same time
Recordset	Recordset object	Returns the Recordset object for the report

Continues

Property	Data Type	Description
RecordSource	String	Used to specify the source of the data for the report
RecordSourceQualifier	String	Returns or sets a string indicating the SQL Server owner name of the record source for the report
Report	Report object	Used to refer to the report associated with a subreport
ScaleHeight	Single	Specifies the number of units for the vertical measurement of the page when the Circle, Line, Pset, or Print methods are used when a report is printed
ScaleLeft	Single	Specifies the units for the horizontal coordinates that reference the location of the left edge of the page when the Circle, Line, Pset, or Print methods are used when a report is printed
ScaleMode	Integer	Specifies the unit of measurement for coordinates on a page when the Circle, Line, Pset, or Print methods are used when a report is printed
ScaleTop	Single	Specifies the units for the vertical coordinates that reference the location of the top edge of a page when the Circle, Line, Pset, or Print methods are used on a report
ScaleWidth	Single	Specifies the number of units for the horizontal measurement of the page when the Circle, Line, Pset, or Print methods are used when a report is printed
Section	Section object	Used to identify a section of a report
ServerFilter	String	Used to specify a subset of records displayed when a server filter is applied
Shape	String	Specifies the shape command corresponding to the sorting and grouping of the report
ShortcutMenuBar	String	Specifies the shortcut menu that appears when you right-click a report
Tag	String	Stores extra information about a report
Toolbar	String	Specifies the toolbar used for a report
Top	Long	Specifies the report's top coordinates

Continues

Property	Data Type	Description
UseDefaultPrinter	Boolean	Determines whether the report uses the system's default printer
Visible	Boolean	True when the report isn't minimized
Width	Integer	Width of the report in twips
WindowHeight	Integer	Specifies the height of a report in twips
WindowLeft	Integer	Indicates the screen position in twips of the left edge of the report relative to the left edge of the Access window
WindowTop	Integer	Specifies the screen position in twips of the top edge of the report relative to the top edge of the Access window
WindowWidth	Integer	Sets the width of the report in twips

Methods of the Report Object

The methods of the Report object are listed in the following table.

Method	Arguments	Description
Circle	Flags, X, Y, radius, color, start, end, aspect	Draws a circle, ellipse, or an arc on a report when the print event occurs
Line	Flags, x1, y1, x2, y2, color	Draws lines and rectangles on a report when the print event occurs
Move	Left, top, width, height	Moves the report to the specified coordinates on the screen
Print	Expr	Prints text on a report object using the current color and font
PSet	Flags, X, Y, color	Sets a point on a report object to the specified color when the Print event occurs
Scale	Flags, x1, y1, x2, y2	Defines the coordinate system for a report object
TextHeight	Expr	Returns the height of a text string as it would be printed in the current font of a report
TextWidth	Expr	Returns the height of a text string as it would be printed in the current font of a report

Events of the Report Object

The events of the `Report` object are listed in the following table.

Event	Description
Activate	Occurs when a report receives the focus and becomes the active window
Close	Occurs when a report is closed but before it is removed from the screen
Deactivate	Occurs when a report loses focus to another object
Error	Occurs when a runtime error occurs when the report has the focus
NoData	Occurs after a report with no data is formatted for printing but before the report is printed
Open	Occurs when a report is opened but before it is displayed on the screen
Page	Occurs after a page is formatted for printing but before the page is printed

The Screen Object

The `Screen` object refers to whatever form, report, or control currently has the focus within the application. You can use the `Screen` object and its properties to manipulate the active window no matter which form, report, or control is currently displayed.

Properties of the Screen Object

The properties of the `Screen` object are listed in the following table.

Property	Data Type	Description
ActiveControl	Control object	Specifies the control that has the focus
ActiveDataAccessPage	DataAccessPage object	Specifies the data access page that has the focus
ActiveDatasheet	Datasheet object	Specifies the datasheet that has the focus
ActiveForm	Form object	Specifies the form that has the focus
ActiveReport	Report object	Specifies the report that has the focus
Application	Application objecr	References the current Access application
MousePointer	Integer	Specifies the type of mouse pointer currently displayed

Continues

Property	Data Type	Description
Parent	Object	Parent of the object that currently has the focus
PreviousControl	Control object	Specifies the control that previously had the focus

The SmartTag Object

All of Microsoft Office 2003 has the capability to use SmartTags. You can programmatically manipulate the SmartTag object by accessing its properties and methods.

Properties of the SmartTag Object

The properties of the SmartTag object are listed in the following table.

Property	Data Type	Description
Application	Application object	Represents the currently active Access application
IsMissing	Boolean	Returns true if the SmartTag isn't installed or isn't correctly installed
Name	String	Returns the name of the SmartTag
Parent	Object	Refers to the parent object of the SmartTag
Properties	SmartTagProperties collection	Returns the collection of all properties for a particular SmartTag
SmartTagActions	SmartTagActions collection	Returns the collection of all actions available for a specific SmartTag
XML	String	Represents the XML code for a SmartTag

The SmartTag object has only one method, the Delete method.

The SmartTagActions collection and the SmartTagProperties collection have the standard properties associated with any collection (Application, Count, Item, and Parent). The individual SmartTagAction object has one method you can utilize within your code, the Execute method. This method performs the specified SmartTag action. The SmartTagProperty object only has one method, the Delete method.

The SubForm Object

When designing Access forms, you can embed a subform within your main form. That subform has some of the same properties as any other Access form object. However, there are some differing properties as well. Rather than force you to return to the Form properties table and determine which of the properties also apply to subforms, all properties for a subform object are listed in the following table.

Properties of the SubForm Object

Property	Data Type	Description
AddColon	Boolean	Specifies whether a colon follows the text in labels for new controls
Application	Application object	Returns the currently active application object
AutoLabel	Boolean	Specifies whether labels are automatically created and attached to new controls
BorderColor	Long	Specifies the color of a control's border
BorderStyle	Byte	Specifies the type of border and border elements for the form
BorderWidth	Byte	Specifies the width of a control's border
CanGrow	Boolean	Specifies whether the subform can grow to accommodate all the data
CanShrink	Boolean	Specifies if the subform can shrink to avoid empty space with no data
Controls	Controls collection	Returns the collection of all controls on the subform
ControlType	Byte	Specifies the type of control on a subform
DisplayWhen	Byte	Specifies which of a subform's sections or controls you want displayed on the screen or in print
Enabled	Boolean	Returns the status of the conditional format in the FormatCondition object
EventProcPrefix	String	Specifies the prefix portion of an event procedure name
Form	Form object	Returns the form associated with the current subform
Height	Integer	Specifies the height of the subform in twips
InSelection	Boolean	Specifies whether a control on a subform in design mode is selected
IsVisible	Boolean	Specifies whether a control on a subform is visible
LabelAlign	Byte	Specifies text alignment within labels on new controls
LabelX	Integer	Specifies the placement of the label for a new control

Continues

Property	Data Type	Description
LabelY	Integer	Specifies the placement of the label for a new control
Left	Long	Specifies the subform's location on a form
LinkChildFields	String	Specifies field on subform that links the subform with the master form
LinkMasterFields	String	Specifies field on master form that links the subform with the master form
Locked	Boolean	Specifies whether you can enter data in a subform
Name	String	Specifies the name of the subform
OldBorderStyle	Byte	Specifies the unedited value of the BorderStyle property for a subform
OnEnter	String	Indicates which macro, event procedure, or user-defined function runs when the OnEnter event occurs
OnExit	String	Indicates which macro, event procedure, or user-defined function runs when the OnExit event occurs
Parent	Form object	The parent of a subform is the master form
Properties	Properties collection	Represents the entire properties collection for the subform
Report	Report object	Refers to the report associated with a subreport control
Section	Section object	Identifies a section on a subform
SourceObject	String	Specifies the form that is the source of the subform
SpecialEffect	Byte	Specifies whether special formatting applies to a subform
StatusBarText	String	Specifies the text displayed in the status bar when a subform is selected
TabIndex	Integer	Specifies a subform's place in the tab order on a form
TabStop	Boolean	Specifies whether you can use the *Tab* key to set the focus to a subform
Tag	String	Stores extra information about the subform
Top	Long	Specifies the subform's location within a form
Visible	Boolean	True if the subform is displayed on the screen
Width	Integer	Specifies the width of the subform in twips

Methods of the SubForm Object

A subform also has its own methods and events. These are detailed in the following tables.

Method	Arguments	Description
Move	Left, Top, Width, Height	Moves the subform to the coordinates specified
Requery	None	Updates the controls on the subform by requerying the data source
SetFocus	None	Moves the focus to the subform
SizeToFit	None	Sizes the subform to fit the data it contains

Events of the SubForm Object

Event	Description
Enter	Occurs immediately before the subform receives the focus
Exit	Occurs immediately before the subform loses the focus to another control or subform

The SubReport Object

Much like forms and subforms, reports can also contain subreports. There are no methods for the SubReport object. The events for the SubReport object are the same as the events for the SubForm object.

Properties of the SubReport Object

The SubReport object contains only four properties. These are listed in the following table.

Property	Data Type	Description
Application	Application object	Returns the currently active application object
Form	Form object	Refers to the form associated with a subreport object
Parent	Various	Refers to the parent of the selected subform
Report	Report object	Refers to the report associated with a subreport control

Other Helpful Information

We've provided you with a lot of information about the Access object model in this appendix. In addition to the basic objects you'll manipulate on a daily basis, you'll need to know some of the myriad of arguments you can use with some of these objects. The following tables detail some of the arguments for a few selected objects and methods.

Application.SetOption Method

The `SetOption` method of the `Application` object allows you to control all of the options you can see by selecting `Tools | Options` from the main Access window. The following tables detail the string arguments for the options available on each tab. For example, to control the visibility of the Status Bar within your Access application, you'd use the following code.

```
Application.SetOption "Show Status Bar", True
```

The arguments you'll need to manipulate the `SetOption` method are broken down by the tab of the `Options` dialog box on which they appear.

View Tab

Option text	String argument
Show, Status bar	Show Status Bar
Show, Startup Task Pane	Show Startup Dialog Box
Show, New object shortcuts	Show New Object Shortcuts
Show, Hidden objects	Show Hidden Objects
Show, System objects	Show System Objects
Show, Windows in Taskbar	ShowWindowsInTaskbar
Show in Macro Design, Names column	Show Macro Names Column
Show in Macro Design, Conditions column	Show Conditions Column
Click options in database window	Database Explorer Click Behavior

General Tab

Option text	String argument
Print margins, Left margin	Left Margin
Print margins, Right margin	Right Margin
Print margins, Top margin	Top Margin

Continues

Option text	String argument
Print margins, Bottom margin	Bottom Margin
Use four-year digit year formatting, This database	Four-Digit Year Formatting
Use four-year digit year formatting, All databases	Four-Digit Year Formatting All Databases
Name AutoCorrect, Track name AutoCorrect info	Track Name AutoCorrect Info
Name AutoCorrect, Perform name AutoCorrect	Perform Name AutoCorrect
Name AutoCorrect, Log name AutoCorrect changes	Log Name AutoCorrect Changes
Recently used file list	Enable MRU File List
Recently used file list, (number of files)	Size of MRU File List
Provide feedback with sound	Provide Feedback with Sound
Compact on Close	Auto Compact
New database sort order	New Database Sort Order
Remove personal information from file properties on save	Remove Personal Information
Default database folder	Default Database Directory

Edit/Find Tab

Option text	String argument
Default find/replace behavior	Default Find/Replace Behavior
Confirm, Record changes	Confirm Record Changes
Confirm, Document deletions	Confirm Document Deletions
Confirm, Action queries	Confirm Action Queries
Show list of values in, Local indexed fields	Show Values in Indexed
Show list of values in, Local nonindexed fields	Show Values in Nonindexed

Continues

Option text	String argument
Show list of values in, ODBC fields	Show Values in Remote
Show list of values in, Records in local snapshot	Show Values in Snapshot
Show list of values in, Records at server	Show Values in Server
Don't display lists where more than this number of records read	Show Values in Limit

Datasheet Tab

Option text	String argument
Default colors, Font	Default Font Color
Default colors, Background	Default Background Color
Default colors, Gridlines	Default Gridlines Color
Default gridlines showing, Horizontal	Default Gridlines Horizontal
Default gridlines showing, Vertical	Default Gridlines Vertical
Default column width	Default Column Width
Default font, Font	Default Font Name
Default font, Weight	Default Font Weight
Default font, Size	Default Font Size
Default font, Underline	Default Font Underline
Default font, Italic	Default Font Italic
Default cell effect	Default Cell Effect
Show animations	Show Animations
Show SmartTags on Datasheets	Show SmartTags on Datasheets

Keyboard Tab

Option text	String argument
Move after enter	Move After Enter
Behavior entering field	Behavior Entering Field

Continues

Option text	String argument
Arrow key behavior	Arrow Key Behavior
Cursor stops at first/last field	Cursor Stops at First/Last Field
Auto commit	Ime Autocommit
Datasheet IME control	Datasheet Ime Control

Tables/Queries Tab

Option text	String argument
Table design, Default field sizes - Text	Default Text Field Size
Table design, Default field sizes - Number	Default Number Field Size
Table design, Default field type	Default Field Type
Table design, AutoIndex on Import/Create	AutoIndex on Import/Create
Query design, Show table names	Show Table Names
Query design, Output all fields	Output All Fields
Query design, Enable AutoJoin	Enable AutoJoin
Query design, Run permissions	Run Permissions
Query design, SQL Server Compatible Syntax (ANSI 92) - This database	ANSI Query Mode
Query design, SQL Server Compatible Syntax (ANSI 92) - Default for new databases	ANSI Query Mode Default
Query design, Query design font, Font	Query Design Font Name
Query design, Query design font, Size	Query Design Font Size
Show Property Update Options buttons	Show Property Update Options buttons

Forms/Reports Tab

Option text	String argument
Selection behavior	Selection Behavior
Form template	Form Template

Continues

Option text	String argument
Report template	Report Template
Always use event procedures	Always Use Event Procedures
Show SmartTags on Forms	Show SmartTags on Forms
Show Windows Themed Controls on Forms	Themed Form Controls

Advanced Tab

Option text	String argument
DDE operations, Ignore DDE requests	Ignore DDE Requests
DDE operations, Enable DDE refresh	Enable DDE Refresh
Default File Format	Default File Format
Default open mode	Default Open Mode for Databases
Command-line arguments	Command-Line Arguments
OLE/DDE timeout (sec)	OLE/DDE Timeout (sec)
Default record locking	Default Record Locking
Refresh interval (sec)	Refresh Interval (sec)
Number of update retries	Number of Update Retries
ODBC refresh interval (sec)	ODBC Refresh Interval (sec)
Update retry interval (msec)	Update Retry Interval (msec)
Open databases using record-level locking	Use Row Level Locking

Pages Tab

Option text	String argument
Default Designer Properties, Section Indent	Section Indent
Default Designer Properties, Alternate Row Color	Alternate Row Color
Default Designer Properties, Caption Section Style	Caption Section Style

Continues

Option text	String argument
Default Designer Properties, Footer Section Style	Footer Section Style
Default Database/Project Properties, Use Default Page Folder	Use Default Page Folder
Default Database/Project Properties, Default Page Folder	Default Page Folder
Default Database/Project Properties, Use Default Connection File	Use Default Connection File
Default Database/Project Properties, Default Connection File	Default Connection File

Spelling Tab

Option text	String argument
Dictionary Language	Spelling dictionary language
Add words to	Spelling add words to
Suggest from main dictionary only	Spelling suggest from main dictionary only
Ignore words in UPPERCASE	Spelling ignore words in UPPERCASE
Ignore words with numbers	Spelling ignore words with number
Ignore Internet and file addresses	Spelling ignore Internet and file addresses
Language-specific, German: Use post-reform rules	Spelling use German post-reform rules
Language-specific, Korean: Combine aux verb/adj	Spelling combine aux verb/adj
Language-specific, Korean: Search misused word list	Spelling use auto-change list
Language-specific, Korean: Process compound nouns	Spelling process compound nouns
Language-specific, Hebrew modes	Spelling Hebrew modes
Language-specific, Arabic modes	Spelling Arabic modes

International Tab

Option text	String argument
Right-to-Left, Default direction	Default direction
Right-to-Left, General alignment	General alignment
Right-to-Left, Cursor movement	Cursor movement
Use Hijri Calendar	Use Hijri Calendar

Error Checking Tab

Option text	String argument
Settings, Enable error checking	Enable Error Checking
Settings, Error indicator color	Error Checking Indicator Color
Form/Report Design Rules, Unassociated label and control	Unassociated Label and Control Error Checking
Form/Report Design Rules, New unassociated labels	New Unassociated Label Error Checking
Form/Report Design Rules, Keyboard shortcut errors	Keyboard Shortcut Errors Error Checking
Form/Report Design Rules, Invalid control properties	Invalid Control Properties Error Checking
Form/Report Design Rules, Common report errors	Common Report Errors Error Checking

RunCommand Method Arguments

One of the easiest ways to perform a variety of functions in Microsoft Access is through use of the RunCommand method. You can use this anywhere within your code. The RunCommand method takes a single argument, the acCommand constant. All of the available acCommand constants are listed in the following table. For convenience, they are listed in two columns. Each of these arguments represents some command in Access that is accessible from a menu or toolbar.

Argument	Argument
acCmdAboutMicrosoftAccess	acCmdPivotChartDrillOut
acCmdAddInManager	acCmdPivotChartMultiplePlots

Continues

Argument	Argument
acCmdAddToNewGroup	acCmdPivotChartMultiplePlotsUnifiedScale
acCmdAddWatch	acCmdPivotChartShowLegend
acCmdAdvancedFilterSort	acCmdPivotChartType
acCmdAlignBottom	acCmdPivotChartUndo
acCmdAlignCenter	acCmdPivotChartView
acCmdAlignLeft	acCmdPivotCollapse
acCmdAlignmentAndSizing	acCmdPivotDelete
acCmdAlignMiddle	acCmdPivotDropAreas
acCmdAlignRight	acCmdPivotExpand
acCmdAlignToGrid	acCmdPivotRefresh
acCmdAlignTop	acCmdPivotShowAll
acCmdAlignToShortest	acCmdPivotShowBottom1
acCmdAlignToTallest	acCmdPivotShowBottom10
acCmdAnalyzePerformance	acCmdPivotShowBottom10Percent
acCmdAnalyzeTable	acCmdPivotShowBottom1Percent
acCmdAnswerWizard	acCmdPivotShowBottom2
acCmdApplyDefault	acCmdPivotShowBottom25
acCmdApplyFilterSort	acCmdPivotShowBottom25Percent
acCmdAppMaximize	acCmdPivotShowBottom2Percent
acCmdAppMinimize	acCmdPivotShowBottom5
acCmdAppMove	acCmdPivotShowBottom5Percent
acCmdAppRestore	acCmdPivotShowBottomOther
acCmdAppSize	acCmdPivotShowTop1
acCmdArrangeIconsAuto	acCmdPivotShowTop10
acCmdArrangeIconsByCreated	acCmdPivotShowTop10Percent
acCmdArrangeIconsByModified	acCmdPivotShowTop1Percent
acCmdArrangeIconsByName	acCmdPivotShowTop2
acCmdArrangeIconsByType	acCmdPivotShowTop25
acCmdAutoCorrect	acCmdPivotShowTop25Percent

Continues

Argument	Argument
acCmdAutoDial	acCmdPivotShowTop2Percent
acCmdAutoFormat	acCmdPivotShowTop5
acCmdBackgroundPicture	acCmdPivotShowTop5Percent
acCmdBackgroundSound	acCmdPivotShowTopOther
acCmdBackup	acCmdPivotTableClearCustomOrdering
acCmdBookmarksClearAll	acCmdPivotTableCreateCalcField
acCmdBookmarksNext	acCmdPivotTableCreateCalcTotal
acCmdBookmarksPrevious	acCmdPivotTableDemote
acCmdBookmarksToggle	acCmdPivotTableExpandIndicators
acCmdBringToFront	acCmdPivotTableExportToExcel
acCmdCallStack	acCmdPivotTableFilterBySelection
acCmdChangeToCheckBox	acCmdPivotTableGroupItems
acCmdChangeToComboBox	acCmdPivotTableHideDetails
acCmdChangeToCommandButton	acCmdPivotTableMoveToColumnArea
acCmdChangeToImage	acCmdPivotTableMoveToDetailArea
acCmdChangeToLabel	acCmdPivotTableMoveToFilterArea
acCmdChangeToListBox	acCmdPivotTableMoveToRowArea
acCmdChangeToOptionButton	acCmdPivotTablePercentColumnTotal
acCmdChangeToTextBox	acCmdPivotTablePercentGrandTotal
acCmdChangeToToggleButton	acCmdPivotTablePercentParentColumnItem
acCmdChartSortAscByTotal	acCmdPivotTablePercentParentRowItem
acCmdChartSortDescByTotal	acCmdPivotTablePercentRowTotal
acCmdClearAll	acCmdPivotTablePromote
acCmdClearAllBreakpoints	acCmdPivotTableRemove
acCmdClearGrid	acCmdPivotTableShowAsNormal
acCmdClearHyperlink	acCmdPivotTableShowDetails
acCmdClearItemDefaults	acCmdPivotTableSubtotal
acCmdClose	acCmdPivotTableUngroupItems
acCmdCloseWindow	acCmdPivotTableView

Continues

Argument	Argument
acCmdColumnWidth	acCmdPreviewEightPages
acCmdCompactDatabase	acCmdPreviewFourPages
acCmdCompileAllModules	acCmdPreviewOnePage
acCmdCompileAndSaveAllModules	acCmdPreviewTwelvePages
acCmdCompileLoadedModules	acCmdPreviewTwoPages
acCmdCompleteWord	acCmdPrimaryKey
acCmdConditionalFormatting	acCmdPrint
acCmdConnection	acCmdPrintPreview
acCmdControlWizardsToggle	acCmdPrintRelationships
acCmdConvertDatabase	acCmdProcedureDefinition
acCmdConvertMacrosToVisualBasic	acCmdPromote
acCmdCopy	acCmdProperties
acCmdCopyDatabaseFile	acCmdPublish
acCmdCopyHyperlink	acCmdPublishDefaults
acCmdCreateMenuFromMacro	acCmdQueryAddToOutput
acCmdCreateRelationship	acCmdQueryGroupBy
acCmdCreateReplica	acCmdQueryParameters
acCmdCreateShortcut	acCmdQueryTotals
acCmdCreateShortcutMenuFromMacro	acCmdQueryTypeAppend
acCmdCreateToolbarFromMacro	acCmdQueryTypeCrosstab
acCmdCut	acCmdQueryTypeDelete
acCmdDataAccessPageAddToPage	acCmdQueryTypeMakeTable
acCmdDataAccessPageBrowse	acCmdQueryTypeSelect
acCmdDataAccessPageDesignView	acCmdQueryTypeSQLDataDefinition
acCmdDataAccessPageFieldListRefresh	acCmdQueryTypeSQLPassThrough
acCmdDatabaseProperties	acCmdQueryTypeSQLUnion
acCmdDatabaseSplitter	acCmdQueryTypeUpdate
acCmdDataEntry	acCmdQuickInfo
acCmdDataOutline	acCmdQuickPrint

Continues

Argument	Argument
acCmdDatasheetView	acCmdQuickWatch
acCmdDateAndTime	acCmdRecordsGoToFirst
acCmdDebugWindow	acCmdRecordsGoToLast
acCmdDelete	acCmdRecordsGoToNew
acCmdDeleteGroup	acCmdRecordsGoToNext
acCmdDeletePage	acCmdRecordsGoToPrevious
acCmdDeleteQueryColumn	acCmdRecoverDesignMaster
acCmdDeleteRecord	acCmdRedo
acCmdDeleteRows	acCmdReferences
acCmdDeleteTab	acCmdRefresh
acCmdDeleteTable	acCmdRefreshPage
acCmdDeleteTableColumn	acCmdRegisterActiveXControls
acCmdDeleteWatch	acCmdRelationships
acCmdDemote	acCmdRemove
acCmdDesignView	acCmdRemoveFilterSort
acCmdDiagramAddRelatedTables	acCmdRemoveTable
acCmdDiagramAutosizeSelectedTables	acCmdRename
acCmdDiagramDeleteRelationship	acCmdRenameColumn
acCmdDiagramLayoutDiagram	acCmdRenameGroup
acCmdDiagramLayoutSelection	acCmdRepairDatabase
acCmdDiagramModifyUserDefinedView	acCmdReplace
acCmdDiagramNewLabel	acCmdReportHdrFtr
acCmdDiagramNewTable	acCmdReset
acCmdDiagramRecalculatePageBreaks	acCmdResolveConflicts
acCmdDiagramShowRelationshipLabels	acCmdRestore
acCmdDiagramViewPageBreaks	acCmdRowHeight
acCmdDocMaximize	acCmdRun
acCmdDocMinimize	acCmdRunMacro
acCmdDocMove	acCmdRunOpenMacro

Continues

Argument	Argument
acCmdDocRestore	acCmdSave
acCmdDocSize	acCmdSaveAllModules
acCmdDocumenter	acCmdSaveAllRecords
acCmdDropSQLDatabase	acCmdSaveAs
acCmdDuplicate	acCmdSaveAsASP
acCmdEditHyperlink	acCmdSaveAsDataAccessPage
acCmdEditingAllowed	acCmdSaveAsHTML
acCmdEditRelationship	acCmdSaveAsIDC
acCmdEditTriggers	acCmdSaveAsQuery
acCmdEditWatch	acCmdSaveAsReport
acCmdEncryptDecryptDatabase	acCmdSaveLayout
acCmdEnd	acCmdSaveModuleAsText
acCmdExit	acCmdSaveRecord
acCmdExport	acCmdSelectAll
acCmdFavoritesAddTo	acCmdSelectAllRecords
acCmdFavoritesOpen	acCmdSelectDataAccessPage
acCmdFieldList	acCmdSelectForm
acCmdFilterByForm	acCmdSelectRecord
acCmdFilterBySelection	acCmdSelectReport
acCmdFilterExcludingSelection	acCmdSend
acCmdFind	acCmdSendToBack
acCmdFindNext	acCmdServerFilterByForm
acCmdFindNextWordUnderCursor	acCmdServerProperties
acCmdFindPrevious	acCmdSetControlDefaults
acCmdFindPrevWordUnderCursor	acCmdSetDatabasePassword
acCmdFitToWindow	acCmdSetNextStatement
acCmdFont	acCmdShowAllRelationships
acCmdFormatCells	acCmdShowDirectRelationships
acCmdFormHdrFtr	acCmdShowEnvelope

Continues

Argument	Argument
acCmdFormView	acCmdShowMembers
acCmdFreezeColumn	acCmdShowNextStatement
acCmdGoBack	acCmdShowOnlyWebToolbar
acCmdGoContinue	acCmdShowTable
acCmdGoForward	acCmdSingleStep
acCmdGroupByTable	acCmdSizeToFit
acCmdGroupControls	acCmdSizeToFitForm
acCmdHideColumns	acCmdSizeToGrid
acCmdHidePane	acCmdSizeToNarrowest
acCmdHideTable	acCmdSizeToWidest
acCmdHorizontalSpacingDecrease	acCmdSnapToGrid
acCmdHorizontalSpacingIncrease	acCmdSortAscending
acCmdHorizontalSpacingMakeEqual	acCmdSortDescending
acCmdHyperlinkDisplayText	acCmdSortingAndGrouping
acCmdImport	acCmdSpeech
acCmdIndent	acCmdSpelling
acCmdIndexes	acCmdSQLView
acCmdInsertActiveXControl	acCmdStartupProperties
acCmdInsertChart	acCmdStepInto
acCmdInsertFile	acCmdStepOut
acCmdInsertFileIntoModule	acCmdStepOver
acCmdInsertHyperlink	acCmdStepToCursor
acCmdInsertLookupColumn	acCmdStopLoadingPage
acCmdInsertLookupField	acCmdSubdatasheetCollapseAll
acCmdInsertMovieFromFile	acCmdSubdatasheetExpandAll
acCmdInsertObject	acCmdSubdatasheetRemove
acCmdInsertPage	acCmdSubformDatasheet
acCmdInsertPicture	acCmdSubformDatasheetView
acCmdInsertPivotTable	acCmdSubformFormView

Continues

Argument	Argument
acCmdInsertProcedure	acCmdSubformInNewWindow
acCmdInsertQueryColumn	acCmdSubformPivotChartView
acCmdInsertRows	acCmdSubformPivotTableView
acCmdInsertSpreadsheet	acCmdSwitchboardManager
acCmdInsertSubdatasheet	acCmdSynchronizeNow
acCmdInsertTableColumn	acCmdTabControlPageOrder
acCmdInsertUnboundSection	acCmdTableAddTable
acCmdInvokeBuilder	acCmdTableCustomView
acCmdJoinProperties	acCmdTableNames
acCmdLastPosition	acCmdTabOrder
acCmdLayoutPreview	acCmdTestValidationRules
acCmdLineUpIcons	acCmdTileHorizontally
acCmdLinkedTableManager	acCmdTileVertically
acCmdLinkTables	acCmdToggleBreakpoint
acCmdListConstants	acCmdToggleFilter
acCmdLoadFromQuery	acCmdToolbarControlProperties
acCmdMacroConditions	acCmdToolbarsCustomize
acCmdMacroNames	acCmdTransferSQLDatabase
acCmdMakeMDEFile	acCmdTransparentBackground
acCmdMaximiumRecords	acCmdTransparentBorder
acCmdMicrosoftAccessHelpTopics	acCmdUndo
acCmdMicrosoftOnTheWeb	acCmdUndoAllRecords
acCmdMicrosoftScriptEditor	acCmdUnfreezeAllColumns
acCmdMoreWindows	acCmdUngroupControls
acCmdNewDatabase	acCmdUnhideColumns
acCmdNewGroup	acCmdUpsizingWizard
acCmdNewObjectAutoForm	acCmdUserAndGroupAccounts
acCmdNewObjectAutoReport	acCmdUserAndGroupPermissions
acCmdNewObjectClassModule	acCmdUserLevelSecurityWizard

Continues

Argument	Argument
acCmdNewObjectDataAccessPage	acCmdVerticalSpacingDecrease
acCmdNewObjectDiagram	acCmdVerticalSpacingIncrease
acCmdNewObjectForm	acCmdVerticalSpacingMakeEqual
acCmdNewObjectFunction	acCmdViewCode
acCmdNewObjectMacro	acCmdViewDataAccessPages
acCmdNewObjectModule	acCmdViewDetails
acCmdNewObjectQuery	acCmdViewDiagrams
acCmdNewObjectReport	acCmdViewFieldList
acCmdNewObjectStoredProcedure	acCmdViewForms
acCmdNewObjectTable	acCmdViewFunctions
acCmdNewObjectView	acCmdViewGrid
acCmdObjBrwFindWholeWordOnly	acCmdViewLargeIcons
acCmdObjBrwGroupMembers	acCmdViewList
acCmdObjBrwHelp	acCmdViewMacros
acCmdObjBrwShowHiddenMembers	acCmdViewModules
acCmdObjBrwViewDefinition	acCmdViewQueries
acCmdObjectBrowser	acCmdViewReports
acCmdOfficeClipboard	acCmdViewRuler
acCmdOLEDDELinks	acCmdViewShowPaneDiagram
acCmdOLEObjectConvert	acCmdViewShowPaneGrid
acCmdOLEObjectDefaultVerb	acCmdViewShowPaneSQL
acCmdOpenDatabase	acCmdViewSmallIcons
acCmdOpenHyperlink	acCmdViewStoredProcedures
acCmdOpenNewHyperlink	acCmdViewTableColumnNames
acCmdOpenSearchPage	acCmdViewTableColumnProperties
acCmdOpenStartPage	acCmdViewTableKeys
acCmdOpenTable	acCmdViewTableNameOnly
acCmdOpenURL	acCmdViewTables
acCmdOptions	acCmdViewTableUserView

Continues

Argument	Argument
acCmdOutdent	acCmdViewToolbox
acCmdOutputToExcel	acCmdViewVerifySQL
acCmdOutputToRTF	acCmdViewViews
acCmdOutputToText	acCmdVisualBasicEditor
acCmdPageHdrFtr	acCmdWebPagePreview
acCmdPageNumber	acCmdWebPageProperties
acCmdPageProperties	acCmdWebTheme
acCmdPageSetup	acCmdWindowArrangeIcons
acCmdParameterInfo	acCmdWindowCascade
acCmdPartialReplicaWizard	acCmdWindowHide
acCmdPaste	acCmdWindowSplit
acCmdPasteAppend	acCmdWindowUnhide
acCmdPasteAsHyperlink	acCmdWordMailMerge
acCmdPasteSpecial	acCmdWorkgroupAdministrator
acCmdPivotAutoAverage	acCmdZoom10
acCmdPivotAutoCount	acCmdZoom100
acCmdPivotAutoFilter	acCmdZoom1000
acCmdPivotAutoMax	acCmdZoom150
acCmdPivotAutoMin	acCmdZoom200
acCmdPivotAutoStdDev	acCmdZoom25
acCmdPivotAutoStdDevP	acCmdZoom50
acCmdPivotAutoSum	acCmdZoom500
acCmdPivotAutoVar	acCmdZoom75
acCmdPivotAutoVarP	acCmdZoomBox
acCmdPivotChartByRowByColumn	acCmdZoomSelection
acCmdPivotChartDrillInto	

Windows API Reference Information

In this appendix you will find information about the Windows API to support the tutorials in Chapter 13.

So now you probably know enough about using the Win32 API to get yourself into some serious trouble. The trick now is to find information about the APIs that are available for use, and how to use them with VBA.

Unlike programming languages, information about the Windows API is somewhat harder to find. As there are literally hundreds of API functions included in the Windows operating system, the information that is available is mostly incomplete. There are also quite a few API functions that Microsoft hasn't publicly documented, for whatever reason. We haven't yet found a single resource that includes everything, so we recommend using several resources.

API Viewer

Microsoft Office 2000 and XP offered a Developer Edition that contained many resources specifically aimed at the developer. In versions prior to that, developer tools were packaged in a separate product called the Developer Toolkit. These products included a utility called the *API Viewer*, which provided detailed information about the Windows APIs, including function, type, and constant declarations. With the release of Office 2003, Microsoft provides the Developer Extensions Toolkit, which unfortunately, does not include the API Viewer (at least that's the case with the beta version I have). You can use the API Viewer from previous versions, or from Visual Basic 6.0.

Finding information about the API is difficult, especially detailed information about how to use it with Visual Basic. There are only two Win32 API viewers that we would recommend for download from the Internet, and at the time of writing, both of these viewers are free. There are probably others around, but we have found the following two to be the best:

❑ The DX21 Web site provides a free online API viewer at the following address:
   http://www.dx21.com/VISSTUDIO/WIN32API/INDEX.ASP?ST=Declarations

❑ The AllAPI Web site provides a good range of information, but the noteworthy point as far as this section is concerned, is that they offer a good (and free) API Viewer for download at the following Web site: http://www.mentalis.org/agnet/apiviewer.shtml

Be advised that, as with many Web sites, you can never guarantee how long a Web site will remain in existence.

Web Sites

There are many Web sites dedicated to the Win32 API, each of which has its good and bad points. Most, however, do not provide a complete API list.

The Microsoft MSDN Web site is, in our opinion, difficult to use when you don't know what you're looking for. If you know the exact name of the API function you want, you can find excellent references to it on the MSDN site, including information and *how to* articles. But finding a complete list of the Windows API is very difficult. The general consensus is that even Microsoft does not publish documentation for the entire API.

The following short list represents those Internet-based resources that I feel are worth a look:

❑ MSDN—search for "Win32 API" or the specific API function name http://search.microsoft.com/search/search.aspx?st=a&View=en-us

❑ Microsoft DLL Help Database http://support.microsoft.com/default.aspx?scid=/servicedesks/fileversion/dllinfo.asp

❑ MSDN—Win32 API declarations download http://www.microsoft.com/downloads/details.aspx?displaylang=en&familyid=1DB32433-87DD-45D9-A4EC-7C7973D7C94B

❑ The ALLAPI Network http://www.mentalis.org/apilist/apilist.php

Books

In addition to the extremely fine book you're currently reading, there are only two other API-related books that we would recommend:

❑ Dan Appleman's *Visual Basic Programmer's Guide to the Win32 API*, ISBN 0-672-31590-4, published by SAMS.

❑ Steven Roman's *Win32 API Programming with Visual Basic*, ISBN 1-56592-631-5, published by O'Reilly.

Some Useful API Functions

Apart from the SetFormIcon function described in Chapter 13, this section is devoted to demonstrating how to use some useful API functions.

Play a Sound in Access

Rather than accept the default DoCmd.Beep to notify users of some event, you can offer something bit more interesting and perhaps meaningful by playing any sound file you happen to have.

```
Public Declare Function sndPlaySound Lib "winmm.dll" _
    Alias "sndPlaySoundA" (ByVal lpszSoundName As String, _
    ByVal uFlags As Long) As Long

Public Const SND_ASYNC = &H1        'The sound is played asynchronously
                                    'and the function returns immediately
                                    'after beginning the sound.
                                    'To terminate an asynchronously played
                                    'sound, call sndPlaySound with
                                    'lpszSoundName set to NULL.
Public Const SND_LOOP = &H8         'The sound plays repeatedly until
                                    'sndPlaySound is called again with the
                                    'lpszSoundName parameter set to NULL.
                                    'You must also specify the SND_ASYNC
                                    'flag to loop sounds.
Public Const SND_MEMORY = &H4       'The parameter specified by
lpszSoundName
                                    'points to an image of a waveform sound
                                    'in memory.
Public Const SND_NODEFAULT = &H2    'If the sound cannot be found, the
                                    'function returns silently without
                                    'playing the default sound.
Public Const SND_NOSTOP = &H10      'If a sound is currently playing, the
                                    'function immediately returns FALSE,
                                    'without playing the requested sound.
Public Const SND_SYNC = &H0         'The sound is played synchronously and
                                    'the function does not return until the
                                    'sound ends.

Public Sub PlayAnySound(lpszSoundName As String)
    Dim retVal As Long
    On Error Resume Next
    retVal = sndPlaySound(lpszSoundName, SND_NODEFAULT)
End Sub
```

Find the Position of a Form

Access does not expose the current *xy* position of a form, so there is no built-in way of determining where it is on the screen. The following example demonstrates how to use an API (specifically GetWindowRect) to return the form's screen position in pixels.

Create a small form containing a single command button, and add the following code:

```
Option Compare Database
Option Explicit

Private Type RECT
    left As Long
    top As Long
    right As Long
    bottom As Long
End Type

Private Declare Function GetWindowRect Lib "user32" _
    (ByVal hwnd As Long, lpRect As RECT) As Long

Private Sub cmdShow_Click()
    Dim FormDims As RECT

    If GetWindowRect(Me.hwnd, FormDims) Then
        MsgBox "The form is located at:" & _
            vbCrLf & "Left: " & vbTab & FormDims.left & _
            vbCrLf & "Top: " & vbTab & FormDims.top & _
            vbCrLf & "Right: " & vbTab & FormDims.right & _
            vbCrLf & "Bottom: " & vbTab & FormDims.bottom
    End If
End Sub
```

Now open the form and click the button. A message box, as shown in Figure F-1, is displayed.

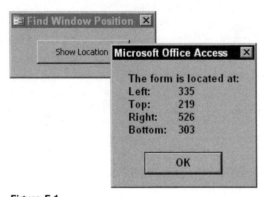

Figure F-1

Find the Temp Directory

The Temp directory is the place where Windows stores temporary files. It is typically C:\Windows\Temp.

```
Declare Function GetTempPath _
    Lib "kernel32" Alias "GetTempPathA" ( _
    ByVal nBufferLength As Long, _
    ByVal lpBuffer As String) As Long
```

```
Private Const MAXLEN = 255

Public Function TempPath() As String
    Dim strPath As String
    Dim lngSize As Long
    Dim lngReturn As Long

    strPath = Space(MAXLEN) & Chr(0)
    lngSize = MAXLEN + 1

    lngReturn = GetTempPath(lngSize, strPath)
    If lngReturn <> 0 Then
        TempPath = left(strPath, lngReturn)
    Else
        TempPath = ""
    End If
End Function
```

Find the Current User's Domain Login Name

This function doesn't mean much unless you are on a network.

```
Private Declare Function GetUserName _
    Lib "advapi32.dll" Alias "GetUserNameA" _
    (ByVal lpBuffer As String, _
    nSize As Long) As Long

Private Const MAXLEN = 255

Function GetLoginName() As String
    Dim strUserName As String
    Dim lngSize As Long
    Dim lngReturn As Long

        strUserName = Space(MAXLEN) & Chr(0)
    lngSize = MAXLEN + 1

    If GetUserName(strUserName, lngSize) <> 0 Then
        GetLoginName = Left(strUserName, lngSize - 1)
    Else
        GetLoginName = ""
    End If
End Function
```

Open or Print Any File

The following procedure allows you to open or print any file, without needing to know what its executable program is. For example, this same procedure can be used to open or print a Word or PDF document, an Excel spreadsheet, or an ASCII text file.

```
Public Const SW_HIDE = 0
Public Const SW_MINIMIZE = 6
```

```
Public Const SW_RESTORE = 9
Public Const SW_SHOW = 5
Public Const SW_SHOWMAXIMIZED = 3
Public Const SW_SHOWMINIMIZED = 2
Public Const SW_SHOWMINNOACTIVE = 7
Public Const SW_SHOWNA = 8
Public Const SW_SHOWNOACTIVATE = 4
Public Const SW_SHOWNORMAL = 1

Public Declare Function ShellExecute Lib "shell32.dll" Alias
"ShellExecuteA" _
    (ByVal hWnd As Long, ByVal lpOperation As String, ByVal lpFile As
String, _
    ByVal lpParameters As String, ByVal lpDirectory As String, _
    ByVal nShowCmd As Long) As Long

Public Sub ExecuteFile(sFileName As String, sAction As String)
    Dim vReturn As Long
    'sAction can be either "Open" or "Print".

    If ShellExecute(Access.hWndAccessApp, sAction, _
            sFileName, vbNullString, "", SW_SHOWNORMAL) < 33 Then
        DoCmd.Beep
        MsgBox "File not found."
    End If
End Sub
```

Naming Conventions

The logic of using a naming convention is about as easy to grasp as the logic of standardizing the look of our alphabet or language. Both structures are intended to make communication easier. And although they provide standards, they also allow plenty of opportunities for customization. Adopting a naming convention sets the framework for building strong code that can be interpreted by the original developer and other developers, while at the same time be implemented by application. Additionally, using a naming convention will help prevent conflicts due to multiple uses of the same name, because a name will only be allowed to have one meaning within an application.

This appendix includes some guidance for naming objects and provides tables of the most commonly accepted names used in VBA. People who choose to create their own naming conventions still benefit from being aware of this material. We all need to read and interpret code used in Access and VBA help files, books, sample applications, and when collaborating with others.

Why Implement Naming Conventions?

No one has to use naming conventions. Developers can and do write applications without applying (or enforcing) naming conventions. However, they can save a lot of time, money, and prevent needless frustrations by making it easier and faster to read and interpret code, whether it is something you wrote last week or last year, or code from another developer.

Naming conventions convey many benefits. As mentioned earlier, they are like sharing a common language. Typically, that is important if the application will be shared, but it may also be applied to the individual developer who has to work with a program that was shelved for a couple of years. Some of the obvious benefits of using a naming convention include the following.

- ❑ They make object names more informative so developers can quickly understand an application's structure and code

- ❑ They provide a standardized vocabulary for team efforts.

- ❏ They minimize conflicts when adding third-party products.

- ❏ They allow code, tools, and code libraries to be shared across various VBA platforms.

- ❏ They group objects and facilitate various sort options.

- ❏ They can provide self-documenting program code.

- ❏ They enhance search and replace capabilities.

- ❏ They allow us to learn, modify, and incorporate code from others, including from magazines, reference books, the Internet, and our peers.

The naming conventions need to be an integral part of the basic design and be fully adopted before one stroke is committed to the database. It takes a little extra time upfront, but the payoff is fast. The return on investment is compounded as the application grows, becomes more complicated, interfaces with other applications, or is used by other developers.

Many developers are careful about naming tables, forms, fields, and even controls that they build. But all too often, the controls that a wizard builds are left with their original names such as `Command65` or `Text58`. Since these names do not indicate what the control really does, they can create confusion and unnecessary conflicts, particularly if code is added. My solution is to let the wizards do their stuff, and then I promptly rename the object so that all future references to it will automatically use the correct name. Please remember that if the wizard generated code, the name of the object needs to be changed both in the object's property and in VBA.

A Brief History

Currently, the most commonly used naming conventions used in Access applications, Microsoft product documentation, and reference books are based on the Hungarian notation. This naming standard was originally created by the Hungarian Charles Simonyi while working at Microsoft in the 1980s. In the Access world, Greg Reddick and Stan Leszynski further developed and popularized the naming convention. Greg published the Reddick VBA (RVBA) Naming Conventions at http://www.xoc.net/standards/rvbanc.asp. The Leszynski Naming Conventions (LNC) and development style are detailed in the Leszynski Naming Conventions for Microsoft solution developers. Stan's materials are available through the Kwery Corporation, http://www.kwery.com/

So much for the history lesson. The critical part is to recognize that the Hungarian notation is pretty much universally recognized, if not adopted. And, that it continues to be adapted (couldn't resist)—to keep up with technology. Some tags are becoming obsolete and new ones are continuously added. But, even though the tags may be retired, there are still programs using it, so it is handy to know where to find a translator (table of tag definitions).

The Fundamentals of the Hungarian Convention

The Hungarian convention has a very straightforward design. It dictates that a name may contain up to five parts, and that they are combined in the order of prefix(es), tag, BaseName, qualifier, and suffix defined below. Although all parts are not required, nearly every name will contain a tag and a BaseName.

❑ A *prefix* precedes a tag to provide clarification. It can describe one or more important properties with one or two lowercase characters.

❑ A *tag* is, by some, considered to be the critical, non-optional element. A tag should be unique and easily differentiated from similarly named tags. A tag is typically three (occasionally four) lowercase characters that identify what the object is, for example, a table, form, or text box. The tag is usually a mnemonic abbreviation, such as "tbl," "frm," and "txt" or the first letter of each word from multiword items. Exceptions are often due to the tag already being assigned for a different purpose, adopting a tag from another program and, of course, it isn't always easy to create an intuitive three-letter abbreviation.

❑ The *BaseName* is a descriptive name that defines the particular object. This could be the layman's term used to concisely identify the subject. Use proper case and be brief but clear.

❑ A *qualifier* is an extension that indicates how the object is being used. Qualifiers should be proper case and as short as practical, without sacrificing comprehension. For example, the qualifier Avg may be added to a query name to indicate that the query calculated the qryStudentGradeAvg (or qsumStudentGradeAvg).

❑ A *suffix* is rarely needed as it's purpose is to differentiate object names that could otherwise be identical. The suffix is written in proper case and should be as short as practical. For example, a series of queries that calculate the average grade for each grade (see the need to make a distinction) could be named qryStudentGradeAvg4, qryStudentGradeAvg5, qryStudentGradeAvg6, indicating the average for the fourth grade, the fifth grade, and the sixth grade class, respectively. And, although we typically avoid using the underscore, some developers like to separate the prefix by using one, as in qryStudentGradeAvg_4.

❑ A *flag* is used to affect where an object appears in lists. You may want to consider flags as a way to put objects at the beginning or the end of a list. Flags and even the object itself may be deleted before deploying the database. Examples of flags and their uses include the following.

  ❑ _ causes the item to be listed before numbers and letters. It is often used for items under development.

  ❑ zh can indicate a system object used for development and maintenance, but it is a hidden object.

  ❑ zs can indicate a system object used for development and maintenance but should not be seen by the end user.

  ❑ zt can indicate a temporary object that is created programmatically, such as a query built by code and not preserved after it has been run.

  ❑ zz can denote an object that you are no longer using and which is waiting to be deleted.

Examples tend to add clarity. So, let's start with a very common and easy to understand example, the name for a table: tblStudent. This example quickly conveys that there are no spaces, that the tag is all lowercase, and that the BaseName is proper case. That is a fairly universally accepted format. Remember, object names should never include special characters or spaces. Other guidelines that you may want to follow are covered later in this appendix, under *Rules for Creating Names—Adding the Personal Touch*.

> **Remember, object names should never include special characters or spaces.**

Rules for Creating Names—Adding the Personal Touch

As developers, we tend to have an independent streak, which often means that we like to do things our own way. Thankfully, in most cases, there are multiple ways of achieving the desired results. That's the case with naming conventions. Even if you choose to adopt existing standards, there are plenty of opportunities to incorporate your own preferences. But before you start customizing things, it's a good idea to understand the rules. The following should help you to both work existing standards and to create standards of your own. You may find that a combination works best.

Starting with the Basics

Naming conventions apply to application objects, such as forms, controls, queries, and user-defined objects, as well as to Jet objects such as containers, databases, fields, `queryDefs`, `tableDefs`, and workspaces.

Consistency is the key. As stated already, you should determine your naming conventions before you create the first object in your database. So, pick your conventions or standards and apply them consistently throughout your application. Remember that even when following an established naming convention, there will be plenty of situations that challenge your interpretation of how to apply it.

Next, you should be thinking short and sweet—for names, that is. Although Access allows up to 64 characters, no one wants to type or read names that are that long. Plus, the application may need to interface with other programs that are more restrictive. And, if your object names aren't compatible with those programs, you will be in for a lot of extra work. For example, prior to SQL Server 6.0, field names needed to be lowercase for upsizing from Access to the SQL Server. Through 6.5, the SQL Server limited field and table names to 30 characters. And prior to 7.0, the SQL Server required an underscore instead of allowing an embedded space. So, just because Access allows 64 characters, doesn't mean it is a good thing to create 64-character names.

> NOTE: By the way, we recently demonstrated that having an excessively long path to a table name will cause Access to close. And, if you are using Windows XP and your database is in a folder in `MyDocuments`, you can automatically add about 50 characters just to get to `MyDocuments`!

> **One of our pet peeves is people putting periods in file names. They don't belong in there! Periods are a special character that can cause your code to break.**

The following are some basic rules and guidelines for both the name and the elements:

- ❑ Can ontain up to 64 characters.
- ❑ Use standard, easy to interpret abbreviations when practical.
- ❑ Include any combination of letters, numbers, spaces.
- ❑ Ttechnically,they can include special characters except period (.) exclamation point (!) accent grave (') , and brackets ([ ]). However, *don't* use special characters.

❑ Do not begin with a leading space.
(Don't use spaces. If readability is an issue, use an underscore.)

❑ Do not include control characters ASCII values 0–31 (remember, that special character thing).
See Appendix H on reserved words to learn about special characters.

❑ Do not duplicate the name of a property or other element used by DAO.

❑ Avoid a series of uppercase letters—these are reserved for formal abbreviations, such as USA.

❑ They should typically be singular rather than plural.

❑ Include the base name of the object(s) that it is built on, when practical and logical.

❑ List multiple base objects left-to-right in descending order of importance.

❑ When complete, the name should be primarily proper case construction, preceded by a lowercase, three-letter tag, such as in `tblStudentClass` or `lblClassDate`.

Some Additional Thoughts about Other Objects

If you are going to venture very far into customizing an existing convention or creating your own, there are several other things that you will want to consider. The following are some of the more common objects that you'll want to have *rules* for handling.

Variables and Routines

The body of a variable or routine name should use mixed case and should be only long enough to describe its purpose; for example, `im FormCount As Integer` returns the number of open forms.

Functions

Function names should begin with a verb. And, it may be worth prefixing functions with type, f for `fnc`, to make it easier to identify the function. Avoid using `fn_` because that is how SQL Server prefixes functions.

Public Function fCloseAllForms

Stored `ProceduresStored` procedure names should begin with a verb. Having a tag precede the base name facilitates sorting. For example, `ins` for insert and `arc` for archive. When applying tags, avoid `sp_`, `dt_`, and `xp_` because they are used by SQL Server.

The BaseName of a constant is often UPPER_CASE with underscores (_) between words. Prefixes like i, s, g, and m can be very useful in understanding the value and the scope of a constant. For example, `gsNEW_LINE` new line character string (g indicates that it is global to entire application and s indicates that this is a string)

Constants

Constants should be prefixed by the scope prefixes m or g for module or global, respectively. A constant is indicated by appending the letter c to the end of the data type or it can have the generic tag `contcDiscount`. g is the scope, `intc` indicates the `datatype` and that it is a constant, with the base name of `Discount`. `conDiscount` names the same constant, but conveys less information. `mdblcPi` indicates module level, double integer constant with the base name `Pi`.

Classes

A class defines a user-defined object. Because this invents a new data type, you will need to invent a new tag for the object. You can add a BaseName to the tag to spell out the abbreviation indicated by the tag.

Menu Items

Menu items should use the tag mnu, followed by BaseName then the location where the menu item falls. For example,

```
mnuFile (File on menu bar)
mnuSave (Save on menu bar)
mnuFileSaveAs (SaveAs on File - popup menu)
mnuFileNew (New on File - popup menu)
mnuFileNewForm (Form on File - New flyout menu)
mnuFileNewReport (Report on File - New flyout menu)
```

More Do's and Don'ts

By now, you'd think that we'd have covered all of the basics. But, of course, there is always more. So, just for good measure, here are a few more do's and don'ts.

❑ When creating a new tag, stick to existing rules and styles for length, case, etc.

❑ Don't redefine an existing tag. Either create a new unique tag or find an existing tag that fits the purpose.

❑ Before creating a new tag, think through the application of existing tags. There is likely a tag that will cover the situation.

❑ Don't use ID as a prefix or suffix.

❑ Since ADO, ADOX, and DAO share some of the same tags, it is a good idea to specify the library name. In addition to avoiding confusion, explicitly naming the library will make the code run faster. For example, to specify that it is an ADO record set, you might write

```
Dim rst As ADODB.Recordset
```

To specify that you are using ADOX, you might write

```
Dim idx As ADOX.Index
```

Tables

The following tables are a compilation of terms and tags from a multitude of sources. They are by no means a comprehensive listing of all the tags currently in use or that have been used, as new tags are generated as programs evolve and as developers create their own objects. That being said, the hope is that having a comprehensive list will save research time while trying to select the right tag or interpret an existing tag.

The following table is a compilation of tags and the objects that they represent. It is in alphabetical order by tag to facilitate looking up a tag to see what it means. Although some developers like to use an *s* to indicate plural, only the singular (more common) form is listed here.

All Objects	
Tag	**Object**
ani	Animated Button
Aob	AccessObject
Aop	AccessObjectProperty
App	Application
Bac	Backup
Bas	Module
bed	Pen BEdit
Bfr	BoundObjectFrame
Bin	Binary
bln/f	Boolean (Yes/No)
Brk	Page break
byt	Byte
Cat	Catalog
cbo	Combo box
Chg	Change
chk	Check Box
Chr	Text (character)
Cht	Chart
Clm	Columns
clms	Column
clp	Picture clip
cmd	Command button
cnn {cnx}	Connection
cnt/con	Container
col	Collection
com	Communications
ctr/ctl	Control (generic)
cur	Currency

Continues

All Objects	
Tag	**Object**
dap	DataAccessPage
dat	Data control
dat/dtm	Date/Time
db	Database
dbc/dbcbo	Data-bound combo box
dbe	DBEngine
dbg/dbgrd	Data-bound grid
dbl	Double
dcm	DoCmd
ddl	Data definition
dec	Decimal
del	Delete
dir	Directory list box
dlg/cdl	Common dialog
dls/dblst	Data-bound list box
doc	Document
drv	Drive list box
dyn/ds	Dynaset
err	Error
exp	Export
f	Flag
fcd	FormatCondition
fd	Field object
fdc	Field collection
fdlg	Form (dialog)
fil	File list box
fld	Field
flt	Filter

Continues

All Objects	
Tag	**Object**
fmnu	Form (menu)
fmsg	Form (message)
fra	Frame
frm	Form
fsfr	Form (subform)
gau/gph	Gauge
glb	Global
gra	Graph
grd	Grid
grl	GroupLevel
grp	Option group
grp/gru	Group
gru	Group
hed	Pen Hedit
hsb	Horizontal scroll bar
hyp	Hyperlink
ID	AutoNumber
idx	Index
ils	ImageList
img/iml	Image
imp	Import
ink	Pen ink
int	Integer
itt	Internet Transfer Control
ix	Index Object
ixc	Index collection
key	Key status
keys	Keys

Continues

All Objects	
Tag	**Object**
lbl	Label
lin	Line
lkp	Lookup
lng	Long
lst	List box
lvw	ListView
mak	Make table
mci	MCI
mcr	macro
mdi	MDI child form
mem	Memo
mmnu	Macro (menu)
mnu	Menu
mpm/msg	MAPI message
mps/ses	MAPI session
msg	MS Flex Grid
mst	MS Tab
new	New
obj	Object
ocx	CustomControl
old	Old
ole	OLE
opt	Option button
out	Outline
pal	PaletteButton
pic	Picture
pl3d	Panel 3D
prb/prg	ProgressBar

Continues

All Objects	
Tag	**Object**
prc	Procedure
prm	Parameter
prp	Property
prt	Printer
qapp	Query (append)
qd	QueryDef Ojbect
qddl	Query (DDL)
qdel	Query (delete)
qdf	QueryDef
qflt	Query (filter)
qlkp	Query (lookup)
qmak	Query (make table)
qry	Query
qsel	Query (select)
qspt	Query (SQL pass-through)
qtot	Query (totals)
qty	Quantity
quni	Query (union)
qupd	Query (update)
qxtb	Query (crosstab)
rdyn	Recordset (dynaset)
ref	Reference
rel	Relation
rpt	Report
rsnp	Recordset (snapshot)
rsrp	Report (subreport)
rst	Recordset
rtbl	Recordset (table)

Continues

All Objects	
Tag	**Object**
rtf	RichTextBox
sbr/sta	StatusBar
scr	Screen
sec	Section
sel	Select
sfr	SubForm
shp	Shape
sld	Slider
sng	Single
snp	Snapshot
sok	Winsock
spn	Spin
spt	Pass through (SQL pass through)
srp	SubReport
stf	String (fixed length)
str	String
sys	System
tab	TabStrip
tb	Table Object
tbl	Table
td	TableDev Object
tdf/tbd	TableDef
tgl	Toggle button
tlb	Toolbar
tlkp	Table (lookup)
tmr	Timer
tre	TreeView
trx	transaction

Continues

All Objects	
Tag	**Object**
txt	Text box
typ	Type—User-Defined
uctl	Control (user)
udoc	Document (user)
udt	User-defined type
uni	Union
upd	UpDown
usr	User
val	Validate
var/vnt	Variant
vsb	Vertical scroll bar
vw	View
wrk/wsp	Workspace
xtb	Crosstab
Ysn	Yes/No

The following table lists the Access Object Variables and their most common tags. Please note that many developers prefer to use only the singular form for tags. This table is alphabetical by the Object Variable name.

Access Object Variable Tags	
Tag	**Object Variable**
aob	AccessObject
aops	AccessObjectProperties
aop	AccessObjectProperty
app	Append
app	Application
bac	Backup
bfr	BoundObjectFrame

Continues

Access Object Variable Tags	
Tag	**Object Variable**
chg	Change
chk	CheckBox
cbo	ComboBox
cmd	CommandButton
ctl	Control
xtb	Crosstab
ocx	CustomControl
ddl	Data definition
dat	Data entry
dap	DataAccessPage
del	Delete
dcm	DoCmd
exp	Export
flt	Filter
frm	Form
fcd	FormatCondition
fcds	FormatConditions
frms	Forms
grl	GroupLevel
hyp	Hyperlink
img	Image
imp	Import
lbl	Label
lin	Line
lst	ListBox
lkp	Look up
mcr	Macro
mak	Make table

Continues

Access Object Variable Tags	
Tag	**Object Variable**
bas	Module
new	New
ole	ObjectFrame
old	Old
opt	OptionButton
fra	OptionGroup (frame)
brk	PageBreak
pal	PaletteButton
spt	Pass through (SQL pass through)
prps	Properties
qty	Quantity
shp	Rectangle
ref	Reference
refs	References
rpt	Report
scr	Screen
sec	Section
sel	Select
sfr	SubForm
srp	SubReport
sys	System
tab	TabControl
tbl	Table
tlkp	Table (lookup)
txt	TextBox
tgl	ToggleButton
trx	Transaction
uni	Union

Continues

Access Object Variable Tags	
Tag	**Object Variable**
usr	User
val	Validate

The following table lists the common ADOX tags. This includes the plural forms although most developers stick to the singular. The list is in order by ADOX object.

ADOX Objects	
Tag	**ADOX Object**
Cat	Catalog
clms	Column
Clm	Columns
Cmd	Command
Grp	Group
Grps	Groups
Idx	Index
Idxs	Indexes
Key	Key
keys	Keys
prc	Procedure
prcs	Procedures
prps	Properties
prp	Property
tbl	Table
tbls	Tables
usr	User
usrs	Users
vw	View
Vws	Views

The following table lists the common ADO tags. Again, these include plural forms although most developers stick to singular forms. The list is in order by ADO object.

ADO Object	
Prefix	**ADO Object**
Cmd	Command
Cnn/cnx	Connection
Err	Error
Errs	Errors
Fld	Field
Flds	Fields
Prm	Parameter
Prms	Parameters
Prps	Properties
Prp	Property
Rst	Recordset

The following table lists the common DAO tags. Again, these include the plural forms although most developers stick to singular forms. The list is in order by DAO object.

DAO Object	
Prefix	**DAO Object**
cnt/con	Container
Db	Database
dbe	DBEngine
doc	Document
Ds	dynaset
err	Error
fld	Field
Fdc	Field collection
Fd	Field object

Continues

DAO Object	
Prefix	**DAO Object**
grp/gru	Group
idx	Index
Ixc	Index collection
Ix	Index Object
Int	Integer
Lng	Long
Obj	Object
prm	Parameter
Prp	Property
qry	Query
Qdf	QueryDef
Qd	QueryDef Object
rst	Recordset
Rdyn	Recordset (dynaset)
Rsnp	Recordset (snapshot)
Rtbl	Recordset (table)
rel	Relation
Sng	Single
Snp	Snapshot
Str	String
tbl	Table
Tb	Table Object
Tdf	TableDef
Td	TableDev Object
usr	user
Var	Variant
Wsp	Workspace

The following table lists the common VB Object tags. Again, these include the plural forms although most developers stick to singular forms. The list is in order by VB object.

VB Objects	
Tag	**VB Object**
App	App
Chk	CheckBox
Clp	Clipboard
Cbo	ComboBox
Cmd	CommandButton
Ctl	Control
Dat	Data
Dir	DirListBox
Drv	DriveListBox
Fil	FileListBox
Frm	Form
Fra	Frame
Glb	Global
Hsb	HScrollBar
Img	Image
Lbl	Label
lics	Licenses
lin	Line
lst	ListBox
mdi	MDIForm
mnu	Menu
ole	OLE
opt	OptionButton
pic	PictureBox
prt	Printer
prp	PropertyPage
scr	Screen
shp	Shape

Continues

VB Objects	
Tag	**VB Object**
txt	TextBox
tmr	Timer
uctl	UserControl
udoc	UserDocument
vsb	VscrollBar

The following table lists the common Data Type tags in order by data type.

Data Type	
Prefix	**Data Type**
ID	AutoNumber
Bin	Binary
bln/f	Boolean (Yes/No)
byt	Byte
col	Collection
cur	Currency
dat/dtm	Date/Time
dec	Decimal
dbl	Double
err	Error
int	Integer
lng	Long
mem	Memo
obj	Object
ole	Ole
sng	Single
str	String
stf	String (fixed length)

Continues

Data Type	
Prefix	**Data Type**
Chr	Text (character)
udt	User-defined type
var/vnt	Variant

The following table lists the common scope prefixes. A scope prefix typically precedes the tags for functions and constants.

Scope	
Prefix	**Scope**
(none)	Local, procedural level lifetime
C	Constants
G	Global (public) object lifetime
M	Module-level, private object lifetime
S	Static variable, static, object lifetime

Field tags are truly optional. They provide the extra bit of detail when added to an otherwise complete name. Think "self-documenting." Notice that many of the field tags are also the same as the data type tags for other objects.

Field Tags	
Field Tag	**Field Object Type**
lng	Autoincrementing (either sequential or random) Long (used with the suffix Cnt)
bin	Binary
byte	Byte
cur	Currency
date	Date/time
dbl	Double

Continues

Field Tags	
Field Tag	**Field Object Type**
guid	Globally unique identified (GUID) used for replication Autoincrement fields
int	Integer
lng	Long
mem	Memo
ole	OLE
sng	Single
str	Text
bool	Yes/No

Tag suffixes are another optional detail. These explicitly identify the type of object.

Tag Suffixes with Objects		
Tag	**Suffix**	**Object**
tlkp	Lookup	Table (lookup)
qsel	(none)	Query (select)
qapp	Append	Query (append)
qxtb	Xtab	Query (crosstab)
qddl	DDL	Query (DDL)
qdel	Delete	Query (delete)
qflt	Filter	Query (filter)
qlkp	Lookup	Query (lookup)
qmak	MakeTable	Query (make table)
qspt	PassThru	Query (SQL pass-through)
qtot	Totals	Query (totals)
quni	Union	Query (union)
qupd	Update	Query (update)
fdlg	Dlg	Form (dialog)

Continues

Tag Suffixes with Objects		
Tag	Suffix	Object
fmnu	Mnu	Form (menu)
fmsg	Msg	Form (message)
fsfr	SubForm	Form (subform)
rsrp	SubReport	Report (subreport)
mmnu	Mnu	Macro (menu)

Flags are prefixes used primarily to determine the placement or sort order of database objects within the database windows.

Flags	
Flags	Indicates
_(underscore)	Moves object to top of the list—for development
Zh	Hidden system object used for development
Zs	System object used for development—not hidden
Zt	Temporary object built by code
Zz	Object pending deletion

Reserved Words and Special Characters

There are numerous words that should not be used to name fields, objects, and variables. For the most part, these are called *reserved words*. Reserved words have a specific meaning to Microsoft Access, the Microsoft Jet database engine, or in conjunction with SQL Server or ODBC drivers. It may be easy to start a list of reserved words by thinking of the list of all the properties of database objects, all Visual Basic keywords, and all third-party and user-defined names and functions.

Using reserved words often creates error messages that do not indicate the source of the problem. For example, it is far from intuitive that the error message "The wizard was unable to preview your report, possibly because a table needed by your report is exclusively locked" was triggered by the use of a reserved word. Consequently, a developer may spend time troubleshooting and going down the wrong path. So in an application that uses reserved words, if it is at all possible and feasible, rename database objects—particularly tables and fields—which use reserved words. If it is not possible or practical to rename the offending object, then be sure to enclose the names in brackets when they are called in code. The following example shows the name of the table in brackets because the term tableName is a reserved word.

```
SELECT fieldX
FROM [tableName]
```

When writing code, it is often handy to use the IntelliSense feature and just select from the available list of objects and actions. This requires the use of Me. rather than Me! However, if the name of a field is a reserved word that could be the objects property, the code will not compile. As shown in the following image, the debugger will stop and highlight the problem object. In this instance, merely changing the syntax to use Me! (bang) instead of Me. (dot) will allow the code to compile. And, simply not compiling the code is not a shortcut. This merely ensures that the code will break and stop the application from running.

> We've developed a practice of debugging promptly after making changes to any code. It works to catch errors promptly and prevents them from being repeated or compounding.

Considering all the things that can go wrong, and the propensity for something to go wrong at the worst times, why tempt fate? There are utilities such as Speed Ferret that are ideal for the task of finding and replacing the offending word(s).

> **Ever hear of Naming Conventions?** In looking at the lists of reserved words, it is clear that if they are causing a problem with a database, then it is worth enforcing naming conventions. Check the appendices to learn about some of the well-accepted naming conventions.

What Are the Sources of Reserved Words?

In addition to the lists of reserved words that are directly associated with Access 2002, Access 2003, Jet 4, and Visual Basic, there are additional words to avoid that have special meaning to ActiveX Data Objects (ADO), OLE DB, Open Database Connectivity (ODBC), and any DLL (dynamic-link library) referenced in your application. Just by setting a reference to a type library, an object library, or an ActiveX control, all the reserved words for the referenced items become reserved words for the Access application. And the list keeps growing. All built-in function names and user-defined names also become reserved words.

It can get even hairier. The reserved words for a given application will vary depending on what mode the Jet database engine is running in. This is determined by whether Jet is called from Microsoft Access, the Microsoft OLE DB Provider for Microsoft Jet, a Data Access Object, or the Microsoft Access ODBC driver. The list is further impacted by whether Jet is running in ANSI mode or non-ANSI (traditional) mode. So, a query that works under one scenario may fail when the database application is opened in a different mode.

It is possible to find lists of reserved words by using the online help feature in Access, by searching for reserved words using various online search engines, and by pouring through reference books. Regretfully, any given list is not going to be comprehensive. This is another obvious endorsement for implementing naming conventions.

The potential list of reserved words can seem a bit overwhelming. That is why this appendix contains a table of reserved words. The table is a compilation of words from a variety of sources and it includes the reserved words for ANSI mode. So it should save developers significant research time. Please keep in mind that it is not an exhaustive list and that it specifically does not include additional words associated with third-party add-ins.

Reserved Words

The following terms should be in the list.

Omitted Reserved Words from "SQL Reserved Words" Topic

```
CONTAINS
FROM Clause
INSERT INTO
SMALLDATETIME
SMALLMONEY
SYSNAME
```

Omitted Reserved Words from KB Article Q286335 (http://support.microsoft.com/?id=286335)

```
Application
CompactDatabase
CreateDatabase
CreateField
CreateGroup
CreateIndex
CreateObject
CreateProperty
CreateRelation
CreateTableDef
CreateUser
CreateWorkspace
CurrentUser
Description
Document
Echo
Eqv
Error
Exit
Field, Fields
FillCache
Form, Forms
FUNCTION
Idle
If
Indexes
InsertText
LastModified
Macro
Move
NAME
NewPassword
OFF
OpenRecordset
Parameter
Property
Queries
Query
Quit
```

```
Recalc
Recordset
Refresh
RefreshLink
RegisterDatabase
Relation
Repaint
RepairDatabase
Report
Reports
Requery
SCREEN
SetFocus
SetOption
TableDef, TableDefs
Type
Workspace
YES
```

Reserved Words	
ABSOLUTE	AUTOINCREMENT
ACTION	AVG
ADD	BAND
ADMINDB	BEGIN
ALL	Between
ALLOCATE	BINARY
Alphanumeric	BIT
ALTER	BIT_LENGTH
ALTER Table	BNOT
And	BOOLEAN
ANY	BOR
Application	BOTH
ARE	BXOR
AS	BY
ASC	BYTE
ASSERTION	CASCADE
AT	CASCADED
AUTHORIZATION	CASE

Continues

Reserved Words	
CAST	CreateDatabase
CATALOG	CREATEDB
CHAR	CreateField
CHAR_LENGTH	CreateGroup
CHARACTER	CreateIndex
CHARACTER_LENGTH	CreateObject
CHECK	CreateProperty
CLOSE	CreateRelation
CLUSTERED	CreateTableDef
COALESCE	CreateUser
COLLATE	CreateWorkspace
COLLATION	CROSS
COLUMN	CURRENCY
COMMIT	CURRENT
COMP	CURRENT_DATE
CompactDatabase	CURRENT_TIME
COMPRESSION	CURRENT_TIMESTAMP
CONNECT	CURRENT_USER
CONNECTION	CurrentUser
CONSTRAINT	CURSOR
CONSTRAINTS	DATABASE
CONTAINER	DATE
CONTAINS	DATETIME
CONTINUE	DAY
CONVERT	DEALLOCATE
CORRESPONDING	DEC
COUNT	DECIMAL
COUNTER	DECLARE
CREATE	DEFAULT

Continues

Reserved Words	
DEFERRABLE	Exit
DEFERRED	EXTERNAL
DELETE	EXTRACT
DESC	FALSE
DESCRIBE	FETCH
Description	Field, Fields
DESCRIPTOR	FillCache
DIAGNOSTICS	FIRST
DISALLOW	FLOAT
DISCONNECT	FLOAT4
DISTINCT	FLOAT8
DISTINCTROW	FOR
Document	FOREIGN
DOMAIN	Form, Forms
DOUBLE	FOUND
DROP	FROM
Echo	FROM Clause
ELSE	FULL
END	FUNCTION
END-EXEC	GENERAL
Eqv	GET
Error	GLOBAL
ESCAPE	GO
EXCEPT	GOTO
EXCEPTION	GRANT
EXCLUSIVECONNECT	GROUP
EXEC	GUID
EXECUTE	HAVING
EXISTS	HOUR

Continues

Reserved Words	
IDENTITY	INTERVAL
Idle	INTO
IEEEDOUBLE	IS
IEEESINGLE	ISOLATION
If	JOIN
IGNORE	KEY
IMAGE	LANGUAGE
IMMEDIATE	LAST
Imp	LastModified
IN	LEADING
In	LEFT
INDEX	Level
INDEXCREATEDB	Like
Indexes	LOCAL
INDICATOR	LOGICAL
INHERITABLE	LOGICAL1
INITIALLY	LONG
INNER	LONGBINARY
INPUT	LONGCHAR
INSENSITIVE	LONGTEXT
INSERT	LOWER
INSERT INTO	Macro
InsertText	MATCH
INT	MAX
INTEGER	MEMO
INTEGER1	MIN
INTEGER2	MINUTE
INTEGER4	Mod
INTERSECT	MODULE

Continues

Reserved Words	
MONEY	OPTION
MONTH	Or
Move	ORDER
NAME	OUTER
NAMES	OUTPUT
NATIONAL	OVERLAPS
NATURAL	OWNERACCESS
NCHAR	PAD
NewPassword	Parameter
NEXT	PARAMETERS
NO	PARTIAL
NONCLUSTERED	PASSWORD
Not	PERCENT
NOTE	PIVOT
NTEXT	POSITION
NULL	PRECISION
NULLIF	PREPARE
NUMBER	PRESERVE
NUMERIC	PRIMARY
NVARCHAR	PRIOR
OBJECT	PRIVILEGES
OCTET_LENGTH	PROC
OF	PROCEDURE
OFF	Property
OLEOBJECT	PUBLIC
ON	Queries
ONLY	Query
OPEN	Quit
OpenRecordset	READ

Continues

Reserved Words	
REAL	SET
Recalc	SetFocus
Recordset	SetOption
REFERENCES	SHORT
Refresh	SINGLE
RefreshLink	SIZE
RegisterDatabase	SMALLDATETIME
Relation	SMALLINT
RELATIVE	SMALLMONEY
Repaint	SOME
RepairDatabase	SPACE
Report	SQL
Reports	SQLCODE
Requery	SQLERROR
RESTRICT	SQLSTATE
REVOKE	StDev
RIGHT	StDevP
ROLLBACK	STRING
ROWS	SUBSTRING
SCHEMA	SUM
SCREEN	SYSNAME
SCROLL	SYSTEM_USER
SECOND	TABLE
SECTION	TableDef, TableDefs
SELECT	TableID
SELECTSCHEMA	TEMPORARY
SELECTSECURITY	TEXT
SESSION	THEN
SESSION_USER	TIME

Continues

Reserved Words	
TIMESTAMP	USAGE
TIMEZONE_HOUR	USER
TIMEZONE_MINUTE	USING
TINYINT	VALUE
TO	VALUES
TOP	Var
TRAILING	VARBINARY
TRANSACTION	VARCHAR
TRANSFORM	VarP
TRANSLATE	VARYING
TRANSLATION	VIEW
TRIM	WHEN
TRUE	WHENEVER
Type	WHERE
UNION	WITH
UNIQUE	WORK
UNIQUEIDENTIFIER	Workspace
UNKNOWN	WRITE
UPDATE	Xor
UPDATEIDENTITY	YEAR
UPDATEOWNER	YES
UPDATESECURITY	YESNO
UPPER	ZONE

What Are Special Characters?

Special characters are characters that are interpreted by Access, SQL Server, and VBA as field type delimiters, the introduction of a comparison function, or other instructions. Therefore, special characters and control characters (ASCII values 0 through 31) should not be used as part of the name of a database field, object, variable, procedure, or constant. (OK, we do concede that there are different guidelines for naming VB procedures, variables, and constants than for database objects and field names, but it may not hurt to apply the union of the two sets of rules to both situations.)

Looking at the list of special characters, it can be obvious why some should be avoided. For example the "." (period) can be dastardly combined with a reserved word.

Given a field Name in table Students, the syntax Students.Name would return the value of the table's Name property instead of the value in the Name field.

Similarly, putting an apostrophe in a field name will cause the VBA to choke as it will interpret the single quote as the beginning or end of a string. Obviously, since it is being used as an apostrophe, there is nothing to close the string.

In addition to the following two lists of characters to avoid, there are a couple more seemingly innocent things that can turn into gotcha's. We strongly recommend avoiding spaces in field names and starting field or column names with a numeric character. For example, field names such as 2ndPhone and Area Code could cause unexpected hiccups. For people stuck on separating words, the underscore is a grudgingly acceptable option. Keep in mind that an object or field name can't begin with a space. For those of us with short memories or prone to typos, Access will immediately advise us of the error in our ways if we try to put certain special characters in a field name. The following image shows the error message generated by trying to create a field name with a leading space. Notice that Access accepted other special characters within the field name. This might create a false sense of well-being. As pointed out before, if the name contains a special character it will require special treatment throughout the application.

> *An extra tip:* Special characters not only wreak havoc in code, they can cause problems if they are in text and memo fields. Most of these special characters will put the breaks on a word search. So, an application that has been working fine for months may suddenly throw error messages when the user runs a search on a text field. For example, Kim's Curry House, as the name of a business will likely stop a search. The apostrophe will cause the SQL interpreter to "think" that a string has been initiated or ended. *Solution:* Use code to prevent users from entering special characters into text and memo fields. See the code example at the end of this appendix.

Special Characters to Avoid		
Key	**ASCII**	**Name**
,	44	Comma
.	46	Period
;	59	Semicolon
:	58	Colon
`	96	Acute
'	39	Apostrophe (single quote)

Continues

843

Special Characters to Avoid		
Key	**ASCII**	**Name**
"	34	Quote (double quote)
?	63	Question
/	47	Solidus (slash)
>	62	Greater than
<	60	Less than
[	91	Left square bracket
]	93	Right square bracket
{	123	Left curly brace
}	125	Right curly brace
\	92	Reverse solidus (backslash; aka: whack)
|	124	Vertical bar (pip)
~	126	Tilde
!	33	Exclamation
@	64	Commercial at
#	35	Number (pound, hash)
$	36	Dollar
%	37	Percent
	94	Carot
&	38	Ampersand
*	42	Asterisk
(	40	Left parenthesis
)	41	Right parenthesis
=	61	Equal
+	43	Plus

ASCII Characters Names to Avoid

ASCII is often referenced, but it is seldom spelled out. So, here it is in plain English: American Standard Code for Information Interchange. Computers are number-driven, and ASCII code is the numeric representation of a character or action. The first 32 ASCII characters are actions or nonprinting characters. This explains why using any of these characters as a name of an object, function, and so on, would be interpreted as an instruction and wreak havoc with an application. Most developers recognize ESC, CAN, NUL, LF, CR, and TAB, but many of the others have been forgotten. So, having the following table may be a handy tool for not only knowing what to avoid, but for intentionally including an action in your VBA.

ASCII Characters 0 through 31				
DEC	Hx	Oct	Char	Function
0	0	000	NUL	(null)
1	1	001	SOH	(start of heading)
2	2	002	STX	(start of text)
3	3	003	ETX	(end of text)
4	4	004	EOT	(end of transmission)
5	5	005	ENQ	(enquiry)
6	6	006	ACK	(acknowledge)
7	7	007	BEL	(bell)
8	8	010	BS	(backspace)
9	9	011	TAB	(horizontal tab)
10	A	012	LF	(NL line feed, new line)
11	B	013	VT	(vertical tab)
12	C	014	FF	(NP form feed, new page)
13	D	015	CR	(carriage return)
14	E	016	SO	(shift out)
15	F	017	SI	(shift in)
16	10	020	DLE	(data link escape)
17	11	021	DC1	(device control 1)
18	12	022	DC2	(device control 2)
19	13	023	DC3	(device control 3)
20	14	024	DC4	(device control 4)
21	15	025	NAK	(negative acknowledgement)
22	16	026	SYN	(synchronous idle)
23	17	027	ETB	(end of transmission block)
24	18	030	CAN	(cancel)
25	19	031	EM	(end of medium)

Continues

ASCII Characters 0 through 31				
DEC	Hx	Oct	Char	Function
26	1A	032	SUB	(substitute)
27	1B	033	ESC	(escape)
28	1C	034	FS	(file separator)
29	1D	035	GS	(group separator)
30	1D	036	RS	(record separator)
31	1F	037	US	(unit separator)

Bonus Code Example

When users enter data via a form (and that is certainly the preferred avenue), it is possible to prevent the user from entering certain characters. By setting the form's KeyPreview property to Yes, an even procedure can be used to essentially ignore selected character entries. This is accomplished by using an event procedure for the control's OnKeyPress property.

Using the ASCII character numbers listed in the preceding table, "Special Characters to Avoid," the following example will prevent the database from entering a period, apostrophe, or ampersand in the text box txtBusinessName.

```
Private Sub txtBusinessName_KeyPress(KeyAscii As Integer)

    Select Case KeyAscii
        Case 46, 39, 38 ' Period, apostrophe, ampersand
            KeyAscii = 0
    End Select
End Sub
```

So, if the user entered Kim & John's Café, the table would actually store Kim Johns Café. The specified ASCII characters are essentially eliminated since the ASCII character 0 is null. This code example can be modified to fit many situations and an infinite combination of characters. Obviously, error trapping needs to be added, but it was left out here for the sake of simplicity.

Tips and Tricks

Here is a selection of tips, tricks, technique, and advice to help you build better, stronger, and cooler Access applications.

Visual Interface Standards

No matter how good your application is under the covers, people won't believe it if it doesn't look good. On the other hand, if your application looks great, people will think it is a good application. This reality about your user's perception of your Access application might not be fair, but you are going to have to deal with it. Luckily, it isn't too hard to make your application look as great on the outside as you made it inside.

Use Businesslike Colors

Please take our advice: Don't use a lot of colors on your Access forms. If you want your applications to look like they fit right in the Windows environment, you should use the colors that Windows uses. For the venerable Windows Standard color scheme, this means gray. However, you should actually make the colors of your forms adapt to the Windows scheme automatically.

For the background color of almost everything (forms, buttons, read-only text boxes, and so on), use the Windows default background color (which defaults to gray in Windows Standard). The numeric color value is −2147483633. Use white (color value 16777215) for the background of changeable fields.

> *Magic numbers:* Access color properties use regular, positive numbers for normal static colors. All the "Windows" colors (that change automatically when the Windows scheme changes) are negative numbers.

To test your colors and make sure they aren't hard-coded to a certain color, change your Windows color scheme to something different (like Lilac or Maple) and look through your screens to make sure there isn't any gray still showing.

Use red sparingly. You can use red (255) for the Fore Color of the Exit button and any dangerous buttons you might have, but don't use it anywhere else. If you overuse it, it will lose its special purpose as a warning or danger color.

Provide a Well-Marked Exit

Provide an easy, but safe, exit from most of your screens. You should put an Exit button on most screens, always in the same place, like the lower-right corner. It should call a function that asks if the user really wants to exit the application. Users seem to like this a lot, because it gives them an easy way to exit the application without them feeling like they are circumventing something. Don't put this button on a screen where the user hasn't completed a particular action, like in the middle of a wizard or in a pop-up screen where they are adding some detailed level of information.

Here is some code you can call from the On Click event of the Exit button in any form. It can be placed in any Module.

```
Sub ExitProgram()
On Error GoTo Error_Handler

    Dim response As Variant
    If MsgBox("Are you sure you want to exit " & "My Application" _
    & "?", vbOKCancel, "My Application") = vbOK Then
        DoCmd.Quit
    End If

Exit_Procedure:
    Exit Sub
Error_Handler:
    MsgBox "An error has occurred in this application. " _
    & "Please contact your technical support person and tell " _
    & "them this information:" _
    & vbCrLf & vbCrLf & "Error Number " & Err.Number & ", " _
    & Err.Description, _
    Buttons:=vbCritical, title:="My Application"
    Resume Exit_Procedure
    Resume
End Sub
```

With this code, you can give your users a chance to stay in the application in case they didn't mean to exit all the way out. Since applications often take several seconds to start back up, they'll appreciate the chance you gave them to think about whether they really intend to exit.

Watch Your Punctuation

Most Access applications are used in a business setting, so it's best to keep a professional tone in your application. Proper punctuation is especially important, as it shows a level of polish and thoroughness.

For example, use exclamation points very sparingly. Don't kid yourself; it's unlikely that anything in your application is exciting enough to warrant one. Don't let the user think you excite easily.

It's much more professional to say: `"All product records were imported successfully."` than `"All product records were imported successfully!"`

Also, always end sentences and statements with periods. It looks more polished to say: `"Products sales forecast calculations have been completed."` than `"Products sales forecasts have been completed"`

If you keep your punctuation correct and your tone businesslike, your users will perceive your application as a competent business tool.

Use Consistent Button Placement

Be consistent with button placement, size, and color. `Close` and `Exit` buttons should always be in the same places on the screen. The "drill-down" form the user opens by double-clicking on a row should also be available by clicking the left-most button at the bottom of the screen. See Figure I-1.

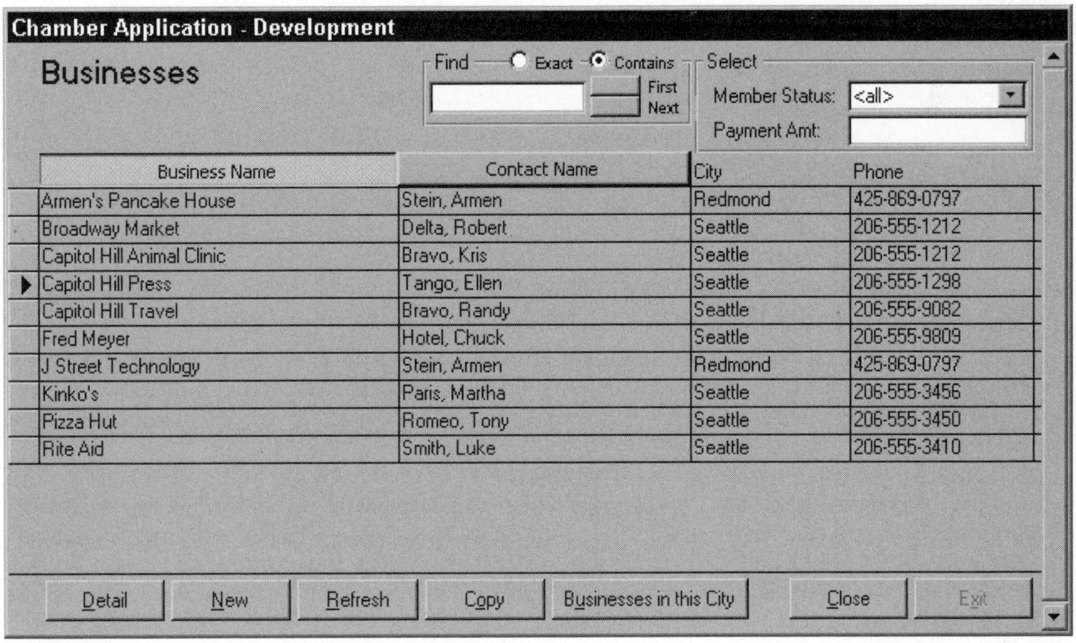

Figure I-1

Also, provide *Alt* keys for your buttons. It's easy: In the caption of each button, add an ampersand (&) before the letter you want to use for the *Alt* key combination. Try to make them consistent across all your forms, and make sure that you don't use the same letter for two different buttons.

> If you really want to use an ampersand (&) in your button text, use two ampersands in a row (&&).

849

Hide Higher Level Forms

Hide previous forms as you drill down, unless the next one is directly related to the previous one and you open the next one in Dialog mode. Don't let the user click between open forms; they may get lost or take actions you didn't plan for in your code. See the Daisy-Chaining topic later in this appendix for a method to do this.

Use Read-Only "Index" Forms

When your user needs to open a table or recordset to modify data, don't just dump the user straight into the detail form where the poor "alphabetically first" record always appears. This is very unprofessional looking, and it forces the user to constantly navigate to the desired record. In the meantime, they can mistakenly change the wrong record.

Instead, build an in-between index form showing all the records, read-only, in default Windows gray, in continuous form view (see the previous section *Use Businesslike Colors*). When the user double-clicks on a row or clicks the Detail button, show only that particular detail record by setting the WhereCondition on the OpenForm command to the key of the selected record, like this:

```
DoCmd.OpenForm FormName:="frmBusiness", _
wherecondition:="BusinessKey = " & Me!BusinessKey
```

> **Double-Click Anywhere:** If you allow double-click on a row, make sure that the user can click on any field in the row, plus the record selector itself. The technique for this is shown in Chapter 8, under section *Drilling Down with Double-Click.*

A good way to distinguish between your index form and the detail form is this: Name the index form with the plural form, and the index with the singular form. For example, you can have frmBusinesses (read-only index form showing multiple records) and frmBusiness (editable detail form showing only one record).

Another advantage of using an index form (in case you need another one!) is that you can get some performance improvements by showing just a few fields on the index form and only opening up the whole editable record (often with performance-costly combo boxes, and so on) when the user drills down on it. This is especially noticeable if you are building a client/server application using SQL Server for the back-end database.

Check Your Table Linkage

You already have a database that has a separate front-end application and back-end database, right? Well, don't let the user see an invalid table message if the back-end database isn't in the location that it was last time. Check your table links every time you start your application. There are some common routines on the Internet or in other books to check table links, or you can write your own. Either way, if you handle your linked tables before your user sees a problem, your application will look a lot more professional.

Translate Default Delete Messages

Depending on how slick you want your application to be, you may want to replace the messages Access gives you when you delete records with a friendlier version of your own. You can confirm deletions for each record or for a whole group, and you can prevent the default Access messages from appearing. This takes a bit more work, but it looks more professional. (See Chapter 8 for more information about using the `Delete` and `Before Delete Confirm` events). Use wording like: `Are you sure you want to delete product Widget125?`

Showing your own message before deleting a record is especially helpful when you have enabled Cascade Deletes in back-end relationship. You may want to use wording like: `Are you sure you want to delete business Joe's Tire Shop? This will also delete all the Payments made by this business.`

By using your own friendly warning messages instead of the default Access messages, your application will look more professional and will be easier for your users to understand.

Looking Good

Remember that your users can't see your great code or beautiful database structure. They can only see your user interface—the forms and reports in your application. Much of their perception of your application will be determined by how it looks, so it's important to pay special attention to these areas.

Now that we have your applications looking good, let's explore some techniques that you can use to make your applications more powerful and easy to use.

Daisy Chain Your Forms

When your user navigates from one form to another, one of your jobs as an application developer is to keep things simple. When users have the ability to click between multiple open forms, they can lose track of their current form, or perform actions that you fail to handle properly. A safer approach is to carefully control which forms are visible at any one time.

Controlling the visibility and flow of one form to another is often called "daisy chaining." There are a few different types of daisy chaining. They involve two main choices: whether to hide the calling form, and whether to open the called form in Dialog mode. Let's call the calling form "Form A" and the called form "Form B."

If Form A needs to requeried after Form B is closed, then you should open Form B in Dialog mode to have Form A's code wait until the user is finished with Form B. This often occurs when Form A is an index form showing multiple records, and Form B is a detail form where the user can create, change, or even delete one of the records.

If Form A provides some contextual information that would be handy for the user to see while Form B is open (like which record they are currently working with), then you can leave Form A visible while Form B is open. However, in order to prevent the user from clicking between the two and possibly obscuring Form B, you should also use our old friend Dialog mode to prevent them from clicking on Form A.

If Form A does not need to be visible, nor does it need to be requeried when Form B closed, then the easiest form of daisy chaining is just to hide Form A when Form B is opened, then make Form A visible again when Form B closes. This is the most common form of daisy chaining and it works well when traversing menu or "switchboard" forms.

> **Dialog mode—the end of the line:** When you daisy chain a form and use Dialog mode, you are committed to using Dialog mode for each level thereafter unless you hide the calling form. This is because a form opened in Dialog mode will not allow any non-Dialog Mode form to come to the forefront or to accept input. Also, if you open a report while a form is open and visible in Dialog Mode, the report will appear behind the Dialog Mode form, and will also not accept any input.

The main VBA components of the "hiding and showing" aspects of daisy chaining code fall into the following sections.

Form A Opens Form B

When Form A opens Form B, Form A also needs to "hide itself." However, to make Form A visible again, Form B needs to remember which form opened it. In order to remember this, Form A uses a global variable to "pass in" its own name. See Figure I-2.

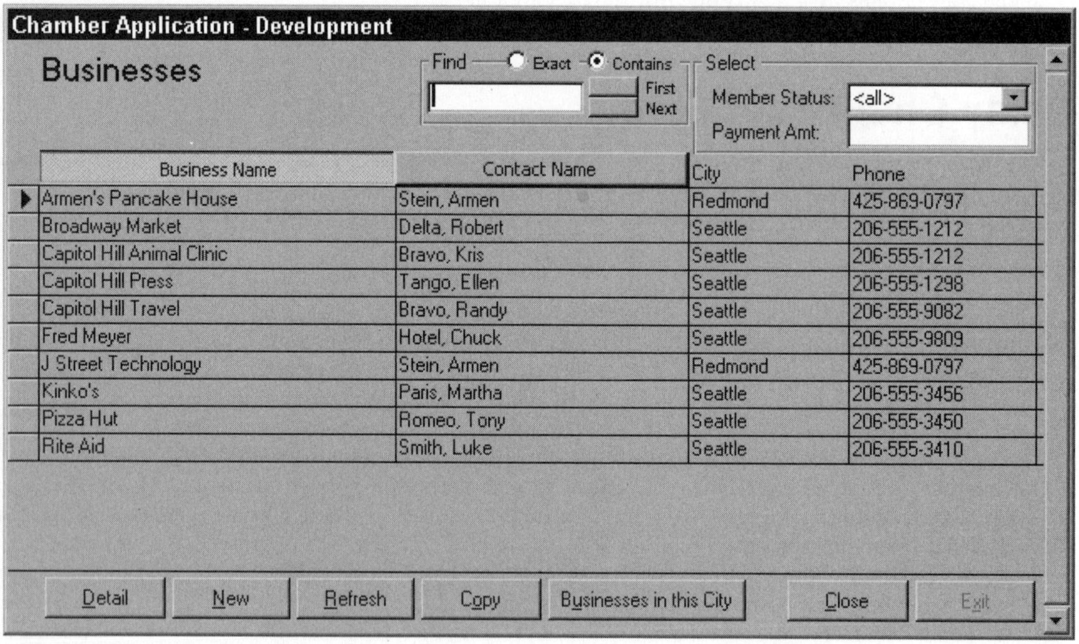

Figure I-2

> **Alternatives to Globals:** Most professional developers avoid using Global variables, as they don't always retain their values when the code stops due to an error condition or during debugging. However, if they are used for a very short time (like to bridge this gap between Form A and Form B), then they are an acceptable choice. Alternatives include using `OpenArgs` (but this is just one text property which needs to be parsed if more than one value must be passed), and a hidden form to store these "global values" as text boxes.

Here is some example code in `frmBusinesses` (an index form showing many businesses) to open `frmBusiness` (a detail form to modify a single business).

```
Private Sub cmdDetail_Click()
On Error GoTo Error_Handler

    Dim stLinkCriteria As String

    If IsNull(Me!BusinessKey) Then
        EnableDisableControls
        GoTo Exit_Procedure
    End If

    gstrCallingForm = Me.Name
    stLinkCriteria = "[BusinessKey]=" & Me![BusinessKey]
    DoCmd.OpenForm FormName:="frmBusiness", _
        wherecondition:=stLinkCriteria
    Me.Visible = False
Exit_Procedure:
    On Error Resume Next
    Exit Sub
Error_Handler:
    MsgBox "An error has occurred in this application. " _
    & "Please contact your technical support person and tell " _
    & "them this information:" _
    & vbCrLf & vbCrLf & "Error Number " & Err.Number & ", " _
    & Err.Description, _
    Buttons:=vbCritical, title:="My Application"
    Resume Exit_Procedure
    Resume

End Sub
```

Note that before `frmBusiness` is opened, the name of the current form (`Me.Name`) is loaded into the global variable `gstrCallingForm`.

```
gstrCallingForm = Me.Name
```

Then, after the line to open `frmBusiness`, the current form is hidden using `Me.Visible = False`.

```
Me.Visible = False
```

At this point, the first form is hidden and only the second form is visible, as shown in Figure I-3.

Form B Opens

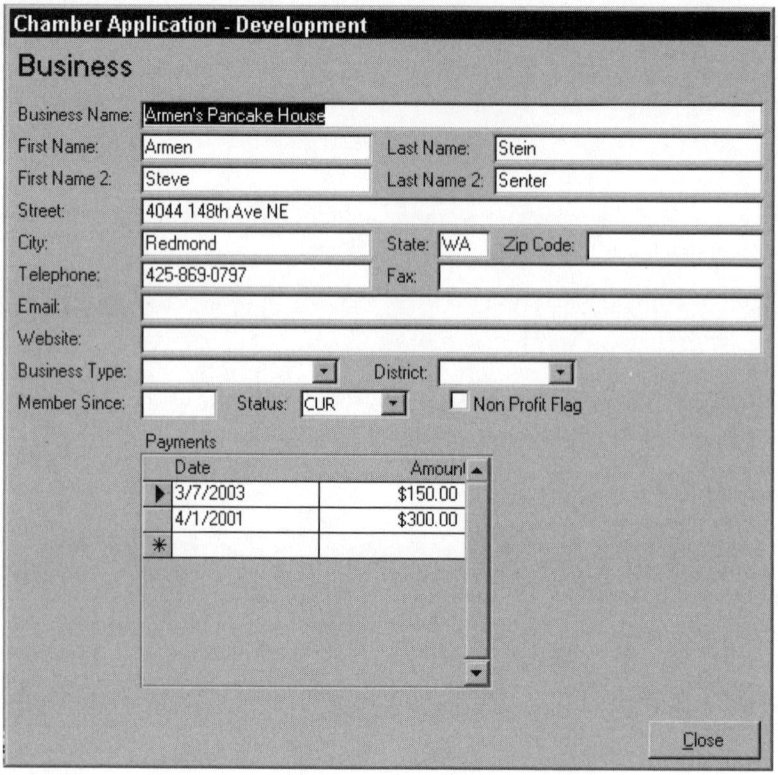

Figure I-3

When Form B wakes up, it has a little housekeeping to do before anything else happens. In the `On Open` event, it needs to remember the name of the form that called it. Later, when Form B closes, it will use that name to make Form A visible again.

```
Private Sub Form_Open(Cancel As Integer)
On Error GoTo Error_Handler

    Me.Caption = AppGlobal.ApplicationNameAndDB()
    mstrCallingForm = gstrCallingForm
    gstrCallingForm = ""

Exit_Procedure:
    Exit Sub
Error_Handler:
    MsgBox "An error has occurred in this application. " _
    & "Please contact your technical support person and tell them this
information:" _
    & vbCrLf & vbCrLf & "Error Number " & Err.Number & ", " &
Err.Description, _
    Buttons:=vbCritical, title:="My Application"
```

```
        Resume Exit_Procedure
        Resume
End Sub
```

To remember the name, the value in `gstrCallingForm` is placed safely into `mstrCallingForm`.

```
mstrCallingForm = gstrCallingForm
```

This module level variable (indicated with the `"m"` prefix) is declared at the top of the Form B's module, like this:

```
Option Compare Database
Option Explicit
Dim mstrCallingForm As String
```

Notice that `gstrCallingForm` is set to an empty string right after its contents are saved into `mstrCallingForm`:

```
gstrCallingForm = ""
```

There is no programming logic reason for doing this; it's really just a message to other programmers that we are completely done with using the global variable, so we are clearing its value. It has done its job well (for the last few milliseconds) and can go back to being an empty string now that it has transferred its contents to the local module variable.

At this point, Form B is ready to continue opening and perform whatever functions it is designed to do. It will remember the name of the calling Form A until Form B closes.

Form B Closes

During the whole time that Form B (`frmBusiness`) is open, Form A (`frmBusinesses`) remains hidden. However, when the user closes Form B, we need to make sure that Form A becomes visible again. The following code is in the `On Close` event of Form B:

```
Private Sub Form_Close()
On Error GoTo Error_Handler

    If mstrCallingForm <> "" Then
        Forms(mstrCallingForm).Visible = True
    End If

Exit_Procedure:
    Exit Sub
Error_Handler:
    If Err = 2450 Then
        ' ignore error if calling form is no longer loaded
        Resume Next
    Else
        MsgBox "An error has occurred in this application. " _
        & "Please contact your technical support person and tell them
```

```
this information:" _
        & vbCrLf & vbCrLf & "Error Number " & Err.Number & ", " &
Err.Description, _
        Buttons:=vbCritical, title:="My Application"
        Resume Exit_Procedure
        Resume
    End If
End Sub
```

The operative code here is:

```
Forms(mstrCallingForm).Visible = True
```

This code uses the `Forms` collection (a collection of all currently open forms in the database) to locate the form with the name stored in `mstrCallingForm` and make it visible.

However, there are two other sections of code that are there just for you, the developer. The first is a check to make sure that `mstrCallingForm` actually has a value before attempting to make it visible. This is to allow you to open Form B directly during development (instead of from Form A), and not have to deal with the resulting error every time Form B closes.

```
If mstrCallingForm <> "" Then
    Forms(mstrCallingForm).Visible = True
End If
```

Along the same lines, the error handler code contains an exception for `Error 2450`. This error will occur if the calling form is no longer loaded—again, this is to allow you, in development mode, to close Form A while Form B is open without seeing an error when Form B closes.

```
If Err = 2450 Then
    ' ignore error if calling form is no longer loaded
    Resume Next
```

When Form B closes and makes Form A visible again, Form B's link in the daisy chain is complete.

When Form A Is a Subform

Sometimes Form A is a subform. In this case, you cannot send `Me.Name` into Form B, because a subform cannot be made visible or hidden directly. Instead, the parent form name needs to be specified.

This is easy to do. Instead of setting the global variable and making the current form hidden, like this:

```
gstrCallingForm = Me.Name
Me.Visible = False
```

send use the name of the parent form, like this:

```
gstrCallingForm = Me.Parent.Name
Me.Parent.Visible = False
```

The calling form will never know the difference. When it closes, the parent form will be made visible again.

Find Records

Access provides a way to search for records, but it leaves a lot to be desired. The binoculars button pops up a dialog box with several search options, but most users don't know how to use it properly. The problem is that it is has too many options, when your user probably just wants to find a record containing a certain text value.

Instead of the dreaded binoculars, you can include a quick and easy way for your user to find records. Figure I-4 shows a form with a built-in technique to find records.

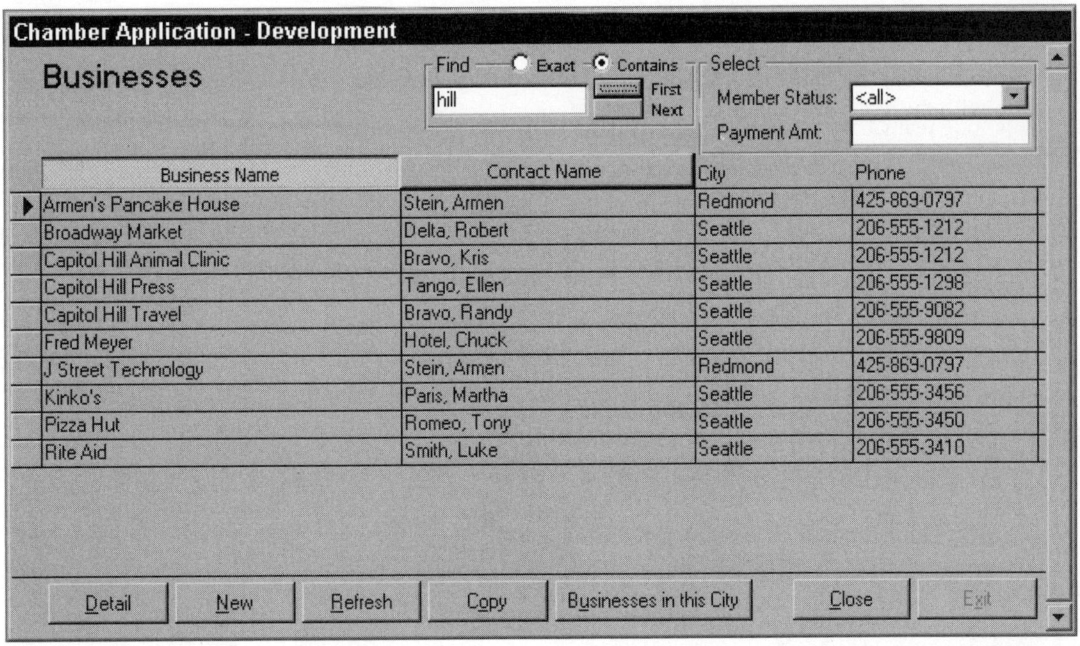

Figure I-4

This record finding technique allows any phrase to be entered in the text box, then finds the first (or next) record that contains that phrase anywhere in the displayed fields. Alternatively, the user may use the radio buttons to switch to an *exact* match instead of a *contains* search, where the entire field must match the phrase. This *exact* mode is not used very often, but it can be handy in searching for exact codes or numbers (such as membership or account numbers).

Calling the Record Finder Code

The On Click event of the Find button (shown in Figure I-4) includes this code:

```
Private Sub cmdFirst_Click()
On Error GoTo Error_Handler

    FindRecordLike "first"
```

```
Exit_Procedure:
    On Error Resume Next
    Exit Sub
Error_Handler:
    MsgBox "An error has occurred in this application. " _
    & "Please contact your technical support person and tell " _
    & "them this information:" _
    & vbCrLf & vbCrLf & "Error Number " & Err.Number & ", " _
    & Err.Description, _
    Buttons:=vbCritical, title:="My Application"
    Resume Exit_Procedure
    Resume

End Sub
```

This code really has only one operative line:

```
FindRecordLike "first"
```

The code behind cmdNext_Click() is almost identical. Instead of using "first" as the parameter for FindRecordLike, it sends in "next":

```
FindRecordLike "next"
```

Now, let's take a look at the code for the subroutine FindRecordLike. This code also resides in the same index form that contains the record finder controls (shown in Figure I-3). It looks like this:

```
Private Sub FindRecordLike(strFindMode As String)
On Error GoTo Error_Handler

Call ww_FindRecord(frmCallingForm:=Me, _
        ctlFindFirst:=Me!cmdFirst, _
        ctlFindNext:=Me!cmdNext, _
        ctlSearchText:=Me!txtFind, _
        ctlSearchOption:=Me!optFind, _
        strFindMode:=strFindMode, _
        strField1:="BusinessName", _
        strField2:="LastName", _
        strField3:="FirstName", _
        strField4:="City")

Exit_Procedure:
    On Error Resume Next
    Exit Sub
Error_Handler:
    MsgBox "An error has occurred in this application. " _
    & "Please contact your technical support person and tell them this
information:" _
    & vbCrLf & vbCrLf & "Error Number " & Err.Number & ", " &
Err.Description, _
    Buttons:=vbCritical, title:="My Application"
    Resume Exit_Procedure
    Resume
End Sub
```

This Sub accepts a parameter strFindMode of "first" or "next", which it passes directly on to the ww_FindRecord procedure. In fact, pretty much all this procedure does is call ww_FindRecord. The interesting part is the set of parameters that is passed to ww_FindRecord, many of which are explained the next section. However, we'll first take a look at the parameters strField1, strField2, strField3, and strField4.

In order for the record finder routine to know which fields to search for our user's phrase, we need to make it known. We can do this by sending in up to 10 field names. These must be names of fields that appear in the Recordsource for the form. Although they don't technically have to appear on the form itself, it will seem strange to the user to find records containing a phrase that they can't see.

> **Why not automate the list of fields?** It would be possible to use VBA to cycle through all of the fields displayed on the form, using the form's Controls collection, and send their names to the ww_FindRecord procedure automatically. However, this wouldn't necessarily be desirable, as you may not want all the fields to be searchable. By sending them yourself using this simple code, you can carefully control which fields are searched.

In this example, we are only sending in four field names to be searched, but we could have specified up to 10. Fields 2 through 10 are optional parameters, and are explained later in this chapter.

Record Finder Code

In order to make this code easy to implement, we want to reuse as much code as possible. The key to this technique is to pass references to the controls on this form (the text box, buttons, even the form itself) to a reusable Record Finder function. Note that this code has a "ww" prefix (for Wiley-Wrox) to reduce conflicts with any other public procedures.

```
Option Compare Database
Option Explicit

'Record Finder

'Accepts references from a continuous form with Record Finder
'controls, finds the first/next record containing the search
'text in one of the passed-in field names, and repositions the
'form to that record.

Public Function ww_FindRecord(frmCallingForm As Form, _
        ctlFindFirst As Control, _
        ctlFindNext As Control, _
        ctlSearchText As Control, _
        ctlSearchOption As Control, _
        strFindMode As String, _
        strField1 As String, _
        Optional strField2 As String, _
        Optional strField3 As String, _
        Optional strField4 As String, _
        Optional strField5 As String, _
        Optional strField6 As String, _
```

```
            Optional strField7 As String, _
            Optional strField8 As String, _
            Optional strField9 As String, _
            Optional strField10 As String)

On Error GoTo Error_Handler

Dim recClone As Recordset
Dim intBookmark As String
Dim strAllFields As String
Dim strSelection As String

' Field delimiter is used to separate concatenated
' field values below. This prevents text from being
' matched across adjacent fields. It may be changed
' to any text value that is unlikely to appear in the fields.
Const FIELDDELIMITER = "@%%@"

' If there is no string to search for set the focus back to
' the text box.
If ctlSearchText & "" = "" Or strField1 & "" = "" Then
    ctlSearchText.SetFocus
    Exit Function
End If

DoCmd.Hourglass True

ww_FindRecord = False
```

This next section of code handles the search if the user has specified the Contains mode. This is the default search and the most flexible, as it will find the phrase anywhere in any of the specified fields.

```
'Test search option
If ctlSearchOption = 1 Then 'Contains search

    ' build string to concatenate all fields together
    strAllFields = "[" & strField1 & "]"
    If strField2 <> "" Then
        strAllFields = strAllFields & " & """ & FIELDDELIMITER & _
        """ & [" & strField2 & "]"
    End If
    If strField3 <> "" Then
        strAllFields = strAllFields & " & """ & FIELDDELIMITER & _
        """ & [" & strField3 & "]"
    End If
    If strField4 <> "" Then
        strAllFields = strAllFields & " & """ & FIELDDELIMITER & _
        """ & [" & strField4 & "]"
    End If
    If strField5 <> "" Then
        strAllFields = strAllFields & " & """ & FIELDDELIMITER & _
        """ & [" & strField5 & "]"
    End If
```

```
            If strField6 <> "" Then
                strAllFields = strAllFields & " & """ & FIELDDELIMITER & _
                """ & [" & strField6 & "]"
            End If
            If strField7 <> "" Then
                strAllFields = strAllFields & " & """ & FIELDDELIMITER & _
                """ & [" & strField7 & "]"
            End If
            If strField8 <> "" Then
                strAllFields = strAllFields & " & """ & FIELDDELIMITER & _
                """ & [" & strField8 & "]"
            End If
            If strField9 <> "" Then
                strAllFields = strAllFields & " & """ & FIELDDELIMITER & _
                """ & [" & strField9 & "]"
            End If
            If strField10 <> "" Then
                strAllFields = strAllFields & " & """ & FIELDDELIMITER & _
                """ & [" & strField10 & "]"
            End If


            Set recClone = frmCallingForm.RecordsetClone

            ' if find First button was used
            If strFindMode = "first" Then
                recClone.FindFirst strAllFields & " Like ""*" & _
                Replace(ctlSearchText, """", """""") & "*"""
                If recClone.NoMatch Then
                    MsgBox "No matches found.", vbOKOnly, "Record Finder"
                    ctlSearchText.SetFocus
                Else
                    frmCallingForm.Bookmark = recClone.Bookmark
                    ctlFindNext.SetFocus
                    ww_FindRecord = True
                End If
            Else
                ' if find Next button was used
                If strFindMode = "next" Then
                    recClone.Bookmark = frmCallingForm.Bookmark
                    recClone.FindNext strAllFields & " Like ""*" & _
                    Replace(ctlSearchText, """", """""") & "*"""
                    If recClone.NoMatch Then
                        MsgBox "No more matches found.", vbOKOnly, _
                        "Record Finder"
                        ctlFindFirst.SetFocus
                    Else
                        frmCallingForm.Bookmark = recClone.Bookmark
                        ctlFindNext.SetFocus
                        ww_FindRecord = True
                    End If
                End If

            End If
        End If
Else
```

Now, we move on to the search if the user specified Exact mode. This mode checks the exact contents of each of the specified fields to see if they equal the user's search phrase.

```
'ctlSearchOption = 2 'Exact Search

    strSelection = "CStr(" & strField1 & " & """") = """ & _
    Replace(ctlSearchText, """", """""") & """"
    If strField2 <> "" Then
        strSelection = strSelection & _
        " OR CStr(" & strField2 & " & """") = """ & _
        Replace(ctlSearchText, """", """""") & """"
    End If
    If strField3 <> "" Then
        strSelection = strSelection & _
        " OR CStr(" & strField3 & " & """") = """ & _
        Replace(ctlSearchText, """", """""") & """"
    End If
    If strField4 <> "" Then
        strSelection = strSelection & _
        " OR CStr(" & strField4 & " & """") = """ & _
        Replace(ctlSearchText, """", """""") & """"
    End If
    If strField5 <> "" Then
        strSelection = strSelection & _
        " OR CStr(" & strField5 & " & """") = """ & _
        Replace(ctlSearchText, """", """""") & """"
    End If
    If strField6 <> "" Then
        strSelection = strSelection & _
        " OR CStr(" & strField6 & " & """") = """ & _
        Replace(ctlSearchText, """", """""") & """"
    End If
    If strField7 <> "" Then
        strSelection = strSelection & _
        " OR CStr(" & strField7 & " & """") = """ & _
        Replace(ctlSearchText, """", """""") & """"
    End If
    If strField8 <> "" Then
        strSelection = strSelection & _
        " OR CStr(" & strField8 & " & """") = """ & _
        Replace(ctlSearchText, """", """""") & """"
    End If
    If strField9 <> "" Then
        strSelection = strSelection & _
        " OR CStr(" & strField9 & " & """") = """ & _
        Replace(ctlSearchText, """", """""") & """"
    End If
    If strField10 <> "" Then
        strSelection = strSelection & _
        " OR CStr(" & strField10 & " & """") = """ & _
        Replace(ctlSearchText, """", """""") & """"
    End If

    Set recClone = frmCallingForm.RecordsetClone
```

```
            If strFindMode = "first" Then
                recClone.FindFirst strSelection
                If recClone.NoMatch Then
                    MsgBox "No matches found.", vbOKOnly, "Record Finder"
                    ctlSearchText.SetFocus
                Else
                    frmCallingForm.Bookmark = recClone.Bookmark
                    ctlFindNext.SetFocus
                    ww_FindRecord = True
                End If
            Else
                ' if find Next button was used
                If strFindMode = "next" Then
                    recClone.Bookmark = frmCallingForm.Bookmark
                    recClone.FindNext strSelection
                    If recClone.NoMatch Then
                        MsgBox "No more matches found.", vbOKOnly, _
                        "Record Finder"
                        ctlFindFirst.SetFocus
                    Else
                        frmCallingForm.Bookmark = recClone.Bookmark
                        ctlFindNext.SetFocus
                        ww_FindRecord = True
                    End If

                End If
            End If
        End If

        DoCmd.Hourglass False

Exit_Procedure:
        Exit Function

Error_Handler:
        DoCmd.Hourglass False
        MsgBox "An error has occurred in this application. " _
        & "Please contact your technical support person and tell " _
        & "them this information:" _
        & vbCrLf & vbCrLf & "Error Number " & Err.Number & ", " _
        & Err.Description, Buttons:=vbCritical, title:="My Application"
        Resume Exit_Procedure
        Resume
End Function
```

There are several techniques in this code that are worth a closer look. They are explained in the next few sections.

Passing Control and Form References to a Function

This function does not reside behind any form, but rather in a separate module. In order for it to be usable from any index form, it needs to be able to interact with that form. To do so, we pass object references from our form in addition to actual parameter values. These reference parameters are:

❑ frmCallingForm (the actual form itself, to build a RecordsetClone and to set the Bookmark)

❑ ctlFindFirst (the First button, to set focus)

❑ ctlFindNext (to Next button, to set focus)

❑ ctlSearchText (the text box with the search phrase, to use for searching and to set focus)

❑ ctlSearchOption (the radio button group of Exact/Contains, to determine which kind of search to perform)

The key thing to remember here is that these are not values themselves; they are pointers to the controls on the original form, so they give us direct access to those controls as if this code were in that form itself.

The rest of the parameters are values, such as the Find mode (first or next matching record) and the names of up to 10 fields to search.

Optional Parameters

This function uses *optional parameters*, meaning that when you call this function, you can choose whether or not to specify them. In this case, the optional parameters are strField2 through strField10. Optional parameters are very useful in this case, because they give you the flexibility of specifying any number of fields to search, from 1 to 10. If we didn't use optional parameters in this procedure, we would have to specify all 10 field names every time we called it, sending in empty strings for the ones we didn't need.

Using the RecordsetClone

A RecordsetClone is a recordset based on a form's recordset, but with full search capabilities and a different record cursor. We use a RecordsetClone of the form to find a matching record, and then use its Bookmark property to position the form to the matching record. We do all this with the passed in Form reference:

```
Set recClone = frmCallingForm.RecordsetClone
frmCallingForm.Bookmark = recClone.Bookmark
```

Remember, the form reference was passed in as a parameter to this procedure, so the RecordsetClone being searched is the same as the recordset currently displayed on the index form that called our record finder procedure.

Searching Multiple Fields Using Concatenation

In order to search multiple fields, this function takes a different approach than you might be familiar with. Instead of building a complex SQL string that searches each specified field in the recordset with OR statements, it concatenates all the desired fields from the recordset into one large string (strAllFields). Then it searches this large text field for the search phrase.

There's one problem with this approach, however. The search phrase may be discovered using the end of one field and the beginning of another. For example, if the fields for City and State are concatenated together, they may look like this:

```
SeattleWA
```

If your user searches for the phrase "lew", this record will be found, even though "lew" doesn't appear in any one field.

To avoid this problem, we use the FIELDDELIMETER constant. It is set to "@%%@", a value that's unlikely to occur in any search phrase. When we concatenate the desired fields together into the one big field, they are separated by this delimiter value, like this:

```
Seattle@%%@WA
```

By doing this, we separate the two words and prevent a search for "lew" from finding this record.

Handling Quotes in the Search Phrase

There's a potential problem when the user types a quote (") in the search phrase, as shown in Figure I-5.

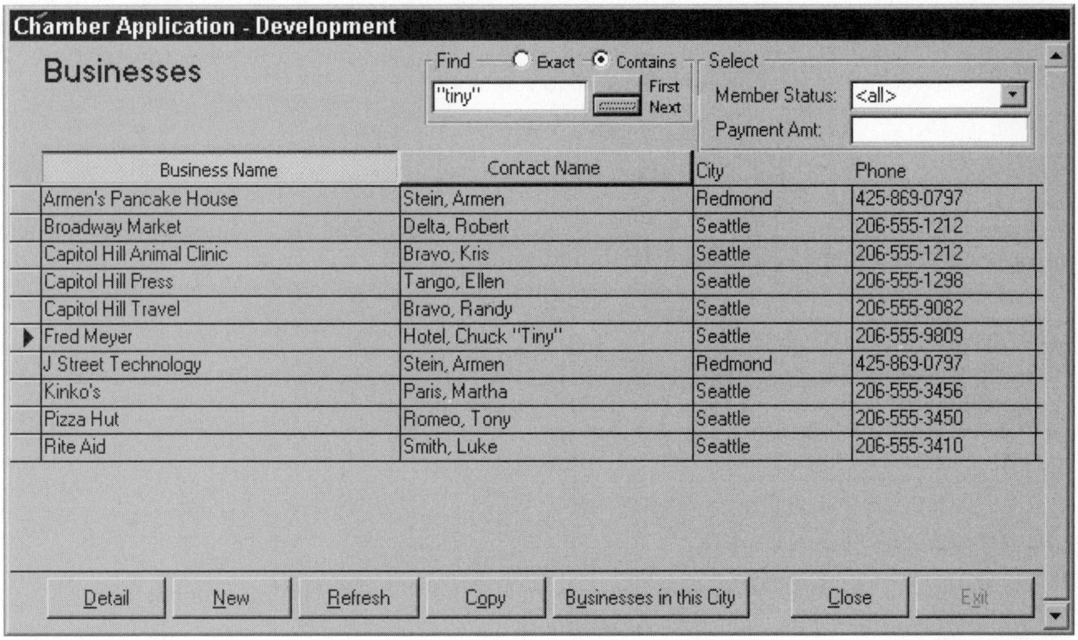

Figure I-5

Since we build strings using quotes in the code, these extra quotes supplied by the user can cause errors. To guard against this, we need to replace each quote in the user's search phrase with two quotes (there's a full discussion of string handling techniques in Chapter 14, "SQL and VBA").

To perform the quote replacement, we use the VBA Replace function in this rather strange-looking code:

```
Replace(ctlSearchText, """", """""")
```

This takes every instance of a quote (") in ctlSearchText and replaces it with two quotes (""). Then, when we build search strings with it, those doubled-up quotes will "collapse" back into solo quotes. It's weird, but it works.

Setting Focus from Afar

To help the user use the Find routine efficiently, we control the focus so that keystrokes make sense. For example, if the user clicks the First button and no match is found, we know that they are probably going to want to change the search phrase to something else. To help them in this regard, we set the focus to the Search Text control.

```
If recClone.NoMatch Then
    MsgBox "No matches found.", vbOKOnly, "Record Finder"
    ctlSearchText.SetFocus
```

Remember, this code is not in the form the user is viewing—we are controlling focus from this procedure using a reference to the control on the index form that called ww_FindRecord.

Similarly, in order to facilitate cycling through all the matching records, we set focus to the Next button when a record is found, and to the First button after no more records are found. This allows the user to continue to press the *Enter* key on the keyboard to repeatedly loop through all the matching records. This sort of convenience feature adds a lot of polish to your applications.

Split Your Application

You've probably heard it many times: Your application should be split into a front-end application and a back-end database. The benefits are many, including the ability to easily switch back-end databases (for example, between Production and Test) and to deliver new versions of the application without disturbing the user's data.

Access provides a wizard to split databases, but it's easy to do yourself if you follow these steps. Also, it will improve your understanding of what splitting a database really does.

1. Make a backup.

2. Copy your MDB to another MDB, named something like "MyApp Data.MDB".

3. Rename the first MDB "MyApp Application.MDB".

4. In the Data MDB, delete all objects except the tables. You can also delete configuration tables that you know will be in the front-end database.

5. In the Application MDB, delete the tables (except any local tables). Then, use File..Get External Data..Link Tables to link all the tables from the Data MDB.

Now that your database is split, you can relink tables using the Linked Table Manager under the Tools..Database Utilities menu, or you can install one of the many Access table relinker functions available on the Internet or in other books.

Display Informative Form Captions

If you don't set your own form Captions, Access will just display the form name there, as shown in Figure I-6.

This is a sure sign of a novice developer. You need to at least replace the Caption with the name of your application. One nice additional feature for the Caption is to indicate which back-end database you are currently using. That way, your user knows instantly whether they are in the Production or Test database, for example.

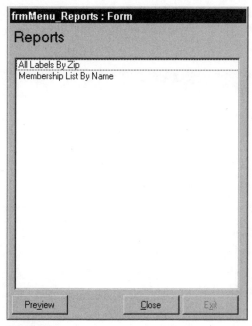

Figure I-6

You'll need a table in the back-end database to store system-wide configuration values. In this example, it is named tsysConfig_System, and it contains a field containing the name of the database (see Figure I-7).

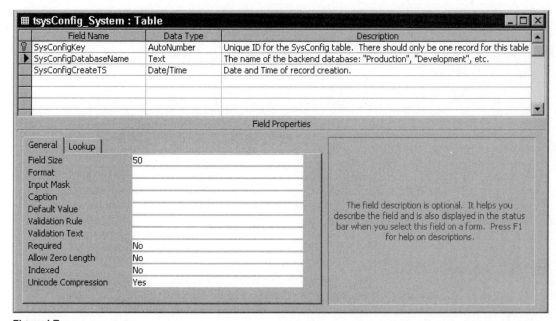

Figure I-7

You'll also need a local table in the front-end MDB to store static values for the application itself, as shown in Figure I-8. In our example, one of the fields is the name of the application, suitable for showing on various forms throughout the system.

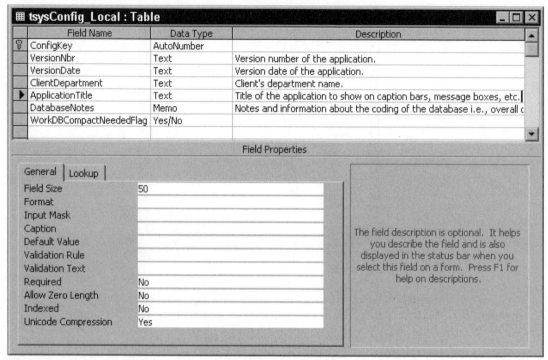

Figure I-8

The code to set the Caption is easy. It belongs in the Open event code behind every form:

```
Me.Caption = DLookup("ApplicationTitle", "tsysConfig_Local") _
& " - " & DLookup("SysConfigDatabaseName", "tsysConfig_System")
```

Now, when each form opens, you can set the Caption to the title of the application, concatenated with the name of the back-end database, as in Figure I-9.

By setting the caption of every form, you avoid the rookie move of showing an internal form name like "frmBusinesses" in the caption. And by using a configuration table to supply the application name, you avoid hard-coding it in every form. This will make your job a lot easier for each application you develop, as you won't have to change this code in every table—only the value in the one table.

Preload Records

Sometimes, you'll have a problem when you open a detail form for a brand new record. If there is a subform with child records on the detail form, your user will encounter an error if they try to create a child record before they have entered any data for the parent (master) record, as shown in Figure I-10.

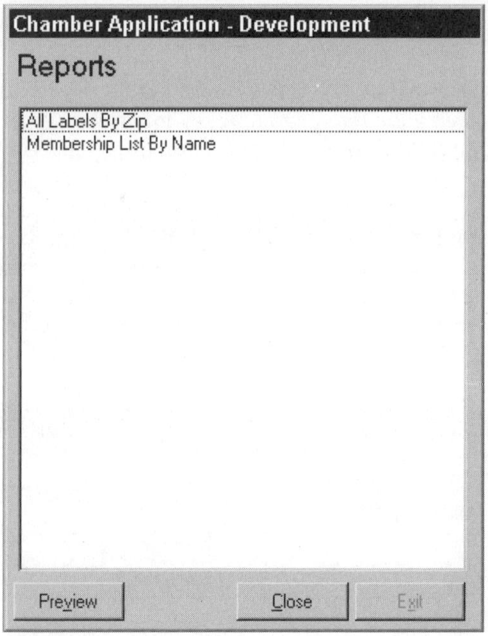

Figure I-9

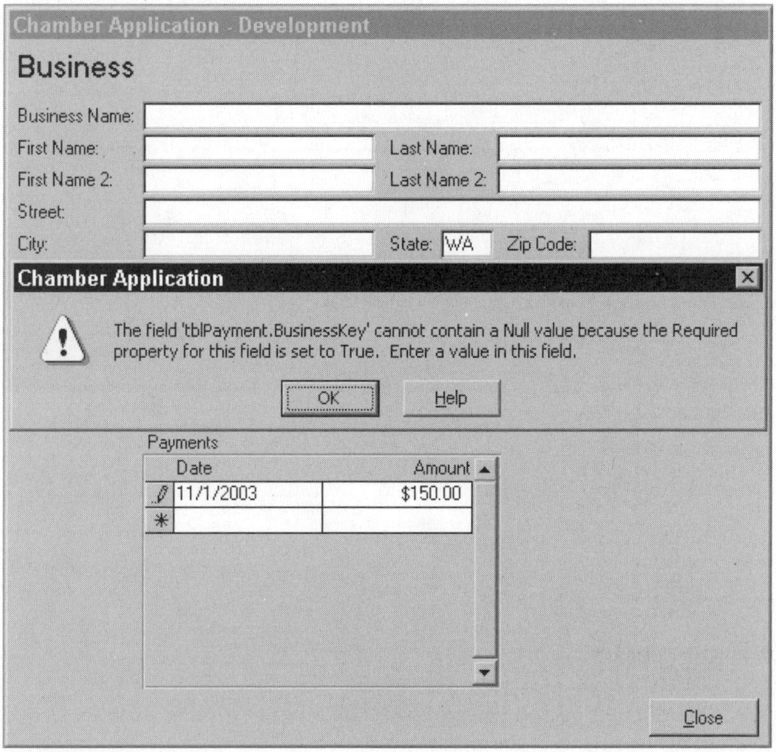

Figure I-10

This is because the parent key still has a Null key, and the child record has a required foreign key for the parent `Business` record. Even if the foreign parent key in the child record isn't set to `Required`, there will be another problem: The child record will have a null foreign parent key, making it an orphan record with no parent.

One way to prevent this error is to create an empty record before opening the `Detail` form. This way, the parent record already has a primary key and can accept related child records. During this preloading operation, you can specify a default name for the new record, such as `"<New Business>"`. This gives your user a clear indicator that they have just created a new record and allows them to add child records immediately. The new record is shown in Figure I-11.

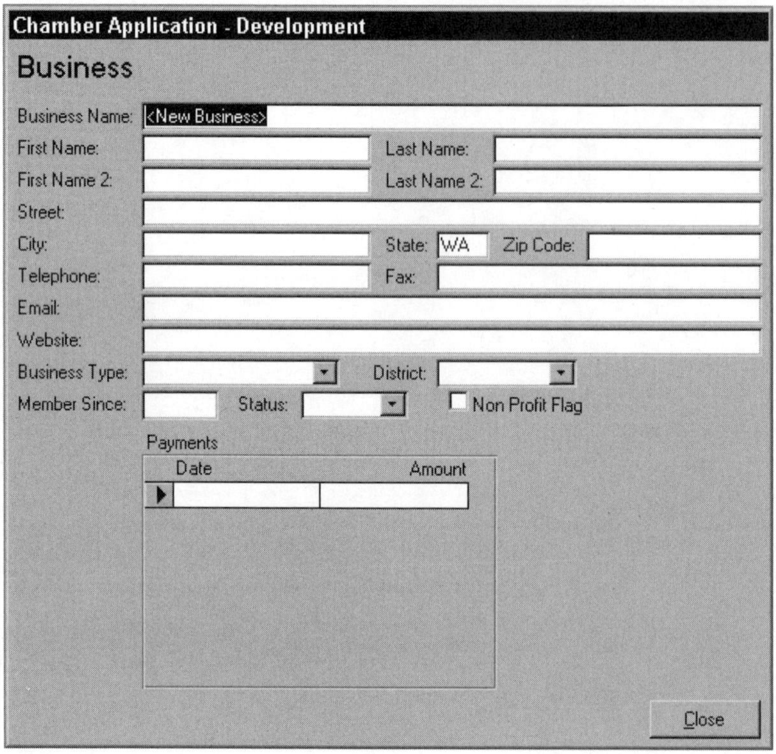

Figure I-11

The code to preload the record is in the index form `"frmBusinesses"`, in the `Click` event of the `New` button:

```
Private Sub cmdNew_Click()
On Error GoTo Error_Handler

    Dim rs As Recordset
    Dim strDocName As String
    Dim strLinkCriteria As String

    'Open form to new record
```

```
        gstrCallingForm = Me.Name
        strDocName = "frmBusiness"
        strLinkCriteria = "[BusinessKey]=" & NewBusinessKey()
        Me.Visible = False
        DoCmd.OpenForm FormName:=strDocName, _
        wherecondition:=strLinkCriteria, Windowmode:=acDialog

        'Requery index form to pick up the new record, then
        'set the bookmark to this new record.
        Me.Requery
        Set rs = Me.RecordsetClone
        If Me.RecordsetClone.RecordCount > 0 Then
            'If first new record was cancelled, would fail.
            rs.FindFirst strLinkCriteria
            If Not rs.EOF Then
                Me.Bookmark = rs.Bookmark
            End If
        End If

Exit_Procedure:
    On Error Resume Next
    rs.Close
    Set rs = Nothing
    Exit Sub
Error_Handler:
    MsgBox "An error has occurred in this application. " _
    & "Please contact your technical support person and tell" _
    & " them this information:" _
    & vbCrLf & vbCrLf & "Error Number " & Err.Number & ", " & _
    Err.Description, Buttons:=vbCritical, title:="My Application"
    Resume Exit_Procedure
    Resume

End Sub
```

Notice that after Business form is closed, this Business form is requeried, and then positioned to the new Business record so the user gets visual feedback that the record they just added is indeed now in the list.

Also note that the Business form is opened with a key specified as NewBusinessKey(). This function to generate the new Business record looks like this:

```
Public Function NewBusinessKey() As Long
On Error GoTo Error_Handler
'This function creates a new Business record and returns the key.

    Dim db As Database
    Dim rec As Recordset
    Set db = CurrentDb
    Set rec = db.OpenRecordset("tblBusiness")

    'Add the record, storing new key value as variable and
    'passing it out as the function name
    With rec
```

```
            .AddNew
            NewBusinessKey = rec!BusinessKey
            !BusinessName = "<New Business>"
            .Update
            .Close
        End With

        Set rec = Nothing

Exit_Procedure:
        Exit Function
Error_Handler:
        MsgBox "An error has occurred in this application. " _
        & "Please contact your technical support person and tell" _
        & " them this information:" _
        & vbCrLf & vbCrLf & "Error Number " & Err.Number & ", " & _
        Err.Description, Buttons:=vbCritical, title:="My Application"
        Resume Exit_Procedure
        Resume
End Function
```

Now, there's only one more issue to handle. If the user tries to leave the Business Name as
"<New Business>", we need to prompt them to see whether we should clean up the record, as shown
in Figure I-12.

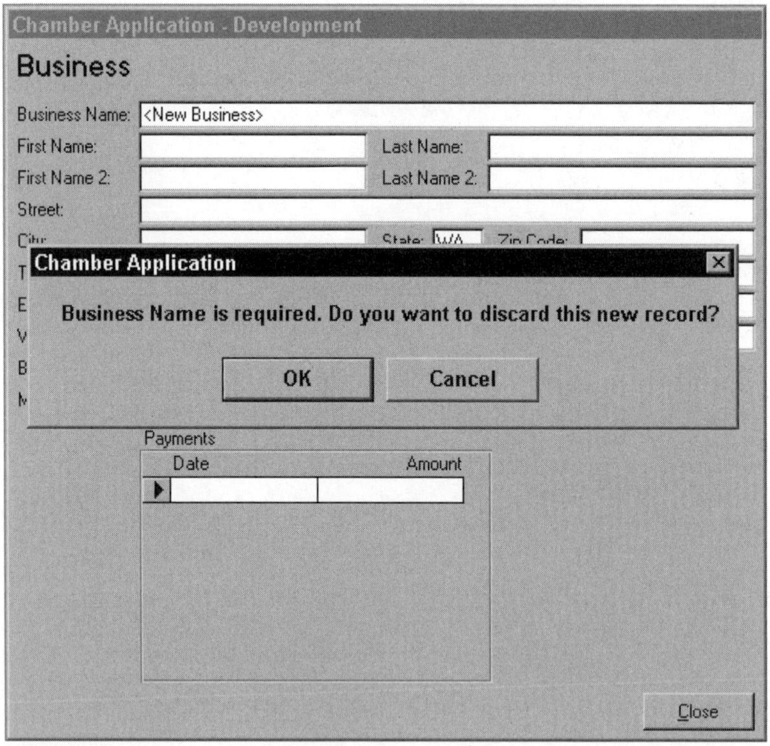

Figure I-12

Notice that we use the word "discard" instead of "delete". Even though we know that we have created a new record, the user doesn't know that. To them, this record hasn't been fully created yet, so using the word "delete" may be confusing.

The code for this cleanup is in the Unload event of the Business form:

```
Private Sub Form_Unload(Cancel As Integer)
On Error GoTo Error_Handler

Dim strSQL As String
Dim bDelete As Boolean

bDelete = False

'If user has not changed preloaded record, or if there is no name,
'delete the record.
If (Me!BusinessName = "<New Business>") Then
    If MsgBox("Business Name is required. Do you want to " _
        & "discard this new record?", vbOKCancel, _
        DLookup("ApplicationTitle", "tsysConfig_Local")) = vbOK Then
        'Delete the record
        bDelete = True
    Else
        'Yes delete the record, return to the form
        Cancel = True
    End If
End If

If Me!BusinessName & "" = "" Then
    If MsgBox("Business Name is required. Would you like to " _
        & "delete this record?", vbOKCancel, _
        DLookup("ApplicationTitle", "tsysConfig_Local")) = vbOK Then
        'Delete the record
        bDelete = True
    Else
        Cancel = True
    End If
End If

If bDelete = True Then
    strSQL = "DELETE * FROM tblBusiness WHERE BusinessKey = " _
    & Me!BusinessKey
    DoCmd.SetWarnings False
    DoCmd.RunSQL strSQL
    DoCmd.SetWarnings True
End If

Exit_Procedure:
    Exit Sub
Error_Handler:
    DoCmd.SetWarnings True
    MsgBox "An error has occurred in this application. " _
    & "Please contact your technical support person and tell" _
    & " them this information:" _
```

```
            & vbCrLf & vbCrLf & "Error Number " & Err.Number & ", " & _
            Err.Description, Buttons:=vbCritical, title:="My Application"
            Resume Exit_Procedure
            Resume
      End Sub
```

If the user clicks OK, we delete the record and close the form. If they click Cancel, we cancel the Unload event and return to this record.

Note that this code actually does use the word "delete" if the Business Name is blank. This is because some users are unsure of how to delete a record, and will try to do so by clearing out the main name field. This code will recognize this situation and offer to delete the record.

Use a Splash Screen

You can display a custom logo (instead of the Access logo) while the Access program loads. Name a bitmap the same name as your mdb file (YourAppName.bmp) and put it in the same folder as the MDB. This bitmap image will be displayed instead of the Access startup logo when you launch your application.

Now, with a fast computer, you probably won't notice this logo since it will only be displayed for a fraction of a second. So, you need another splash screen. The first screen of your application should always be a splash screen that shows at least the application name, client's company name, version number, and your company name. This single feature says, "this is a professional application."

When your application starts, it should show a Splash screen with a logo (either yours or your client's) and some basic application information, as shown in Figure I-13.

Figure I-13

Example code for displaying the Splash screen for a specified number of seconds (3 or 4 seconds seems like a good duration) can be found on the Microsoft Knowledgebase article 101374.

Pop-Up Memo Workspace Form with Spell-Check

Sometimes you want to give your user more room to enter long text into a memo field. Instead of using the built-in Access zoom feature, you can include a workspace feature to zoom into a memo field, allow the user to OK or Cancel their changes, and even invoke the Word spell-checking feature (if Word is installed on their PC). This feature is shown in Figure I-14.

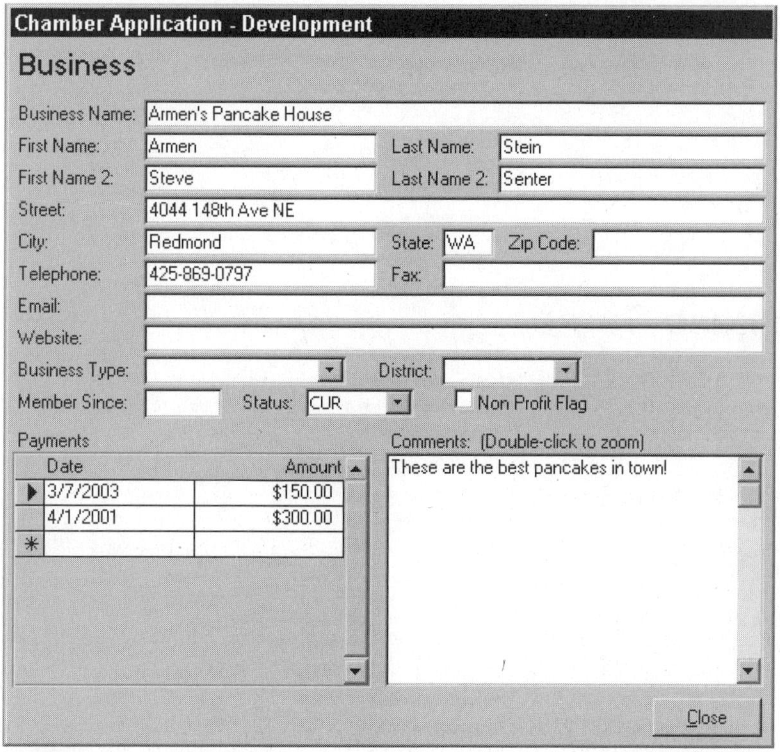

Figure I-14

The code in the double-click event of the memo field is simple:

```
Private Sub BusinessComments_DblClick(Cancel As Integer)
On Error GoTo Error_Handler

    Workspace Me.ActiveControl, Me

Exit_Procedure:
    Exit Sub
Error_Handler:
    DoCmd.SetWarnings True
    MsgBox "An error has occurred in this application. " _
    & "Please contact your technical support person and tell" _
    & " them this information:" _
    & vbCrLf & vbCrLf & "Error Number " & Err.Number & ", " & _
    Err.Description, Buttons:=vbCritical, title:="My Application"
    Resume Exit_Procedure
    Resume

End Sub
```

The code in the Workspace procedure looks like this:

```
Sub Workspace(ctl As Control, CallingForm As Form)
On Error GoTo Err_Workspace

        CallingForm.Refresh
        'Save any data which may have been entered into memo field

        Set gctlWorkspaceSource = ctl

        If ctl.Locked Or Not ctl.Enabled Then
            DoCmd.OpenForm "frmWorkspace", WindowMode:=acDialog, _
            OpenArgs:="ReadOnly"
        Else
            DoCmd.OpenForm "frmWorkspace", WindowMode:=acDialog
        End If

        If IsLoaded("frmWorkspace") Then
            gctlWorkspaceSource = Forms.frmWorkspace.txtWorkspace
            DoCmd.Close acForm, "frmWorkspace"
        End If

Exit_Workspace:
    Exit Sub
Err_Workspace:
    Select Case Err
        Case 3163 'Too much data for field
            MsgBox "The field is too small to accept the amount " _
            & "of data you attempted to insert. As a result, " _
            & "the operation has been cancelled.", vbExclamation, _
            DLookup("ApplicationTitle", "tsysConfig_Local")
            Resume Next
        Case Else
            MsgBox Err.Number & ", " & Err.Description
            Resume Exit_Workspace
    End Select
End Sub
```

Notice that if the original text box control is locked, the Workspace form is passed OpenArgs of "ReadOnly". This will cause the Workspace form to display the data in a gray, locked text box.

Also, the text on the original form is updated by the Workspace text if the Workspace form is still open. After that, the Workspace form is closed.

When the Workspace form opens, it looks like Figure I-15.

The code in the Workspace form looks like this:

```
Option Compare Database
Option Explicit
'Note: Uncomment the mode you want to support:
'Const conSpellCheckOption = 0 'No Spell Checking,
Const conSpellCheckOption = 1 'Default Spell Checking
```

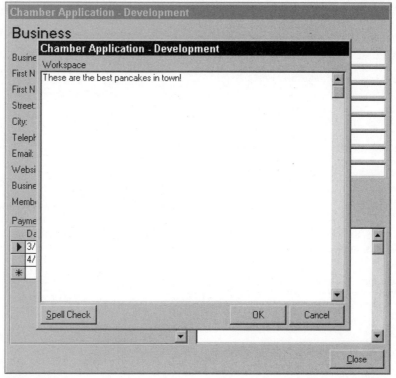

Figure I-15

```
'Const conSpellCheckOption = 2 'Word Grammer
'Const conSpellCheckOption = 3 'Word Grammer with Options
```

Options, options: This code is written so that you, the programmer can decide which level of spell checking you want to provide. You can try the different types of spell checking to see which one you want to provide to your users, or turn it off entirely using a value of 0.

```
Private Sub cmdCancel_Click()
On Error GoTo Err_cmdCancel_Click

    DoCmd.Close acForm, ObjectName:=Me.Name

Exit_cmdCancel_Click:
    Exit Sub
Err_cmdCancel_Click:
    MsgBox Err.Number & ", " & Err.Description
    Resume Exit_cmdCancel_Click
    Resume
End Sub
```

If the `Cancel` button is clicked, the Workspace form is closed. That will prevent any changes from making it back to the calling form.

```
Private Sub cmdOK_Click()
On Error GoTo Err_cmdOK_Click

    Me.Visible = False

Exit_cmdOK_Click:
    Exit Sub
Err_cmdOK_Click:
    MsgBox Err.Number & ", " & Err.Description
    Resume Exit_cmdOK_Click
    Resume
End Sub
```

Notice that if OK is clicked, the Workspace form is merely hidden. It was opened in Dialog mode, so the calling code was paused until now.

```
Private Sub cmdSpellCheck_Click()
On Error GoTo Err_cmdSpellCheck_Click

    Dim intTemp As Integer

    Select Case conSpellCheckOption
        'This is set in the frmWorkspace declarations section above
        Case 1 'Use default spell checker
            intTemp = fnCheckSpelling(Me!txtWorkspace, False)
        Case 2, 3 'Use MS Word grammer checker
            intTemp = fnCheckSpelling(Me!txtWorkspace, True)
    End Select

Exit_cmdSpellCheck_Click:
    Exit Sub
Err_cmdSpellCheck_Click:
    MsgBox Err.Number & ", " & Err.Description
    Resume Exit_cmdSpellCheck_Click
    Resume

End Sub
```

Depending on which option is set in the constant, the spell check is performed.

```
Private Sub cmdSpellOptions_Click()
On Error GoTo Err_cmdSpellCheck_Click

    Call subSetWordSpellingOptions

Exit_cmdSpellCheck_Click:
    Exit Sub
Err_cmdSpellCheck_Click:
    MsgBox Err.Number & ", " & Err.Description
```

```
            Resume Exit_cmdSpellCheck_Click
            Resume
    End Sub
```

If the Spell Options button is visible, the user can click it to change spell-checking options.

```
    Private Sub Form_KeyDown(KeyCode As Integer, Shift As Integer)
    On Error GoTo Err_Form_KeyDown

        If KeyCode = vbKeyF7 Then
            KeyCode = 0
            If Me!cmdSpellCheck.Visible And Me!cmdSpellCheck.Enabled Then
                Me.cmdSpellCheck.SetFocus
                Call cmdSpellCheck_Click
            End If
        End If

    Exit_Form_KeyDown:
        Exit Sub
    Err_Form_KeyDown:
        MsgBox Err.Number & ", " & Err.Description
        Resume Exit_Form_KeyDown
        Resume
    End Sub
```

To support the standard usage of the *F7* key to check spelling, this code traps the *F7* keystroke, and if the spell-checking button is enabled, runs its code.

```
    Private Sub Form_Load()
    On Error GoTo Err_Form_Load

        Dim ctl As Control

        'Setup SpellChecker Options
        Select Case conSpellCheckOption
            'This is set in the frmWorkspace declarations section above
            Case 0 'Spell Checker OFF
                Me!cmdSpellCheck.Visible = False
                Me!cmdSpellOptions.Visible = False
            Case 1, 2 'Default Spell Checker, Word Grammer Checker
                Me!cmdSpellCheck.Visible = True
                Me!cmdSpellOptions.Visible = False
            Case 3 'Word Grammer Checker with Options
                Me!cmdSpellCheck.Visible = True
                Me!cmdSpellOptions.Visible = True
        End Select

        'Import data into workspace
        Me!txtWorkspace = gctlWorkspaceSource

        If Me.OpenArgs = "ReadOnly" Then
            Set ctl = Me!txtWorkspace
            With ctl
                .EnterKeyBehavior = False 'Sets to Default / No new line
```

```
                .Locked = True
                .BackColor = vbButtonFace
            End With
            Set ctl = Nothing

            Me!cmdSpellCheck.Enabled = False
            Me!cmdSpellOptions.Enabled = False
        End If

Exit_Form_Load:
    Exit Sub
Err_Form_Load:
    MsgBox Err.Number & ", " & Err.Description
    Resume Exit_Form_Load
    Resume
End Sub
```

When the Workspace form loads, the option constant is used to show the appropriate spell-checking buttons. Then the text from the original form is loaded into the text box, and the whole thing is locked down if the original text box was locked.

```
Private Sub Form_Open(Cancel As Integer)
On Error GoTo Err_Form_Open

    Me.Caption = DLookup("ApplicationTitle", "tsysConfig_Local") _
    & " - " & DLookup("SysConfigDatabaseName", "tsysConfig_System")

Exit_Form_Open:
    Exit Sub
Err_Form_Open:
    MsgBox Err.Number & ", " & Err.Description
    Resume Exit_Form_Open
    Resume
End Sub
```

This is just the normal form caption setting as described earlier in this appendix.

```
Private Sub txtWorkspace_GotFocus()
On Error GoTo Err_txtWorkspace_GotFocus

    Dim varX As Variant

    ' jump to end of existing text instead of leaving it
    'all highlighted.
    varX = Len(Me!txtWorkspace.Text & "")
    If Not IsNull(varX) And varX > 0 Then
        Me!txtWorkspace.SelStart = Len(Me!txtWorkspace)
        Me!txtWorkspace.SelLength = 0
    End If

Exit_txtWorkspace_GotFocus:
    Exit Sub
```

```
Err_txtWorkspace_GotFocus:
    MsgBox Err.Number & ", " & Err.Description
    Resume Exit_txtWorkspace_GotFocus
    Resume
End Sub
```

When the Workspace text box receives focus, we make sure that the insertion point jumps to the end of the text, instead of highlighting the whole field. This helps to prevent the user from inadvertently changing of the entire field.

When the Spell button is clicked, the text on the Workspace form is checked for spelling errors, as shown in Figure I-16:

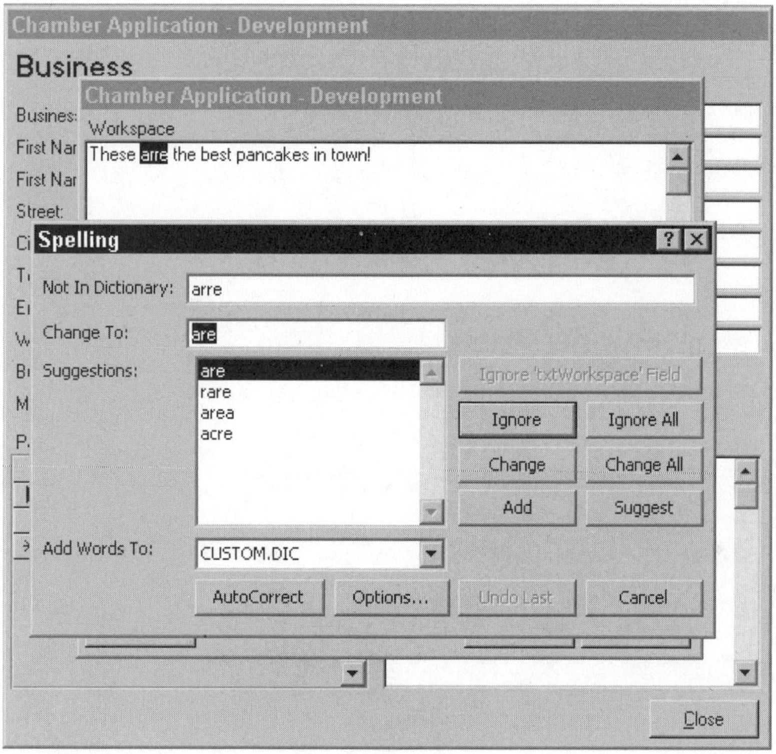

Figure I-16

The code in the Spell Checking module looks like this:

```
Option Compare Database
Option Explicit

Public Function fnCheckSpelling(ctl As Control, _
    bUseWordSpellChecker As Boolean) As Boolean
On Error GoTo Err_fnCheckSpelling
```

```
'This procedure checks spelling with either the Word Spell
'Checking/Grammar Checking window or the Access default Spell
'Checking only window. Both methods require Word 97 or later
'to work, because the dictionary is used. The Word method
'gives the user more functionality with the addition of the
'grammar checking capability. The downside is that the
'Word checker takes longer to load and unload.

Dim wrdApp As Object
Dim wrdDoc As Object

DoCmd.Hourglass True
'This function is meant for textbox controls only.
Select Case ctl.ControlType
    Case acTextBox
        If Not ctl.Enabled Or ctl.Locked Then
            'Text in control can not be updated.
            GoTo Exit_fnCheckSpelling
        ElseIf IsNull(ctl) Then
            'Nothing to check
            GoTo Exit_fnCheckSpelling
        End If
    Case Else
        GoTo Exit_fnCheckSpelling
End Select

If bUseWordSpellChecker Then
    'Use Word 97's default spell checker (with grammer checker)
    Set wrdApp = CreateObject("Word.Application")

    wrdApp.Visible = False
    Set wrdDoc = wrdApp.Documents.Add

    wrdApp.Selection.Text = ctl
    DoCmd.Hourglass False
    'wrdApp.WindowState = 2 'wdWindowStateMinimize
    wrdApp.Visible = False
    wrdApp.Dialogs(828).Show
    'wdDialogToolsSpellingAndGrammar = 828
    wrdApp.Visible = False
    DoCmd.Hourglass True

    'The cancel button on the Word Spell Checker was NOT pressed.
    If Len(wrdApp.Selection.Text & "") <> 1 Then
        ctl = wrdApp.Selection.Text

        wrdApp.ActiveDocument.Close 0 'wdDoNotSaveChanges = 0
        Set wrdDoc = Nothing
        wrdApp.Quit
        Set wrdApp = Nothing

        fnCheckSpelling = True
        MsgBox "The spelling check is complete.", vbInformation
    End If
```

```
        Else 'Use Access's default spell checker (without grammer)
            ctl.SetFocus
            ctl.SelStart = 0
            ctl.SelLength = Len(ctl.Text & "")
            If ctl.SelLength <> 0 Then
                DoCmd.Hourglass False
                RunCommand acCmdSpelling
                ctl.SelLength = 0
                fnCheckSpelling = True
            End If
        End If

Exit_fnCheckSpelling:
    On Error Resume Next
    DoCmd.Hourglass False
    If Not (wrdApp Is Nothing) Then
        If Not (wrdDoc Is Nothing) Then
            wrdApp.ActiveDocument.Close 0 'wdDoNotSaveChanges = 0
            Set wrdDoc = Nothing
        End If
        wrdApp.Quit
        Set wrdApp = Nothing
    End If
    Exit Function
Err_fnCheckSpelling:
    DoCmd.Hourglass False
    Select Case Err.Number
        Case 429 'Word not installed
            MsgBox "Microsoft Word 97 (or later) must be " _
            & "installed for the spell checking option to " _
            & "function.", vbExclamation, _
            DLookup("ApplicationTitle", "tsysConfig_Local")
        Case Else
            MsgBox Err.Number & ", " & Err.Description
    End Select
    Resume Exit_fnCheckSpelling
    Resume
End Function
```

Notice that by setting `wrdapp` as Object, we are using *late binding*. Even if Word is not installed on this PC, this code will still compile. When the code attempts to create the Word object at run time, a trappable error will occur and we'll tell the user that Word is required.

If we had used *early binding*, the `Dim` statement for `wrdApp` would have looked like this:

```
Dim wrdApp As Word.Application
```

The problem with early binding is that if the object specified (in this case, Word) is not installed on the PC, the VBA code will not even compile. This will prevent your user from using your application at all. That's why it's usually best to use late binding when you are developing applications that will run on other PCs where you don't necessarily know which other programs are installed.

Now we move on to the code to allow the users to set their own spelling options:

```
Public Sub subSetWordSpellingOptions()
On Error GoTo Err_subSetWordSpellingOptions

    Dim wrdApp As Object
    Dim wrdDoc As Object

    DoCmd.Hourglass True

    Set wrdApp = CreateObject("Word.Application")

    wrdApp.Visible = False
    Set wrdDoc = wrdApp.Documents.Add

    DoCmd.Hourglass False
    wrdApp.Dialogs(211).Show
    'wdDialogToolsOptionsSpellingAndGrammar = 211
    wrdApp.Visible = False
    DoCmd.Hourglass True

Exit_subSetWordSpellingOptions:
    On Error Resume Next
    DoCmd.Hourglass False
    If Not (wrdApp Is Nothing) Then
        If Not (wrdDoc Is Nothing) Then
            wrdApp.ActiveDocument.Close 0 'wdDoNotSaveChanges = 0
            Set wrdDoc = Nothing
        End If
        wrdApp.Quit
        Set wrdApp = Nothing
    End If
    Exit Sub
Err_subSetWordSpellingOptions:
    DoCmd.Hourglass False
    Select Case Err.Number
        Case 429 'Word not installed
            MsgBox "Microsoft Word 97 (or later) must be " _
            & "installed before the spell checking options can " _
            & "be set.", vbExclamation, _
            DLookup("ApplicationTitle", "tsysConfig_Local")
        Case Else
            MsgBox Err.Number & ", " & Err.Description
    End Select
    Resume Exit_subSetWordSpellingOptions
    Resume
End Sub
```

This is the code that, if the button is enabled, allows the user to change the built-in options for the spell-checking utility.

By adding an area for your users to enter more text and check the spelling, you make your application more powerful and easy to use. Plus, when you add this capability, you don't have to make your memo field text boxes as large, which saves valuable real estate on your forms.

Determine the User Name

Often, you'll need to know the current user of the application. This might be to determine what activities they are allowed to do or to stamp records with change logging information. There are two user names that you'll be concerned with: the current Access user and the current Windows user.

The Current Access User

The current Access user is determined using the built-in `CurrentUser` function. However, if you are not using Access security and requiring the user to log in with a `User Name` and `Password`, this user name will always be the default Access user of "Admin". This isn't too descriptive, so you may need to know the name of the user that is currently using this PC.

The Current Windows User

To determine the currently logged in Windows user, you can use this code. First, in the module declaration section, include this code:

```
Global Const ERRORMOREDATA = 234
Global Const ERR_SUCCESS = 0

Private Declare Function WNetGetUser Lib "mpr" Alias _
"WNetGetUserA" (ByVal lpName As String, _
ByVal lpUserName As String, lpnLength As Long) As Long
```

Then, create a function with this code:

```
Public Function WinUserName() As String
    Dim lUserNameLen As Long
    Dim stTmp As String
    Dim lReturn As Long

    Do
        ' Set up the buffer
        stTmp = String$(lUserNameLen, vbNullChar)

        lReturn = WNetGetUser(vbNullString, stTmp, lUserNameLen)

        ' Continue looping until the call succeeds or the buffer
        ' can't fit any more data
    Loop Until lReturn <> ERRORMOREDATA

    If lReturn = ERR_SUCCESS Then
        WinUserName = Left$(stTmp, InStr(1, stTmp, vbNullChar, _
        vbBinaryCompare) - 1)
    End If

End Function
```

You can use this Windows user name anywhere you like, including displaying it on forms, using it to allow or disallow certain features, or including the user name whenever a record is changed or created.

ADO Object Argument Information

In this appendix you will find information relating to Chapter 7, "Using ADO to Access Data."

Connection.Execute Method Options

The following tables list the values you can specify for the Command.Execute method's options argument.

CommandTypeEnum Values

The CommandTypeEnum values specify how the Connection.CommandText argument is to be interpreted.

Constant	Value	Description
AdCmdUnspecified	-1	Hidden. No command type is specified.
AdCmdText	1	The CommandText argument is a command or the name of a stored procedure.
AdCmdTable	2	The *CommandText* argument is the name of a table.
AdCmdStoredProc	4	The CommandText argument is the name of a stored procedure.
AdCmdUnknown	8	Default. The type of command in the CommandType argument is unknown.

Continues

Constant	Value	Description
AdCmdFile	256	The CommandText argument is the name of a stored Recordset (Recordset.Open or Requery methods only).
AdCmdTableDirect	512	The CommandText argument is the name of a table (Recordset.Open or Requery methods only). This option cannot be combined with adAsyncExecute.

ExecuteOptionEnum Values

The ExecuteOptionEnum values specify how the provider is to execute the Connection.CommandText argument.

Constant	Value	Description
AdOptionUnspecified	-1	Hidden. The command is not specified.
AdAsyncExecute	16	The command executes asynchronously. This option cannot be combined with adCmdTableDirect.
AdAsyncFetch	32	The rows that remain to be retrieved after those specified by the CacheSize property are to be retrieved asynchronously.
AdAsyncFetchNonBlocking	64	The main thread never blocks while retrieving data, so if the requested row has not been retrieved, the current row automatically moves to the end of the file.
		This setting is ignored if the adCmdTableDirect option is used, or if you open a recordset from a stream that contains a persistently stored recordset.
AdExecuteNoRecords	128	The CommandText argument is a command or stored procedure that does not return records.
AdExecuteStream	1024	Return the results of a command operation as a Stream (Command.Execute only).
AdExecuteRecord	2048	Hidden. The CommandText argument is a command or stored procedure that returns a single row as a Record object.

Note: For information about how to view hidden objects in the Object Browser, refer to Chapter 2.

Recordset.Open Method Options

There are 30 Win32 Registry functions that you can use from VBA. This section describes only 25 of them, because the remaining five require specialist knowledge of Windows security, which is well beyond the scope of this book.

CursorType Argument Options (CursorTypeEnum Values)

Constant	Value	Description
AdOpenUnspecified	-1	Hidden. No cursor type is specified.
AdOpenForwardOnly	0	Default. Specifies a forward-only cursor. This is similar to a static cursor, except that you can only scroll forward through the records.
AdOpenKeyset	1	Specifies a *keyset cursor*. This is similar to a dynamic cursor, except that records added by other users are not reflected in your recordset; however, records that other users delete are inaccessible in your recordset.
AdOpenDynamic	2	Specifies a *dynamic cursor*. In this cursor type, all additions, deletions, and modifications made by other users are visible in your recordset, and all types of row movement are allowed. If the provider supports bookmarks, they too are allowed.
AdOpenStatic	3	Specifies a *static cursor*. This cursor type is read-only, and additions, deletions, and modifications made by other users are invisible in your recordset.

LockType Argument Options (LockTypeEnum Values)

Constant	Value	Description
AdLockUnspecified	-1	Hidden. A lock type is not specified. Clones are created with the same lock type as their original.
AdLockReadOnly	1	Specifies a read-only recordset.
AdLockPessimistic	2	Specifies *pessimistic locking* at record-level.
AdLockOptimistic	3	Specifies pessimistic locking at record-level. The record is locked only when you call the Update method.
adLockBatchOptimistic	4	Specifies *optimistic locking* for batch updated.

Options Argument (Constant Values)

The Options argument can be one or more of the following constant values.

Constant	Value	Description
CommandTypeEnum values		
adCmdUnspecified	-1	Hidden. No command type is specified.
AdCmdText	1	The Source argument is a command or the name of a stored procedure.
AdCmdTable	2	The Source argument is the name of a table.
AdCmdStoredProc	4	The Source argument is the name of a stored procedure.
AdCmdUnknown	8	Default. The type of command in the Source argument is unknown.
AdCmdFile	256	The Source argument is the name of a stored Recordset.
adCmdTableDirect	512	The Source argument is the name of a table. This option cannot be combined with adAsyncExecute.
ExecuteOptionEnum values		
adOptionUnspecified	-1	Hidden. The command is not specified.
AdAsyncExecute	16	The command executes asynchronously. This option cannot be combined with adCmdTableDirect.
AdAsyncFetch	32	The rows that remain to be retrieved after those specified by the CacheSize property are to be retrieved asynchronously.
adAsyncFetchNonBlocking	64	The main thread never blocks while retrieving data, so if the requested row has not been retrieved, the current row automatically moves to the end of the file. This setting is ignored if the adCmdTableDirect option is used, or if you open a recordset from a stream that contains a persistently stored recordset.
adExecuteNoRecords	128	The Source argument is a command or stored procedure that does not return records.
AdExecuteRecord	2048	Hidden. The Source argument is a command or stored procedure that returns a single row as a Record object.

Note: For information about how to view hidden objects in the Object Browser, refer to Chapter 2.

Connection.OpenSchema Method Options

The following tables list the values you can specify for the `Command.OpenSchema` method's `schema` and `restrictions` argument.

Schema Argument Values

The `Schema` argument specifies the type of information to return and its values are defined in the following table.

We have included only those values that have meaning in Access. The four remaining values, *adSchemaActions*, *adSchemaCommands*, *adSchemaFunctions*, and *adSchemaSets* relate specifically to the Microsoft OLE DB Provider for OLAP Services library. For more information about these values, refer to the Microsoft KnowledgeBase.

Option	Value	Description
AdSchemaAsserts	0	Returns the constraints defined in the catalog. Unsupported by the Jet provider.
AdSchemaCatalogs	1	Returns the catalogs that are accessible from the database. Unsupported by the Jet provider.
AdSchemaCharacterSets	2	Returns the character sets defined in the catalog. Unsupported by the Jet provider.
AdSchemaCheckConstraints	4	Returns the check constraints (validation rules) defined in the catalog.
AdSchemaCollations	3	Returns the sort orders defined in the catalog. Unsupported by the Jet provider.
AdSchemaColumnPrivileges	13	Returns the privileges on columns that are available to, or granted by, a given user. Unsupported by the Jet provider.
AdSchemaColumns	4	Returns the columns of tables and views that are accessible to a given user.
adSchemaColumnsDomainUsage	11	Returns the columns that are dependent on a domain that is owned by a given user. Unsupported by the Jet provider.
adSchemaConstraintColumnUsage	6	Returns the columns used by referential constraints, unique constraints, check constraints, and assertions.

Continues

Option	Value	Description
adSchemaConstraintTableUsage	7	Returns the tables that are used by referential constraints, unique constraints, check constraints, and assertions for a given user. Unsupported by the Jet provider.
adSchemaCubes	32	Returns information about the available cubes (multidimensional data) in a schema (or the catalog, if the provider does not support schemas). Unsupported by the Jet provider.
adSchemaDBInfoKeywords	30	Returns a list of provider-specific keywords
adSchemaDBInfoLiterals	31	Returns a list of provider-specific literals (quotes and escape characters) used in text commands.
adSchemaDimensions	33	Returns information about the dimensions in a cube; one row per dimension. Unsupported by the Jet provider.
adSchemaForeignKeys	27	Returns the foreign key columns defined in the catalog.
adSchemaHierarchies	34	Returns information about the hierarchies available in a cube dimension. Unsupported by the Jet provider.
adSchemaIndexes	12	Returns the indexes defined in the catalog.
adSchemaKeyColumnUsage	8	Returns the columns that are defined in the catalog as keys.
adSchemaLevels	35	Returns information about the levels available in a cube dimension. Unsupported by the Jet provider.
adSchemaMeasures	36	Returns information about the available cube measures. Unsupported by the Jet provider.
adSchemaMembers	38	Returns information about the available cube members. Unsupported by the Jet provider.
adSchemaPrimaryKeys	28	Returns the primary key columns defined in the catalog.
adSchemaProcedureColumns	29	Returns information about the columns in stored procedures. Unsupported by the Jet provider.

Continues

Option	Value	Description
adSchemaProcedureParameters	26	Returns information about the parameters and return codes of stored procedures. Unsupported by the Jet provider.
adSchemaProcedures	16	Returns the procedures defined in the catalog. Unsupported by the Jet provider.
adSchemaProperties	37	Returns information about the available properties for each level of the cube dimension. Unsupported by the Jet provider.
adSchemaProviderSpecific	-1	Returns schema information for a provider that defines its own nonstandard schema queries.
adSchemaProviderTypes	22	Returns the base datatypes supported by the provider.
adSchemaReferentialConstraints	9	Returns the referential constraints (relationships) defined in the catalog.
adSchemaSchemata	17	Returns the schemas (database objects) that are owned by a given user. Unsupported by the Jet provider.
adSchemaSQLLanguages	18	Returns the levels of ANSI SQL conformance, options and dialects supported in the catalog. Unsupported by the Jet provider.
adSchemaStatistics	19	Returns the catalog statistics.
adSchemaTableConstraints	10	Returns the table constraints (validation rules) defined in the catalog.
adSchemaTablePrivileges	14	Returns the privileges on tables that are available to, or granted by, a given user. Unsupported by the Jet provider.
adSchemaTables	20	Returns the tables and views defined in the catalog.
adSchemaTranslations	21	Returns the character translations defined in the catalog. Unsupported by the Jet provider.
adSchemaTrustees	39	Returns the users and groups defined in the catalog.
adSchemaUsagePrivileges	15	Returns the USAGE privileges on objects that are available to, or granted by, a given user. Unsupported by the Jet provider.

Continues

Option	Value	Description
adSchemaViewColumnUsage	24	Returns the columns included in views. Unsupported by the Jet provider.
adSchemaViews	23	Returns the views defined in the catalog.
adSchemaViewTableUsage	25	Returns the tables included in views. Unsupported by the Jet provider.

Restrictions Argument Values

The optional Restrictions parameter allows you to filter the output. For example, you can filter the recordset to return only a single table or view. The available values are listed in the following table.

Option	Constraint columns
AdSchemaAsserts	CONSTRAINT_CATALOG CONSTRAINT_SCHEMA CONSTRAINT_NAME
AdSchemaCatalogs	CATALOG_NAME
AdSchemaCharacterSets	CHARACTER_SET_CATALOG CHARACTER_SET_SCHEMA CHARACTER_SET_NAME
AdSchemaCheckConstraints	CONSTRAINT_CATALOG CONSTRAINT_SCHEMA CONSTRAINT_NAME
AdSchemaCollations	COLLATION_CATALOG COLLATION_SCHEMA COLLATION_NAME
AdSchemaColumnPrivileges	TABLE_CATALOG TABLE_SCHEMA TABLE_NAME COLUMN_NAME GRANTOR GRANTEE
AdSchemaColumns	TABLE_CATALOG TABLE_SCHEMA TABLE_NAME COLUMN_NAME

Continues

Option	Constraint columns
AdSchemaColumnsDomainUsage	DOMAIN_CATALOG DOMAIN_SCHEMA DOMAIN_NAME COLUMN_NAME
AdSchemaConstraintColumnUsage	TABLE_CATALOG TABLE_SCHEMA TABLE_NAME COLUMN_NAME
AdSchemaConstraintTableUsage	TABLE_CATALOG TABLE_SCHEMA TABLE_NAME
AdSchemaCubes	CATALOG_NAME SCHEMA_NAME CUBE_NAME
AdSchemaDBInfoKeywords	\<None\>
AdSchemaDBInfoLiterals	\<None\>
AdSchemaDimensions	CATALOG_NAME SCHEMA_NAME CUBE_NAME DIMENSION_NAME DIMENSION_UNIQUE_NAME
AdSchemaForeignKeys	PK_TABLE_CATALOG PK_TABLE_SCHEMA PK_TABLE_NAME FK_TABLE_CATALOG FK_TABLE_SCHEMA FK_TABLE_NAME
AdSchemaHierarchies	CATALOG_NAME SCHEMA_NAME CUBE_NAME DIMENSION_UNIQUE_NAME HIERARCHY_NAME HIERARCHY_UNIQUE_NAME
AdSchemaIndexes	TABLE_CATALOG TABLE_SCHEMA INDEX_NAME TYPE TABLE_NAME
AdSchemaKeyColumnUsage	CONSTRAINT_CATALOG

Continues

Option	Constraint columns
	CONSTRAINT_SCHEMA CONSTRAINT_NAME TABLE_CATALOG TABLE_SCHEMA TABLE_NAME COLUMN_NAME
AdSchemaLevels	CATALOG_NAME SCHEMA_NAME CUBE_NAME DIMENSION_UNIQUE_NAME HIERARCHY_UNIQUE_NAME LEVEL_NAME LEVEL_UNIQUE_NAME
AdSchemaMeasures	CATALOG_NAME SCHEMA_NAME CUBE_NAME MEASURE_NAME MEASURE_UNIQUE_NAME
AdSchemaMembers	CATALOG_NAME SCHEMA_NAME CUBE_NAME DIMENSION_UNIQUE_NAME HIERARCHY_UNIQUE_NAME LEVEL_UNIQUE_NAME LEVEL_NUMBER MEMBER_NAME MEMBER_UNIQUE_NAME MEMBER_CAPTION MEMBER_TYPE Tree operator (For more information, see the OLE DB for OLAP documentation.)
AdSchemaPrimaryKeys	PK_TABLE_CATALOG PK_TABLE_SCHEMA PK_TABLE_NAME
AdSchemaProcedureColumns	PROCEDURE_CATALOG PROCEDURE_SCHEMA PROCEDURE_NAME COLUMN_NAME
AdSchemaProcedureParameters	PROCEDURE_CATALOG PROCEDURE_SCHEMA PROCEDURE_NAME PARAMETER_NAME

Continues

Option	Constraint columns
AdSchemaProcedures	PROCEDURE_CATALOG
	PROCEDURE_SCHEMA
	PROCEDURE_NAME
	PROCEDURE_TYPE
AdSchemaProperties	CATALOG_NAME
	SCHEMA_NAME
	CUBE_NAME
	DIMENSION_UNIQUE_NAME
	HIERARCHY_UNIQUE_NAME
	LEVEL_UNIQUE_NAME
	MEMBER_UNIQUE_NAME
	PROPERTY_TYPE
	PROPERTY_NAME
AdSchemaProviderSpecific	\<Provider specific\>
AdSchemaProviderTypes	DATA_TYPE
	BEST_MATCH
AdSchemaReferentialConstraints	CONSTRAINT_CATALOG
	CONSTRAINT_SCHEMA
	CONSTRAINT_NAME
AdSchemaSchemata	CATALOG_NAME
	SCHEMA_NAME
	SCHEMA_OWNER
AdSchemaSQLLanguages	\<None\>
AdSchemaStatistics	TABLE_CATALOG
	TABLE_SCHEMA
	TABLE_NAME
AdSchemaTableConstraints	CONSTRAINT_CATALOG
	CONSTRAINT_SCHEMA
	CONSTRAINT_NAME
	TABLE_CATALOG
	TABLE_SCHEMA
	TABLE_NAME
	CONSTRAINT_TYPE
AdSchemaTablePrivileges	TABLE_CATALOG
	TABLE_SCHEMA
	TABLE_NAME
	GRANTOR
	GRANTEE
AdSchemaTables	TABLE_CATALOG
	TABLE_SCHEMA

Continues

897

Option	Constraint columns
	TABLE_NAME
	TABLE_TYPE
AdSchemaTranslations	TRANSLATION_CATALOG
	TRANSLATION_SCHEMA
	TRANSLATION_NAME
AdSchemaTrustees	\<None\>
AdSchemaUsagePrivileges	OBJECT_CATALOG
	OBJECT_SCHEMA
	OBJECT_NAME
	OBJECT_TYPE
	GRANTOR
	GRANTEE
AdSchemaViewColumnUsage	VIEW_CATALOG
	VIEW_SCHEMA
	VIEW_NAME
AdSchemaViews	TABLE_CATALOG
	TABLE_SCHEMA
	TABLE_NAME
AdSchemaViewTableUsage	VIEW_CATALOG
	VIEW_SCHEMA
	VIEW_NAME

Group or User.SetPermissions Method Options

The SetPermssions method of both the Group and User objects allows you to specify the permissions a group or user has to a database object.

ObjectType Values

The ObjectType option specifies the type of object to which the permission will be applied.

Constant	Value	Description
AdPermObjColumn	2	The object is a column.
AdPermObjDatabase	3	The object is a database.
adPermObjProcedure	4	The object is a procedure.

Continues

Constant	Value	Description
adPermObjProviderSpecific	-1	The object type is defined by the provider. If you specify this value, you must also supply an ObjectTypeID
AdPermObjTable	1	The object is a table.
AdPermObjView	5	The object is a view.

Action Values

The Action option specifies what you intend to do with the permission to the specified object.

Constant	Value	Description
adAccessDeny	3	Deny the specified permissions.
adAccessGrant	1	Grant the specified permissions. The permissions specified are added to those that have already been granted.
adAccessRevoke	4	Revoke all permissions.
adAccessSet	2	Set the specified permissions. Only the specified permissions will be in force.

Rights Values

The Rights option specifies the actual rights, or permissions, that you are denying, granting, revoking, or setting.

Constant	Value	Description
AdRightCreate	16384	The user/group has permission to create a new object of the specified type.
AdRightDelete	65536	The user/group has permission to delete data from the specified object. For objects such as tables, the user also has permission to delete data.
AdRightDrop	256	The user/group has permission to remove objects from the catalog.
AdRightExclusive	512	The user/group has permission to access the object exclusively.

Continues

Constant	Value	Description
AdRightExecute	536870912	The user/group has permission to execute the object.
AdRightFull	268435456	The user/group has all permissions on the object.
AdRightInsert	32768	The user/group has permission to insert the object. For objects such as tables, the user also has permission to insert data.
adRightMaximumAllowed	33554432	The user/group has the maximum number of permissions allowed by the provider.
AdRightNone	0	The user/group has no permissions for the object.
AdRightRead	-2147483648	The user/group has permission to read the object. For objects such as tables, the user also has permission to read its data.
AdRightReadDesign	1024	The user/group has permission to read the object's design.
adRightReadPermissions	131072	The user/group can view, but not change, the specific permissions for an object in the catalog.
AdRightReference	8192	The user/group has permission to reference the object.
AdRightUpdate	1073741824	The user/group has permission to update the object. For objects such as tables, the user also has permission to update its data.
AdRightWithGrant	4096	The user/group has permission to grant permissions on the object to other users.
AdRightWriteDesign	2048	The user/group has permission to modify the object's design.
AdRightWriteOwner	524288	The user/group has permission to modify the object's owner.
adRightWritePermissions	262144	The user/group has permissions to modify the specific permissions for an object in the catalog.

Inherit Values

The Inherit option specifies how the specified object inherits permissions.

Constant	Value	Description
AdInheritBoth	3	The objects and containers contained by the primary object inherit the permissions.
AdInheritContainers	2	Other objects contained by the primary object also inherit the permissions.
AdInheritNone	0	Default. Do not inherit permissions.
AdInheritNoPropagate	4	The adInheritObjects and adInheritContainers flags are not inherited.
AdInheritObjects	1	Objects outside the container inherit the permissions.

Access Wizards, Builders, and Managers

Access provides many tools that do a lot of work for developers. These tools not only save us time and prevent or minimize errors, but they are also a great resource for teaching ourselves how to do things. But many developers may not even know that some of these wizards exist. So, if we don't know about them, we aren't likely to be using them to our advantage.

Hopefully, the tables in this appendix will expand your use of the tools built into Access. We've tried to list all of the wizards, builders, and managers that are in Access 2003, along with a very short explanation of what they do. And, for your convenience, we even tried to find out which ones had been recently added or enhanced.

Access Wizards

As you can tell from the extensive list of enhanced wizards, Access is getting more user-friendly all the time.

Wizard	Description	New or Enhanced in 2002 or 2003
AutoDialer	Adds an AutoDialer control to a form, datasheet, or toolbar. The wizard incorporates modem information and dials the number	
AutoForm	Creates a form automatically based on the selected table or query. Well, the end result is enhanced to the extent that forms themselves are enhanced	Enhanced*

Continues

Wizard	Description	New or Enhanced in 2002 or 2003
AutoFormat	Applies a predefined style and format to a form or report, and allows creation of custom styles	
AutoPage	Creates a data access page that can be used on the Web or Intranet. A DAP can also get data from other sources, such as Excel.	
AutoReport	Creates a report automatically. Again, enhanced due to report features being enhanced	Enhanced*
Chart/Graph*	Adds a chart to a form or report based on the data in a table or query	Enhanced
Combo Box	Creates a combo box control on a form. Check this out AGAIN, this now includes sort options!	Enhanced
Command Button	Creates a command button control on a form	
Conflict Resolver	Resolves conflicts between replicated databases at synchronization time	
Crosstab Query	Creates a query that summarizes data in a compact, spreadsheet-like format	
Database Splitter*	Splits databases into data and interface portions, so that one or more users can have local copies of the interface connected to the data on a server	
Database	Creates an entirely new database for a variety of uses	Enhanced
Documenter*	Generates an Access report that displays the design characteristics of database objects, including the tables, queries, forms, reports, pages, macros, and modules	
Export to Windows SharePoint Services	Exports to Windows SharePoint Services	New 2003
Export Text	Exports data to a text file	
Find Duplicates Query*	Creates a query that finds records that have duplicate field values and are in a single table or query	
Find Unmatched Query*	Creates a query that finds records in one table and which have no related records in another table	
Form	Creates a new form. Enhancements include incorporating many of the features available for forms	Enhanced

Continues

Wizard	Description	New or Enhanced in 2002 or 2003
Import Exchange/Outlook	Imports an Exchange or Outlook folder to a table in a Microsoft Access database	Enhanced
Import HTML	Imports HTML tables and lists from the Internet and intranet site into an Access table. A great way to start building interfaces with Web-based databases	Enhanced
Import from Windows SharePoint Services	Imports from Windows SharePoint Services	New 2003
Import Spreadsheet	Imports a Microsoft Excel or other spreadsheet into a Microsoft Access table. Better import specification opportunities	Enhanced
Import Text	Imports a text file into a Microsoft Access table	Enhanced
Input Mask Wizard*	Creates an input mask for a field that you choose in a table	Enhanced
Label Wizard	Creates mailing labels in standard and custom sizes	Enhanced
Link Exchange/Outlook	Links an Exchange or Outlook folder to a table in a Microsoft Access database	Enhanced
Link HTML	Links an HTML table or list on the Internet or an intranet to a Microsoft Access table	Enhanced
Link to Windows SharePoint Services	Link to Windows SharePoint Services	New 2003
Link Spreadsheet	Links spreadsheet data to a Microsoft Access table. Can pull in SmartTags	Enhanced
Link Table*	Links to tables in Access projects. Can be used to create connections to multiple Access files. And in 2003 included horizontal scrolling and ability to copy a linked table locally	Enhanced
Link Text	Links a text file to a Microsoft Access table	
List Box	Creates a list box control on a form, now includes sort options	Enhanced
Lookup	Creates a lookup column in a table, which displays a list of values the user can choose from. Includes a sort option	Enhanced
Macro To Module Converter*	Converts macros to Visual Basic code	

Continues

Wizard	Description	New or Enhanced in 2002 or 2003
Microsoft Access Mail Merge	Manages mail merge operations for merging tables, views, functions, or stored procedure into Microsoft Word documents	Enhanced
Microsoft SQL Server Database*	Creates a new Microsoft SQL Server Database that a new Microsoft Access project is connected to	Enhanced
Microsoft Word Mail Merge	Manages mail merge operations by using letters that are stored in Microsoft Word and addresses that are stored in Microsoft Access	Enhanced
Option Group*	Creates a group of option buttons on a form	
Page Combo Box	Creates a drop-down control on a data access page	Enhanced
Page Command Button	Creates a command button control on a data access page	Enhanced
Page List Box	Creates a list box control on a data access page	Enhanced
Page	Creates a new data access page, allows determining a distinct recordsource	Enhanced
Partial Replica Wizard*	Creates or modifies a partial replica. This will build a replica that only contains a subset of the records that a full replica would have	New 2002
Performance Analyzer*	Analyzes the efficiency of a database and produces a list of suggestions for improving its performance	Enhanced
PivotTable	Places a Microsoft Excel PivotTable on a Microsoft Access form. PivotTables and PivotCharts are now optional views for tables, queries, forms, views, and stored procedures	Enhanced
Print Relationships	Creates a report that diagrams the relationships in a Microsoft Access database	Enhanced
Report	Creates a report that is based on a table or query. Now incorporates new report features	Enhanced
Simple Query Wizard	Creates a select query from the fields that you pick	
Subform/Subreport Field Linker*	Links fields in a main form and a subform, or in a main report and a subreport, based on shared fields or established relationships	Enhanced

Continues

Wizard	Description	New or Enhanced in 2002 or 2003
Subform/Subreport*	Creates a new subform or subreport on a form or report	Enhanced
Table Analyzer*	Takes a table with a lot of duplicate data and splits it into related tables for more efficient storage	Enhanced
Table	Creates a new table	Enhanced
Upsizing*	Upsizes a Microsoft Access database to a Microsoft SQL Server database	Enhanced
User-Level Security*	Creates a new, encoded database, with regulated user access, from an existing database. Regulates user access to the current database and creates an unsecured backup copy of the database.	

Access Builders

Access uses builders to guide developers through a process. We are all familiar with the Query Builder. There are also some builders, such as the Color Builder, that are available in other Office programs.

Builder	Description
Color Builder	Displays a palette for creating customized colors
Expression Builder	Creates expressions for macros, queries, and property sheets
Field Builder	Creates fields in tables
ODBC Connection String Builder*	Creates the correct syntax for a connection to an ODBC database. The wizard walks you through establishing a connection to an external data source
Picture Builder	Creates bitmap images for forms and reports
Query Builder	Creates the correct syntax for a query
Smart Tags Builder	Displays a list of available smart tags and their actions. Smart tags allow you to perform tasks within Access that you otherwise would have needed to open in other programs. Smart tags can be attached to a file in a table or query or to controls on a form, report, or data access page

Access Managers

In addition to builders and wizards, Access has three very powerful managers. We don't know what we would do without the Linked Table Manager to quickly link or re-link to data files. Granted, we could create our own tools or use add-ins to provide these functions, but for the most part, these do an incredible job. I admit that I often create my own main menu, but there are still plenty of instances in which a switchboard is ideal.

These managers are consistent, they work, and they are quick and easy to use.

Manager	Description	Location
Add-In Manager*	In addition to installing and uninstalling wizards, builders, and add-ins, the Add-In Manger helps to create wizards and install your own add-in	Tools | Add-Ins
Linked Table Manager*	Allows linking and changing links to tables in external databases as well as through some ODBC connections, such as with Excel.	Tools | Database Utilities
Switchboard Manager	Creates and manages switchboard forms for applications	Tools | Database Utilities

Windows Registry Information

In this appendix you will find information about the Windows Registry to support the tutorials in Chapter 18, including Windows Registry data types, functions, and constant and user-defined Type declarations.

Windows Registry Data Types

In the same way that database table fields, variables, and API parameters require data of specific types, the kind of data the Registry can store is also defined in terms of data types. The following data types are supported under Windows 2000.

REG_BINARY

This data type specifies raw binary data. Most hardware information is stored with this data type, which can be displayed and entered in binary or hexadecimal format.

REG_DWORD

This data type is a 32-bit (4-byte) number, which is used to store `Boolean` values and information about many device drivers and services. `REG_DWORD` values can be displayed and edited as binary, hexadecimal, or decimal format.

REG_DWORD_LITTLE_ENDIAN

This data type is the same as `REG_DWORD`, a 32-bit number, but it is used to store values in a specific way. In `REG_DWORD_LITTLE_ENDIAN`, the most significant byte contains the high-order byte (leftmost). This is the most common format for storing numbers in Windows 98 and 2000.

REG_DWORD_BIG_ENDIAN

The only difference between this data type and REG_DWORD_LITTLE_ENDIAN is that this data type stores the most-significant byte as the low-order byte (rightmost). This is the opposite order in which bytes are stored in the REG_DWORD_LITTLE_ENDIAN data type.

REG_EXPAND_SZ

This data type is a variable-length text string, and is used to store variables that are resolved when an application or service uses the data. For example, some values include the variable Systemroot. When a service or application references the data in this data type, it is replaced by the name of the directory containing the Windows system files.

REG_LINK

This data type is used to store a symbolic link between system or application data, and a registry value. REG_LINK supports both ANSI and Unicode characters.

REG_MULTI_SZ

This data type is used to store multiple strings that are formatted as an array of null-terminated strings, the last of which is terminated by an extra null character. This means the entire array is terminated by two null characters.

The values in this data type can be separated by spaces, commas, or other characters.

REG_SZ

This data type is a fixed-length string. Boolean values and short-text strings are usually stored with this data type.

REG_FULL_RESOURCE_DESCRIPTOR

This data type is used to store a series of nested arrays, for resource lists (often for hardware components or drivers). These data types are declared as constants using the VBA Const keyword. For convenience, we have included these constant declarations a little later in this chapter.

Registry Function Declarations

There are 30 Win32 Registry functions that you can use from VBA. This section describes only 25 of them, because the remaining 5 require specialist knowledge of Windows security, which is well beyond the scope of this book. The functions are arranged in alphabetical order and a brief description of what each function does is given. It also lists the functions declarations, and describes each of their parameters and their return values.

The following API functions are not included in this section:

- ❑ `RegDisablePredefinedCache`: This API function disables the specified handle table for a process's `HKEY_CURRENT_USER` key.

- ❑ `RegOpenCurrentUser`: This API function returns a handle to `HKEY_CURRENT_USER` for the user for whom the current thread is impersonating.

- ❑ `RegOpenUserClassesRoot`: This API function returns a handle to `HKEY_CLASSES_ROOT` for the specified user.

- ❑ `RegOverrridePredefKey`: This API function maps one key to another.

- ❑ `RegQueryMultipleValues`: This API function returns the type and data of the values of an open key.

Some functions have been extended to provide more programming flexibility over their predecessors. Such functions are preferred in 32-bit Windows and are distinguished from the former version by a trailing `Ex` in their name, for example, `RegCreateKeyEx`.

RegCloseKey

Description	This API function closes a registry key.
Declaration	`Declare Function RegCloseKey Lib "advapi32.dll" _` `    (ByVal hKey As Long) As Long`
Parameters	**Parameter** **Description**
	`Hkey` `Long Integer`—The handle of the key to close.
Return value	`Long Integer` Zero (`ERROR_SUCCESS`) on success. All other values are the specific error code.

RegConnectRegistry

Description	This API function connects to one of two specific registry keys on a remote computer.

Declaration	`Declare Function RegConnectRegistry Lib "advapi32.dll" _`
	`    Alias "RegConnectRegistryA" ( _`
	`    ByVal lpMachineName As String, _`
	`    ByVal hKey As Long, _`
	`    phkResult As Long) As Long`

Continues

Parameters	Parameter	Description
	`lpMachineName`	`String`—The name of the system to connect to. This is in the form `\\computername`
	`HKey`	`Long Integer`—The handle of the hive to connect to. This can only be HKEY_LOCAL_MACHINE or HKEY_USERS
	`phkResult`	`Long Integer`—A variable that is loaded with a handle to the specified key.
Return value	Long Integer Zero (`ERROR_SUCCESS`) on success. All other values are the specific error code.	

RegCreateKeyEx

Description	This API function creates a new registry key under the one you specify, but if the key already exists, it opens that key. This is a more sophisticated function thant `RegCreateKey`, and is recommended for use on Win32.

Declaration	```Declare Function RegCreateKeyEx Lib "advapi32.dll" _```
	``` Alias "RegCreateKeyExA" (_```
	``` ByVal hKey As Long, _```
	``` ByVal lpSubKey As String, _```
	``` ByVal Reserved As Long, _```
	``` ByVal lpClass As String, _```
	``` ByVal dwOptions As Long, _```
	``` ByVal samDesired As Long, _```
	``` lpSecurityAttributes As SECURITY_ATTRIBUTES, _```
	``` phkResult As Long, _```
	``` lpdwDisposition As Long) As Long```

Parameters	Parameter	Description
	`Hkey`	`Long Integer`—The handle of the open key, or one of the hive constants listed above.
	`LpSubKey`	`String`—The name of the new subkey to create.
	`Reserved`	`Long Integer`—This is a reserved parameter. Set it to zero
	`LpClass`	`String`—A class name for the key. This can be `vbNullString`.
	`DwOptions`	`Long Integer`—Set to either zero or `REG_OPTION_VOLATILE`.

Continues

	SamDesired	Long Integer—One or more KEY_??? Constants that combine to define the operations that are allowed for this key.
	lpSecurityAttributes	SECURITY_ATTRIBUTES—A user-defined Type that defines the security attributes for this key. Security attributes are quite a complex subject and most of its features only work on Windows NT. In any case, they are rarely used, so the examples provided at the end of this chapter re-declare this parameter as ByVal lpSecurityAttributes as Long, and pass a Null (0&). For more information about security, refer to the Microsoft Win32 SDK.
	PhkResult	Long Integer—A variable that is loaded with a handle to the new subkey.
	LpdwDisposition	Long Integer—A variable that is loaded with one of the following constants. REG_CREATED_NEW_KEY, or REG_OPENED_EXISTING_KEY.
Return value	Long Integer Zero (ERROR_SUCCESS) on success. All other values are the specific error code.	

RegCreateKey

Description	This API function creates a new registry key under the one you specify, but if the key already exists, it opens that key. The previous function, RegCreateKeyEx, is recommended on Win32.

Declaration	`Declare Function RegCreateKey Lib "advapi32.dll" _`
	`    Alias "RegCreateKeyA" ( _`
	`    ByVal hKey As Long, _`
	`    ByVal lpSubKey As String, _`
	`    phkResult As Long) As Long`

Parameters	**Parameter**	**Description**
	Hkey	Long Integer—The handle of the open key, or one of the hive constants listed above.
	LpSubKey	String—The name of the new subkey (or subkeys) to create.

Continues

		You can create multiple subkeys at the same time by separating the names with backslashes. For example, `newkey1\newkey2\newkey3`.
	phkResult	`Long Integer`—A variable that is loaded with a handle to the new subkey.
Return value		`Long Integer` Zero (`ERROR_SUCCESS`) on success. All other values are the specific error code.

RegDeleteKey

Description	This API function deletes the specified subkey.

Declaration	`Declare Function RegDeleteKey Lib "advapi32.dll" _`
	`    Alias "RegDeleteKeyA" ( _`
	`    ByVal hKey As Long, _`
	`    ByVal lpSubKey As String) As Long`

Parameters	**Parameter**	**Description**
	HKey	`Long Integer`—The handle of the open key, or one of the hive constants listed above.
	lpSubKey	`String`—The name of the subkey to delete.
Return value		`Long Integer` Zero (`ERROR_SUCCESS`) on success. All other values are the specific error code.

RegDeleteValue

Description	This API function deletes a value under the specified subkey.

Declaration	`Declare Function RegDeleteValue Lib "advapi32.dll" _`
	`    Alias "RegDeleteValueA" ( _`
	`    ByVal hKey As Long, _`
	`    ByVal lpValueName As String) As Long`

Parameters	**Parameter**	**Description**
	HKey	`Long Integer`—The handle of the open key, or one of the hive constants listed above.

Continues

	lpValueName	String—The name of the value to delete. To delete the key's default value, use vbNullString or an empty string.
Return value	Long Integer Zero (ERROR_SUCCESS) on success. All other values are the specific error code.	

RegEnumKeyEx

Description	This API function enumerates the subkeys for a given key (hive). This is a more sophisticated function than RegEnumKey, and is recommended for use on Win32.

Declaration	```Declare Function RegEnumKeyEx Lib "advapi32.dll" _```
	``` Alias "RegEnumKeyExA" (_```
	``` ByVal hKey As Long, _```
	``` ByVal dwIndex As Long, _```
	``` ByVal lpName As String, _```
	``` lpcbName As Long, _```
	``` lpReserved As Long, _```
	``` ByVal lpClass As String, _```
	``` lpcbClass As Long, _```
	``` lpftLastWriteTime As FILETIME) As Long```

Parameters	Parameter	Description
	HKey	Long Integer—The handle of the open key, or one of the hive constants listed above.
	DwIndex	Long Integer—The index of the subkey to retrieve. This value is zero-based, that is, the first subkey index is zero.
	LpName	String—A null-terminated buffer that is loaded with the name of the key whose index is specified by dwIndex.
	lpcbName	Long Integer—A variable that you load with the length of lpName (including the terminating Null character). When the function returns, this variable contains the number of characters actually loaded into lpName.
	lpReserved	Long Integer—This is a reserved parameter. Set it to zero.
	LpClass	String—A null-terminated variable that will be loaded with the class name for the key. This can be vbNullString.

Continues

	lpcbClass	Long Integer—A variable that you load with the length of lpClass (including the terminating Null character). When the function returns, this variable contains the number of characters actually loaded into lpClass.
	lpftLastWriteTime	FILETIME—A user-defined Type that will contain the last time that the specified subkey was modified.
Return value	Long Integer Zero (ERROR_SUCCESS) on success. All other values are the specific error code.	

RegEnumKey

Description	This API function enumerates the subkeys for a given key (hive). The previous function, RegEnumKeyEx, is recommended on Win32.	

Declaration	Declare Function RegEnumKey Lib "advapi32.dll" _
	    Alias "RegEnumKeyA" (_
	    ByVal hKey As Long, _
	    ByVal dwIndex As Long, _
	    ByVal lpName As String, _
	    ByVal cbName As Long) As Long	

Parameters	**Parameter**	**Description**
	HKey	Long Integer—The handle of the open key, or one of the hive constants listed above.
	dwIndex	Long Integer—The index of the subkey to retrieve. This value is zero-based, that is, the first subkey index is zero.
	lpName	String—A null-terminated buffer that is loaded with the name of the key whose index is specified by dwIndex.
	cbName	Long Integer—A variable that you load with the length of lpName (including the terminating Null character). When the function returns, this variable contains the number of characters actually loaded into lpName.
Return value	Long Integer Zero (ERROR_SUCCESS) on success. All other values are the specific error code.	
Comments	To discover the length of the buffer needed to hold the longest key that can be returned by this function, use RegQueryInfoKey.	

RegEnumValue

Description	This API function enumerates the values for a given subkey.

Declaration	`Declare Function RegEnumValue Lib "advapi32.dll" _`
	`    Alias "RegEnumValueA" ( _`
	`    ByVal hKey As Long, _`
	`    ByVal dwIndex As Long, _`
	`    ByVal lpValueName As String, _`
	`    lpcbValueName As Long, _`
	`    ByVal lpReserved As Long, _`
	`    lpType As Long, _`
	`    lpData As Byte, _`
	`    lpcbData As Long) As Long`

Parameters

Parameter	Description
Hkey	Long Integer—The handle of the open key, or one of the hive constants listed above.
DwIndex	Long Integer—The index of the value to retrieve. This value is zero-based, that is, the first value index is zero.
lpValueName	String—A null-terminated buffer that is loaded with the name of the value whose index is specified by dwIndex.
lpcbValueName	Long Integer—A variable that you load with the length of lpValueName (including the terminating Null character). When the function returns, this variable contains the number of characters actually loaded into lpValueName.
lpReserved	Long Integer—This is a reserved parameter. Set it to zero.
LpType	Long Integer—The key value type (from the constant list above)
LpData	Byte—A buffer that is loaded with the data for the specified value.
lpcbData	Long Integer—A variable that you load with the length of lpData. When the function returns, this variable contains the number of bytes actually loaded into lpData.

Return value	Long Integer Zero (ERROR_SUCCESS) on success. All other values are the specific error code.

RegFlushKey

Description	This API function writes flushes the cache changes made to a key and its subkeys, to disk.
Declaration	`Declare Function RegFlushKey Lib "advapi32.dll" _` `    (ByVal hKey As Long) As Long`

Parameters	Parameter	Description
	Hkey	Long Integer—The handle of the key to flush, or one of the hive constants listed above.

Return value	Long Integer Zero (ERROR_SUCCESS) on success. All other values are the specific error code.
Comments	To improve performance, some operating systems delay writing changes to disk; instead of holding them in a cache, to be written to disk (flushed) later. The problem with this approach is that in the event of a power failure, all the cached changes are lost. This function forces the operating system to immediately write those changes to disk, but doing so may degrade system performance.

RegGetKeySecurity

Description	This API function retrieves security information about the specified key.

Declaration	`Declare Function RegGetKeySecurity Lib "advapi32.dll" ( _`
	`    ByVal hKey As Long, _`
	`    ByVal SecurityInformation As Long, _`
	`    pSecurityDescriptor As SECURITY_DESCRIPTOR, _`
	`    lpcbSecurityDescriptor As Long) As Long`

Parameters	Parameter	Description
	Hkey	Long Integer—The handle of the key whose security information is to be retrieved, or one of the hive constants listed above.
	SecurityInformation	Long Integer—A flag that indicates the security information to retrieve.
	PSecurityDescriptor	SECURITY_DESCRIPTOR—A user-defined Type that will contain the security information for the specified key.
	lpcbSecurityDescriptor	Long Integer—A variable that you load with the length of pSecurityDescriptor.

Continues

		When the function returns, this variable contains the number of bytes actually loaded into `pSecurityDescriptor`.
Return value	`Long Integer` Zero (`ERROR_SUCCESS`) on success. All other values are the specific error code.	

RegLoadKey

Description	This API function creates a new subkey (whose information is loaded from a file that was created using the `RegSaveKey` function) under the specified key.

Declaration	`Declare Function RegLoadKey Lib "advapi32.dll" _`
	    `Alias "RegLoadKeyA" ( _`
	    `ByVal hKey As Long, _`
	    `ByVal lpSubKey As String, _`
	    `ByVal lpFile As String) As Long`

Parameters	Parameter	Description
	`hKey`	`Long Integer`—HKEY_LOCAL_MACHINE, HKEY_USERS, or the handle of a key returned by the `RegConnectRegistry` function.
	`lpSubKey`	`String`—The name of the new subkey to create.
	`lpFile`	`String`—The path and name of the file to load.

Return value	`Long Integer` Zero (`ERROR_SUCCESS`) on success. All other values are the specific error code.

RegNotifyChangeKeyValue

Description	This API function provides the mechanism to be notified when a Registry key or any of its subkeys is changed.

Declaration	`Declare Function RegNotifyChangeKeyValue Lib "advapi32.dll" ( _`
	    `ByVal hKey As Long, _`
	    `ByVal bWatchSubtree As Long, _`
	    `ByVal dwNotifyFilter As Long, _`
	    `ByVal hEvent As Long, _`
	    `ByVal fAsynchronus As Long) As Long`

Continues

Parameters	Parameter	Description
	hKey	Long Integer—The handle of the key to watch, or one of the hive constants listed above.
	lpWatchSubTree	Long Integer—Boolean flag that indicates whether to watch the subkeys for change. Zero—Do not watch subkeys. True (nonzero)—Watch subkeys.
	dwNotifyFilter	Long Integer—One of the following constants: REG_NOTIFY_CHANGE_ATTRIBUTES—To detect changes to a key's attributes. REG_NOTIFY_CHANGE_LAST_SET—To detect changes to a key's last modification time. REG_NOTIFY_CHANGE_NAME—To detect changes to a key's name, or the creation or deletion of keys. REG_NOTIFY_CHANGE_SECURITY—To detect changes to a key's security information.
	hEvent	Long Integer—A handle to an event. This parameter is ignored if fAsynchronus = False (zero).
	fAsynchronous	Long Integer—Boolean flag that indicates whether the function returns immediately when a change is detected. True (nonzero)—The function returns immediately, but the event specified by hEvent is signalled when a change is detected. False (zero)—The function does not return until a change is detected.
Return value		Long Integer Zero (ERROR_SUCCESS) on success. All other values are the specific error code.
Comments		To use this function, you must understand how to detect and act upon system events, a topic which is beyond the scope of this book.

RegOpenKeyEx

Description	This API function opens an existing key. This is a more sophisticated function than RegOpenKey, and is recommended for use on Win32.
Declaration	`Declare Function RegOpenKeyEx Lib "advapi32.dll" _` `    Alias "RegOpenKeyExA" ( _`

Continues

```
ByVal hKey As Long, _
ByVal lpSubKey As String, _
ByVal ulOptions As Long, _
ByVal samDesired As Long, _
phkResult As Long) As Long
```

Parameters	Parameter	Description
	Hkey	`Long Integer`—The handle of the key to open, or one of the hive constants listed above.
	LpSubKey	`String`—The name of the key to open.
	ulOptions	`Long Integer`—This is a reserved parameter. Set it to zero.
	samDesired	`Long Integer`—One or more `KEY_???` Constants that combine to define the operations that are allowed for this key.
	phkResult	`Long Integer`—A variable that is loaded with a handle to the new key.
Return value		`Long Integer` Zero (`ERROR_SUCCESS`) on success. All other values are the specific error code.

RegOpenKey

Description	This API function opens an existing key. The previous function, `RegEnumKeyEx`, is recommended on Win32.
Declaration	`Declare Function RegOpenKey Lib "advapi32.dll" _` `Alias "RegOpenKeyA" ( _` `ByVal hKey As Long, _` `ByVal lpSubKey As String, _` `phkResult As Long) As Long`

Parameters	Parameter	Description
	Hkey	`Long Integer`—The handle of the key to open, or one of the hive constants listed above.
	LpSubKey	`String`—The name of the key to open.
	PhkResult	`Long Integer`—A variable that is loaded with a handle to the new key.
Return value		`Long Integer` Zero (`ERROR_SUCCESS`) on success. All other values are the specific error code.

RegQueryInfoKey

Description	This API function retrieves information about an existing key.

Declaration	`Declare Function RegQueryInfoKey Lib "advapi32.dll" _`
	`    Alias "RegQueryInfoKeyA" ( _`
	`    ByVal hKey As Long, _`
	`    ByVal lpClass As String, _`
	`    lpcbClass As Long, _`
	`    lpReserved As Long, _`
	`    lpcSubKeys As Long, _`
	`    lpcbMaxSubKeyLen As Long, _`
	`    lpcbMaxClassLen As Long, _`
	`    lpcValues As Long, _`
	`    lpcbMaxValueNameLen As Long, _`
	`    lpcbMaxValueLen As Long, _`
	`    lpcbSecurityDescriptor As Long, _`
	`    lpftLastWriteTime As FILETIME) As Long`

Parameters	Parameter	Description
	Hkey	Long Integer—The handle of an open key, or one of the hive constants listed above.
	LpClass	String—A null-terminated variable that will be loaded with the class name for the key. This can be vbNullString.
	LpcbClass	Long Integer—A variable that you load with the length of lpClass (including the terminating Null character). When the function returns, this variable contains the number of characters actually loaded into lpClass.
	LpReserved	Long Integer—This is a reserved parameter. Set it to zero.
	LpcSubKeys	Long Integer—A variable that will be loaded with the number of subkeys under the selected key.
	lpcbMaxSubKeyLen	Long Integer—A variable that will be loaded with the length of the longest subkey under the selected key, excluding the terminating Null character.
	LpcbMaxClassLen	Long Integer—A variable that will be loaded with the length of the longest class name for the subkeys under the selected key, excluding the terminating Null character.
	LpcValues	Long Integer—A variable that will be loaded with the number of values for the selected key.

Continues

lpcbMaxValueNameLen	Long Integer—A variable that will be loaded with the length of the longest value name for the subkeys under the selected key, excluding the terminating Null character.
LpcbMaxValueLen	Long Integer—A variable that will be loaded with the buffer size required to hold the largest value data for this key.
lpcbSecurityDescriptor	Long Integer—A variable that will be loaded with the length of the selected key's Security Descriptor. When the function returns, this variable contains the number of bytes actually loaded into pSecurityDescriptor.
LpftLastWriteTime	FILETIME—A user-defined Type that will contain the last time that the specified subkey was modified.

Return value Long Integer
Zero (ERROR_SUCCESS) on success.
All other values are the specific error code.

RegQueryValueEx

Description This API function retrieves the value for the specified key.
This is a more sophisticated function that RegQueryValue, and is recommended for use on Win32.

Declaration
```
Declare Function RegQueryValueEx Lib "advapi32.dll" _
    Alias "RegQueryValueExA" ( _
    ByVal hKey As Long, _
    ByVal lpValueName As String, _
    ByVal lpReserved As Long, _
    lpType As Long, _
    lpData As Any, _
    lpcbData As Long) As Long
```

Parameters

Parameter	Description
Hkey	Long Integer—The handle of an open key, or one of the hive constants listed above.
LpValueName	String—The name of the value to retrieve.
LpReserved	Long Integer—This is a reserved parameter. Set it to zero.

Continues

	LpType	Long Integer—The key value type (from the constant list, above)
	LpData	Any—A buffer that is loaded with the data for the specified value.
	LpcbData	Long Integer—A variable that is loaded with the length of lpData. When the function returns, this variable contains the number of bytes actually loaded into lpData.
Return value		Long Integer Zero (ERROR_SUCCESS) on success. All other values are the specific error code.

RegQueryValue

Description		This API function retrieves the (Default) value for the specified key. The previous function, RegQueryValueEx, is recommended on Win32.

Declaration		`Declare Function RegQueryValue Lib "advapi32.dll" _`
		 `    Alias "RegQueryValueA" ( _`
		 `    ByVal hKey As Long, _`
		 `    ByVal lpSubKey As String, _`
		 `    ByVal lpValue As String, _`
		 `    lpcbValue As Long) As Long`

Parameters	**Parameter**	**Description**
	Hkey	Long Integer—The handle of an open key, or one of the hive constants listed above.
	LpSubKey	String—The name of the subkey whose (Default) value you want to retrieve. To retrieve the (Default) value for the key specified by hKey, use vbNullString.
	LpValue	String—A variable that will be loaded with the value for the specified key.
	LpcbValue	Long Integer—A variable that you load with the length of lpValue. When the function returns, this variable contains the number of characters actually loaded into lpValue.
Return value		Long Integer Zero (ERROR_SUCCESS) on success. All other values are the specific error code.

RegReplaceKey

Description	This API function replaces a subkey with information contained in a file, and creates a backup of the original subkey.

Declaration	`Declare Function RegReplaceKey Lib "advapi32.dll" _`
	`    Alias "RegReplaceKeyA" ( _`
	`    ByVal hKey As Long, _`
	`    ByVal lpSubKey As String, _`
	`    ByVal lpNewFile As String, _`
	`    ByVal lpOldFile As String) As Long`

Parameters	Parameter	Description
	`Hkey`	`Long Integer`—The handle of an open key, or one of the hive constants listed above.
	`LpValueName`	`String`—The name of the subkey to replace. This subkey must be directly under `HKEY_LOCAL_MACHINE` or `HKEY_USERS`.
	`LpNewFile`	`String`—The name of the file (created using `RegSaveKey`) that contains the information with which to replace to selected subkey.
	`LpOldFile`	`String`—The name of the file to which the existing subkey will be backed up.

Return value	`Long Integer` Zero (`ERROR_SUCCESS`) on success. All other values are the specific error code.

RegRestoreKey

Description	This API function restores a subkey with information contained in a file.

Declaration	`Declare Function RegRestoreKey Lib "advapi32.dll" _`
	`    Alias "RegRestoreKeyA" ( _`
	`    ByVal hKey As Long, _`
	`    ByVal lpFile As String, _`
	`    ByVal dwFlags As Long) As Long`

Parameters	Parameter	Description
	`Hkey`	`Long Integer`—The handle of an open key to restore from disk, or one of the hive constants listed above.

Continues

	LpFile	String—The name of the file that contains the information to restore.
	DwFlags	Long Integer—Use zero for a regular restore. Use REG_WHOLE_HIVE_VOLATILE for a temporary restore (which is not saved when the system is restarted), in which case, hKey must point to HKEY_LOCAL_MACHINE or HKEY_USERS
Return value		Long Integer Zero (ERROR_SUCCESS) on success. All other values are the specific error code.

RegSaveKey

Description	This API function saves a key and all its subkeys to a disk file.

Declaration	`Declare Function RegSaveKey Lib "advapi32.dll" _`
	`    Alias "RegSaveKeyA" ( _`
	`    ByVal hKey As Long, _`
	`    ByVal lpFile As String, _`
	`    lpSecurityAttributes As SECURITY_ATTRIBUTES) As Long`

Parameters	Parameter	Description
	Hkey	Long Integer—The handle of an open key, or one of the hive constants listed above.
	LpFile	String—The name of the file into which the key (and its subkeys) will be saved.
	lpSecurityAttributes	SECURITY_ATTRIBUTES—A user-defined Type that defines the security attributes for this key. Security attributes are quite a complex subject and most of its features only work on Windows NT. In any case, they are rarely used, so the examples provided at the end of this chapter re-declare this parameter ByVal SecurityAttributes as Long, and pass a Null (0&). For more information about security, refer to the Microsoft Win32 SDK.
Return value		Long Integer Zero (ERROR_SUCCESS) on success. All other values are the specific error code.

RegSetKeySecurity

Description	This API function sets the security information for the specified key.

Declaration	```Declare Function RegSetKeySecurity Lib "advapi32.dll" (_```
	 ``` ByVal hKey As Long, _```
	 ``` ByVal SecurityInformation As Long, _```
	 ``` pSecurityDescriptor As SECURITY_DESCRIPTOR) As Long```

Parameters	Parameter	Description
	Hkey	Long Integer—The handle of a key, or one of the hive constants listed above.
	SecurityInformation	Long Integer—A flag that defines the security information to save.
	PSecurityDescriptor	SECURITY_DESCRIPTOR—A user-defined Type that contains the security information to save for the specified key.

Return value	Long Integer Zero (ERROR_SUCCESS) on success. All other values are the specific error code.

RegSetValueEx

Description	This API function sets the value for the specified key. This is a more sophisticated function than RegSetValue, and is recommended for use on Win32.

Declaration	```Declare Function RegSetValueEx Lib "advapi32.dll" _```
	 ``` Alias "RegSetValueExA" (_```
	 ``` ByVal hKey As Long, _```
	 ``` ByVal lpValueName As String, _```
	 ``` ByVal Reserved As Long, _```
	 ``` ByVal dwType As Long, _```
	 ``` lpData As Any, _```
	 ``` ByVal cbData As Long) As Long```

Parameters	Parameter	Description
	Hkey	Long Integer—The handle of an open key, or one of the hive constants listed above.
	LpSubKey	String—The name of the subkey whose value is to be set. To set the (Default) value, specify vbNullString. If the value does not exist, it is created.

Continues

	LpReserved	Long Integer—This is a reserved parameter. Set it to zero.
	DwType	Long Integer—REG_SZ.
	LpData	String—The null-terminated data to be written to the value.
	CbData	Long Integer—A variable that you load with the length of lpData, excluding the terminating Null character.
Return value		Long Integer Zero (ERROR_SUCCESS) on success. All other values are the specific error code.

RegSetValue

Description	This API function sets the default value for the specified key. The previous function, RegSetValueEx, is recommended on Win32.

Declaration	`Declare Function RegSetValue Lib "advapi32.dll" _`
	`    Alias "RegSetValueA" ( _`
	`    ByVal hKey As Long, _`
	`    ByVal lpSubKey As String, _`
	`    ByVal dwType As Long, _`
	`    ByVal lpData As String, _`
	`    ByVal cbData As Long) As Long`

Parameters	Parameter	Description
	hKey	Long Integer—The handle of an open key, or one of the hive constants listed above.
	lpSubKey	String—The name of the subkey whose value is to be set. To set the (Default) value, specify vbNullString. If the value does not exist, it is created.
	dwType	Long Integer—REG_SZ.
	lpData	String—The null-terminated data to be written to the value.
	cbData	Long Integer—A variable that you load with the length of lpData, excluding the terminating Null character.
Return value		Long Integer Zero (ERROR_SUCCESS) on success. All other values are the specific error code.

RegUnloadKey

Description	This API function unloads the specified key and all its subkeys.

Declaration	```Declare Function RegUnLoadKey Lib "advapi32.dll" _```
	``` Alias "RegUnLoadKeyA" (_```
	``` ByVal hKey As Long, _```
	``` ByVal lpSubKey As String) As Long```

Parameters	**Parameter**	**Description**
	HKey	Long Integer—HKEY_LOCAL_MACHINE, HKEY_USERS, or the handle of a key returned by the RegConnectRegistry function.
	lpSubKey	String—The name of the subkey (loaded using the RegLoadKey function) to unload.

Return value	Long Integer Zero (ERROR_SUCCESS) on success. All other values are the specific error code.

Registry API Constant and User-Defined Type Declarations

To help you with this book, and so that you won't have to go searching for them, the following is a list of all the Constant and User-Defined Type declarations you'll need when using the Registry APIs.

```
'Key declarations
Const HKEY_CLASSES_ROOT As Long = &H80000000
Const HKEY_CURRENT_CONFIG As Long = &H80000005
Const HKEY_CURRENT_USER As Long = &H80000001
Const HKEY_DYN_DATA As Long = &H80000006
Const HKEY_LOCAL_MACHINE As Long = &H80000002
Const HKEY_PERF_ROOT As Long = HKEY_LOCAL_MACHINE
Const HKEY_PERFORMANCE_DATA As Long = &H80000004
Const HKEY_USERS As Long = &H80000003

'Parameter declarations
Const REG_NOTIFY_CHANGE_ATTRIBUTES As Long = &H2
Const REG_NOTIFY_CHANGE_LAST_SET As Long = &H4
Const REG_NOTIFY_CHANGE_NAME As Long = &H1
Const REG_NOTIFY_CHANGE_SECURITY As Long = &H8
Const REG_CREATED_NEW_KEY As Long = &H1
Const REG_OPENED_EXISTING_KEY As Long = &H2
Const REG_OPTION_BACKUP_RESTORE As Long = 4
Const REG_OPTION_VOLATILE As Long = 1
Const REG_OPTION_NON_VOLATILE As Long = 0
Const STANDARD_RIGHTS_ALL As Long = &H1F0000
```

```
Const SYNCHRONIZE As Long = &H100000
Const READ_CONTROL As Long = &H20000
Const STANDARD_RIGHTS_READ As Long = (READ_CONTROL)
Const STANDARD_RIGHTS_WRITE As Long = (READ_CONTROL)
Const KEY_CREATE_LINK As Long = &H20
Const KEY_CREATE_SUB_KEY As Long = &H4
Const KEY_ENUMERATE_SUB_KEYS As Long = &H8
Const KEY_NOTIFY As Long = &H10
Const KEY_QUERY_VALUE As Long = &H1
Const KEY_SET_VALUE As Long = &H2

Const KEY_READ As Long = (( _
    STANDARD_RIGHTS_READ _
    Or KEY_QUERY_VALUE _
    Or KEY_ENUMERATE_SUB_KEYS _
    Or KEY_NOTIFY) _
    And (Not SYNCHRONIZE))

Const KEY_WRITE As Long = (( _
    STANDARD_RIGHTS_WRITE _
    Or KEY_SET_VALUE _
    Or KEY_CREATE_SUB_KEY) _
    And (Not SYNCHRONIZE))

Const KEY_EXECUTE As Long = (KEY_READ)

Const KEY_ALL_ACCESS As Long = (( _
    STANDARD_RIGHTS_ALL _
    Or KEY_QUERY_VALUE _
    Or KEY_SET_VALUE _
    Or KEY_CREATE_SUB_KEY _
    Or KEY_ENUMERATE_SUB_KEYS _
    Or KEY_NOTIFY _
    Or KEY_CREATE_LINK) _
    And (Not SYNCHRONIZE))

'Key value types
Const REG_BINARY As Long = 3
Const REG_DWORD As Long = 4
Const REG_DWORD_BIG_ENDIAN As Long = 5
Const REG_DWORD_LITTLE_ENDIAN As Long = 4
Const REG_EXPAND_SZ As Long = 2
Const REG_LINK As Long = 6
Const REG_MULTI_SZ As Long = 7
Const REG_NONE As Long = 0
Const REG_RESOURCE_LIST As Long = 8
Const REG_SZ As Long = 1

'API return codes
Const ERROR_ACCESS_DENIED As Long = 5&
Const ERROR_BADDB As Long = 1009&
Const ERROR_BADKEY As Long = 1010&
Const ERROR_CANTOPEN As Long = 1011&
Const ERROR_CANTREAD As Long = 1012&
```

```
Const ERROR_CANTWRITE As Long = 1013&
Const ERROR_INSUFFICIENT_BUFFER As Long = 122
Const ERROR_INVALID_HANDLE As Long = 6&
Const ERROR_INVALID_PARAMETER As Long = 87
Const ERROR_KEY_DELETED As Long = 1018&
Const ERROR_KEY_HAS_CHILDREN As Long = 1020&
Const ERROR_MORE_DATA As Long = 234
Const ERROR_NO_MORE_ITEMS As Long = 259&
Const ERROR_OUTOFMEMORY As Long = 14&
Const ERROR_REGISTRY_CORRUPT As Long = 1015&
Const ERROR_REGISTRY_IO_FAILED As Long = 1016&
Const ERROR_REGISTRY_RECOVERED As Long = 1014&
Const ERROR_SUCCESS As Long = 0&

'User-defined Types
Type SECURITY_ATTRIBUTES
    nLength As Long
    lpSecurityDescriptor As Long
    bInheritHandle As Long
End Type

Type FILETIME
    dwLowDateTime As Long
    dwHighDateTime As Long
End Type

Type ACL
    AclRevision As Byte
    Sbz1 As Byte
    AclSize As Integer
    AceCount As Integer
    Sbz2 As Integer
End Type

Type SECURITY_DESCRIPTOR
    Revision As Byte
    Sbz1 As Byte
    Control As Long
    Owner As Long
    Group As Long
    Sacl As ACL
    Dacl As ACL
End Type
```

Index

Index

Index

Index

Index

Index